EMBODYING ALTERITY

DS25 2018-2025
EDITED BY ALESSANDRO AYUSO & MARY KONSTANTOPOULOU

STUDIO AS BOOK
NO. 10

STUDIO AS BOOK

INTRODUCTION

Studio as Book is a series of publications that tender the extraordinary creative work undertaken in the School of Architecture + Cities design studios— in detail. Each book in the series covers the work of a single design studio, either undergraduate or graduate, and sometimes both, over the course of at least two years. Its objectives are:

- To record, archive, and present the pedagogical programme and creative student outputs of a design studio.
- To position the work of a design studio within a broader intellectual, scientific or aesthetic field.
- To advance the design driven research being undertaken in the School's design studios.
- To provide a reference for future iterations and variations of a design studio.

Compressing the creative output of a multi-year design studio into a single volume, using a pre-designed book template is no easy undertaking, and it is necessarily selective. At the same time, it provides a consistent, sure platform for the wide range of approaches to the discipline of teaching architectural design which characterise the school.

Each *Studio as Book* has been peer-reviewed on the basis of a proposal submitted by the studio's tutors to an editorial committee. In addition to studio briefs and student work, each book includes content that draws out the studio's research and pedagogical agenda. The format that this takes varies from book to book— reflective essays by tutors or past students, interviews, theoretical essays from parallel fields, and so forth.

I wish to acknowledge the contribution of the following in bringing this project to fruition: Lindsay Bremner, Director of Research and Knowledge Exchange, who was the driving force behind the series when it was launched in 2016; Mark Boyce, author of *Sizes May Vary, A workbook for graphic design* (Lawrence King, 2008)— and the designer of *Studio as Book*; Filip Visnjic and Mirna Pedalo, who have given the books a presence on OpenStudioWestminster: http://www.openstudiowestminster.org/studio-as-book/; and the design tutors and students who have given of their time and energy to collate and edit the books into this unique series.

Harry Charrington
Former Head of the School of Architecture + Cities
University of Westminster

EMBODYING ALTERITY

DS25 2018-25
EDITED BY ALESSANDRO AYUSO & MARY KONSTANTOPOULOU

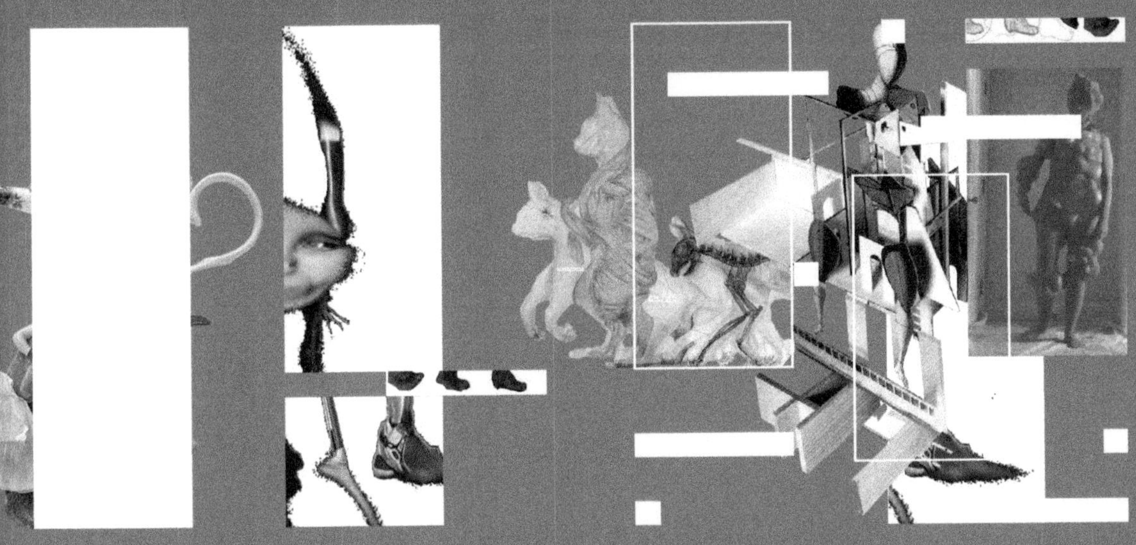

STUDIO AS BOOK
NO. 10

SCHOOL OF ARCHITECTURE + CITIES
UNIVERSITY OF WESTMINSTER

CONTENTS

PREFACE

The collective's bodily composition has shifted over the years as students and co-tutors have moved through it and returned as visitors, critics and supporters.

As a University of Westminster M Arch studio, DS25 defines itself as a collective endeavour working within a supportive and vibrant context. Amidst a broader pedagogical context of arguably increasing conservatism, the studio aspires to be a bastion of speculation, daring, and a source of deep enquiries into architecture's imaginative possibilities. This book discusses the life of DS25 as a platform for spatial and theoretical discovery. One could look at DS25 as a body in itself (fig. 5.01). The individual material and philosophical interests that pass through this body are altered by its internal workings at any given time. The projects and briefs that grow within it shape it and stretch it, providing it with new tentacles, heads or microbial colonies which echo through past skins. The book aims to bring together the speculative spatial experiments that have materialised through its lifespan which have been fundamental to creating this growing assemblage. Pedagogical positions are manifested in briefs and mutated over time through the conversations that each time period enables, thus also mutating the body of DS25.

The collective's bodily composition has shifted over the years as students and co-tutors have moved through it and returned as visitors, critics, and supporters. Students— their personalities, energy, insights, work, and their return to the studio discussion in various capacities— are crucial to the evolution of DS25 as a living body. Their contributions are largely evident through their projects shown and discussed in the pages to come; this preface recognises other crucial contributors through an informal telling of the genesis of the studio.

As a research collective, the studio is based on enquiries; at its initial formation the central one asked: what is the potential of the body as a generator in design? My PhD by Design at the Bartlett first posed the question that the studio has since taken forward in exciting and unexpected directions. The thesis question arose from a frustration with the paucity of represented figures and bodily engagement in the digital design processes predominating architectural practice in the 2000s. The idea of body agents took shape as I examined how the lived body could be actively represented in the digital design process. Already the formal and informal threads of discourse and community were at work: the idea of body agents was meant as an advancement of my former mentor Marco Frascari's idea of metonymic figures (discussed further in chapter two). My own design process, where drawing figures inhabiting buildings was an integral part of design, was cultivated under his guidance. Frascari's ideas about drawing and the body, and his love of narrative, imagination, monsters, magic, and dreams in architecture still pervade the discussions in the studio. In my PhD work, introducing figures into digital design exposed more critical issues and possibilities than I had expected: coming to the fore were questions of intersubjectivity, posthumanism, narrative, and the inherent confrontations with *alterity* entailed in contemporary embodiment.

Coming from practice in New York, the architectural discourse in London, and particularly at the Bartlett, was, for me, a shot in the arm: an intense place humming with rigorous activity, idiosyncratic, fascinating work and a commitment to speculation. My supervisors Professor Jonathan Hill and Dr Marcos Cruz were vital voices at that time. Professor Hill's mode of teaching— one of gentle inquisitiveness and curiosity— became just as influential as the concepts embedded in his notable books such as *Actions of Architecture: Architects and Creative Users* and the spectacular drawings and visions of his students in Unit 12. Dr Cruz's research on disgusting embodiment and architecture's "inhabitable flesh" were sources of great inspiration, as was the collective output of his unit at the Bartlett, Unit 20, co-taught with Dr Marjan Coletti.

At the same time that I started my PhD, I began teaching at the University of Westminster– a short walk away from the Bartlett, and another place buzzing with ideas and energy. There, on the M Arch course, Cruz and Coletti taught another studio; William Firebrace and Gabby Shawcross taught a studio focused on film; Susanne Isa, Professor Murray Fraser and others led studios producing awe-inspiring work. I taught on the new BA Interior Architecture course, working with Dr Ro Spankie and Julia Dwyer. This was an exciting time of shaping a course from the ground up. We approached architecture from the inside out, with an emphasis on the scale of the body, sociocultural dimensions of inhabitation, details, and "filling the void left behind by architecture." In many schools of architecture, Interiors courses are often scoffed at by those ensconced in the architecture department. Yet, outside of the strictures of regulating bodies such as the RIBA and ARB, there are advantages that those looking down on the field miss. Not only do these courses provide a greater freedom to explore spatial propositions, but also, standing slightly outside of the core of the discipline, the

As a research collective, the studio is based on enquiries; at its initial formation the central one asked: what is the potential of the body as a generator in design?

course environment lends itself to both students and tutors developing a critical eye towards current architectural discourse. We questioned the shiny freestanding objects that architects as a whole seemed to be obsessed with, focusing instead on revitalising existing structures; this focus presaged the coming emphasis on adaptive reuse in wider architectural practice.

I joined the M Arch team at the University of Westminster first through leading a Digital Design group; this module was designed to expose first-year M Arch students to a specialisation in digital media. Much like the studio structure, students were presented with an array of thematic groups and chose among them based on their interest. The premise of Group F was to use modelling and animation software to design body agents and then introduce them into the students' studio projects as a way to reveal possibilities in each project. In addition to tutorials on digital skills, Group F involved a history and theory lecture series on embodiment in architecture from me, presentations from the students on precedents and their design projects, and reviews; in short, what the Digital Design group structure allowed for was exciting, but it was at the same time evident that Group F's curriculum was becoming bloated, outgrowing the module structure.

Dr Dan Dream (whom I had met through an introduction by Professor Hill and a shared interest in the work of Michelangelo, Baroque architecture, drawing and painting, and embodiment in architecture) had become a regular Group F critic, and encouraged me to transform the Digital Design group into a studio. The proposal found support and encouragement from the M Arch course administrator, Samir Pandya. For the first and second year of DS25, the team consisted of Dr Dan Dream, Martyna Marciniak, and myself. A graduate of PG24 at the Bartlett, and having just finished a residency at the Bauhaus Foundation, Dessau, where she designed speculative prosthetics for interfacing with an Oskar Schlemmer-designed building, Marciniak brought her own interest in embodiment, through the cinematic and narrative dimensions of architecture. Dr Dan Dream was in the final stages of his PhD, and brought his connoisseur's love of plans, esoterism, perversion and body horror in architecture, as well as an inimitable sense of humour and tough love to his pedagogical approach. The first cohort of students comprised a keen group from the Digital Design group; if one stayed later in the studio space in the Westminster architecture campus, passing by from the mezzanine, the students could be heard below, giggling while inexplicably drawing in the dark at a large table. Reviews at this time were formative moments of discussion, with the studio agenda nascent, and with precious input from Professor Hill, Julia Dwyer, and Dr Mary Vaughan Johnson. I had also begun supervising M Arch Theses at the Bartlett, reinforcing a proxy connection with PG24 taught by Professor Penelope Haralambidou and Michael Tite, due to common research interests leading to my often supervising PG24's students. In addition to Martyna Marciniak, other enduring alliances stemmed from the inspiring and substantive conversations in the thesis supervision meetings.

The third year of the studio was impacted by the pandemic; the teaching team was Dr Fiona Zisch, Dr Dan Dream, and myself. Dr Zisch brought a new dimension to the studio through her expertise in performance interaction design and neuroscience. Teaching was carried out through Zoom and Teams, a frustrating time that students made the best of, drawing and 3d modelling at home. The fourth year of the studio seemed like an interregnum after the Covid-19 shutdowns, with the teaching routine moving towards business as usual. Mary Konstantopoulou joined the team that year: having graduated from PG24 at the Bartlett, she brought her own interest in film, narrative, and a strong ecological awareness and agenda. Working then at Jan Kattein Architects, she infused an interest in considering communities and buildings as tangled assemblages. With an aversion towards buildings that are standalone and separate from their material context, Konstantopoulou gravitated more towards reusing existing buildings and site-specific materiality. Bartlett MPhil/PhD researcher Deniz Özbek was an informal but crucial contributor in our most recent year, bringing her unique knowledge of horror and architectural theory to bear on the discussions, briefs, review panels, and presentations.

This is all to say that studios, as collective bodies of knowledge, engines of research and fora for discussion, don't materialise out of thin air; collaborations, kinships based on common questions or obsessions, and serendipitous alliances all have to fall into place and evolve. From this recounting it is likely very clear that the milieu within which DS25 operates is just as important to its existence as any one aspect of its content or individual contributor; yet it's worth closing by emphasising that colleagues at the University of Westminster have been (and continue to be) invaluable in providing a supportive environment for the studio to thrive. DS25 has at various times overlapped with and benefited from teaching contributions and collaborations at the University of Westminster with BA Interior Architecture, BA Architecture, and the Fabrication Lab. The studio has found strong support and encouragement from M Arch Course Leader Richard Difford as well as fellow tutors who have provided invaluable feedback, input, and encouragement through cross-crits, marking sessions, and discussions. We are indebted to the interest, generosity, and support of all those that have contributed.

- Dr Alessandro Ayuso

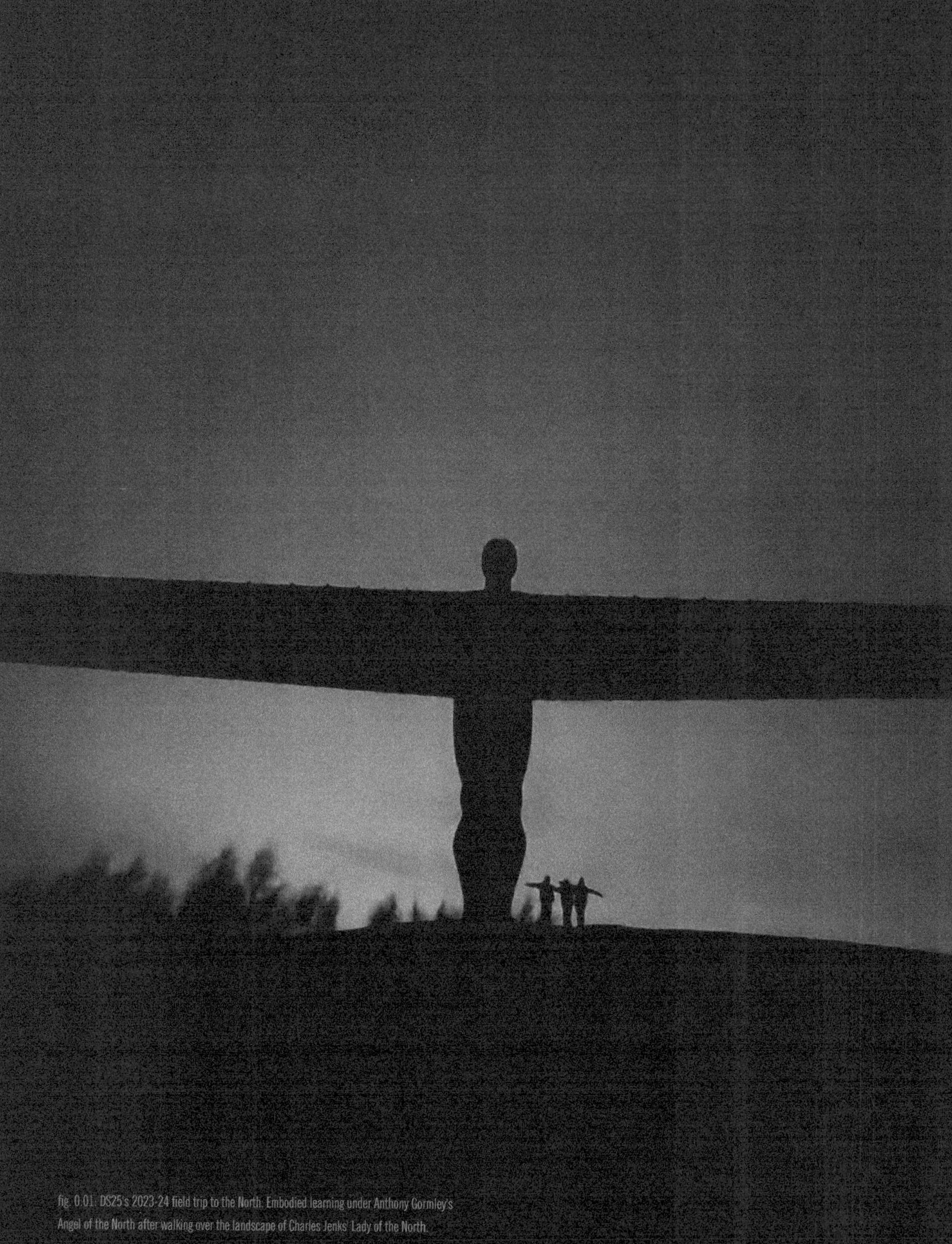

fig. 0.01. DS25's 2023-24 field trip to the North. Embodied learning under Anthony Gormley's Angel of the North after walking over the landscape of Charles Jenks' Lady of the North.

CHAPTER 1: INTRODUCTION TO DS25 & THIS BOOK

THE COLLECTIVE MISSION OF THE STUDIO
THE BOOK
EVOLUTION OF THE STUDIO
DS25'S PEDAGOGICAL APPROACH

by Dr ALESSANDRO AYUSO and MARY KONSTANTOPOULOU

THE COLLECTIVE MISSION OF THE STUDIO

Who are architecture's subjects? Are they architects themselves, with their intentional authorship often diminished from passive design processes, such as by the predominant use of generic corporate software packages? Or are they the occupants of buildings, so often given token representation by architects as generic scale figures to provide "people texture" to final renders?[(01)] Or could they be the myriad entities affected by architecture– wildlife, neighbouring buildings, environmental conditions– rarely lucky enough to be recognised as part of aims for sustainable or contextual design?

Envisioning *alterity*— or otherness— as part of the design process is a way of taking account of architecture's potential subjects. Taken on as an ambitious enquiry, exploring the alterities moving through and affected by architecture likely involves a repositioning of the assumed human subject amidst a constellation of othernesses, affinities, and overlaps. As environmental regeneration becomes more pressing, this task is part of a necessary shift away from the legacy of Humanist hierarchies and towards possibilities of, as multispecies feminist theorist Donna Haraway would put it, "making kin."[(02)]

The architecture design studio is a unique context to explore such pressing issues as an enriching and generative part of pedagogy. Postgraduate studio-based architectural projects are a unique format: steeped in intellectualism, freed from imperatives of profit, undertaken in the spirit of collective discourse, and taking invention as a virtue. With project production taking as long as nine months, and with two years available for students to develop a personal line of enquiry, the projects are meditations on themes, as well as opportunities for experimentation, imagination, and the production of new knowledge. Benefitting from this context and format, DS25 serves as a laboratory to speculate on radical architectural possibilities, with inquiries into the embodied subject— and the narratives that emerge from them— as central to its approach.

The concept of body agents— figures that are alter-egos, protagonists, and agitators, animated and deployed into contexts to challenge preconceived viewpoints— are central to the approach of the studio, both conceptually and methodologically. Through the design process, these invented subjects are endowed with a vicarious agency to affect and direct the course of students' design projects. Through their incorporation into spatial representations, body agents mobilise intentionally-situated subjectivities and impart particularly directed architectural imagination and sensibilities into drawings and materials. Stemming from this premise, DS25 projects allow for the emergence of multiple parallel worlds and their inhabitants. In between realities, the projects straddle an intersection of objective and subjective points of view, giving them a resonance of plausible outrageousness. As each student designs a body agent every year, the studio compiles an ongoing compendium of fantastical subjects and possible architectures that could arise from them.

The DS25 studio platform is meant to provide a supportive environment for each student to find and develop their specific, individual, long-term interest, cultivating an approach that can enrich their design careers past the two years of their M Arch studies. In this aim lies the underlying purpose and possible scope for the future of architectural design pedagogy: working through the actual stuff of models, drawings, material specs, and technicalities; but moving beyond coursework, and beyond buildings.[(03)] The architectural project becomes an ontological and epistemological source of enquiry: reaching through the discipline of architecture and beyond it, uncovering the unconscious, projecting through speculation, and revealing potentials about selves and realities otherwise inaccessible.

Through their incorporation into spatial representations, body agents mobilise intentionally-situated subjectivities and impart particularly directed architectural imagination and sensibilities into drawings and materials.

THE BOOK

This book thematically presents the research of DS25 as a tale narrated by a multiplicity of voices— including students, critics, tutors, and body agents— traced through discussions, teaching methodologies, and student projects over the past seven years of the studio's existence. Portraying a pedagogical approach, the book is meant to reveal a research trajectory probing the query of what could constitute the subjects of architecture, and how adventurous and experimental ideas of the subject can be incorporated into design.

For the most part, the chronology of the studio ties to the emphasis of particular themes, as evidenced by the studio briefs and student projects. Keeping this in mind as a structuring device, the overall organisation of the book presents both briefs and projects largely chronologically, with some looping back and springing forward here and there. When narrated within a collection, the body agents and their architectures reveal a play in four dimensions, stitching and tangling both DS25's real, and the body agents' own imagined, spacetimes. This structure also reflects the studio's thematic direction, where over subsequent years the discussion has emanated from the locale of the more knowable body, towards notions of the more uncanny posthuman body, to nonhuman and monstrous Others, to relational ecosystems and constructed worlds.

As described in Dr Ayuso's note at the start of the book, the studio has been taught by a team of people, all of whom have contributed greatly to the agenda, discussion and pedagogy. Throughout the book, the design tutors involved in a year's teaching are credited at the first mention of the brief for that year; the design tutor team for each project is also credited in a footnote at the first mention of a student project. The expert essays in the book from two studio contributors not only help to situate the chapters but also showcase the vibrancy and diversity of the ongoing studio discussion, one that is reliant not only on students and tutors, but also graduates and visiting critics that could be considered kindred spirits, interested in the embodied, the strange, impure, fascinating, or monstrous in architecture.

Each chapter begins with a vignette designed by Mary Konstantopoulou, spliced with quotes from students, drawings of their body agents, and sketches and photographs from the studio activities relating to the particular theme that the chapter explores. The vignettes bring aspects of the subjects that have emerged through the studio in conversation with each other and reinforce thematic and theoretical links, connecting different time periods, individuals, and briefs (fig. 1.01). Body agents and briefs which experimented with the self and the body populate the vignette that precedes chapter two (Vignette: Ch.2). The recurring rectangle that appears in the vignette is meant as a diagram of the self as a bound entity, stretching towards the Other through its erosion and extension. Fragments of architecture are interspersed among the figures, direct results of their agency. The second vignette introducing chapter three (Vignette: Ch.3) expands the idea of the singular body further. The pages become more populated with bodies found within a constellation of other bodies in ecosystemic relations. The third vignette introduces the theme of chapter four (Vignette: Ch.4). Its background is inverted in comparison to the previous two vignettes. Through voids of the pink ground, glimpses of the previous two vignettes in full colour are visible, as though looking into parallel worlds. Translucent body agents in the foreground of the world reveal projects that have extended out of the fabric of the studio's reality by weaving narratives in every aspect of their project. All of the vignettes are interspersed with text excerpts from the students' portfolios; these speak to aspects of their designs that relate to their body agents' agenda, or are otherwise words spoken by the body agents themselves within portfolios, in an interview-style format, creating an overlaid narrative of associative meanings and connections.

Drawings and models from an array of student projects are shown in the galleries of each chapter, with five to eight projects showcased more extensively to convey their intricacy and depth, and their important contributions into the themes of each chapter and the studio discussion. Rather than grouping by project programme or site location, projects are curated thematically; this does mean that projects and briefs reappear throughout the book, as a single brief or project may be apt for discussion about multiple themes. The vignettes and galleries reflect how student projects constitute a collective body of research solidifying common interests, discussions, and evolving methodologies that develop year to year.

The second chapter's theme is the body itself. Dr Dan Dream's essay preceding it delves into the studio's approach to the body, combining an amalgam of the historically-informed and irreverent, informed to arrive at relevant visions of the body in architecture. Dream sheds light on the studio's glitchy, experimental way of working and gives a sense of the body-related references that inspire the projects.

The second chapter sets out the original question driving the studio research trajectory: How can the body be conceptualised and mobilised as an agent in architecture, particularly taking into account posthuman, non-ideal, non-normative, and even deviant bodies as originators of architecture? The briefs featured in this chapter question the potential of the posthuman body, observed in conditions of technological saturation of the body through digital networks, pharmaceuticals, prosthetics, and technologically-laden environments and practices. This discussion reveals a branching and overlapping phenomena of "body-doubling" that occurs through conditions of embodied subjectivity, further complicated by the act of representing these conditions in the design process. The projects shown respond to discussions in the studio regarding not only the material condition of the posthuman body but also a philosophical understanding of the subject after Humanism. Posthumanism arguably opens the body up to new possibilities for intersubjective exchange and encounters with alterity,[04] properties that are evident in the students' designs. These questions framed in the first two studio briefs discussed in the chapter begin to reveal intangible shadow figures that arise from the innate conditions of living through, with, and in a human body. These shadow bodies can have aspects of ephemerality

How can the body be conceptualised and mobilised as an agent in architecture, particularly taking into account posthuman, non-ideal, non-normative and even deviant bodies as originators of architecture?

BODY

On the one hand, the body, as a singular, whole and bounded entity

stretches from its seemingly known shape and finds itself

invaded by, extending into the

OTHER

opening up the concept that the body sits in conversation with

duplicates

and strangers

in space

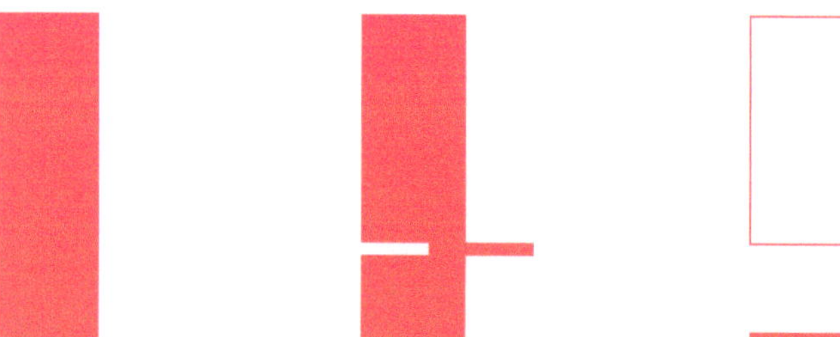

fig. 1.01: The structure of the book reflects the studio's thematic direction, with the vignettes at the beginning of each chapter setting out the themes explored, expanding from the locale of the more knowable body towards notions of the more uncanny posthuman body, to nonhuman and monstrous Others, to relational ecosystems and constructed worlds.
Image by Mary Konstantopoulou.

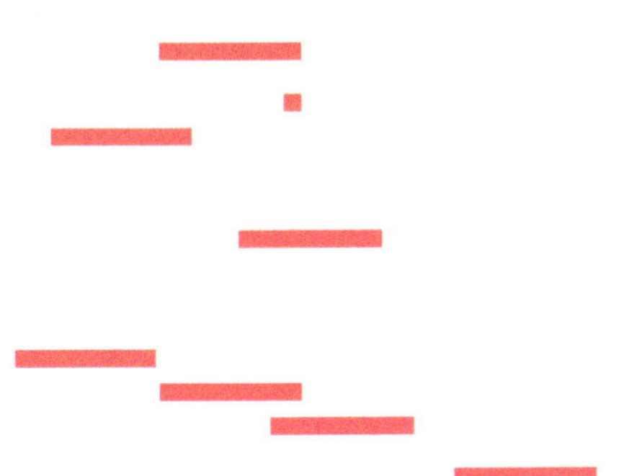

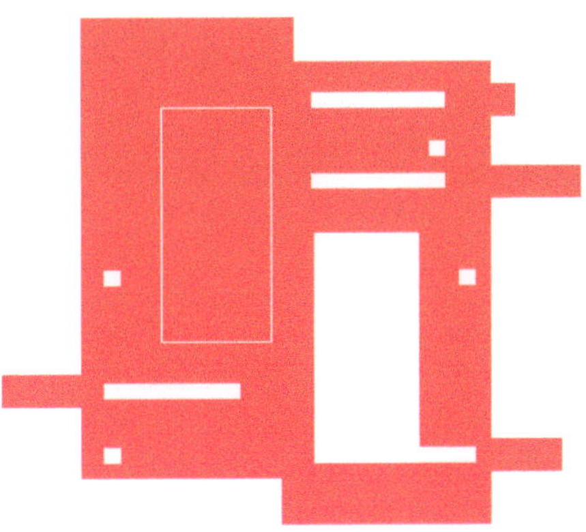

ECOSYSTEM

forming a part in a constellation of entities living in

parallel

WORLD(S)

mirror images of the

stretched-

porous-

tentacular-

shadow-

other-

bodies within

or nonhumanness, making inevitable the consideration of other-than-human bodies.

Expanding the notion of the alterity inherent to embodied subjectivity, the third chapter's focus is on the potential of an array of non-human bodies as agents. The notion of predominantly human-centred agency opens up further through philosophies that question the privileged position of humans as the only validators of truth.[05] Arguably, given the humanist-infused hubris that has given rise to the climate crisis, humans may do well to consider other ontologies and their attendant viewpoints; for example, of those "anaerobes [which] may experience, say, air as a toxic pollutant created by plant life," to follow anthropologist Stefan Helmreich in his essay on extraterrestrial relativism.[06] The human subject as a privileged zenith rather than a fellow actor in a larger scenario is challenged as objects, things, and the dynamics between them are taken as enablers of potential other subjectivities. Most of the body agents discussed in this chapter are assemblages with a foot remaining in the more purely human world, reflecting the innate identity of their designers. As design devices their hybridity gives access to multifaceted ecologies, exposing architecture's reach into often overlooked niches and territories. This chapter moves through categories of non-human bodies, moving steadily away from the human, or even materially-bound notion of embodiment, to probe more radical and imaginative architectural possibilities. Here, the horrific qualities of embodied otherness are embraced. The monstrous, alien, and spectral become means of mobilising desires and fears, of externalising subjective modes, in turn forcing design to take a fuller accounting of relational ecological strands. It is important to acknowledge, however, that, even in these destabilised explorations, the self is an inseparable part of any attempt to shift subjectivities.

Dr Amy Brookes' essay preceding the fourth chapter considers how sci-fi, a recurrent genre in the studio with explicit manifestations in many of the projects, offers potential for seeing architectural futures and responding through design. Brookes' essay highlights that the potential of sci-fi as part of architectural projects can be a way to critically look back at our present.

The introduction of sci-fi more concretely into the book is a fitting way to frame the fourth chapter. The theme of the book here shifts to a more methodological basis, considering the all-encompassing studio interest in narrative. Hinging on protagonists and deuteragonists, narrative is a methodology integral to an approach based on body agents. Innately linked with subject-positions and points of view, it allows for increased empathy and deepening of the visions attained by seeing through first the eyes of the self and then of the imagined Other. As opposed to singular frozen snapshots, storytelling strategies are more suited to communicating the complex manifestations of embodied subjectivities that the projects suppose. This way, subjects can be viewed in motion, moving through architecture, interspersed, and commingling in time. With this working method, narrativised space becomes charged with subjectivity.

As a method, narrative can cut up and restitch spacetime, tangling past, present and future.

The pantemporality of narrative as a method enables thinking through critical histories and weaving together disparate elements between contextualised points of view. Its logic frees up experimental, critical, propositional, and long-term thinking. As a method, narrative can cut up and restitch spacetime, tangling past, present, and future. Finally, as an element of design methodology, narrative is a means for mobilising conceptualisations of embodiment and architecture in non-linear, socially- and ecologically-situated scenarios. The architectural impact of such an approach is evidenced in DS25 projects shown here. Evading classification as standalone building-objects considered at a frozen moment of perfection, the proposals show architectures that form a strand in four-dimensional, multifaceted contexts, created through particularly linked and situated viewpoints.

The conclusion of the book takes stock of two underlying research questions that run through the book: First, given that the body is a fundamental reference for considering how a subject sees and experiences natural and human-made environments, how can questioning the relationship between embodied subjectivity and context lead to an architecture that is considerate of and symbiotic with Earth's long-term inhabitants? Second, given that architecture is designed by architects at one specific moment in time, but otherwise inhabited by far-reaching subjects and entities, how can narrating from considered situated points of view help us to imagine radical spatial and temporal possibilities? Finally, the conclusion considers what DS25's approach and development could implicate for future potential architectural pedagogy and practice.

fig. 1.02: Facing page: Chronological Evolution of DS25. Image by Mary Konstantopoulou.

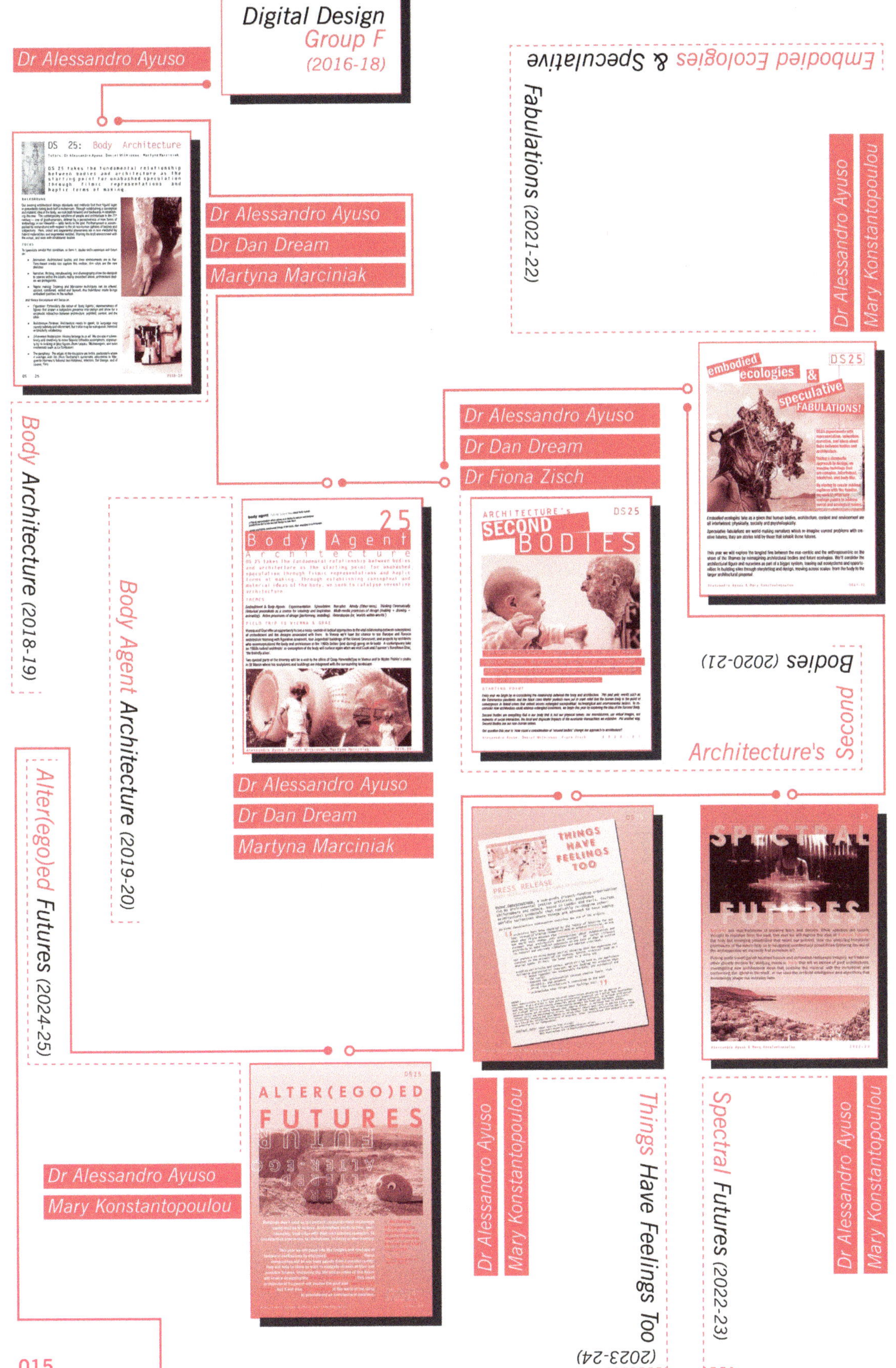
Digital Design
Group F
(2016-18)
Dr Alessandro Ayuso
Body Architecture (2018-19)
Dr Alessandro Ayuso
Dr Dan Dream
Martyna Marciniak
Body Agent Architecture (2019-20)
Dr Alessandro Ayuso
Dr Dan Dream
Martyna Marciniak
Architecture's Second Bodies (2020-21)
Dr Alessandro Ayuso
Dr Dan Dream
Dr Fiona Zisch
Embodied Ecologies & Speculative Fabulations (2021-22)
Dr Alessandro Ayuso
Mary Konstantopoulou
Spectral Futures (2022-23)
Dr Alessandro Ayuso
Mary Konstantopoulou
Things Have Feelings Too (2023-24)
Dr Alessandro Ayuso
Mary Konstantopoulou
Alter(ego)ed Futures (2024-25)
Dr Alessandro Ayuso
Mary Konstantopoulou
DS 25: Body Architecture
Body Agent Architecture
ARCHITECTURE'S SECOND BODIES
embodied ecologies & speculative FABULATIONS!
SPECTRAL FUTURES
THINGS HAVE FEELINGS TOO
PRESS RELEASE
ALTER(EGO)ED FUTURES

DS25'S PEDAGOGICAL APPROACH

"Process, which I here counterpose to system and structure, seeks to grasp existence in the very act of its constitution, definition, and deterritorialization; it is a process of 'setting into being', instituted by sub-sets of expressive ensembles which break with their totalizing frame and set to work on their own account, gradually superseding the referential totality from which they emerge, and manifesting themselves finally as their own existential index, processual lines of flight. . . ."
-Félix Guattari, *The Three Ecologies*[07]

DS25 is one of eleven M Arch studios that sit within the School of Architecture and Cities at the University of Westminster's College of Design, Creative and Digital Industries. The M Arch design studios are taught by two or three collaborating tutors with a mix of specialised agendas and skills, with students selecting one of the diverse offerings that aligns with their own interest. Design studios are supported by a "super module" that covers more specialised areas of digital and technical design, professional practice, building regulations, and history and theory. The studio works within the framework of the RIBA- and ARB-validated Part II, a two-year course where students arrive having already completed their undergraduate Part I degree and participated in at least one year of practical experience.

The shape of a year is structured by three semesters, with the bulk of the teaching and studio meetings taking place in the first two twelve-week semesters, with the third for informal meetings, self-directed production by the students, and end-of-year show preparation. Within this structure, a template linking pedagogical strategy, conceptual development of projects, and overall timing has emerged over the years of DS25. The first semester is typically dedicated to research and generation of possibilities and is more structured by tutors through periodically issued prompts: one- or two-page provocations that ask questions, frame tasks, and give references. The first semester also usually includes a field trip, as well as a number of guided skills-based workshops. The prompts and structure given by tutors at the start of the year provide a collaborative, conversational environment for the year between students, and between students and tutors. The prompts also provide the students with unexpected encounters with topics and precedents, even making strange potentially familiar concepts or processes; they give a gentle nudge to step outside of comfort zones to ask questions with fresh eyes. In the second semester, based on the first semester's research, students write their own brief for a building project; as the students have by then outlined the direction and ambition for their own projects, no further prompts are issued. As the student projects become more specifically focused on building designs, workshops continue but take the form of collaborative working days; individual or small group tutorials become effective companions to these workshops to enable development of the details and particularities of projects.

In a typical year, students have time in the first semester to focus on the body, architecture, and site. The three are introduced sequentially through the first semester prompts, with the aim that the three entities become interrelated and their associated scales and properties mutate into and inform one another. Starting design from the immediacy of the body through the design of their body agents, students move to taking on an embodied subjective viewpoint of an urban situation, and then focus on an architectural fragment that the body interacts with.

Every year, each M Arch studio starts with the issuance of a two-page flyer— essentially the summary of the year's brief— and a "pitch" in the form of a lecture by the tutors that expands on it; both function as a bit of an advertisement for the studio, as students vote for whichever topic presented piques their interest. All the briefs, quoted and referenced throughout the book, were co-written with that year's teaching team.

Once the studio allocation process is complete, each DS25 student selects "ingredients" curated by the tutors. These are precedents or topics for students to research and use to inform their work throughout the year. The ingredients are especially important to catalyse initial explorations and to invite students to step outside of their preconceptions. In the first studio meeting, the ingredients are chosen by the students with a semi-random and playful process. Often, sets of images are pinned to the wall; they are particular, but mostly suggestive, with some more recognisable and some more obscure than others; other times quotes from precedent architects are displayed without showing images of the project itself.[08] The pedagogical aim is to encourage students either to step outside of their comfort zone by making an intuitive decision (assuming they were not entirely sure what specific ingredient the quote or image pertained to), or alternately,

Starting design from the immediacy of the body through the design of their body agents, students move to taking on an embodied subjective viewpoint of an urban situation, and then focus on an architectural fragment that the body interacts with.

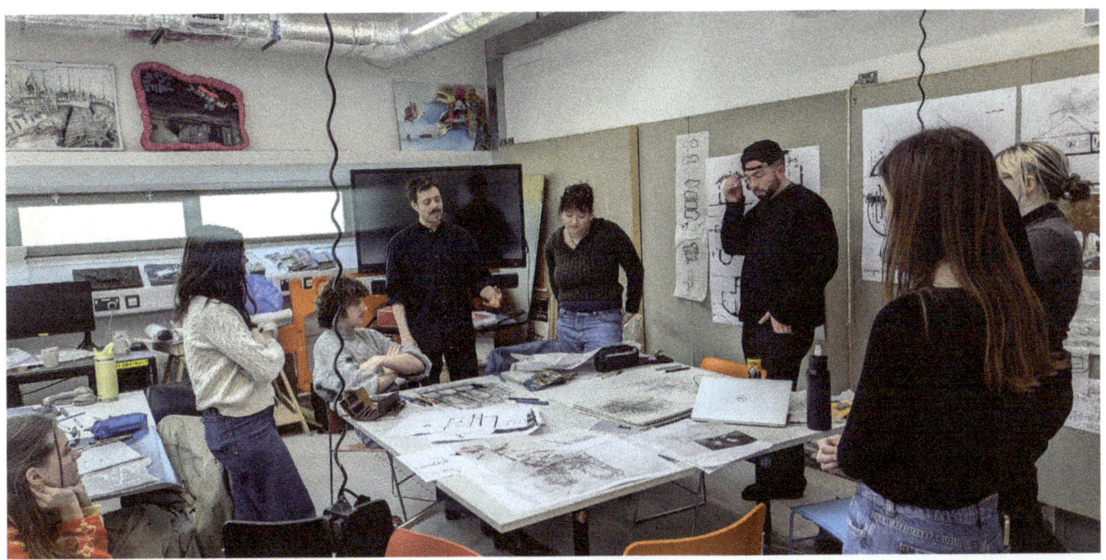

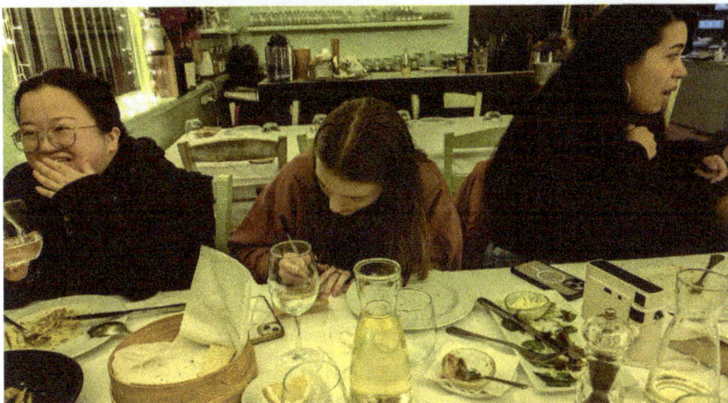

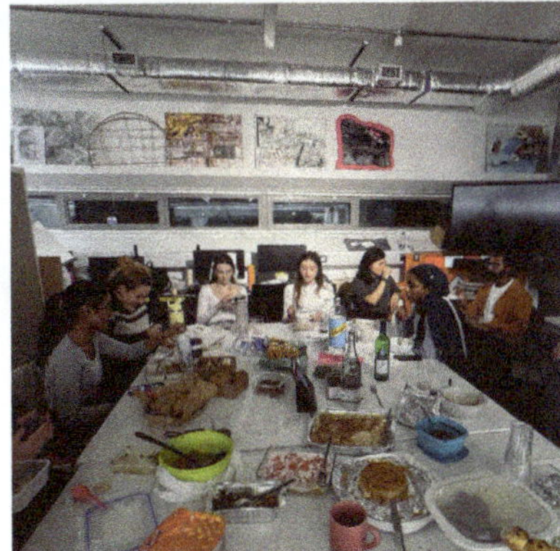

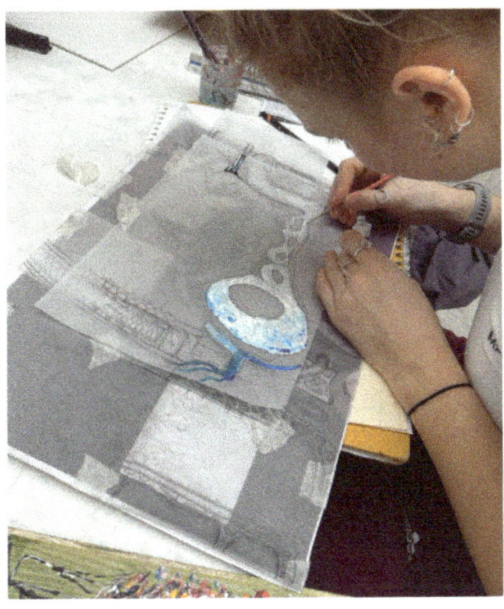

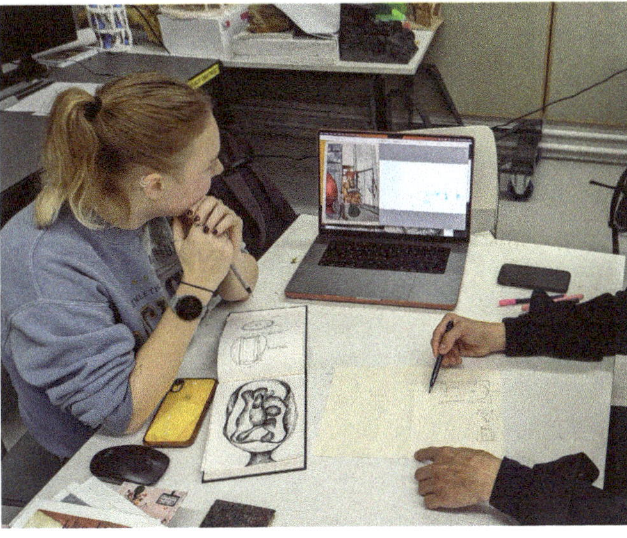

fig. 1.03-1.07: Top-Left to Bottom-Right: "Under Construction" workshop in the DS25 studio space; Exquisite corpse drawing at studio meal during the 2024-25 field trip to Athens; Studio pot-luck dinner; Imogen Power's body agent invading Conrad Daniel Areta's 1:20 detail; Individual tutorials.

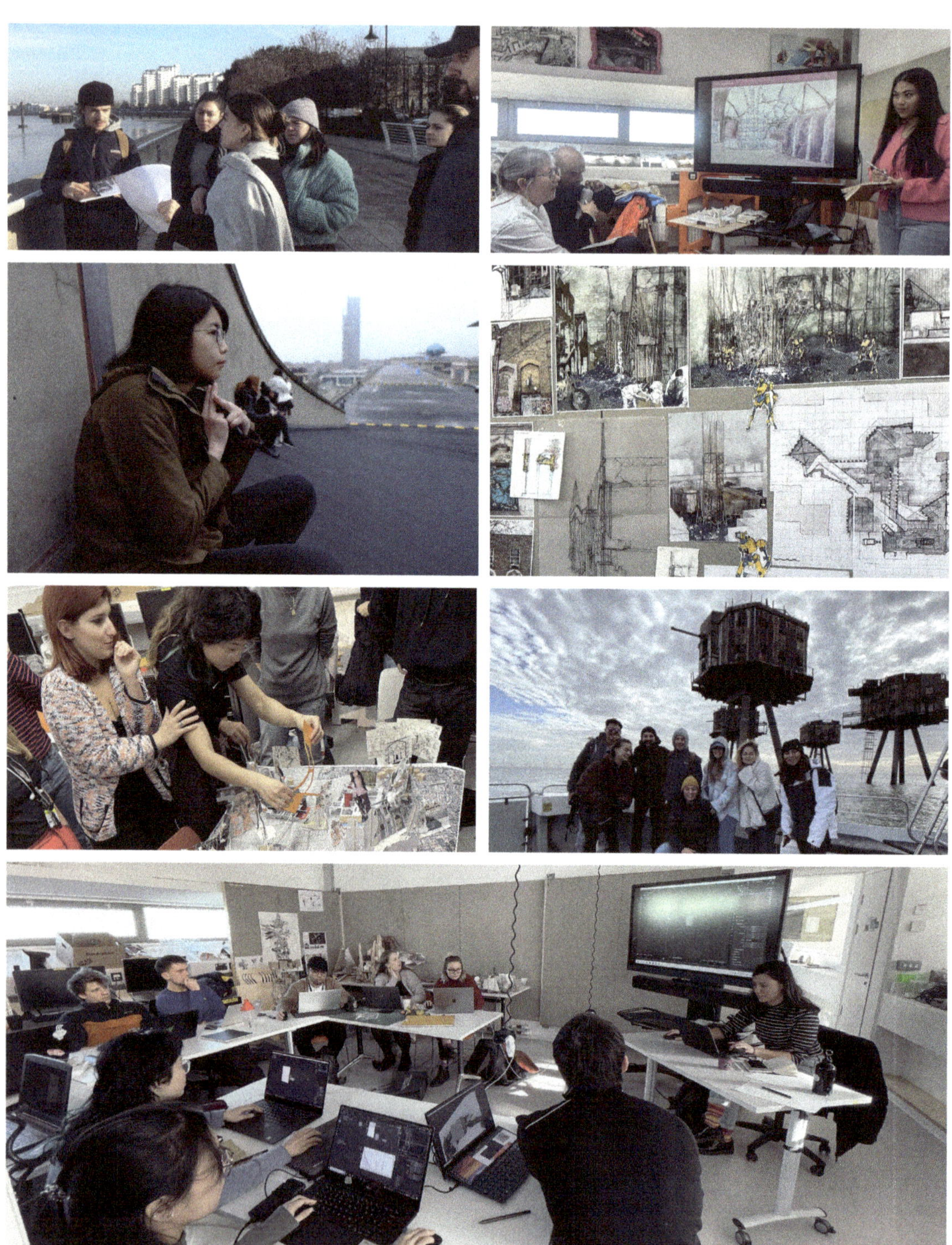

fig. 1.08-1.14: Top-Left to Bottom-Right: On-site project review in Woolwich; Jessica Gabriel presenting her project "Water Bar, Strip Pub & Public Bathrooms" at an M Arch cross review with visiting critics Ro Spankie and Samir Pandya; DS25 2018-19 field trip to Lingotto, Turin; Khushi Patel presenting her project "The Somatics of spaces" at an M Arch cross review; Spectral Making in the DS25 studio; DS25 20221-22 study trip to the Maunsell Forts; In-studio software workshop.

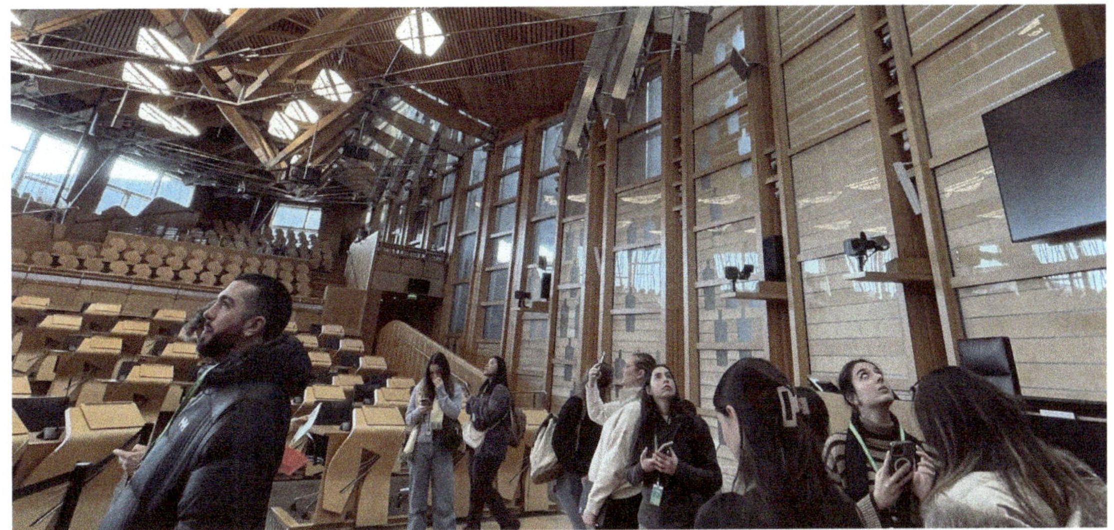

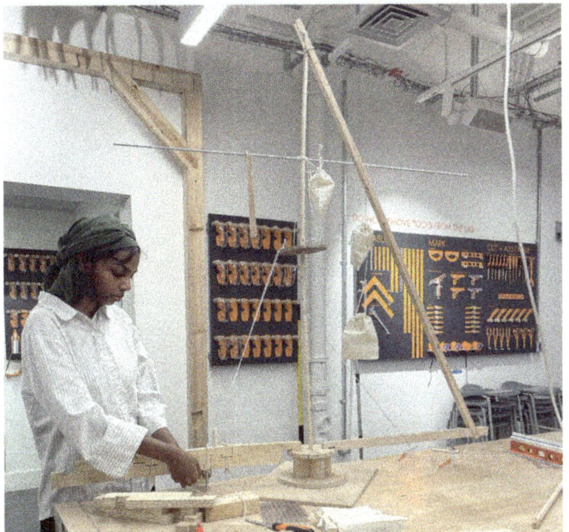

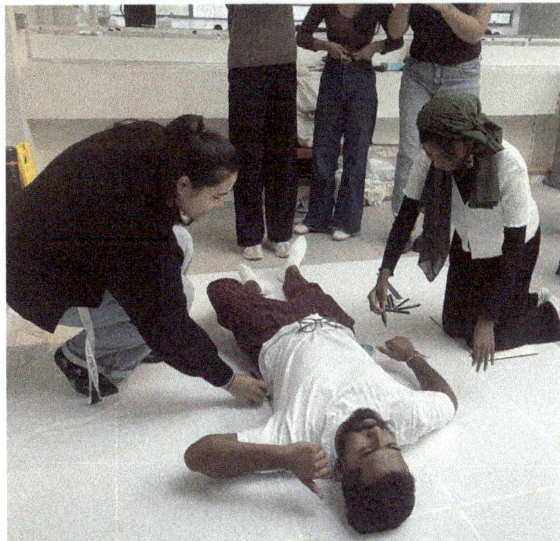

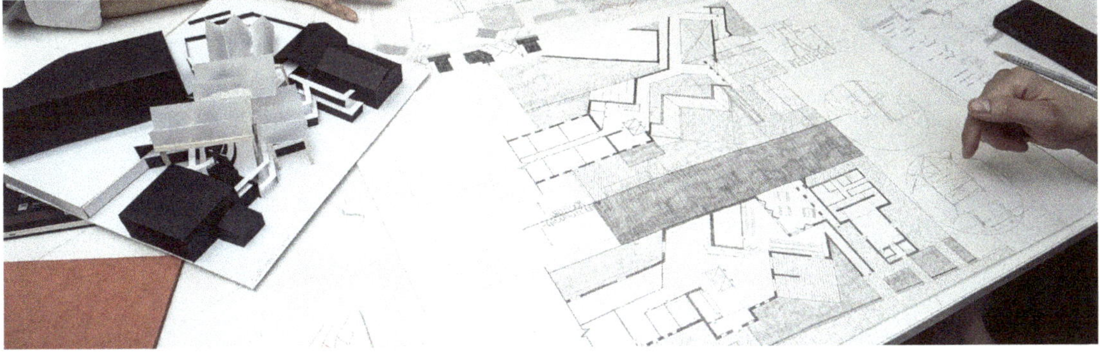

fig. 1.15-1.18: Top-Left to Bottom-Right: DS25 2023-24 field trip to the Scottish Parliament by EMTB; Making day in the Westminster Fabrication Lab; Students drawing 1:1 bodies in the DS25 studio space; Amabelle Aranas' project "Coded Compositions" at individual tutorials.

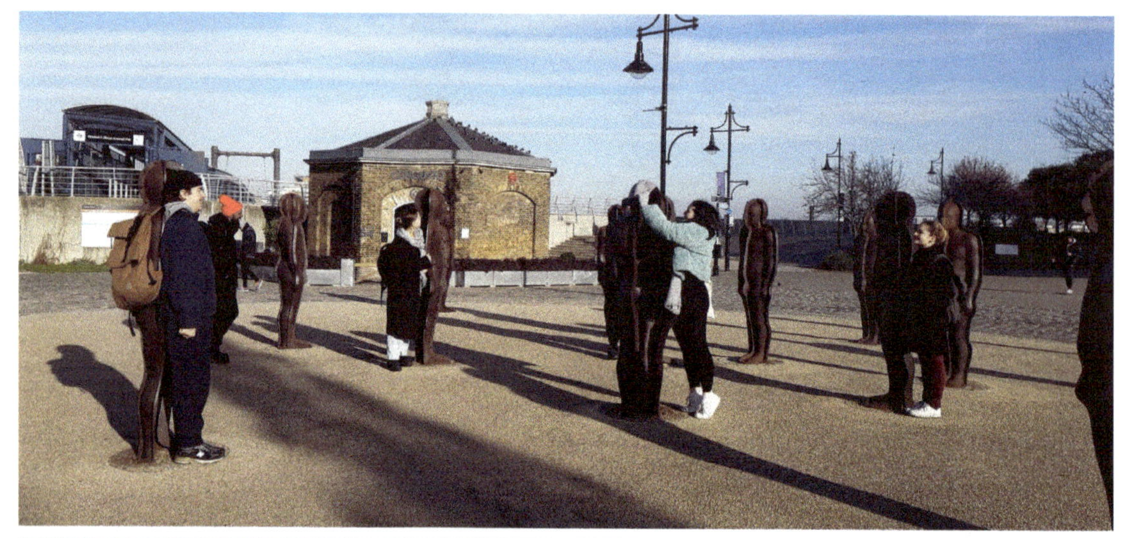

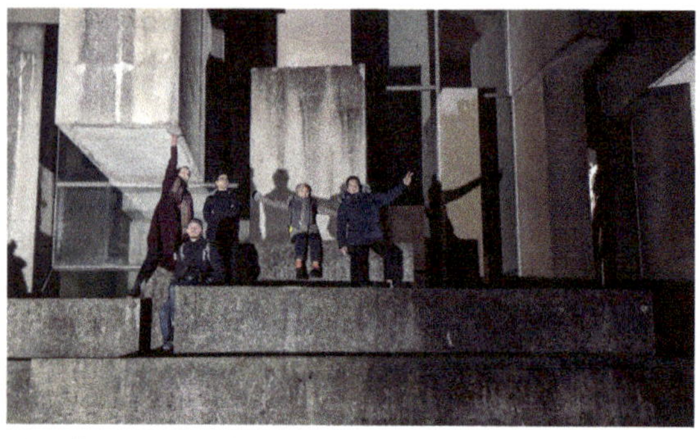

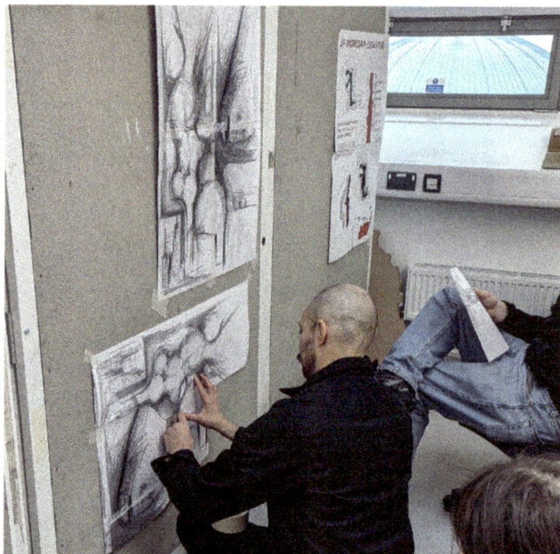

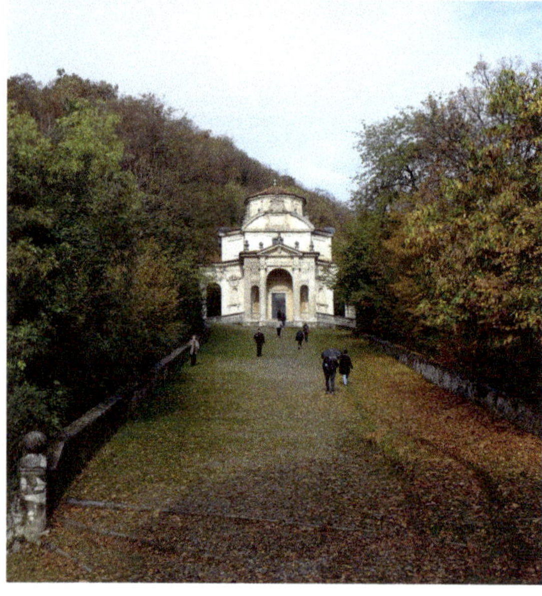

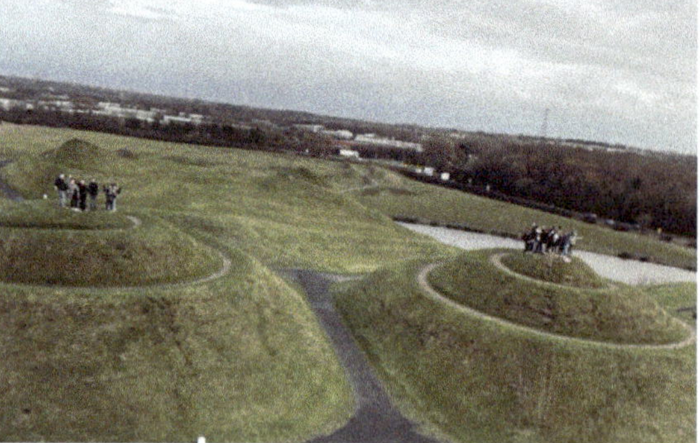

fig. 1.19-1.23: Top-Left to Bottom-Right: Students on a site visit to Woolwich; DS25 2019-20 Field trip to Wotruba Church, Vienna; Orthographic drawing pin-up tutorials; DS25 2018-19 field trip to Sacro Monte di Varese, Italy; DS25 2023-24 field trip to Charles Jenks' Lady of the North, UK.

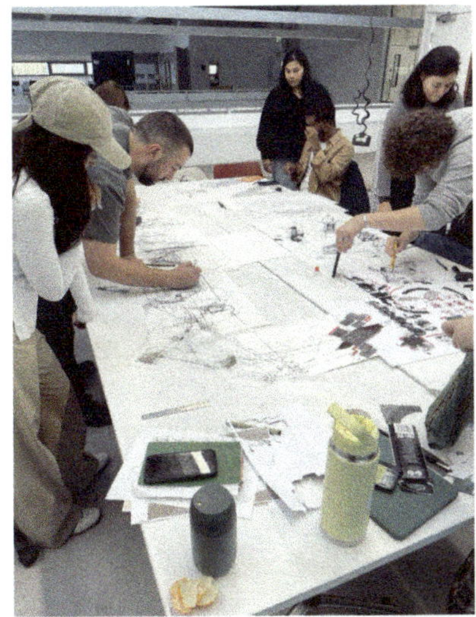

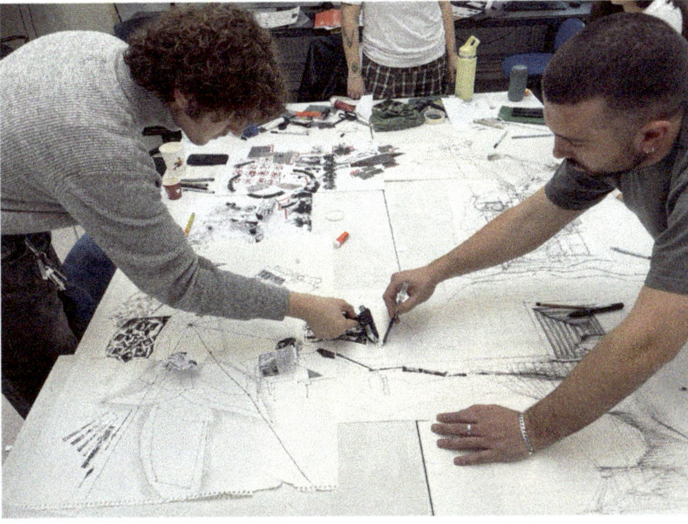

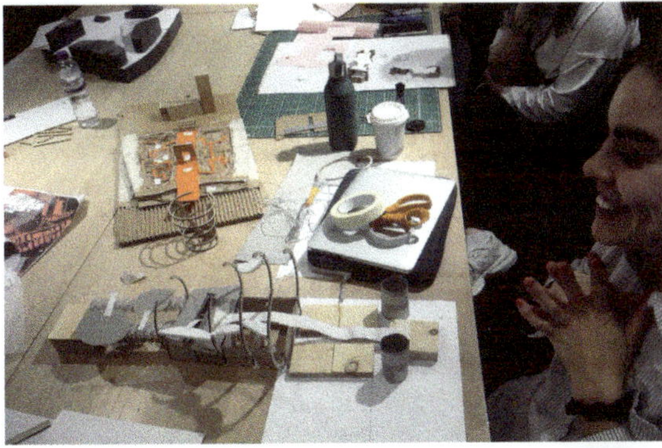

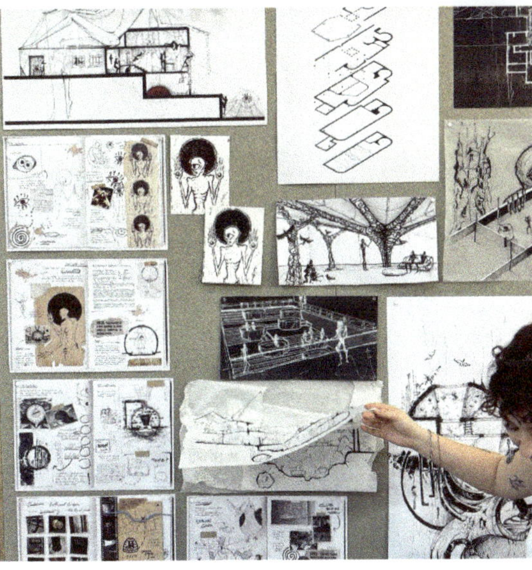

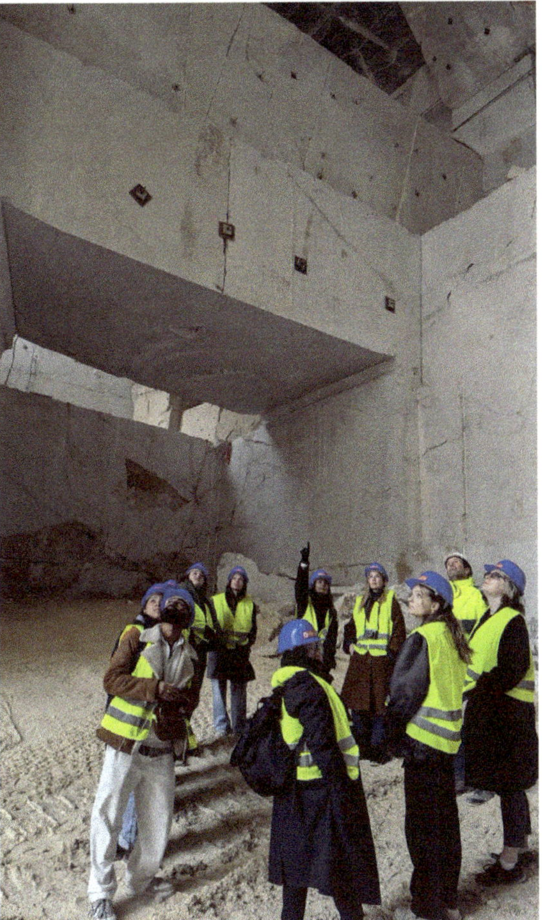

fig. 1.24-1.28: Top-Left to Bottom-Right: Collaborative detail constellation drawing workshop in the DS25 studio space; Students negotiating the connections between their chosen drawing methods; Isabel Mills-Lyle's trash model during a workshop in the Fabrication Lab; Mara Sendroiu presenting her first year project "Pest Sanctuary" at M Arch cross crits; DS25 2024-25 field trip to Dionyssos Marble Quarry in Athens.

making a well-informed, intentional decision (assuming that they recognised and were interested in the quote or image). Students have the assurance that if the ingredient is explored rigorously, they can enrich their preconceptions of architecture and their designs.

Starting the year playfully, with both intuition and intentionality, is important in setting the tone for the year. As Dr Dream describes in his essay, oscillating between the two modes is an important way of working in the studio, one where students can find desires, imagination, and possibility but following it up with critical rigour. In the working method established in DS25, reminiscent of Salvador Dalí's Paranoiac Critical approach, strategies of intuitive decision making are coupled with rigorous criticality, encouraging a speculative form of design as self-directed research.(09) The overall pedagogical approach centres around posing questions without supplying a predetermined outcome. The framing of activities and projects urge students to step outside of their comfort zone. This is meant as a gentle deterritorialisation where known structures begin to give way to process, as Guattari puts it, resulting in "manifesting themselves finally as their own... processual lines of flight."(10)

For DS25, the first week or two of the first semester is typically focused on the development of the body agent design, where the selected ingredients are synthesised as part of a visual assemblage. It is understood that the development of the body agent will continue throughout the year, in reciprocation with the architectural design itself. The design of body agents has speculative and pedagogical value, as the figures can become devices allowing students to mobilise both (newly found and a priori) architectural interests and their autobiographical selves into their design explorations. This twin capability allows students to delve deeply, to criticise, and to question their knowledge of chosen themes. As taking risks in design projects can be a daunting endeavour, passing responsibility to a "versioned" self can allow students to indulge in experimentation and testing that otherwise might be impinged by any number of worries (of failure, being weird, being wrong, etc.).

The specific ideas of the body enacted by the students in DS25 are always personal and subjective, but are all also conceivably considered as nonhuman, posthuman, or even unhuman. This can lead to attendant architectural ideas that even challenge the notion of architecture as an inanimate object, leading to further questions in the studio of both human and non-human inhabitants' relationship with their environments. By embracing hybridity, contingency, and multiplicity of the body, the incorporation of body agents into the design process tends to help expand students' research projects outwards, towards otherwise overlooked objects, elements, and architectural space. Incorporating the inhabitant and the body as critical tools offers students' projects the capacity for a continuous dialogue with sustainability and ecology, among other concepts.

Through the prompts and body agents, interests and questions arise for students that may at first seem unexpected. Ultimately though, the body agents are vessels for students to fill, respond to, and develop in a way that reveals their own interests and aspects of themselves. As much as the prompts and brief topics may frame the activities, the body agents become "the way in" to each student's own agenda, allowing it to thrive within the larger studio brief. The design of body agents not only allows a projection of the embodied self into the figure by way of imagination and empathy, but also often leads to the engagement of the designer's own body in the process, through active modes of designing, such as performance, large-scale drawing, and the design of prosthetics and equipment.

This active mode is particularly important for the studio, extending into the analysis of sites, and the approach to drawing and making. The first brief given in the studio, discussed in chapter two, captured this active approach to digitally-based work in the first semester: "... using the limited time of a semester to our advantage, the inevitable glitches, errors, and oversights which are bound to occur along the way in learning how you'd like to use digital media and materials will become criteria for developments— an attitude we'll encourage over the remainder of the year."(11) The brief went on to state: "... both successes and 'failures' in these experiments are incredibly valuable," capturing an enduring sentiment in the studio approach.

The identification of a site is often closely tied to the "view" of the territory by the body agent envisioned through psychogeographic and filmic techniques. Through the myriad of factors coalescing through a site, this approach allows for intuition and selectivity to inform other site mappings and initial programmatic ideas. For instance, students' mappings, fabricated fragments, and collections of recognised on-site social and architectural conditions can be consolidated in the making of palimpsestic models that define a territory. In the second semester, such models or similarly constructed drawings become the staging grounds for architectural interventions.

Field trips are opportunities for first-hand studying, "living" unfamiliar narratives, tracing paths through a city, meeting people face-to-face, and getting to know places.(12) In the context of the field trip, these methods act as means of questioning top-down, distanced modes of designing, bringing a critical and curious attitude to settings experienced in-person and encouraging discussions and the involvement of a wider community in architecture.

There are some activities that carry through

the whole year: these include tutorials, reviews, and workshops. Tutorials— meetings with tutors to discuss students' ongoing project development— are often done with randomised pairs of students, or as individual one-to-one discussions. Reviews involve more formal and public presentations of work by the students, with practitioners, alumni, tutors from the other M Arch studios, and other experts sitting in to give their specialist feedback; these occur every six weeks in the first two semesters. Workshop timing varies, but occurs roughly every two weeks, focussing on themed days for individual or collaborative development of an aspect of the design relevant to the time of the year.

The studio projects begin with research and experimentation, and culminate in a building proposal; the entire line of enquiry and resolved proposal are presented at the end of an academic year as a single portfolio document. (13) While striving for clear communication in its final form, students explore ideas through drawing, models, and animations. Layers to these are added, subtracted and edited to bring out concepts, narrate particular ideas, find unfamiliar paths, and refine emerging architectural languages. This method of designing provides depth to each project's specific research trajectory and brings to life otherwise potentially tentative conceptual links.

NOTES

(01) Walker writes: "The apparent purpose of these figures is to provide [a] sense of scale, … the more-official names given to these denizens of hypothetical environs, including 'people textures' and 'populating images'." Rob Walker, "Go Figure," in *New York Times Magazine*, published February 4, 2011. Accessed August 12, 2014, http://www.nytimes.com/2011/02/06/magazine/06fob-consumed-t.html?_r=0

(02) Donna J. Haraway, "Making Kin," in *Staying with the Trouble: Making Kin in the Chthulucene*, (Experimental Futures: Technological Lives, Scientific Arts, Anthropological Voices. Durham and London: Duke University Press, 2016), 99.

(03) In 2023 the ARB proposed changes to the RIBA Part 1, 2, and 3 educational structure, focusing instead on what they have identified as 5 "competency areas." They define competence as "a professional's ability to carry out their role successfully, having the relevant knowledge and skills and behaviours necessary to achieve this. These are identified as: "1. Contextual and Architectural Knowledge; 2. Design; 3. Research and Evaluation; 4. Management Practice and Leadership; 5. Professionalism and Ethics." The ARB's five areas indicate that their meaning of "tomorrow" is taken to mean quite literally that a new graduate could sit down at a desk at an established architecture office and seamlessly perform. Architects Registration Board, *Tomorrow's Architects: Competency Outcomes for Architects*, (Architects Registration Board, 2023), 2, https://arb.org.uk/wp-content/uploads/ARB-Competency-outcomes.pdf.

(04) Lisa Blackman, *The Body: The Key Concepts*, English ed., 1. publ, The Key Concepts (Berg, 2008), 117.

(05) Correlationism, "the theoretical tendency to consider the world only in relation to humans," problematised by the philosophical discourse of speculative realism, is discussed further in chapter three. Tania Rossetto and Giada Peterle, "Buildings as Non-human Narrators: Between Post-phenomenological and Object-oriented Architectural Geographies," *Transactions of the Institute of British Geographers* 46, no. 3 (2021): 644, https://doi.org/10.1111/tran.12457.

(06) Stefan Helmreich, "Extraterrestrial Relativism," in *Futures and Fictions*, eds. Henriette Gunkel, Ayesha Hameed and Simon O'Sullivan (London: Repeater Books, 2017), 178.

(07) Félix Guattari, "The Three Ecologies," trans. Chris Turner, *New Formations*, no. 8 (Summer 1989): 131–147, at 136.

(08) This starting point was modelled after the selection process used by Professor Pia Sarpaneva for her "House" Seminar at Virginia Tech ca.1998. The display of quotes rather than images by Sarpaneva was intentional, pre-empting students making decisions based on iconic or stylistic bases.

(09) Dali wrote: "Paranoid-critical activity: spontaneous method of irrational knowledge based on the critical and systematic objectivation of delirious associations and interpretations." Salvador Dalí, "La conquista de lo irracional," *Sí* (Barcelona; Caracas; Mexico City: Ariel, 1977), 17–30. Originally published as "La conquête de l'irrationnel" (1935). Reproduced in *Salvador Dalí: A Panorama of His Art*, ed. A. Reynolds Morse (Cleveland, OH: Salvador Dalí Museum, 1974), 49. Quoted in Ana E. Iribas, "Art as Therapy: Salvador Dalí in

the Light of Psychoanalysis," *Arts-Therapies-Communication, Vol. III. European Arts Therapy: Different Approaches to a Unique Discipline*, ed. Line Kossolapow, Sarah Scoble, and Diane Waller (Münster: LIT Verlag, 2005), 242.

(10) Guattari, "The Three Ecologies," *New Formations*, 136.

(11) The text for the brief for that year was written by the studio team Dr Alessandro Ayuso, Dr Dan Dream, and Martyna Marciniak.

(12) This is evident through multiple studies in experience-based learning, both in the arts and sciences, see for example Berk Kesim and Nilüfer Baturayoğlu Yöney, "Architectural Travelers: The Role of Field Trips in Spatial Design Education," *Periodica Polytechnica Architecture* 52, no. 2 (2021): 155–164. https://doi.org/10.3311/PPar.18861; This is also supported by paragogical teaching methods, enhancing peer-based and self-led learning that begin in the studio environment. Marilyn Herie, "Andragogy 2.0? Introducing emerging frameworks for teaching and learning in the global classroom: Heutagogy and Paragogy," *Global Citizen Digest* 2, no. 2 (2013), https://educateria.com/wp-content/uploads/2012/07/herie-2013-gcd-article.pdf.

(13) "Portfolio submissions will typically include an explanation of project briefs, conventional and exploratory architectural representations of the design proposals (plans, sections, elevations, axonometrics, etc.), physical models or photographs of physical models, digital models, visualisations of the proposal in context, computer animations, initial design sketches and development work, supporting research material, cultural and site analysis, technological and detail studies. … the final design portfolio … should be edited and sequenced to coherently describe the overall project and its development." University of Westminster, *MODULE: 7ARCH022W.Y Architectural Productions II, APII Module Description*, (2025): 6-7.; Further details on the nature of portfolios can be found in: Andreas Luescher, *The architect's portfolio: planning, design, production* (London: Routledge, 2010).

BODYGAMES: FROM ALBERTI TO ROBOCOP

by Dr DAN DREAM

BODYGAMES: FROM ALBERTI TO ROBOCOP

DS25 represents a provocation to the methodological and conceptual norms of architectural practice by asking if the interrogation of bodies, and their relation to spatial experience, can suggest alternative approaches to architectural design. Developed and advanced by its different generations of tutors and students over recent years, this questioning underpins the studio's perpetual reconceptualising of figuration and the figure— concepts which are explored through their applicability to the design process and their depiction in the development of this work. Notably, this approach is multifaceted, drawing on perspectives from diverse fields, both contemporary and historical. Around this, the studio's focus oscillates between material and immaterial concerns, echoing the interplays central to architecture's relatively short history as a clearly defined discipline. The work produced by DS25 thus far demonstrates how a methodological emphasis on the corporeal, in conjunction with factors of narrative and experience, can both critique and expand our understanding of the archetypal image, concerns, and methods of the architect.

VITRUVIUS IN THE CANON: ALBERTI'S DISEMBODIED INFLUENCE

Many aspects of contemporary architecture, including the version of the practitioner that is most commonly subscribed to, can be traced back to Leon Battista Alberti's *De re aedificatori* (On the Art of Building, 1485). In much scholarship over the past 50 years, the impact of Alberti on the Western conception of the arts has been considered as immeasurable. As a part of his emphasis on orthographic drawing as a method to detach the design process from the practicalities of construction, with his vision of the architect being delinked from the building site,[01] Alberti centralized an immaterial and disembodied approach in which ideas would be found in the mind prior to drawing, avoiding issues of presence and materiality.[02] An insistence on Virtruvianism was a central facet of his valorising of the intellect over the physical due to its idealised simplification of the body to a set of numerical relationships. This saw the corporeal subjugated to the flat surface of the page, being explored and communicated through delineated measurements, with the relevance of the figure for architectural design being neatly tidied up through a belief that its ratios could guide harmonious plans.

Although his prescriptions for the discipline were never *fully* implemented in practice, Alberti has "inspired most of Western architecture for the last five centuries."[03] Within the return to the body as a creative concern that marked the Renaissance,[04] during which Alberti's ideas can be firmly placed, his emphasis on orthographic proportions contributed to a paradox at the core of his thought: while a version of the human body was central to his theories through calculated measurements, this was an abstract conception that contributed to the absence of a comprehensive integration of mobile, physical, and felt experience. Alberti's all-encompassing emphasis on drawings as a tool for working at a remove from the muck and effort of the real world had further methodological consequences. Alongside its settling of the role of the nude for architectural design concerns, he also subjugated the architectural model to the surface of the page through its secondary placement in the design process. For Alberti, models were a tool to test plans guided by Vitruvian proportions, to ascertain whether further drawings were needed to resolve oversights. He described best practice as "models [that] are not accurately finished, refined, or highly decorated, but plain and simple, so that they demonstrate the ingenuity of him who conceived the idea, and not the skill of the one that fabricated the model."[05] His emphasis on the planar was extended by advising these models be made from flat wooden sheets and to omit issues of colour and decoration, these being factors that had a contentious position in the Renaissance due to their ability to excite the bodily senses, and with Alberti having insisted that architecture should be painted white.[06]

> *"models [that] are not accurately finished, refined or highly decorated, but plain and simple, so that they demonstrate the ingenuity of him who conceived the idea, and not the skill of the one that fabricated the model."*[05]

BRIDGING HYBRIDITIES: EMBODIMENT AS RESPONSE AND ALTERNATIVE TO ABSTRACTION

Through its exalting of the immateriality of thought over the inexactitudes of experience, Alberti's was an understanding of the body that took place at a distance—an opening in which DS25 oscillates. Importantly, as his prioritising of immaterial and proportional concerns became dominant in the intellectual settling of the Renaissance and the concurrent formalizing of architectural education, other methodologies had existed which would now be considered as "hybrid." Practitioners such as Ghiberti, Donatello, and Michelangelo had worked across disciplines like goldsmithing, painting, and sculpture, alongside architectural design, before the arts were divvied up as a key development of the era. These approaches relied on diverse mediums and distinct conceptions of the human figure, along with specific ways to explore and represent it.[07] While returns to Alberti are somewhat common by contemporary architectural thinkers,[08] with Peter Eisenman having referred to 20th century theory as a game of "capturing the flag of Alberti,"[09] an awareness of the wider framework in which Alberti relied on a cerebral reading of the body can be instructive for placing the designs that emerge from DS25.

This underpinning of the discipline as being tied to just one possible reading of the body is questioned by the agenda of DS25, with the historical intertwining of design with a curated reading of the body having contributed to the visceral and experiential propensities of corporeal experience being absent from the heart of practice. In both concept and methodology, DS25 works through a material-corporeal lens. The intention of this is not to arrive at a set style or fixed values, but to value the entwining of experience as a part of a design process in which multiple hybrid approaches can be explored. The studio acts as a midwife towards this by facilitating this exploration rather than being a dictator of its outcomes, as evidenced by the projects in this volume. In their own distinctly tacit ways, these proposals critique this history by modifying and expanding upon it. As such, DS25's central placement of the corporeal emphasises the role of history, not through rote repetition, but through critical and idiosyncratic engagement. Consequently, this is a twofold approach to the complex issue of embodiment in relation to contemporary architecture. As much as the studio looks to question the valuing of the intellect over the manual during the 15th century, other aspects of its output can be defined against the revering of abstraction that has followed the Modern era's denigrating of figuration. Although the rejection of the body from 20th and 21st century architecture has not been absolute, its occasional returns as a decorative device such as during 1980s postmodernism, have not been able to address the corporeal connections that architecture can foster. Instead, these returns have often relied purely on ornamentation, missing opportunities to explore the rich, tactile relationships between space and the human form. As returned to below, DS25 navigates this gap by re-engaging the body as a vital participant in the design process, ensuring that physicality informs every stage of the project. This means prioritizing hands-on experimentation, where materials are not merely used but are actively engaged with. By allowing for a more visceral exploration of form and space, the studio fosters an environment where the designer-as-body can inform the design, creating spaces that resonate on a deeper level. This sees the studio complement the visual aesthetics of architecture with a methodological commentary on the lived experience of moving through space, by way of numerous hybrid interplays.

EMBODIED IDIOSYNCRASIES: EXPLORING THE NON-VITRUVIAN & THE POPULAR

Key to the foundation of the studio was the absence of a tidy line between history and practice. Also missing was a tidy demarking of the academic weight of scholarly references with popular and cult reimaginings of the body. This saw tutorial conversations fluctuate and bounce between ideas of embodiment that, while not fully aligning, could lead to new insights and reframings of how the ends of this spectrum might be instructive as design drivers. Particular conversations come to mind when thinking back to these first years of the studio, such as Paul Verhoeven's *Robocop* (1987) being discussed alongside the body-games at play in Michelangelo's plan for the Campidoglio, and how these games were informed by a non-Albertian methodology in which a serendipitous hands-on engagement with modelling set the tone for a synthesis of moving flesh and stone mass in a manner unusual for its moment. Much like the bilateral symmetry of the body affords us postures and propulsions away from this condition as its starting point, the Campidoglio is a propelling play of axis and motion, with Michelangelo, as a sculptor, having seen the symmetry of the body (and plan) as a departure point for posture and not as the norm. This results in the rigidity of the project's plan being at odds with the physical propulsions and interactions that take place in three dimensions while navigating its subtle complexities. This tension between the static and the dynamic was reconsidered in a feedback loop with Robocop's hybrid physicality in relation to distinct flows of motion and form. Juxtaposing such concerns allowed for a creative identifying of the contradictions that arise when considering different bodies in different contexts, the relationships between biological and built form, and the parallels that can be found when considering the dynamic stresses and pivots that humanoid and architectural symmetry enables. As such, obliquely, the plays of stasis and movement, and the organic and the built which are at play in the Campidoglio can be echoed in discussions of Robocop, with both examples capable of framing discussions on how the boundaries between the biological and the fabricated can be blurred both conceptually and practically. Perhaps ironically, it was only while writing this piece after stepping aside from DS25 that I discovered Peter Weller, the mime-trained actor who played Robocop, had completed a PhD on Alberti in 2014.[10]

The point of such alternations between the references of architectural academia and popular entertainment was neither to confirm nor complicate the meaning of either. Instead, we looked to extend and effervesce certain examples likely to have been discussed in the other modules of a student's education with more leftfield examples. In a conversation on the practicalities of domestic space, Bachelard's ideas on the attic in *The Poetics of Space* were subverted according to its role in Stuart Gordon's 1986 body horror classic *From Beyond*. Bachelard's idealisation of the attic as being exempt from the mundane, and for the intertwining of memories and dreams, was thrown up against Gordon's use of the space as a breeding ground for horror. The *Poetics* version of the space as a realm for a retreat into the imagination was questioned and modified according to a less romantic conception of the psyche, as demonstrated by *From Beyond*'s linking of the attic with the saturated distorted bodies that are housed there as a representation of the darker side of human ingenuity. Through the creative licence which DS25 thrives on, Bachelard's notion of imagination is taken to its most corporeal extreme in this crossing over, with a domestic space being translated into a scientific abyss. In this, the attic becomes a space that, through technology, feeds on the imagination of its residents as a locus of dread and distorted physical terror. Projects informed by conversations such as these would not be required to adhere to either example. Instead, they would be encouraged to have a foot in both possibilities, often growing a third to place in the space between such conceptual ricochets.

Explorations of, and discussions on, the potential dimensions of idiosyncratic forms of embodiment are used in the development of building designs that display the narratives and procedures that went into their resolving. Sylvester Stallone's contrasting portrayals in *Rocky III* (1982) and *Rambo III* (1988), which relied on different agglomerations and distributions of muscle acted as further theoretical frothers. These examples' intertwining of physique, persona, and psyche, which have one foot in fact and the other in fiction, would indirectly advance conversations on the development of work informed by 15th-17th century sculptural references. By studying the differences in bulk dispersal, along with other factors such as starvation and scarification, ideas of physical imposition could be factored into narrative strategies, with torsos being used as devices to register experience in relation to the portrayal of character through sculpture. Tutorial discussions on the topic explored developments in the image of the male hero, along with the capacity of the body to physically tell of its "building" through resistance and impact. This tied into the aim of revising the contemporary relevance of the body through the development of idiosyncratic and speculative design processes which interwove the physical with the digital. Buoyed up by the visceral joy of the styles and methods employed by other relatives of the studio, such as Bernardo Buontalenti, Félicie de Fauveau, Hermann Finsterlin, and Nikki de Saint Phalle, the studio sought to translate theoretical scholarship on these designers, alongside responses to further examples from popular culture such as Brundlefly and Max Renn, into design concerns.

Juxtaposing such concerns allowed for a creative identifying of the contradictions that arise when considering different bodies in different contexts, the relationships between biological and built form, and the parallels that can be found when considering the dynamic stresses and pivots that humanoid and architectural symmetry enables.

EMBODIED MATERIALITY: THE AESTHETICS OF IMMERSED ENGAGEMENT

The unit's emphasis on the figure extends beyond ornament and style by incorporating the designer's physical presence within the design process, and the visceral responses that can result from engagements with impromptu physical modelling. Through these reactions and excitements, working with preparatory models has often been a catalyst in the studio as a methodological tool for addressing and applying its underlying themes. This sees ideas for designs found in matter being explored in further kinds of drawings and models, digital and otherwise. This corporeal-material emphasis positions DS25's design research within a broader epistemological framework that challenges the historical devaluation of manual activity in favour of supposedly superior intellectual pursuits. Recent publications like Richard Sennett's *The Craftsman* (2010), Peter Korn's *Why We Make Things and Why It Matters* (2017), Matthew B. Crawford's *Shop Class As Soulcraft* (2009), Michael Polanyi's *The Tacit Dimension* (1966), and *The Routledge Companion to Research in the Arts* (2012), edited by Michael Biggs and Henrik Karlsson, all address the marginalization of hands-on, sensorial and preverbal experiences. These texts highlight how the elevation of the mind over the body throughout history, including the Renaissance, has contributed to this marginalization, with a common concern across their respective approaches being the limitations of language for communicating the intimate and experiential nature of practice.

The studio values preverbal material engagements as a driving force for design projects, giving embodied experience agency within the design process. At key points in the year, students are provided interim output-based briefs in which they are guided on how to model fragments of bodies and buildings with a low level of anchorage to anything other than the serendipity of the moments that go into their assembly. In these briefs, materials such as clay, metal, wax, latex, and more have been prescribed before being fortuitously arranged, rearranged and probed in cakey, brittle, and sticky ways— their agglomerations being instinctively shifted and changed. Incipient arrangements would be brought about through a feedback loop with stuff being squeezed, screwed, or joined according to momentary hunches, as a corporeal game of call and response in the material realm. In being worked until they felt "right", these preparations were resolved in a present-tense relationship with the sensations of experience. Articulating these experiences in words can often prove difficult; it would be much easier to provide the materials and have you experience them first hand. Consequently, as a result of their challenge for linguistic description, the vagaries of bodily reaction that frame such an approach have suffered an intellectual neglect,(11) while having also been left out of the canonical architectural treatises.(12) In research on the importance of these felt corporeal states for our daily engagement with the world, it has been identified that feeling occurs, and physical responses begin, prior to rational comprehension; the body comes first.(13) The capacity of visceral flows and rushes to contribute to aspects of the design process are valued by DS25. The languages and ideas that can emerge when reflecting on this often have further consequences for the digital methods of the studio. The last century has seen the drawing board replaced with the computer screen, with the first version of AutoCAD having been released in 1982.(14) Programmes of this kind, and more recent examples such as Rhino, are entwined with rationalized and technical understandings of drawing at the expense of its poetic properties.(15) What the projects included in this volume show is how oscillating between the material world of impromptu modelling and the immateriality of the digital can lead work in more unexpected directions. Students in DS25 have assembled studies out of all kinds of junk, sometimes quite literally, to look for relationships and ideas in a three dimensional and experiential form of sketching.

In research on the importance of these felt corporeal states for our daily engagement with the world, it has been identified that feeling occurs, and physical responses begin, prior to rational comprehension; the body comes first.(13)

AN AFFECTIVE TURN

The aim of this briefest of overviews is not to present Alberti as a strawman for the rationale of DS25. Instead, the studio looks to build upon the conceptual importance of the body at a key moment in history by implicitly questioning the wider implications of Vitruvianism. Within the Albertian canon, countless fascinating designs and buildings have been produced, many of which are also discussed in tutorials. By understanding how the placement of a specific figure could have such comprehensive consequences for a wider disciplinary footing, the unit asks what happens when the defining of a speculative figural rationale becomes an integral part of a methodological process. Around Alberti, other practitioners carried different conceptions of the body into the realm of architectural design, often leading the design process towards notably different relationships between the model and the drawing, ushering in distinctly non-Albertian designs as a result. Predicated on an engagement with the past and the body today, DS25 presents a methodology with a twofold significance for the figure; the first being its corporeal engagement with design, and the second being its depiction of bodies as a fundamental aspect of architectural representation. While Alberti is unlikely to be a regular mention in the everyday negotiations of commercial practice, the stacked and rectilinear traits of much of what is built in London today represent a version of architecture with other interests to the corporeal. Such designs can be seen as resulting from an approach that is indebted to 20th century functionalism and contemporary building regs, and as a shorthand of contemporary norms.(16) The distance between the building site and the design studio that continues in our current moment can be seen as an extension of the Albertian tone of early 20th century Modernism which, while no doubt propelling the key concerns of practice into new territory, did not reexplore the disciplinary footing of the architect as it moved away from the styling of the preceding era.

The work of DS25 contributes to broader conversations about the potential of the embodiment in architectural practice, recognising its physical and conceptual implications for the design process. This aims to establish a continuity with architectural history by way of doing things differently. At its core lie complex interplays between the physical form, changing cultural representations, and the design process. The studio harnesses this as a generative force to explore relationships between the physical and conceptual, and the material and immaterial, while closing the gap between such binaries. As such, DS25 aims to uncover the rich possibilities offered by diverse physical experiences, fostering a more critically embodied and experiential approach to practice. References to various forms of popular culture highlight an interest in exploring the complexities of these factors in relation to contemporary society and storytelling. The importance accorded to the body in the studio is tied to a multitude of social factors. It acts as both a unifying force and a source of potential difference, capable of reflecting different backgrounds in gender, race, age, class, and environment. Ultimately, this approach offers a way to represent the embodied makeup of its participants. DS25 looks to excite and amuse, to engage the intellect and the visceral rushes and effects which define our engagement with the world.

NOTES

(01) The point has been covered extensively, see: Alberti stated that "it is quite possible to project whole forms in the mind without recourse to the material": *Leon Battista Alberti, On the Art of Building in Ten Books*, trans. and eds. Tavernor et al. (Cambridge, MA: The MIT Press, 1991), 7.

(02) John Shannon Hendrix, *The Contradiction between Form and Function in Architecture* (London: Routledge, 2013), 22.

(03) Mario Carpo, "Revolutions: Some New Technologies in Search of an Author," *LOG*, no. 15 (Winter 2009): 49-54. Architectural analyses and translations of Alberti can be found in Zurko (1957), Tavernor (1991) and Parcell (2012).

(04) Kenneth Clark, *The Nude: A Study of Ideal Art* (London: Penguin, 1976), 12.

(05) Alberti, op. cit: 34; "Leon Battista Alberti's System of Human Proportions," Jane Andrews Aiken in *Journal of the Warburg and Courtauld Institutes* 43 (1990): 68- 96.

(06) Alberti's comments on white paint and architecture are presented in: Hall (2000), 133. His architectural treatise gives an account of how to mix the whitest plaster which should "gleam with an amazing sparkle, like white marble"; Mark Wigley, "Chronic Whiteness," E-flux Architecture, published online: https://www.e-flux.com/architecture/sick-architecture/360099/chronic-whiteness.

(07) For various considerations of practitioners who have worked between sculpture, painting and architecture in different ways, see: L.C. (1914), Marceau (1930), Kennedy (1934), Put (1939), Rosci (1962), Spencer (1963), Beck (1967), Zach (1970), Weil (1971), Šilbajoris (1975), Wycherly (1978), Munman (1979), Greene (1979), Rykwert (1982), Davis (1985), Schatborn (1986), Lowry (1988), Ostrow (1988), Kristof (1989), Koortbojian (1991), Shell (1992), Davies (1994), Roll (1994), Jennings (1994), Jones (1997), Cooper (1998), Moskowitz (2001), Waldman (2007), Gossman (2008), Lewis (2008), Vinograd (2009), Abercrombie (2008), Payne (2014), Boucher (2014), Sutera (2014), Lombaerde (2014), Burke (2015).

(08) For examples of Alberti being used to frame contrasting concerns: Paul Emmons, *Drawing Imagining Building: Embodiment in Architectural Design Practices* (London: Routledge, 2019); Mario Carpo, The *Alphabet and the Algorithm* (Cambridge, MA: MIT Press, 2011).

(09) The University of Belgrade, "Peter Eisenman - Session 4: History, Alberti, Palladio (Part 1 of 2)," March 25, 2016, https://www.youtube.com/watch?v=6ppr-0LSij4&t=33s (accessed April 10th, 2024).

(10) Peter Francis Weller, *Alberti Before Florence: Early Sources Informing Leon Battista Alberti's De Pictura* (UCLA, 2014), https://escholarship.org/uc/item/0dm859tj (accessed April 12th, 2024).

(11) This neglect is considered, in relation to different schools of thought, throughout: Leder (1990); Johnson (2012).

(12) Michael Pollan has considered the architectural design process, according to Albertian and Vitruvian terms, in relation the physicality of construction and occupation: Pollan, *A Place of My Own: The Architecture of Daydreams* (London: Penguin, 2008), 248.

(13) Mark Johnson, "Embodied Knowing Through Art," *The Routledge Companion to Research in the Arts*, eds. Michael Biggs and Henrik Karlsson (London and New York: Routledge, 2012), 43.

(14) For the history of AutoCAD versions and release: Shaun Hurley/Autodesk, "Autodesk Release History," https://autodesk.blogs.com/between_the_lines/autocad-releasehistory.html (accessed April 11, 2024).

(15) For an account of mechanised drawing tools in relation to embodied practices: Emmons (2019), 217.

(16) Paul Emmons and Andreea Mihalache, "Architectural Handbooks and the UserExperience," *Use Matters: An Alternative History of Architecture*, ed. Kenny Cupers (New York: Routledge, 2013), 35-50.

CHAPTER 2: BODY DOUBLING

VIGNETTE CH.2: BODY>OTHER>

VICARIOUS BODIES
DRAWING BODIES
BODIES AS BUILDINGS
BODIES IN BUILDINGS
SHADOW BODIES
CONCLUSION

PROJECT IMAGE GALLERY

by Dr ALESSANDRO AYUSO and MARY KONSTANTOPOULOU

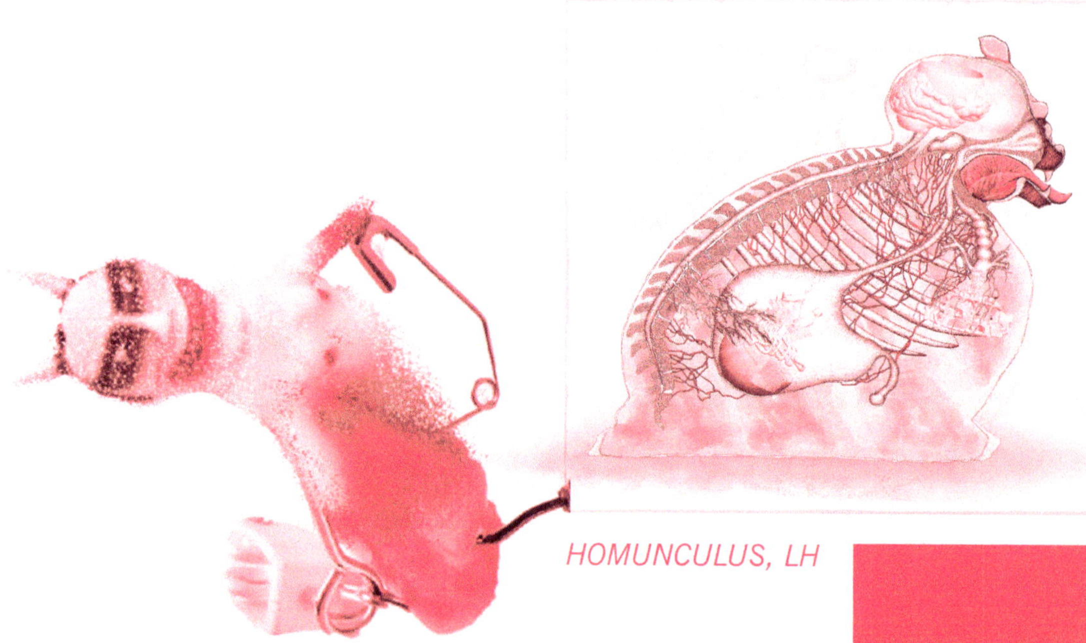

HOMUNCULUS, LH

VIGNETTE: CH.2

BODY

On the one hand, the body, as a singular, whole and bounded entity

stretches from its seemingly known shape and finds itself

invaded by, extending into the

OTHER

opening up the concept that the body sits in conversation with

duplicates

and strangers *in space*

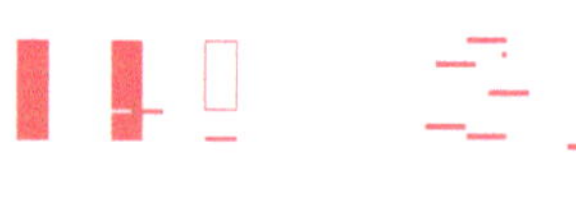

〉BODY 〉OTHER 〉ecosystem 〉world 〉

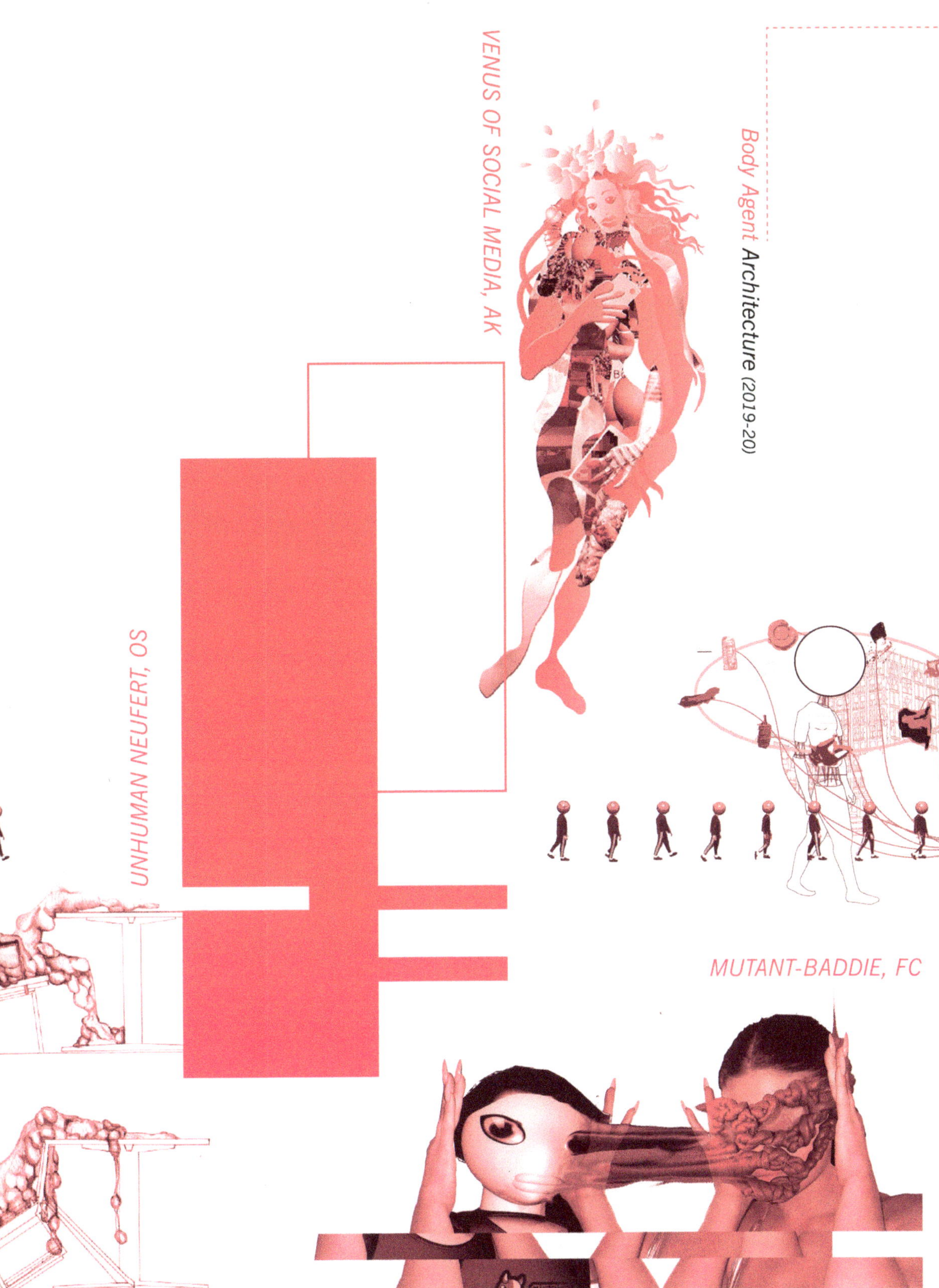
Body Agent Architecture (2019-20)
VENUS OF SOCIAL MEDIA, AK
UNHUMAN NEUFERT, OS
MUTANT-BADDIE, FC

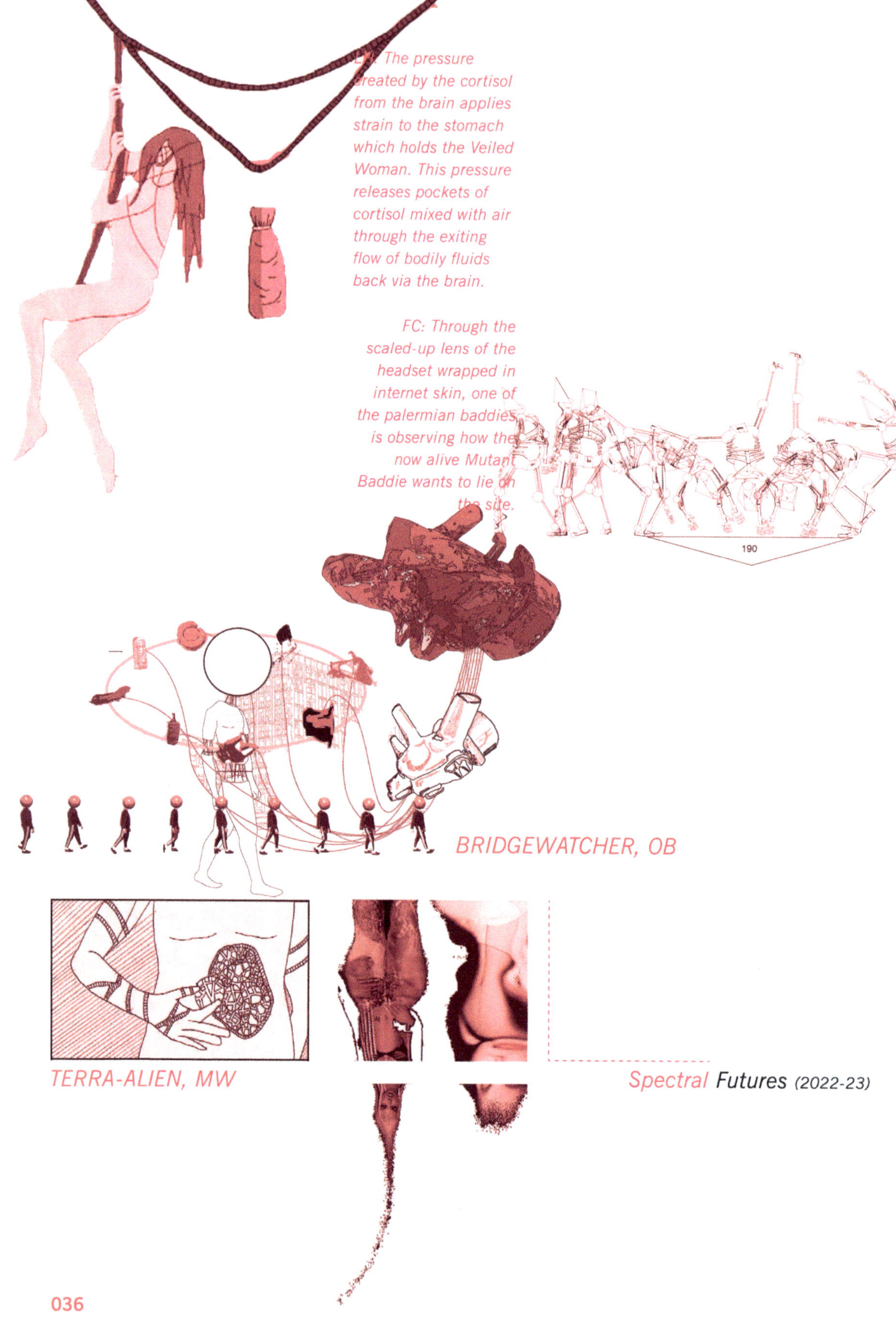

L[illegible]: The pressure created by the cortisol from the brain applies strain to the stomach which holds the Veiled Woman. This pressure releases pockets of cortisol mixed with air through the exiting flow of bodily fluids back via the brain.

FC: Through the scaled-up lens of the headset wrapped in internet skin, one of the palermian baddies is observing how the now alive Mutant Baddie wants to lie on the site.

BRIDGEWATCHER, OB

TERRA-ALIEN, MW

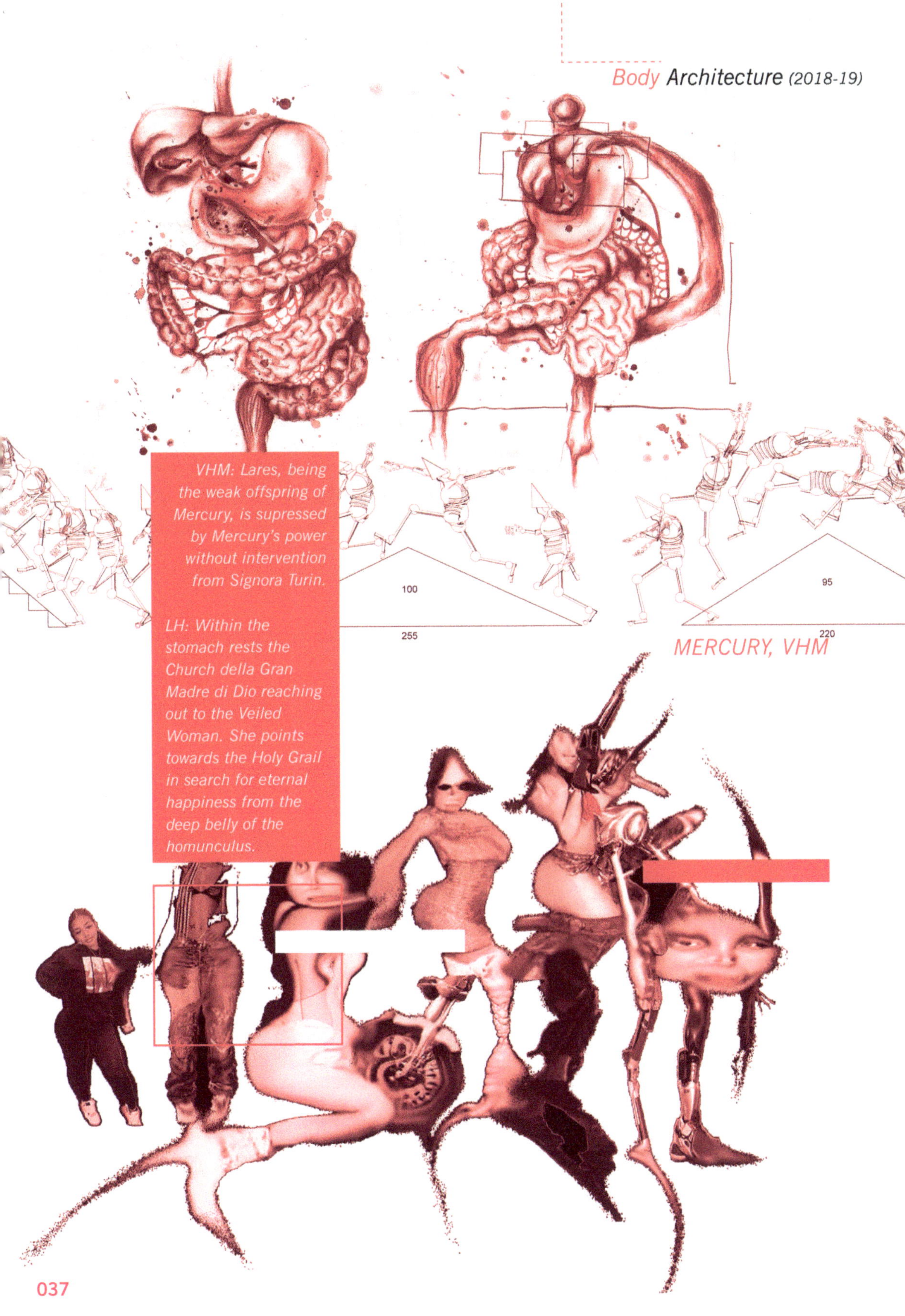

VHM: Lares, being the weak offspring of Mercury, is supressed by Mercury's power without intervention from Signora Turin.

LH: Within the stomach rests the Church della Gran Madre di Dio reaching out to the Veiled Woman. She points towards the Holy Grail in search for eternal happiness from the deep belly of the homunculus.

OB: Along with an interesting array of objects for the Second Body to begin to find measure in, the Second Body was also intrigued by the high social velocity within the area, and how a community had seemingly formed out of the domestic settings of the square.

MW: The eye projection of the second body can affect its vision, creating a distorted

projection of the world in its view and within its mind.. The origin of Gaudi's spirit in their inner eye is attracted to controversy...

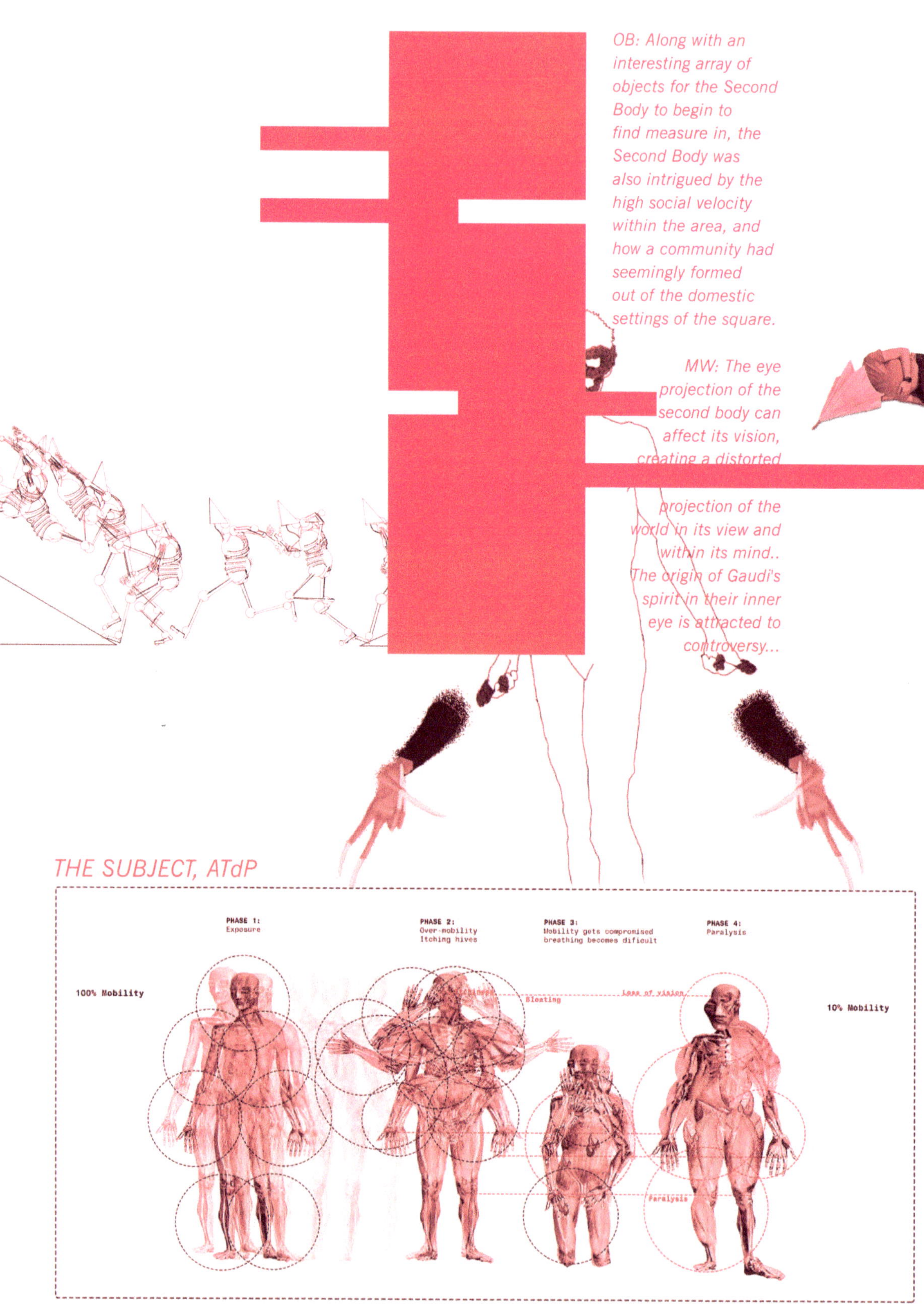

THE SUBJECT, ATdP

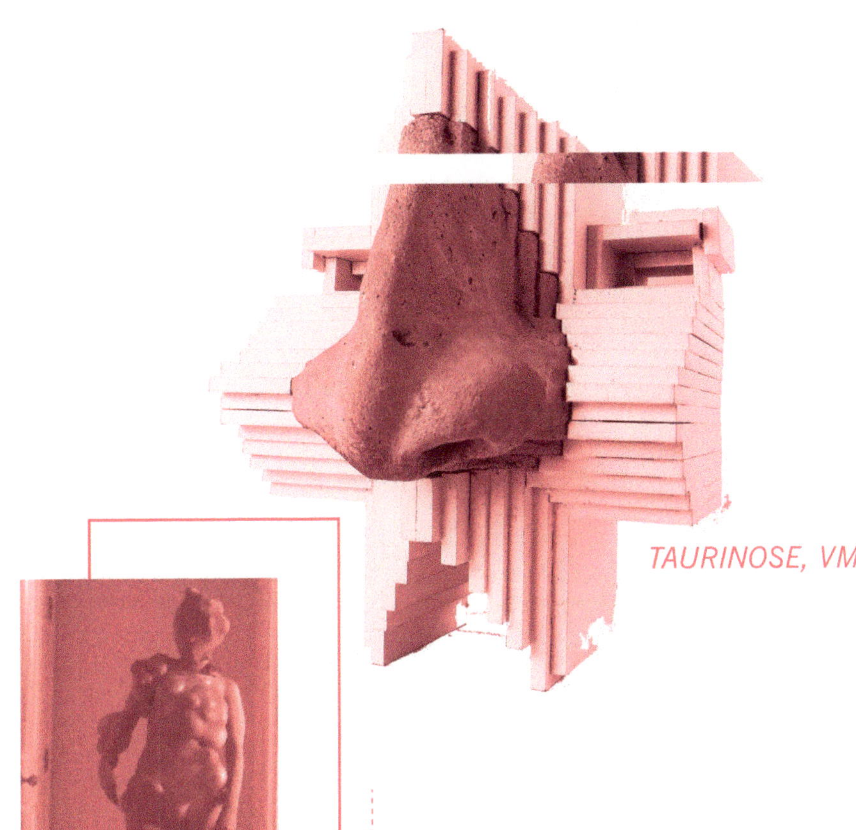

TAURINOSE, VM

Architecture's Second Bodies *(2020-21)*

THE COLOSSAL MOTHER, RK

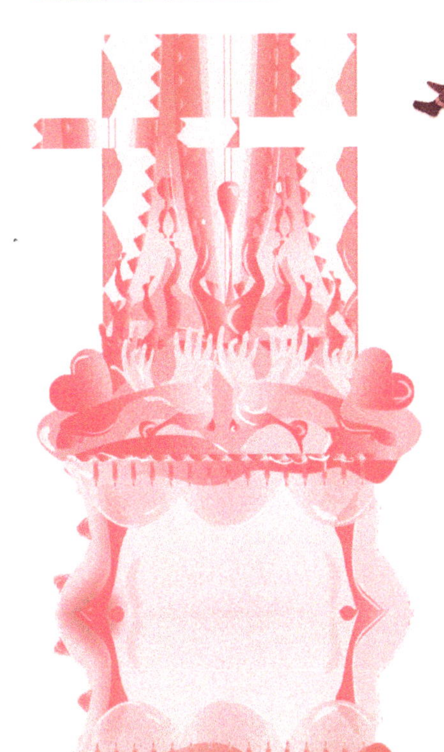

ATdP: I touch the cold porcelain of the model. I want the pollution. I want the allergens. I want to violently filter them through the new Chapel extension.

VM: A manufactured soft machine/creature made by the Taurini cult to record and deploy scents. It inhibits the spirit of the Deus Sensuum to bring it to life.

VICARIOUS BODIES

Outwardly, a body seems like a coherent, singular entity. Yet, certain vantage points on the body can reveal duplications, where corporeal manifestations blur and tangle with multiple versions of themselves. One such doubling can be seen in two bodies that are inexorably tied to architecture.

The first is the tangible body that encounters the world physically; this body inhabits architecture by sensing, seeing, and moving through it via active participation. The mind is part of this physical body; as proponents of Embodied Embedded Cognition theory contend, cognition is based on the interplay between body, mind, and world.[(01)] The centrality of this thinking, feeling body to human understanding makes it a central metaphor— or "metaphor we live by"— that is mentally projected onto the world to derive and construct meaning.[(02)] The predominance of embodiment in perception and cognition makes subjectivity— the condition of arriving at a collection of feelings and thoughts defining an individual— an inevitably embodied process where thinking and corporeal doing are synthesised.[(03)] This conception of embodiment reveals that subjecthood and embodiment are impossible to separate.

The other body is a simulated version of the first. These vicarious bodies are representations that impart corporeal presence into architecture; these represented bodies exist primarily through drawings and simulations. Considering actual, lived bodies, one could say that they tell stories; they accumulate scars, postures, and habits that compile the narrative of their becoming.[(04)] Through their incorporation into design, the represented bodies, reflecting the actual lived ones, are versions of subjects, telling stories through the appearance of their bodies and imprinting stories that situate possibilities of embodied agency for the physical, tangible bodies. Just as the vicarious bodies inject the body itself into design when they stand in for the physical bodies in the simulated arena where design takes place, the vicarious bodies implant an inseparable vicarious subjectivity into architecture.

An architect's drawing of a figure shows a particular conception of subjecthood. Throughout history, architects' drawings of figures even illustrate how the ontology defining subjecthood changed over time. In this respect, in much of Western architectural history, the legacy of the Vitruvian Man looms large in many guises. This idealised representation of a human in the form of the well-known, purportedly well-proportioned man was taken from Vitruvius's description from the first century BC; it informed Francesco di Giorgio Martini's sketches and diagrams in the Renaissance, and its image was then solidified into the famous drawing by Leonardo da Vinci, and then reiterated and adjusted for centuries afterwards by countless architects.[(05)] The ontology advanced by this figure, through its influence and direct representation in architectural drawings and treatises, stems from what we would now call Humanism. Perhaps virtuous in many of its ambitions of achieving harmony and reason, it is plagued by what now can be interpreted as insinuations of overlapping, problematic aspects including "univocalism,"[(06)] patriarchal values, an abstracted idealism, and an exaltation of the human as a divine model apart and above from the rest of the natural world.[(07)]

Another pivotal moment in this strand of architectural history occurred when, in the modernist era, in definitive drawings of the period, the geometrical boundaries once sparsely surrounding an arguable iteration of the Vitruvian man densified around and through the body of scale figures. These vectors became numerically definite, regulating the body as a mechanised entity. The quantification of the body found in these modernist figures make them not only idealised but normativised; data sets underlying the body image make it not just an aspiration or a vision, but rather present an ostensible, statistical truth. Just as the ontology of the Vitruvian man endures through drawing practices as a default body, so too the modernist scale figures stay with architects. For instance, the normative body depicted by Ernst Neufert in his *Architectural Handbook* of 1936 has been propagated through multiple other design handbooks and the standardised practices they engender over many years.[(08)]

Architectural history gives many examples of architects applying rigour to the aim of universalising, instrumentalising, and quantifying the body, treating it as a means to an end. Short-hand or ready-made body images may make design easier in the sense that they are readily available and predictable; the rules of thumb they provide can be a welcome salve to the dizzying array of responsibilities an architect encounters in day-to-day practice. Yet they also propagate a one-size-fits-all meta-subjectivity.[(09)] Often these standardised practices are arguably less about addressing particular subjects or even the body itself; instead, the represented bodies are cramped and deformed to enable an explicit agenda of the architect, or equally often, more inadvertently, their internalised (often unconscious) socio-cultural ideas and mores. To contemporary sensibilities— where subjects are likely considered as physically and ethnically diverse, neurodivergent, differently-abled, and with any number of varying aspirations and ideologies that cannot be presumed too much more beyond an acceptance of variation itself— the implications of imprinting normativity, universalisation, or a default neutrality into the built environment are already problematic enough to warrant a rethink.

There are more reasons to warrant a rethink of the default depictions of human bodies in architecture. The present day is haunted by photoshopped post-production "scalies" in renders as a cosmetic afterthought, utterly failing to meet the moment of imparting subjectivity in a meaningful way into the design process.[10] Furthermore, whether on paper or as built, inhabitable spaces, architecture designed with the figure as an afterthought leaves a lasting, skewed legacy to be further referenced and perpetuated by the architects that follow. The urgency to radically reconsider the representation of the body in architecture mounts when taking into account the changing nature of embodiment in the contemporary era.

Body Architecture, the first DS25 brief issued in the year 2018-19, with the studio teaching team of Dr Alessandro Ayuso, Dr Dan Dream, and Martyna Marciniak, proposed looking both forwards and backwards to establish new conceptual and material ideas of the body. The brief brought up the notion of posthumanism— as philosopher Rosi Braidotti puts it, the "posthumanist agreement" is one where "...contemporary science and biotechnologies affect the very fibre and structure of the living and have altered dramatically our understanding of what counts as the basic frame of reference for the human today."[11] Posthumanism is accompanied by conundrums with respect to the all-too-human spheres of society and subjectivity: social and experiential phenomena are in turn mediated by hybrid materialities and augmented realities, blurring the built environment with the virtual, and even with inhabitants' bodies. The brief asked how posthuman bodies could become agents for design. Spurred by selected precedent architects and artists, the ingredients also included a material and a verb. Students designed their body agents largely through drawing, performance, and animation.

The urgency to radically reconsider the representation of the body in architecture mounts when taking into account the changing nature of embodiment in the contemporary era.

Examples included second-year student Harry Matthews, who, for his body agents, designed satirically testosterone-supplemented body builders.[12] Poking fun at a caricatured, toxic form of hypermasculinity modulated by fitness and cosmetics, Matthews looked to Matthew Barney, his chosen precedent. Barney's *Drawing Restraint* project provided inspiration for a series of large-scale drawings made with prosthetic drawing tools. The process was filmed as a performance in the shared studio space.

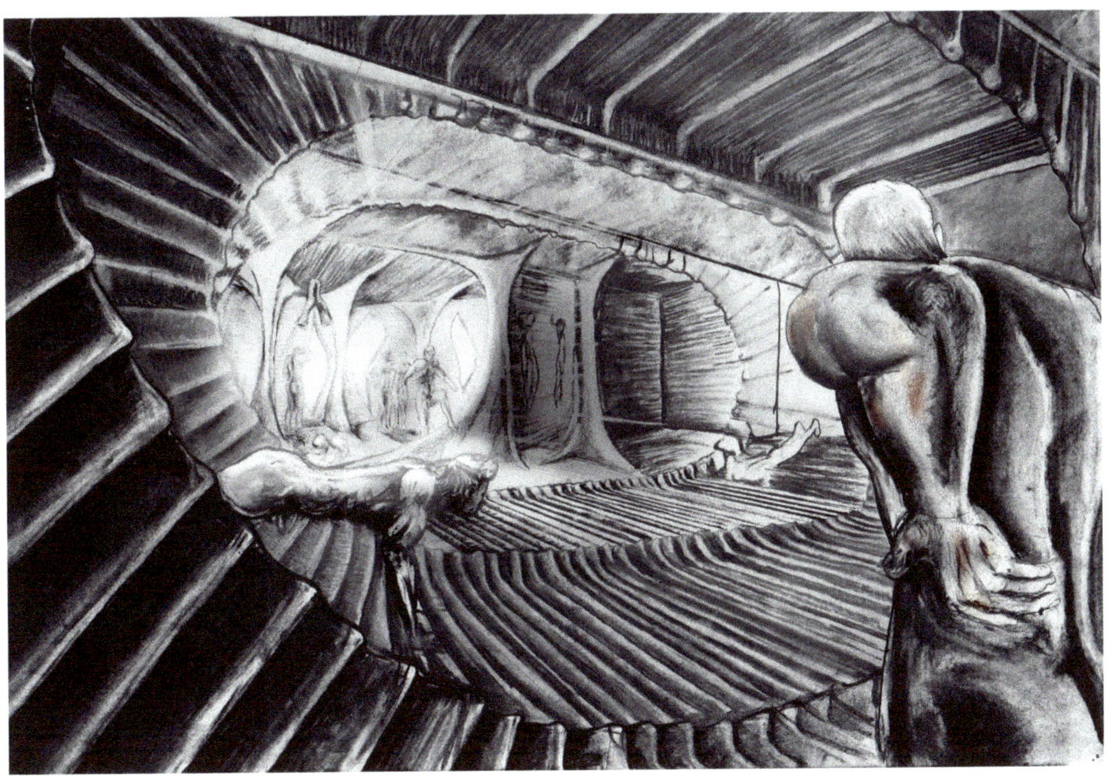

fig. 2.01: Matthews' testosterone-supplemented body-builders in the exhibitionist, hyper-masculine shower rooms of the gym.

The bodies that emerged in the depictions were also informed by those shown in Barney's *Cremaster* cycle, many of which complicated or challenged the hypermasculine ideal. Matthews' architectural proposal was a luxury hotel where the gym— taking the form of a central climbing wall carving a void through the high-rise volume— threatens to take over the building, and where the bustling showers become a place for exhibitionism, while the bar shown in the images remains empty (fig. 2.01). The weird sociability envisioned in the place along with the architectural language evoking musculature, makes for a tongue-in-cheek problematisation of gym culture and masculinity.

Students endeavoured to enact their chosen verb through experimenting with their chosen material; this directly informed the construction of body agent fragments, models that were understood as representing a fragment of their body agent's anatomy. In his project entitled *The Taurini Shrine* that questioned how architecture engaged with predominant historical narratives and probed the intersection of ornament and the body, second-year student Vishal Mistry experimented with cast plaster with the aim of better understanding the construction of the details of his chosen precedent, Carlo Scarpa.[13] Introducing clay into his material repertoire, Mistry made an image of his body agent that hybridised versions of Scarpa's trademark stepped forms with recognizable human anatomy; in this case, noses were especially significant to the overarching narrative in the project (fig. 2.02-2.04). The physical hybridisation of overt anatomy with the concrete, geometrical forms gave an uncanny quality where the human and the architectonic coexisted in a surprising way. Digitally-animating a 3d representation of the model gave it a further vivacious quality, mobilising the figure into Mistry's project site with a particular directionality and personality. The figures' vivacity and strange combinations planted the seeds for Mistry's proposal. Facing the historic Porta Palatina, Mistry's wildly ornate proposed tourist centre doubled as the meeting place for a group of historians dedicated to an alternate telling of the history of the city, emphasising the period where the Taurini, an ancient Celto-Ligurian population, occupied the region.

Students visited buildings alive with interaction between figures and architecture during that year's field trip travelling through Milan to Turin (fig.1.22). This included overt representations of figures dwelling in architectural space, as in the full-scale statues of biblical characters inhabiting the chapels of Sacro Monte di Varese, but also more subtle embodied presences such as those Carlo Mollino endowed in a dense network of interrelated details for his own apartment. Mollino's approach, where he designed sensuous, sculptural, and decorative scenes permeated by a spectral presence of absent, erotic, otherworldly bodies, became an important touchstone for later studio discussions.

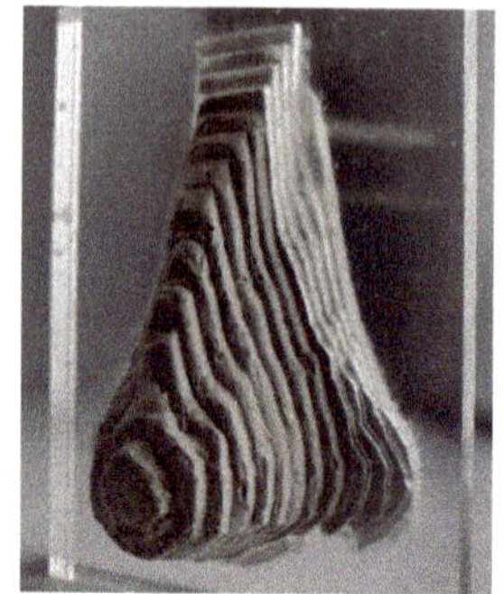

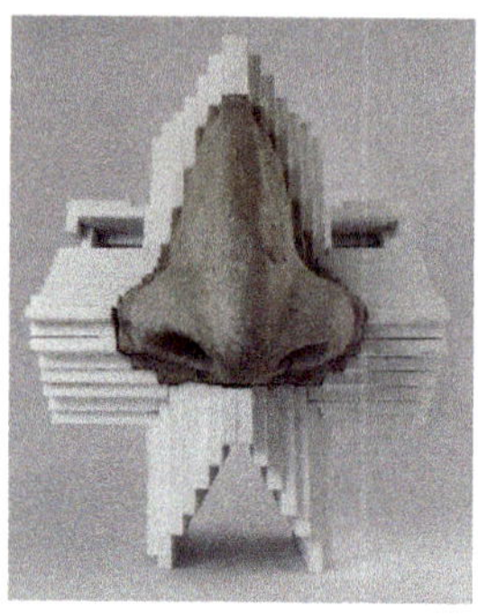

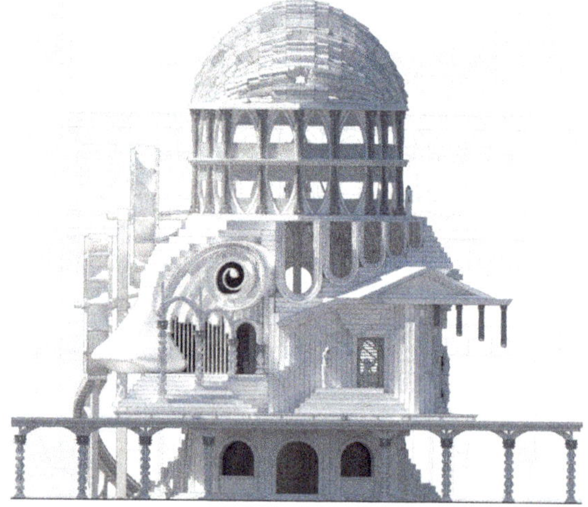

fig. 2.02-2.04: Top: Mistry's Taurinose model-making experiments. Bottom: The Taurini Shrine.

In Turin, students' body agents served as tools to analyse urban space by their deployment into sites via films, mappings, and models; these were crucial transitions from research to the design of urban building projects. In-studio seminars focused on camera tracking, where students' animated body agents entered the reality of their chosen sites through the production of a short film clip. From these, palimpsestic site study models arose, where each student's film stills were spatially layered, making the site reading into something akin to a miniature film set. Students explored the idea of "posthuman programmes"— meaning programmes not only taking into account the imminently technologically saturated future, but also the social and experiential circumstances they would contribute to— looking toward the city and its communities.

In his second-year project (see chapter two project gallery), Stefano Perretti used a variety of tactics to bring his idea of the body to the site and consider programmatic possibilities (fig. 2.05).[14] Perretti constructed a parallel science fiction universe with its own logic and constraints, grounded in an idea of the super-perceiving body, a concept based on the work of his chosen precedent, Haus-Rucker-Co. Perretti animated figures in the setting of the parallel reality of his project and then used the system of constraints derived from it to carry out a series of filmed and montaged urban drifts. Walking and viewing were strictly systematised; Perretti regulated his own bodily movements on-site to produce a film that transferred the parallel reality to Turin, locating points for his catalytic urban interventions (fig. 2.49). His project proposal for a series of parasitic micro-interventions throughout the city was meant to allow further super-perception of the city itself, urging new modes of seeing, occupying, and building (fig. 2.40).

DRAWING BODIES

Drawing, architecture, and the body are profoundly linked. The studio discussion, informed by theorists such as Frascari and Robin Evans, takes as a given that architectural drawings always involve an act of translation, where, through an act of material imagination, lines on paper become (other) physical stuff in the intellect and imagination. As a projection of a building idea, drawings are analogues to larger construction processes. A vicarious sense is inherent to the act of drawing; when a mark is made it activates a haptic sensation, the draughtsperson feels the mark being made on the page, and through it, imagines the feeling— the roughness or smoothness of a texture, the contoured edge of a profile, or the relative weight— of the thing that is being depicted.[15] How— and to what degree— the bodily imagination is involved in drawing depends on the method employed. In a body agent-based method the chiasmatic duality of the body being drawn and the body drawing becomes particularly important with an intensified relationship between the two; the drawn body and the drawing body are in communication through the medium of drawing, responding to one another.[16] In this respect, the choice of drawing tactics gains importance, as particular drawing modes set in motion particular potentialities between

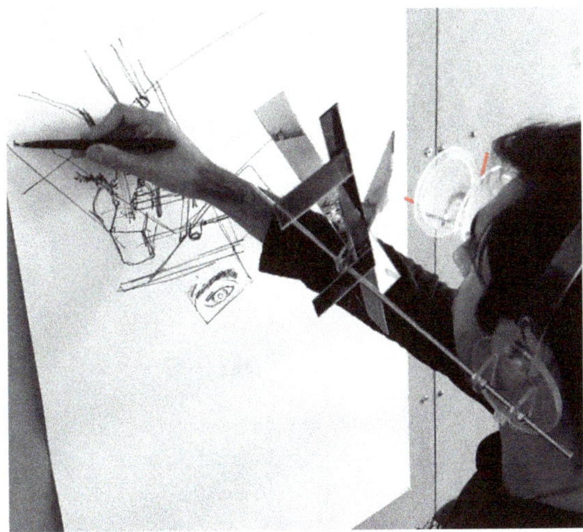

fig. 2.05: Perretti's Superperception Method in use in the DS25 studio space.

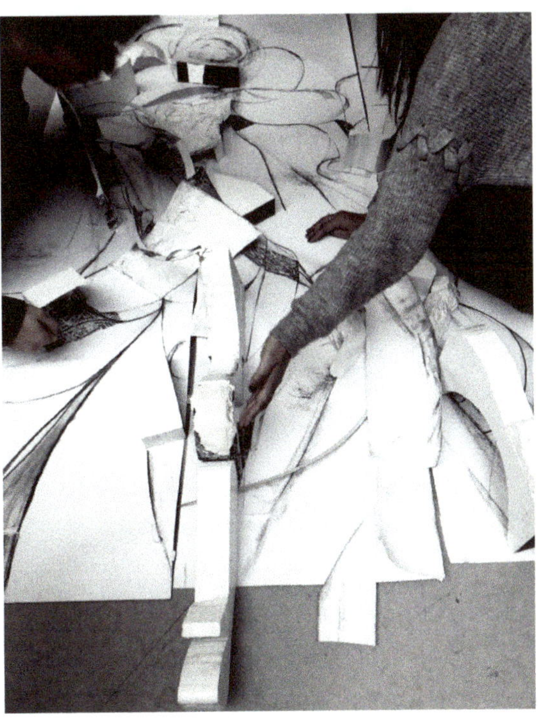

fig. 2.06: Kershaw's full-scale 2D-3D figure interacting with other student-designers in the DS25 studio space.

How— and to what degree— the bodily imagination is involved in drawing depends on the method employed.

architect, body agent, and architecture. Drawing tactics that can intensify this sort of embodied imagination include those that engage performance, play with scale, the design of ergonomic tools, experimentation with mark-making, or physical construction of the drawing.

The latter was exemplified by first-year student Laura Kershaw in her full-scale drawing of her body agent (fig.2.06), where through cutting away and making additions to the paper, her depiction took on physical depth.[17] Influenced by her chosen precedent, *Nude Descending the Staircase* by Marcel Duchamp, Kershaw drew using charcoal and pencil, and then altered her drawing, subtracting with a scalpel and adding volume and mass with folds and attached material. The emergent figure could be seen as both a figure and a landscape. These topographies doubled as a ground upon which to mine spatial possibilities for her building proposal.

BODIES AS BUILDINGS

Within the classification of the vicarious body made above, a further body doubling occurs. For instance, Frascari makes a distinction between two types of figures drawn by architects in the design process. They can either be classified as "metaphoric," meaning that they are models governing arrangement, proportion or form, or they can be embedded in design drawings as what he calls "metonymic" figures, where the depicted figure is drawn moving through and shaping the building.[18]

If the body can be considered as a "metaphor we live by," corporeal metaphors as underlying models for building forms and arrangements in the design process could be considered almost as a given. This argument suggests that as an architect conceives of their design, even at an unconscious level, they are likely projecting the metaphor of the body onto it. Subconsciously, too, the architect's understanding of the world is governed by their own embodied experience within that world, with the metaphor of their own body subsequently entering their designs in addition to generic or standardised understandings of the body.

A conscious tactic of utilising human form as a generator for architectural form, again, can be traced back to antiquity and through Western architectural history from Vitruvius to di Giorgio et al. From the diagramming, drawing, and rhetorical methods employed in all of these intentional design tactics, translating the literal form of the body to that of a building entails some method of abstraction. Through the utilisation of the system of orders, diagrams such as the Vitruvian Man, and treatises outlining the body-building homology, classical architecture in its various permutations supplied a method and vocabulary for this translation.[19]

In the context of classicism, architects strove to find perfect bodies from which to arrive at design form. But with the drive to attain the exemplar of this particular abstraction, both body and building could become distorted to fit the reality of the other. For instance, French Enlightenment era architect Jacques-Francois Blondel found "discordant physiognom[ies]" in Italian Renaissance architect Andrea Palladio's cornice designs, where, what Blondel saw as grotesque profiles of heads combined from many body types were drawn aligning with the contour of Palladio's cornice profiles.[20] Blondel found the underlying bodies imperfect in their apparently mismatched features. The perfect body that can lead to perfect architecture remains ever illusive.

In these instances where the lived body is ignored at the expense of an abstract classical ideal, the representation of the body is meant as a signification of a larger metaphysical order, a cosmological ambition rather than

What myths begin to emerge when lived, or even grotesque bodies, become the metaphor for architecture?

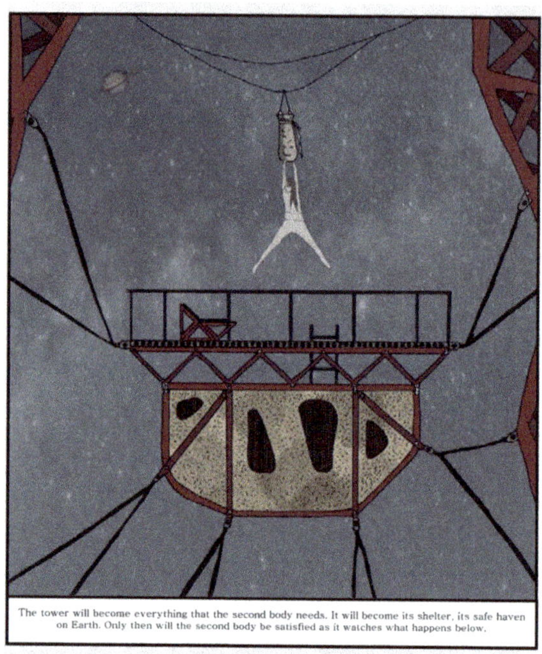

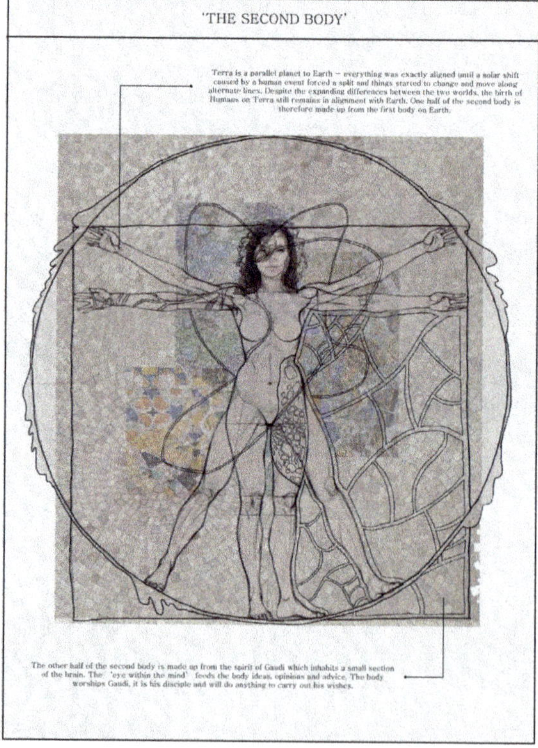

fig. 2.07-2.08: Top: The alien mid-acrobatic swing from tensile cables on Anish Kapoor's Orb. Bottom: Woods' Second Body Vitruvian-Female-Alien diagram.

a literal, lived reality. In a sense, the metaphorical body becomes a mythical body instantiated through tectonics, exerting its influence on the inhabitants of buildings that are based on this mythic corporeality. This prompts the question: for the body to be an intentional metaphorical device for generating building form, do the lived realities of bodies need to be reduced or ignored? What myths begin to emerge when lived, or even grotesque bodies, become the metaphor for architecture?

Students in DS25 have questioned how metaphorical models for the body engage the messiness and contingency of lived embodiment. For instance, in her first-year project, Megan Woods playfully engaged the notion of a universalised metaphysical body by appropriating the Vitruvian diagram (fig. 2.08).[21] In Wood's diagram the patriarchal, idealised figure is replaced by an image of her body agent, which she conceived as "her alien." The figure, ostensibly her, yet understood as an alien, had superhuman properties. The inscribed geometries surrounding the figure hint at the acrobatic paths the alien constructor takes in her leaps and swings as she builds (fig 2.07). Here, the figure is feminised, personal, other, and not so much bound by geometry as created and propelled by it.

In another instance, first-year student Lauriane Hewes designed a body agent inspired by the "homunculus"— a figure visually indicating the sensitivity of corporeal regions through indexically magnifying their size according to sensitivity, exaggerating what would be considered "true" proportions.[22] Hewes designed her body agent homunculus as a creature whose slug-like body, spine, bat-like head, translucent skin and internal organs became the metaphoric basis of the design (fig.2.09). Modelled in latex with its interior structure visible through its skin, the grotesque metaphoric body image resonates less with the idealised metaphors of the Renaissance described above, and more with body images identified with medieval conceptions of the body.[23]

Body images like that of Hewes' homunculus, with its lingering attention to the presence of organs that seem to be on the verge of emerging from the confines of the body, also find common ground with the philosopher Julia Kristeva's idea of the abject. Kristeva describes a decisively non-canonical vision in the consideration of the substances cast aside by the body.[24] Challenging the immutability of the idea of the "body proper," i.e. the notion of the body as a skin-bound, discrete entity, these substances are both of and out of the body, disgusting in their status as in-between the external world and the body.[25] Although the abject is an inevitable aspect of embodiment, the canonical body cannot account for it, and in fact might be canonical in part *because* of the omission. Following this line of thought, the reality of bodies is one comprised of disgusting, unpredictable, lumpy, fragile, and fluctuating moments. It is one of flux and growth, but also of an ultimate and absolute decline. Bodies are messy, aged, and scarred.

the reality of bodies is one comprised of disgusting, unpredictable, lumpy, fragile, and fluctuating moments.

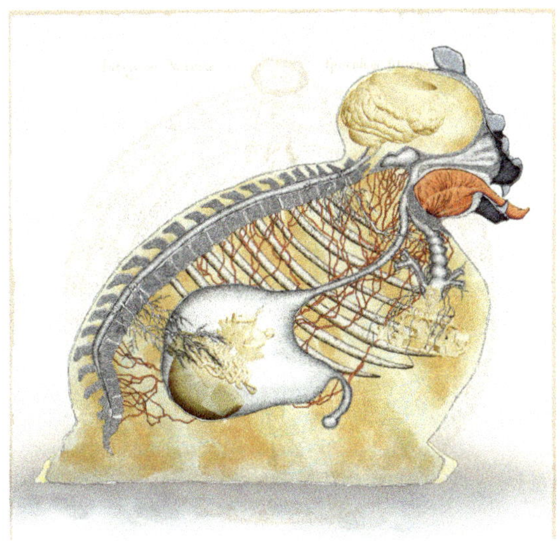

fig. 2.09: Hewes' "homunculus" body agent.

Whether intentionally conveyed by the architect or not, buildings, like real bodies, defy perfection, and in their lifetimes succumb to asymmetries, decay, ageing, and even— like posthuman bodies— to prosthetic enhancement and makeovers. Building waste can be found in all states of construction— for instance, through demolished debris and excess materials cast aside. It can also be found in buildings' occupations— for instance, through human waste channelled through pipes or into bins, and exhaust and rainwater funnelled outside. Therefore, to find buildings that reflect lived bodies one needs to look past shiny and perfect renders— more often than not being the main design process/outputs for the western-influenced built reality— and to acknowledge the body and the building in their lived realities. Could these dimensions of embodiment be embraced to generate new building homologies that relate to the subjects they intend to care for? Could these non-ideal qualities be allowed to flourish, and allow buildings themselves to engage the reality of the world that they sit within?

The brief for the second year of the studio's life, entitled *Body Agent Architecture* issued in the year 2019-20, and taught by the studio teaching team of Dr Alessandro Ayuso, Dr Dan Dream, and Martyna Marciniak, shifted the focus even more to the potentiality of the body agents as generative devices. Students were asked to draw their body agent at full-scale, bringing their own bodies into a more immediate dialogue with the one brought to life on paper. In one of the following first-semester prompts, students made what were referred to as Spatio-Temporal Recordings, which graphically combined urban mapping and interpretations of the speculative spatio-temporal perception of the site from the viewpoint of their body agent. These were enriched through haptic, material experimentations which led to the design of what were referred to as "Body Agent Monuments." The BAMs were meant to be examples of *kleinarchitektur*, structures that straddle the lines between model, object, and building. [26] *Kleinarchitektur*'s relatively small size makes it prone to interface with the body directly through its proximity and accessibility. Unburdened by much of the functional requirements and programmatic complexity of large buildings, *kleinarchitektur* can more readily distil an architectural language and even proclaim an agenda. In this sense, in their most successful iterations, the BAM designs could contain the DNA for the larger building project.

The field trip to Austria was particularly important in allowing students to see buildings alive with interaction between figures, bodies, ornament, and architecture. A tour of Vienna led by architect Evelyn Zisch included a look inside the interior of a post office designed by Otto Wagner, its entrance framed by two figures on the parapet of the five-storey tall facade, a visit to what was originally the Retti Candle Shop designed by Hans Hollein (with a facade that is arguably a visage), a drink nestled in the banquette seats of Adolf Loos' American Bar (a micro-interior relating to the body through its materiality and ergonomics), and examples of secession-era architecture. The visit to artist-architect Walter Pichler's farm was extraordinary. Pichler's drawings— where fragile, prosthetically-laden figures merge and interact with landscapes and other figures— [27] were already important references for the studio discussion. The new and renovated vernacular outbuildings housing Pichler's own figural sculptures sited in the farm were exquisite examples of *kleinarchitektur*, as well as the interrelation of both actual and represented bodies and buildings. Students were able to visit the Pichler-designed MAK courtyard door (fig. 2.10), the drawings of which were studied that year in the studio, in which the figures are drawn as dynamic agents, both taking part in and physically relating to the design process. In Graz, a visit to the Cook- and Fournier- designed Kunsthaus Graz foreshadows a studio interest in "friendly aliens." There, students also visited the Vito Acconci-designed artificial island of Murinsel, an organ-like composition with capsule bathrooms that brought up intriguing ideas about body-building analogies and interactions.

The final projects in the studio that year, sited in

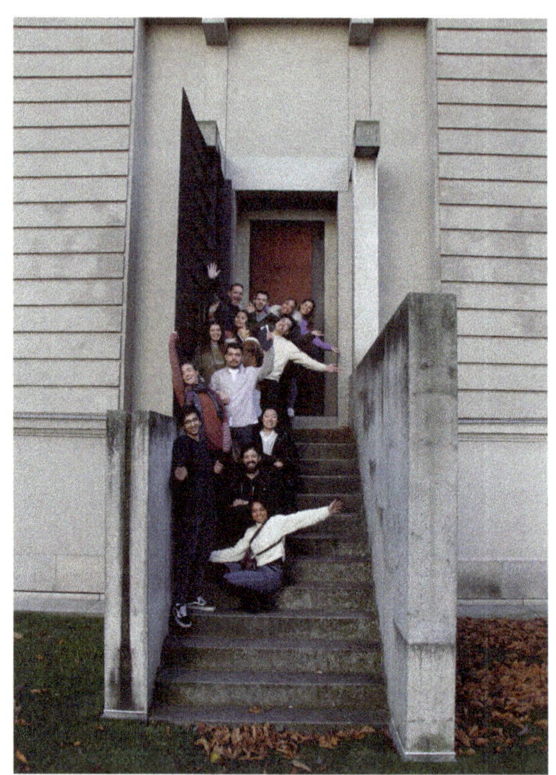

fig. 2.10: DS25 students in front of the door to the MAK courtyard designed by Pichler, Vienna.

and around Mile End Park, were purposefully holistic with respect to their programmes, styles, and media, and were driven by each student's individual investigation. For instance, Hewes' second-year project (see chapter three project gallery) considered a posthuman realignment of animal-human relationships using a series of ergonomic details as the starting point for a show-home targeted at families of single "parents" and their prosthetically-augmented ailuranthropic cats (fig. 3.37).[28] Exploring the therapeutic potential of architecture, second-year student Daniel Buban Ngu's project (see chapter four project gallery) melded surrealism and high modernism to imagine an Alzheimer's patients' home where figurative architecture evokes memories and aids in navigation (fg. 4.24).[29]

Inspired by nineteenth century flaneur culture and research on London's past culture of sex cinemas, Alexandros Tzortzis de Paz's first-year project (see chapter two project gallery) probed architecture's potential to provide pleasure, envisioning a hidden, doll-burlesque theatre where the architecture plays a role in seducing visitors to venture ever deeper into its hedonistic and fetishistic world (fig. 2.11-2.13, 2.18).[30] Tzortzis de Paz looked into the perverse puppets of Hans Bellmer; noting their crustacean qualities, he began considering fleshy architecture augmented by integuments and exoskeletons, which he brought to life through detailed pencil hand drawings.

Ryan Kyberd explored the lived body-building analogy in his first-year project.[31] Inspired by the paintings and animations of Madelon Vriesendorp, where buildings are personified and even imagined having illicit affairs, Kyberd considered colossal buildings that could give birth. Inspired by Frascari's writings on the etymological association between the words angle and angel,[32] Kyberd constructed a template with the profile of an angel drawn by Scarpa to draw 1:1 scale parts of a colossal body. He placed the drawings to scale in the Westminster studios, with the eye near the lecture theatre and the foot on the other end of the building (fig. 2.19). Kyberd proposed that a building is born, just like a human child, as a combination of its ancestors and the context it is found in. Kyberd imagined two buildings as parents to his gestating building proposal. He acted out the birthing process, imagining the landscape of Mile End Park as a maternal figure pregnant with an underground building (fig. 2.20). Kyberd's sectional physical model of the plaster-cast pregnant belly of the site uncovered underground chambers of the womb with the yet unborn baby-building inside. The latter— made of bent metal, wood, and paper parts— hinted at the DNA of the mother-building which seems to have collapsed on the site, its ruins in time becoming consumed by the landscape (fig. 2.14). In this case, *kleinarchitectur* was the child-building which contained both the genetic, ancestral references and the new, combined language for the adult-building proposed in the second semester. Kyberd's experiment questioned the influence that architects' personal identities exert on the designs of buildings, whether consciously or unconsciously, mirroring architectural trends and financial and regulatory challenges.

The building's growth referenced organic ageing processes, as Kyberd explains in his project portfolio: "…in each phase of construction the part of the building will be closed off with a flexible latex covering, like a scab covering an open wound, ready for the next phase of growth."[33] In Kyberd's performance of the birth the swollen landscape topography became the pregnant abdomen. In the association of architectural genesis and pregnancy,

Could these non-ideal qualities be allowed to flourish, and allow buildings themselves to engage the reality of the world that they sit within?

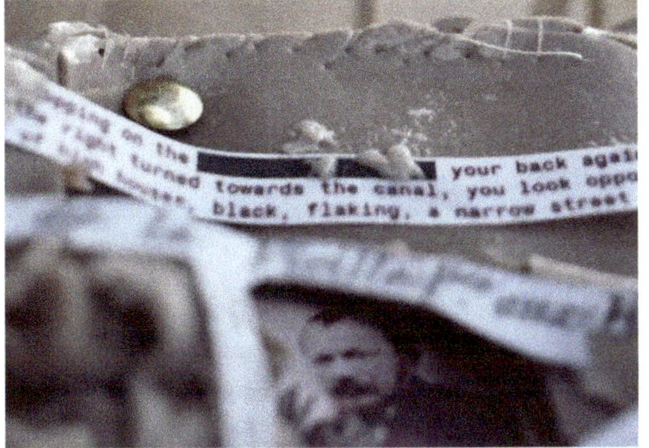

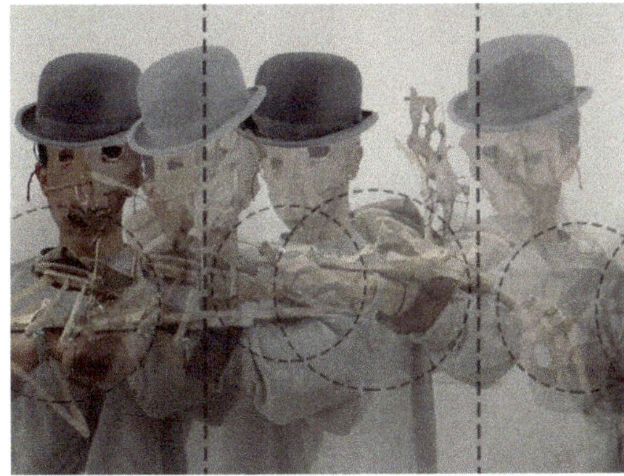

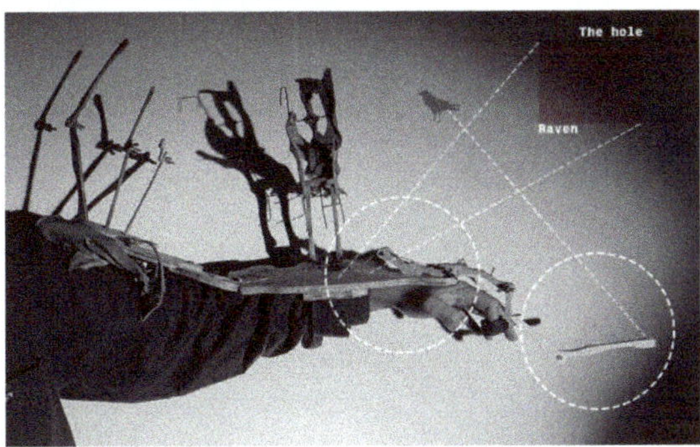

fig. 2.11-2-13: Tzortzis de Paz's poetic prosthetic and latex mask designed to help him become the Flaneur on his site drift guided by a cut up poem by Alexandre Dumas.

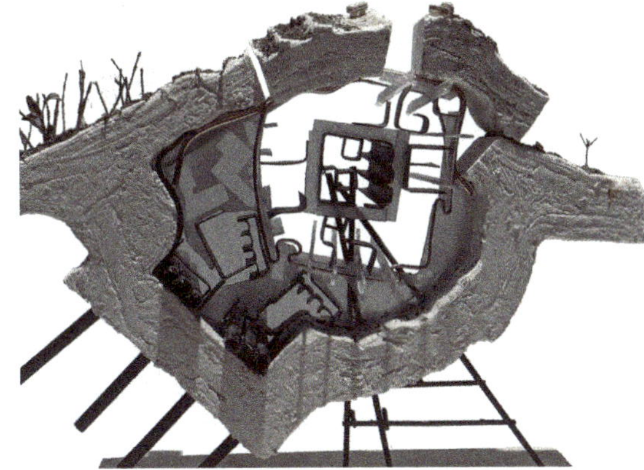

fig. 2.14: Kyberd's cast of the ground filled with the architecture plans of the mother and the baby. The growth of the baby has pressed on the spine / cores of the mother distorting the plan.

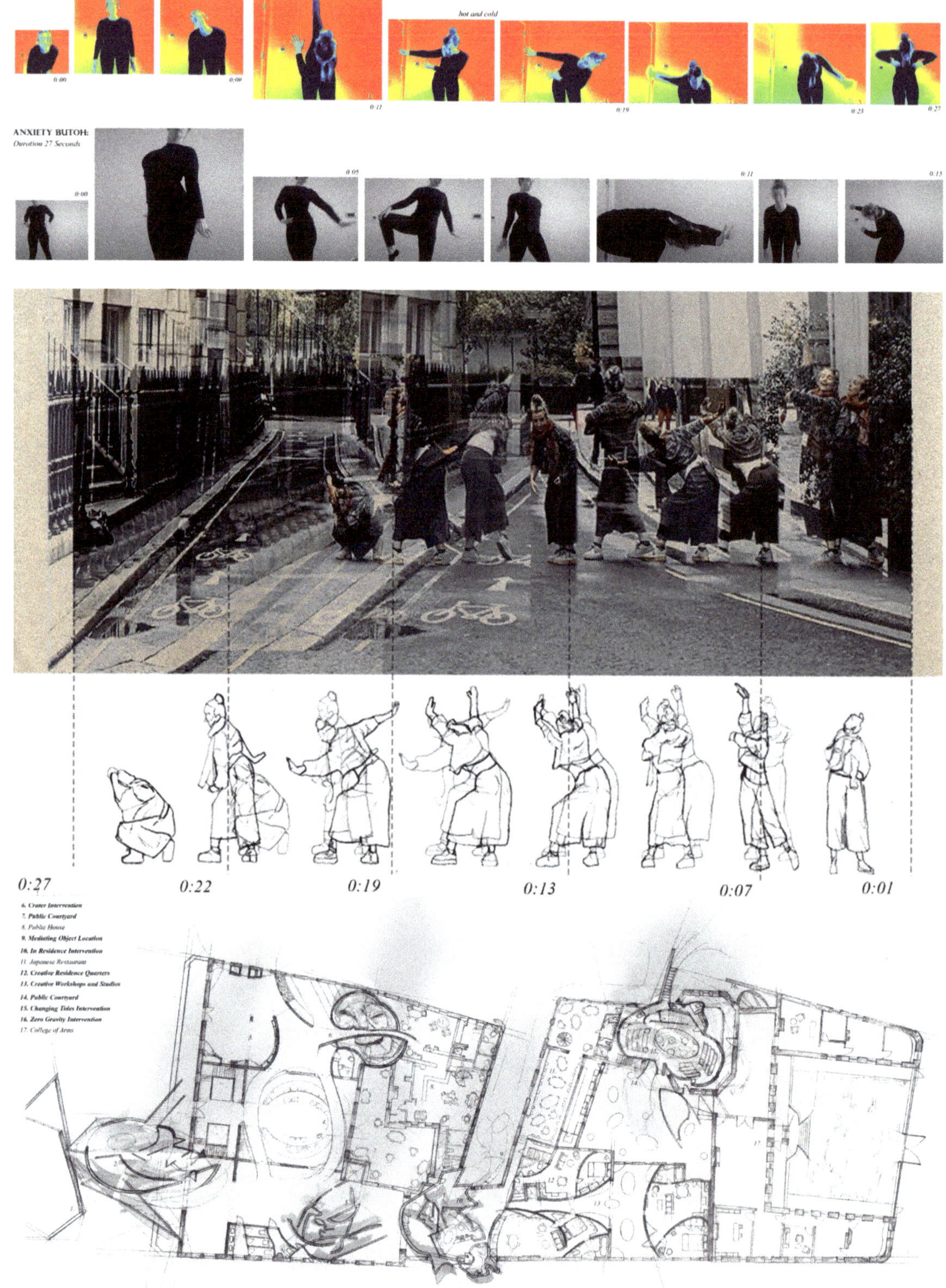

fig. 2.15-2.18: Kershaw's architecture was influenced by her body's recorded movements of dance on site. Facing page: Tzortzis de Paz's interior view of the Doll Stage.

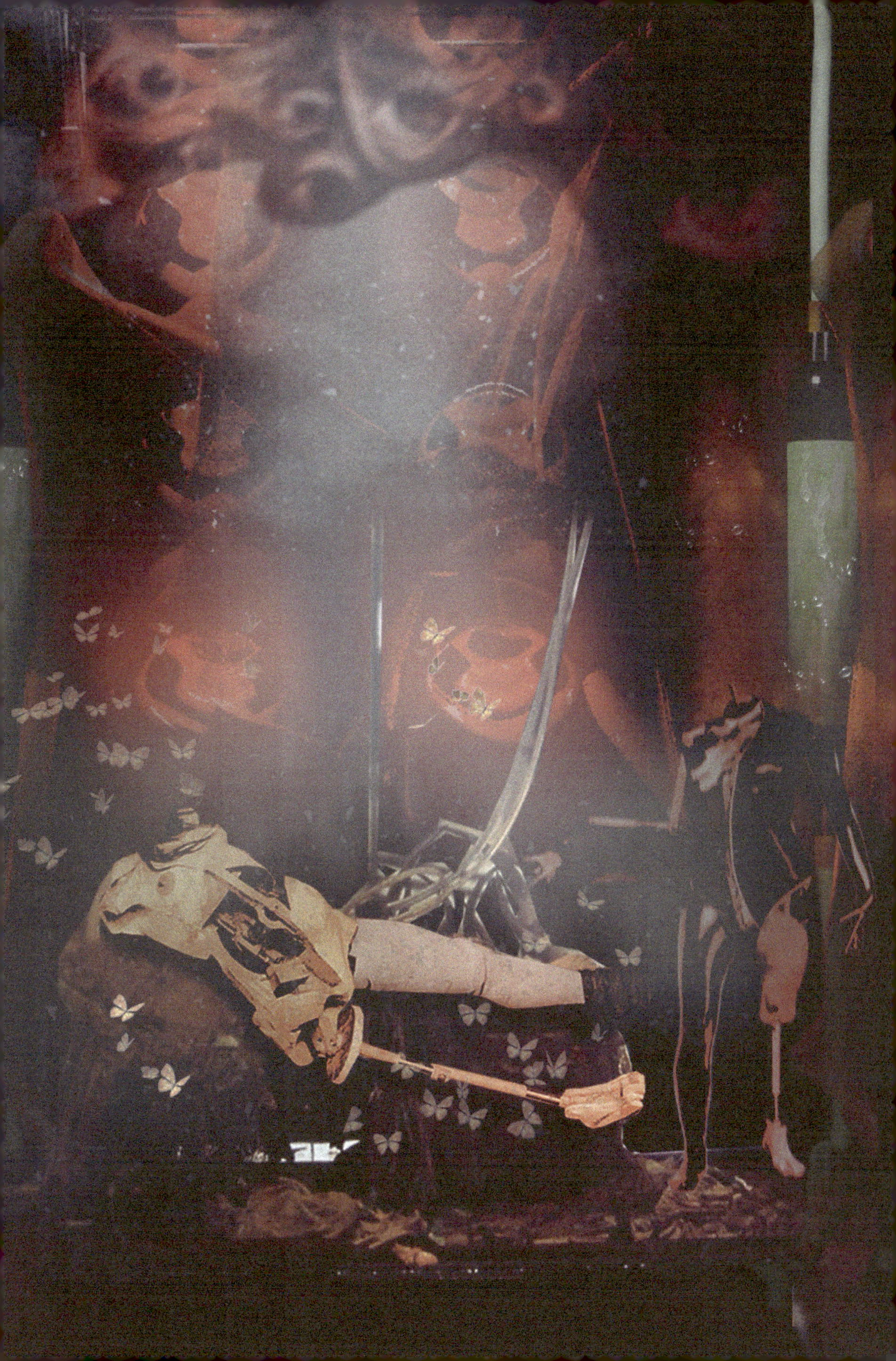

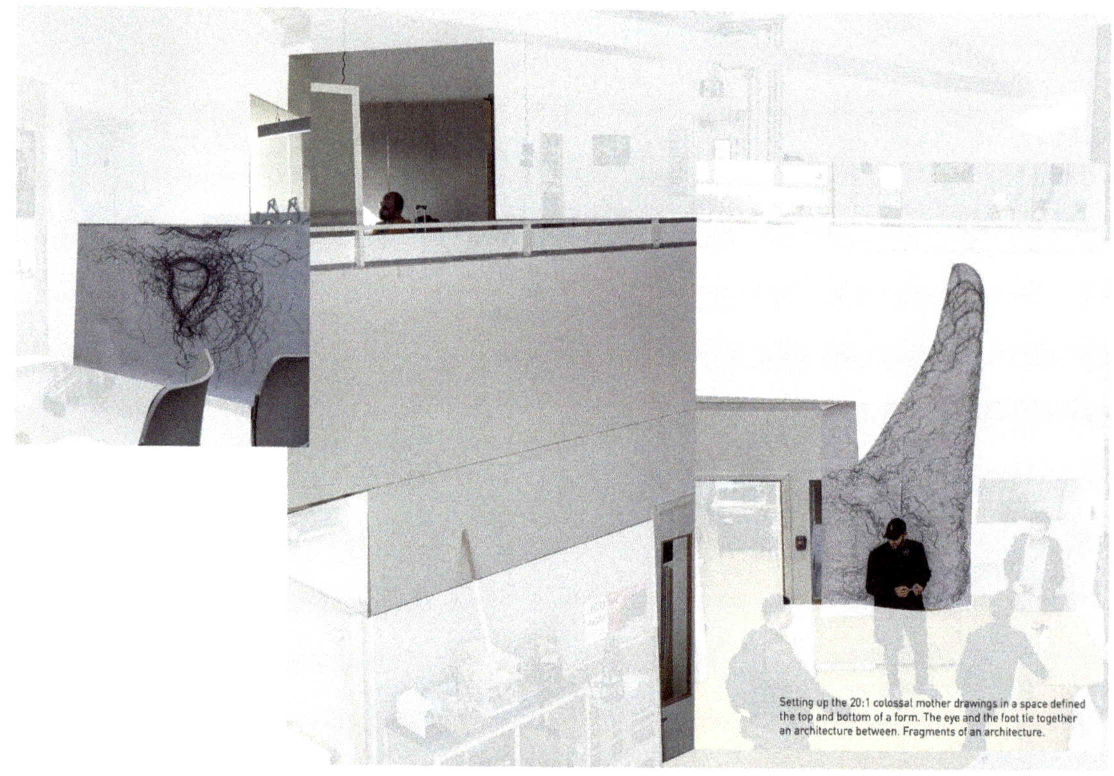

fig. 2.19: Kyberd's Colossus in the studio, drawn from angle/angels using his customised drawing tool based on Frascari's methodologies.

Kyberd's project brings to mind the Renaissance architect Filarete, who in his *Trattato di Architettura*, written in 1464, likened the architect to a pregnant mother.

BODIES IN BUILDINGS

For Frascari, the metonymic figure is one that is drawn moving through architecture; as the architect responds to their depiction of the figure, the metonymic figure catalyses design changes, effectively shaping the design.(34) Frascari points out the existence of a cast of characters in Scarpa's drawings— from self portraits to nude dancers— whose roles and reappearances are consistent through his sets of drawings for a series of projects.(35) Frascari notes that, in instances when there was the design of a detail that needed particular concentration, Scarpa drew his floating profile looking at that detail.(36) In such moments, the architect intentionally projects their own bodily sensibility into the drawn figure. The intentional inclusion of the self and groups of protagonists as specifically imagined relational others are techniques that turn drawn figures into enablers of imaginal and empathetic connections between the designer's body, inhabitants or users, and the building. Through the act of drawing them in burgeoning designs and investing them with meaning, they aid in the weaving of a continuous thread of experience, tectonics, and time in the imagination of the architect.

Scarpa's practice suggests that each figure is meant to bring a particular sensibility or subjectivity to bear on the design. Body agents take this assumption further: the figure becomes an alter-ego, a methodological device of a cultivated persona that allows an author to access an expanded, alternate viewpoint or set of parameters. Alter-egos are not so much a detachment from the self as they are a multiplying or versioning of it.

As alter-egos, body agents often mirror the author's body, evoking an uncanny quality, where the drawn body appears as a version of the self. This is more than a depiction of an Other imprinted with characteristics of the author's physical and psychical self. The medium stretches the designer's body into a new materialisation in two-dimensional space, making the image of a new being tied to the designer in particular ways. In the process of drawing throughout a project, as the body agent is depicted moving across drawings of different scales, media, and projection types, the figure's outline shifts, developing its contours to respond to evolving spatial parameters. These shifts are dependent on the time and tools that the designer's "actual" body activates to bring the figure to life. The figure's changes track the designer's thought process, mood,

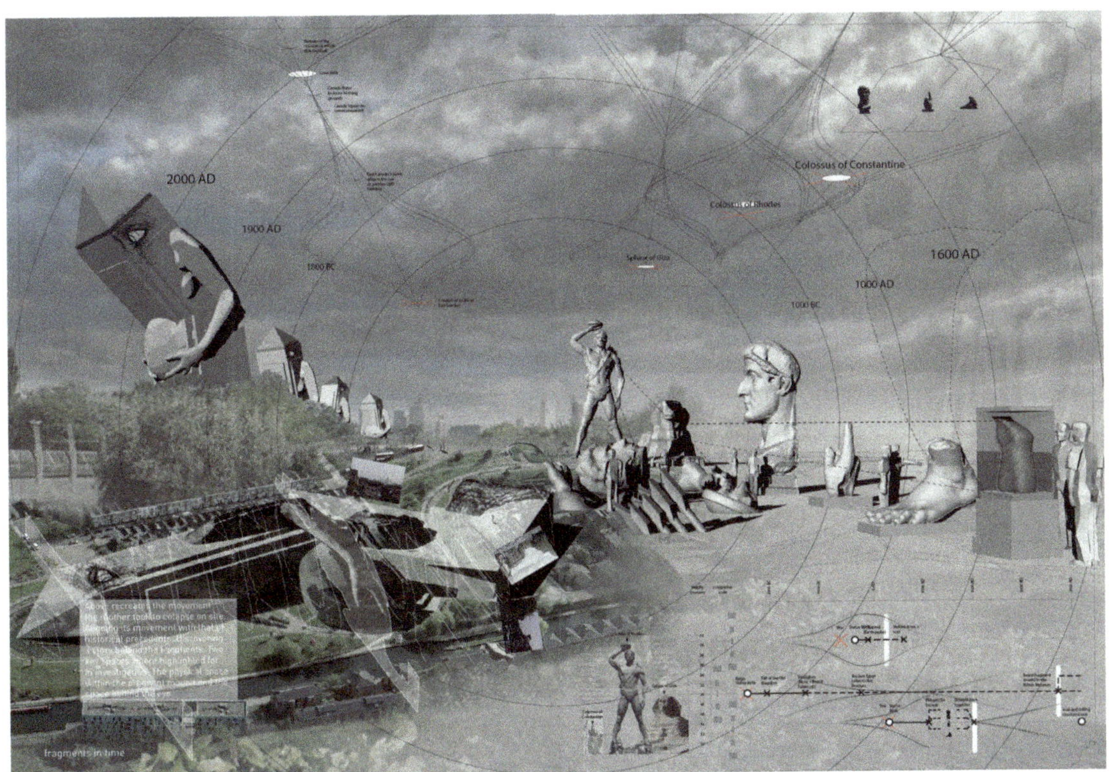

fig. 2.20: "Fragments in time," Kyberd's composite drawing of the mother-colossus on Mile End Park.

Alter-egos are not so much a detachment from the self as they are a multiplying or versioning of it.

posture, and deepened understanding of themselves and of their body agent at a particular moment. The figure need not always be visible, but from the moment of its birth in relation to an architectural problem, it leaves residual traces from how it imprints its presence on the designed space.(37)

The drawn figure could be thought to behave like a shadow; not always fully seen and sensed, but always mirroring the shape of the "real" body. With a material ambiguity akin to a shadow that exists perceptibly and materially, yet is fleeting and ungraspable, the drawn figure assumes its role. By consciously attempting to decipher the figure's hazy qualities and sharpen its fuzzy edges, the uncanny quality of real bodies emerges, and the essence of the designer's duplicate might appear out of the corner of their eye— a materialisation of the character Lorna's statement in Russel Hoban's novel *Riddley Walker*: "theres some thing in us it dont have no name … it aint us but yet its in us."(38)

To cultivate an alter-ego involves investing the represented figure with intensified meaning; one way to do this is to intentionally write the figure's backstory, allowing the narrative of the figure to take on more substance and affect. The representation, writing, and animating of an other body to some extent will always be a mirroring of the author's body, imparted into the image of the Other, as also occurs in the relationship between architect and building during the design process discussed in the "Bodies as Buildings" subchapter above. If this process is taken to its utmost, through layered and rigorous production methods, as Dr Dream's essay notes, an interchangeability of viewpoints and experiences begins to occur, where the boundary between the self and the imagined Other becomes reflexive. Philosopher Gilles Deleuze recognized a "double-becoming" inherent to the creation of this imagined Other, where, as the imagined Other is developed, so too is the self.(39) Designing with a body agent can enable realisation and a delving into specific aspects of the self, but the idea of double-becoming suggests the methodology even involves an expansion of the scope of the self. Leading towards a stepping outside of the self, the cultivation of alter-egos can become a tool used to avoid succumbing to a neutral, global point of view, or as a tool for defamiliarisation.

For example, in Hewes' second-year project (discussed above and further in chapter four), the alternate version of herself portrayed in her project helped to problematise and personalise the issue of animal-human relationships. Hewes drew a human figure with a cultish devotion to her cats; a cat owner and millennial, the figure was reminiscent of herself (fig. 3.09). Hewes designed anthropomorphic prosthetics for the cats, as they became increasingly like "children" for their doting "parent" (fig. 2.21). In the narrative images, the figure also donned accoutrements that made her appear more catlike. The architectural language of the domestic showroom was devoted to the exaltation of the ailuranthropic lifestyle and the cats themselves, instantiating a double-becoming in the design of both body and architecture.

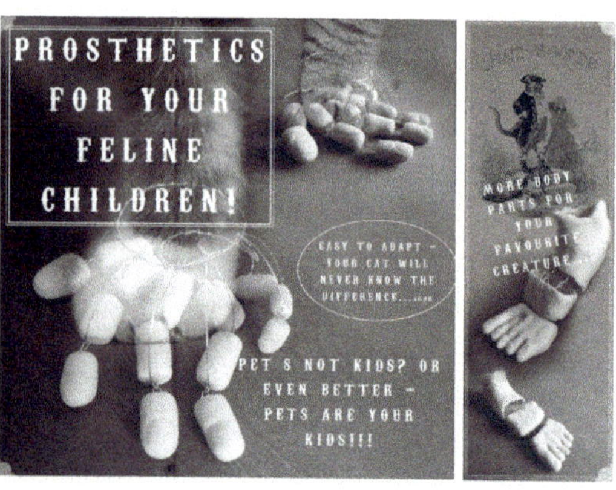

fig. 2.21: Hewes' feline-human prosthetics advertised in that week's Meowspaper.

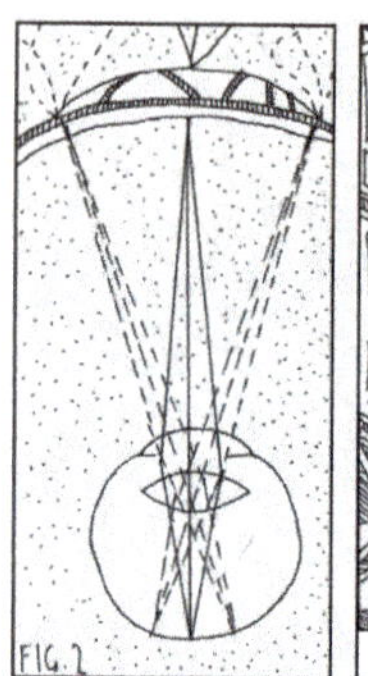

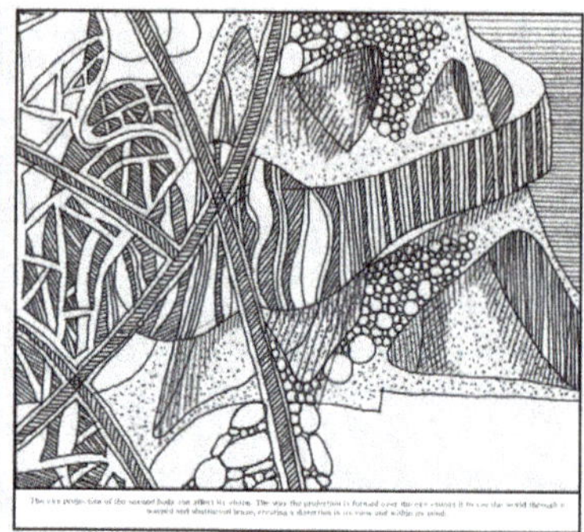

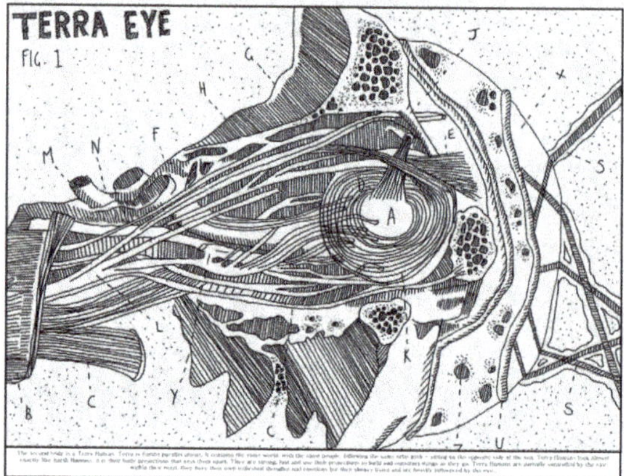

fig. 2.22: Woods' Terra-eye, Gaudi's Eye in the anatomy of the Terra-Human.

In her first-year project, Woods' alter-ego alien, called the "Terra-Human," became a device for defamiliarisation. In vignettes that described a journey by the two through Stratford, the "real" Woods explained the site to "alien" Woods. The origin story of Woods' alien also embedded architectural precedents into the work, the premise of the alien's backstory being linked to its home planet, where the architectural ethos of Antoni Gaudi was a socially foundational myth. The "Gaudi eye" was also embedded in the alien's bodily composition, in organs through which it understood the world, choosing and altering sites on "real" Woods' earth based on its internal images (fig. 2.22). The alien acrobatically constructed structures, incorporating cables arranged in catenary curves as the basis for the design.

SHADOW BODIES

Body agents are always inflected by digital media. In the design environments of cosmopolitan practices and universities, digital production is inevitable: arguably, the presence of the digital is globally ubiquitous. The technological turn provided another set of tools available for drawing architecture, and for selecting types of representation to communicate the designer's ideas, ostensibly reducing the time required to complete them, often with a commercialised veneer. Yet, digital drawing is not just a timesaving or aestheticising tool; in fact, it complicates the correlation between physicality and image-making discussed above. The digital drawing process is often much more physically passive and detached than a more traditional one, and in a digital design environment, many of the inherent analogies between physical construction and traditional drawing are absent.[40] Still, it is not quite right to condemn digital drawings as being simply disembodied. Instead, the dematerialised sense of embodiment epitomised by many digital drawing methods could be considered as yet another dimension of embodiment. With the ubiquity of digital media, people have incorporated digital sensibilities into their sensorimotor schema, and digitally-inflected spatiality into their bodies' proprioception.[41]

When digital media changes the tactile and motile participation entailed in the act of drawing, it injects posthuman qualities into the drawing process, changing the nature of the represented body images. Like any other entity in the virtual, digital space of design, representations of figures are subjected to the digital operations of morphing, animating, and transforming. Digitally-represented bodies

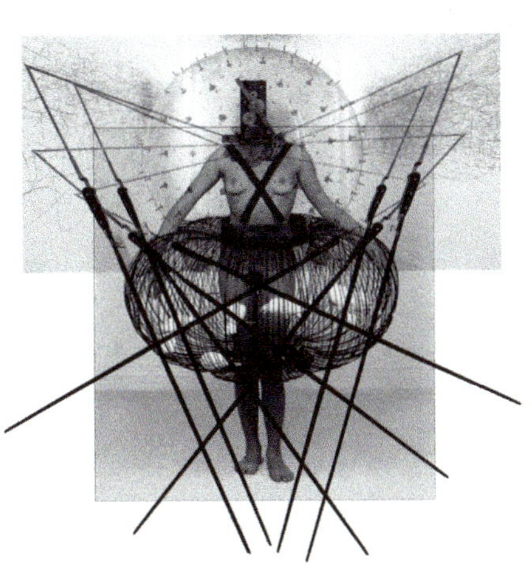
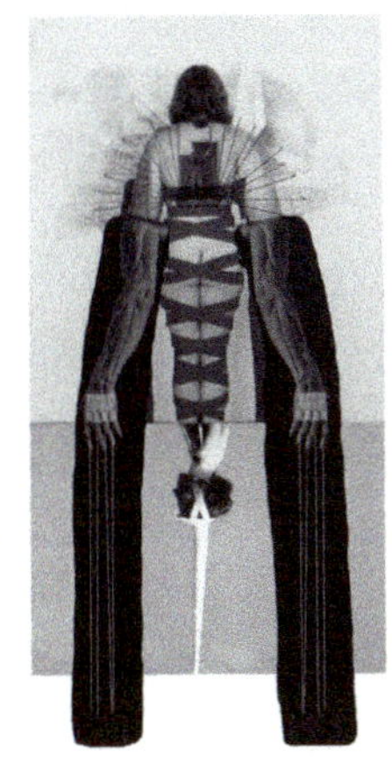
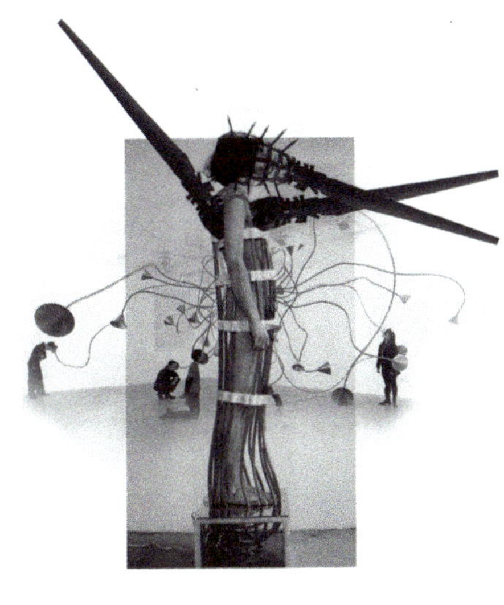

fig. 2.23: Man's collages of Rebecca Horn's body extensions.

are visualised in ways inherent to digital media, as point clouds, meshes, or (often uncanny) renders; both the operational and visual contingency exerted on the body disturb the stability of the body as a reference point. The limitless zoom functions in digital media break down scale distinctions of the body, making the delineation between a metaphoric body— often a gargantuan-scaled body encompassing an entire building— and the metonymic body— often the size of a typical scale figure, inside architecture— more contingent.

In this way, being digital is part of contemporary architects' bodily sense, arguably creating another bodily duplication, or sometimes a shadow body comprised of digital mediation and extension. Digital drawing is facilitated through electrical synapses between the computer's nerve endings, resulting in a pixel-inscribed picture. The mouse and keyboard, in direct contact with the designer's hands, take on a sensorial seamlessness with the body. This happens to the point that, taking from the parallel that Joanna Zylinska notes with regards to the camera in the hands of the photographer, the common understanding of the computer as just another tool could be inverted, with the body becoming an extension of the computer.[42]

In the time it takes to inscribe a click into a pixel, calculations, signals, and processes take place in the hardware and software of a computer, leaving traces of the designer's actions inside a digital datascape. Even the most code-savvy designer is not party to most of those computations, only presented with the final result, bringing up a complicated authorship. On the one hand, an Other, immaterial body is conducting the designer's actions for them, acting as an intermediary. On the other hand, these computations could not occur without the designer initiating them, making them an amplification of the designer's intentions. In this way, the digitisation of drawing implies a further, more complicated, sense of shadowing, mirroring, or duplication, of the real.

In digital representations of bodies, where the body is potentially ever-transforming and posthuman, the body could be considered as an original prosthetic, or an armature, for augmentation.[43] In this posthuman reading, the body becomes hybrid and extended— a cyborg, invoking Haraway's figuration of a reinvented, "leaky" creature that blurs boundaries between seeming dichotomies such as between organic and inorganic. Given the indeterminate nature of figures represented with digitally-saturated methods, it is important to recognise that body agents— as an *idea* of the body— are also meant to be fluid, where the concepts they enact can extend through metaphorical and metonymic modalities.

A potential conceptualisation of the body that can inform how the perplexing corporeality of perpetual variability begot by digitality might be represented can be found in Deleuze's notion of the figural. Building from ideas put forward by philosopher Jean-Francois Lyotard, Deleuze traced a body in the midst of becoming in the paintings of Francis Bacon. In Bacon's portraits, Deleuze saw bodies that were at once in flux and physically concrete, making them able to transmit sensation to the viewer in a directly affective, or pre-cognitive, way; Deleuze even argues that representation itself is bypassed.[44] In this way, the figural body eschews more passive contemplation and the semiotic decoding typically involved in viewing images of classical canonical bodies. The figural body addresses an arguably fundamental aspect of lived (and perhaps, specifically, digitally-inflected) embodiment, in its emphasis on sensation and perpetual becoming. The potentially ever animate, blurred, morphing, and contingent bodies that can be produced in digital space seem to hold properties in common with Deleuze's figural examples that were ever-becoming and defying representation.

Anastasia Tsamitrou's second-year project questioned the relationship between the physical body and its possible digital shadow.[45] In the imagery resulting from her process, she showed how the figural and the digital could coincide (fig. 2.24). In the film she made at the start of her project, Tsamitrou portrayed a classical sculpture disintegrating into voxels amidst Roman ruins. This scene was followed by footage of her own hands touching building surfaces near her site. Portrayed as an animated point cloud, her tactile body was also a fleeting one; as it felt stone and concrete, it was contingent to algorithmic shifts. For Tsamitrou, this exploration catalysed an idea for a museum project where elements of the Roman past of London were exhibited in a setting in which the virtual and real, and fantastical and actual overlap, opening up reconsideration of the nature of the past and present realities.[46]

being digital is part of contemporary architects' bodily sense, arguably creating another bodily duplication, or sometimes a shadow body comprised of digital mediation and extension.

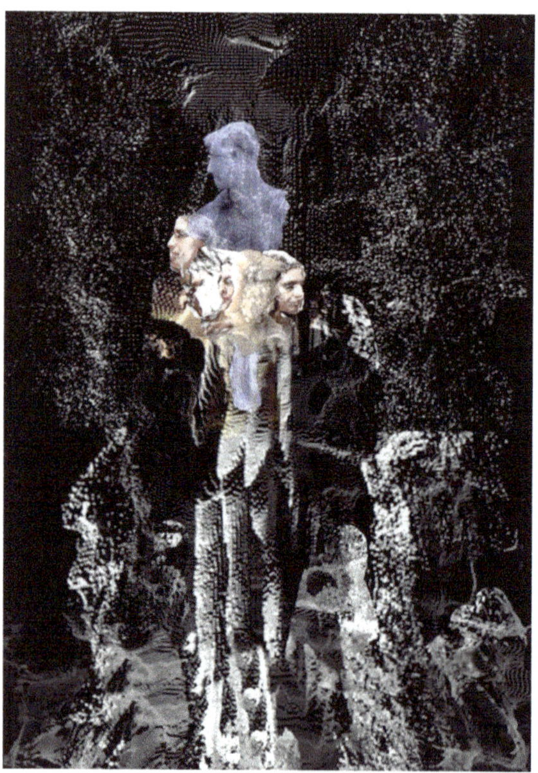

fig. 2.24: Tsamitrou's body agent creation as a combination of photographs of herself within a point cloud of a 3D-scanned classical sculpture.

Filippo Cocca's second-year project (see chapter two project gallery) explored how digitality in the form of doom-scrolling can be linked to processes of identity formation and the alteration of the posthuman, queer body.[47] Influenced by Ettore Sottsass' *Planet as Festival* and McKenzie Wark's *Hacker Manifesto*, Cocca invented "the mutant baddie," a figure channelling technology's ability— and influence— to alter the body and its presentation. The baddie's shadow digital body, glimpsed through the edges of square Instagram posts in an AI-assisted collage of trendy digital body imagery extending the frame, interwove with its manifestation in meatspace. Augmentations and interventions through prosthetics and attire developed in both the virtual and actual realms, leaving traces and building up a continuous cultural identity exchange across both spheres. The architectural intervention that arose from this exploration was a rave and artists' residency building in Palermo's Piazza Garraffello, where revellers would augment themselves through tangible attire and virtual layers visible through headsets. The experience of the mycelium-clad structure intertwined among existing buildings offered a range of experiences integrating both real and virtual space and body identities, from a rooftop mycelium garden to pods where participants immersed themselves completely in a virtual setting. Resembling organs without a body, the building announced itself as a living prosthetic to the urban fabric, helping to regenerate and produce culture and identity.

From the notion of bodies as ever mutable, and merging with prosthetics, architecture, pixels, and digital networks, the studio discussion led to more expansive notions of what a body could be and do. The body agent designs by students— often evoking violated, doubled or contaminated bodies— led to further discussions about how the condition of embodiment extends beyond the body proper. Picking up on these notions, the brief for the year 2020-21, taught by the teaching team of Dr Alessandro Ayuso, Dr Dan Dream, and Dr Fiona Zisch, entitled *Architecture's Second Bodies*, posited that what defines the human body inevitably mingles with nonhuman elements and that the actualisation of embodiment is as much nonhuman as human. This idea became more concrete as a theme through discussions of Daisy Hildyard's concept of the *second body*.[48] Hildyard sees the second body as a kind of shadow body comprised of everything that is our body that is not our physical selves; in the studio, this was taken to mean everything from our virtual images to the local and disparate impacts of the economic transactions we establish. In studio discussions, the Second Body was considered as the imprint and extension of a body's interaction with the world, including the tapestry of organic life and nonorganic entities that are integrated with physical selves, as well as the complex web of tangible and intangible economic and social relationships that emanate from them.(49) As a microbiome, it is highly localised as an integral part of each person, and as a manifestation of humans' relationship with the modern, digitised world, it is global in its reach. Put another way, second bodies were considered as our non-human selves.

Formulating the brief for that year, dramatic current events foregrounded the framing. The Coronavirus pandemic and the Black Lives Matter protests put in stark relief the notion that the human body is a key point of convergence in linked crises that extend across connected sociopolitical, technological, and environmental factors. The idea of the second body was a way to catalyse possibilities as to how architecture could address these entangled conditions. Visualising and designing with second bodies held potential to externalise hidden aspects of the body. The brief asked students the question: How could designing with second bodies change our approach to architecture in a way that responds to what is under the surface or outside the frame?

Expanding beyond Hildyard's concept, the first prompt of the year asked students to aim towards designing Second Body Agents that could help them speculate and imagine. The Second Body Agents were discussed as hybrid assemblages, combinations of ingredients of a nonhuman element (from zombies to chloroplasts), an architectural element (from a wide range of examples from Pharaoh Dental Clinic by Shin Takamatsu to Piranesi's Santa Maria del Priorato) and a part of the students' selves (be that a material, e.g. organs, or immaterial, e.g. a dream or desire).

Expanding the notion of the Second Body into an exercise in imaginative possibilities, the surrealist paintings of Remedios Varo were discussed. For example, in *The Opposite Shadow*, in an oneiric inversion, the figure's shadow is transformed into the primary body, and the literal body becomes the ephemeral imprint on the floor surface. During the year, co-tutor Fiona Zisch ran workshops on photogrammetry and spatial choreography driven by bodily movements, looking to precedents such as choreographer William Forsythe. Forsythe's mappings of bodily movement suggest an edifying structure left in the wake of motions and gestures, another idea of a second body that students picked up on. Students were asked to construct a specification drawing of their Second Body Agent in the vein of the figures in Neufert's *Architects' Data*. Neufert's figures are normative, represented to aid in the production of normative architecture; with the discussion of speculation, surrealism, and imagination in the studio, it was clear that the students' figures would be anything but. Students were asked to question the format of the specification as they questioned the representation and possibilities of the body itself.

For example, in her Second Body Agent specification drawing, second-year student Akmaral Khassen imagined a figure beleaguered by consumerism.(50) She portrayed her Second Body Agent as physically and psychologically inundated with mediated messages of commerce. The figure, shown in a pose reminiscent of a Renaissance Venus, clutches her phone with a weary expression, with imagery from consumerist culture coursing through her and comprising her body (fig. 2.25).

the digitisation of drawing implies a further, more complicated, sense of shadowing, mirroring, or duplication, of the real.

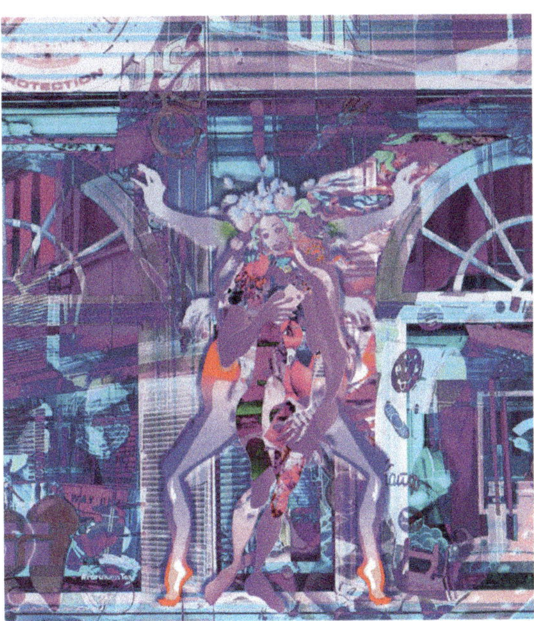

fig. 2.25: Khassen's Modern Venus tries to attach herself to the existing facade of Fortnum & Mason during her drift, West End.

For the next step of the project, students took urban drifts to locate and initially assess sites in London. The tactic recommended took from the post-war French art collective the Situationists: to reveal unconscious desires, they developed a psychogeographic practice called the *dérive*, or, the drift, which involved wandering the city to see it from a new, psychologically-attenuated, often euphoric, vantage point. For the DS25 students, the strategy for defamiliarisation involved walking along a predetermined, given line through London; this ensured a certain decision-making process along the route.(51)

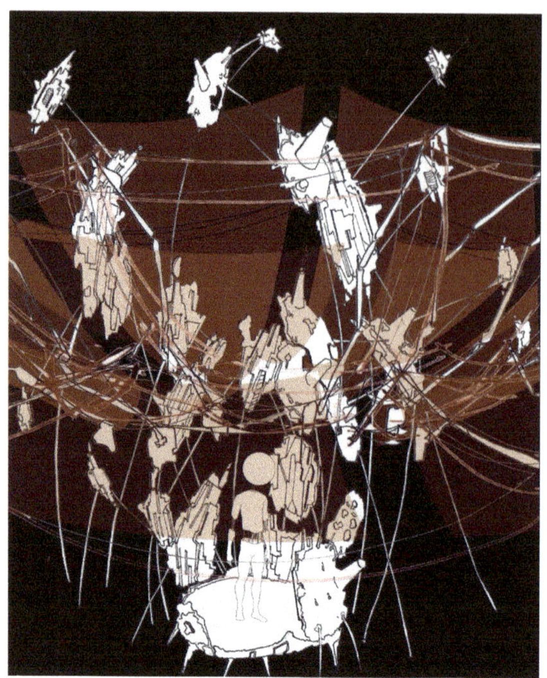

fig. 2.26: Brown's body agent establishing himself in reality. The Second Body remains in the centre of the mediating object. The structure and the objects begin to become increasingly similar to each other while the canopies continue to react to the qualitative values of the site.

Traversing through boundaries, grains, and textures in the urban fabric, the strategy for the drift also relied on walking, looking, and listening, as a Second Body Agent. For this, students used photography, filming, and sketching to get into character, looking to channel their Second Body Agents' desires, proclivities, and attractions.

For example, in his urban drift, first-year student Oscar Brown imagined his Second Body Agent as an archaeologist-storyteller.(52) Through the making of films and panoramic drawings he showed his Second Body Agent obsessively cataloguing and analysing objects found in the site area. Objects were shown orbiting around the Second Body Agent as it moved through the site; as it collected and curated, it created a visual conversation between body and world (fig. 2.26).

Asking how the body and site could be further mediated through a design intervention, students embarked on the design of Mediating Objects, catalytic insertions that were meant to mediate between the student's Second Body Agent and the site. The Mediating Object was discussed as having properties of both a body-extension and a building prosthetic; it was thought of as an architectural fragment, and as potentially dynamic and interactive, similar to an instrument. The aim of the Mediating Object was meant to further intensify the Second Body Agent's interaction with the site.(53) This could mean heightening the Second Body Agent's experience of the site or setting the stage for some future act or appropriation by the Second Body Agent. It could otherwise mean allowing for the Second Body Agent to dwell in the site, or move through the site in a particular way, or view, or sense, or daydream, or communicate, or collect data or objects in particular ways: in short, whatever students determined their Second Body Agent desired which could be realised by architecture. A final note on the brief read: "The Mediating Object should be fetishistic, in that it should be irrationally, obsessively, singularly, and likely flamboyantly devoted to its particular purpose."

To design her Mediating Object, second-year student Olga Smoili's project explored links between culture and sustainability and was driven by a Second Body Agent who was a cyborgian reincarnation of JMW Turner.(54) Her Mediating Object, an elastic, clothed interior with immersive atmospheric conditions, was a first step towards proposing a public space and energy plant adjacent to Somerset House (fig. 2.27). In her project, weather conditions were curated and harnessed for aesthetic and sensorial effects, engaging and educating the public on the potential for weather elements to generate sustainable energy.

In his project, first-year student Aaron John Spiers-Reed devised an android Second Body Agent programmed by the architects Arakawa and Gins.(55) His Second Body Agent was portrayed in vignettes exploring Stratford, where it was shown looking for spatial situations that correlated with Arakawa and Gins' *Reversible Destiny* concept, which holds that corporeally engaging— even

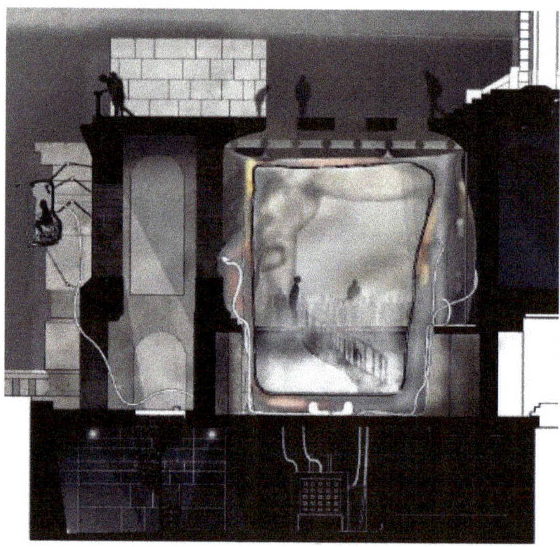

fig. 2.27: Smoili's mediating object was a combination of JMW Turner, the Second Body (extraskeleton) and London's weather. It takes place in the maisonette of Sommerset House but it involves the whole building. Its aim is to communicate to the viewers his admiration for the extreme weather phenomena of London and understand the impact of weather to their bodies but also their moods.

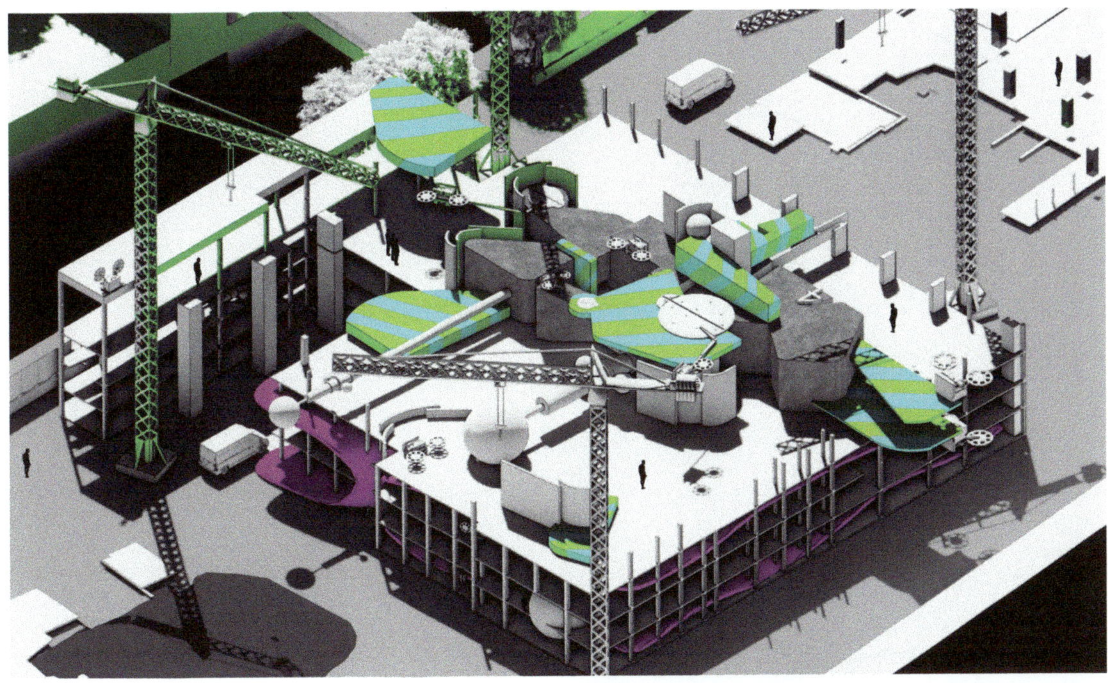

fig. 2.28: Spiers-Reed's mediating object starts to distribute its findings into the construction and surrounding context, preparing for the kinaesthetic connection to the grid.

challenging— environments could extend life and, in their view, even make one immortal.[56] For the design of the Mediating Object, the Second Body Agent was shown settling into a construction site, altering the course of the ongoing construction (fig. 2.28).

In his second-year project (see chapter two project gallery), Tzortzis de Paz questioned the notion of purity in architecture.[57] Tzortzis de Paz's Mediating Object was designed as a kind of architectural equipment used by the two Second Body Agents in his project: "The Subject," a character with a fetish for allergens, and "The Handler," the enabler of the Subject's erotic events. Harnesses and tubes channelling pollutants out of the interior of St Paul's cathedral allowed the Subject to be ceremoniously hoisted and exposed to allergens in a ritualistic (and to the two characters, erotic) event (fig. 2.29). The epidermal layers of The Subject became a model for the layered assembly of the building (fig. 2.31). The project also brought grotesque and abject body concepts to bear on the design of the bathrooms of air purification and chapel for St Paul's Cathedral. Here, urine and water runoff from the roof collected in channels inscribed on the floor, intermingling the discharged fluids of the human body and the material comprising the body of the building; impurities became an ornamental atmospheric presence unifying body and building (fig. 2.30).

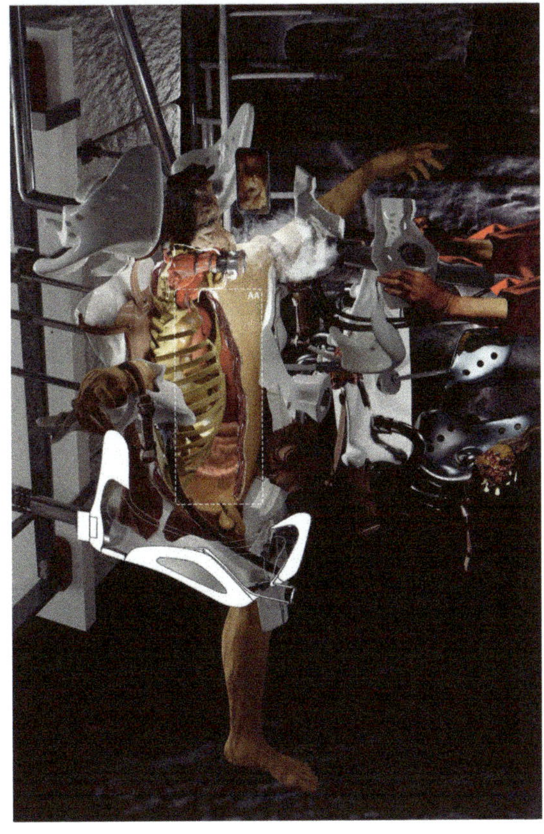

fig. 2.29: Tzortzis de Paz's sectional view of the "Subect's" body as it is being covered in dust particles by the "Handler," generating an allergenic reaction.

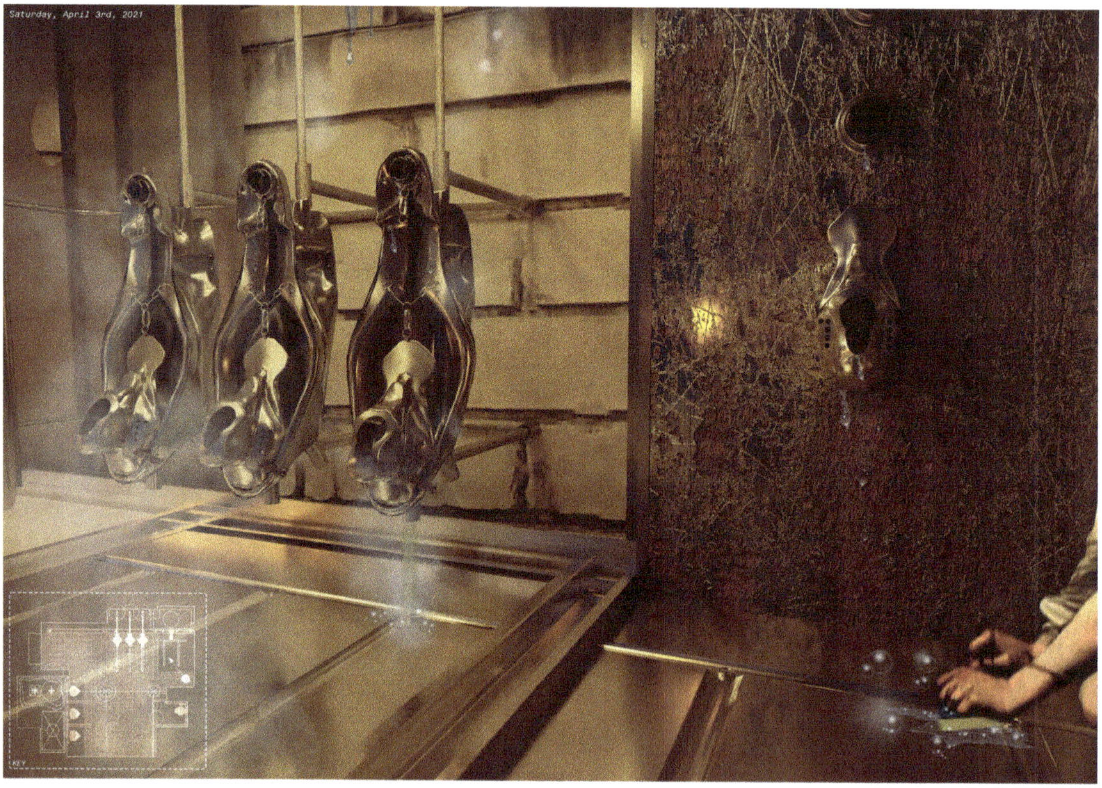

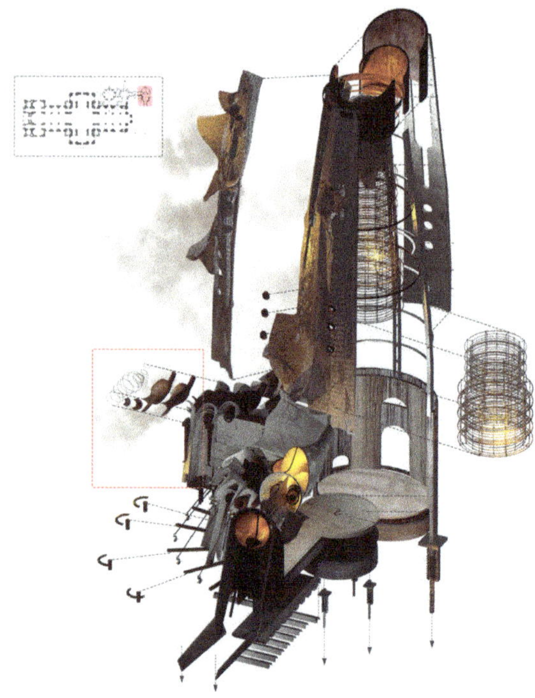

CONCLUSION

As design tools, body agents introduce unexpected variables into design. They are meant not only to shape architecture but to be shaped by it, purposefully evolving with the designs they are drawn in. They are meant to intentionally communicate ideas stemming from autobiography, biography, and history to mobilise these ideas and allow them to be thought through and embedded in both architecture and world.

The act of designing with and through body agents destabilises ideas of bodily integrity, amplifying doublings that are already inherent to the condition of embodiment. The burgeoning of body-doublings described in this chapter become more complicated with subsequent convergences, cominglings, and further bifurcations. In these many manifestations, the body is revealed as innately other. While unsettling and beguiling in many ways, it is in these taxonomic branch's overlaps and gaps that embodiment becomes a productive zone of enquiry. Grappling with questions of how the body can be understood and represented in architectural design brings to bear fundamental issues and opens up new possibilities of how architecture can relate to subjects.

fig. 2.30-2.31: Top: Tzortzis de Paz's urinal room within the Air Purification Chapel. Bottom: Exploded axonometric of the Chapel and Air Filtering Tower.

NOTES

(01) Francisco J. Varela et al., *The Embodied Mind: Cognitive Science and Human Experience* (MIT press, 1993), 172–73.

(02) Hight summarises how Lakoff and Johnson "placed the projection of bodily experience at the core of what it means to be human and of our understanding of the world created through such metaphoric operations." Christopher Hight, *Architectural Principles in the Age of Cybernetics*, (Routledge, 2007), 20, https://doi.org/10.4324/9780203086568. The quoted text refers to one of Lakoff and Johnson's seminal texts: George Lakoff and Mark Johnson, *Metaphors We Live By* (Chicago: University of Chicago Press. 1980).

(03) This is a notion that goes back to Aristotle's theory on the soul, the latter explained as an innate part of a very specific body, and one which cannot exist otherwise. This brings forth the question of whether architecture can then perform as a generic shell, if architecture is innately created by and for specific bodies. "η ψυχή είναι κατά κυριολεξίαν εκείνο με το οποίο ζούμε και αισθανόμαστε και σκεπτόμαστε ... και δεν είναι όπως έλεγαν οι παλαιότεροι, που την προσάρμοζαν σε σώμα, χωρίς καθόλου να προσδιορίζουν σε τι σώμα και ποιάς λογής, ενώ είνει φανερό πως το οποιοδήποτε πράγμα δεν δέχεται το ότιδήποτε." Αριστοτέλης, translated from the original Ancient Greek by Β. Τατάκης. "Περί Ψυχής [On the Soul]," in *Περί Ψυχής - Μικρά Φυσικά*, (Βιβλιοθήκη Αρχαίων Συγγραφέων 11. Athens: Ε. & Μ. Ζαχαροπούλου Ε.Π.Ε., 1954.), 89.

(04) There are a number of theoretical references that could support this assertion, some of which are elaborated below. However, arguably one only need to look at a painting by artists such as Lucien Freud or Jenny Saville to see how lived bodies tell a story by virtue of their collected experiences registering in and on the body itself.

(05) The sequential developments leading to the creation of this figure are described in: Toby Lester, *Da Vinci's Ghost: Genius, Obsession, and How Leonardo Created the World in His Own Image* (Free Press, 2012).

(06) María Luisa Palumbo, *New Wombs: Electronic bodies and Architectural Disorders* (Basel: Birkhauser, 2000), 22.

(07) Philosopher Rosi Braidotti describes this as "an ideal of bodily perfection which, in keeping with the classical dictum *mens sana in corpore sano*, doubles up as a set of mental, discursive and spiritual values." Rossi Braidotti, *The Posthuman* (Cambridge: Polity Press, 2013), 13.

(08) Paul Emmons and Andreea Mihalache, "Architectural Handbooks and the User Experience," in *Use Matters: An Alternative History of Architecture* (Routledge, 2013), 35.

(09) Professor of Architecture and Spatial Culture Penelope Haralambidou's 2020 project, *City of Ladies*, is often discussed in the studio with regards to alternative and feminist practices that question this narrow notion of the subject in the designs of spaces. Penelope Haralambidou, "The Female Body Politic: Enacting the Architecture of The Book of the City of Ladies," *Architecture and Culture* 8 (2020), (3–4): 385–406. doi:10.1080/20507828.2020.1794146.

(10) Rob Walker, "Go Figure."

(11) Braidotti, *The Posthuman*, 40.

(12) Project done under the supervision of the studio teaching team of Dr Alessandro Ayuso, Dr Dan Dream, and Martyna Marciniak.

(13) Project done under the supervision of the studio teaching team of Dr Alessandro Ayuso, Dr Dan Dream, and Martyna Marciniak.

(14) Project done under the supervision of the studio teaching team of Dr Alessandro Ayuso, Dr Dan Dream, and Martyna Marciniak.

(15) This concept can be understood also for example in practices such as Yukinori Yanagi's solo exhibition "Wandering Position," where the artist traces the position of an ant on a paper in red chalk. The journey is here felt both through vision and movement, but also through the act of tracing and recording through drawing whereby the position in time and space is transferred from the pencil, to the hand, and to the mind of the artist. Yukinori Yanagi, "Wandering Position 1988-2021," Exhibition Space. Anomaly Tokyo (blog), published April 3, 2021. https://anomalytokyo.com/en/exhibition/wandering-position-1988-2021/.

(16) Marco Frascari, *Eleven Exercises in the Art of Architectural Drawing: Slow-Food for the Architect's Imagination* (Routledge, 2011), 79, https://doi.org/10.4324/9780203835852.

(17) Project done under the supervision of the studio teaching team of Dr Alessandro Ayuso, Dr Dan Dream, and Martyna Marciniak.

(18) Body Agents are meant to be able to operate in both modalities; this is discussed further below.

(19) This can be seen in illustration where types of columns were thought to embody types of figures, epitomised by the illustrations in John Shute's *The first and chief groundes of architecture* of 1563.

(20) Marco Frascari, "The Body and Architecture in the Drawings of Carlo Scarpa," *Res: Anthropology and Aesthetics* 14 (September 1987): 128, https://doi.org/10.1086/RESv14n1ms20166778.

(21) Project done under the supervision of the studio teaching team of Dr Alessandro Ayuso, Dr Dan Dream, and Dr Fiona Zisch.

(22) Project done under the supervision of the studio teaching team of Dr Alessandro Ayuso, Dr Dan Dream, and Martyna Marciniak. The spelling of the word "homunculus" was intentional in Hewes' project.

(23) Marcos Cruz, *The Inhabitable Flesh of Architecture, Design Research in Architecture* (Routledge, 2016), 10–11, https://doi.org/10.4324/9781315238982.

(24) Julia Kristeva et al., "Powers of Horror: An Essay on Abjection," Nachdr., *European Perspectives* (Columbia Univ. Press, 2010).

(25) Margaret Lock and Judith Farquhar, eds., *Beyond the Body Proper: Reading the Anthropology of Material Life* (Durham, NC: Duke University Press, 2007), 2.

(26) Alina Alexandra Payne, *From Ornament to Object: Genealogies of Architectural Modernism* (Yale University Press, 2012), 147.

(27) Alessandro Ayuso, *Experiments with Body Agent Architecture: The 586-Year-Old Spiritello in Il Regno Digitale* (UCL Press, 2022), 145, https://doi.org/10.14324/111.9781800081703.

(28) Project done under the supervision of the studio teaching team of Dr Alessandro Ayuso, Dr Dan Dream, and Martyna Marciniak.

(29) Project done under the supervision of the studio teaching team of Dr Alessandro Ayuso, Dr Dan Dream, and Martyna Marciniak.

(30) Project done under the supervision of the studio teaching team of Dr

Alessandro Ayuso, Dr Dan Dream, and Martyna Marciniak.

(31) Project done under the supervision of the studio teaching team of Dr Alessandro Ayuso, Dr Dan Dream, and Martyna Marciniak.

(32) Marco Frascari, "A New Angel/Angle in Architectural Research: The Ideas of Demonstration," *Journal of Architectural Education* 44, no. 1 (1990): 11, https://doi.org/10.1080/10464883.1990.11102663.

(33) Ryan Kyberd, *Discovery by investigation of an aNatomical & architectural response to pregnAncy*, 2019-20.

(34) Frascari, "The Body and Architecture in the Drawings of Carlo Scarpa," 125.

(35) Frascari, "The Body and Architecture in the Drawings of Carlo Scarpa."

(36) Ibid., 131.

(37) Ibid., 125.

(38) Russel Hoban, *Riddley Walker* (UK: Penguin Classics, 2021, orig. pub. 1980), 6; Alain Robbe-Grillet's nouveau roman novel *La Reprise*, plays with the idea of second / shadow bodies as the manifestations of fears threatening or revealing the protagonists' true identities, which are hidden even from themselves.

(39) "The author takes a step towards his characters, but the characters take a step towards the author: double-becoming." Gilles Deleuze quoted in David Burrows and Simon O'Sullivan, *Fictioning: The Myth-Functions of Contemporary Art and Philosophy* (Edinburgh: Edinburgh University Press, 2019), 20.

(40) Frascari, *Eleven Exercises in the Art of Architectural Drawing*, 106.

(41) Nancy Katherine Hayles, "Unfinished Work: From Cyborg to Cognisphere," in *Architectural Theories of the Environment: Posthuman Territory* (Routledge, 2013), 38, https://doi.org/10.4324/9780203084274.; Philosopher Andy Clark also describes this condition: "when the coupling with key tools and technologies is robust and reliable, so that the brain learns to simply expect the presence of those resources, …, we become (I'll argue) extended minds– cyborg or hybrid minds created without the need for invasive implants." Andy Clark, *The Experience Machine: How Our Minds Predict and Shape Reality* (UK: Penguin Books, 2024), 148.

(42) "rather than the camera functioning as our prosthesis, helping us see and capture things, we humans become a prosthetic attachment for the camera-led acts of cutting the world by discretizing the flow of particles passing through it as images, and by giving them names, identities, and functions in our cultural repertoire of objects and behaviors." Joanna Zylinska, *The Perception Machine: Out Photographic Future between the Eye and AI* (Cambridge, MA and London: MIT Press, 2023), 130, https://doi.org/10.7551/mitpress/14471.001.0001

(43) Nancy Katherine Hayles, *How We Became Posthuman: Virtual Bodies in Cybernetics, Literature, and Informatics* (University of Chicago Press, 2010), 3.

(44) Project done under the supervision of the studio teaching team of Dr Alessandro Ayuso, Dr Dan Dream, and Dr Fiona Zisch.

(45) Tsamitrou's proposal is reminiscent of Alexandra Daisy Ginsberg's installation view for the *Eco-Visionaries* exhibition at the Royal Academy titled "The Substitute," where a Deep Mind-generated, pixelated, extinct Rhinoceros is placed in a perfectly square digital room extending the physical gallery space. Oliver Wainwright, " Eco-Visionaries review – the salt flats will die and the jellyfish shall rise," in *The Guardian*, published November 21, 2019; https://www.theguardian.com/artanddesign/2019/nov/21/eco-visionaries-review-royal-academy-london-jellyfish-salt-plains; Eco-Visionaries: Confronting a planet in a state of emergency, Exhibition at the Royal Academy of Arts, London, November 23, 2019 until February 23, 2020, https://www.royalacademy.org.uk/exhibition/architecture-environment-eco-visionaries

(46) Gilles Deleuze, *Francis Bacon: The Logic of Sensation*, trans. Daniel W. Smith (Univ. Minnesota Press, 2005), 26.

(47) Project done under the supervision of the studio teaching team of Dr Alessandro Ayuso and Mary Konstantopoulou.

(48) Daisy Hildyard, *The Second Body* (Fitzcarraldo Editions, 2023).

(49) Clark uses the term "leaky system," a term referred to earlier in the chapter, to explain the human mind as "a system apt to lean on the surrounding world in heavy and sometimes unexpected ways," moving on to describe that for these types of systems, "brain, body, pencil, and notepad act as a new and potent whole." Clark, *The Experience Machine*, 151.

(50) Project done under the supervision of the studio teaching team of Dr Alessandro Ayuso, Dr Dan Dream, and Dr Fiona Zisch.

(51) This is a method of structuring student *dérives* was used by Professor Francisco Sanin in his M Arch II Florence teaching ca. 2003.

(52) Project done under the supervision of the studio teaching team of Dr Alessandro Ayuso, Dr Dan Dream, and Dr Fiona Zisch.

(53) Architect Madeline Gins explains hers and her partner Shusaku Arakawa's definition of the "Architectural Body" as the "Body Proper plus Architectural Surround," "as the minimal unit to be taken into consideration when trying to determine what lives as a human being." Léopold Lambert, "Arakawa + Madeline Gins," *The Funambulist Pamphlets* 8 (Brooklyn, NY: punctum books, 2014): 36. https://library.oapen.org/bitstream/id/4e471c84-c1a6-48cb-be7d-d875d13cebc0/1004541.pdf; In an interview excerpt, Gins explains this again: "Architectural Body Theory suggests that you are not just the body proper. You are the body proper plus the architectural surround." Madeline Gins, "Interview with Madeline Gins from Documentary Film: We, Madeline Gins," excerpt posted by Reversible Destiny Foundation, August 14, 2025, YouTube, 5:01, https://youtu.be/pevznEPi5tY?si=eOI8JDz18c_RrN4b

(54) Project done under the supervision of the studio teaching team of Dr Alessandro Ayuso, Dr Dan Dream, and Dr Fiona Zisch.

(55) Project done under the supervision of the studio teaching team of Dr Alessandro Ayuso, Dr Dan Dream, and Dr Fiona Zisch.

(56) An example of this is Arakawa+Gins' 2008 project *Bioscleave House*, which "fundamentally proposes an architecture of viability that helps to sustain one throughout life, and even extend human lifespan indefinitely.": "Bioscleave House (Lifespan Extending Villa)," in *Reversible Destiny* Foundation, Arakawa and Madeline Gins, founded 2022, https://www.reversibledestiny.org/bioscleave-house-lifespan-extending-villa/

(57) Project done under the supervision of the studio teaching team of Dr Alessandro Ayuso, Dr Dan Dream, and Dr Fiona Zisch.

CHAPTER 2: PROJECT IMAGE GALLERY

THE CAMPODIGLIO CHOCOLATE COLLECTIVE
SUPERPERCEPTION
THE BADDIEVERSE
THE BECOMING
RASHES & HIVES

THE CAMPIDOGLIO CHOCOLATE COLLECTIVE

by
VICTOR MAN

BRIEF *Body Architecture*

YEAR *2018-19*

TUTORS *Dr Alessandro Ayuso, Dr Dan Dream, Martyna Marciniak*

THEMES

Shadow Duplicate Body

Active Body

Animate Body

Prosthetics

Body Agent Techniques (Cast of Characters)

Performance (Actual Body on Site)

"How can bodily movement be used to generate architecture?

The Body Agent has an extension of limbs and leaves traces as he moves, therefore he translates site-specific movement into space, revealing a layer of information within a site.

The fictional narrative of the project revolves around Body Agent Mercury and Campidoglio. Ever since Turin's heavy decline in the manufacturing industry in the past decades, Mercury relinquishes his title as God of Commerce and vents his frustrations by adopting the "God of movement" personality. Body Agent Mercury moves through Campidoglio leaving traces of glulam beams every night. Signor Doglio, a master chocolatier realises that genus name for the chocolate plant, Theobroma translates to "food for the Gods" and that an offering of hot chocolate for Mercury every evening will calm his rampage. Making use of the glulam structures coded through movements made by Mercury, the residents set out to create a chocolate workshop in their courtyards, that aim to establish a physical and social link in their communities. They re-establish the courtyard as a workshop space and create a blurred fabric of factory and living.

The Campidoglio Chocolate Collective factory becomes a pretext for community involvement."

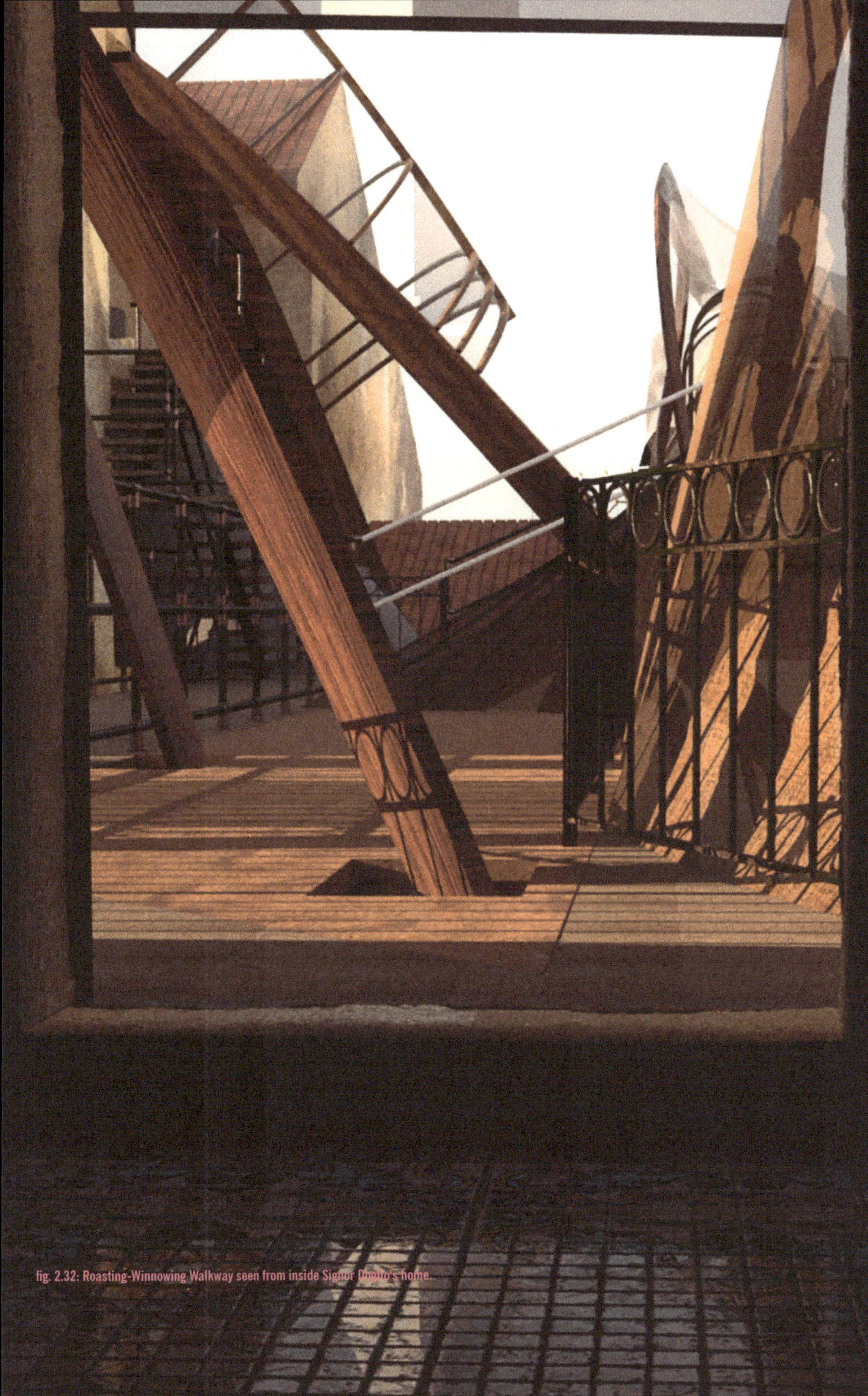

fig. 2.32: Roasting-Winnowing Walkway seen from inside Signor Doglio's home.

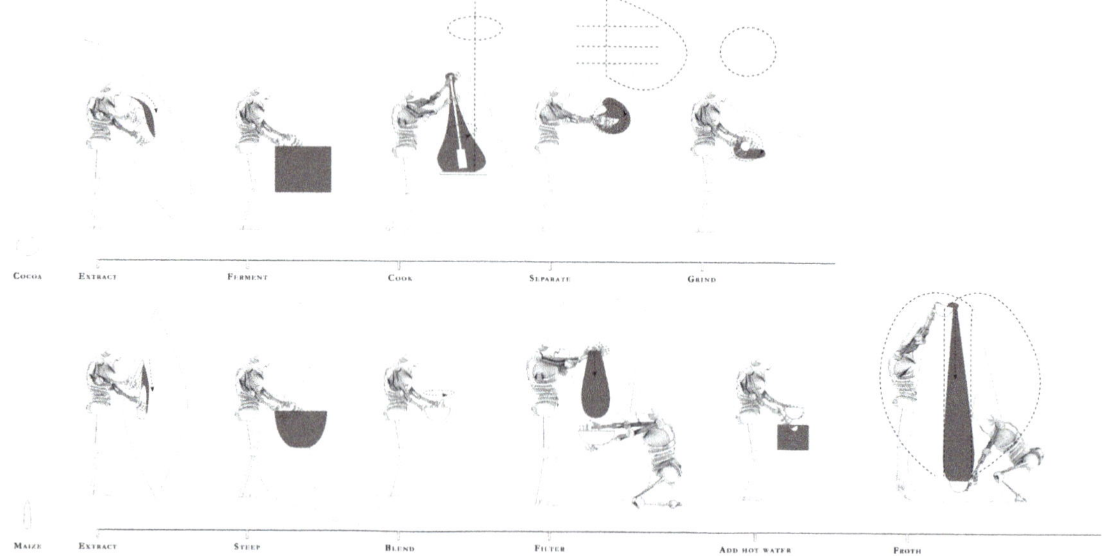

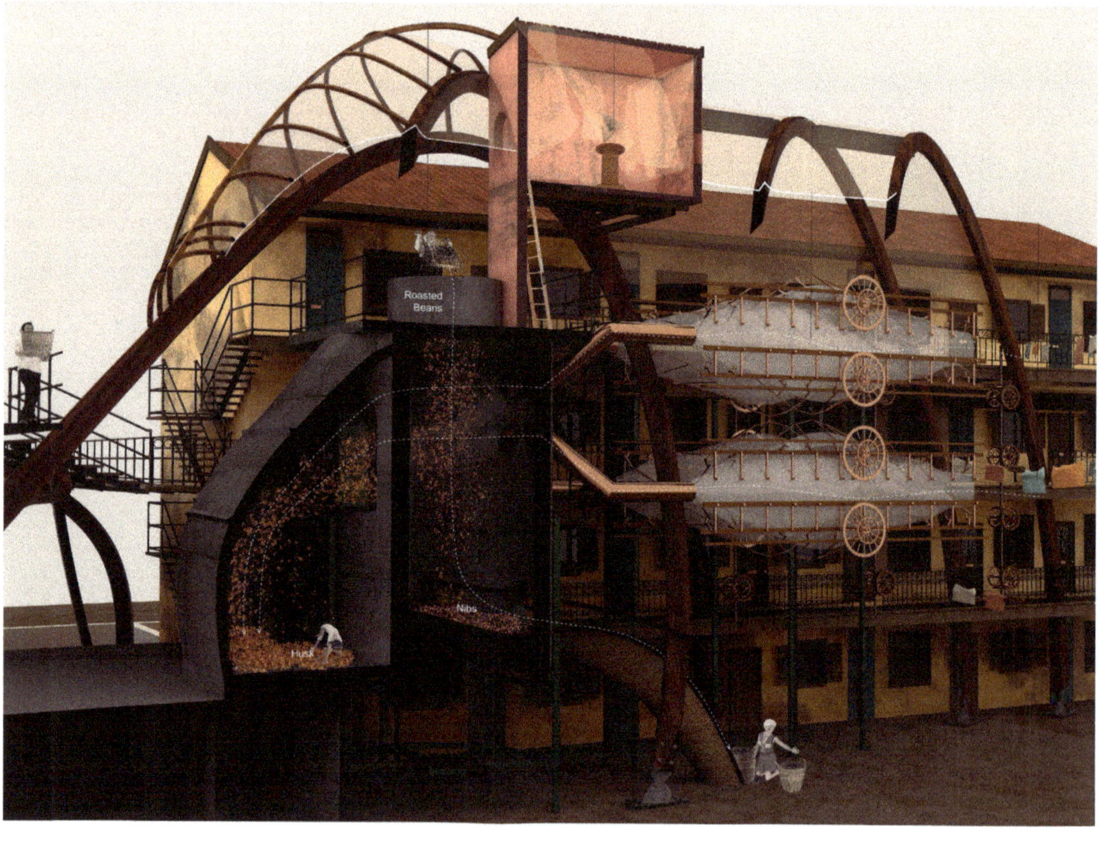

fig. 2.33-2.34: Top: The project focuses on cocoa making as a traditional, artisan craft and a ritual of choreography. Modern day chocolate uses industrialised processes to create an anauthentic product removed from its traditions. The oldest ways of chocolate making involves steps of strenuous motion to create a hot, frothy chocolate drink ground straight from the bean. Bottom: Winnowing station.

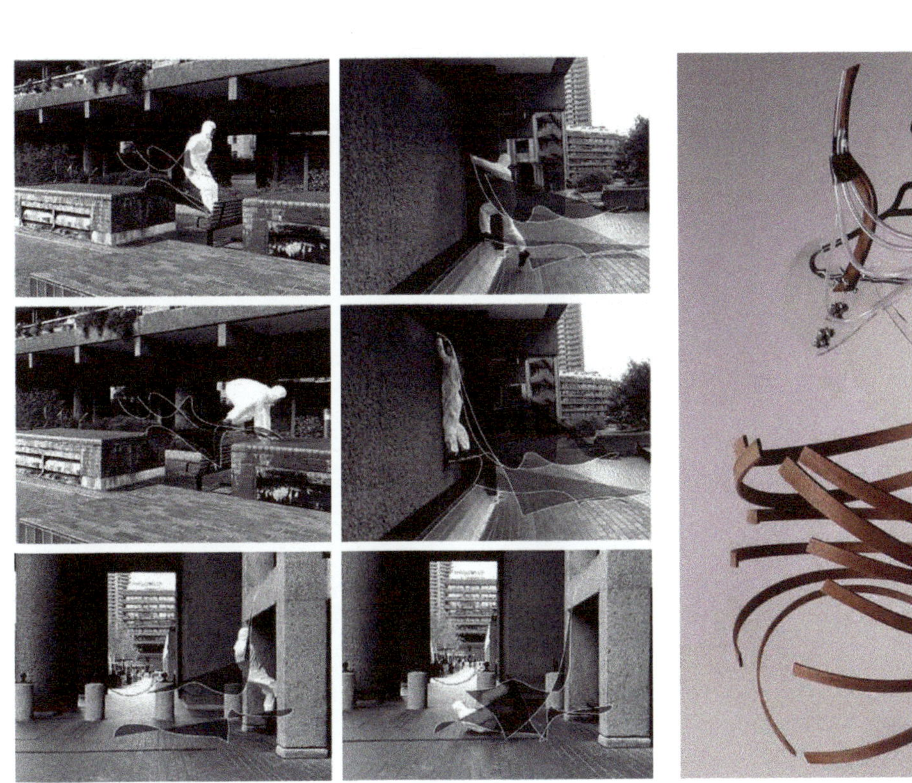

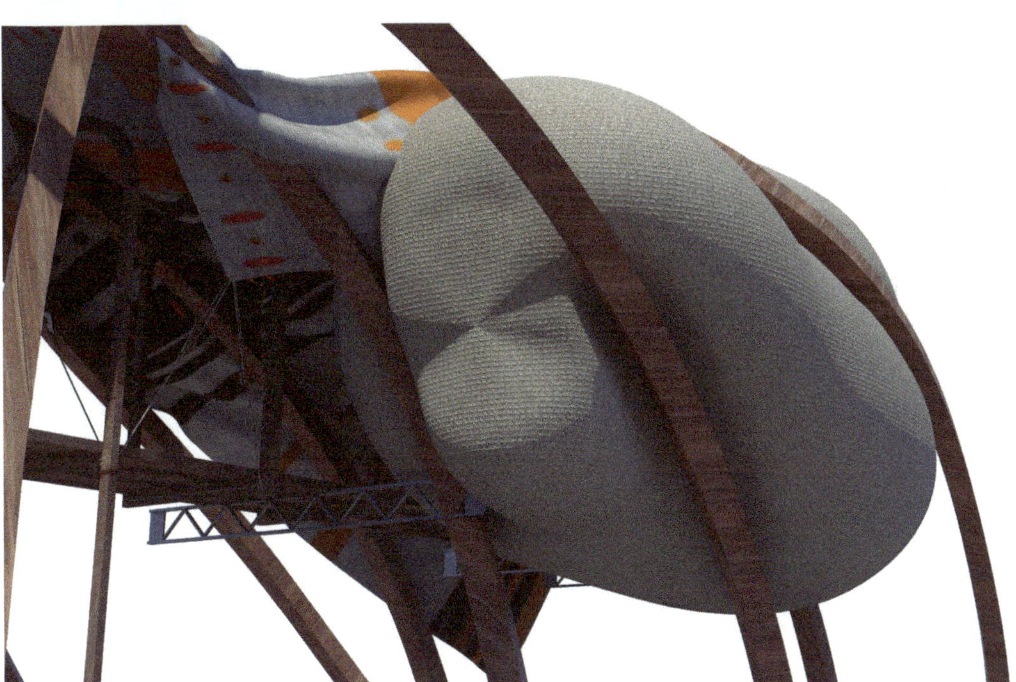

fig. 2.35-2.37: Top-Left to Bottom-Right: Man's "bad parkour" performance filmed on site; The torso of the body agent fragment uses laminated strips of wood veneer and plexiglass. It embraces the wearer's body and face providing a framework for the pipework and outlets for the pigment to spray out; Lares, being the weak offspring of Mercury, is supressed by Mercury's power without intervention from Signora Turin.

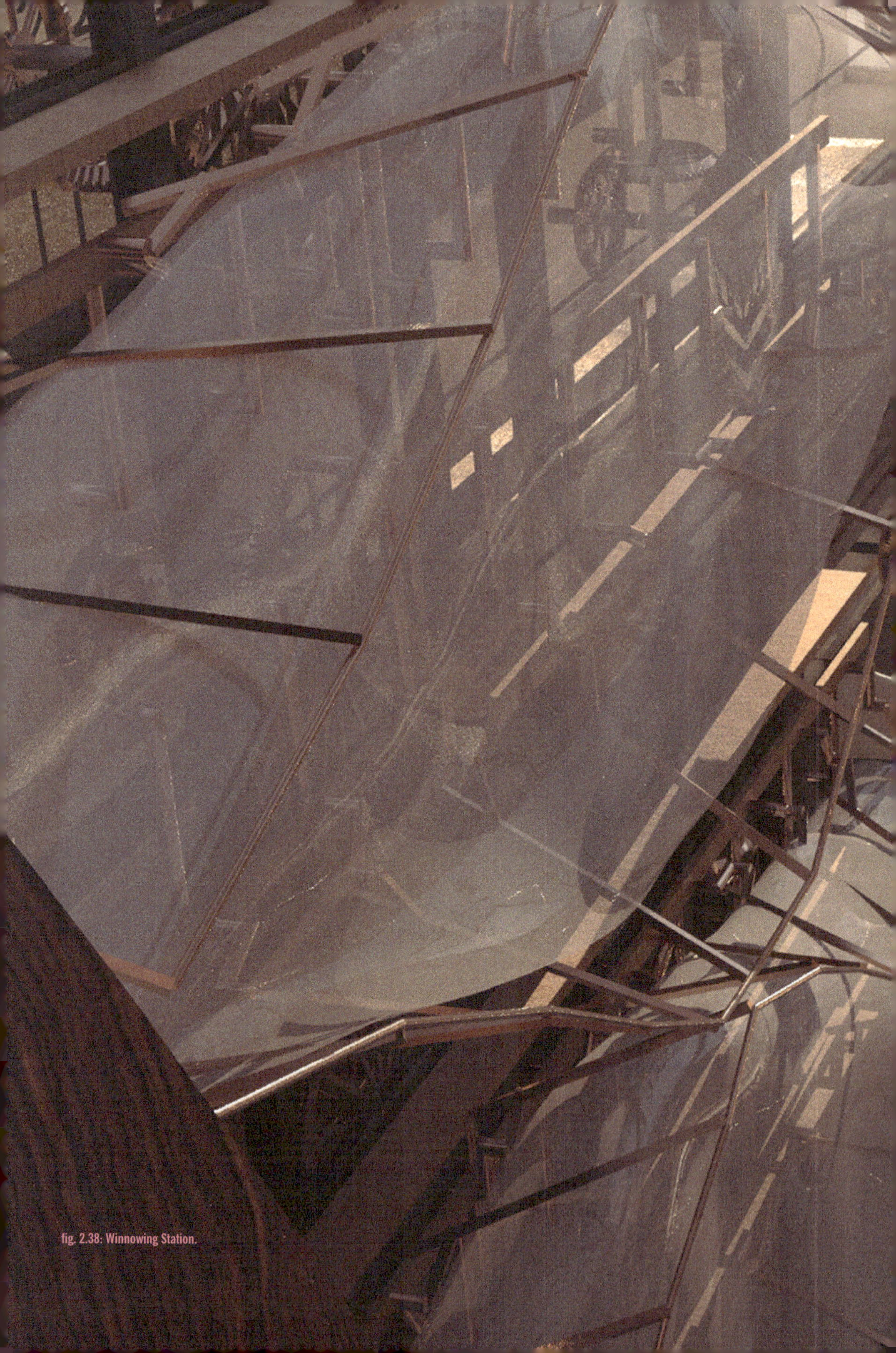

fig. 2.38: Winnowing Station.

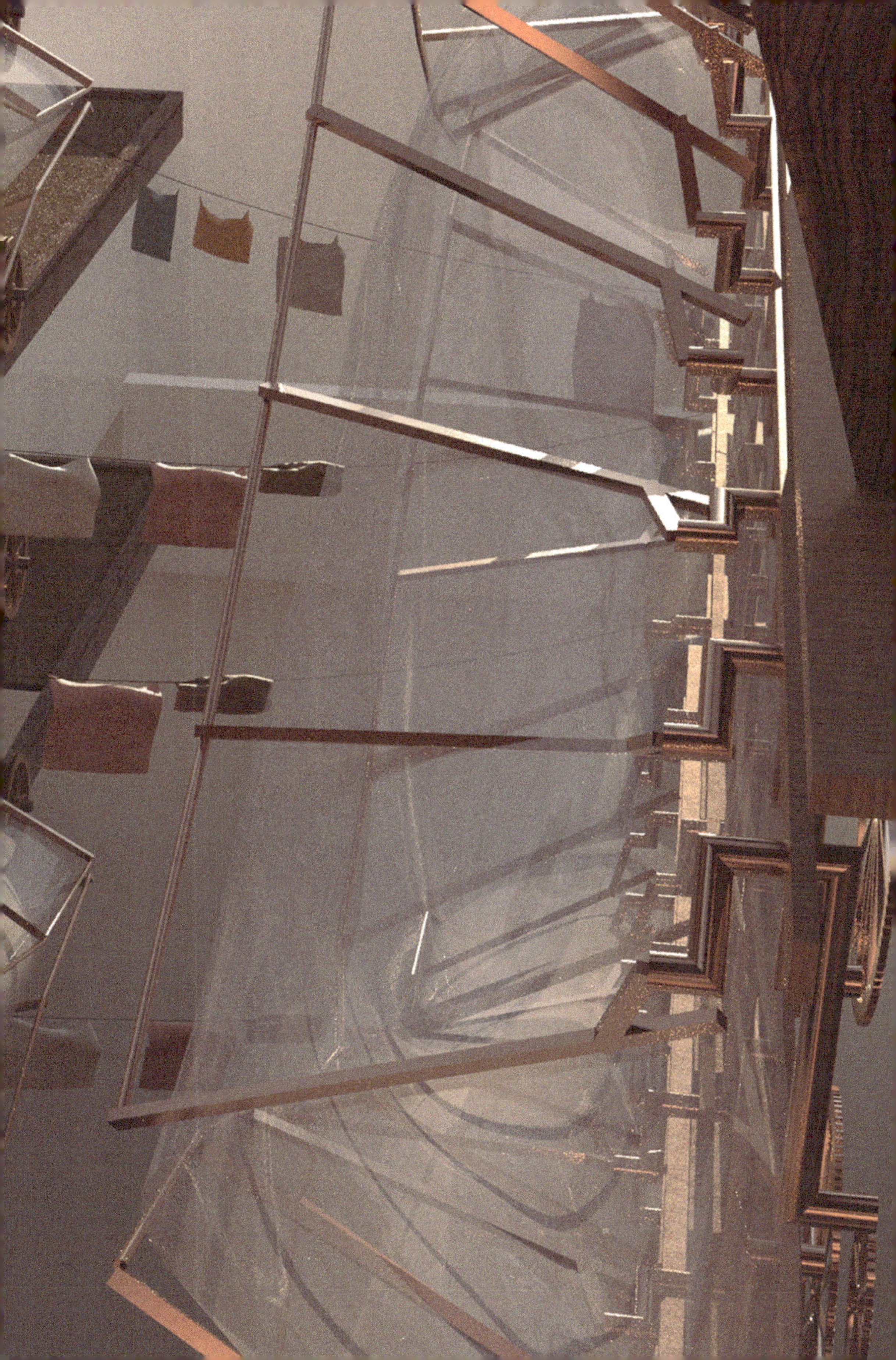

SUPERPERCEPTION

by
STEFANO PERRETTI

BRIEF *Body Architecture*

YEAR *2018-19*

TUTORS *Dr Alessandro Ayuso, Dr Dan Dream, Martyna Marciniak*

THEMES

Performative Drawing

World Building (Parallel Sci-fi Universe)

Prosthetics

Chance Operations

Urban Strategies (Parasites)

"I am the body agent. I am the system. I was deployed in Turin. This is my perception of Turin.

There are two critical approaches undertaken to escape the normative and the preconceived understanding of the body and its encompassing environments; the system and the content. The 'system' explores the relations between art and architecture. It is an experimental method in which the analogue and digital tools for design (drawing, models, CAD, film, narrative) are produced, questioned, laminated and re-laminated to explore different perceptions. For example, a drawing is seen as not just a drawing, but also a tool, a model, a fictional world, a film or a narrative. This perception applies to all the media. The thresholds between these tools are blurred and hybridized, building the foundation to perceive Turin in the same manner.

This investigation aims to examine how a fragmented city can be interconnected, re-stitched or re-laminated through a lens of perception and augmentation. Specifically, between the thresholds of fictional and non-fictional narratives as design generators, coined as superperception in this work."

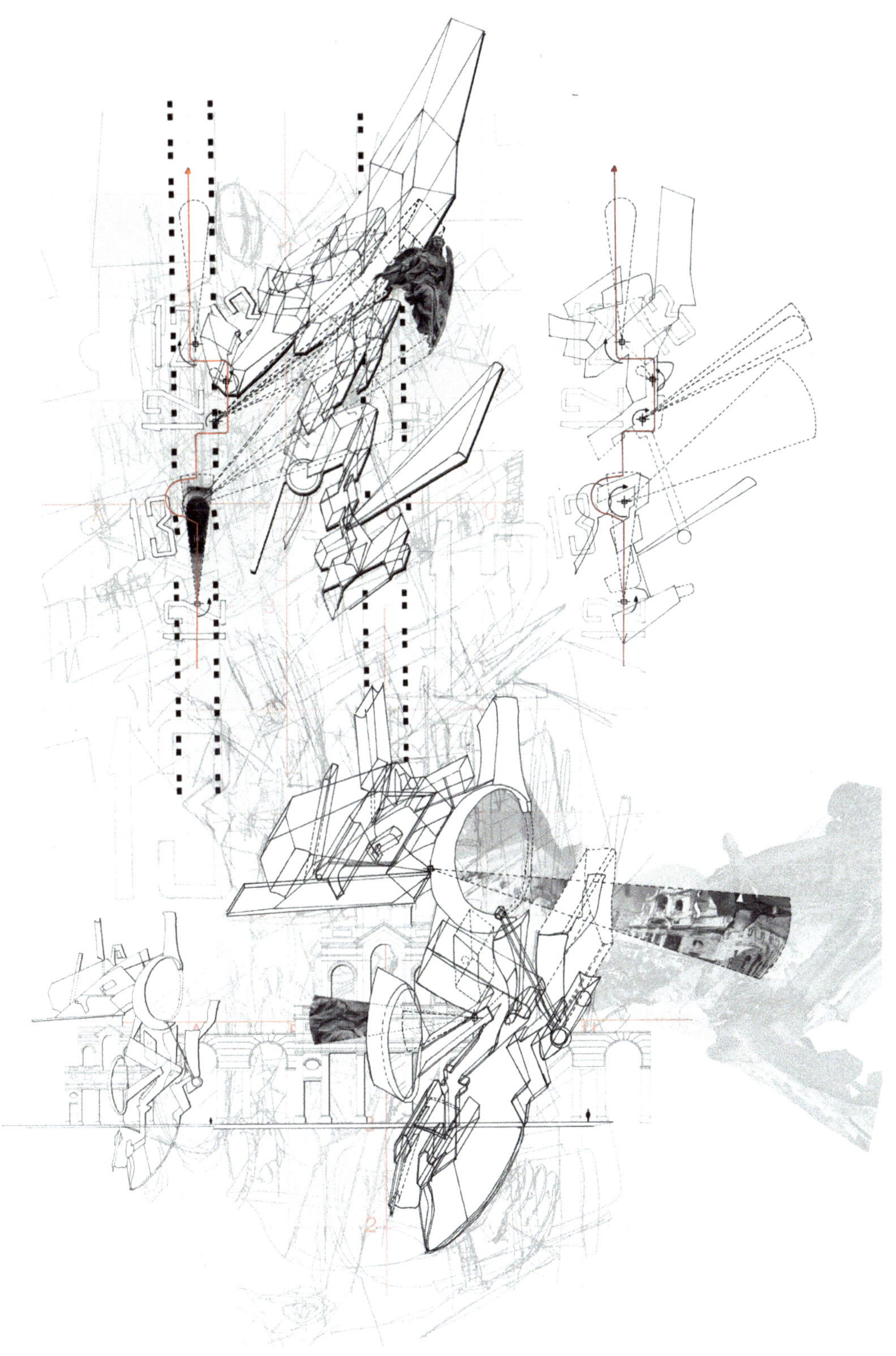

fig. 2.39: An initial study of laminating previous "Superperception Drawings" to explore architectural opportunities.

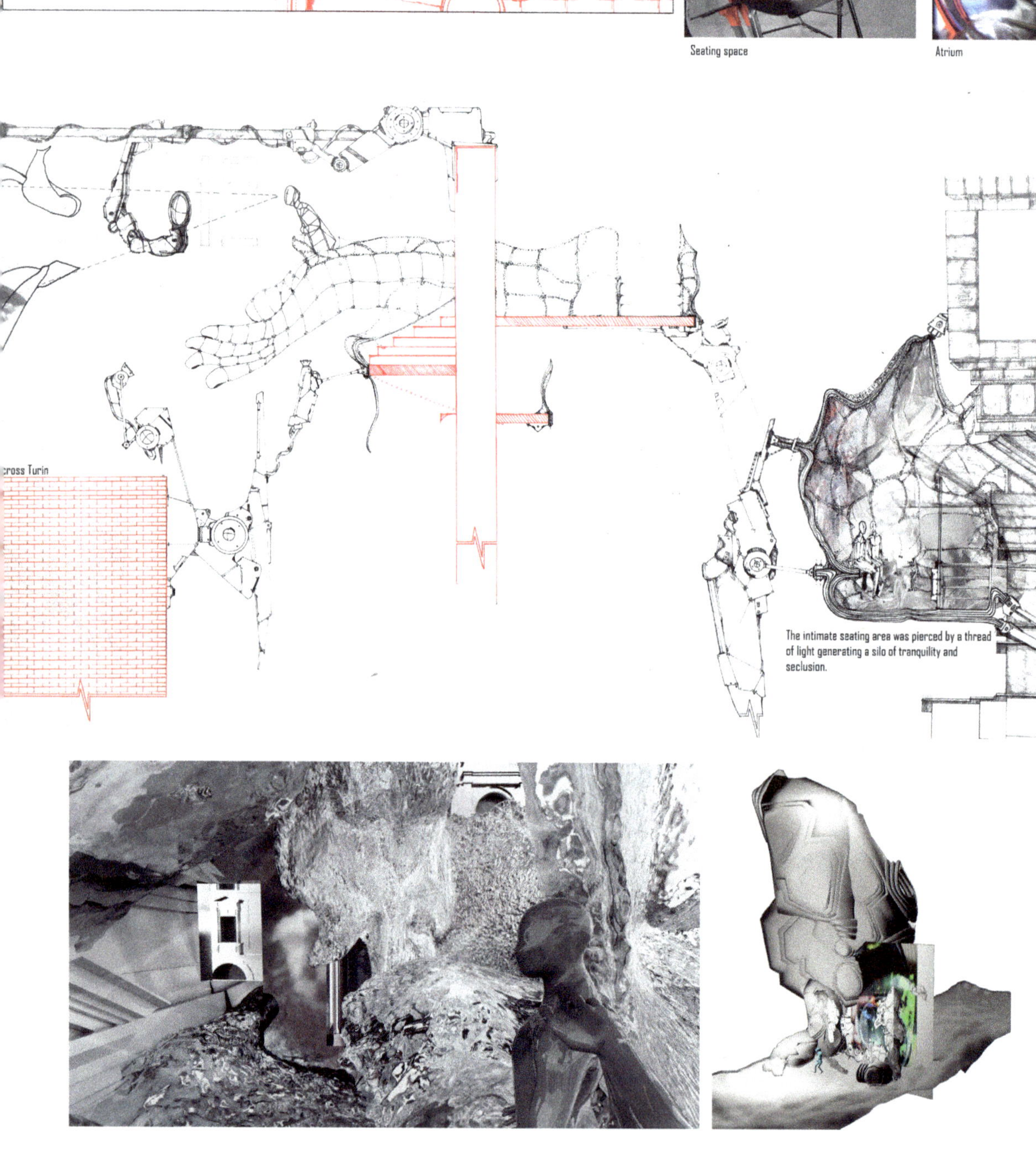

fig. 2.40-2.42: Top to Bottom: The future vision of the Catalytic Silos in which they provide new visual axes across the city in a supercomposite drawing; The visual devices distort the perception of distance and magnify architectural elements from across the city, assembling the architectural values that were once fragmented; An imagined SF World set in the light dimension, where the buildings and the vehicles are not victim of Earth's gravitaty, due to the speed at which they move.

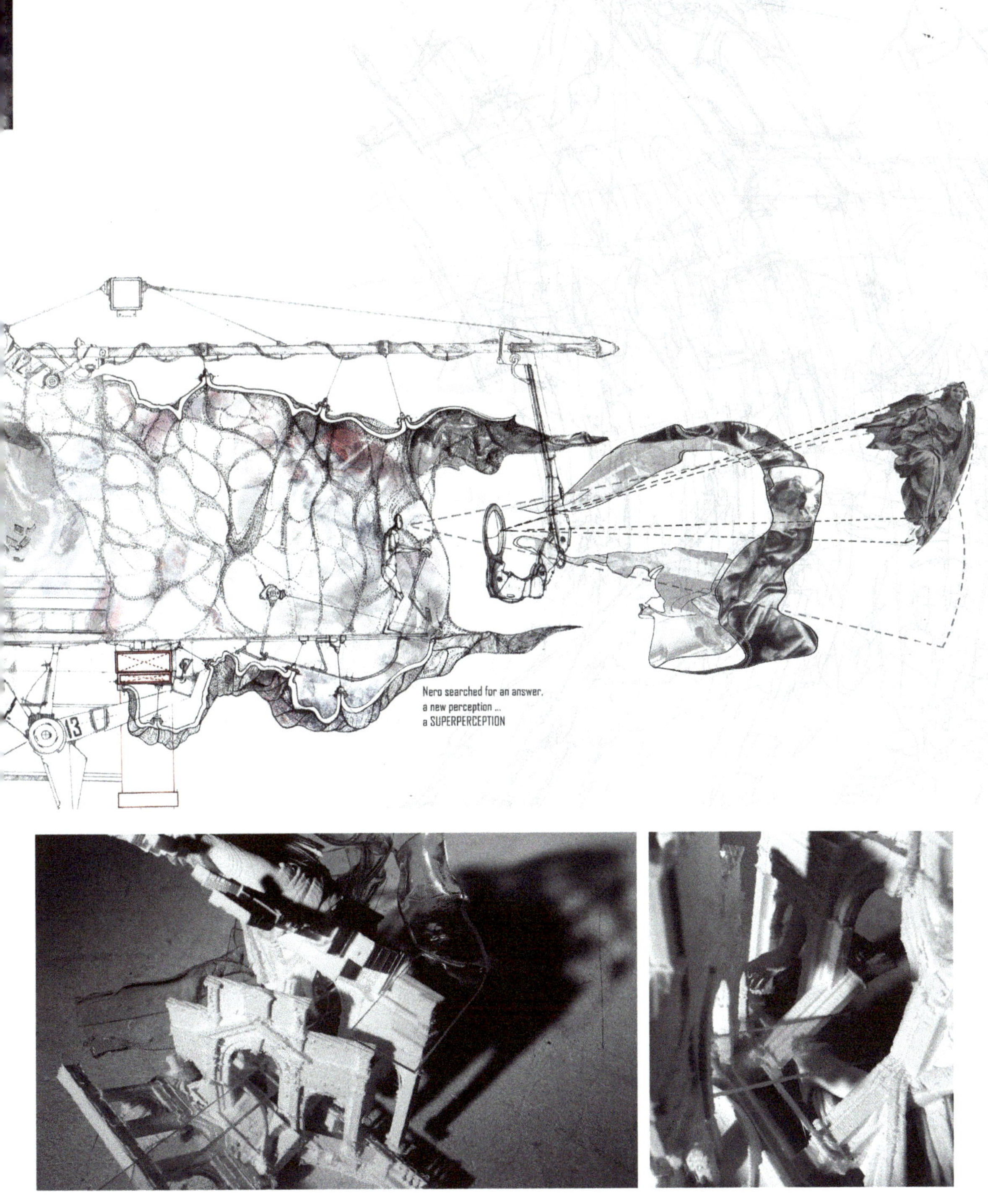

fig. 2.43-2.44: Bottom: Perretti's Plastic Intervention & Expression, physical & digital model compositions as experimental fictional landscapes of plastics penetrating the existing building in Via Po.

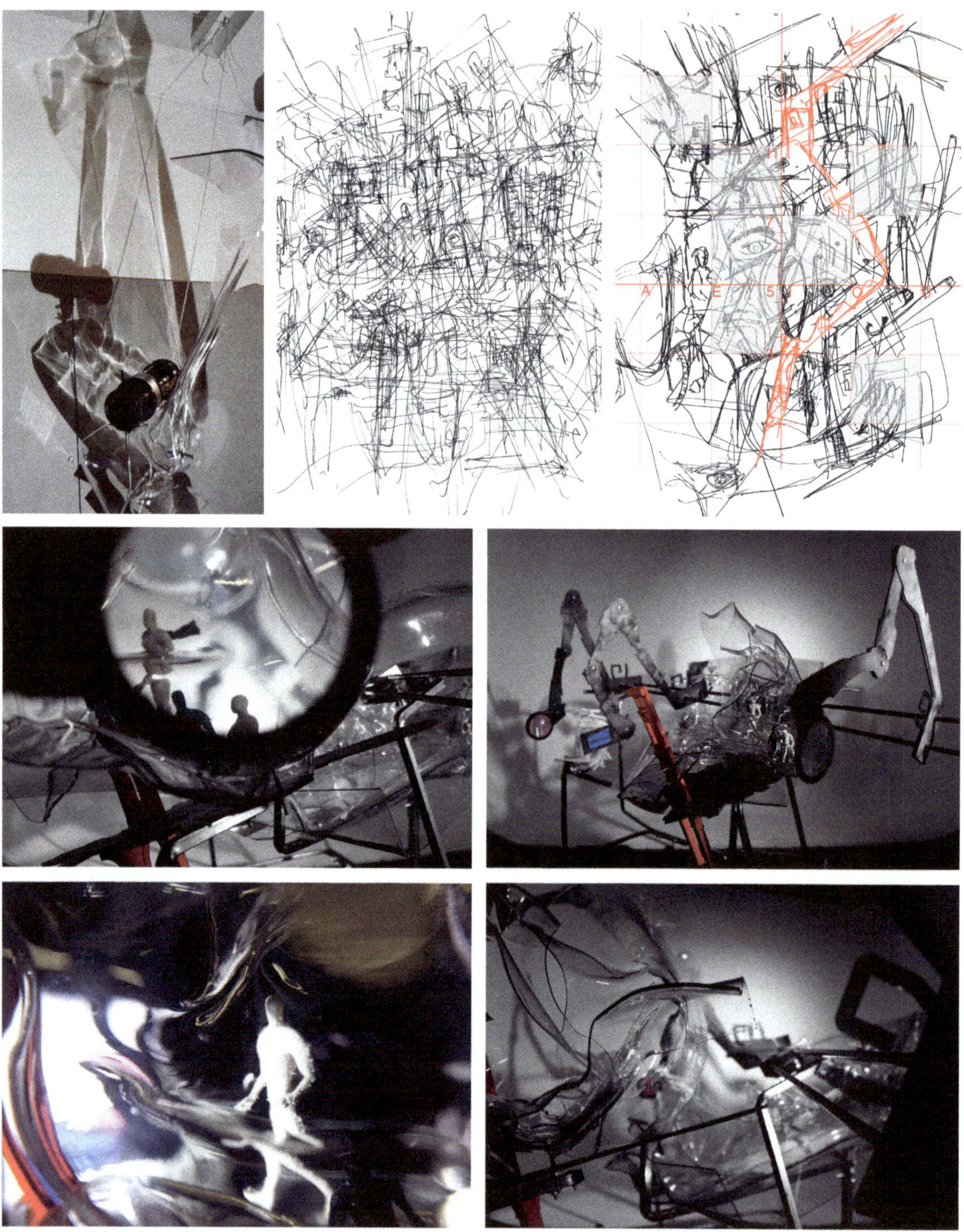

fig. 2.45-2.48: Top-Left to Bottom-Right: Perretti's plastic distortion model showing a Superperception lens, where the "dark" is a product of distortion of the true reality of the material; The application of the term "laminate" as a process of altering the perception of the drawing from solely being a visual production into one that indicates the next iteration of the Superperceptor apparatus; Superperception Model - filming a physical model introduced a dynamic first person experience of the fictional landscape.

fig. 2.49: Facing Page: Perretti's introduction of the science fiction narrative was used as a means to generate a physical effect on the drawing. Breaking thresholds and creating new opportunities to be exploited by the superperception devices to re-tie the narrative of the drawing and, by extension, Turin.

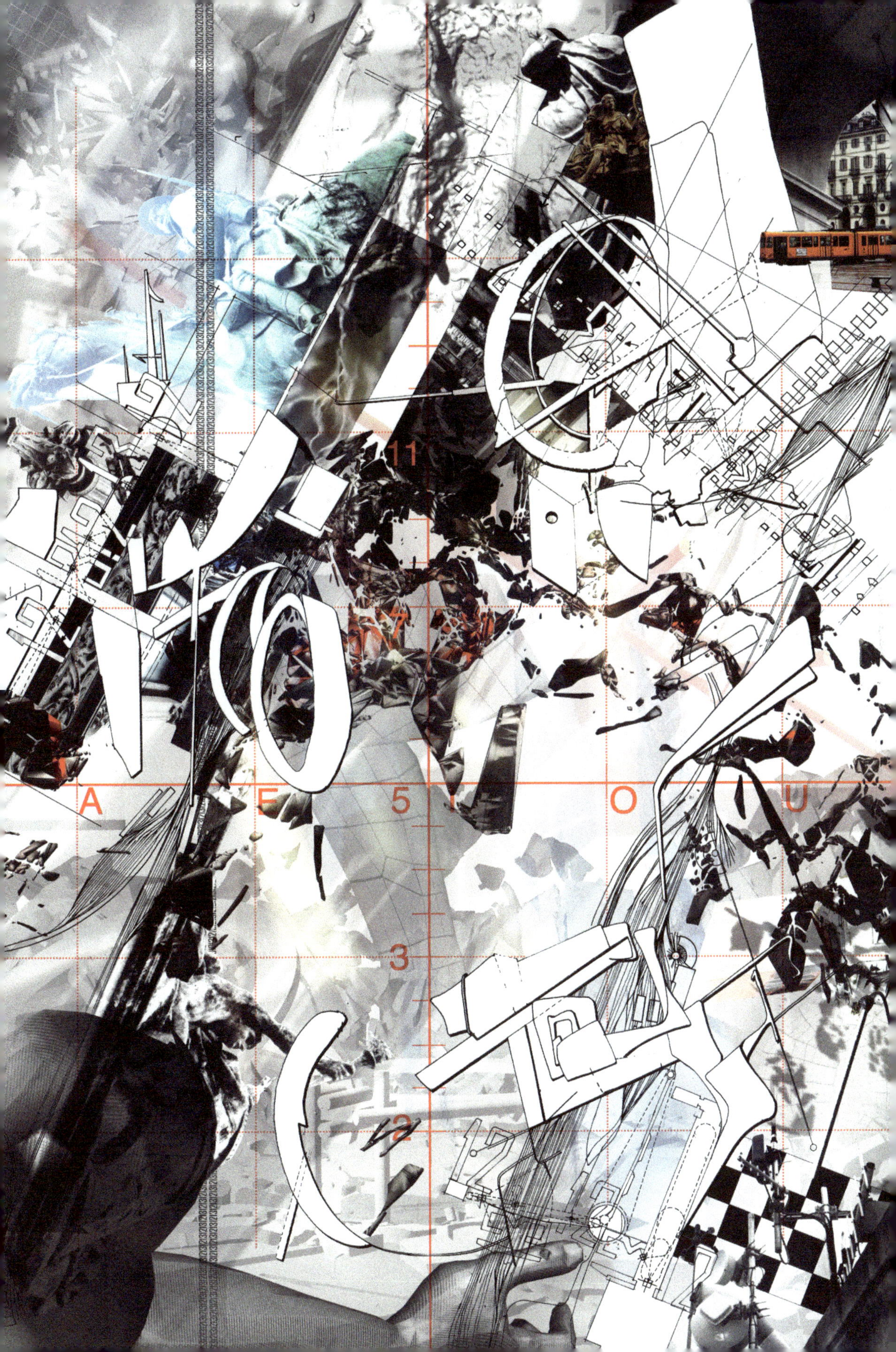
11
A
E
5
O
U
3
2

THE BADDIEVERSE

by
FILIPPO COCCA

BRIEF *Spectral Futures*

YEAR *2022-23*

TUTORS *Dr Alessandro Ayuso, Mary Konstantopoulou*

THEMES

Posthuman Body

Virtual / IRL Body

Sociocultural Dimension of Embodiment (Fashion & Tech)

Organs Without Bodies

Queer Community Identity Enabled by Tech "Hacking"

*"In the abandoned reality of Palermo subjected to the virtual, the Future Ghost is a virtual shapeshifter who has subsumed the Baddie as one of the possible manifestations of its individual expression. It lives at the stretched threshold between, in McKenzie Wark's words, the Actual and the Virtual. It repurposes abandoned objects of the actual, amongst which its body, using the virtual. It's a real b*d b^*@h!*

The Mutant-Baddie's first manifestation was the Internet Skin. In its phenomenological development, the more the Mutant-Baddie expresses itself virtually, the more objects it accumulates and needs actually. What are the possible actual existing 'environments' that can be repurposed?

A semi-real, semi-digital environment of digital unlabour that explores the unlimited power of the virtual as instrument of the queers to heal from trauma through the Rave. The only digital cultural place dedicated to the codification of a new non-commodified expressive language outside the 'male gaze image complex'."

fig. 2.50: Facing Page: Cocca's Shell-of-the-Ghost as "the Intenet Skin" inspired by McKenzie Wark's *Hacker Manifesto*.

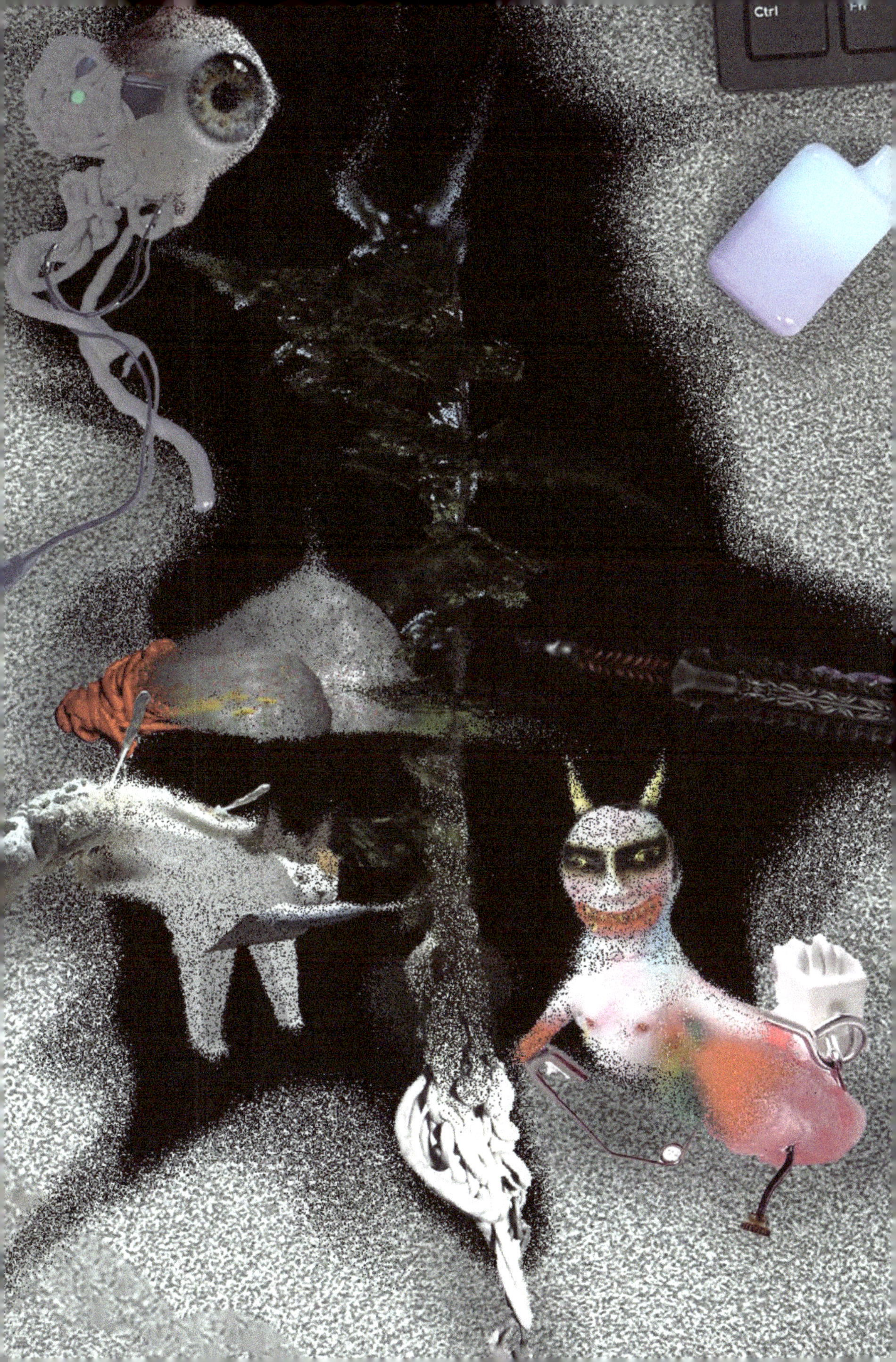
Ctrl

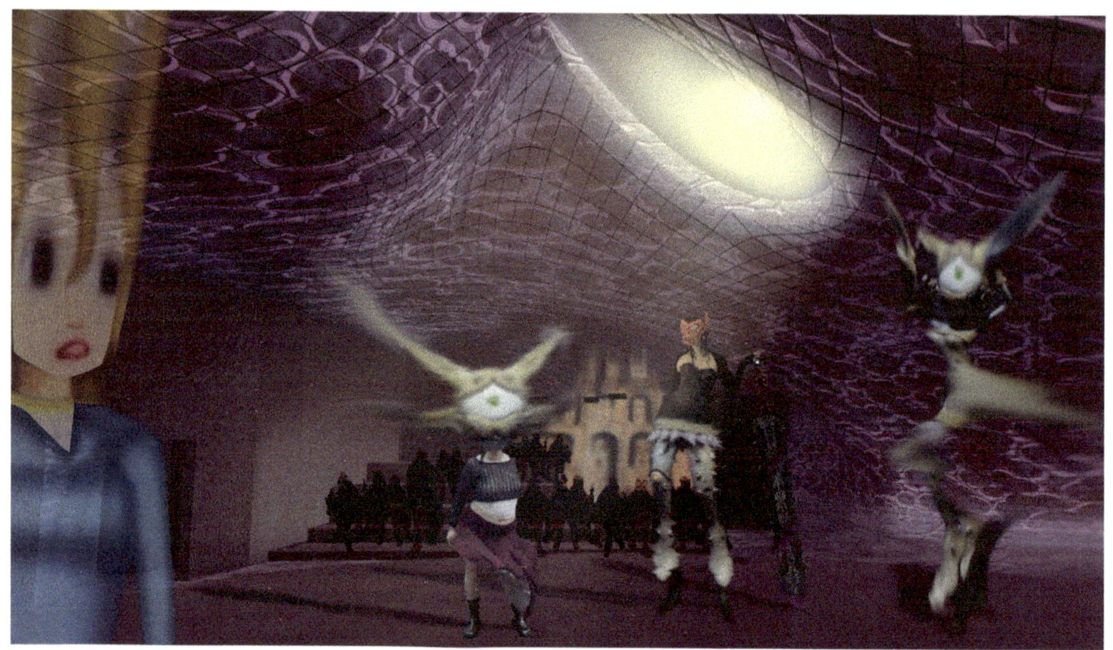

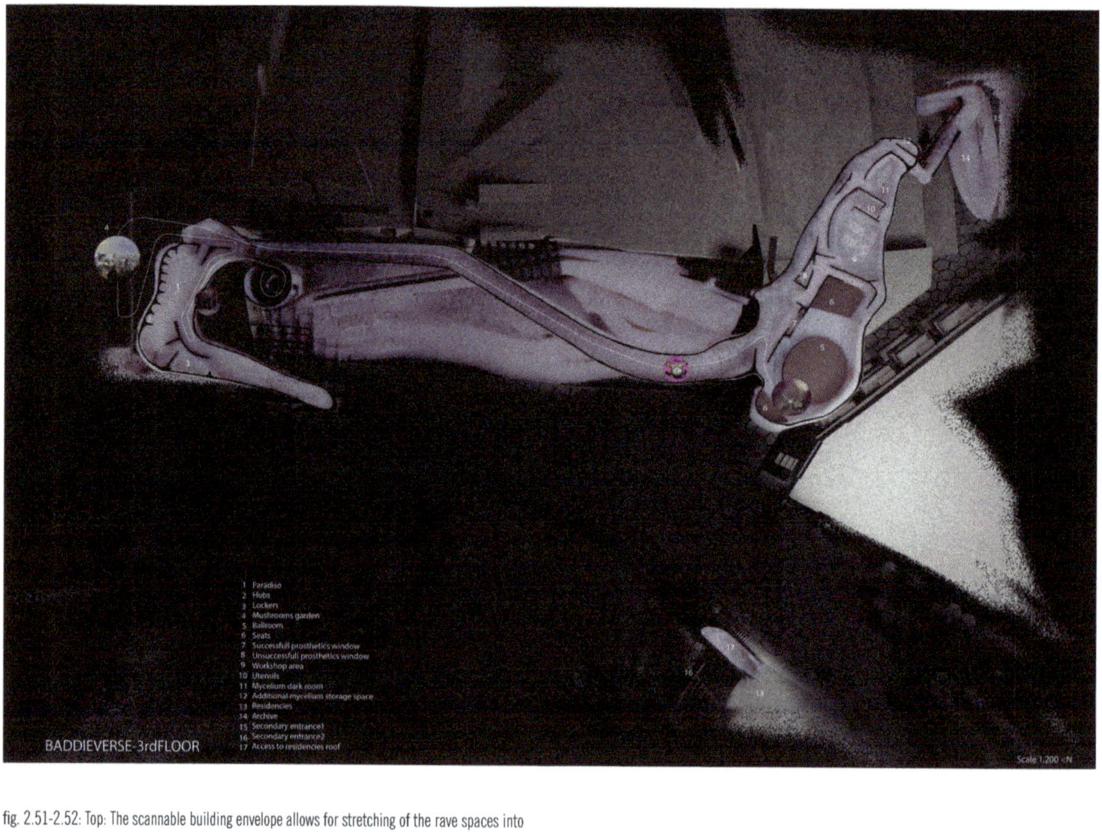

BADDIEVERSE-3rdFLOOR

1 Paradiso
2 Hubs
3 Lockers
4 Mushrooms garden
5 Ballroom
6 Seats
7 Successfull prosthetics window
8 Unsuccessfull prosthetics window
9 Workshop area
10 Utensils
11 Mycelium dark room
12 Additional mycelium storage space
13 Residencies
14 Archive
15 Secondary entrance1
16 Secondary entrance2
17 Access to residencies roof

Scale 1:200

fig. 2.51-2.52: Top: The scannable building envelope allows for stretching of the rave spaces into mixed reality experiences - 02:35 - "Lmao I look huge don't I? Yea just wanted everybody to see my new lil dress. Well have fun and if u need anything...well...u see me."; Bottom: Baddieverse - 3rd Floor plan, containing successful and unsuccessful prosthetics windows, workshops, mycellium dark rooms, access to residencies rooftop.

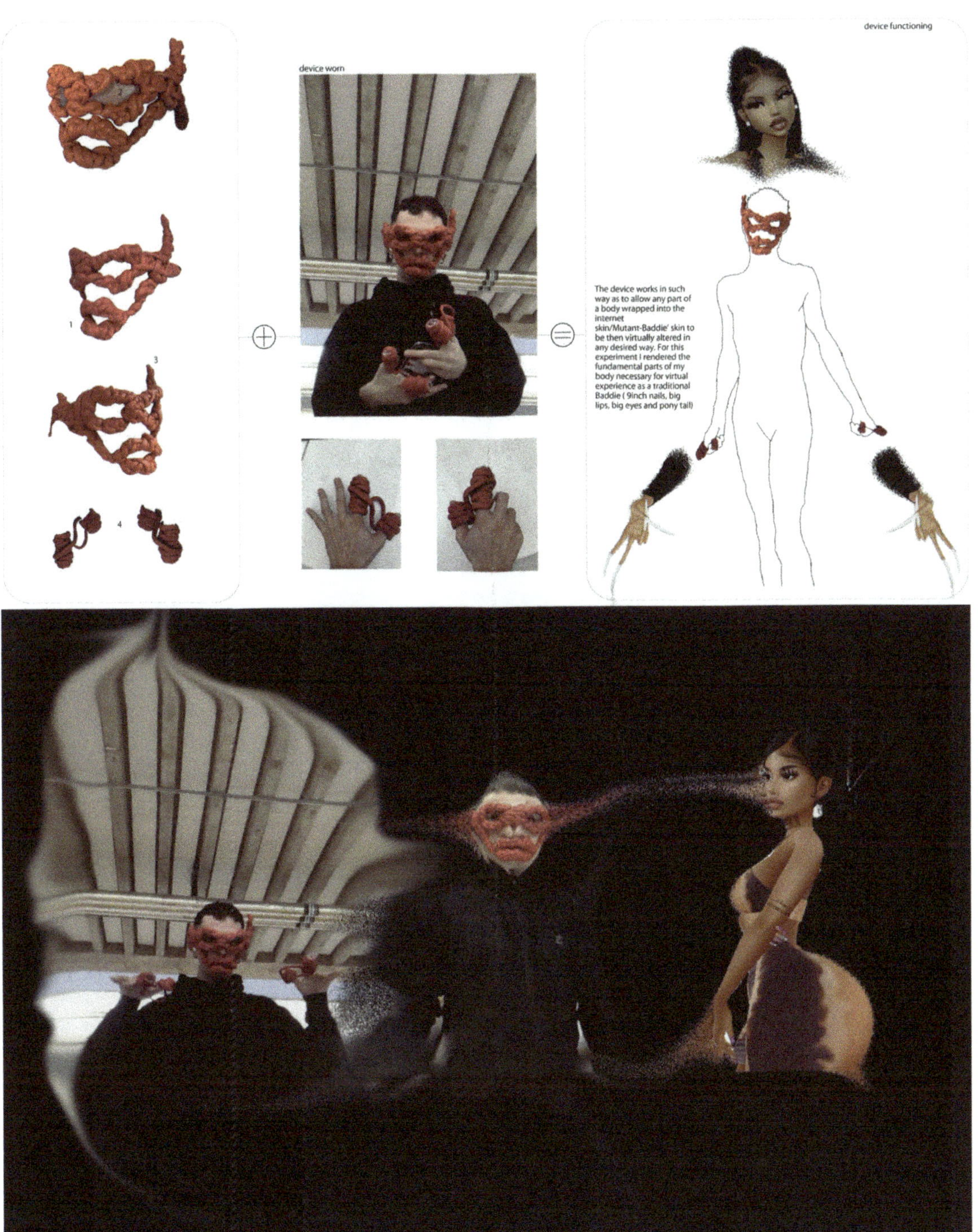

fig. 2.53: Cocca's Shell-of-the-Ghost was designed as "a device that uses the fundamental parts of my body necessary for virtual experience as a traditional Baddie (9inch nails, big lips, big eyes and ponytail)."

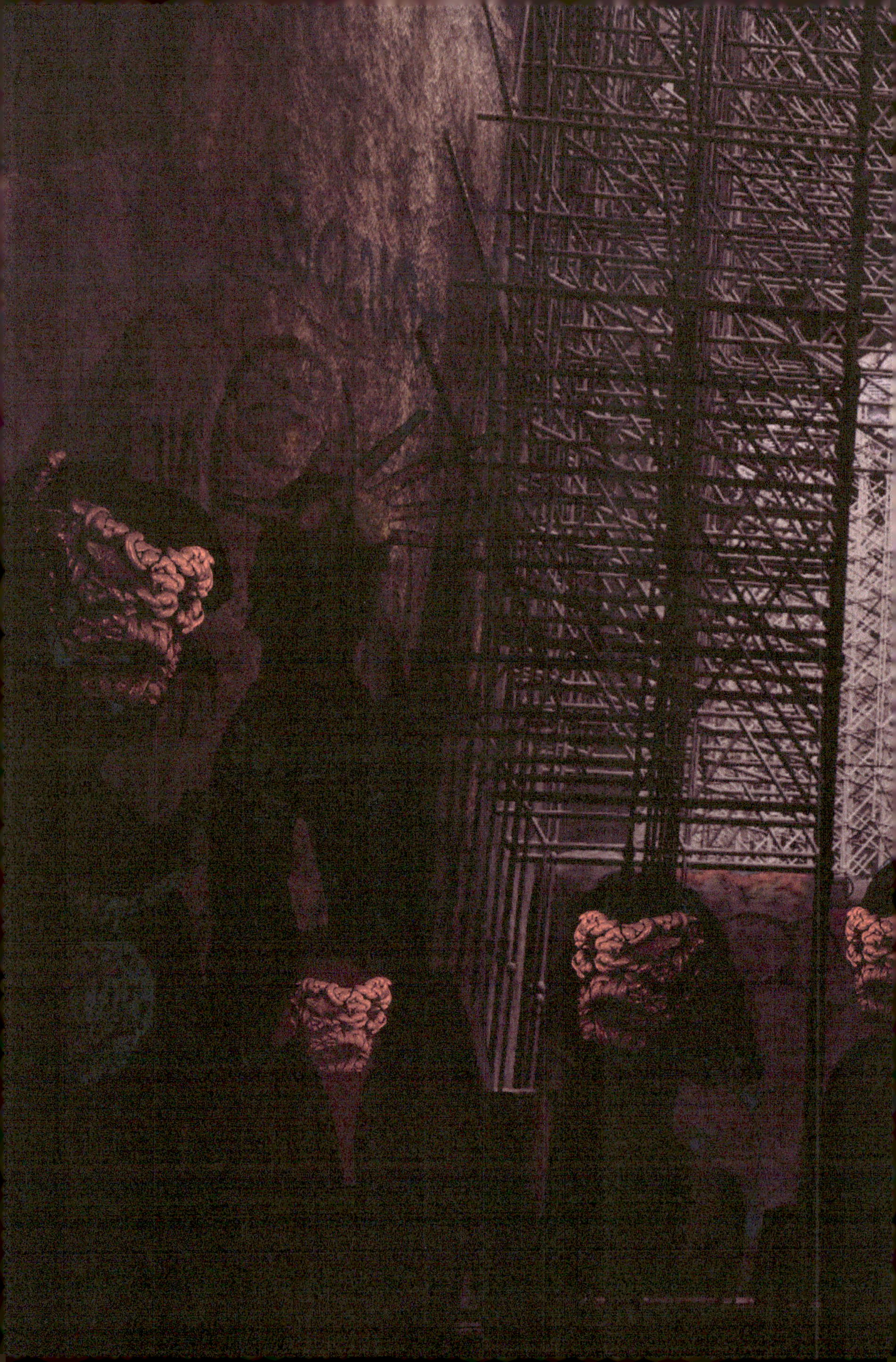

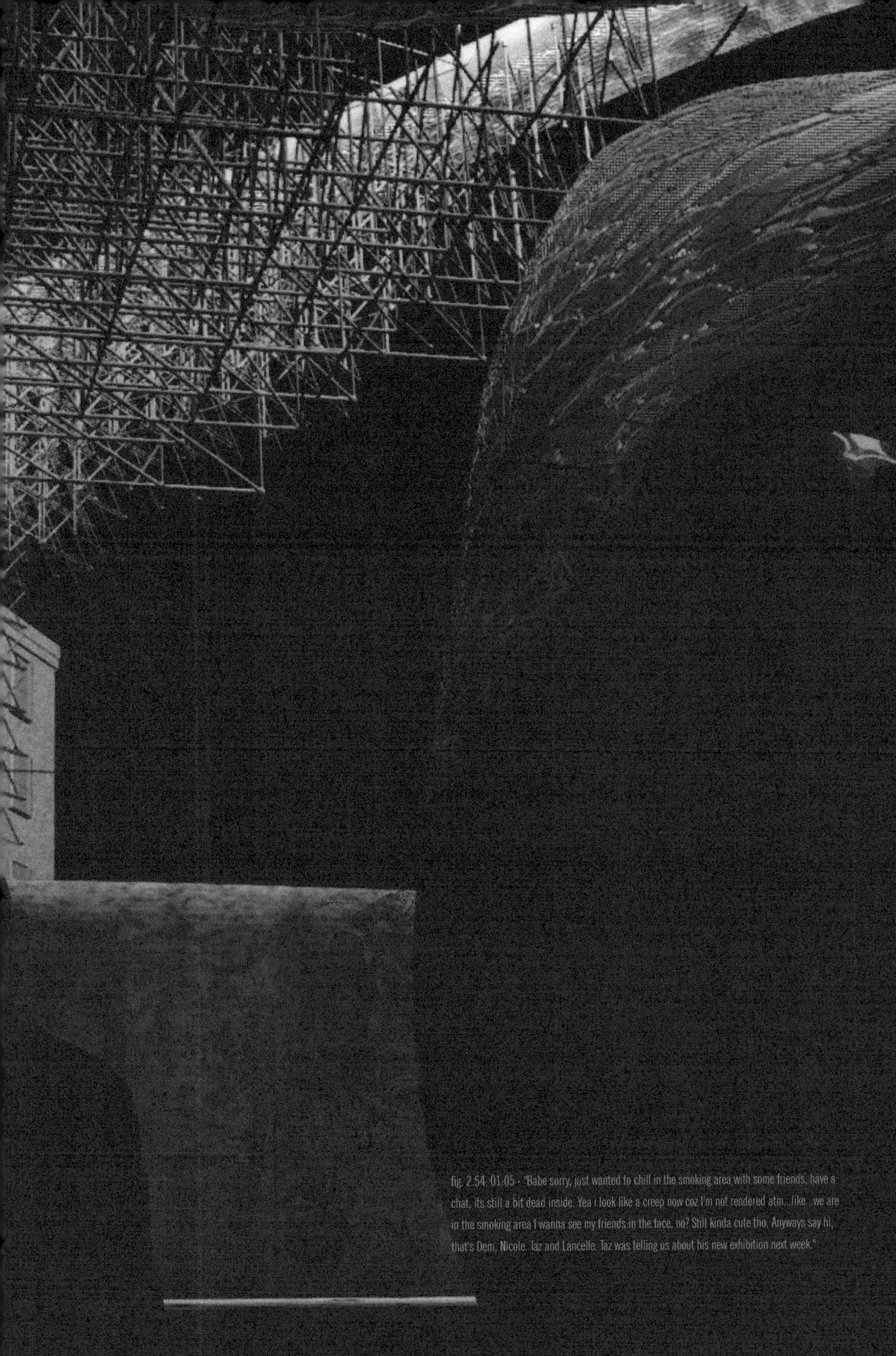

fig. 2.54: 01:05 - "Babe sorry, just wanted to chill in the smoking area with some friends, have a chat, its still a bit dead inside. Yea i look like a creep now coz I'm not rendered atm...like...we are in the smoking area I wanna see my friends in the face, no? Still kinda cute tho. Anyways say hi, that's Dem, Nicole, Taz and Lancelle. Taz was telling us about his new exhibition next week."

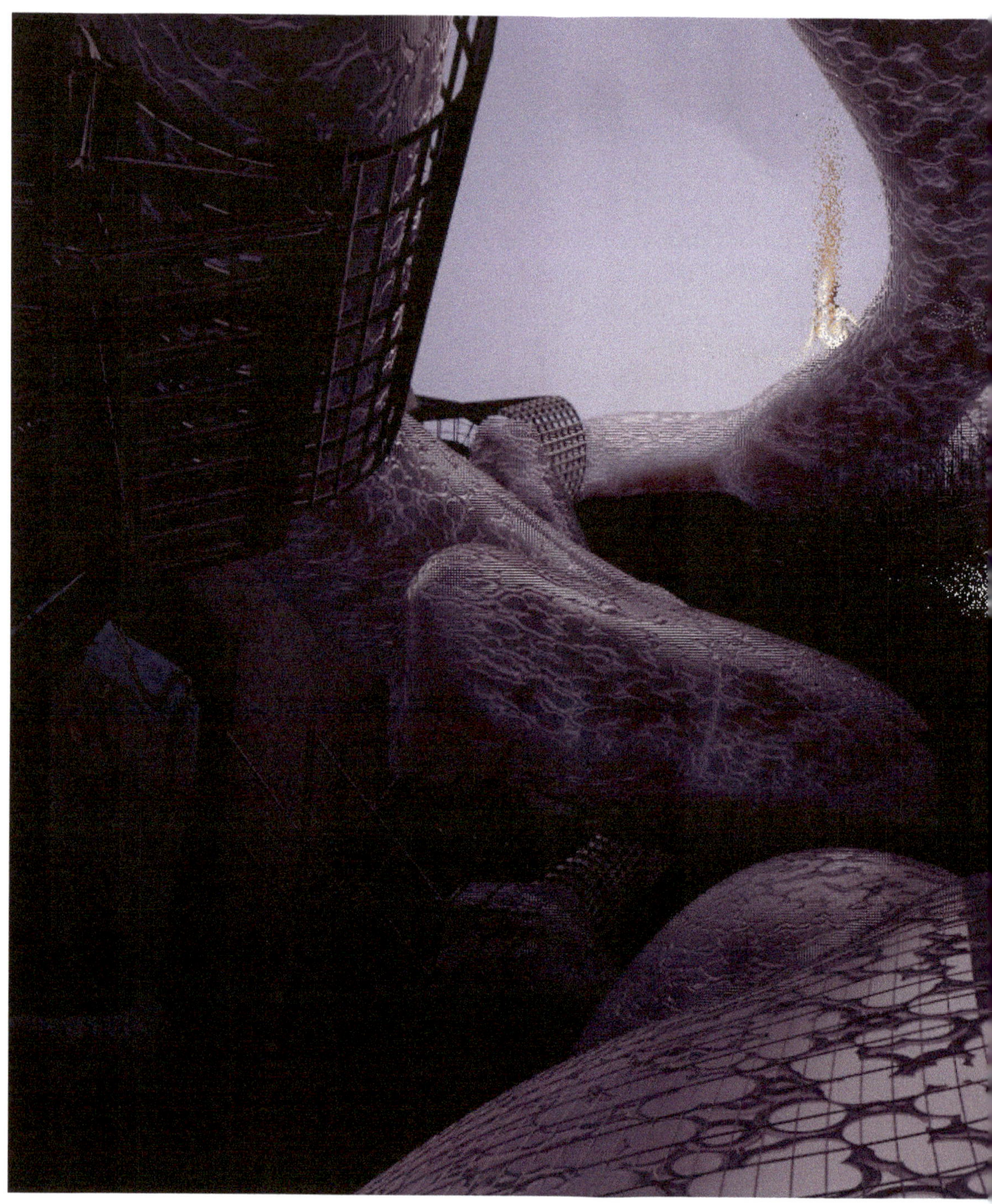

fig. 2.55-2.58: Top-Left to Bottom-Right: The Baddieverse mixed reality exterior; Mutant-Baddie cause of death: the iPhone's health app. Although the queers resident in the Baddieverse enforced a strict no-photo policy, the European branch of Apple Inc. noticed an unusual drastic increase in steps in the ruins of la Kalsa, Palermo. They bought the site, sold the data and replaced the Mutant-Baddie with an Apple Store; 23:55 - "Hey queen, it's Bea now. Sick right?! Yea that's Mark, we hate him around here...like...why are you so obsessed with me?"; 05:20 - "Omg it's always so nice to come up here! So here is where we grow the mushrooms to make our prosthetics."

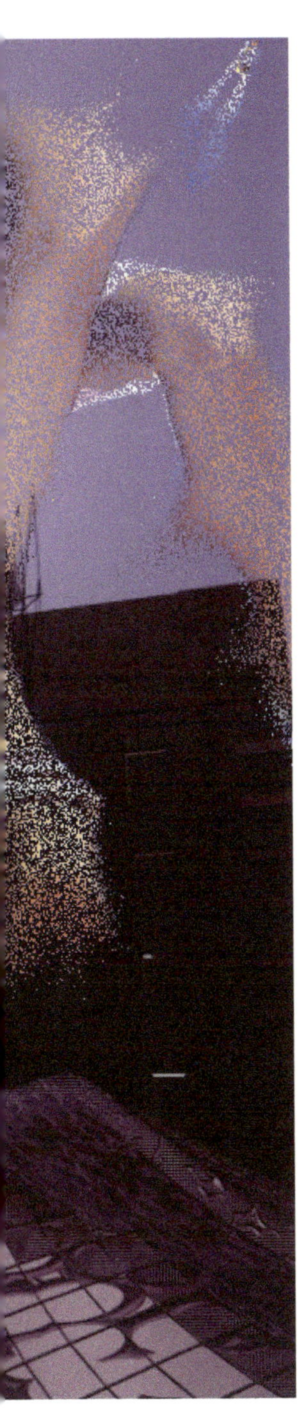
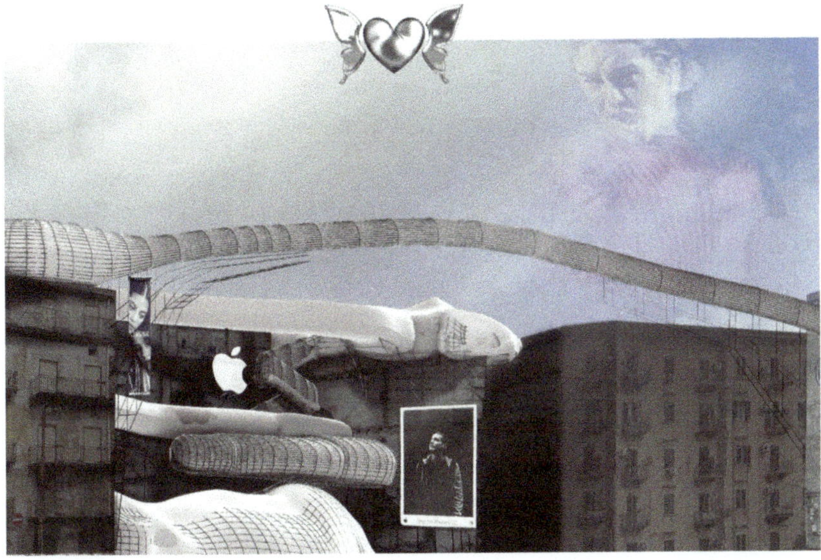
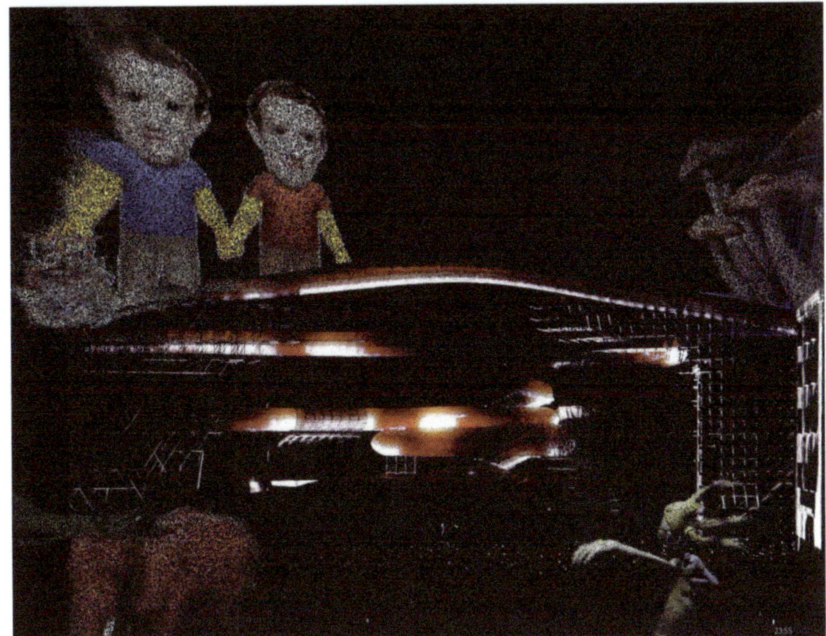
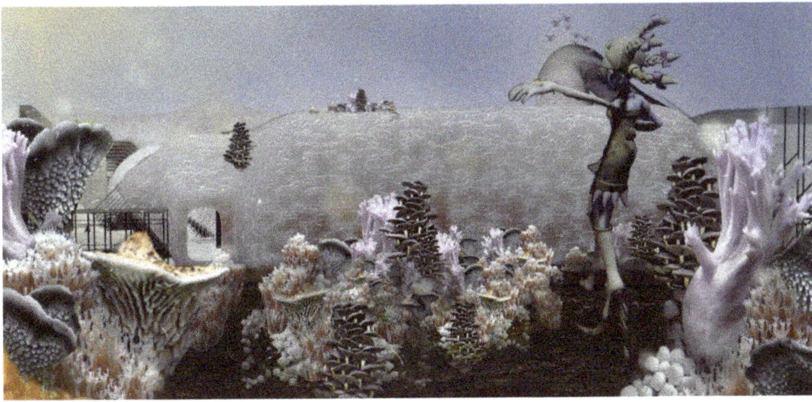

THE BECOMING: The Story of the Flaneur and the Doll Theatre

by
ALEXANDROS TZORTZIS DE PAZ

BRIEF *Body Agent Architecture*

YEAR *2019-20*

TUTORS *Dr Alessandro Ayuso, Dr Dan Dream, Martyna Marciniak*

THEMES

Flaneurism

Hedonistic Body

Doll-Burlesque

Puppet Theatre

Fleshy Architecture

Building as Protagonist

"After the Suicide of Gerard de Nerval ,the original flaneur, on the 26th January 1855, his lobster pet escaped. Traces of the incident and where it took place are embedded in the lobster's memory.

London, 2020: 'I have been looking for the lobster... the legend says it made its way from the Seine river in Paris all the way to Mile End, London, in search for a new master. I must begin by separating the different parts of A. Dumas' poem of the incident based on the main architectural elements referred in it, deleting the geographical details of Paris.'

The flaneur created a device that spoke to him phrases from the poem while he took his drift around Mile End in search of the lost lobster.When he eventually finds the lobster, the flaneur realises that he needs to become anatomically more like a male lobster in order to interact with the dormant one on site.

Mimicking the lobster's anatomy, the monument that the flaneur constructs has a harsh crustacean shell cladding and a soft skin on the inside. The site begins to shed its shells like a lobster on a regular basis, leaving thee buildings fragile until it has regenerated."

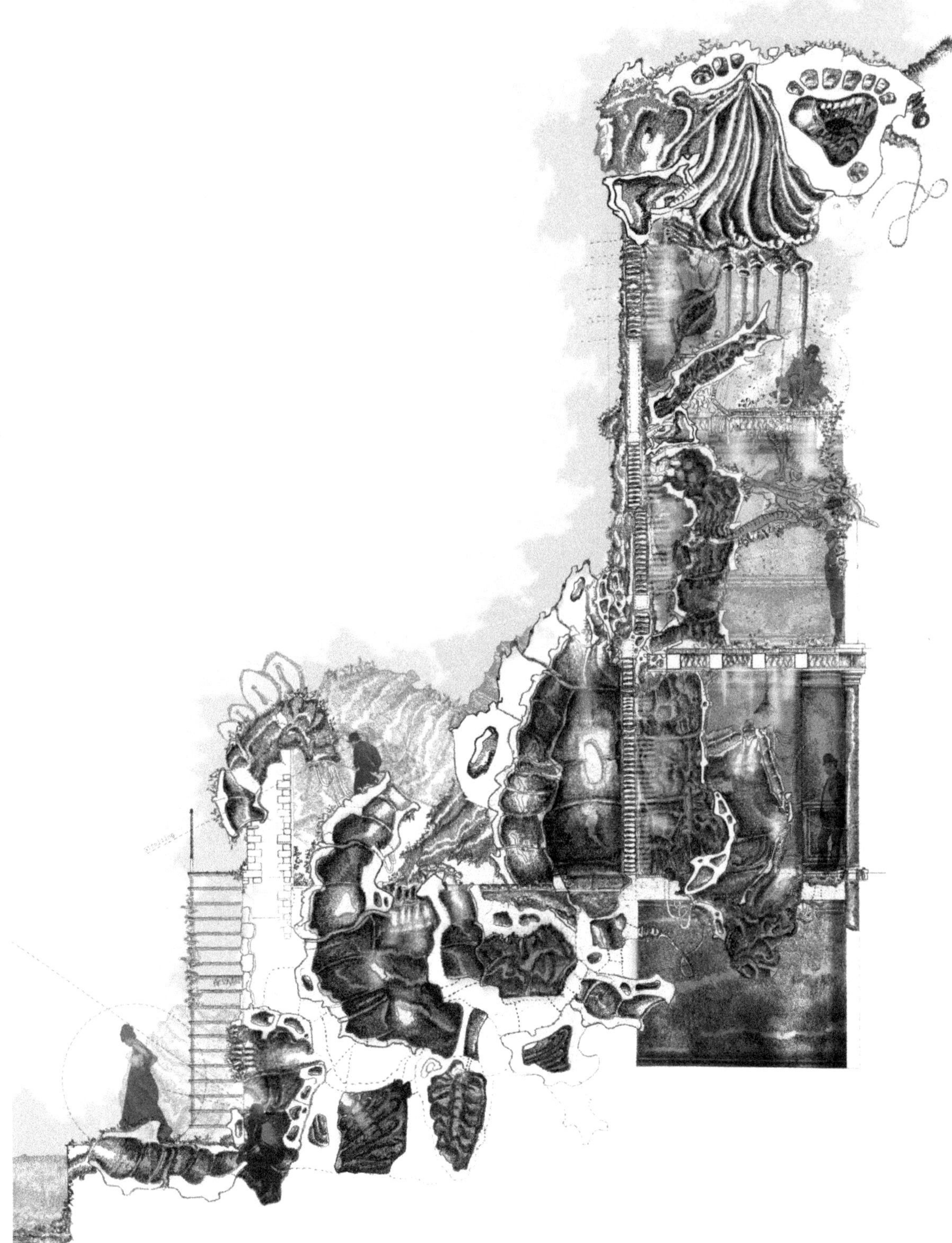

fig. 2.59: A new zone of flaneurism: The 1:20 section explored an initial intervention into Mile End Park. The lobster and the master have been reunited. As the lobster sheds its many shells, it creates a labyrinthine landscape of carcasses, in which the modern-day flaneur can indulge in their impulses. The hybrid flaneur inhabits the head of the lobster. Flaneurs are encouraged to get lost in the voyeristic landscape, watch, stroll and observe.

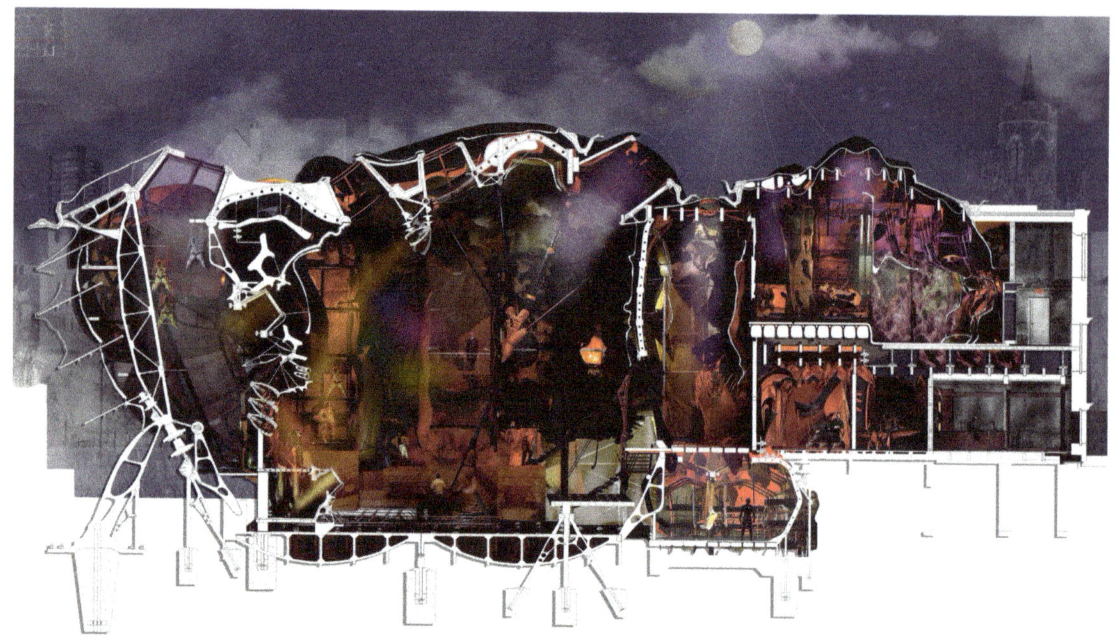

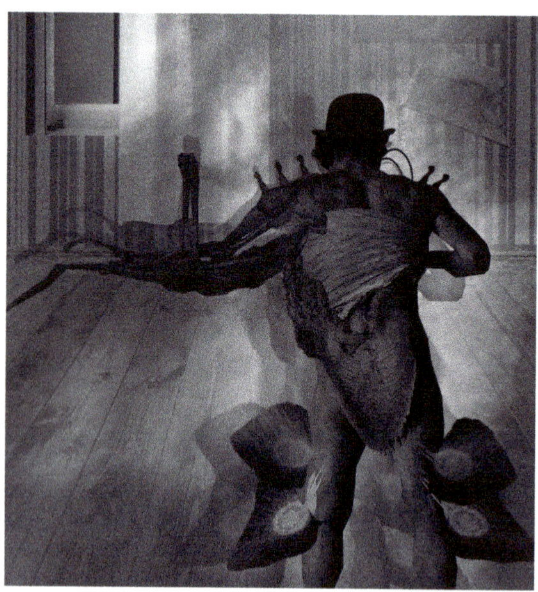

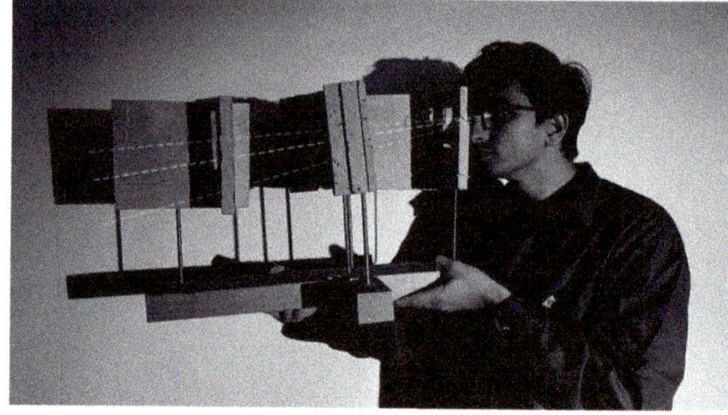

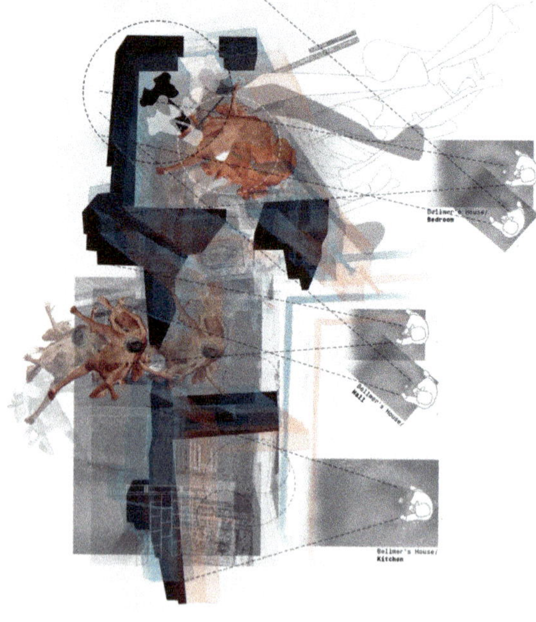

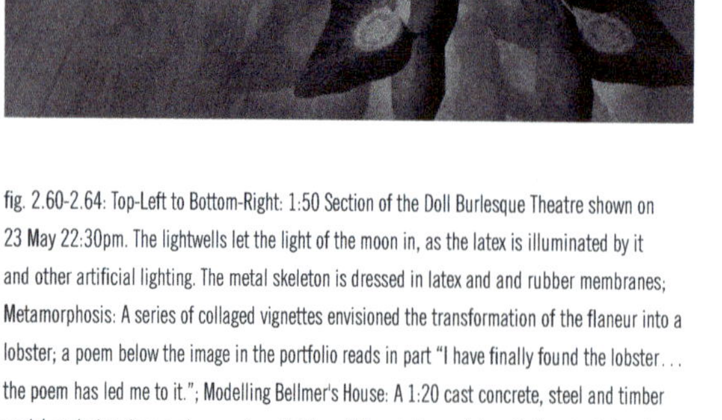

fig. 2.60-2.64: Top-Left to Bottom-Right: 1:50 Section of the Doll Burlesque Theatre shown on 23 May 22:30pm. The lightwells let the light of the moon in, as the latex is illuminated by it and other artificial lighting. The metal skeleton is dressed in latex and and rubber membranes; Metamorphosis: A series of collaged vignettes envisioned the transformation of the flaneur into a lobster; a poem below the image in the portfolio reads in part "I have finally found the lobster... the poem has led me to it."; Modelling Bellmer's House: A 1:20 cast concrete, steel and timber model analysing views and spaces in artist Hans Bellmer's house (where Bellmer took the photos of his doll-manequin sculptures). Facing page: The Molting Facade: Inspired by lobsters' ability to shed their shells, Tzortzis de Paz constructed a latex study model of the facade in a post-molting condition, where the facade is though to be made from what he called carapace, membrane, skin and building.

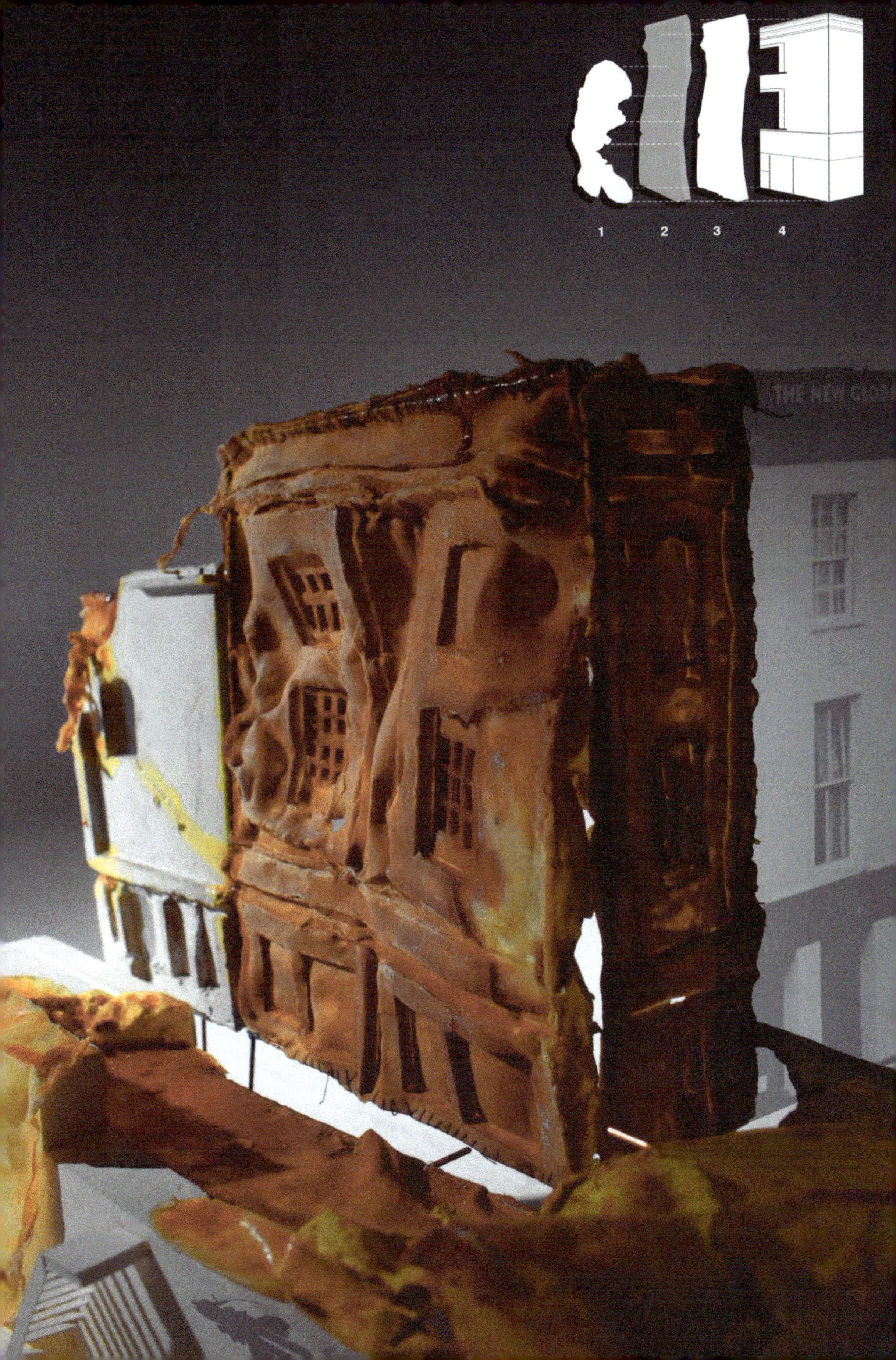

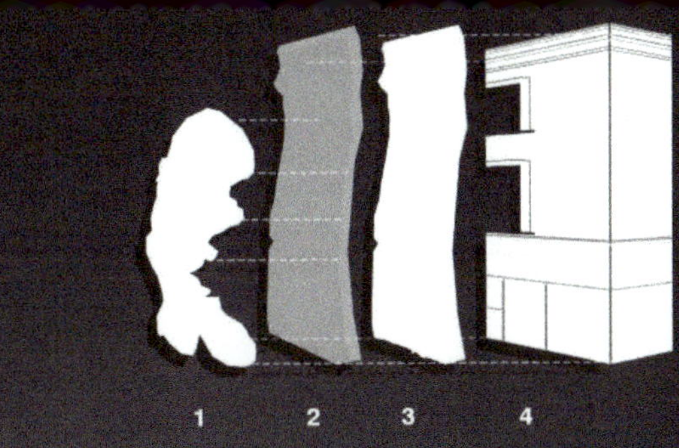
1
2
3
4

RASHES & HIVES: Allergenic Architecture, Stimulatory Instruments & a New Purification Chapel for St. Paul's Cathedral

by
ALEXANDROS TZORTZIS DE PAZ

BRIEF *Architecture's Second Bodies*

YEAR *2020-21*

TUTORS *Dr Alessandro Ayuso, Dr Dan Dream, Dr Fiona Zisch*

THEMES

Microscale of the Body (Epidermal Layers)

Metaphoric Body / Grotesque

Erotic / Ceremonial Body

Abject

Body-Building Mirror Through Narrative

Purity & Fetish as Design Generators

"The City of London is one of the most polluted urban centres in the world. Monuments need to start being modified in order to assist the city with its air cleaning. The proposed filtration system that attaches to St Paul's Cathedral is one of them. The mediating object takes the form of a porcelain suit that attaches to the facade of the Cathedral. A network of particle collectors is already in place waiting for the suit to be assembled and plugged in. Once in place the second body is inserted into it, as the handler increasingly adds its layers.

A headline on The City of London Observer newspaper on the 14th January 2021 notes:

St. Paul's Cathedral moves on with new air filtration plan.

After much controversy, the first filtration systems were installed on the most polluted area of the cathedral's facade. In a bid to protect the Cathedral's facade and filter the polluted atmosphere of London, officials decided to greenlight the system. Official sources state the system filters the air from dust, pollen and pollution particles, but its exact use is still a mystery."

fig. 2.65: Facing page: 1:1 anatomical hand drawing of the body combined with cross sections of the existing cathedral with the air filtering devices attached in the "Handler's" atelier.

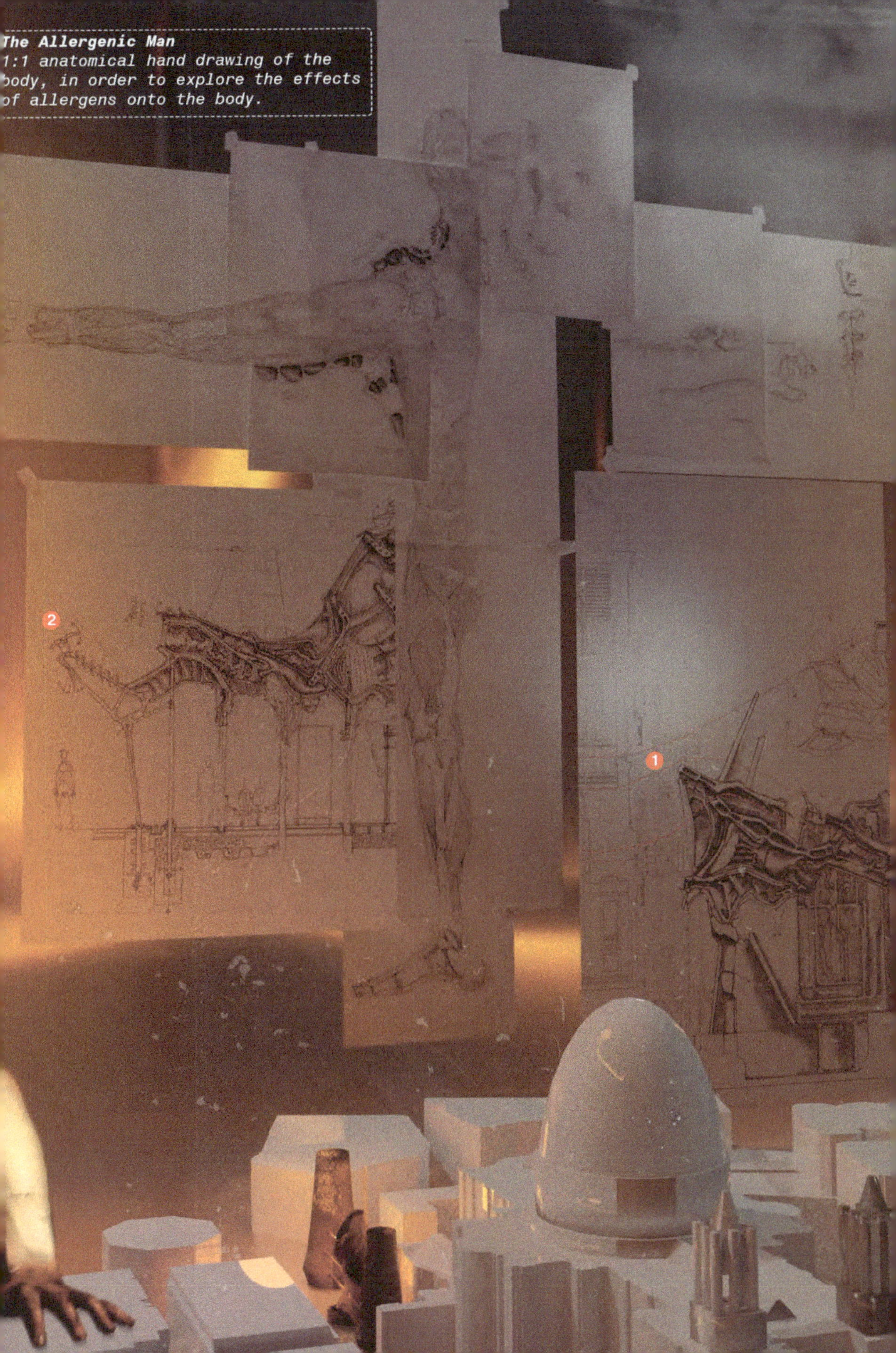

The Allergenic Man
1:1 anatomical hand drawing of the body, in order to explore the effects of allergens onto the body.

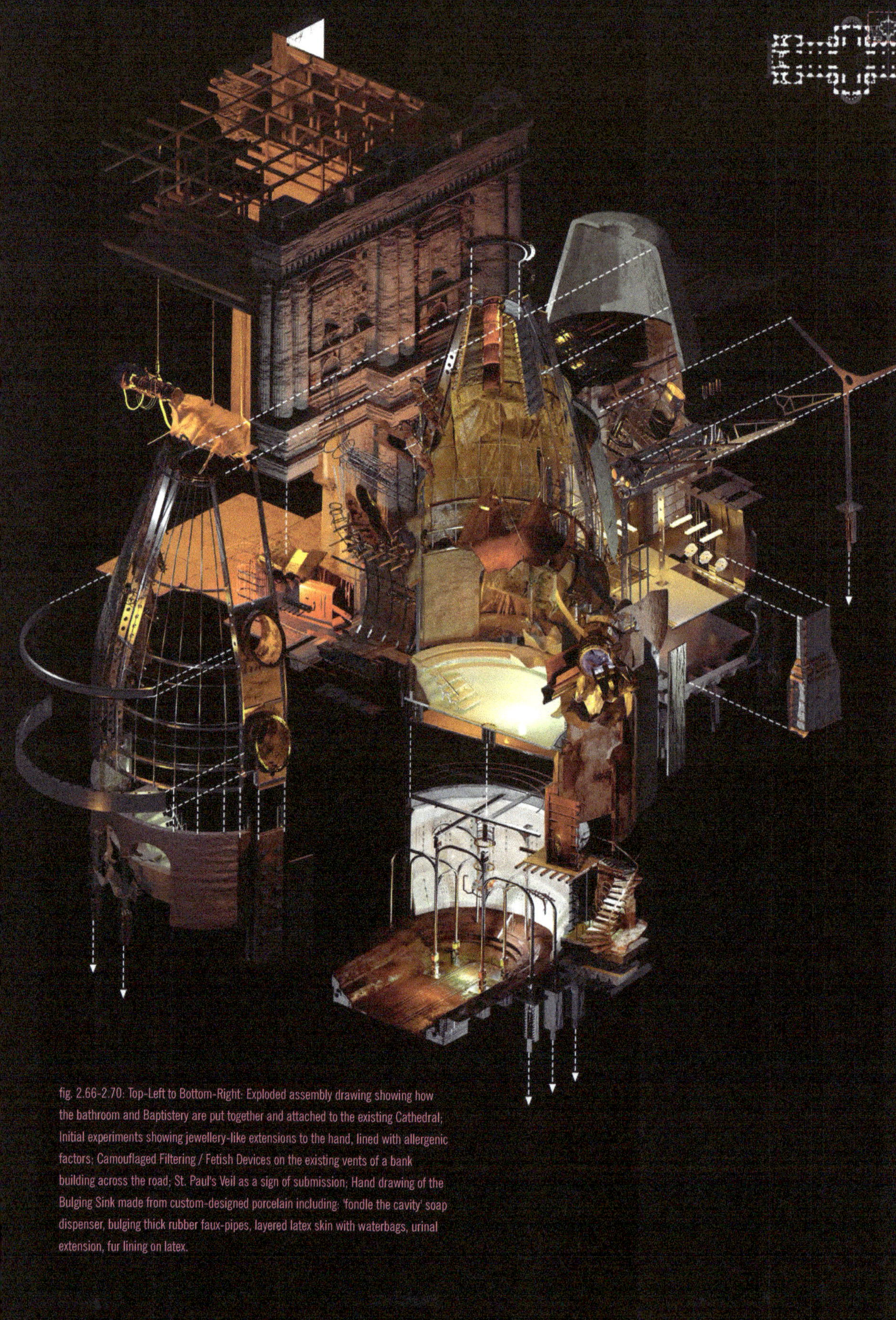

fig. 2.66-2.70: Top-Left to Bottom-Right: Exploded assembly drawing showing how the bathroom and Baptistery are put together and attached to the existing Cathedral; Initial experiments showing jewellery-like extensions to the hand, lined with allergenic factors; Camouflaged Filtering / Fetish Devices on the existing vents of a bank building across the road; St. Paul's Veil as a sign of submission; Hand drawing of the Bulging Sink made from custom-designed porcelain including: 'fondle the cavity' soap dispenser, bulging thick rubber faux-pipes, layered latex skin with waterbags, urinal extension, fur lining on latex.

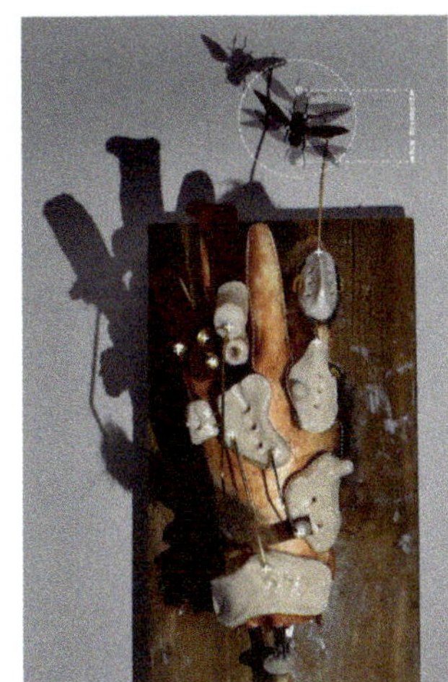

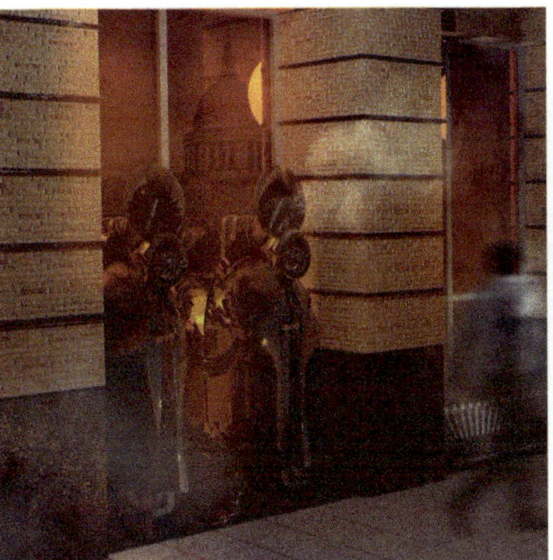

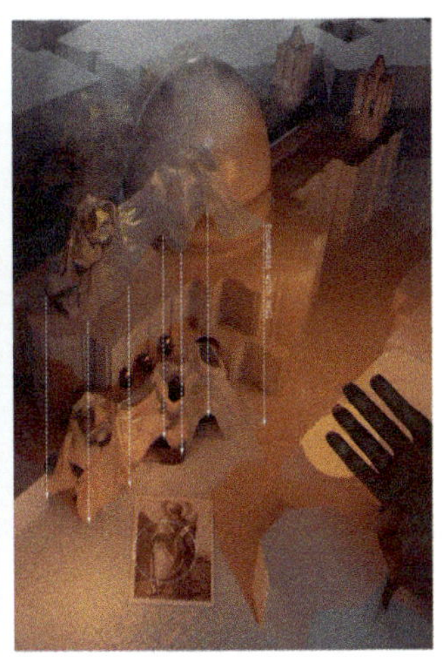

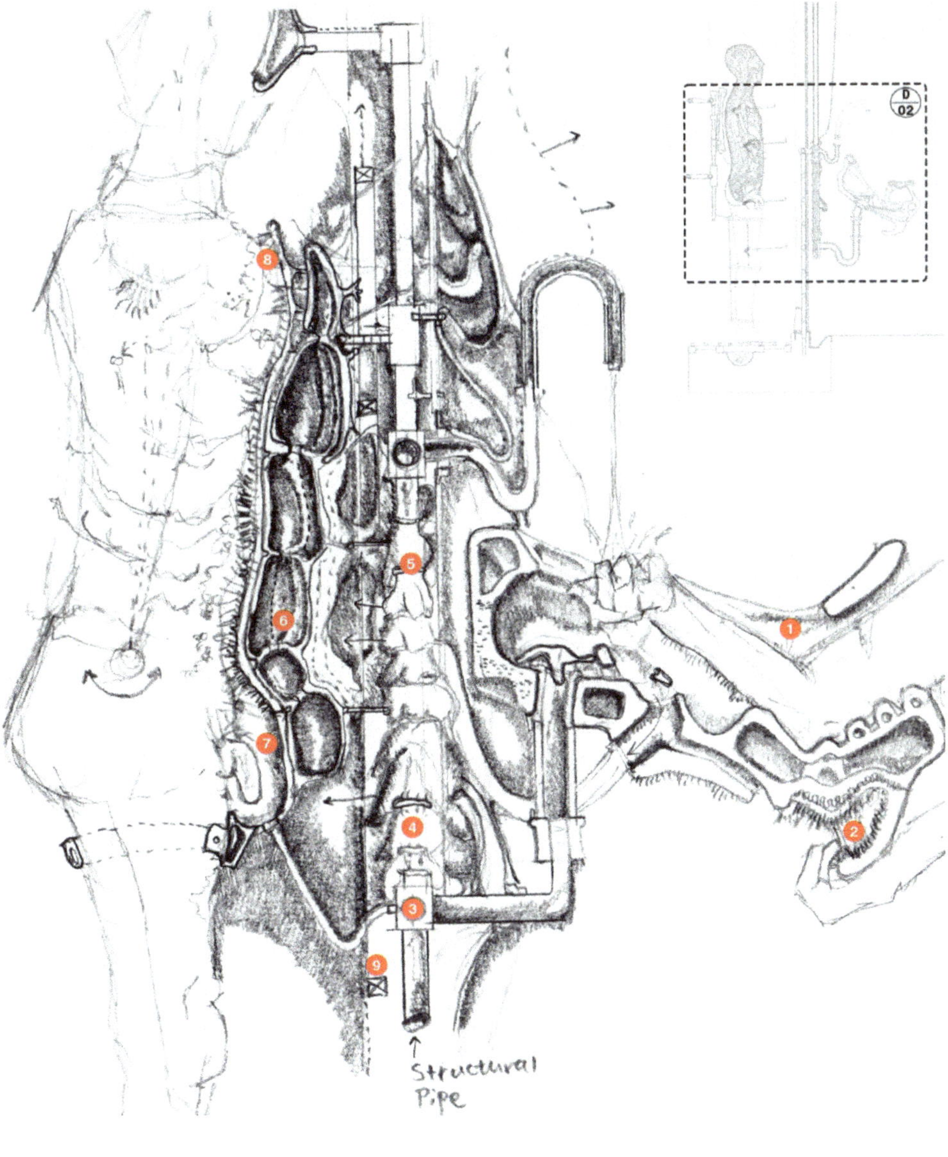

D
02

8
5
6
1
7
4
2
3
9

Structural
Pipe

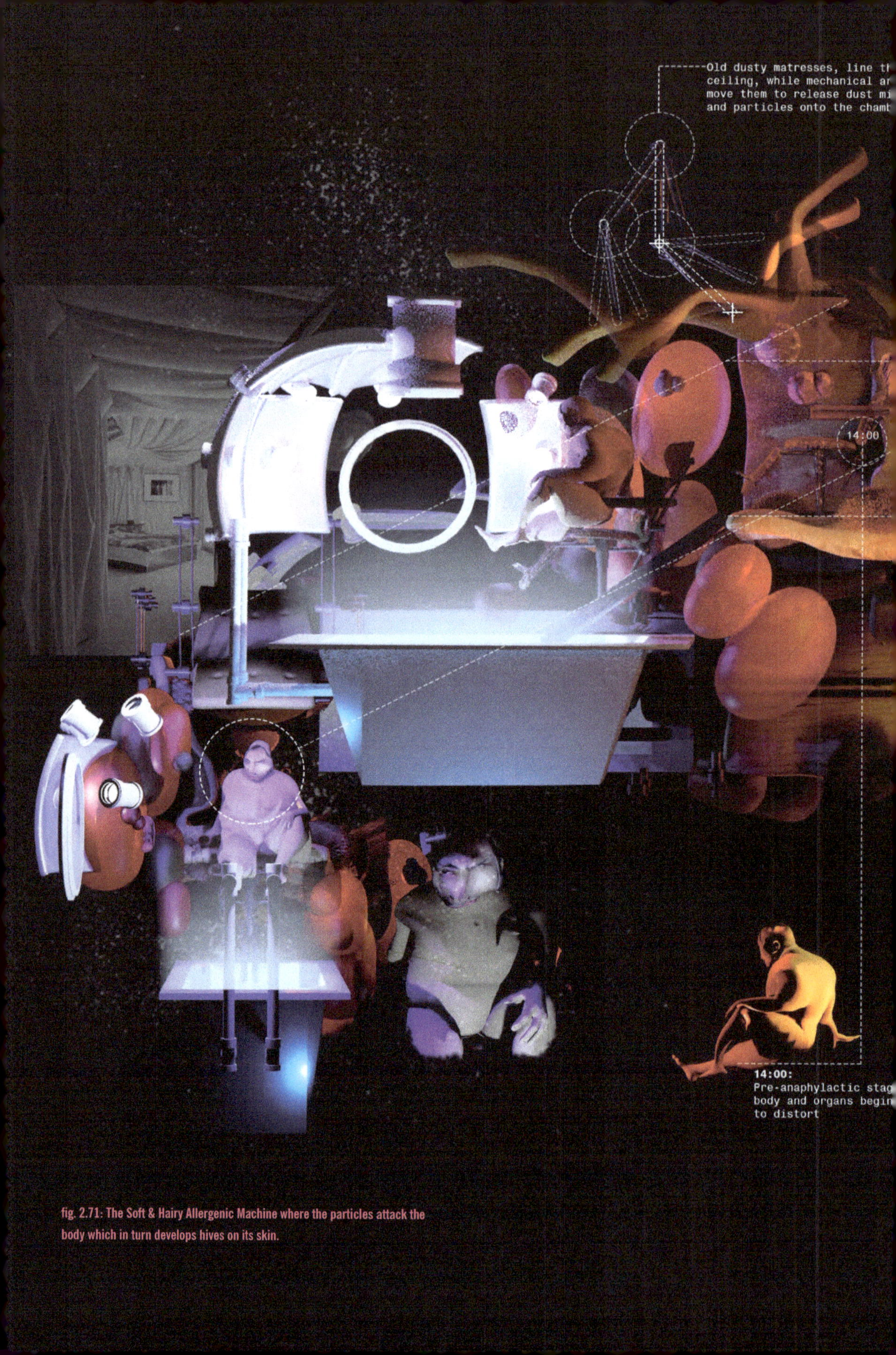

Old dusty matresses, line th
ceiling, while mechanical ar
move them to release dust mi
and particles onto the chamb

14:00

14:00:
Pre-anaphylactic stag
body and organs begin
to distort

fig. 2.71: The Soft & Hairy Allergenic Machine where the particles attack the body which in turn develops hives on its skin.

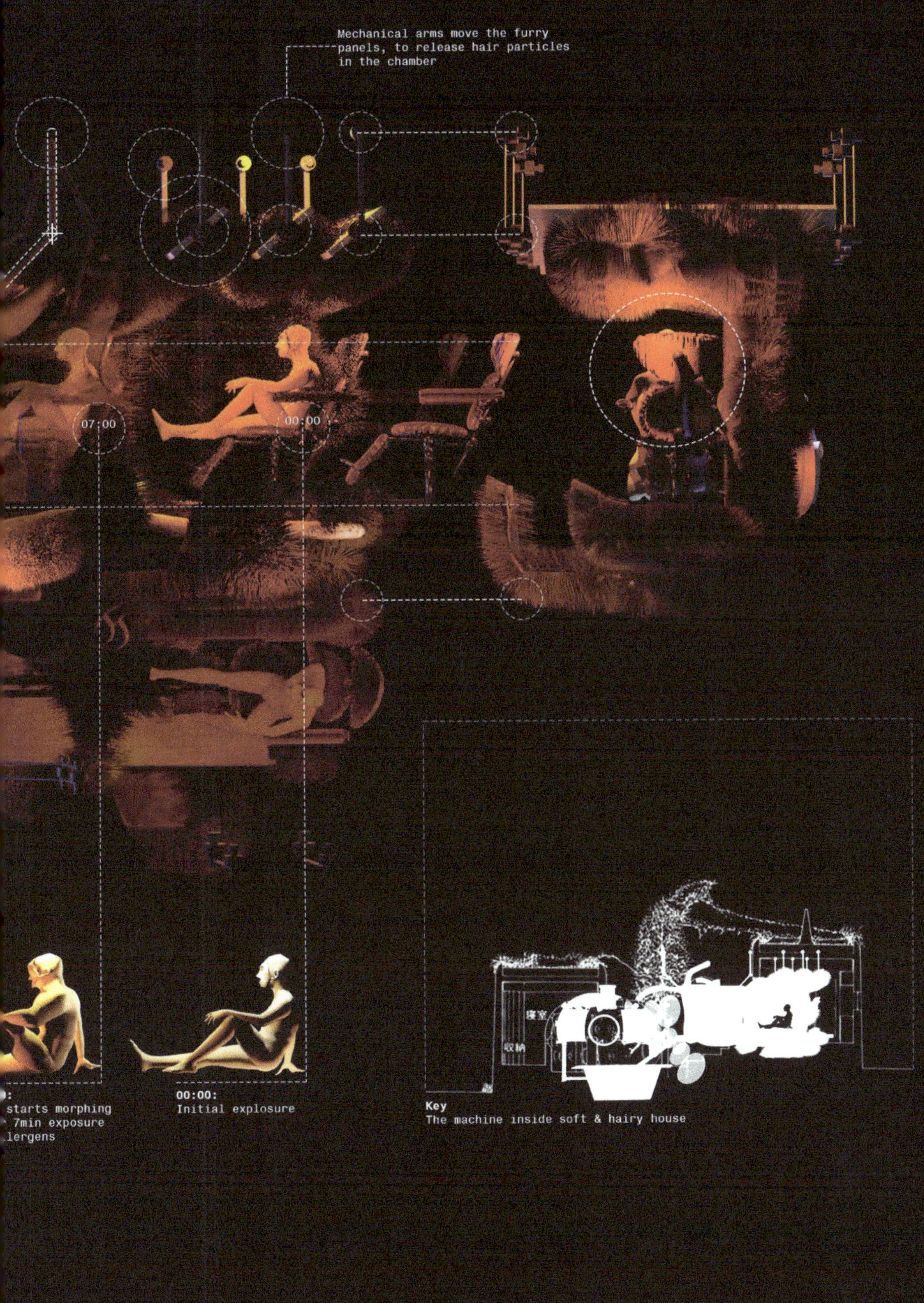
Mechanical arms move the furry panels, to release hair particles in the chamber
07:00
00:00
:
starts morphing
7min exposure
lergens
00:00:
Initial explosure
Key
The machine inside soft & hairy house

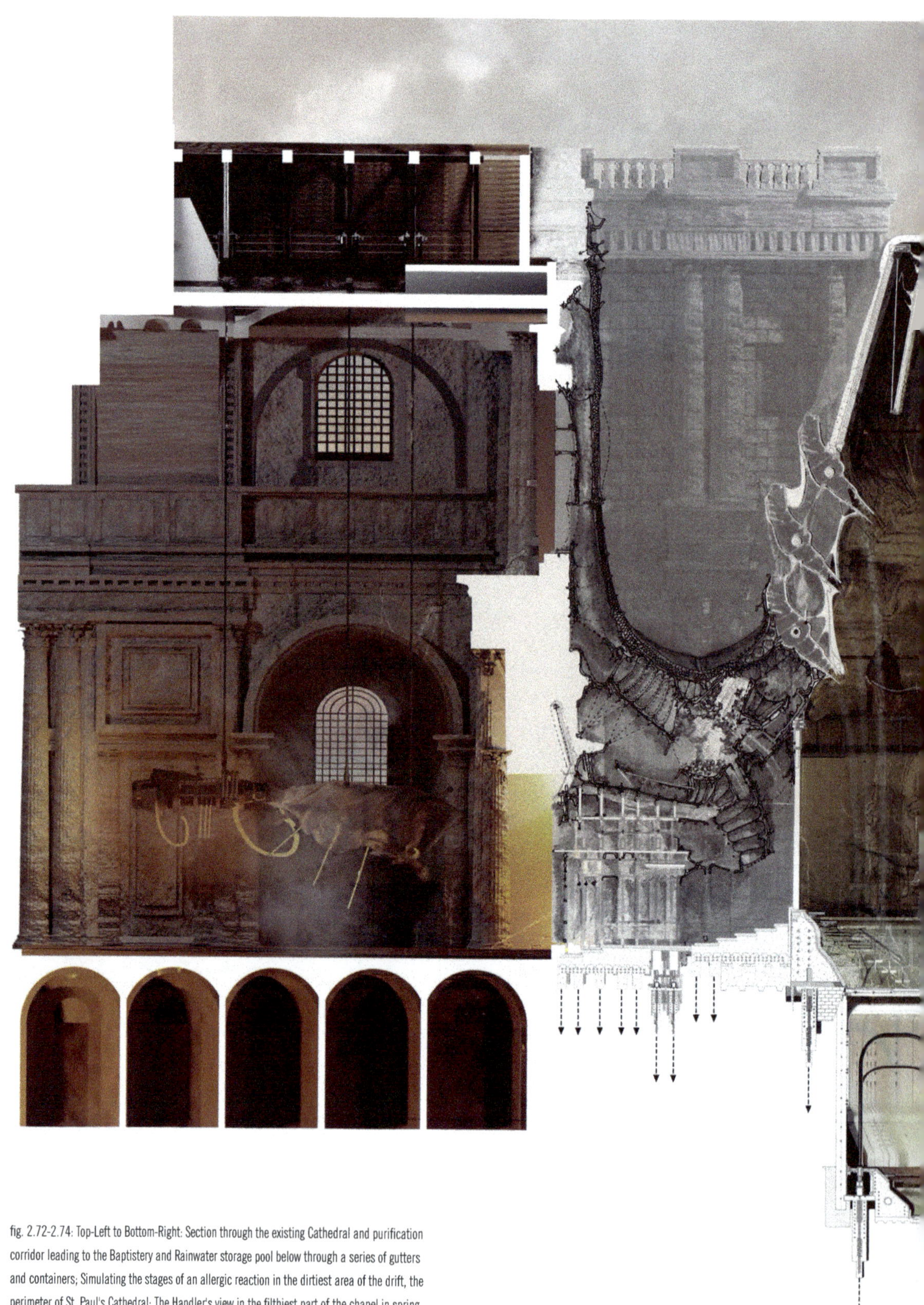

fig. 2.72-2.74: Top-Left to Bottom-Right: Section through the existing Cathedral and purification corridor leading to the Baptistery and Rainwater storage pool below through a series of gutters and containers; Simulating the stages of an allergic reaction in the dirtiest area of the drift, the perimeter of St. Paul's Cathedral; The Handler's view in the filthiest part of the chapel in spring.

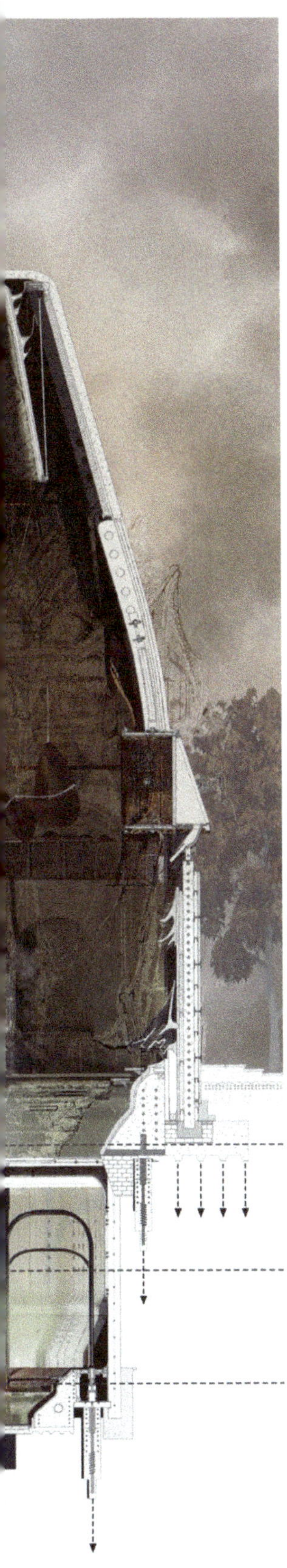

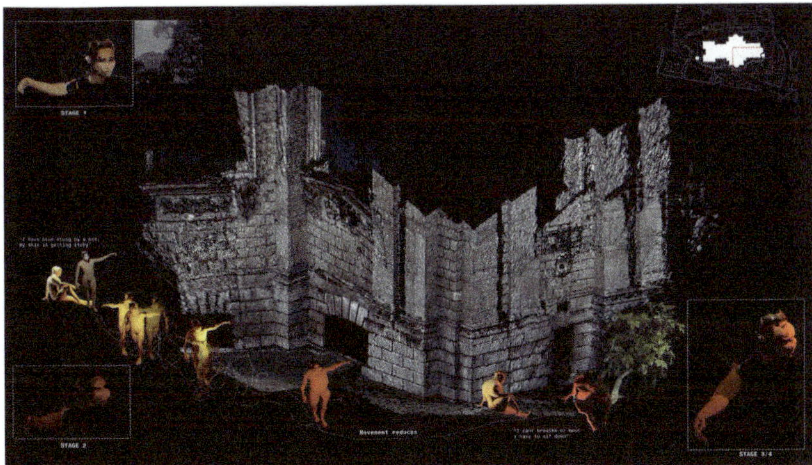
STAGE 1
STAGE 2
Movement reduces
STAGE 3/4

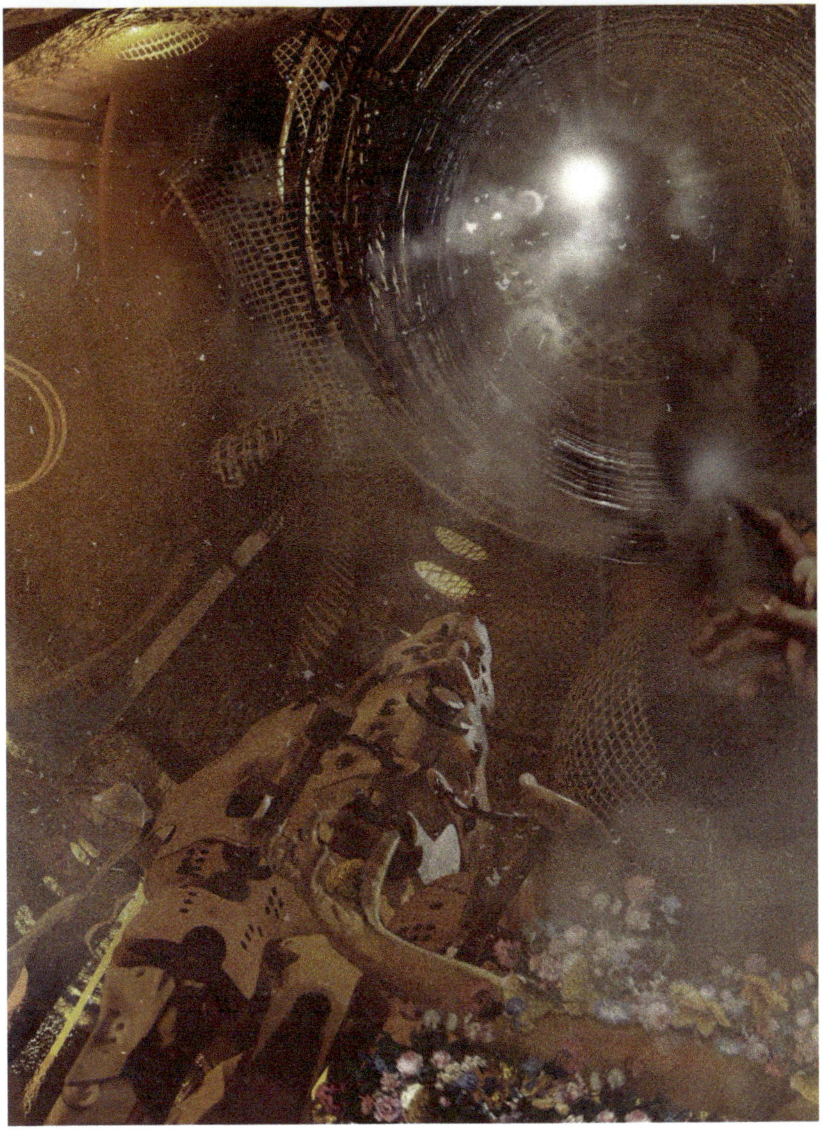

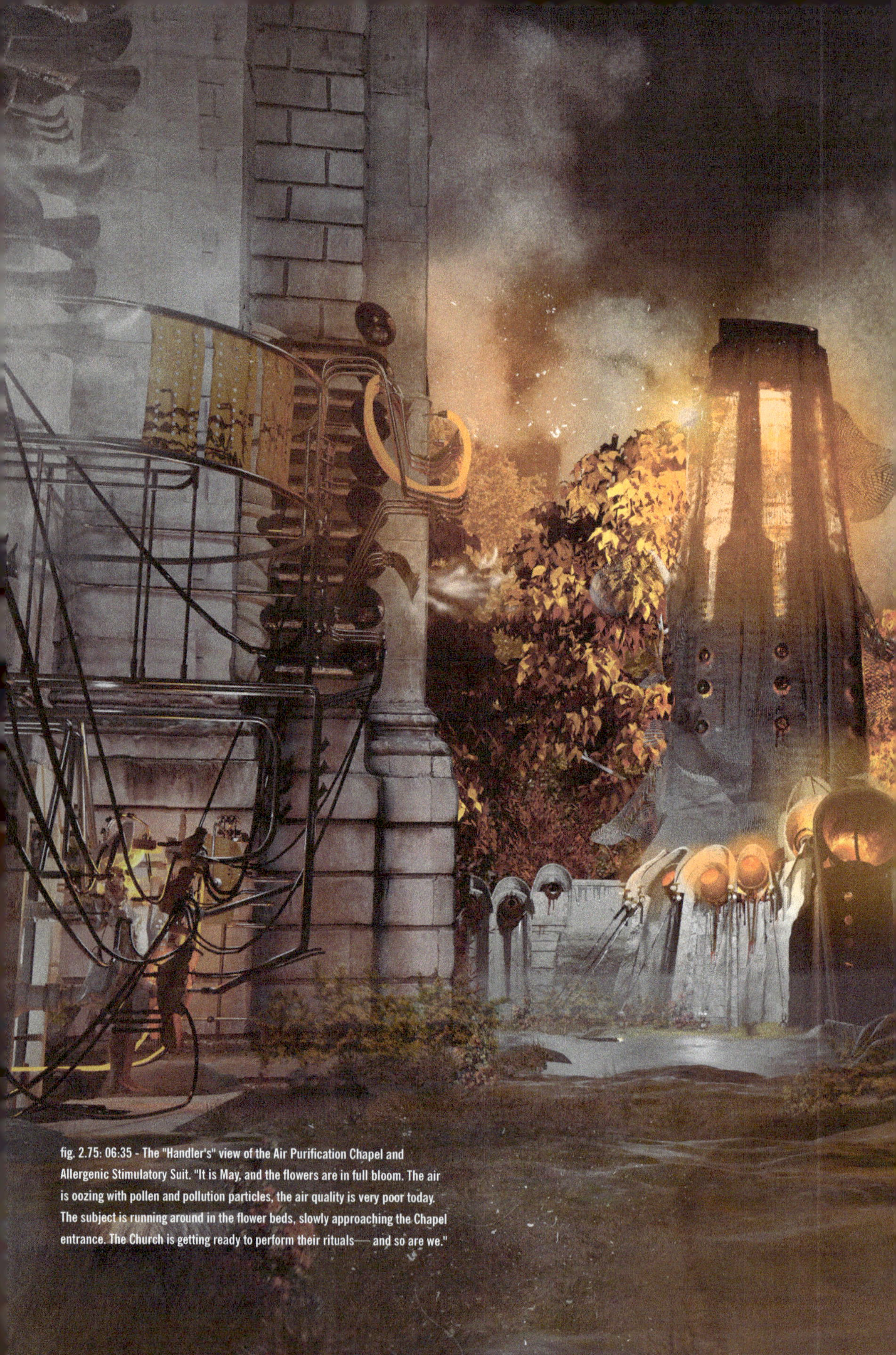

fig. 2.75: 06:35 - The "Handler's" view of the Air Purification Chapel and Allergenic Stimulatory Suit. "It is May, and the flowers are in full bloom. The air is oozing with pollen and pollution particles, the air quality is very poor today. The subject is running around in the flower beds, slowly approaching the Chapel entrance. The Church is getting ready to perform their rituals— and so are we."

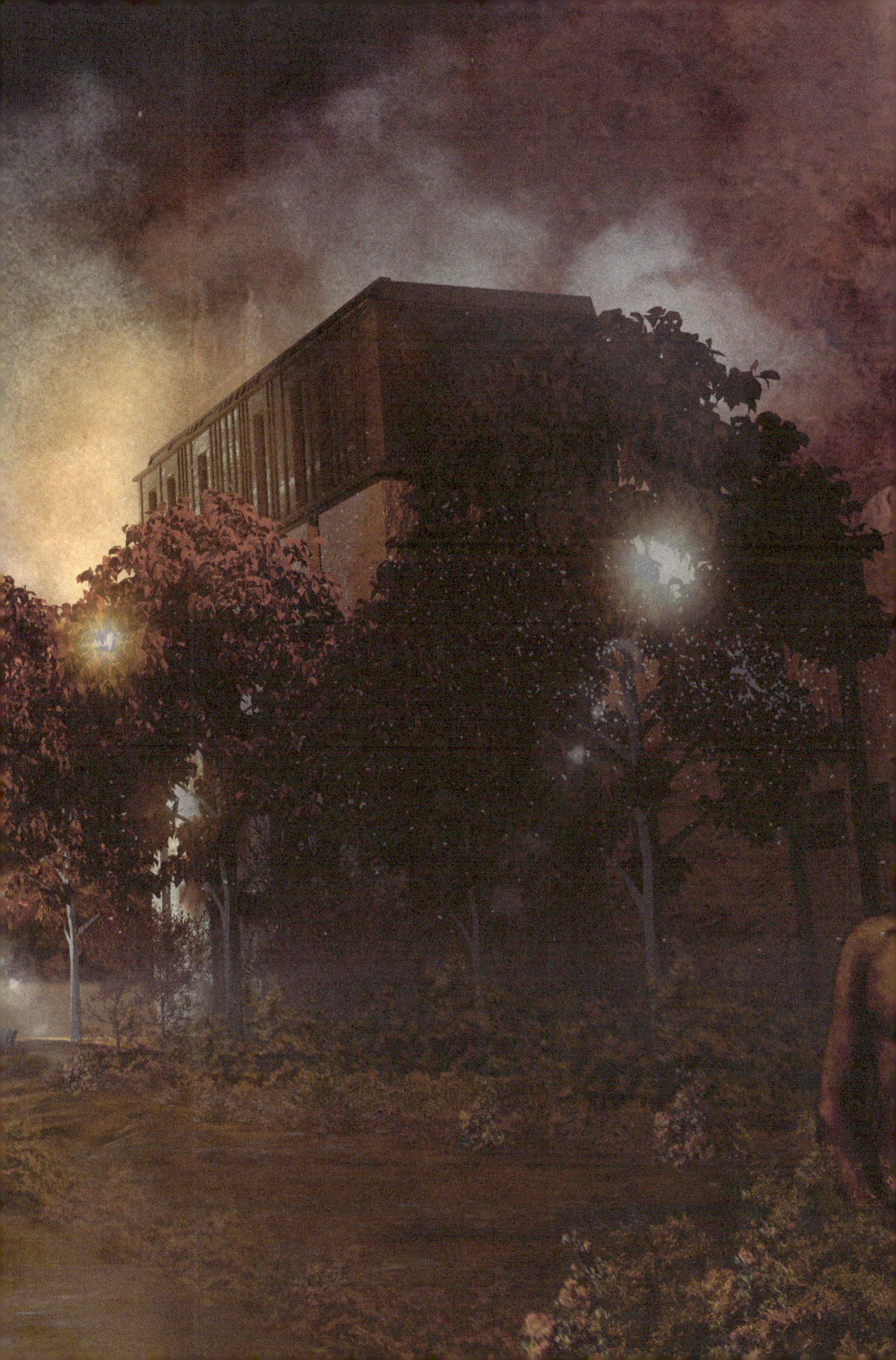

CHAPTER 3:
ANIMALS, MONSTERS & APPARITIONS

VIGNETTE CH.3: >ECOSYSTEM>

MOVING AWAY FROM ANTHROPOCENTRIC DESIGN: EXPANDED SUBJECTIVITY
ANIMALS
MONSTERS
APPARITIONS
A CONCLUDING NOTE REGARDING ALIENS

PROJECT IMAGE GALLERY

by MARY KONSTANTOPOULOU and Dr ALESSANDRO AYUSO

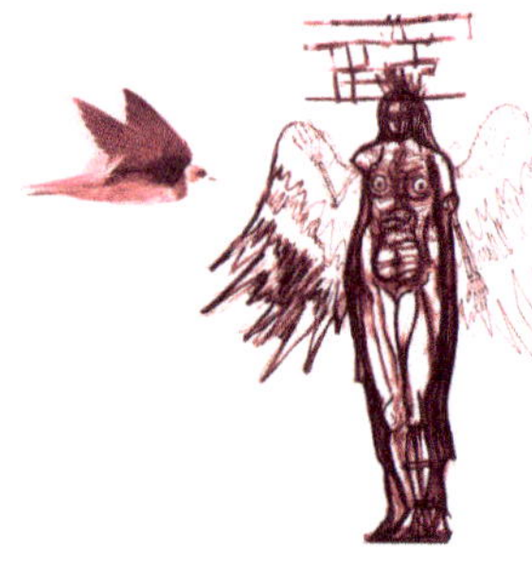

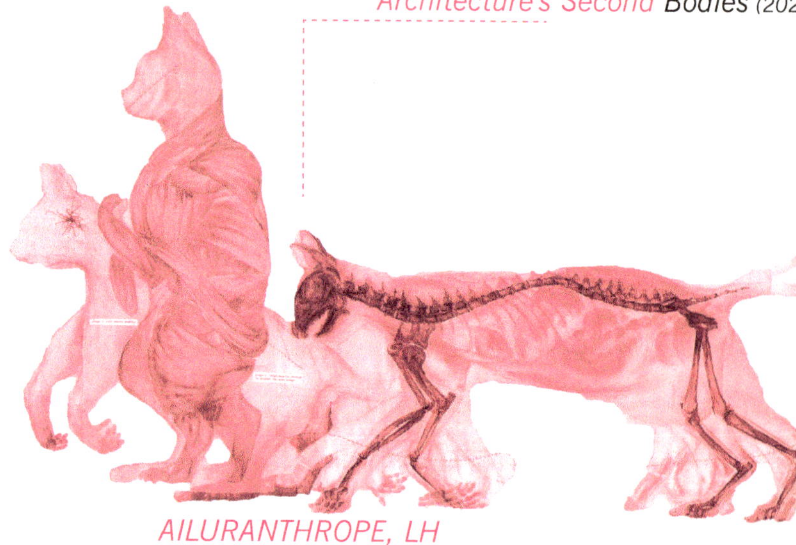

AILURANTHROPE, LH

THE CARECROW, CRP

VIGNETTE: CH.3

OTHER

opening up the concept that the body sits in conversation with

duplicates

and strangers in space

ECOSYSTEM

forming a part in a constellation of entities living in

parallel

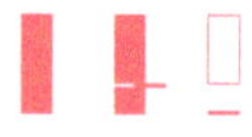

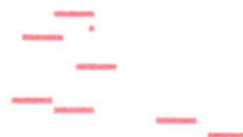

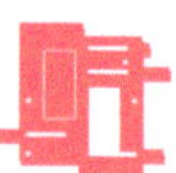

-⟩ BODY ⟩ OTHER ⟩ ECOSYSTEM ⟩ world ⟩-

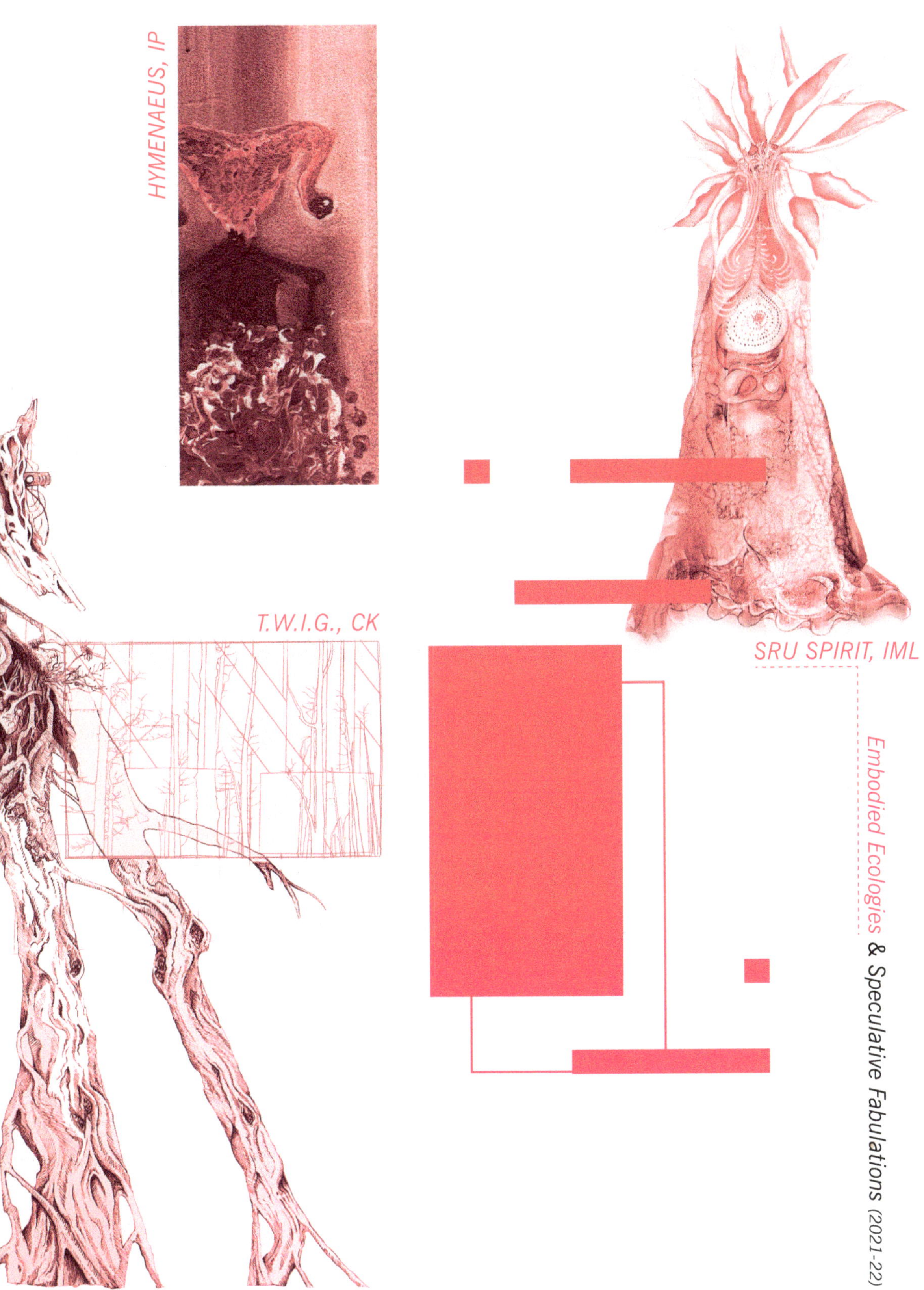
HYMENAEUS, IP
T.W.I.G., CK
SRU SPIRIT, IML
Embodied Ecologies & Speculative Fabulations (2021-22)

MA'WOOLY, AK

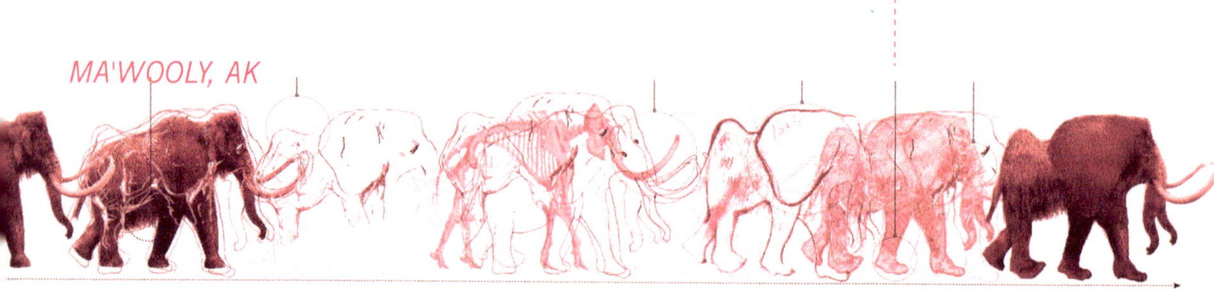

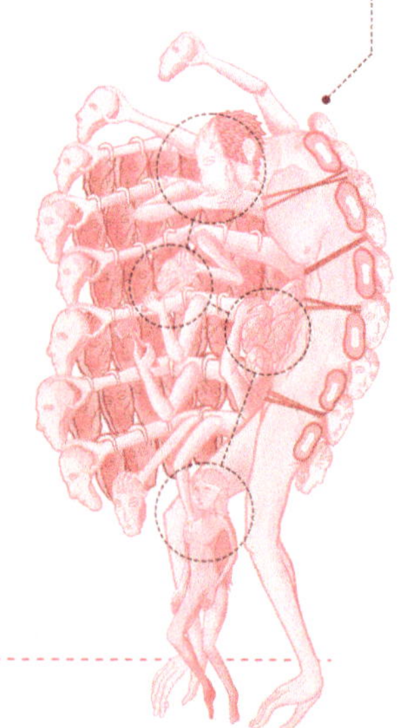

POLYCEPHALIC, AB

IP: The Hymenaeus character is born out of exploring the female form and its history in painting. She starts as a non-sentient being, having a womb for a head and various discarded mechanical parts as a body.

MW: She had another shapeshifting episode overnight, where she altered her appearance and surrounding space...

AW: The Odradek is drawn to the financial district of canary wharf. Unsure of the monolithic enclosed structures, the Vessel connects to their homogeneous glass facade, trying to break in and understand their inner workings.

AW: Correcting the construction industry's contribution to global emissions is taking too long, and the Cloud is here to change this...

CDA: [Creating Clipping Plane, generating meshes, establishing neural links...linking site taste to River Thames]

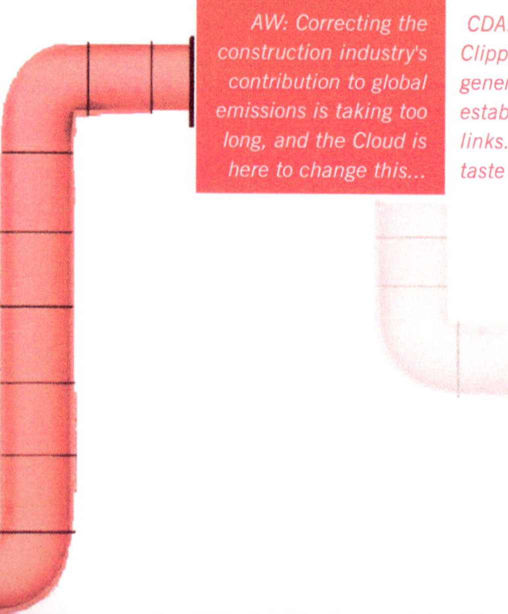

THE VESSEL, AW

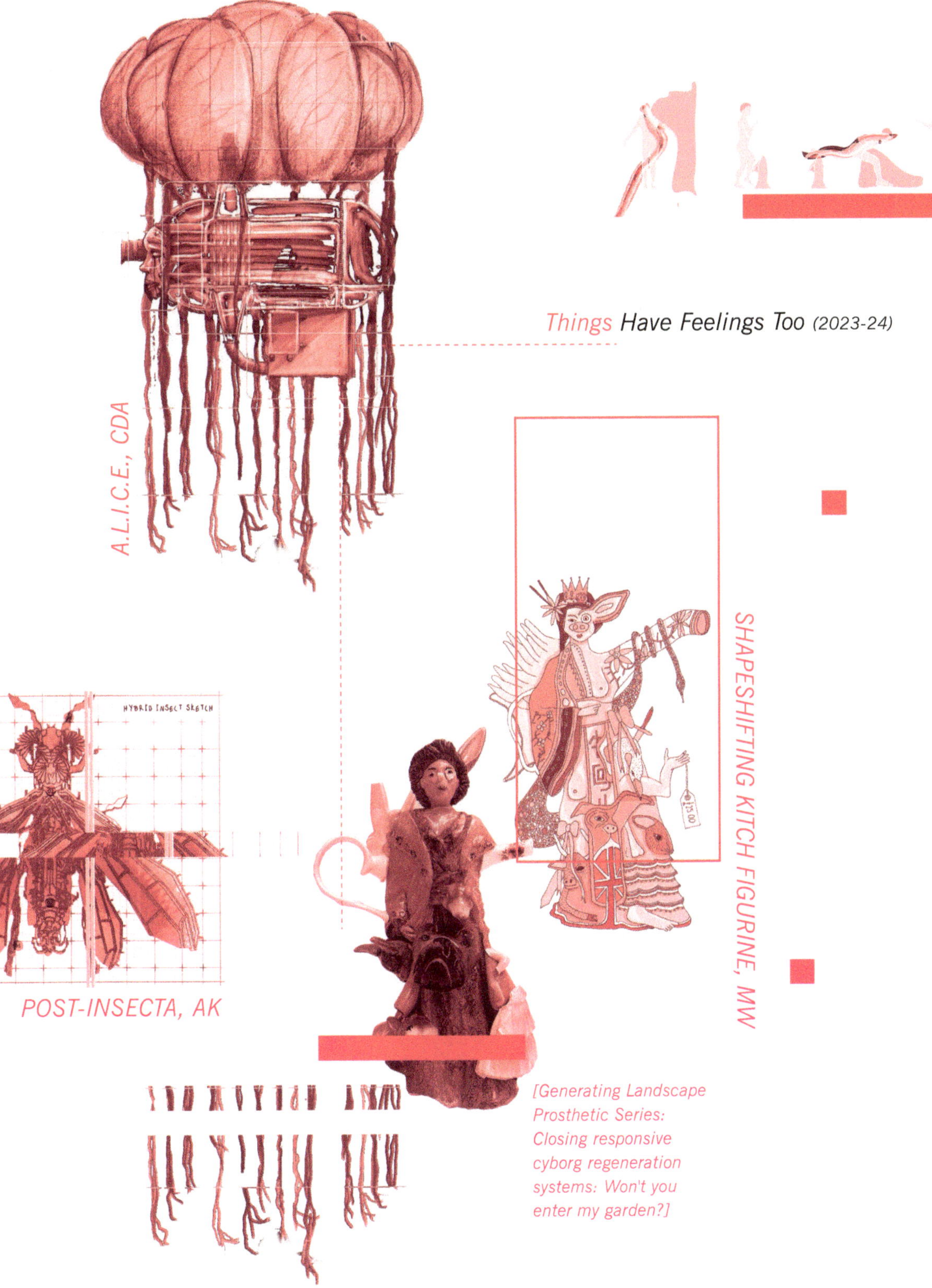

Things Have Feelings Too (2023-24)

A.L.I.C.E., CDA

SHAPESHIFTING KITCH FIGURINE, MW

POST-INSECTA, AK

[Generating Landscape Prosthetic Series: Closing responsive cyborg regeneration systems: Won't you enter my garden?]

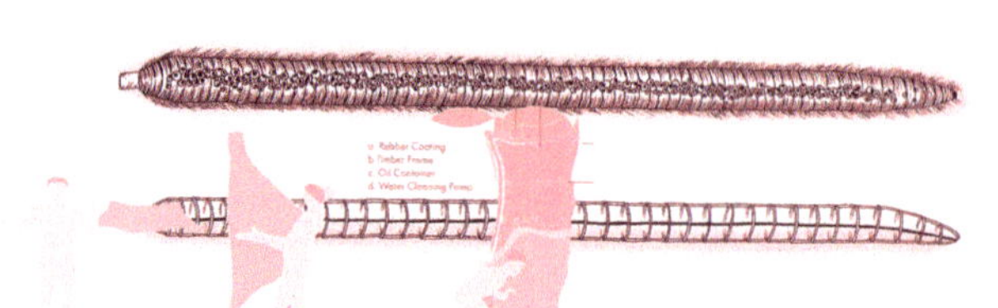

THE VERMIS, AL

JB: He indicated textures on the site, that did indeed resemble the body of a creature.

AL: The Vermis is a worm-like cyborg designed by Other Constructions as a digital accessory, which collects the user's digital data. The public believe it is a naturally evolved worm, native to isle of dogs.

LLT: The following shows the Court where M.O.L.A.R. intended to gather material to fuse with its body in an attempt to grow, then utilise for the constrcuction of its 'intervention' within the Plaintiff's development already on site.

AJ: 01:12, 10th March, 1958, The birds that make regular visits to my caves over time began to construct nests above the ground using the material produced by The Greebles, clothing whole human buildings in their constructions.

Alter Ego(ed) Futures *(2024-25)*

REPAIRER & OBSERVER, AJ

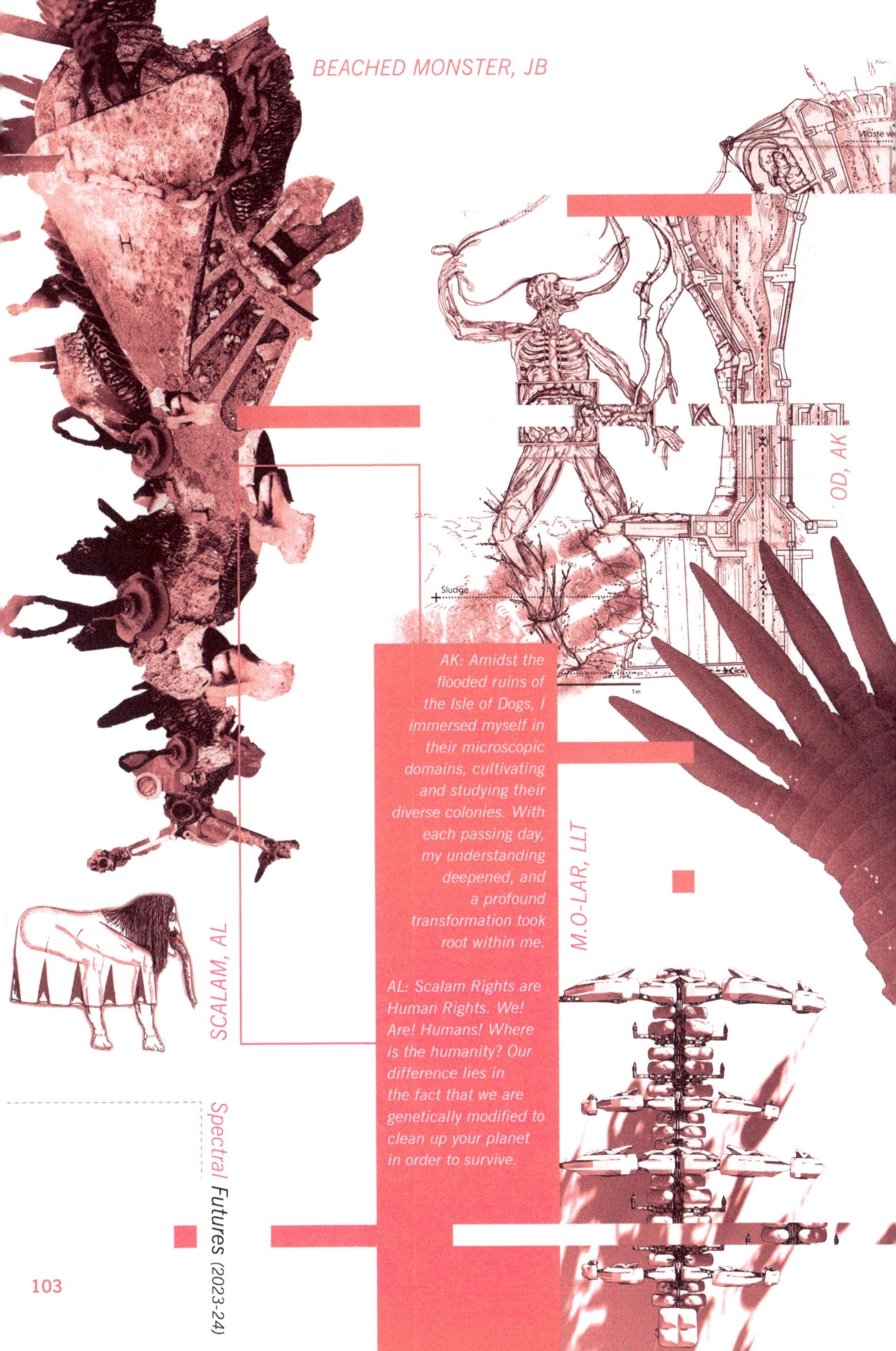

BEACHED MONSTER, JB

OD, AK

M.O-LAR, LLT

SCALAM, AL

AK: Amidst the flooded ruins of the Isle of Dogs, I immersed myself in their microscopic domains, cultivating and studying their diverse colonies. With each passing day, my understanding deepened, and a profound transformation took root within me.

AL: Scalam Rights are Human Rights. We! Are! Humans! Where is the humanity? Our difference lies in the fact that we are genetically modified to clean up your planet in order to survive.

MOVING AWAY FROM ANTHROPOCENTRIC DESIGN: EXPANDED SUBJECTIVITY

As the DS25 briefs evolved over the years, the interest in the body has moved further beyond the anchor point of the purely human. Moving outward from the human-centred subject and asking what this could mean for the creation of architectural space, this chapter focuses on an expanded conception of embodiment that developed through the studio discourse. The projects discussed in the second chapter showed the human body stretched, doubled, and combined with space and technology, yet still maintaining the human body proper as its grounding point.

What might such new conceptions of relationality do to change the body of a person or a constructed body, and what architecture could arise from this change?

TINKERING

The student work shown in this third chapter differs in that it departs further from this grounding. In the projects shown, this question is explored first through tinkering with the body itself. Xenofeminist collective Laboria Cuboniks argue that "...to say that...nothing is transcendent or protected from the will to know, to tinker and to hack, is to say that nothing is supernatural."(01) Tinkering with the body renders the body hackable, in turn extending outward to the immediate space around it, even splicing the surrounding context with the body. Tinkering renders the body open to consideration as an accumulation of forces that move through and coalesce at a particular locale, becoming a locus of relational forces intertwined with material and immaterial strands. For example, the body's constituent parts or organs might be considered as interconnected extensions to other systems; its soul or other immaterial affects of the body's actions, fears, and desires might be considered as manifestations connected to wider systems, timelines, and phenomena. What might such new conceptions of relationality do to change the body of a person or a constructed body, and what architecture could arise from this change?

THE ANTHROPOCENE

In the most broad sense, the Anthropocene era foregrounds all current relational potentials; acknowledging that human activities have affected changes on a planetary scale— and will continue to do so— drastically and differently positions the human relative to previous eras.(02) Philosopher Timothy Morton suggests that the conscious Western human is ever more ecologically paranoid; this paranoia is understandable, as the global situation requires

The emphasis on the question of subjectivity with respect to emergent ecologies creates degrees of inquiry, asking: who is the protagonist? For who— and by who— does architecture exist in the end?

urgent solutions and the problems looming in the future become increasingly more daunting.(03) Following on from the Anthropocene's implication that human beings have managed to disproportionately shape the material world, one could posit, following philosopher Andy Clark's observations, that the more the human body's habits are encouraged, the more the world is transformed to fulfil them.(04) For example, in Edward Burtynsky's film-essay *Manufactured Landscapes* (2006)— a reference frequently discussed in the studio— the manufacturing of the products that make habitual behaviours of humans possible is shown to significantly alter ecologies and terrains on a global scale. Under this premise, architecture itself is a continuation of the human body, made to serve its desires; architecture is centred around the human, made and affected by bodily agency.(05) In this sense, the world, both material and immaterial, can then be seen as a mirror image of the body: the human body exerts itself on the world, remaking the world according to the body, imposing a reflection. Yet, as Burtynsky's films show, the mirroring has detrimental effects, scarring the planet on which humans rely with the byproducts of industrial processes, and presenting incomprehensibly monotonous and sterile settings; ironically, the extensive imprinting of the human onto their environment becomes the very thing that alienates them.

If the human body brings with it an embodied subjectivity, and if, as an imprinting device the human body fails our current moment, how else could the subject be conceived? Guattari argues that "...with the increasing development of the machines of production of signs, images, syntax, and artificial intelligence, the question of enunciation of subjectivity will pose itself ever more forcefully."(06) The emphasis on the question of subjectivity with respect to emergent ecologies creates degrees of inquiry, asking: who is the protagonist? *For who*— and *by who*— does architecture exist in the end?

The work in chapter two suggests that perhaps this protagonist is the cyborg; yet, even Haraway's recent statements imply that such a posthumanist conception of the subject, with its alterations and extensions of the unfettered human, remains inadequately tied to foundational humanist paradigms to allow for this reconsideration.(07) The cyborg remains tethered to some degree to the human body as an "original prosthetic,"(08) and therefore to the ontological legacies that go with it. Haraway writes: "We are compost, not posthuman; we *if humans are just another critter in a symbiotic tangle, architecture's responsibilities extend far beyond the human.*

inhabit the humusities, not the humanities. Philosophically and materially, I am a compostist, not a posthumanist. Critters— human and not— become-with each other, compose and decompose each other, in every scale and register of time and stuff in sympoietic tangling, in ecological evolutionary developmental earthly worlding and unworlding."(09)

Rather than a central or apex position of the human, implicit in the term *Anthropo*-cene, Haraway suggests considering tentacular, tangled, dynamic networks of symbiotic critters— of which humans are themselves one— enmeshed, and becoming from and through earth.(10)

For architectural practices and aims, the turn away from anthropocentrism implies a radical shift: if humans are just another critter in a symbiotic tangle, architecture's responsibilities extend far beyond the human. Part of enacting a paradigm shift premised on relationality rather than exhausted anthropocentric hierarchies entails taking on different tactics. The anthropocentrism ingrained in architecture's practices and agendas makes surpassing the anthropocentric model that much more difficult.(11)

ASSEMBLAGES

Thinking holistically, Haraway suggests that "... Species Man does not make history [and] ... [t]hat History must give way to geostories, to Gaia stories, to symchthonic stories."(12) For Haraway, since forming an assemblage entails creating situated links between its components, assemblages become important tools for thinking through the recuperation between beings.(13) At the same time, when read as a whole, each assemblage surfaces as a new bounded entity; the assemblage's components can no longer be read as separate from one another, having to always be questioned in relation to their neighbour, and in relation to the system as a whole.(14) In a similar vein, theorist Jane Bennet notes that "each member and proto-member of [an] assemblage has a certain vital force, but there is also an effectivity proper to the grouping as such: an agency of the assemblage."(15)

TIME HORIZONS

A reconsideration of materiality as part of an extended time horizon also follows as a concern that is pivotal to formulating new tactics. Considering architectural space as "philosophically and materially" compost implies that architecture participates in geological and biological processes of change.(16) This concept provides students with a way to question architecture's effects on its context beyond the intended purpose imposed on it by clients and policymakers, which are ultimately driven by finite budgetary constraints and short time horizons.(17) As one of the things humans construct and the things humans leave behind, architecture as compost can be thought to both destroy life but also to engender other ways of life. Living things, remnants, and processes that operate in slower registers can become narrators, exposing architecture's reach and responsibilities.

TIME

Considering animals, monsters, and apparitions as potential agents for architecture can produce alternative timeflows.(18) In her book *A Land*, archaeologist Jacquetta Hawkes illustrates the epiphanies enabled by acknowledging this other temporal stream through the observation of her own material and immaterial connections to the earth and its critters. Delving into geological time while lying on the ground in her garden, she writes:

"Every being is united both inwardly and outwardly with the beginning of life in time and with the simplest forms of contemporary life. 'Me' is a fiction, though a convenient fiction and one of significance to the consciousness of which I am the temporary home."(19)

Living things, remnants, and processes that operate in slower registers can become narrators, exposing architecture's reach and responsibilities.

SUBJECTIVITY & TIME

Both Hawkes and Haraway propose that the idea of subjectivity, and specifically collective human subjectivity, is not— and in fact has never been— the only story. In order to "question the tissues of one's knowings and ways of knowing," and to "respond to non-anthropocentric difference,"(20) projects developed in DS25 attempt to begin to understand this subjective, fictional "home," first experimenting with the idea of the human self as a subject and the fiction of the self, and then by looking through the lens of other subjects.(21)

Embodying and designing through subjects other than human, however, is a large and unthinkable task: how might one see as anything other than their own lived and living self, in the skin and eyes one has worn since birth, and with all the attached environmental, parental, contextual, time-sensitive influences?

Simon O'Sullivan, professor of Art Theory and

fig. 3.01: Next page: Kyberd's "Squirrel Perspective" drawing showing the Tree-Body-Building in the year 2221. A combination of nutrient injections, graftings, weights and new supports encouraged the growth of a new branch of structural capabilities.

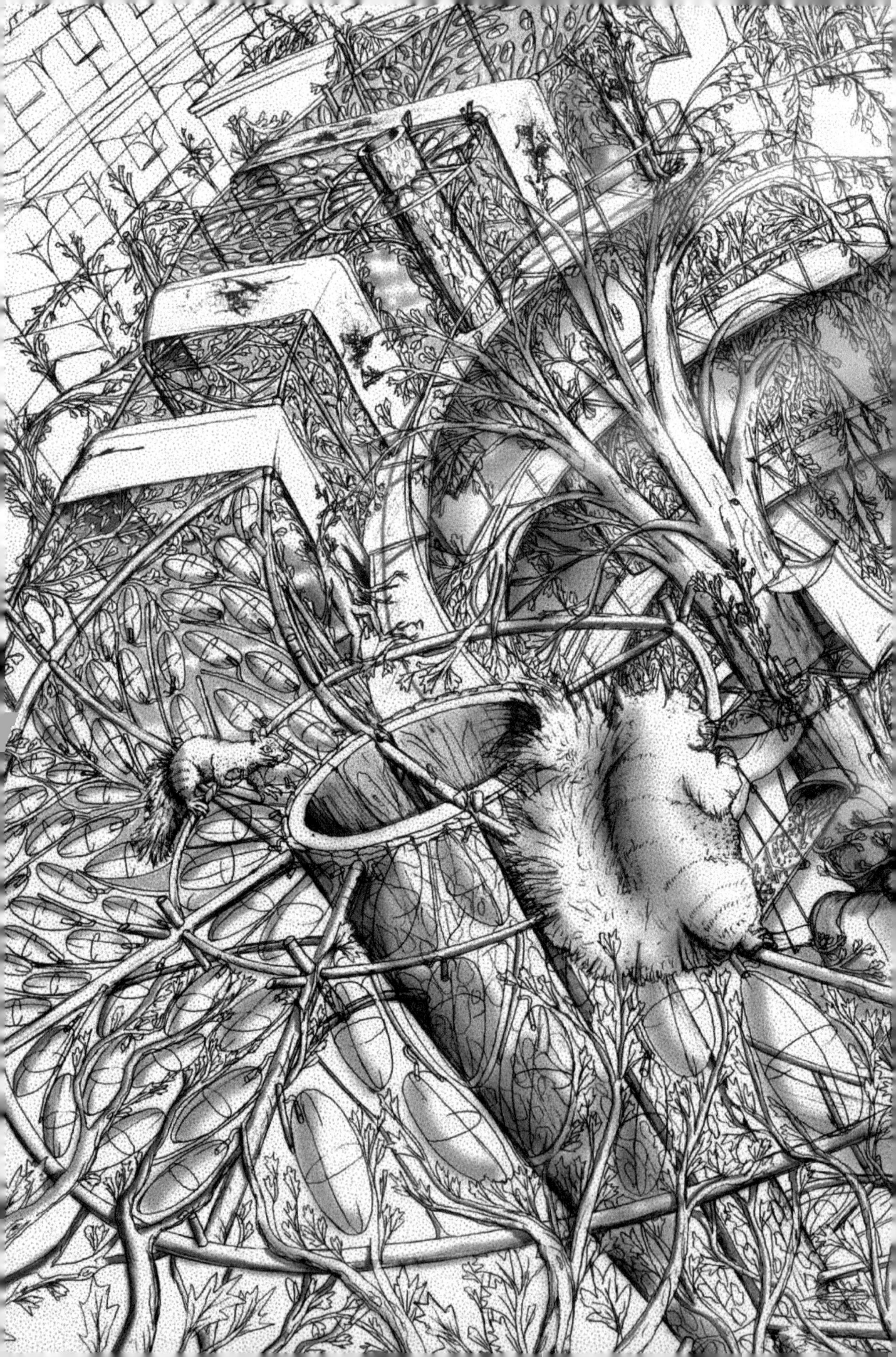

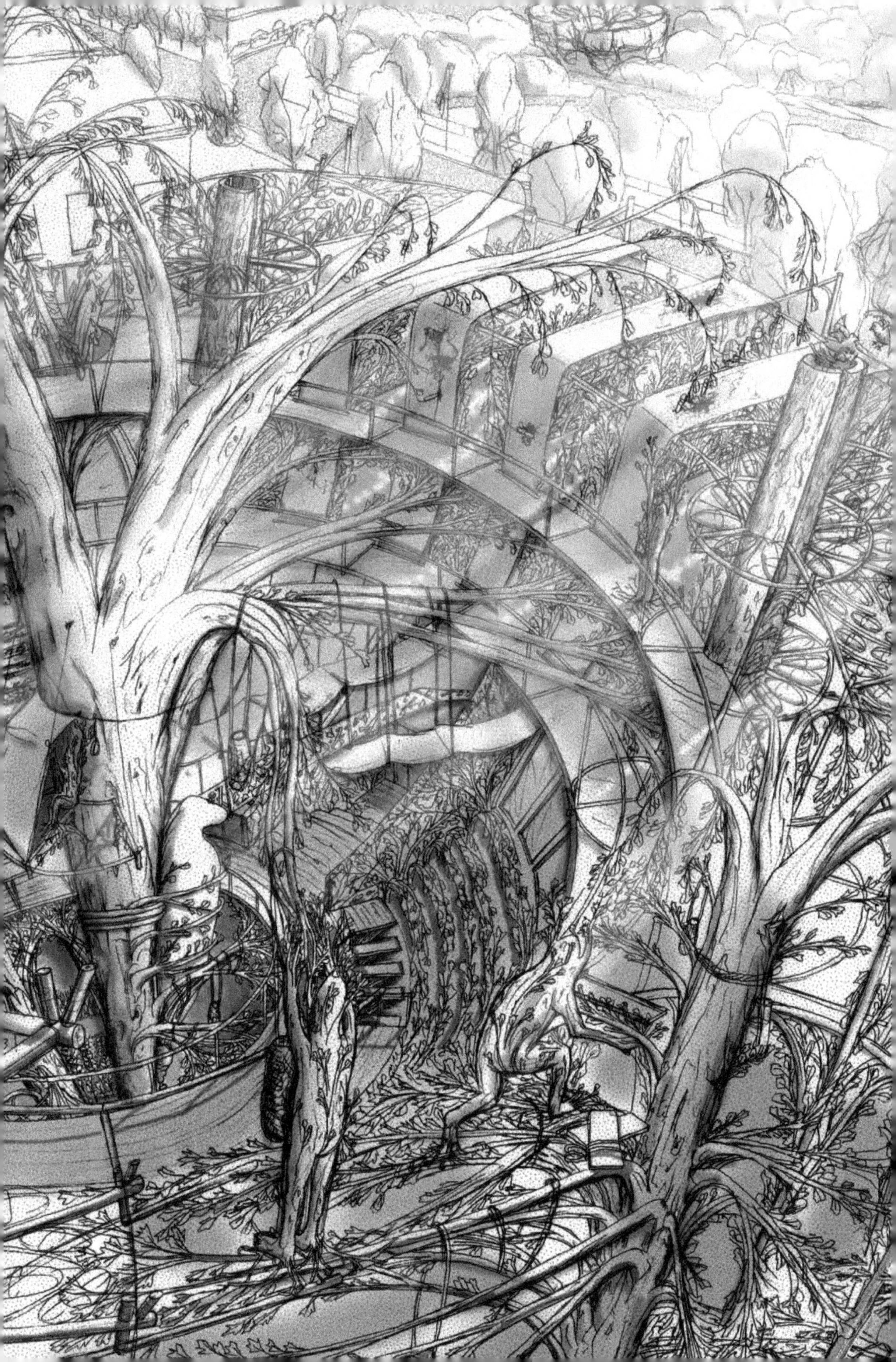

Practice at Goldsmiths University, and founder of art collective Plastique Fantastique explains this predicament:

"Non-human or part-part human entities of inhuman social imaginaries do not necessarily share a sense of historical time with humans— possibly having perspectives devoid of human-historical subjectivity. Furthermore, they do not necessarily share human conceptions of space and time, or recognise what humans take for reality as reality. ... history itself involves a species-specific conception of time."[22]

Projects in more recent years in DS25 increasingly experiment with breaking out of one's human self and attempting to include Others into the equation of the design process. Within the briefs and projects, a question reverberates: through degrees of estrangement and defamiliarisation, how far can intersubjective senses be stretched?

ZOE

In DS25, the exploration of stretching intersubjective sense moves forward via types of Other bodies, moving through a relational network to radically reconsider the role of architects in this expanded field, or *zoe*, that which comprises all that is traditionally considered in the nonhuman realm.[23] The task is to escape the drowsy repetition of the now and the known, and to stretch the imagination into possibilities where the presumed idea of the human might not exist.[24] Such a perspective acknowledges that nature is strange, that nature experiments, and that nature produces relations that are both beneficial and destructive. When confronted with questions such as animal rights, ethics in genetic science, or scientific meddling in ecologies and biodiversity,[25] in order to grapple with emerging complexities, it is necessary to expand experimentation past the current paths of general understanding, past the known human-centric stories, accepting all options as plausible and equally important.[26] Doing so means progressing outside of the self-perpetuating storyline; the current notion of the human and the body may not necessarily always be central.

ANIMALS

REVEALING THE ANIMAL DIMENSION

With concepts such as *zoe* in mind, the world can be considered as a place where a nearly infinite taxonomy of bodies reside and exert influence, including the human. This suggests that perhaps a more productive model of the human body could be as a world made up of all sorts of other bodies. Thinking this way, a vision of an infinite zoom takes shape, moving through bodies and worlds by changing scales. Manoeuvring through this body comprised of other bodies, the idea of the human body as complete is destabilised. The human body becomes open to examination and play with its form, changing the understanding of its self-made (autopoietic) or made-with (sympoietic) qualities, in turn affecting the hierarchies of the world it operates within.[27] In this alternative definition of the body-world relationship, body and world are viewed together at once, from the micro to the macro, from bacteria to ecosystems.

THE PERCEPTION OF ANIMALS

Animals are part of the everyday human reality, occupying niches hidden within the human everyday. The animals that are not hidden from humans could be perceived by humans as companions, urban or rural pests, background noise, edible or usable produce, produce-making creatures, or spectacle. In many ways, the human perception of an animal is of a being that is perpetuated by stereotypes and distanced from the self. The amount of encounters a human might have had with these and other creatures, including stories one hears about them in documentaries, films, or news articles, might draw humans closer to understanding animals in some respects; in other ways encounters could provide a set of preconceptions that prevent humans from being able to fully embody that creature. For example, a human living in London might encounter an urban fox or pigeon, and based on their preconceptions, see them as unwanted pests, meeting them with disgust, while others with different backgrounds may greet their presence with wonder or fascination.

Adding to these complications of the human perception of animals is the human intervention with them, as most of the animals that humans may encounter (or arguably, any animals at all) are not pure manifestations of nature but are to some degree partly human-fabricated or influenced. For instance, foxes and pigeons in London have adapted to human-made societal rhythms and infrastructure; more overtly, dogs and cats have been bred over millennia for human use and companionship.

BECOMING AND BECOMING-WITH ANIMALS

Through projects that engage with the concept of *animal*, specific questions arise on the generative potential of attempting to *be* animal: is it, for example, even possible to think that fully embodying a bird, an eel, or a bacterial form could also entail being human? Would humans really be able to understand the world as a slimy, underwater, wriggling, armless and legless creature such as an eel (fig. 3.02)— a thing some humans eat, or more frequently try to steer clear of— in both living and processed form? How about crossing notional biological boundaries and considering the lifespans of plant life? Would someone with over twenty years of human experience be able to

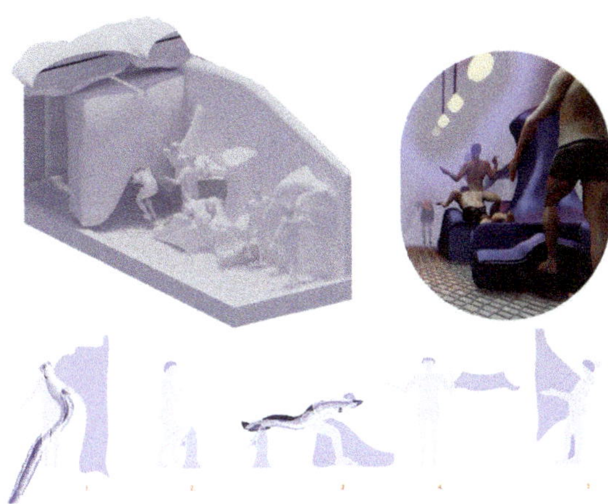

fig. 3.02: Mills-Lyle's design for the "Strigil Room" which reinterprets the ancient practice of scraping oils and dirt off the body before bathing using a strigil. The strigil apparatus is spatially configured so that the user mimicks the movements of an eel.

through degrees of estrangement and defamiliarisation, how far can intersubjective senses be stretched?

substantially embody a tree? Would they not fidget, being burdened with human ideas of fast action in contrast with the new, slow rhythms one is supposed to live in within the tree's existence?[28]

As Thomas Nagel argues in his seminal essay on the mind-body problem "What is it Like to be a Bat?," possessing subjectivity entails a particular consciousness that prevents a full understanding of another subjectivity; we can never really know what it is like to be a bat. [29] Human subjectivity, further complicated by the preconceptions discussed above, prevents a designer from fully embodying other living beings; a premise that DS25 projects relating to animals attempt— against the philosophical odds— to defy.

And then again, one might ask, what use would it be for people to attempt to live life like a fox or a tree? What would one do with the knowledge of geological time without the ability of returning to their human body? As Braidotti writes, to operate in the Anthropocene era, navigating these subjective challenges is actually a necessity of the age: "The collapse of the nature-cultural divide requires that we need to devise a new vocabulary with new figurations to refer to the elements of our posthuman embodied and embedded subjectivity."[30]

Further to this discussion are important concepts by Deleuze, Guattari, and Haraway. Deleuze and Guattari put forward the concept of "becoming-animal"; following their eschewing of representation in favour of affect, and their interest in deterritorialisation, they see becoming-animal as a "line of escape" from the confines of human subjectivity.[31] In a sense agreeing with Nagel, they do not see the viability of truly taking on an animal's point of view, but instead see a productive "zone of indiscernibility," an in-between space achieved between humans and animals through artistic practices.[32] Countering the idea of "becoming-animal," Haraway puts forward the idea of "becoming-with" animals, an idea of innate kinship captured by her term "companion species," where humans and animals have an intrinsic mutuality. [33] Haraway suggests that it would be more useful to consider humans and animals in all their evolutionary taxonomies as "partners ... species of all kinds [which] are consequent upon worldly subject- and object-shaping entanglements."[34]

DS25 projects involve experiments in becoming-animal and becoming-with animals. In order for architectural space to consider the core of what an animal subjectivity might be, the body agents in DS25 projects allow their authors to employ ways to experiment with unfamiliar territories and embodiments. In these projects, students can find themselves productively conflicted with their existence as human; the empirical and imagined experiences mix, and conflicts between possible subjectivities become apparent; taken on as subjects, animals reveal their connections and disjunctions with the human realm in cosmological tangles.

While not dealing with animals per se— but perhaps approaching the "zone of indiscernibility" adjacent to them—, DS25 projects such as second-year student Cara Kinzelmann's *The Nursery* (fig. 3.03) entered the realm of the biological nonhuman by attempting to explore and design for a new paradigm that shakes up the relationships between humans, human habitats, and trees.[35] Kinzelmann's idea for her body agent, T.W.I.G., was imagined as drawn first by the hands of a human child, made up of tree bark, human anatomy, mechanical equipment, and projected images. This conception of this vegetal-anatomical-mechanical-electrical-photonic hybrid allowed Kinzelmann to explore the reciprocal relationships of ecosystems from an ecologically-centred child's perspective, as the narrative of the project was told through conversations between the child and the tree-monster (fig. 3.03). The result was a growing, living nursery for both human children and plants on the shores of the Thames which considered extended time spans that related to the central willow tree's life, furthering her first-year explorations on the constraining effects of architecture on nature (fig. 3.27-3.28).

ANIMALS AS AGENTS

In other DS25 projects, the introduction of animals is another parameter contributing to something akin to

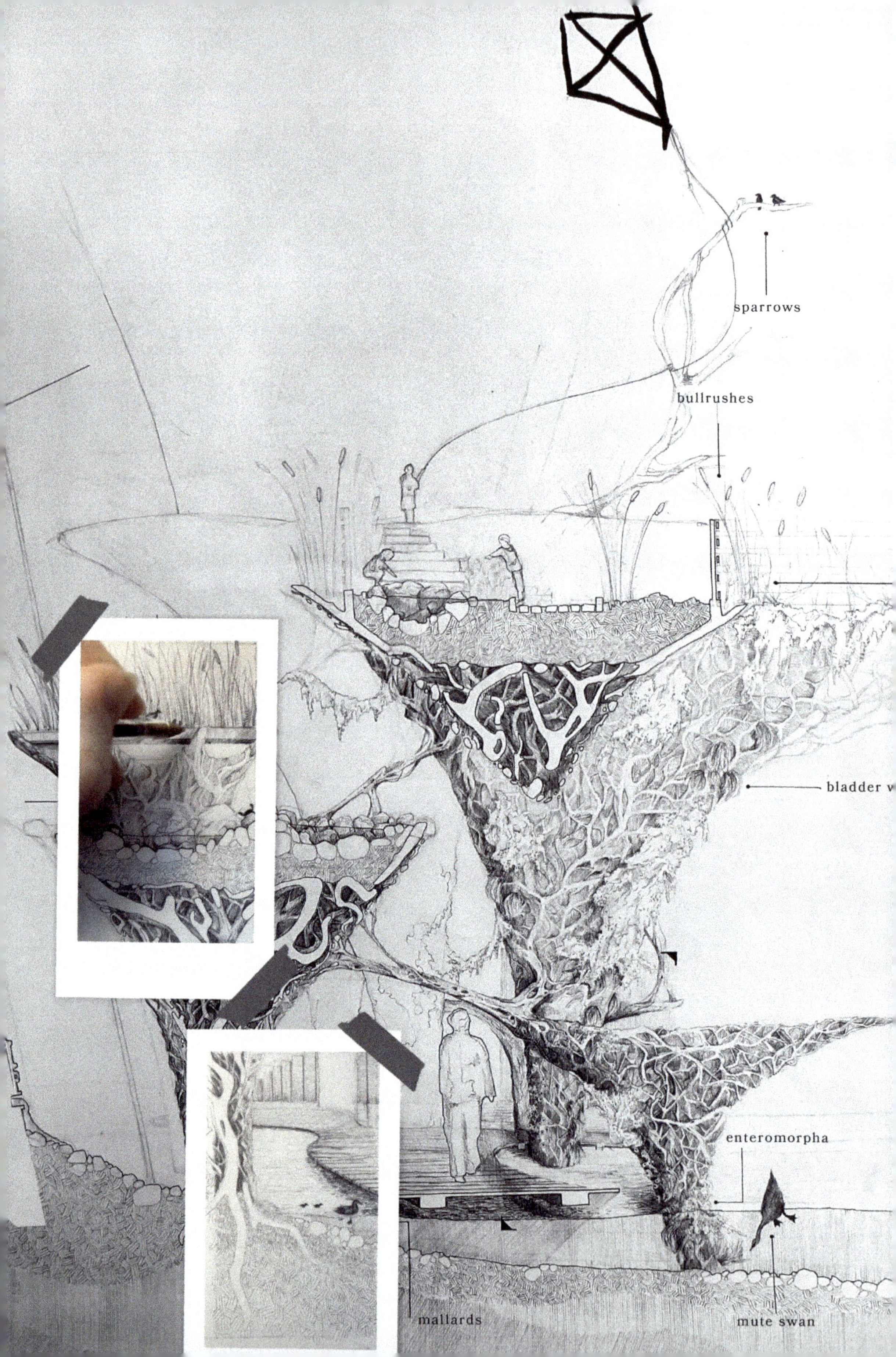
sparrows
bullrushes
bladder w
enteromorpha
mallards
mute swan

taken on as subjects, animals reveal their connections and disjunctions with the human realm in cosmological tangles.

chance operations; non-human bodies become devices for the generation of relations which can challenge the human-centred environment. Taken rigorously, animal logic imagined by humans is not random, yet it often operates so differently than usual human thought process in design that the strange logic can open up playful dimensions of design. As Haraway recognizes, "It is in the realm of play, outside the dictates of teleology, settled categories, and function, that serious worldliness and recuperation become possible."(36)

An example of playfulness in this vein can be found in the short film by Bi Gan titled *A Short Story*, where the viewer is taken through a journey of discovery through the point of view of a cat.(37) The film asks the viewer to suspend their disbelief when, in order to capture the "soul" of the cat in its quest, the filmmaker hides the subject within a human trenchcoat and hat. Through the magic and alternative points of view this in-between being allows for, a possibility of new relations emerges between the subject and the world.(38) Similar to Gan's "cat," the methodology encouraged in DS25 briefs is one where body agents are hybrids, assemblages that are not quite completely animal and not quite completely human either, allowing the designer to move through levels of defamiliarisation from the known body into that of an Other.

In the 2021-22 brief, *Embodied Ecologies & Speculative Fabulations*, taught by the design teaching team of Dr Alessandro Ayuso and Mary Konstantopoulou, students were tasked with exploring the tangled line between the eco-centric and the anthropocentric on the shore of the Thames by reimagining architectural bodies and future ecologies. Following Joshua LaBare, Haraway defines the term "speculative fabulation" as a "mode of attention, a theory of history and a practice of worlding";(39) in another passage, she describes speculative fabulations as stories in which enmeshed, multispecies players "... redo ways of living and dying attuned to still possible finite flourishing...."(40) The first prompt that year asked for the creation of a "Body Monster Terminus Figure" (BMTF), a hybrid assemblage made of ingredients from four categories which provided a melting pot for what Braidotti would call "visualiz[ing] the subject as a transversal entity encompassing the human, our genetic neighbours the animals and the earth as a whole.... "(41)

fig. 3.03: Kinzelmann's T.W.I.G. was an assemblage of many parts and a kind-hearted recluse. Despite being perceived by the child as a "monster," through befriending the child, it was able to intervene on the Isle of Dogs. In an area deprived of space to pause, T.W.I.G. grew a forest school in the quiet of the pier.

Termes, an ancient Greek typology, are architectural column fragments comprised of a human head atop a tapering column; they were understood as boundary markers and portrayals of Terminus, the Roman god of boundaries. The first ingredient students chose was one Terme figure from Hughues Sambin's *Oeuvre de la Diversite des termes*, written and illustrated in 1572. Sambin's illustrations of Termes are wildly hybrid, blending human, animal, earthly, mythical, and architectural elements; a reinterpretation of them incorporating the other three ingredients— a material, an ecology, and some aspect stemming from the students' own interest— allowed for a re-imagining of BMTFs as more-than-human, and as potential liaisons with the animal world. To design their BMTF, the students examined the body of the Terme they chose, adding their ingredients to it, recomposing the ingredients of their chosen, original Terme.

This methodology for tackling the problem of the Humanist story accepts that embodiment can occur only in new and unexpected ways, where humans exist as a constituent part of other entities. Because the BMTF designs consisted of a combination of components, the consideration of relations between components forced entirely unfamiliar readings. This idea of embodiment is one where preconceptions are either acknowledged and questioned or become irrelevant as new forms of embodiment are discovered. While no methodology can completely remove the human self from the human (yet), methodologies such as that put forward in the brief are at the very least meant to encourage an understanding of the human role in their inhabited and perpetuated fictions and realities. This is a move towards acknowledging human responsibility towards human connections with one another and other worldly beings, extending to the spaces and conditions architects create.

As BMTFs, Termes became new ecosystemic fields, placing the human figure among other critters and inviting students to question the natural order. In the Actor-Network Theory posed by Bruno Latour, all actors within a network exert influence within their bounded field. Sambin's figures could be thought of as a model for this network, challenging the humanist qualities of the Karyatids upon which they were based. The human figures are infiltrated, and at times completely overshadowed, by nonhuman elements of architecture, earth, sediment, and encrustations of animals and animal parts. In this sense, the figure of the Karyatid becomes an animalistic creature, keeping a foot (or a face, or an arm) in the human realm. In some of the projects, placing the non-human fruits, fauns, birds, snakes, and other things among differently-scaled human figures provoked a re-reading of the worldly hierarchies. Using Haraway's terminology, animals are placed in a "hot compost pile" of relations— or, unexpected collaborations

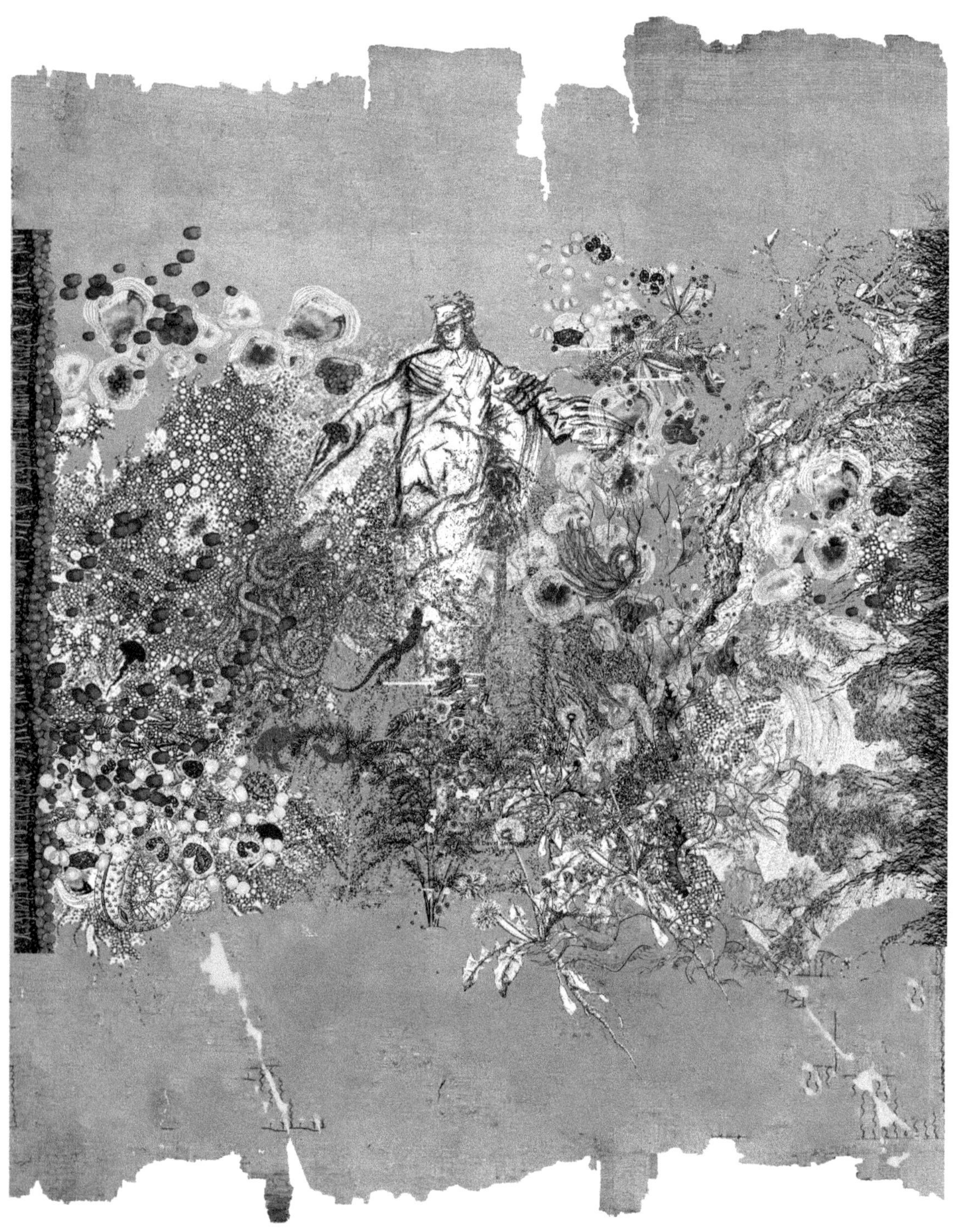

fig. 3.04: Koksal's collage on Shoshanah Dubiner's painting "Endosymbiosis: Homage to Lynn Margulis" showing how the Fossils & Monster's Foundation imagined the Terme as part of a micro-ecology. CE 2019. FMF was founded to make scientific research with limitless imagination on the fossil-monster-animal triangle.

This methodology for tackling the problem of the Humanist story accepts that embodiment can occur only in new and unexpected ways, where humans exist as a constituent part of other entities.

and combinations to make "oddkin." Within the speculative BMTF, and re-imagining and researching into its elements, students pulled on the relative strands that were formed. [42] Through this process, an architecture began to emerge in the projects that destabilised the presumption of *whom* it was being built for, providing the designer with a previously unexplored network of actors.

Considering the architectural figures and selves as part of a larger system invited students to test the concept of "string figures"— or as Haraway describes, "threads of reciprocating energies of biologies, arts, and activisms for multispecies resurgence" that form patterns and are similar to stories by "enact[ing] patterns for participants to inhabit."[43] The students teased out ecosystems and opportunities in building sites through storytelling and design across scales, from the body to the larger architectural proposal. The ingredients that year were a selection of images and themes, posted on an Instagram account as a mix of squares, encouraging students to create actor-network relations without predetermined trajectories. As in every year, selection was encouraged as an intuitive process, yet it was also informed by the sentiment behind Gregory Bateson's notion that "there is an ecology of bad ideas, just as there is an ecology of weeds."[44]

For instance, in Asena Koksal's second-year project (see chapter four project gallery),[45] the Terme figure— a human bust of the primitive Tuscan order— was placed into an altered version of Shoshanah Dubiner's painting *Endosymbiosis* (fig. 3.04).[46] Koksal's collage envisioned this lonely architectural figure in a microscopic actor-network, as one among many hairy critters. This initial exercise upturned the human-animal hierarchy, bringing to life a re-animated and adapted, modern Woolly Mammoth as the main character of the project in the form of the saviour against climate catastrophe. Koksal's project evokes what Haraway might recognise as "[t]he order ... reknitted: human beings are with and of the earth, and the biotic and abiotic powers of this earth are the main story."[47] This type of design experimentation shows that one can engage with the idea that humans cannot be considered or really exist as separate to their nonhuman kin. In what Haraway calls autopoiesis, or, systems that are "self-forming, boundary maintaining, contingent, dynamic, and stable under some conditions but not others," ecologies are an inherent part of the spaces architects create, and are in a sense created by them.[48] Importantly for designers that wish to intervene in a relational scenario, Haraway also discusses the related concept of sympoiesis, or, "making-with" others, where humans could have more of a role, through a "yoke for becoming with, for staying with the trouble... [and] telling the tale of still possible recuperation."[49] Recounting the Project Pigeon Watch story, in which schoolchildren were invited to observe and record urban pigeons and their characteristics, children are seen adopting an attitude of familiarity and respect towards these creatures different to their initial preconceptions of them as "rats with wings," a phrase which suggests further ingrained preconceptions towards rats themselves. [50] Haraway's point reminds us that designers have preconceived ideas about animals they live near to, shaped by a designer's past encounters with animals, along with their education, context, and a multitude of other influences.[51]

For the design of her BTMF in her first-year project, Romana Pop created the "Carecrow," an esoteric, silent giant that communicated with and provided for migratory birds.[52] Inventing the Carecrow, Pop was faced with the problem of how migratory birds could be effectively understood, particularly given their constantly transient lives. Pop researched the types of birds, their flight paths,

Through this process, an architecture began to emerge in the projects that destabilised the presumption of whom it was being built for, providing the designer with a previously unexplored network of actors.

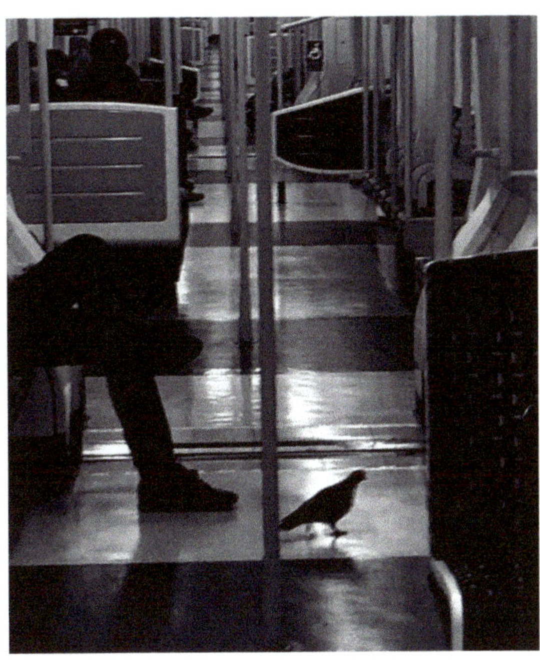

fig. 3.05: Photograph of a pigeon in a London tube carriage by Pop, setting the tone for the project by including it in the first page of the portfolio: "Something really surprising happened to me the other day...I actually got to have a real conversation on the tube! I was minding my business, as everyone does, and this pigeon comes and sits next to me. The usual "Where are you headed?" question came up. It told me that the other birds can't stop talking about this Carecrow, so it's going to Woolwich to see it with its own eyes."

their resting spots, lifespans, and preferred foods. Crucially however, after taking a photograph of a pigeon seemingly happily riding a tube carriage she was travelling on, Pop decided to narrate her project as a conversation between a pigeon and a designer-commuter (fig. 3.05). This led to a more speculative idea that the Carecrow existed not just as a figure, but as a place, an avian oasis in a human-centred city that all birds were "talking" about. From this narrative technique, an ethical stance was established where the animal's lives gained importance and particularity. The hybrid body agent as a mediator allowed for a taking account of animals as a way to question who is speaking, who can speak, and in turn, who can have agency in design.

Pop's use of drawing and sketching as a method for translating intuitive thought-links, her strong storytelling capabilities, her humour, and her sensitivity to confronting an unexplained human fear of the species of animal she chose to work closely with for the year, resulted in a specific form of embodying the creatures and spaces she created. Pop proposed intervening on the shore of the Thames by developing intuitive sketches as she was composing the conversations between herself and the pigeon. She worked through multiple scales, exploring material conditions for human-animal communication. At the same time, a reading of the site emerged through the eyes of an animal, with the site plan being not only from the omnipotent designer's point of view, but from a bird's as well, flying high above the site. This relationship was further exaggerated through the oversaturation of specific chromatic site conditions, as well as the scaling-up of creatures that would likely be magnified in the birds' perceptions, such as worms and dragonflies.

The hybrid body agent as a mediator allowed for a taking account of animals as a way to question who is speaking, who can speak, and in turn, who can have agency in design.

This method was translated further through the frame of the Esquisse, a drawing technique based on an exercise that was part of the École des Beaux-Arts' curriculum.[53] In the version put forward by the prompt that year, students were asked to present their work in a "silent crit," where a single A1-sized composition of orthographic and experimental drawings at different scales would "speak" for them and communicate their idea to visiting critics. Pop used this frame to propose an interstitial wall-hostel-waterfront path that would host

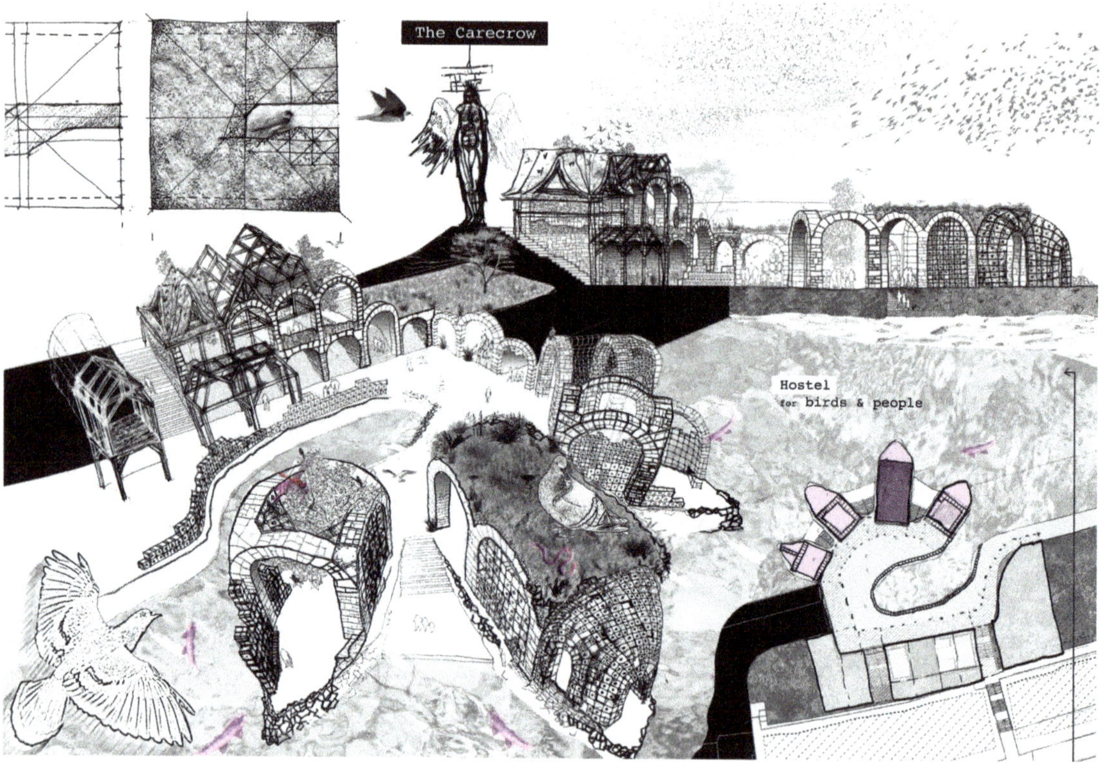

fig. 3.06: Pop's "esquisse" of her Ecology Enabler Element. "'A place where you are allowed to feed the birds' the pigeon added." This drawing was preceded by mapping experiments of Woolwich riverside captioned: "Caution: Map suitable for bird vision."

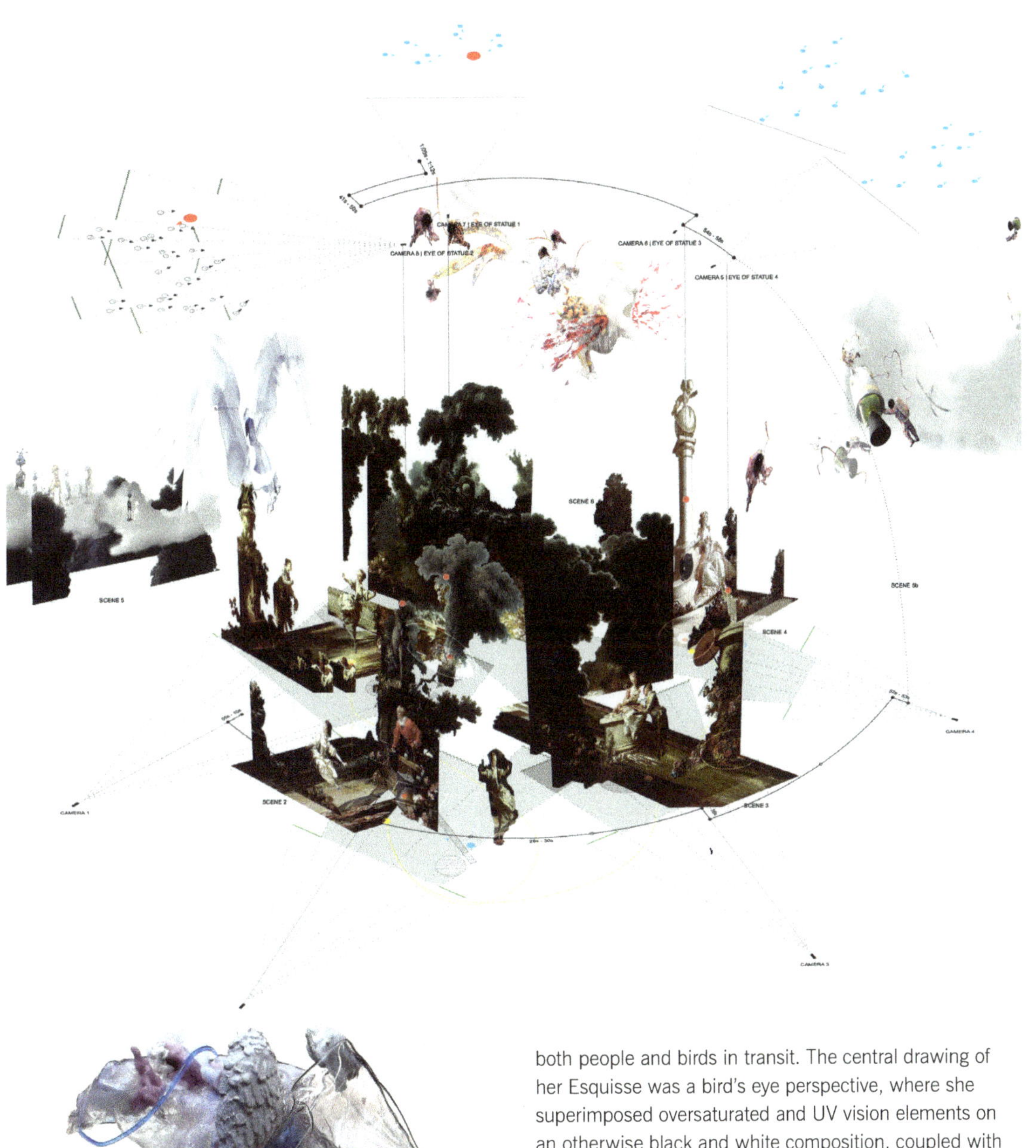

fig. 3.07-3.08: Top: Man created a set as a nature documentary. According to the core narrative of the project, Mile End park would be guarded and watched through a camera system that functions as the guardian Sphynx's eyes. The system used this outdoor studio to produce a documentary of the park's animal dwellers' daily lives, and of the interactions between them and the human visitors; Bottom: Tsamitrou's experimental model used techniques to capture a cloud's thingly inhabitation on a physical site.

both people and birds in transit. The central drawing of her Esquisse was a bird's eye perspective, where she superimposed oversaturated and UV vision elements on an otherwise black and white composition, coupled with details of bird nesting studies (fig. 3.06). The precision with which the drawing was composed was not scientifically accurate, but took certain everyday assumptions and distorted elements of the drawing to bring out an *other* experience, one which is at once understandable by a human eye, and which at the same time displaces the viewer, making them question for what kind of being this drawing is made.

First-year student Lingezzi Man's project engaged these debates in her project that intermingled animal, technological, and social spheres.[54] The proposal involved a rethinking of the Mile End Ecology pavilion as an arena for nature documentaries. Considering the animal habitats as scenographic elements, and the habits of the animals as scenes or vignettes, in Man's project architecture became infrastructure for choreographing, filming, and layering landscape and machines (fig. 3.07). The project took a sympoietic attitude, piercing and manipulating the seemingly autopoietic system of Mile End, bringing up questions about who was the performer and who the observer.

Another way of tinkering with the interrelations between human and animal bodies is by substituting known parts between the two. This practice appears in art-science practices such as Daniel Lee's series of digital paintings, *Manimals,* where human and animal features are blended seamlessly in composite portraits. Another example discussed in the studio is Max Ernst's *Figures*, where ambiguous, zoomorphic, yet uncannily "human" beings are portrayed. Another example often cited in the studio is the Chapman Brothers' *Exquisite Corpse* drawings, where a chimeric creature unfolds literally from the folded panels of the page; this is a drawing game which inevitably enters any DS25 field trip dinner through folded place mats passed around the table (fig. 1.04, 5.01). Yet another example often cited in the studio discussions are the paintings of Francis Bacon, whose retrospective "Man and Beast" at the Royal Academy fortuitously occurred during the year of the *Embodying Ecologies* brief. Through gestural brushstrokes that capture fleeting flesh and sporadic anatomies, Bacon's paintings envision subjects that evoke Deleuze's notion of "becoming-animal" and, through the relationship of portrayed flesh and bone, the closely associated idea of "becoming meat" where "...meat is the common zone between man and the beast."[(55)]

Partly to explore his own dual nationality, in his paintings, Lee developed a typology between human and animal, setting the two against each other as separate categories and at the same time blending their characteristics. Bacon's range of blending— from seamless to violently colliding— show a subject in upheaval. On the other hand, Lee's work suggests that as nature-culture divisions dissolve, the animal-human distinction becomes seamless, inviting a questioning of the validity of taxonomic boundaries.

Blending human-animal embodiment was explored early on in DS25 in 2019, when Hewes questioned animal-human relationships by considering humans living with cats, asking: what does it mean to be a domestic cat living with humans, and what is the line between cat and human? Engaging with the concept of ailuranthropy, Hewes imagined how pet cats would become more human through anthropomorphising prosthetics. Painting what seemed an uncanny self portrait, she imagined that the parents themselves would also become more feline as the lifestyle became almost cult-like. In a mirroring of this relationship, her *Cat Belly House* was filled with details which swapped

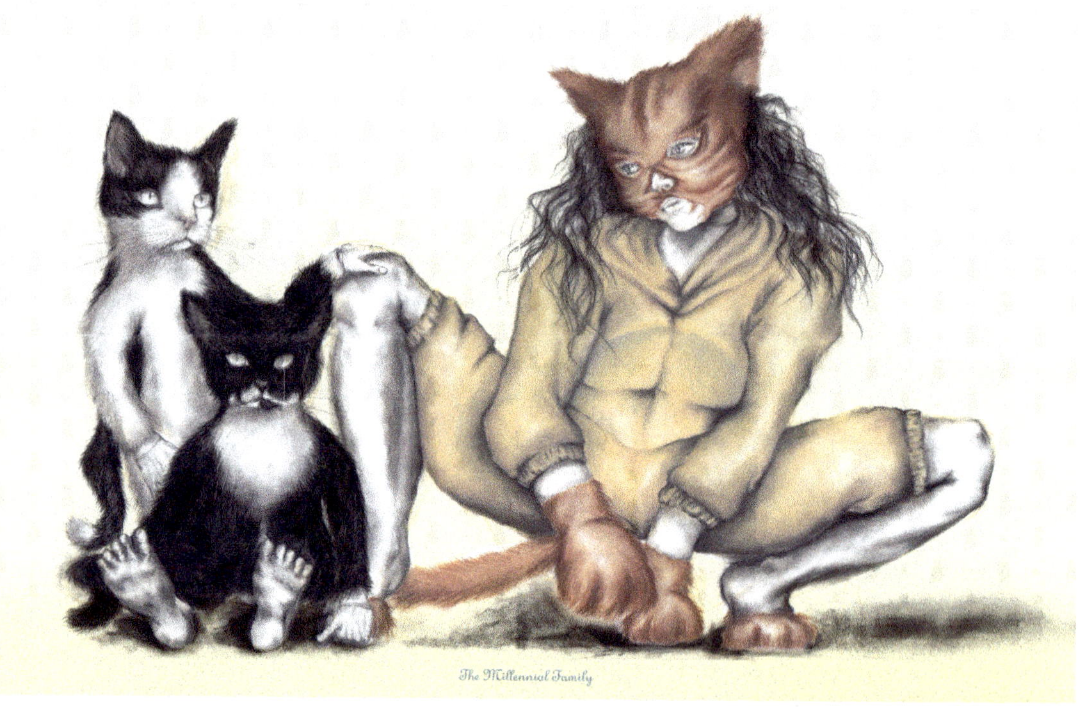

fig. 3.09: Hewes' uncanny self-portrait of "The Millennial Family," showing the ailuranthropy concept where humans use cat-anatomy prosthetics and vice-versa.

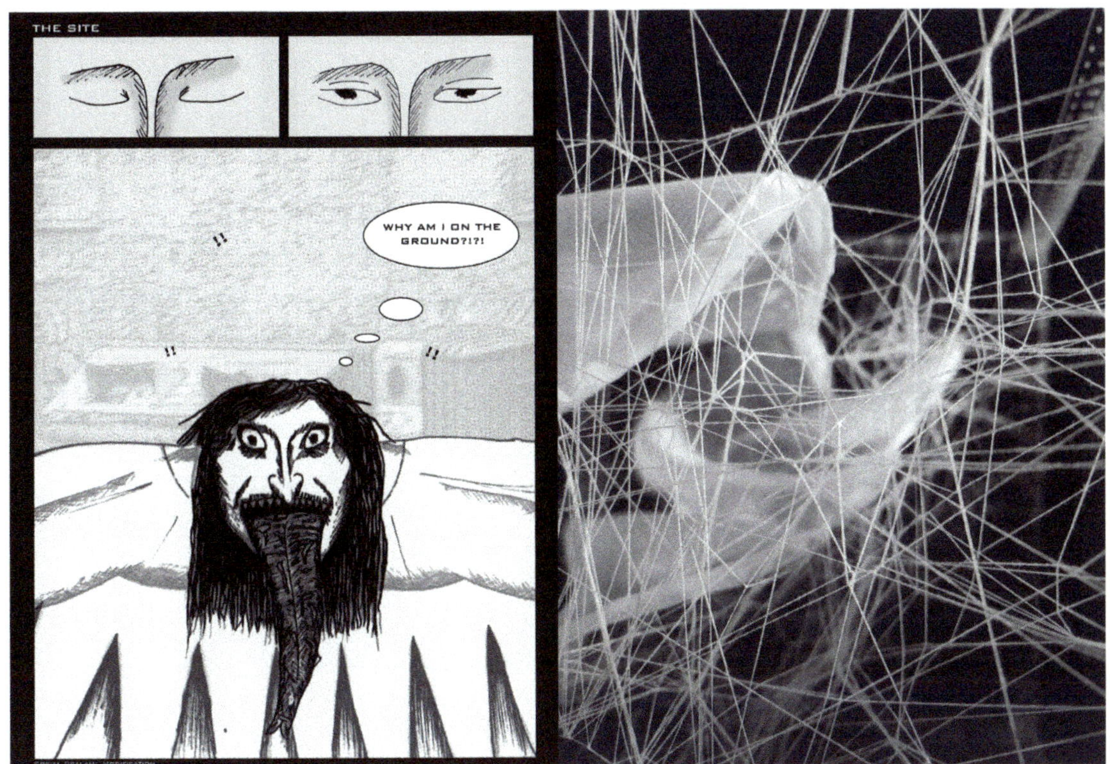

fig. 3.10: Lo's Scalams were narrated through a manga-style graphic novel. The Scalams made their Shell-of-the-Ghost as an open-air above-ground parasitic commune where the community interacted and rested after cleaning the air pollution.

Here, utopia is in the eye of the beholder.

the presumed hierarchy of cat and human (see chapter three project gallery). For instance, the "cat-baby," wearing human-hand and foot prosthetics could sit on a highchair whose headrest featured a human-baby head prosthetic, cradling the cat in a seated human position.

Alcina Lo's first-year project entitled *Social Scalam: The Modification and Conservation of the Human Race* also explored a possible future for animal-human relationships (see chapter three project gallery).[56] Tackling the subject of genetic engineering, Lo questioned the limits of the notion of the human as perceived by a dominant iteration of the human species. In the project, known features of the human body are reassembled to fulfil the interests of non-genetically-modified humans. The "Scalams" were imagined as eight-legged, cat-sized creatures with human heads. Inspired by manga imagery and Japanese folklore, similar to *Samara*,[57] a type of *yōkai*, or supernatural figures from Japanese folklore, Scalams were thought to have disturbingly long tongues.[58]

In Lo's project, Scalams are small, ignorable, marginalised creatures, lost in the background like a spider in the corner of a room. However, inspired by sci-fi, such as Adrian Tchaikovsky's 2015 sci-fi novel *Children of Time* discussed in tutorials, Lo imagined the Scalams' agency to be outsized, overlapping with the human in some ways, but exceeding it in others. Scalams retained certain *habitus*— or humanly-understood cultural habits of the body—[59] such as taking off their shoes before entering a house (fig. 3.46). At the same time, Scalams were thought to have been engineered distinctly beyond humans in their bodily capabilities; for instance, Lo imagined Scalams were created by humans to clean Palermo's air by weaving strands of thread to capture and eat pollutants from the atmosphere. Through this mixture of familiar and approachable traits— but also uncanny, uncomfortable, and unhuman ones—, the Scalams enabled a critical vantage point to question advances in genetic engineering and the financial, societal, and ethical divides it engenders.

With spiders and webs in mind, and informed by Frei Otto's tensile structures, Lo tested differently-scaled models, from a 1:200 site model to a 1:20 suspended interior space to explore techniques of blending spiders' weaving methods (fig. 3.10). The boundary between animals and humans began to be spatially blurred in the initial design of the domestic space of the Scalams. As these hybrid creatures were imagined creating and inhabiting Lo's experimental webs, new spatial conditions began to emerge which challenged the notion of a boundary separating human and other (fig. 3.43).

Burrows and O'Sullivan propose the idea of "fictioning," practices that "...mark out trajectories different to those engendered by the dominant organisations of life currently in existence... exploring those fictions that involve potential realities to come as well as the more general idea of fiction as an intervention in, and augmentation of, existing reality."[60] Through these experiments, Lo "fictioned" habitats for the Scalams in an imagined future setting where the interstitial spaces of the city became covered in a woven cocoon. Lo's allegorical project imagined that in the far-future, the Scalams would curate a taxidermy museum of human evolution, encouraging non-genetically-modified visitors to navigate nets and tensile membranes to experience exhibitions provoking a reconsideration of the presumed social hierarchy (fig. 3.43).

The Scalams engaged with a strand of our reality and the spectral futures that loom over it. With one foot in the human and another in the animal realm, the Scalam became an estranged being, even though it retained certain familiar characteristics. One could even go on to say that because of this, it had a foot in the realm of the monstrous: its image twists the known human form, placing the human in conversation with the unknown, in turn personifying a confrontation with certain collective fears induced by specific human actions.

Looking at body-world hierarchies from the macro to the micro scale is another way of further estranging the human and the self from their definition of their body as complete. The concepts developed in 2024 by Anastasia Kolioliou in her first-year project, *Bacteria Sanctuary,* engaged with two major theoretical frameworks: firstly, the agency of non-human critters in shaping material habitats, and secondly, the idea of the body as a porous field and a habitat for other creatures (see chapter four project gallery).[61] As discussed above, Haraway points out that no living being is a singular organism: "to be animal is to become-with bacteria."[62] Using these frameworks, Kolioliou engaged with the site by bringing to life OD, an obsessive biologist who travelled around the canals of Canary Wharf in search of conditions favourable to bacterial growth. In the framework of the studio's briefs, Kolioliou used film as a generator for defining OD's agenda, visualising the play between the imagery she created, spliced with a voice reminiscent of nature documentary narrator David Attenborough. He says: "I want to *be* the bacteria..."

For Kolioliou, OD's obsession became a way of reading the site through specific parameters, concentrating on pollution and designing speculative tools for finding ideal habitats. Through multiple levels of analysis, chance mappings, and suturings of differently-scaled drawings, Kolioliou's imagination of OD's point of view helped her identify the site of a disused sugar refinery as an ideal condition for OD's laboratory-garden for bacterial growth. In the project narrative, OD is imagined as a solitary individual, but in the story his obsession begins to transform him into a more socially-minded leader, as he created possibilities for a grandiose vision of a flourishing utopia for microorganisms (fig. 4.51). OD is shown planning for the effects his designs will have on both man-made and natural ecosystems with full faith in their beneficial promise. OD's mutant body, born out of exposure to existing bacterial conditions, became a constantly evolving model for the world which he sets out to create, foreshadowing its effects: as the project progresses, his arm and hand are seen becoming invaded with bacterial growths, with oily handprints saturating the pages of the fictitious report comprising the portfolio (fig. 4.49).

Aside from the aspects of this project which relate to the importance of narrative in design, discussed in the fourth chapter, these devices allowed for Kolioliou to immerse herself in a different form of embodiment. Playing with scale, her drawings combined the scale of the fibres of the material in which bacterial growth can take place with that of a room, making it difficult to distinguish which spaces within the section are habitable by humans and which by microorganisms. Incorporating this in her design methodology allowed her to engage with an imagined *umwelt*— or, species-specific perception of the world— of bacteria and ask, "what is bacteria architecture?" This in turn brought to the foreground the question of who the main inhabitant of the spaces she designed really would be. In Kolioliou's words, underlying the seemingly utopian proposal lies "a subversive agenda ... envisioning humanity as a 'boundary crossing entity,' seamlessly integrated with the microbial world."[63] The project was comprised of programmatic spaces that would clearly be beneficial for humans, such as facilities for water purification and waste biodigestion. At the same time, the visual means of communication that Kolioliou employed in instances where bacteria are used by humans asks the question of whose utopia the project is: bacteria, humans, or a new hybrid species? Here, utopia is in the eye of the beholder.

MONSTERS

While body and world become more conceptually unified in a scenario where the human body is extensively imprinted onto the environment, a byproduct could be that the body ironically becomes estranged from itself. Moving to increasingly intensified degrees of estrangement, the monstrous and the Other can have ominous and enticing affects, destabilising the position of the human in assumed ontological hierarchies. In the DS25 projects, degrees of

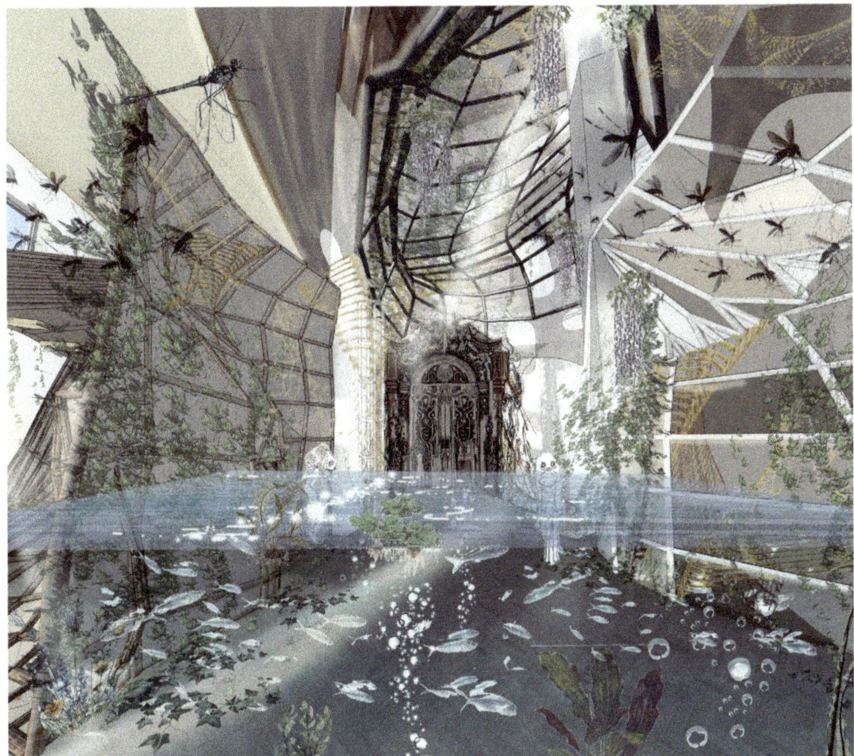

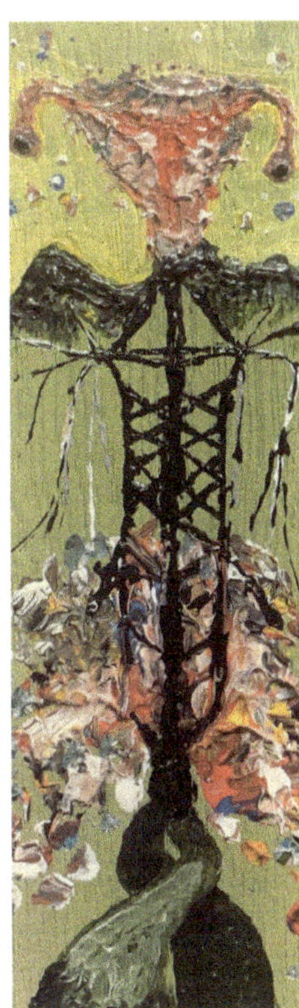

fig. 3.11-3.12: Left to Right: Rama's Chitin building inhabited by fish-scientists and insects in a far-future setting; Power's "Hymenaeus" painting on a found piece of timber.

In those moments where interrogation is provoked, passive assumption of the body as a given condition is ruptured, giving way to the monstrous.

defamiliarisation moving away from the known human world force confrontations with what most humans would believe to be familiar, including the human body itself. As the human body is interrogated and mixed with others, hybrid assemblages give birth to monsters of all kinds, which exaggerate this defamiliarisation.

Philosopher and critic Dylan Trigg notes that "we seldom feel the need to interrogate how our body works and what our body is."[64] In those moments where interrogation is provoked, passive assumption of the body as a given condition is ruptured, giving way to the monstrous. Analogously, architectural space is similarly taken as given and seldom interrogated by its inhabitants or designers. In practice, this passivity relates to complex established policies, standards, and ideals, all deeply ingrained within the historical fabric, which in reality are often questioned only superficially mostly due to budgetary and time constraints.

The definition of what constitutes a monster is elusive. Looking to monsters from the mediaeval period James Elkins notes that "...monsters were formed by conjoining nameable parts taken from nameable creatures."[65] Materially, monsters could appear when tinkering manifests a combination of beings. When a being understood as known— including a human— turns out to be someone or something else, this can also be considered as monstrous.

While as plot devices in narratives monsters often assume hostile, seemingly simplistically antagonistic roles, their roles as signifiers is more complex. As signifiers of difference, monsters stand in for a fear of things their audience cannot comprehend, or versions of themselves that may seem impossible to live with. Monsters are the vilified notions of human non-normative thoughts and actions, created as Others in order for the audience to exorcise fears, creating disturbing questions and feelings, and setting the norm in stark relief with the unusual. Human viewers may find animals themselves to appear monstrous when something about the animal is out of the ordinary. In all the cases, a heightened sense of danger— itself an innately animal sense— is provoked, and it is through self-reflection that the existence of the "monstrous" dimension in the Other is established.

The monster is usually the villain in the story. In nuanced narratives from literature and film, however, the idea of a clear-cut villain, an enemy, or a monster is challenged and complicated, revealing that such denominations are dependent on perspective. Such storylines show that the nomenclature of monster is therefore subjective, brought to life when difference arises that requires confrontation. Taking into account the body-world relationships set out in the beginning of the chapter, the monster could also be thought of as a distorted mirror image of the body. In this sense, the monstrous body can appear frightening or threatening, as the direct enemy to the immutability of the integral human form. However, becoming-monstrous could also be thought to liberate the body, opening up the prospect of experimentation with re-arranged, extended, and intensified body-world relationships.

The proposition of creating monsters allows not only for a tinkering with the human body and a displacement of the protagonist's perspective, but also for experimentation with core understandings and standards which dominate a specific setting, in turn questioning "normal" practices and their effects on a wider context. An example of this questioning through monstrosity can be found in the lyrics and video clip of the song *Arch Enemy* created by animator and songwriter Jonathan Higgs, where the search for a modern religion mixes with "a congregation of greed, toxicity and waste, in the form of a sentient fatberg in the sewer."[66] The feelings of both disgust and awe come from the realisation that what the monster is made of is not supernatural goo, but an ever-growing accumulation of real, tangible discards of centuries of human activity, hidden away from view and impossible to grasp. The confrontation with the known reality as a formed creature allows for one to stand face-to-face with the scale of the issue, and at the same time provides a form of "staying with the trouble."[67] In *The Monster Leviathan: Anarchitecture*, architecture critic Aaron Betsky finds moments of confrontation with vast and disturbing creations of modern industry in "..the beauty and gory glory of the modern environments we have built for ourselves,... the incredible waste of resources and the violence."[68] He looks to Frank Lloyd Wright's narrating of Chicago as a "sprawling industrious city" but also a "beast, an animal that has flesh and sinews [:] the city, the machine, technology, us as human beings, all rolled into a technoorganic being, ... a mythic other to the environment in which we find ourselves."[69]

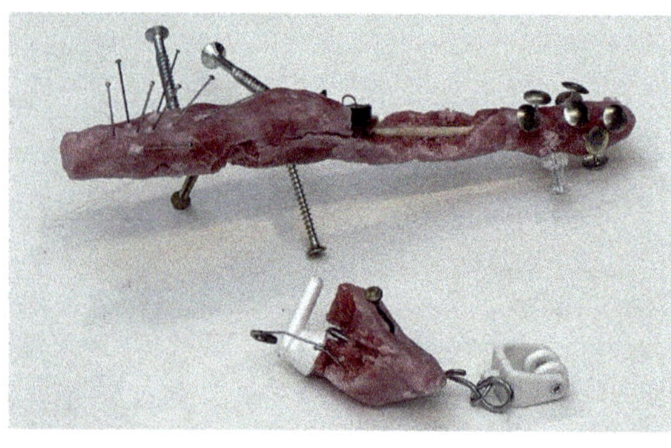

fig. 3.13: Cocca's "internet skin" material experiments.

Monsters dominate both new and old myths, such as in Jorge Luis Borges' collection in the *Book of Imaginary Beings*, where he catalogues mythical beings through modern and ancient sources including Greek myths, bestiaries, and literature, whose pages were intended to be read "at random."[70] Monsters are pictured in *terra incognita* to explain otherwise unexplainable phenomena in 16th century cartography such as the *Carta Marina* by Olaus Magnus.[71] More adventurously hybrid and wide-ranging than the cyborg, which extends the human, monsters are often based on and comprised of more extremely unlikely parts, such as inanimate and animate components, technological attributes, fictitious features, human limbs or organs, and animal appendages.

As assembled entities, monsters are a multifaceted playground for invention, incorporating thing, human, animal, and environment. In these ways, as figurations, monsters offer the opportunity to provide the consideration of a wide range of interfaces with ecologies, producing combined subjectivities. While monster anatomy can be incredibly fantastical, incorporating recognisable parts or elements into their creation can give them particular efficacy as devices to rethink human predicaments.

This can be seen in Cocca's project (see chapter two project gallery) where he started with a crude assemblage of Sottsass-designed products (his chosen precedent), as well as repurposed car tyres, motorbike frames and chains, wrapped with fabrics and plastics (his chosen material). Cocca's "cooking [of] the ingredients" fused them with anatomical parts of staged generalised "Instagram" faces, legs and torsos (his chosen "ecology" of zombie scrolling). [72] This enabled Cocca to question the ideal bodies presented by social media, extending them beyond the Instagram square, taking their existence into "meatspace" (fig. 3.13). The hybrid assemblages that emerged provided him with a design language that challenged the normative body-image, which in turn influenced his design of a rave and artists' residency building resembling human bodily organs (fig. 2.52).

Another example of a monster-assemblage that proved productive for imagining combined subjectivities was the body agent in Xhesika Rama's first-year project, called the "Morphyte."[73] Developed as a combination between the ancient Greek shapeshifting water-deity Proteus, Neri Oxman's experiments with robotically fabricated Chitin structures, and monoprint drawing techniques, Morphyte was designed as an underwater

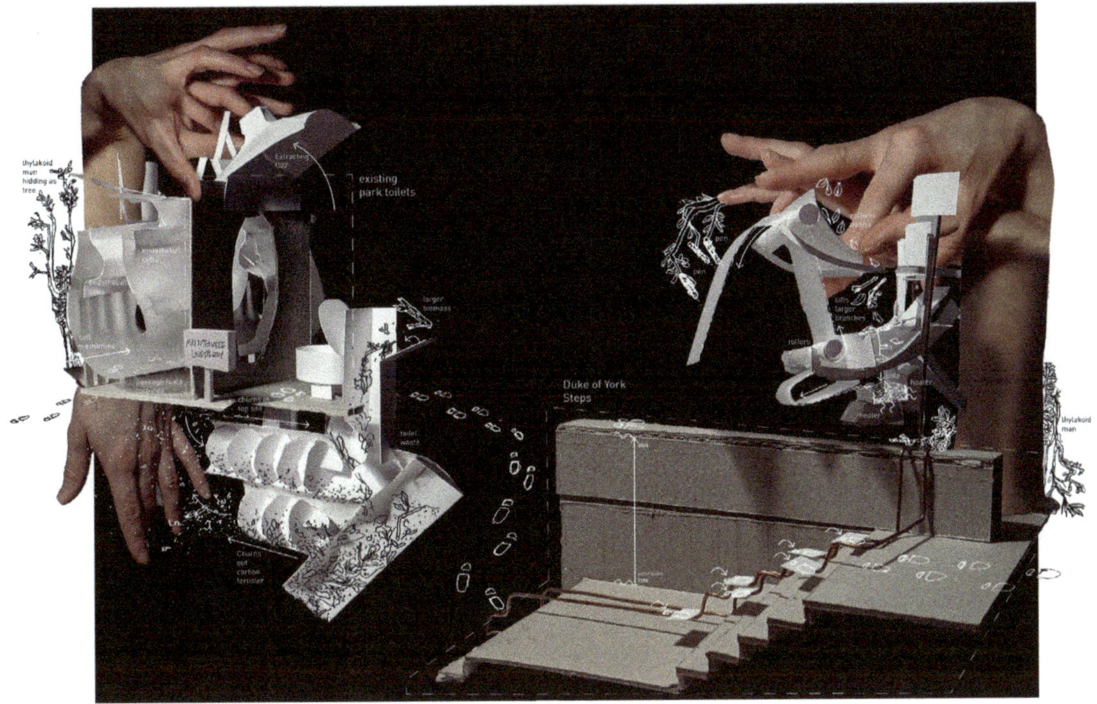

fig. 3.14: Kybrer's "Thylakoid Man" second-year project physical model.

creature with mechanised ribs that would craft shells over its decaying half-human body using collected fish scales and bones from the canal bed. Her project was narrated by mutant half-fish half-human scientists (mutants created in a catastrophic accident in the lab in its far-future) who encouraged circular material processes such as reuse of dead organic material to grow a structure that would be inhabited by the ecologies of London's canal creatures (fig. 3.11).

STRADDLING BOUNDARIES

DS25 briefs often ask for ways to test and experiment with unexpected collaborations between beings by shifting the generative potential of body agents from the singular human body to one of assemblages of multiple entities. In DS25 projects, the starting point of selecting ingredients makes the key presence of assemblages almost inevitable, since it leads to a composition of seemingly disparate things (often including nonhuman elements) to form the body agents and catalyse architectural thinking. Since the *Architecture's Second Bodies* brief, and developing through the BMTF prompt in 2021, each brief has further confronted the human as one of many other actants. This approach, where ingredients prompt the invention of assemblages as a starting point, provides the student-designer with parameters that themselves act as a set of string figures.(74) Generating new body-world relations, the student-designer can then hone their field of study and produce unexpected responses, made-with other, combined forms of embodiment.(75)

Sambin's Termes, straddling boundaries between deities, mortals, animals, and architecture, with the human figure as a central recognisable reference, could be defined as monstrous. The Termes, also referred to as Terms or Terminus, are composed of recognisable, referential elements, including human form and proportions; these referents give the viewer a handhold on the familiar. Sambin designed his Termes in such a way that the assembled elements seem to form a new biological interweaving of known elements; because of this, the familiar elements of the figure take on estranged qualities.

In *The Lost Meaning of Classical Architecture*, architectural historian George Hersey writes that the first century BC Greek historian "Dionysius of Halicarnassus… says that when Targquin wanted to purge the Capitoline of all divinities, he was successful with all but this god, who could take any form, human, animal, or vegetable or, especially, all three. In short, he could be a composite monster, a concretion of heads, thighs, flowers and bones… caryatids— like the temples with which they were associated, might be draped, bound, hung with such offerings. But Terminus could actually be comprised of such things."(76) Hersey goes on to write that "[The Terrminus's] monstrosity is a tribute to Nature's abundance and creativity, her infinite combinatorial powers."(77)

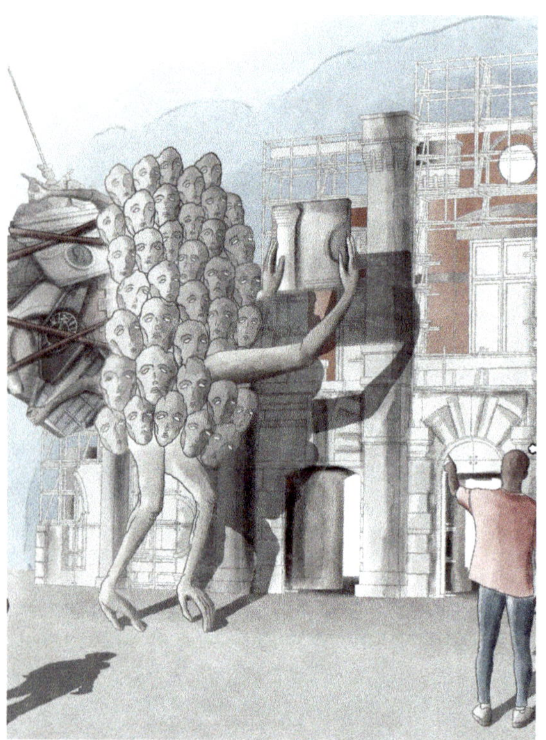

fig. 3.15-3.16: Baldwin's "Urban Polycephalic" BMTF stitching together the Ecology Enabler Element from fragmented facade pieces gathered from across Woolwich in an attempt to conserve its identity. Facing Page: Woods' figurine's drift through the domestic spaces of Woolwich were narrated through a graphic novel format. As she moved through different flat interiors she baffles residents as they wake up to see her not only having grown parts of nearby kitch figurines on the mantlepiece, but also monstrous ceramic extensions to the flats she resides in.

Viewing monstrous assemblages such as Sambin's Termes could provoke a defamiliarisation with the self, and, in turn, the world. Karyatids invite an empathic connection to the viewer of a specific type of human supporting a pediment; they may perhaps spur wonder at the apparent transubstantiation of flesh to stone in the anthropomorphisation of the column.(78) In the case of Sambin's Termes, the substitutions and transpositions are more extreme. Sambin not only substituted building elements for bodies; human body parts are multiplied, or transformed into cornucopias of fruit, plants, other beings, and masks. The human body is presented as a microcosm of a world where architectural conditions are mixed with organic and inorganic elements in infinite combinations, defining the parameters of the world within and outside of the figure. The world Sambin evokes is itself monstrous, with its systems relating to anatomical elements found within the body but recombining and deforming them.

Tinkering with the Termes resulted in imaginative ideas about the material possibilities of the body; for example, in his second-year project, Adriaan Baldwin took his chosen material, stone, as an integral part of the organic body of his BMTF.(79) Also inspired by Baldwin's interest in manga drawing styles and themes, the BMTF that emerged was a found human body covered by a contradictory shell of multiple stone masks held by steel hooks from a carved stone arm (fig. 3.15).

Taking the body agent a step further away from the animal towards becoming a composite subject, or assemblage, allowed it to become monstrous, in turn providing a point of confrontation with the familiar. Like monsters, body agents across various years of the studio arguably expressed unconscious desires and fears of their authors. In 2021, for Koksal, Spiers-Reed (fig. 3.17), and Woods respectively, these surfaced as anxieties regarding ecological crisis, social obsession with self-image, and identity with respect to dual nationality; in projects from 2023, for Lo's second-year project (see chapter three project gallery), Alannah Wilson's second-year project, *Hydropolis: A Civic Revival*(80) (see chapter three project gallery), and Imogen Power's second-year project *The Hymanaeus Collection*(81) (fig. 3.12), respectively, anxieties grappled with included fear of losing one's agency amidst data and media-driven digital culture, the effects of capitalist consumerism, and female safety. The monstrous body agents designed by the students often challenged comforting notions of embodiment, at times even evoking a sense of dread in the deformation and reconfiguration of the body. In this sense, when attempting to understand the non-human and find ways to design architecture for it or with it, projects such as Kolioliou's speculate on embodied ecologies; in the case of her project, the porous human skin was the first point of interrogation.

In the studio work, one aspect that most evoked this sense of dread was the integration of architecture and other technologies into the body. As discussed in chapter two, such transgressions of the body could be considered as an inevitable byproduct of posthumanism, where the body becomes a duplicate Other. The state of continuous becoming is arguably an inevitable condition of embodiment. Body agents are also continuously transforming, as the design of the figure continues over the course of iterations throughout the year. To figure out the workings of the figure, and how the bodily processes play a role in these transformations, often the anatomy of the figure is revealed, drawn, and altered, as a vicarious anatomical tinkering, making for visual representations that can seem to disturb the sanctity of the body's integrity.

becoming-monstrous could also be thought to liberate the body, opening up the prospect of experimentation with re-arranged, extended, and intensified body-world relationships.

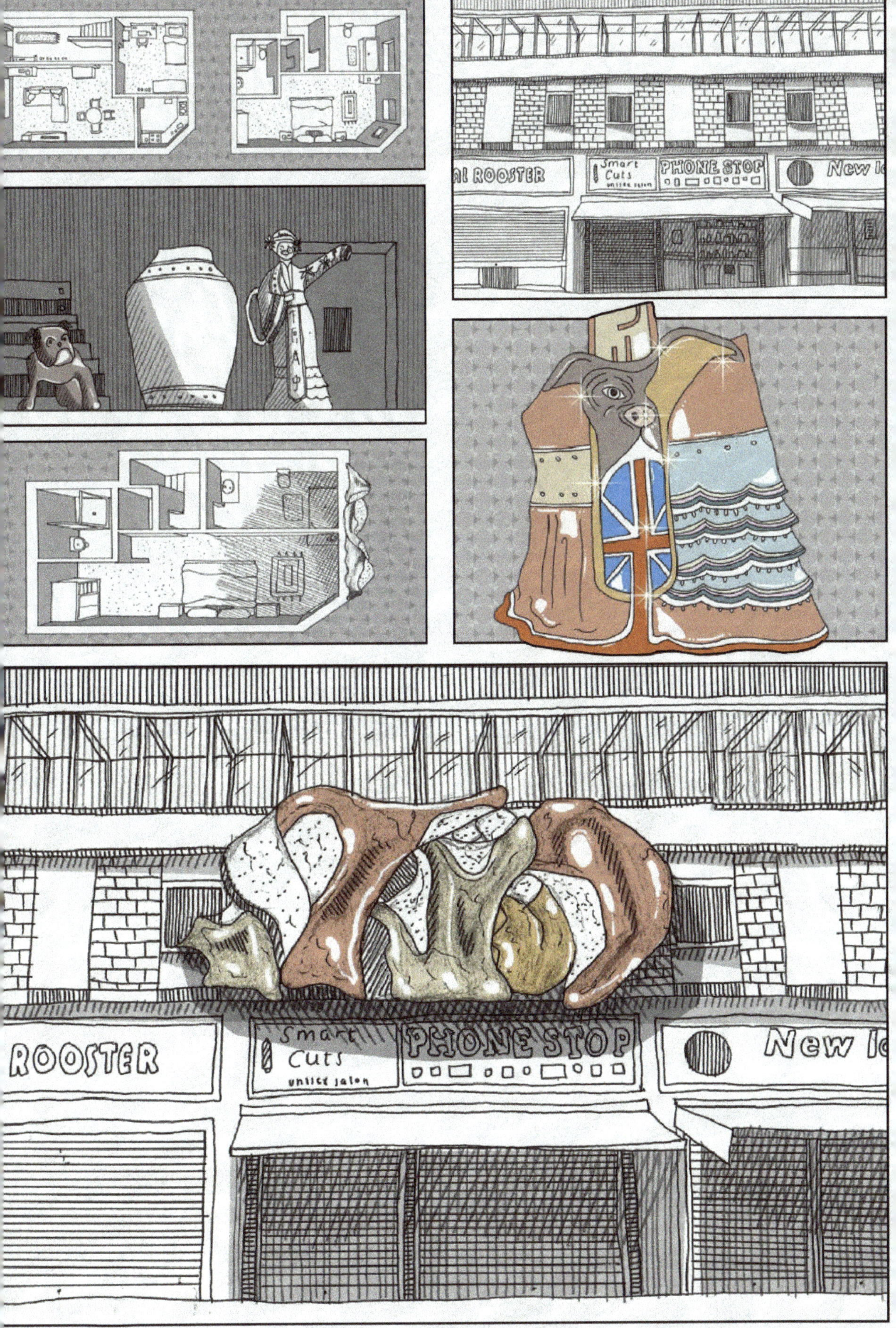

ROOSTER
Smart Cuts
unisex salon
PHONE STOP
New
ROOSTER
Smart Cuts
unisex salon
PHONE STOP
New

In the case of body horror, these expressions work through transformations of the body, violating the sense of security and stability associated with it. In a lecture on the subject, Trigg says: "...in moments of anxiety and horror, you will reflect yourself on where your body begins and where it ends. What if you were to replace your hands with that of a stranger's? ... At which point do you cease to be you?"[(82)] When a body is familiar and has an identity, and its identity is one that can relate to other beings and bodies around it, it is a point of reference within a specific world, and a reflection of social relations. If, however, this body is placed among other beings that have familiar shapes or characteristics but whose ambiguous identity one cannot pin down, or which are decidedly different in appearance to the body itself, that body cannot find points of reference among its context, or else the points of reference are blurred with the unknown or unidentified. In this sense, the body is out of place, requiring examination as something other: "the body is defined at the intersection of the I and the non-I."[(83)] Experimenting with the perception of the subject, the studio also worked with Trigg's ideas concerning how the mere recognition of our own body as a thing that we inhabit can incite uncanny feelings. In his lecture, he goes on to note that the body is at once a familiar and irreducible frame of reference, an orientation within a specific world to a specific and singular subject. The body is "doubled, by an anonymous body which is...not my own."[(84)] Trigg suggests that one cannot exist as one is in the world without their body, yet one's body can and does exist within the world without, before or after them, as self-organising matter. Roman Polanski's film *The Tenant* (1976), captures a similar contradictory— even unsettling— bodily condition where "at one point, [the protagonist]'s own hands begin to strangle him." Over the course of the film the protagonist's body is continuously reinforced as "a body distributed through space without ever fully belonging to [him]."[(85)]

THINGLY AGENCY

With the 2023-24 brief *Things Have Feelings Too*, taught by the studio teaching team of Dr Alessandro Ayuso and Mary Konstantopoulou, the studio moved further from the human body in its consideration of who— or what— architecture's subjects could be. The brief for the year was announced via a fictional press release:

> *"Open call for architects to make radical proposals. Other Constructions, a non-profit project-funding organisation run by environmental justice activists, posthuman philosophers and others, based in London and Paris, invites architectural proposals that radically re-imagine other-worldly narratives where Things are assumed to have agency.*

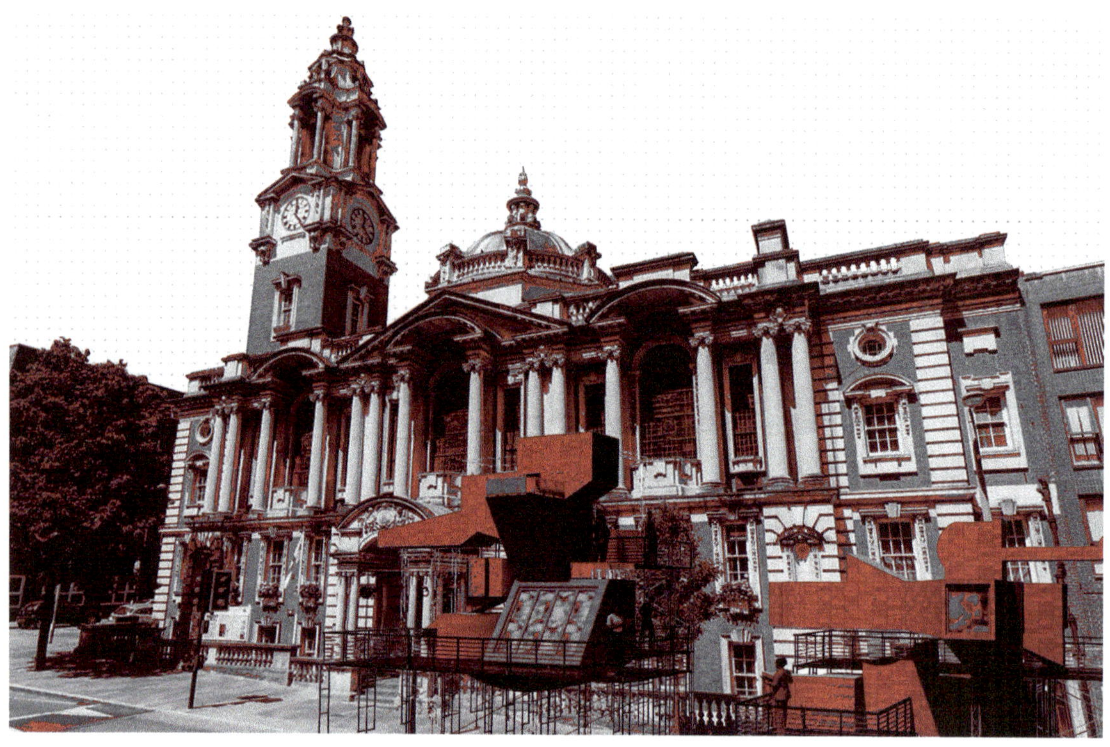

fig. 3.17: Spiers-Reed's "[Un[Selfie Factory's" first step of the procession. The Ecology Enabler Element establishing itself as a Trojan Horse outside Woolwich Town Hall.

An Other Constructions spokesperson describes the aim of the project:

Architects have been shackled by the legacy of humanism for too long. Instead of placing themselves atop an assumed hierarchy, we ask them: What if you assumed that Things have feelings too?
How would this change your presumptions about inhabitation and ecology? What architecture would emerge? We invite visionary architects to make radical proposals on the Isle of Dogs to rethink its natural and man-made ecosystems and embrace otherness.
Our emphasis on Thing-based spatial thinking does not supersede our interest on the primacy of the (cyborg, hybrid, visceral) body as a spatial agent. In fact, the human body is a Thing too."

The press release went on to explain the identity of the organisers:

"Other Constructions is a fictitious non-profit organisation advocating for an embrace of otherness. With a mission to fund daring architectural proposals and a belief that (post)humans must find new ways of positioning themselves amidst complex ecologies, OC believes architecture has a unique ability to enact new relationships between the human and non-human, physically engaging bodies and narrative threads that comprise places. OC believes that to address current social and environmental crises, the humanist legacy must shift to embrace a more non-hierarchical paradigm and give agency to things other than humans. Envisioning the Isle of Dogs as a locale for catalysing ecologies of otherness, Other Constructions also advocates for the re-assertion of its independence."

The premise of the body agents within this brief was linked with Franz Kafka's 1919 story, *Cares of a Family Man*, in which a family engages with a strange bundle of inanimate things called the Odradek, which seems to have a life of its own. "Odradek," writes Walter Benjamin in his 1934 essay titled Franz Kafka, "is the form which things assume in oblivion. ... Odradek's significance lies in where it appears: the attic, the staircase, the corridors, the hall. 'It prefers', he claims, 'the same places as the court of law which investigates guilt'."(86) Things with their own uncanny existence is a concept explored in the constantly reproducing useless junk termed *kipple* by Philip K Dick in his 1968 sci-fi novel *Do Androids Dream of Electric Sheep?*.

To mediate between the human and thingly realms in architectural exploration, each student began the year by designing what the studio called an Odradek Body, a sentient figure assembled from a collection of objects with a subjective point of view. As Bennet notes, "assemblages are ad hoc groupings of diverse elements, of vibrant materials of all sorts"; they are "living, throbbing confederations that are able to function despite the persistent presence of energies that confound them from within."(87)

These figures became catalysts for each project, raising critical issues, bringing up imaginative possibilities, and informing architectural languages. The in-studio discussion considered that as much as we could understand things from our own anthropocentric perspective, in some respects they could be thought to live lives outside of our grasp.(88) Yet, the discussion brought up that perhaps we have more of an affinity with things than we think: as Trigg's comments suggest, at times we may perceive our bodies as things as well. With a starting point being the understanding of parts of the body as things, the studio explored this horrific feeling which is expressed in the short story *Skeleton* written by sci-fi author Ray Bradbury, first published in the September 1945 issue of *Weird Tales*. The narrative takes us through the life of a man who begins to understand his skeleton as an entity apart from himself, that he discovers anew, and that he notices is trying to come out of his skin as parts such as teeth and fingernails. The narrator dissociates with vital parts of his own body, examining parts of himself which he no longer accepts as familiar, but which he clearly sees as an *other* parasitic body existing alongside or within himself. This uncanny perception is described by the "unhuman" condition, epitomised by moments where the body becomes a stranger even to itself.(89)

Acknowledging this aspect of the human body, the Odradek Body was meant to be a hybrid figure that could mediate between the human and nonhuman worlds. Constructed from things— whole objects, fragments, and even elements of human or animal bodies— an Odradek Body could be anthropomorphic, taking the guise of a cyborg. It could also depart radically from human form, perhaps more similar to Deleuze and Guattari's idea of a "body without organs," where non-human assemblages or even abstract systems could be considered as bodies.(90)

The Odradek Bodies were assembled from a choice of six things by each student individually, considering the junctions between parts, composition, proportion, the functionality of how it would move, imagining how it would sense, perceive. The brief specified the six things:

- *"One Thing of yours (important to you)*
- *One Architectural component (a detail such as a joint, fixture, assembly, etc.) from a list of architectural precedents*
- *One Thing from a terrestrial place chosen by a*

random street view generator

- *One Thing from your daily walk to the public transport you use*
- *One anatomical system or body part (nerves, eyes, skin, intestines, microbiome, etc. — preferably form your body, but could be an anonymous body, or the body of a particular architect, sculpture, or artist)*
- *One Thing from the Marylebone Campus (a design tool, a bit of the building itself, part of a person inhabiting the building, etc.)"*

Later in the semester, as part of the site study, students were also asked to integrate a Thing from the Isle of Dogs into the composition of their Odradek Body.

The Odradek Bodies were unleashed into Isle of Dogs via animations and films that set their stories in motion in selected sites. To enrich the outlook, the studio visited the Cosmic House designed by Charles Jencks and saw fascinating objects by Vriesendorp on display (fig. 3.18-3.19). The field trip was to Edinburgh, Dundee, and Newcastle, to visit projects such as the Oak room (fig. 3.20) and Hill House by Charles Rennie Mackintosh, and the Scottish Parliament by EMBT (fig. 1.15). Different approaches to monumental figuration were apparent on visits to the Angel of the North by Anthony Gormley and the Lady of the North by Charles Jencks et al. (fig. 1.23). The students transversed and conversed with landscapes as personified figures, or exaggerated figures acting within the landscape which they explored on-site. The Other Constructions organisation created by the tutors was up for interpretation by each student, echoing Bennet in wanting to "...encourage more intelligent and sustainable engagements with vibrant matter and lively things...," thingly vitality being "...the capacity of things - edibles, commodities, storms, metals - not only to impede or block the will and designs of humans but also to act as quasi agents or forces with trajectories, propensities, or tendencies of their own."[91] The fiction of Other Constructions, and theoretical discourse on the object-agency was accompanied throughout the year by studying objecthood through literary examples such as Stanislaw Lem's *Solaris*, where a sentient ocean affects a human subject in mysterious and powerful ways. Examples from film were discussed, such as the short film *Afterlives*, directed by Michael Heindl and presented in the London Short Film Festival 2023, an event that the students were encouraged to visit. Heindl's film shows man-made objects placed in humanly-uncomfortable settings: for instance, a tennis ball stuck on the door of a commuter train keeping the automatic mechanism from fully closing and therefore preventing the train from leaving the platform. The viewer presumes the potentially infuriating effect of this on the human train users; the latter, however, are absent throughout the film's duration.[92]

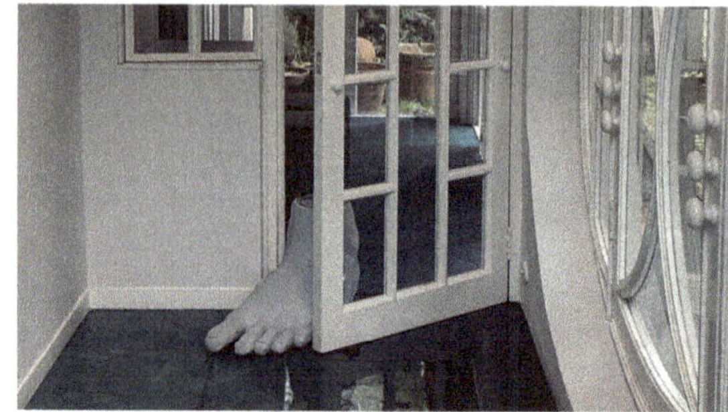

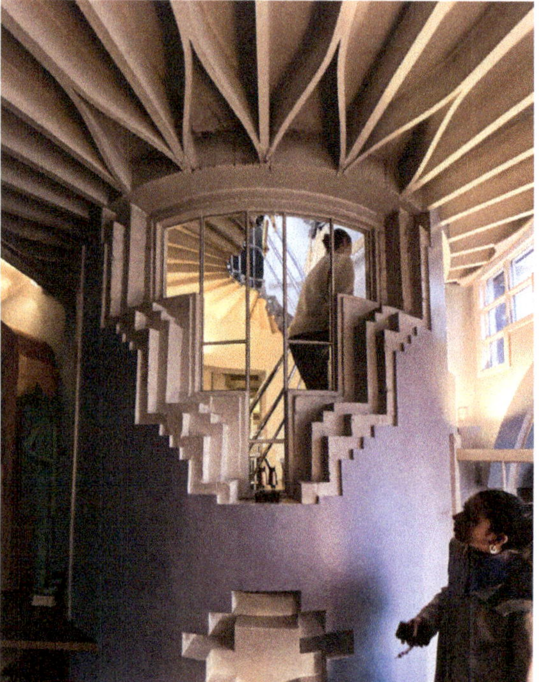

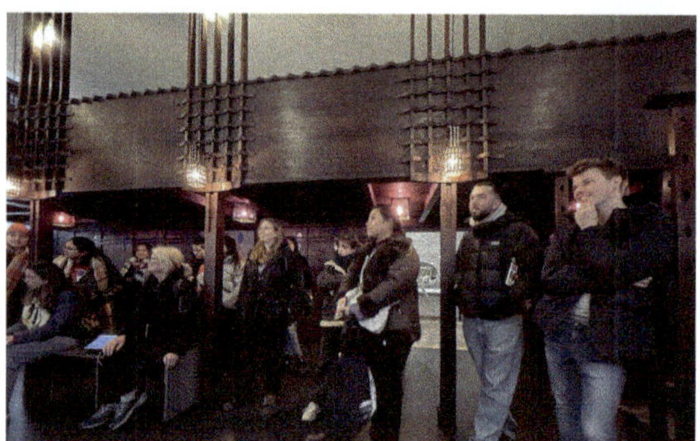

fig.3.18-3.20: Top to Bottom: DS25's 2023-24 field trip to Charles Jenks' Cosmic house during Vriesendorp's exhibition, including a papier-mache foot holding open a door and other creatures inhabiting the spaces; DS25's 2023-24 field trip to the V&A Dundee Mackintosh Oak Room.

A DS25 project which holistically engaged with this idea of object or thingly agency was second-year

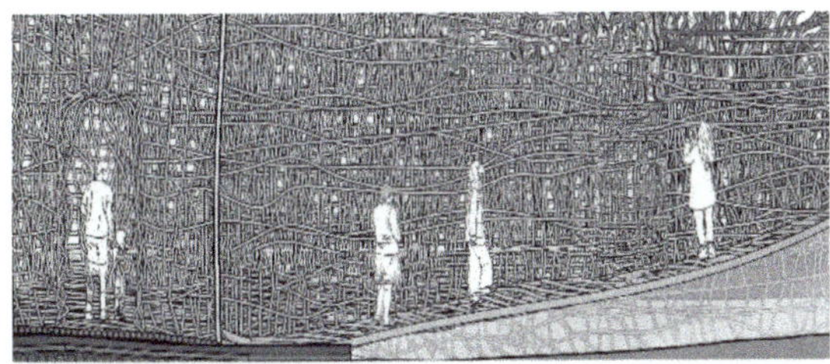

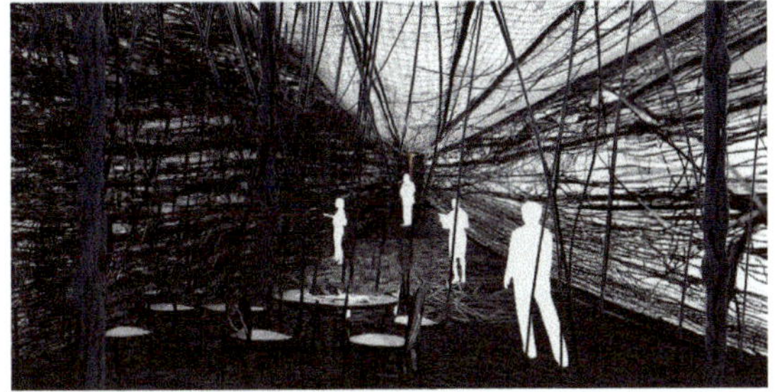

fig. 3.21-3.22: Kwietniewska's unhuman Piezoelectricity Experience spaces inside her "Harmony of Power" building made up of wires and cables using the language of the tangles of wires of her Odradek. The building was supported by the business "Other Constructions" to use in corporate worker-health campaigns.

student Aleksandra Kwietniewska's,[93] where her Odradek appeared as a bundle of wires, as with Bennet's observation of the affective bodies forming the assemblage of the electrical power grid.[94] Kwietniewska's architectural proposal emerged as an exaggeration of the human-made, in rooms woven out of black plastic electrical and piezoelectric wire, threads and string, shown in contrast with a luxury reception desk made of laminated wood panelling, and brushed stainless steel lift doors. Along with the human bodies collaged into the scene, all the furnishings seemed entirely out of place in a setting where indoor room walls merge into flexible floors, steps, outside terraces, and undefined inclining nets (fig. 3.21-22). Kwietniewska employed both tangible and time-based methods for exploring thingly architecture, allowing herself to become her body agent. She created physical models to test and feel space through complex tangles in which tension, weave, and incline are the driving languages, as well as used animation to communicate flexible cause-and-effect architectural conditions.

Looking at things also allows for a further exploration of what Guattari calls "the monstrous system of … Integrated World Capitalism" in his *Three Ecologies*,[95] expanded on by Bennet as a "complex assemblage [that] works to manufacture the particular psychosocial self in the interest of which environmentalism is initially pursued."[96] In the same vein one could deploy a "careful course of anthropomorphization" to "help reveal that vitality" in understanding things such as the Great Pacific Garbage Patch as an assemblage which has "matter-energy" and is "continually doing things," affecting the world.[97] This latter notion is additionally emergent in the fields of evolutionary biology and neuroscience. In attempting to understand the boundaries of bodies, these fields define task-specific "synergies"— acted tasks or events, whether material or immaterial— between a group of certain beings or conditions such as language, or a whirlpool, as transient beings in themselves.[98] Comparative physiologist and evolutionist J. Scott Turner puts forward another way of approaching the tangled relationship between beings. He questions whether animal-built structures such as the termite mounds could be considered as living organs, positing that "for a human, what is inside the body is pretty clear, but for the termite colony, 'inside' includes the nest environment." Turner sees environments as organisms or extended aggregates of the organisms' physiology.[99]

For example, in his first year, in response to the *Things Have Feelings Too* brief, student Jake Bone became fascinated by the textures of decaying parts of human-made structures on the banks of the river Thames.[100] Half-buried in sand and seaweed, Bone imagined a monster-building that lay dormant underneath the surface of the beach (fig. 3.24). In this sense, Bone's project explored the notion of a building as a monster, created from a reading of the site through the lens of a demented actor in a mirroring of Miguel de Cervantes' novel *Don Quixote*. In Bone's project, the building's monstrosity was communicated through his drawing methods and narrative passages, through which one could understand the insides of the brewery as the belly of the monster, drinking in the Thames and processing it into beer, but where also however, rubbish and other forms of pollution in the water would accumulate. The materiality and site analysis additionally originated from a fascination with the beach and the tide, and a bucket full of stuff including a teddy bear and a broom, which, read as an Odradek in itself drove the gritty, cave-like interiors and scratchy exteriors of the being-building (fig. 3.23, 3.25).

APPARITIONS

Through its mere existence, the body leaves traces that conjure absent presences. These imprints of life and actions appear in unexpected ways, as in the planetary transformations left from the timeline of anthropocentric climate change. With this ephemeral imprint, the body-world relationship stretches to the immaterial realm. This stretching and its corporeal manifestations are explored in the video game *Death Stranding* by Hideo Kijoma, where the living and the dead are physically and psychically connected through amniotic cord-like strands that bridge between their two overlapping worlds. The world and the body create parallels which are not disconnected

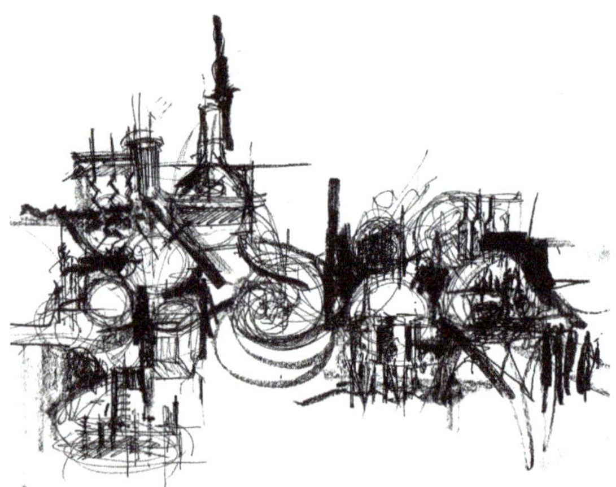

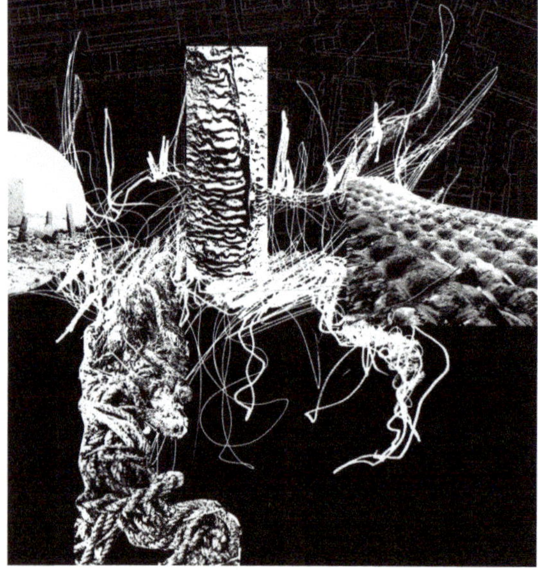

fig. 3.23-3.24: Top to Bottom: Bone's "Architect Sketch" of a monstrous brewery section iteration; Bone's composite site studies depicting the site as the monster, titled in the narrative "How the Knight set free many miserable Creatures."

Ghostly presences haunt architectural drawings.

but exist in the same space and at the same time, also connecting very distant spaces and times. This idea was more explicitly explored in the DS25 2022-23 brief entitled *Spectral Futures*, taught by the studio teaching team of Dr Alessandro Ayuso and Mary Konstantopoulou. The brief was predicated on the idea that body agents that were intentionally designed as Future Ghosts could set in motion ways to speculate on future architectural possibilities addressing looming social and ecological issues.(101)

The spectral— in the form of a present absence, or a fleeting sense of a presence from another time— is a dimension evident in nearly every building. For instance, hauntings occur in material traces and patinas on surfaces of buildings, evoking absent inhabitants and processes; everyday ephemeral phenomena filtering through buildings such as light and heat are immaterial, fleeting substances beyond grasp; and anachronistic architectural styles, strange plan configurations, and idiosyncratic details conjure the presence of the architects that designed them, ghosts that have left their mark. The same could apply to phases of building, in the form of scaffolding, the setup of construction sites, MEP systems, and ruins.(102) References studied in the studio that year included designs by Swiss architect Philippe Rahm, who describes architecture as "a thermodynamic mediation between the macroscopic and the microscopic, between the body and space, between the visible and the invisible, between meteorological and physiological functions,"(103) and South Korean artist Do Ho Suh, whose studio's intricately woven, ghostly installations consider "home as both a physical structure and a lived experience."(104)

Ghosts, as figurations embodying the spectral, have inherently architectural properties: as characters in novels and films they often haunt particular buildings, activating strange corners, in-between spaces, and routes.(105) Ghostly presences haunt architectural drawings. In architectural drawings, the spectral is present in manifold properties: aspects such as traces in the form of erased lines and adjusted solutions and ambiguous forms in layered sketches leave a lingering presence; even the tools that make the drawing could be seen as ghostly presences leaving their trace. Figures are often ghostly presences in drawings. The metonymic aspects of these figures can give them a further spectral quality. How the body is drawn as part of the design process, as it shapes space and moves through architecture in the simulacrum of the drawing, can make it fleetingly physical. Walter Pichler's ephemeral figures are an example, with their ghostly limbs and transparent flesh. For Pichler these attributes are not only an expression of a fragile human condition but also enhanced tools for calibrating space, where the frozen frames of a proto-cinematic movement and a transparency of the flesh are ways to imagine and calibrate architecture relative to the body.(106) In this sense, body agents are always ghostly, haunting drawings and tracing paths through buildings.

Elaborating beyond the trope of Victorian novels, theories of the spectral expand the potentiality of spectres as agents. For instance, Jacques Derrida identified the spectre of Marxism, finding the unfinished business of Karl Marx lingering insistently in the present.(107) Mark Fisher expanded this notion of hauntology, recognising that haunting in the 21st century is a "...confrontation with a cultural impasse: the failure of the future."(108) This lost future permeates not only digital media's regurgitation of the

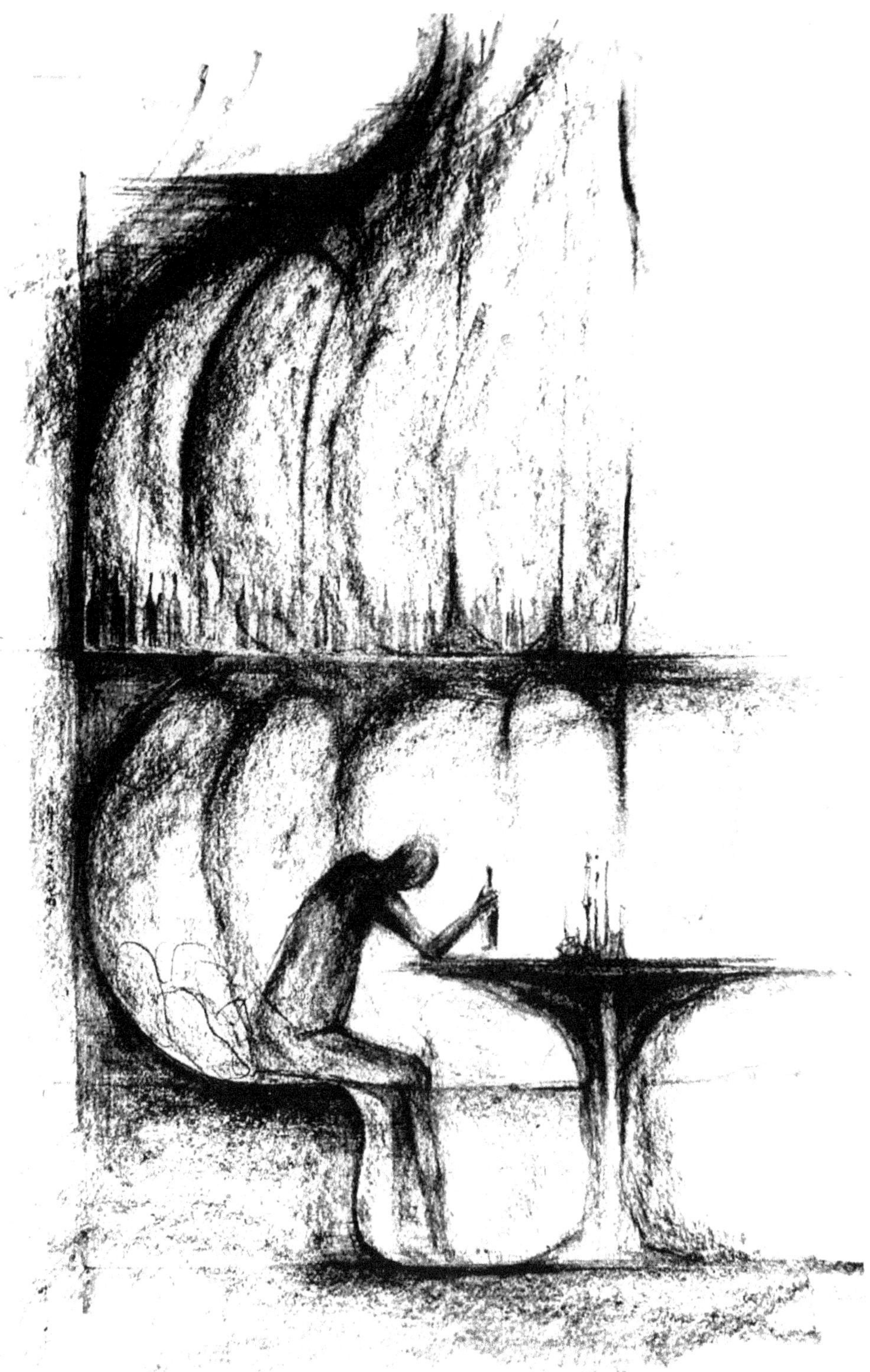

fig. 3.25: Bone's charcoal drawing of the interior of the Brewery monster-building: "Looking back through my journal, I found this drawing of the Knight sat in our new 'brewery' with a letter to the Knight that summarised our journey so far. I still haven't given it to him." The letter contained excerpts from the novel *Don Quixote*, describing the many monsters the Knight would slay.

past but contemporary architectural settings as well, such as ubiquitous non-places identified by Mark Augee, where the coherence and identity of space is eroded.(109) With this spatio-temporal transience, haunting becomes a tool, not only to address the past but to interrogate the future.(110)

These ghostly traces can also be explored in terms of geologic time, which connects spectres of all sorts of beings through science-art practices, such as the work of geologist, palaeontologist and storyteller Dougal Dixon, sci-fi author JG Ballard, and archaeologist Hawkes. As the Father of Speculative Zoology, Dixon operates in what Haraway calls "art science worldings," a term which she deems exceedingly important for creating productive visions of the future.(111) Dixon's *After Man*, an educational resource into grounded speculative futures visualises the evolution of animals post human extinction or near-extinction, 50 million years from now, referring to geologic time, of which we humans have experienced only a miniscule proportion.(112) In his *Drowned World* novel, referenced in discussions with Wilson during her second-year project mentioned earlier in the chapter, JG Ballard traces a future London setting and climate following the current climatic predictions through fictioning a return of the flora and fauna from the Jurassic Period.(113) Ballard further tangles this faraway time with the life of the human characters in the story: "Those so affected share a recurrent dream in which they appear to be reversing the process of their birth, losing their identity in a warm sea that is at once the uterine fluid and the primeval ocean from which life emerged."(114) Hawkes also draws on the traces of geologic time in her autobiographical narrative through the land of England, in which she attempts to "advance a synthetic cosmogony of consciousness, culture and geology," (115) describing for example how the "coiled shells" of "the water snail Viviparus ... accumulated in vast numbers to form the dark green Purbeck marble that the medieval masons loved to cut and polish into slender columns. So Jurassic water snails, their individual lives commemorated by murky scribings on the surface of the marble, helped medieval Christians to praise their God."(116) Shifts in time are difficult to acknowledge, but they are critical to seeing differently and appreciating beings other-than-human, and the spectres that remain or loom around them.

How the body is drawn as part of the design process, as it shapes space and moves through architecture in the simulacrum of the drawing, can make it fleetingly physical.

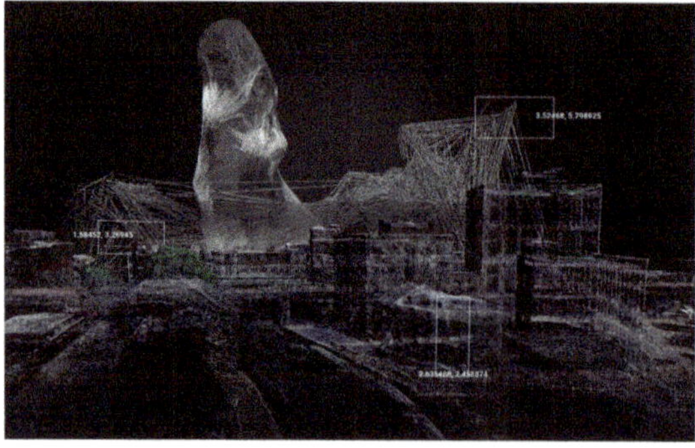

fig. 3.26: Chloe Pegeot's 2024-25 second-year project the "Dreamweaver" over Bethnal Green.

ECOLOGIES & THE SPECTRAL

The *Embodied Ecologies* brief asked students to consider from whose subjective point of view places are constructed, lived in and perceived. Continuing the studio enquiry into agency in design and positing that beings other than humans may in fact be more than mere companions in the linearly perceived pathway of human time, the studio examined the intertwined concepts of social, mental, and environmental ecologies through the creation of the BMTF. This brief more explicitly took as a given that human bodies, architecture, context, and environment are all intertwined, physically, socially, and psychologically. Confronted with the task of embodying an ecology, students created monstrous body agents, allowing for an exploration of wide-ranging definitions of body-world relationships, and building a richer set of relations by "following" these figures.

In the first studio prompt of the year, the design of the Future Ghosts was framed by questions such as:

- *"What is the uncanny fear, desire, trauma or lost/looming opportunity that your FG reveals, warns of, or suggests solutions to? Ghosts have agendas and obsessions, they beckon people, warn them, badger them to acknowledge and act on their agenda. They are often focused on past sins, mistakes, injustices, and return to the present (or future) to address them.*
- *What is your FG's architectural obsession or critique?*
- *How does your FG occupy and/or inhabit spaces? Where do they live, where do they appear, why do they appear? Ghosts are inhabitants of architecture; they are familiar with particular rooms, zones, and paths; they dwell in architecture and move through it parallel to human inhabitants. Ghosts typically have territories, boundaries and routes which might not always match our own current, tactile ones.*
- *How does the ghost manifest; is it tangible, visible, physical, sonic, etc? Ghosts have a meta-materiality, engaging with physicality in a contingent way: moving through walls, coupling and extending bodies, affecting substance in surprising (sometimes horrific) ways."*

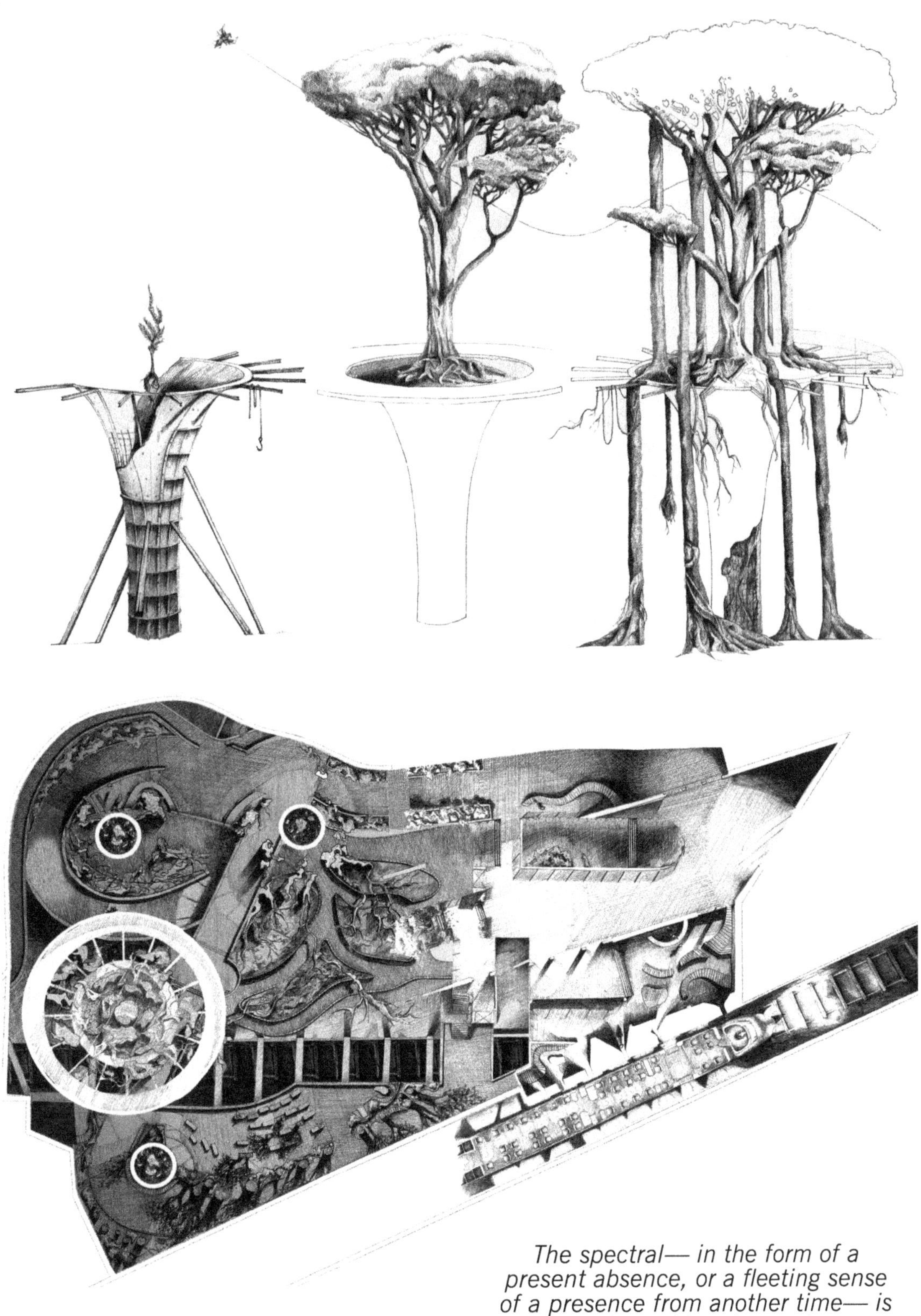

The spectral— in the form of a present absence, or a fleeting sense of a presence from another time— is a dimension evident in nearly every building.

fig. 3.27-3.28: Top to Bottom: Kinzelmann's Strangler Tree Concrete Cradle column over time; "Crown" level plan of the educational facility showing the tree cradle and train passing by.

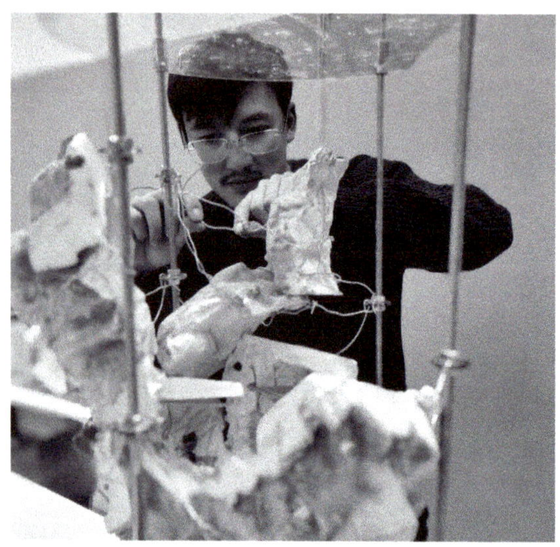

fig. 3.29: Kevin Ferenzena's Spectral Making of Palermian geology and volcanic landforms.

In addition to the architectural precedents such as those discussed above, the studio conversation was further elaborated through references. The possibilities of the visual framing of spectres in architectural space was informed by films such as *Meshes of the Afternoon* directed by Maya Deren (1943) and *Nosferatu* directed by FW Murnau (1922), where the spectral presence in the former is fleetingly visible as a faceless apparition glimpsed through windows or doorways, and in the latter as a distorted, ominous shadow cast onto the wall of a stairwell. The monstrous hauntings of *yōkai* were discussed as they show spectral presences that are at once wildly chimeric and responding to culturally-situated anxieties grounded in particular places. Students were invited to visit *Living with Ghosts* at Pace Gallery, an exhibition dealing with the spectre of colonialism, showing work such as Abraham Oghobase's *Constructed Reality* collage from 2022. *Ghost in the Shell*, directed by Mamoru Oshii (1995) and reinterpreted by director Rupert Sanders (2017), served as entry points into questions of technology's spectral presence in everyday life and in the future, particularly the idea of the posthuman body itself as a spectre. In this context, Midjourney, recently unveiled, could be seen as an instance where algorithmic processes mimic and enhance human cognition as ghostly extensions. To engage this latter issue further, students were asked to collaborate with Midjourney by testing iterations of their Future Ghost with it.

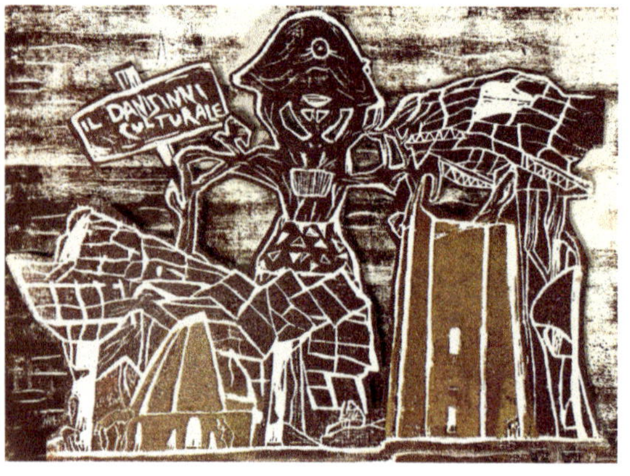

fig. 3.30: De Abreu Viriato's lino cut of Aruanda, the African-Sicilian clay ghost of the Danisinni neighbourhood of Palermo.

The study trip that year was to Sicily, where students explored Palermo's Danisinni neighbourhood (fig. 3.31, 3.33), the ghost town Poggioreale Antica, (fig. 3.34) the newly created towns of Poggioreale Nuova and Gibellina Nuova (fig. 3.32), and Alberto Burri's Cretto Memorial. The students used photography and drawings to attempt to look through the eyes of their Future Ghosts for clues about future possibilities in the traces and visions of the past. Through drawings, storyboards, and materially-based models, students imagined how their Future Ghosts would haunt Palermo, and designed Shells-of-the-Ghosts, architectural fragments on chosen sites, as first forays into mediating the scale of the body and city, a place that the Future Ghost inhabits but also an exploration of "Spectral Making," engaging both the tangible and the fleeting qualities of a chosen material (fig. 3.13, 3.29). The results were adventurous architectural proposals situated in narratives of Palermo's possible futures. For instance, Cocca's project follows "the Mutant Baddie," a Future Ghost constructing their identity through augmented reality technology, proposing a parasitical augmentation of abandoned buildings that would give a presence and place for the local queer community (fig. 2.54).(117) Second-year student Soraia de Abreu Viriato's project *Aruanda: A Cultural Revolutionary Ghost of Argilla Culturale Living Museum and Workshop*, was told from the point of view of a clay ghost that navigates modernist and vernacular architecture, seeking to preserve cultural heritage; considering the proposed building as a continuous piece of the city fabric, the project proposes an accessible ceramics workshop where African and Palermian vernacular building methods could be researched and taught under a ceramic-clad canopy (fig. 3.30).(118)

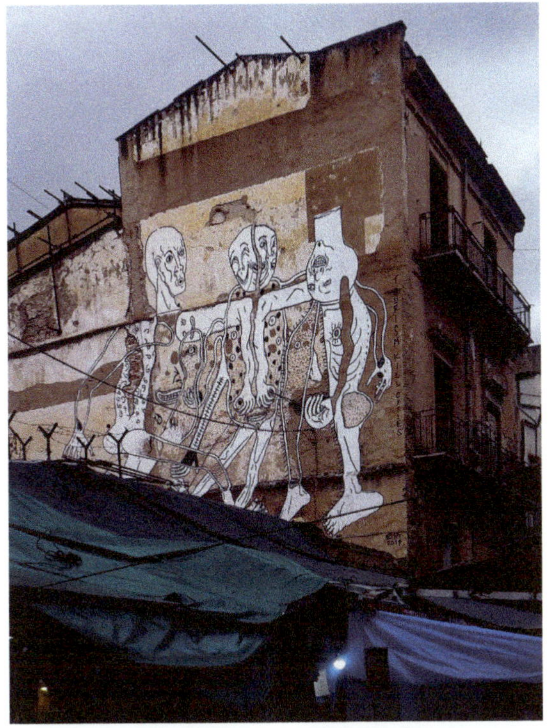

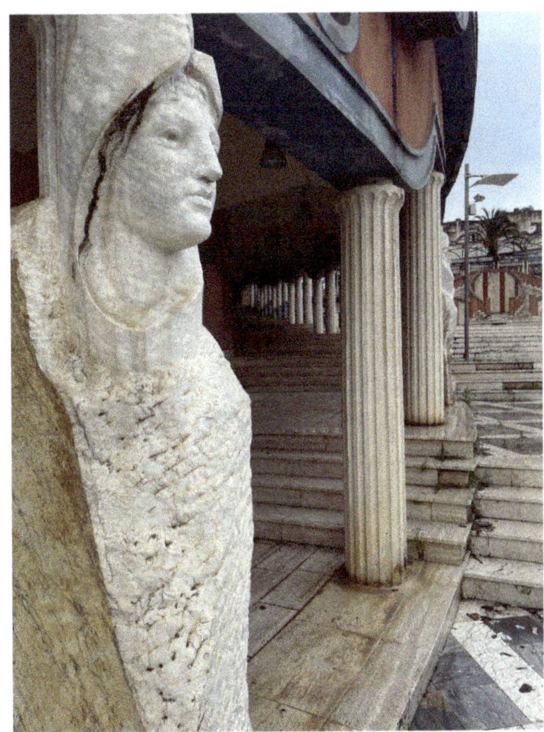

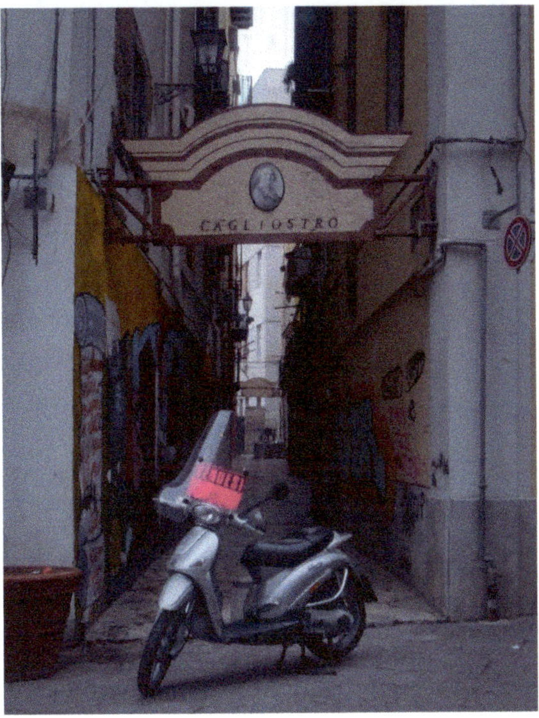

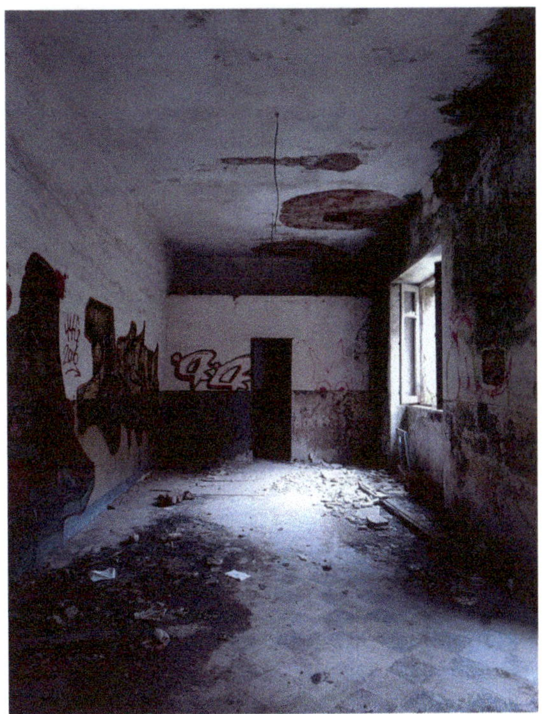

fig. 3.31-3.34: Photographs by Alcina Lo during the DS25 2022-23 field trip to Sicily. Top to Bottom: Graffitti on a Palermo party wall near Mercato Ballarò; Karyatid column of the circular collonade around the empty central square of the ghost town of Gibellina Nuova (photograph by Alessandro Ayuso); Palermo side street; House interior in the ghost town of Poggioreale.

A CONCLUDING NOTE REGARDING ALIENS

Visions of aliens can depart so entirely from an anthropomorphic basis that, as speculative devices, they can provide radically utopic or jolting visions of utter otherness.

The Alien is another category of fantastical Other that has surfaced in the repertoire of body agents in DS25 projects. Alien bodies populated the studio work from its earliest days. With almost every body agent that was designed, alien properties were evident in the figure. As suggested above in the discussion of the unhuman, the possibility of an alien dimension of the human body is arguably an inherent condition of being human but becomes intensified in the posthuman body. Visions of aliens can depart so entirely from an anthropomorphic basis that, as speculative devices, they can provide radically utopic or jolting visions of utter otherness.

Woods' body agent in her first-year project, discussed in chapter two, was one of the first intentionally-designed alien body agents in the studio. In Wood's project, illustrated as a graphic novel, she told the backstory of her alien, a being that appeared as her doppelgänger, but was from a planet where the architecture of Gaudi was a pervasive presence and basis for the alien culture. In the story, Woods' alien becomes stranded in Stratford's Olympic Park. Sequences of images showing Woods explaining phenomena she and her alien discovered in the Olympic Park show how this playful device allowed for a defamiliarisation, playfully making strange of the mundane, and providing a way of slowing down to look more closely at the site (fig. 3.36). The imaginative backstory of her alien also provided Woods with a way to engage in the architectural precedent, not only as a matter of historical research, but— as her alien had the capability to acrobatically construct catenary arches, and had an in-depth understanding of Gaudi's architecture— it also allowed Woods to enact elements of architectural doing derived from the precedent (fig. 3.35).

The studio discussion supporting the *Things Have Feelings Too* brief was driven by another conception of the alien. Informed by Objected Oriented Ontology, part of a philosophical movement called speculative realism, the discussion problematised correlationism, a term coined in 2006 by the French philosopher Quentin Meillassoux which describes the theoretical tendency to consider the world only in relation to humans.(119) By rejecting correlationism, proponents of OOO such as Graham Harman claim the defence of "...the autonomy of the world from human access, but in a spirit of imaginative audacity."(120) A vision of a world of relationality that even extends agency to things arises in OOO discourse. Ian Bogost extends this thought further, acknowledging the ultimate inaccessibility of the lives of things, writing "...the alien is not limited to another *person*, or even another *creature*. The alien is anything— and everything— to everything else... The true alien recedes interminably even as it surrounds us completely."(121) Looking to techniques developed by Latour, as well as photography by fine artists, and drawing techniques by designers, Bogost puts forward a number of possible tactics to close the seemingly insurmountable gap between human and alien ontologies. The narrative strategies discussed in the next chapter could be thought to extend such a list of tactics, where designing with deepening relational understandings and other points of view, embraces alien alterities.

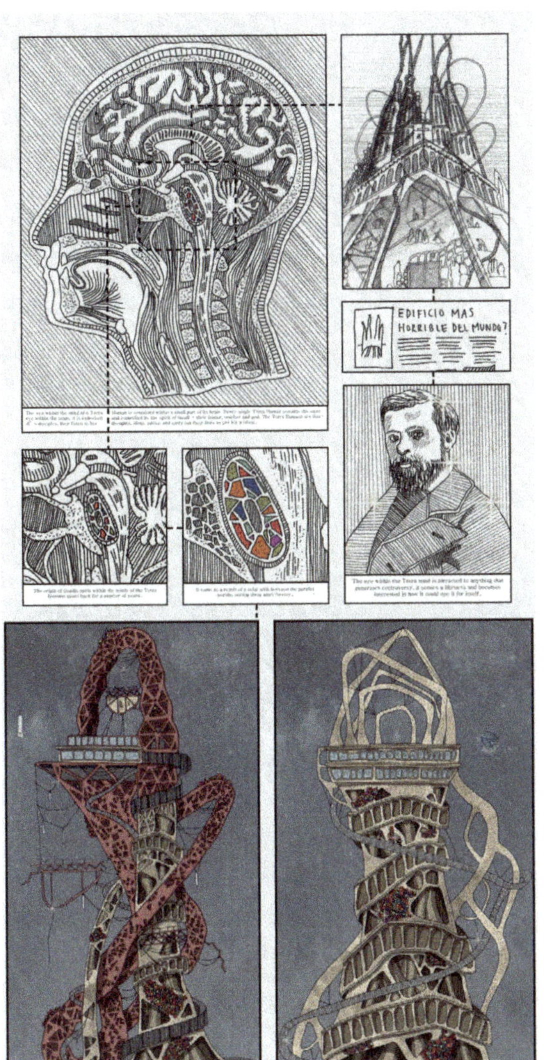

fig. 3.35-3.36: Top to Bottom: Woods' "Gaudi Eye" narrative sequence; Wood's Terra-Human's architecture engulfing Anish Kapoor's Orb in the Olympic Park, London.

NOTES

(01) Laboria Cuboniks, *The Xenofeminist manifesto: A Politics for Alienation* (London and Brooklyn: Verso, 2018), 65.

(02) "The word Anthropocene comes from the Greek terms for human ('anthropo') and new ('cene').": Katie Pavid, "What is the Anthropocene and why does it matter?," Natural History Museum, accessed August 11, 2025, https://www.nhm.ac.uk/discover/what-is-the-anthropocene.html; "The fact that our geological era is known as the "anthropocene" stresses both the technologically mediated power acquired by Anthropos and its potentially lethal consequences for everyone else." Braidotti, *The Posthuman*, 66.

(03) Timothy Morton, *Being Ecological* (UK: Pelican Books, 2018), 211. Morton also highlights this idea in his conclusion to the book: "Snared in the urgency of ecological awareness and the horror of extinction and global warming, it's so incredibly difficult to miss the key point." He goes on mentioning the "intensity of our reactions to the data input (oceans acidifying! Climate warming! Species going extinct!).", Ibid., 214-215.

(04)"Predictive processing speaks to… the nature of the relationship between our minds and reality.…Contrary to the standard belief that our senses are a kind of passive window onto the world, what is emerging is a picture of an ever-active brain that is always striving to predict what the world might currently have to offer. Those predictions then structure and shape the whole human experience." Clark, *The Experience Machine*, xiii; this is expanded on further in the book with regards to the actions of the predictive processing of the human mind: "actions come about because we mentally represent the completed effects of the action.", Ibid., 71; and later on "To act is to alter the world to bring it into line with some of those predictions.": Ibid., 213.

(05) Hans Hollein, "Everything is Architecture," *Bau Magazine*, Issue ½ (1968): 460. https://peripheralfocus.net/ace/Arch+Electronics/readings/HansHollein_EverythingIsArchitecture.pdf.

(06) Guattari, *The Three Ecologies*, 34.

(07) Haraway, *Staying with the Trouble*, 50.

(08) Hayles, *How We Became Posthuman*, 3.

(09) Haraway, *Staying with Trouble*, 97.

(10) "The Anthropocene has now officially been dated as starting in 1945. …can you think of anything more uncanny than realising that you are in a whole new geological period, one marked by humans becoming a geophysical force on a planetary scale?": Morton, *Being Ecological*, 43.

(11) "We are so habituated to living and thinking on a very small range of timescales that students who train as geologists say that they have to go through a process of acclimatizing to much vaster tracts of time." Morton, *Being Ecological*, 63.

(12) Haraway, *Staying with the Trouble*, 49.

(13) "… it is past time to practice better care of kinds-of-assemblages (not species one at a time). Kin is an assembling sort of word. All critters share a common "flesh," laterally, semiotically, and genealogically." Haraway, "Making Kin," in *Staying with the Trouble*, 99-103, at 103; also see: "Like Stengers and like myself, Latour is a

thoroughgoing materialist committed to an ecology of practices, to the mundane articulating of assemblages through situated work and play in the muddles of messy living and dying. ... Alignment in tentacular worlding must be a seriously tangled affair!": Ibid., 42.

(14) Bogost describes a method of analysing these relational units through a concept he calls "unit operations": Ian Bogost, "Alien Phenomenology, or What It's like to Be a Thing," *Posthumanities* 20 (University of Minnesota press, 2012): 25.

(15) Jane Bennet, *Vibrant Matter: A Political Ecology of Things* (Durham: Duke University Press, 2010), 24.

(16) Haraway, *Staying with Trouble*, 97.

(17) This counters current standards of constructing spaces to last for the next 50 or so years, as evidenced by structural and other building systems warranties. As highlighted in the Design Buildings website, "BS EN 1990, Eurocode - Basis of structural design, (Eurocode 0) gives indicative design lives for various types of structure.": "Design life," Design Buildings Ltd, last edited April 27, 2022, http://designingbuildings.co.uk/wiki/Design_life.

(18) "... from grasses to gorillas to gargantuan black holes, everything has its own time, its own temporality." Morton, *Being Ecological*, 64.

(19) Jacquetta Hawkes, *A Land*, introduction by Robert Macfarlane (London: HarperCollins, 2012; orig. pub. 1951), 32.

(20) Haraway, *Staying with Trouble*, 122.

(21) David Burrows and Simon O'Sullivan discuss the idea that the 'self' is a fiction and practices that relate to its "unmasking ... through experimentation— alternative fictions of other possible and multiple selves." in Burrows and O'Sullivan, "Overcoming the Fiction of the Self," in *Fictioning*, 49-62, at 60.

(22) Ibid., *Fictioning*, 281.

(23) Braidotti defines *zoe* as "life in its non-human aspects." Braidotti, *The Posthuman*, 66.; Braidotti's idea of zoe differs from that posed by Giorgio Agamben as "bare life," turning instead to work "within a Spinozist framework" and preferring "to emphasize the politics of life itself as a relentlessly generative force including and going beyond death.": Braidotti, *The Posthuman*, 121.

(24) Burrows and O'Sullivan, *Fictioning*, 4.

(25) Ginsberg identifies such scientific interventions as already happening behind-the-scenes in current social and political trends: Marcus Fairs, "Rewilding with synthetic creatures could 'save nature' says Alexandra Daisy Ginsberg," in *Dezeen*, Published November 13, 2013, https://www.dezeen.com/2013/11/13/synthetic-creatures-could-save-nature-says-alexandra-daisy-ginsberg/#:~:text=Alexandra%20Daisy%20Ginsberg%3A%20There's%20a,re%20too%20close%20to%20reality.; The Royal Society in London holds various projects, talks and publications on "research that involves the design and construction of novel artificial biological pathways," including symposia in 2011 and 2012 on the subject of synthetic biology with the "Royal Academy of Engineering and the national academies of science and engineering in China and the USA": "Synthetic Biology," *The Royal Society*, Accessed August 18, 2025, https://royalsociety.org/news-resources/projects/synthetic-biology/

(26) Laboria Cuboniks, *The Xenofeminist Manifesto*, 65.

(27) Haraway, *Staying with the Trouble*, 58.; also, quoting a M. Beth Dempster's term "sympoiesis for 'collectively producing systems that do not have self-defined spatial or temporal boundaries'.": Ibid., 61.

(28) Attempts at this include Marshmallow Laser Feast's immersive VR installation at the Saatchi Gallery in 2018-19 titled "We Live in an Ocean of Air," where one would be "transported to an ancient forest and witness the majestic power of the largest organism to ever exist— the giant Sequoia tree.": Marshmallow Laser Feast, *We Live in an Ocean of Air*, exhibited in Salon 009, Saatchi Gallery, London, July 12, 2018 - May 5, 2019. https://www.saatchigallery.com/exhibition/salon_009__we_live_in_an_ocean_of_air

(29) Thomas Nagel, "What is it like to be a bat?," *The Philosophical Review* 83, No. 4 (1974): 435-450.

(30) Braidotti, *The Posthuman*, 82.

(31) Gilles Deleuze et al., *A Thousand Plateaus: Capitalism and Schizophrenia*, Athlone Contemporary European Thinkers (Continuum, 1988), 249.

(32) Deleuze, *Francis Bacon*, 16.

(33) Haraway, *When Species Meet* (London and Minneapolis: University of Minnesota Press: 2008), 38

(34) Haraway, *Staying with the Trouble*, 13.

(35) Project done under the supervision of the studio teaching team of Dr Alessandro Ayuso and Mary Konstantopoulou.

(36) Haraway, *Staying with the Trouble*, 23-24.

(37) *A Short Story* [orig. title in Mandarin *Po sui tai yang zhi xin*], directed by Bi Gan (Film Fest Gent and Festival de Cannes, 2022), 15:00, https://mubi.com/en/gr/films/a-short-story-2022.

(38) Swapnil Dhruv Bose, "'A Short Story' Review: Exploring Bi Gan's latest surreal fable," in Far Out, Published February 3, 2023 https://faroutmagazine.co.uk/a-short-story-review-exploring-bi-gans-latest-surreal-fable/

(39) Haraway, *Staying with the Trouble*, 213n8.

(40) Ibid., 10.

(41) Braidotti, *The Posthuman*, 82.

(42) Haraway, *Staying with the Trouble*, 4.

(43) Ibid., 5.; Haraway also uses Baila Goldenthal's painting titled *Cat's Cradle / String Theory*, to demonstrate her meaning of the term "string figures": Ibid., 35.; Ibid., 10.

(44) Gregory Bateson, "Pathologies of Epistimology," in *Steps to an Ecology of Mind* (1972), 484, quoted in Félix Guattari, *The Three Ecologies*, trans. Ian Pindar and Paul Sutton (Bloomsbury Revelations, London: Bloomsbury Academic, 2014), 17.

(45) Project done under the supervision of the studio teaching team of Dr Alessandro Ayuso and Mary Konstantopoulou.

(46) Shoshanah Dubiner, *Endosymbiosis: Homage to Lynn Margulis*, published February 13, 2012, online blog, https://www.cybermuse.com/blog/2012/2/13/endosymbiosis-homage-to-lynn-margulis.html

(47) Haraway, *Staying with the Trouble*, 55.

(48) Ibid., 43-44.

(49) Ibid. 125.

(50) Ibid., 24.

(51) Ibid., 25.

(52) Project done under the supervision of the studio teaching team of Dr

Alessandro Ayuso and Mary Konstantopoulou.

(53) Basile Baudez and Maureen Cassidy-Geiger, "The Beaux-Arts Tradition," in *Drawing Matter*, April 29, 2021, https://drawingmatter.org/the-beaux-arts-tradition/.

(54) Project done under the supervision of the studio teaching team of Dr Alessandro Ayuso, Dr Dan Dream, and Martyna Marciniak.

(55) Deleuze, *Francis Bacon*, 17.

(56) Project done under the supervision of the studio teaching team of Dr Alessandro Ayuso and Mary Konstantopoulou.

(57) *The Ring*, directed by Gore Verbinski, (2002).

(58) "Yōkai, 妖怪, are strange, supernatural creatures and phenomena from Japanese folklore. The word is a combination of the characters 妖 (yō–attractive, bewitching, calamity) and 怪 (kai–mystery, wonder).": "Introduction to Yōkai," in Yokai.com, Accessed August 26, 2025, https://yokai.com/introduction/

(59) Marcel Mauss, "Techniques of the Body (1934)," *Incorporations*, 2. print, Zone 6 (ZONE, 1995).

(60) Burrows and O'Sullivan, *Fictioning*, 1-2.

(61) Project done under the supervision of the studio teaching team of Dr Alessandro Ayuso and Mary Konstantopoulou.

(62) Haraway, *Staying with the Trouble*, 65.

(63) Anastasia Kolioliou, "Bacteria Sanctuary," in University of Westminster Degree Shows, https://degree-shows.westminster.ac.uk/project/bacteria-sanctuary

(64) "Philosophy of (Body) Horror with Dylan Trigg" by Romancing the Gothic, February 15, 2021, video presentation, 40:08, https://youtu.be/AGKwBexOX_4?si=d9RR7D_99dAJC_Ip.

(65) James Elkins, "On Visual Desperation and the Bodies of Protozoa," *Representations*, No. 40, Special Issue: Seeing Science. (Autumn, 1992), 32.

(66) Jonathan Higgs, "Everything Everything detail fifth album and release new song 'Arch Enemy'," interview by Tom Skinner in NME, published May 13, 2020, https://www.nme.com/news/music/everything-everything-detail-upcoming-fifth-album-and-release-new-track-arch-enemy-2667901

(67) Haraway, *Staying with the Trouble*, 1.

(68) "Aaron Betsky: Utopia, monster, city." by A is for Architecture, May 1, 2024, podcast interview, 53:40. at 17:27. https://youtu.be/AvyGMsihC-8?si=MjWfBnl4wauXT70u

(69) "Aaron Betsky: Utopia, monster, city." by A is for Architecture, May 1, 2024, podcast interview, 53:40. at 17:27. https://youtu.be/AvyGMsihC-8?si=MjWfBnl4wauXT70u

(70) Jorge Luis Borges and Margarita Guerrerro, *The Book of Imaginary Beings* (Penguin Books, 1947, orig. pub. Buenos Aires: 1967), 12.; Borges also says: "We are ignorant of the meaning of the dragon in the same way that we are ignorant of the meaning of the universe.": Ibid., 12.

(71) Emilie Lucchesi, "This 16th-century map is teeming with sea monsters. Most are based on a real mammal," in *National Geographic*, published December 28, 2023, https://www.nationalgeographic.com/history/article/carta-marina-renaissance-sea-monsters

(72) Filippo Cocca, *Baddieverse*, 2022-23.

(73) Project done under the supervision of the studio teaching team of Dr Alessandro Ayuso and Mary Konstantopoulou with support from Deniz Özbek.

(74) Haraway, *Staying with Trouble*, 35.

(75) Haraway explains: "sympoiesis is a simple word; it means 'making-with'. Nothing makes itself; nothing is really autopoietic or self-organizing." Haraway, *Staying with Trouble*, 58.

(76) George L. Hersey, *The Lost Meaning of Classical Architecture: Speculations on Ornament from Vitruvius to Venturi*, 2. print (MIT Press, 1988), 129.

(77) Hersey, *The Lost Meaning of Classical Architecture*, 134.

(78) "Erechtheion. Karyatid. Kore B," in *The Acropolis Museum*, Accessed August 26, 2025, https://www.theacropolismuseum.gr/en/erechtheion-karyatid-kore-b

(79) Project done under the supervision of the studio teaching team of Dr Alessandro Ayuso and Mary Konstantopoulou.

(80) Project done under the supervision of the studio teaching team of Dr Alessandro Ayuso and Mary Konstantopoulou.

(81) Project done under the supervision of the studio teaching team of Dr Alessandro Ayuso and Mary Konstantopoulou.

(82) "Philosophy of (Body) Horror with Dylan Trigg" by Romancing the Gothic, February 15, 2021, video presentation, 40:08, https://youtu.be/AGKwBexOX_4?si=d9RR7D_99dAJC_Ip.

(83) Ibid.

(84) Ibid.

(85) Dylan Trigg, "A prehistory of the Apartment," *Log*, no. 42 (Anyone Corporation, 2018): 170-180, at 178.

(86) Walter Benjamin quoted in Matthew Rana, "Odradek: The Form Which Things Assume Oblivion," in *Frieze*, article for the "Odradek" exhibition in Malmo Konsthall, 2018, Accessed August 26, 2025, https://www.frieze.com/article/odradek-form-which-things-assume-oblivion-2018-review

(87) Bennet, *Vibrant Matter*, 23-24.

(88) This concept is discussed further below with reference to Ian Bogost's notion of the alien. Bogost, *Alien Phenomenology, or What It's like to Be a Thing*, 34.

(89) Dylan Trigg, *The Thing: A Phenomenology of Horror* (Zero Books, 2014), 5.

(90) Margaret M. Lock and Judith Farquhar, eds, *Beyond the Body Proper: Reading the Anthropology of Material Life, Body, Commodity, Text* (Duke Univ. Press, 2007), 387–88.

(91) Bennet, *Vibrant Matter*, vii.

(92) *Afterlives*, directed by Michael Heindl, 3:25, https://www.sixpackfilm.com/en/catalogue/2823/

(93) Project done under the supervision of the studio teaching team of Dr Alessandro Ayuso and Mary Konstantopoulou.

(94) Bennet, *Vibrant Matter*, 24.

(95) Guattari, *The Three Ecologies*, 20.

(96) Bennet, *Vibrant Matter*, 113.

(97) "matter-energy": Ibid., 54.; Ibid., 122.

(98) "synergy (the combined effects produced by two or more elements, parts or individuals)": Peter A. Corning, "The Co-operative Gene: On the Role of Synergy in Evolution," *Evolutionary Theory* 11 (1996):

183-207, at 184.; also at 192, in describing honey bee hives: "A second type of synergy involves 'emergent phenomena' … situations in which two or more 'parts' merge in such a way that a new 'whole' arises with distinctive new chemical or physical properties."

(99) J Scott Turner, "A Superorganism's Fuzzy Boundaries," in Natural History (2002): 63-68, at 66; also see "The Theory of the Organism-Environment System," in The Library of Consciousness, published October 1998. https://www.organism.earth/library/document/theory-of-organism-environment-system#part-1

(100) Project done under the supervision of the studio teaching team of Dr Alessandro Ayuso and Mary Konstantopoulou.

(101) The year's brief was developed around the same time when Pace Gallery in London was exhibiting Kojo Abudu's curated group of artworks for Living With Ghosts: "These 'ghosts' are the unseen but deeply felt forces— at once dead and alive, visible and invisible, past and present, future and past— that continually disturb individual and collective relations within the African postcolony and throughout the world, leaving behind melancholic traces in archival materials, architecture, landscapes, and subjectivities." Pace Gallery, "Living With Ghosts," London, July 8 - August 5, 2022, https://www.pacegallery.com/exhibitions/living-with-ghosts-london/

(102) Learning with Ghosts collective, led by artist Lucille Leger, and architect Jacques Marie Ligot, during the 2025 Lisbon Architecture Trienalle examined the typology of Lighthouses along European coasts as ghostly spaces connecting scattered architectural territories: https://www.trienaldelisboa.com/programme/hors-serie/Learningghosts-pt

(103) Philippe Rahm architectes, in "Out There: Architecture Beyond Building" international architecture exhibition curated by Aaron Betsky, Venice, Italy, 2008, http://www.philipperahm.com/data/projects/digestiblegulfstream/index.html

(104) "Do Ho Suh: Breathing Home | Recent Drawings," exhibition at Victoria Miro Venice, 2025, https://online.victoria-miro.com/do-ho-suh-venice-2025/

(105) Examples include *The Others* (2001) by Alejandro Amenábar, and *Beetlejuice* (1988) by Tim Burton, which use the trope of the ghost family in a domestic environment invaded by new residents, and *The Shining* (1980) by Stephen King, where the remote hotel setting strings together timelines of past and present, bringing out ghosts linked to particular rooms.

(106) Ayuso, *Experiments with Body Agent Architecture*, 155.

(107) Jacques Derrida, *Specters of Marx*, trans. Peggy Kamuf (New York: Routledge, 2006).

(108) Fisher writes: "What haunts the digital cul-de-sacs of the twenty-first century is not so much the past as all the lost futures that the twentieth century taught us to anticipate.": Mark Fisher, "What is Hauntology?," *Film Quarterly* 66, no. 1 (2022): 16-24, at 16.

(109) Ibid.

(110) Hauntological tactics could be considered as "...intrinsically resistant to the contraction and homogenization of time and space.": Ibid., 19.

(111) Haraway, *Staying with the Trouble*, 67.

(112) Dougal Dixon, *After Man: A Zoology of the Future*, introduction by Desmond Morris, (London: Breakdown Press, 2018); reproduced from 1st ed. (UK: Granada Publishing; USA: St Martin's Press, 1981). This concept is explored also in his subsequent book *Man After Man*, where through scientific imagination and detailed illustrations he fictions the distant evolution of human animals.

(113) JG Ballard, *The Drowned World*, 2nd ed. (London: Fourth Estate, 2012; orig. pub. 1962).

(114) Kingsley Amis, "Review of The Drowned World by JG Ballard – archive, 27 January 1963," in The Guardian, January 20, 2019, https://www.theguardian.com/books/2019/jan/20/back-pages-the-drowned-world-jg-ballard-review-archive.; "He lay back, … the soothing pressure of the water penetrating his suit so that the barriers between his own private blood-stream and that of the giant amnion seemed no longer to exist. The deep cradle of silt carried him gently like an immense placenta, infinitely softer than any bed he had ever known." Ballard, "The Pool of Thanatos," in *The Drowned World*, 109-10.

(115) Robert Macfarlane, introduction to *A Land* by Jacquetta Hawkes, (London: HarperCollins, 2012), xi.

(116) Hawkes, *A Land*, 71.

(117) Project done under the supervision of the studio teaching team of Dr Alessandro Ayuso and Mary Konstantopoulou.

(118) Project done under the supervision of the studio teaching team of Dr Alessandro Ayuso and Mary Konstantopoulou.

(119) Rossetto and Peterle, "Buildings as Non-human Narrators," 644.

(120) Ibid.

(121) Bogost, *Alien Phenomenology, or What It's like to Be a Thing*, 34.

CHAPTER 3:
PROJECT IMAGE GALLERY

CAT BELLY HOUSE
SOCIAL SCALAM + THE VIRTUAL VERMIS CHURCH
CAGLIOSTRO'S PARANORMAL CASE FILES
HYDROPOLIS

CAT BELLY HOUSE

by
LAURIANE HEWES

BRIEF *Body Agent Architecture*

YEAR *2019-20*

TUTORS *Dr Alessandro Ayuso, Dr Dan Dream, Martyna Marciniak*

THEMES

Prosthetics

Non-human Agency

Mirroring of Body & World

Grotesque / Hybrid Body

World-building (Allegory)

"Is it a crisis the younger members of society are reconsidering their rights to parenthood or finding a more appealing lifestyle through pet-owning?

This project is a study of primarily the cat psychology and physical attributes in an environment where they are slowly re-established as playing a human child's role. This is reasoned based on a study of articles written on the 'modernising' millennial outlook towards pet owning. Altered architectural environments are critiqued as well as the intervention of prosthetics placed on the cats triggering these architectural changes.

Disclaimer:

This topic touches on some ethically questionably arguments and may raise the odd eyebrow. As a fellow 'cat-person', the ethical rationality will be present. However, the nature of the project will pursue an openness to the harshness of this trending alteration in a human household.

No cats shall be harmed in this process. This project is formed out of a fictional probability in a factual world."

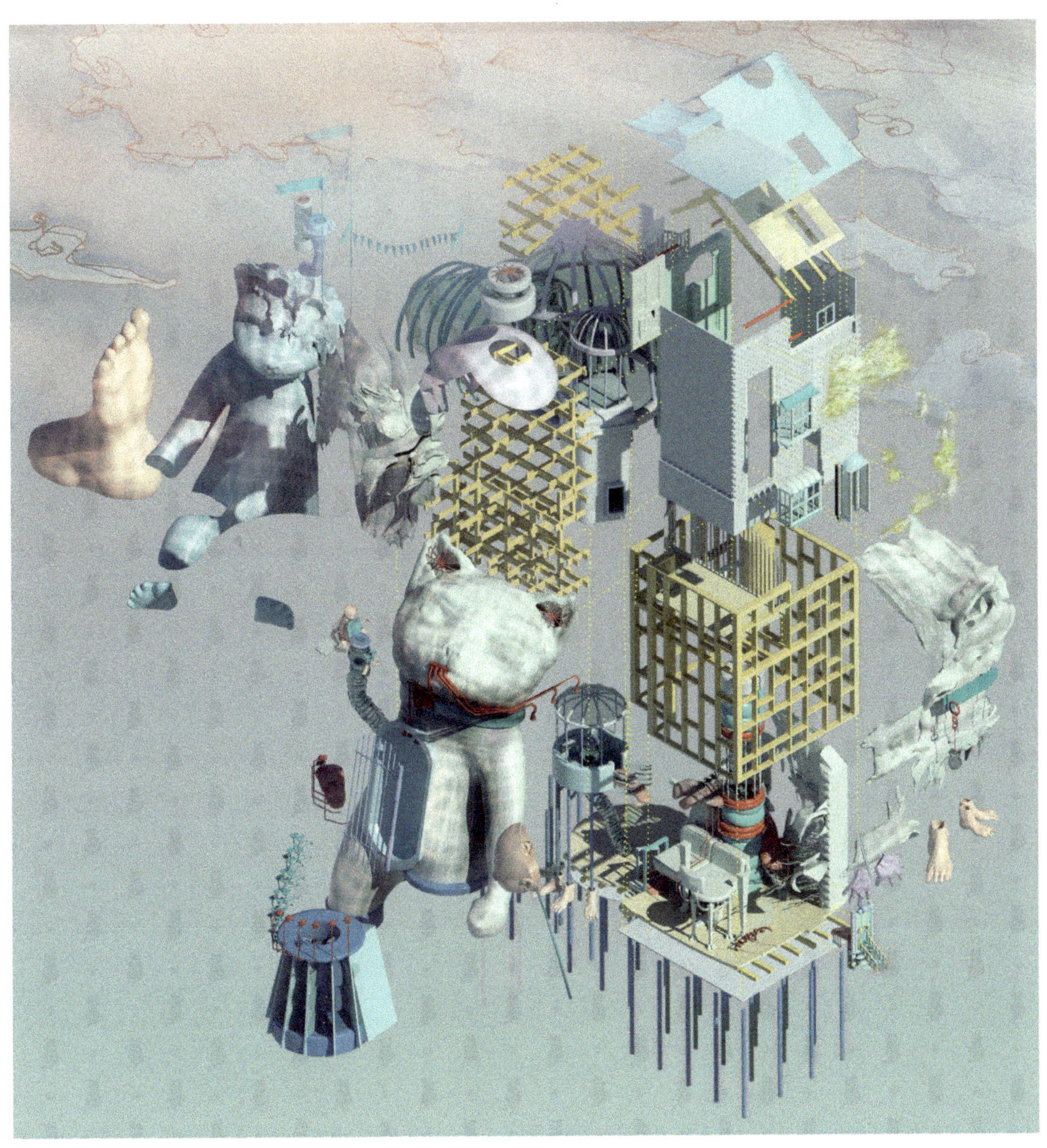

fig. 3.37: Hewes' "Cat Belly House" exploded axonometric.

"Definition of Ailuranthropy:

Ailuranthropy comes from the Greek words ailouros meaning 'cat', and anthropos, meaning 'human' and refers to human/feline transformations, or to other beings that combine feline and human characteristics. Ailuranthrope is a lesser-known term that refers to a feline therianthrope."

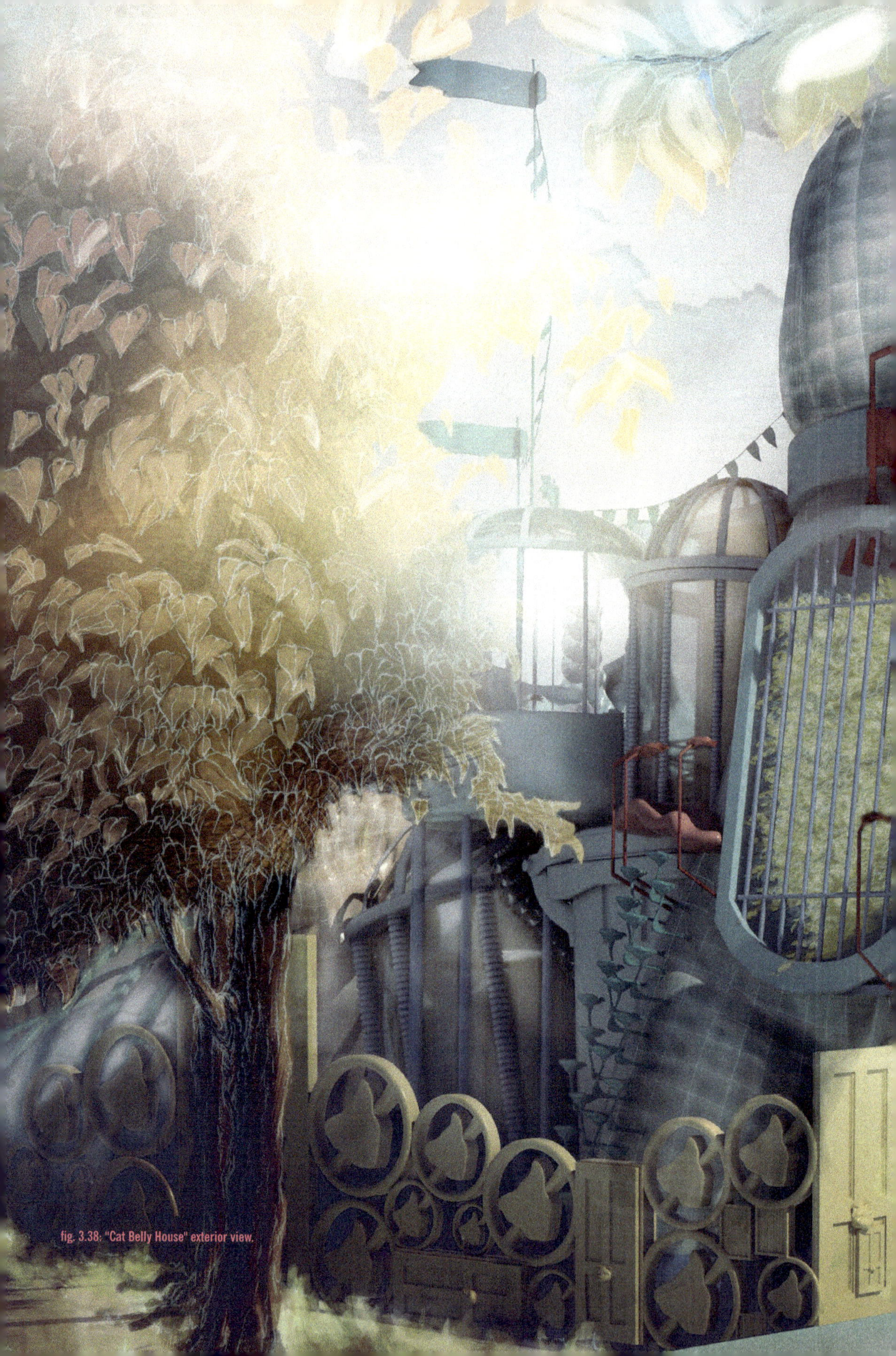

fig. 3.38: "Cat Belly House" exterior view.

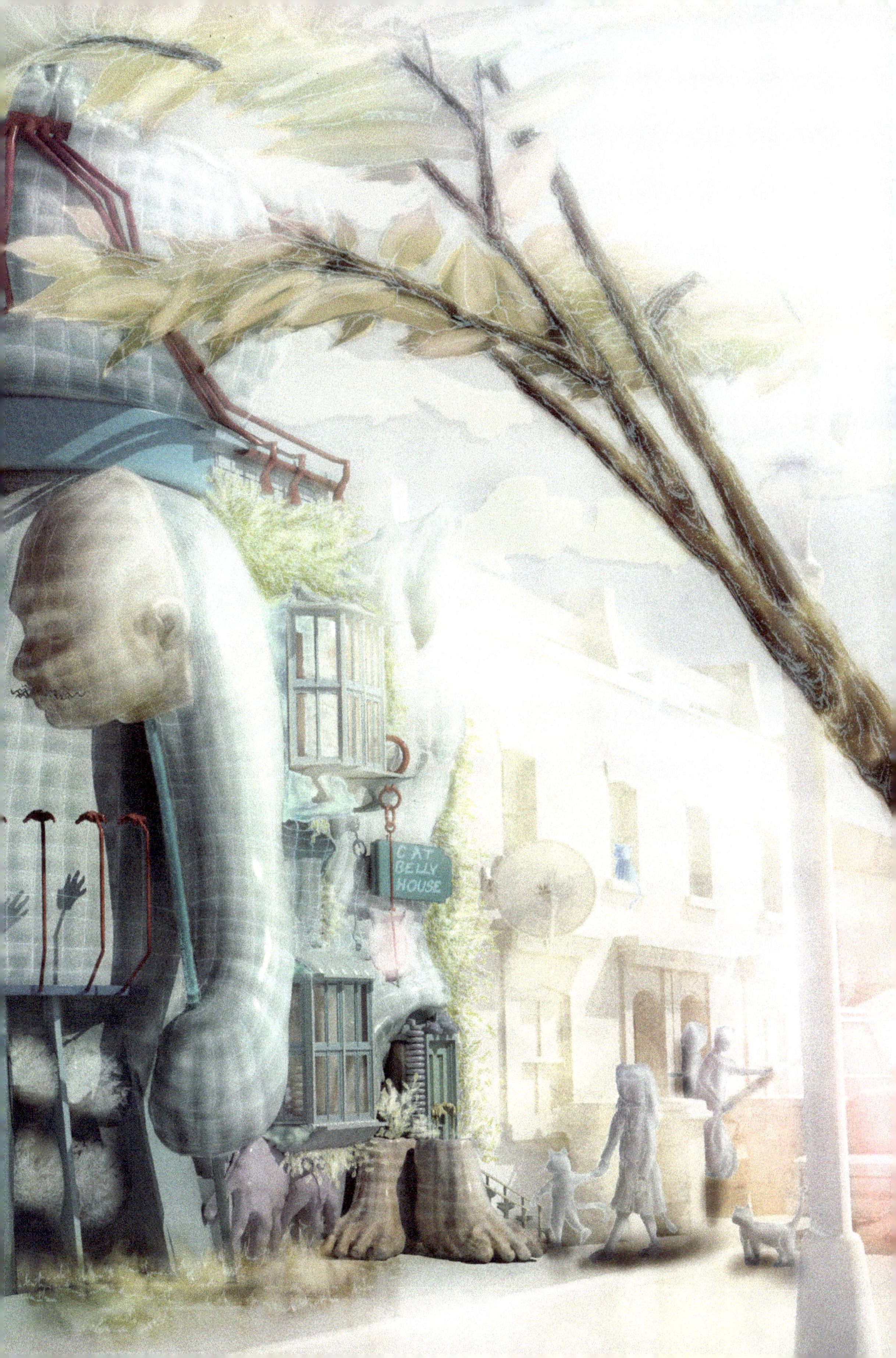
CAT
BELLY
HOUSE

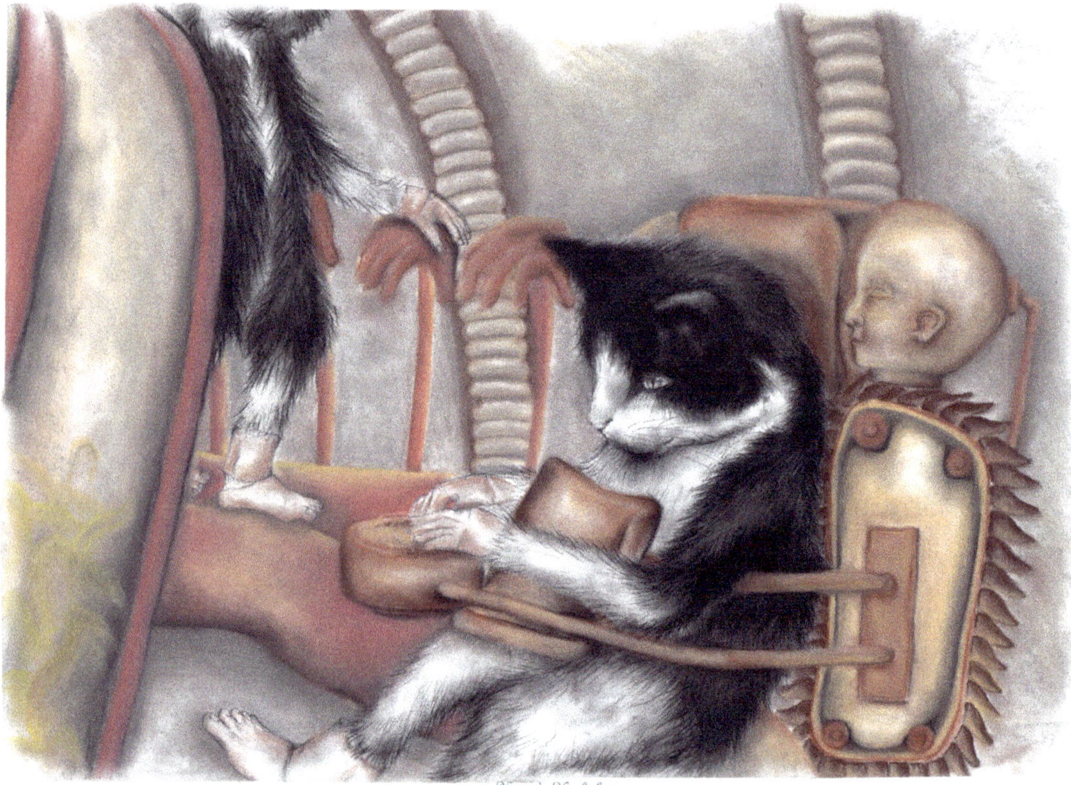

Hector's Highchair

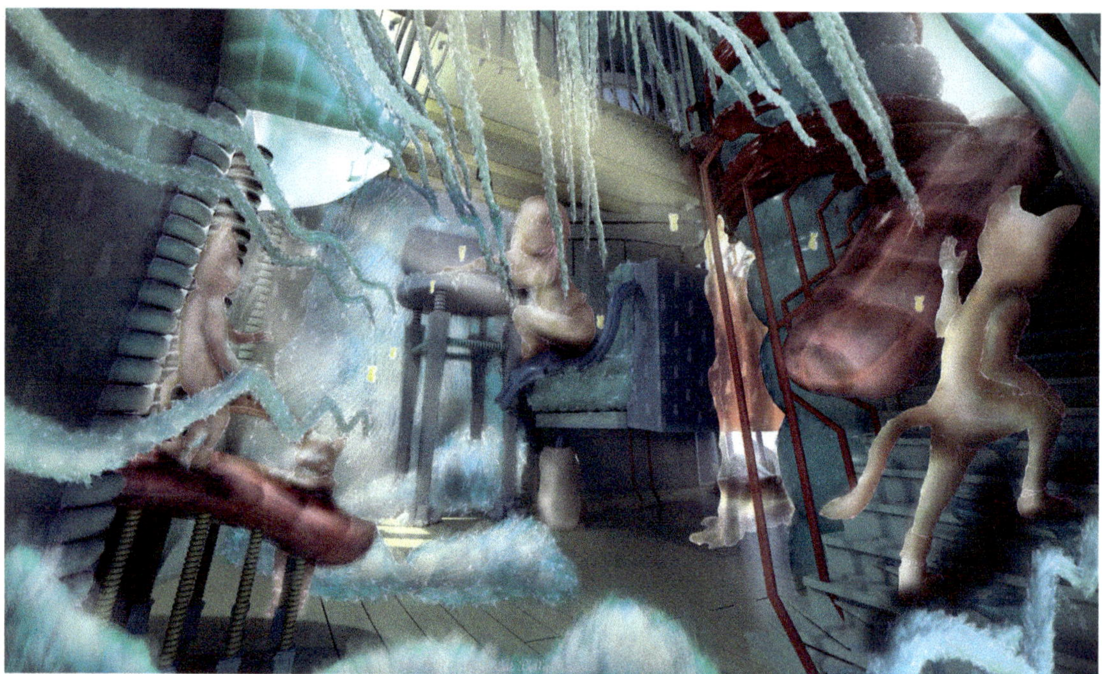

fig. 3.39-3.42: Top-Left to Bottom-Right: Painting of Hector using his High Chair; Cat's perspective interior view of the staircase. Facing Page: Render of Bronson's crib, titled "Ailuranthropic Bedtime"; View of "Cat Belly House" from a cat's perspective underneath a parked car.

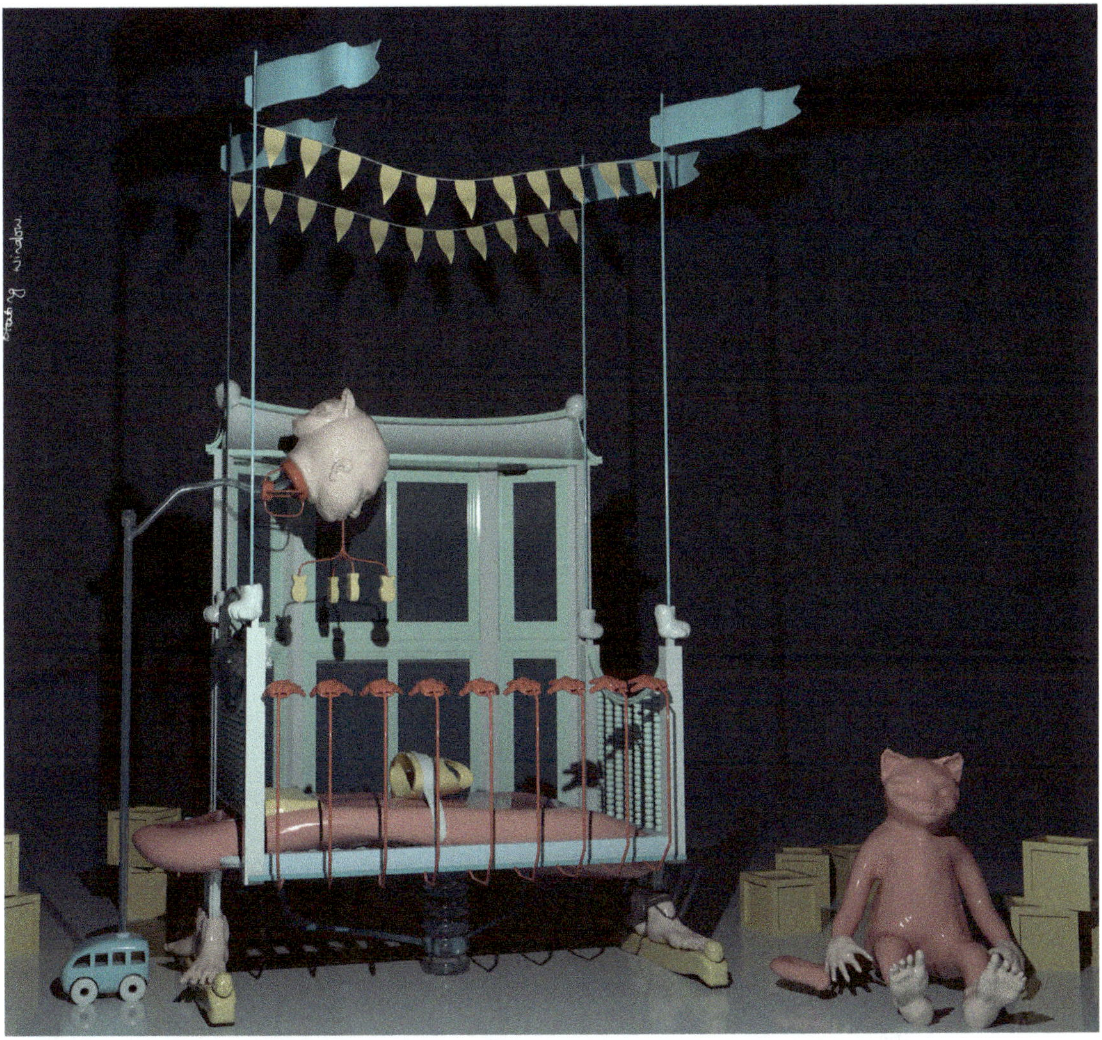

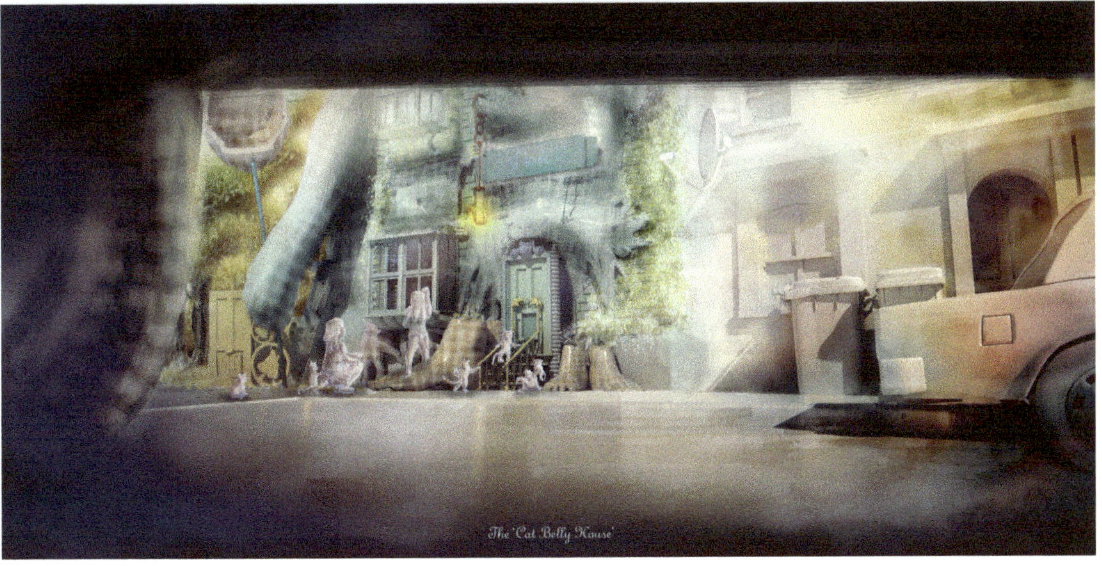

The 'Cat Belly House'

SOCIAL SCALAM: The Modification And Conservation Of The Human Race

and

TERMS + CONDITIONS OF THE VIRTUAL VERMIS CHURCH

by
ALCINA LO

BRIEF *Spectral Futures, Things Have Feelings Too*

YEAR *2022-23, 2023-24*

TUTORS *Dr Alessandro Ayuso, Mary Konstantopoulou*

THEMES

Non-human Agency

Grotesque / Hybrid Body

World-building (Sci-fi Parallel Reality)

Object Agency

Allegory

Mediated Architecture

"The Social Scalam is an allegory on the class hierarchy in society and the responsibility of saving the environment, narrated through a Scalam and a visitor of Palermo in 3000AD.

Scalam [SCAY-LUM]

Noun, Plural Sca-Lams

1. A genetically modified arachnid-like human which eats air pollution. Native to Palermo."

"The Virtual Vermis is a political allegory on digital consent, technology, and religion. The narrative initially follows three realities (virual reality, our reality and the reality of the agenda), until the separation of the realities blurs.

Vermis [VER-MES]

Noun, Plural VER-MISES. Animal.

2. A worm-like cyborg, naturally evolved to be a digital accessory. Native to Isle of Dogs.

*The Vermis is designed by Other Constructions to collect digital information unbeknownst to the users, who believe it is a natural species of worm, native to the area. [the Vermis App discrete terms and conditions read: *By joining you surrender all digital data and control to Other Constructions Co.>>INSTALL]"*

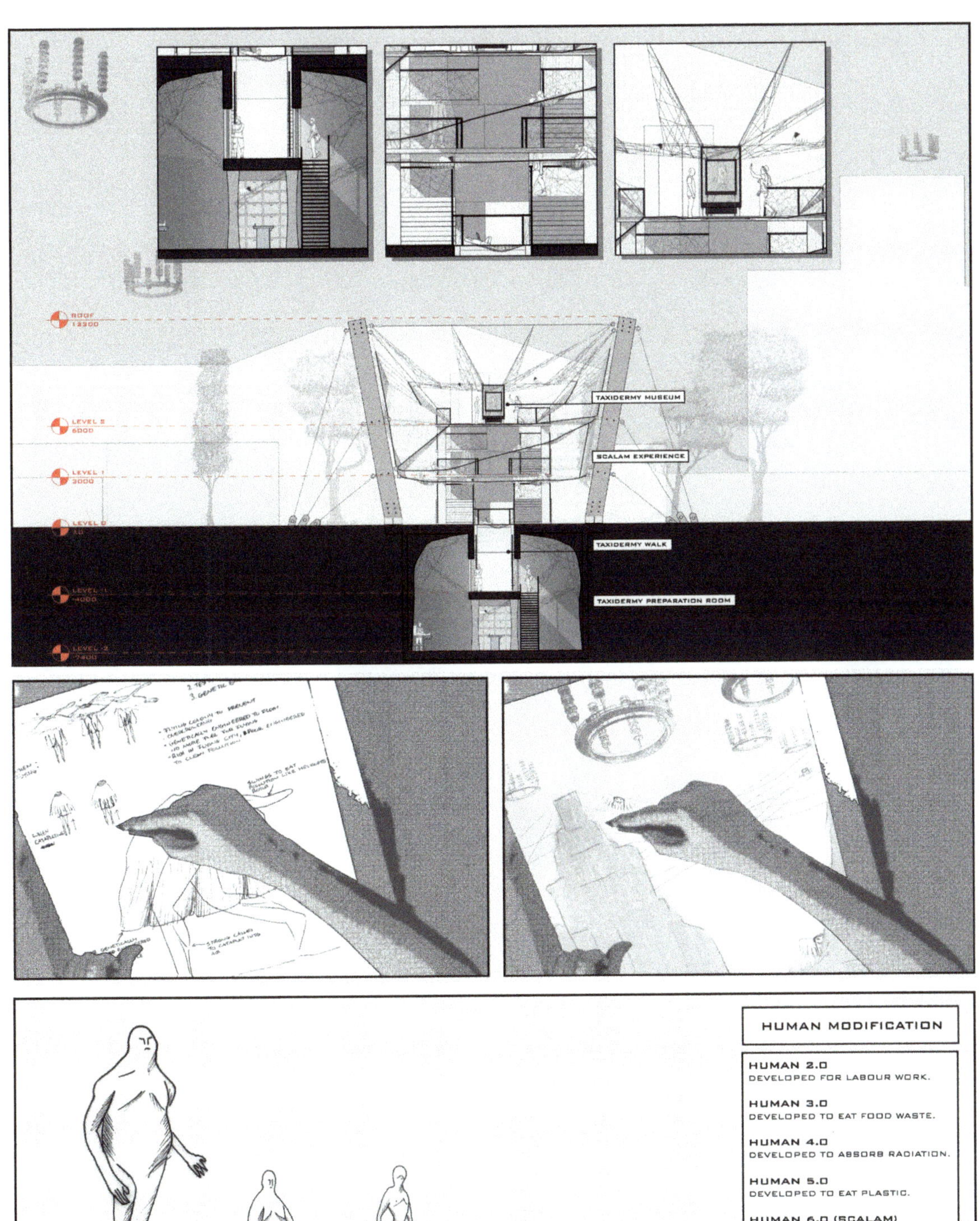

fig. 3.43-3.45: Top to Bottom: Cross section of the Taxidermy Museum; Scalam habitats developed through study sketches of Krutikov's "Flying City" 1928; Human evolution / modification timeline.

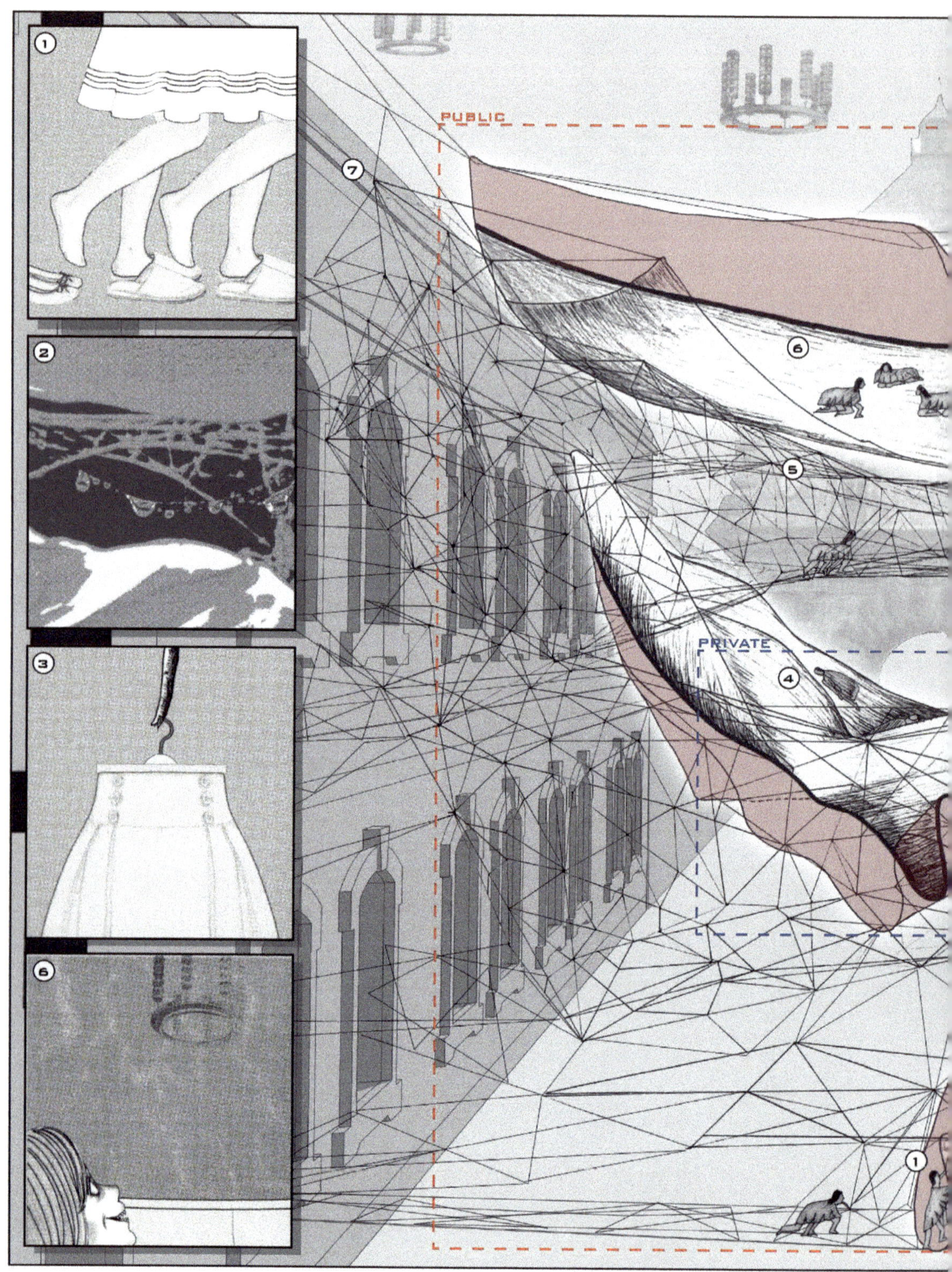

fig. 3.46: Scalam web habitat section constructed across a Palermian street showing behavioural details such as the Scalams taking off their shoes before entering.

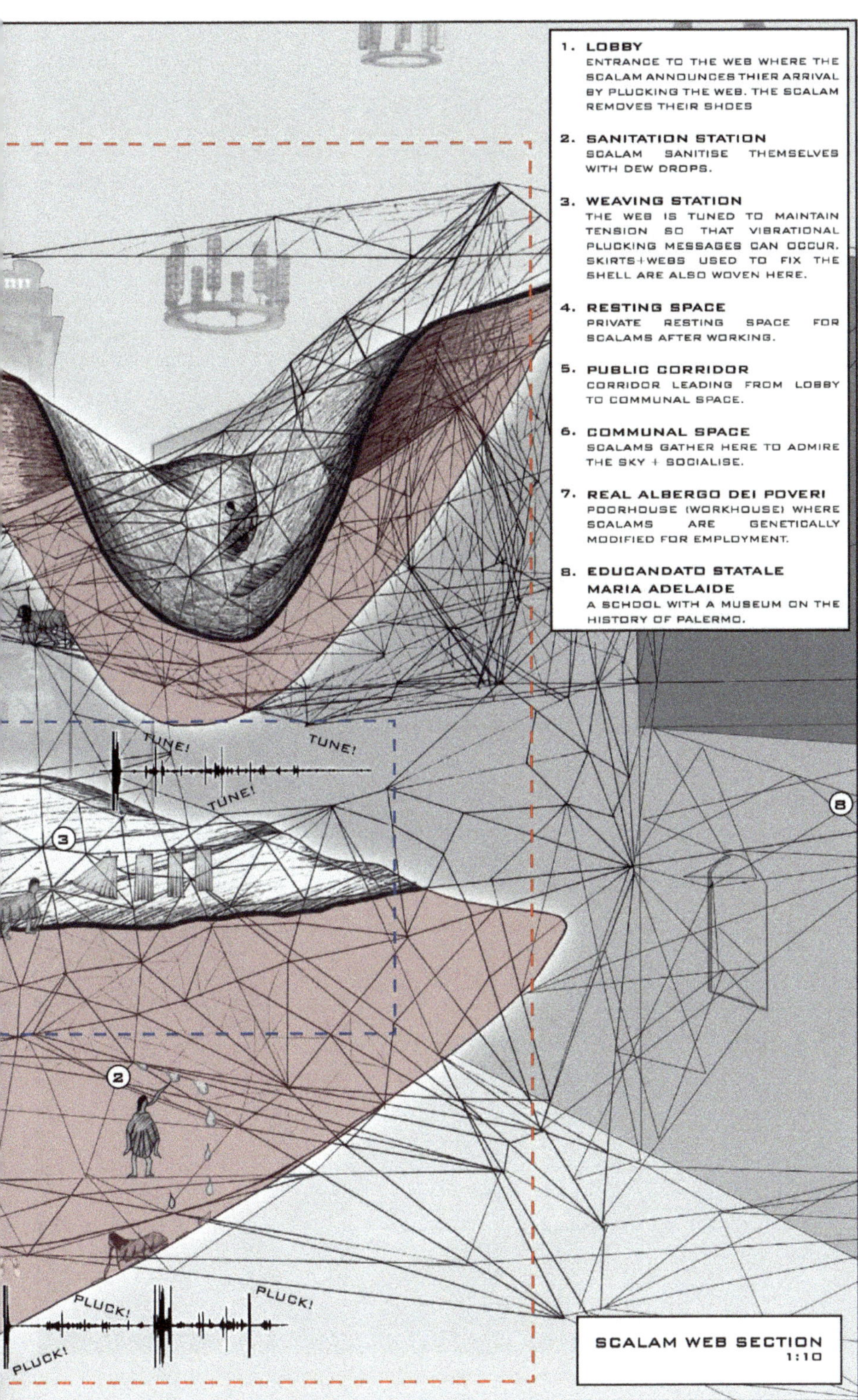
1. LOBBY
ENTRANCE TO THE WEB WHERE THE SCALAM ANNOUNCES THIER ARRIVAL BY PLUCKING THE WEB. THE SCALAM REMOVES THEIR SHOES
2. SANITATION STATION
SCALAM SANITISE THEMSELVES WITH DEW DROPS.
3. WEAVING STATION
THE WEB IS TUNED TO MAINTAIN TENSION SO THAT VIBRATIONAL PLUCKING MESSAGES CAN OCCUR. SKIRTS+WEBS USED TO FIX THE SHELL ARE ALSO WOVEN HERE.
4. RESTING SPACE
PRIVATE RESTING SPACE FOR SCALAMS AFTER WORKING.
5. PUBLIC CORRIDOR
CORRIDOR LEADING FROM LOBBY TO COMMUNAL SPACE.
6. COMMUNAL SPACE
SCALAMS GATHER HERE TO ADMIRE THE SKY + SOCIALISE.
7. REAL ALBERGO DEI POVERI
POORHOUSE (WORKHOUSE) WHERE SCALAMS ARE GENETICALLY MODIFIED FOR EMPLOYMENT.
8. EDUCANDATO STATALE MARIA ADELAIDE
A SCHOOL WITH A MUSEUM ON THE HISTORY OF PALERMO.
TUNE!
TUNE!
TUNE!
3
8
2
PLUCK!
PLUCK!
PLUCK!
SCALAM WEB SECTION
1:10

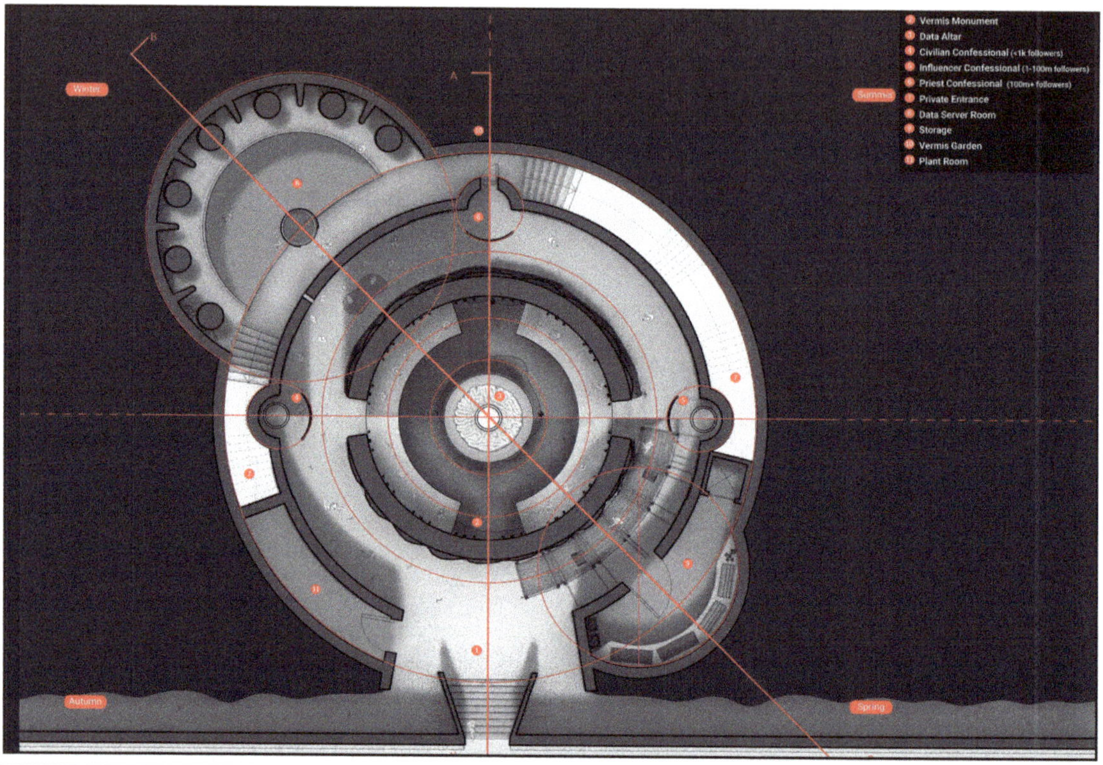

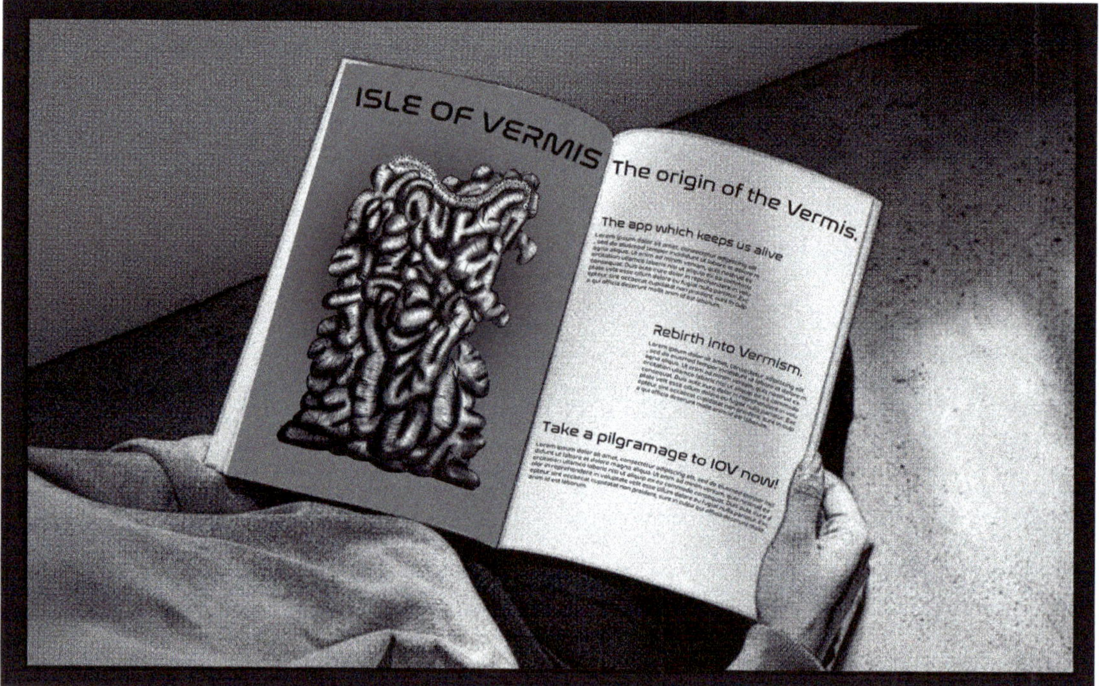

fig. 3.47-3.48: Top to Bottom: Church of Vermis plans - the entrance and spaces around the monument create worm-like tunnels for the visitors. The separation of the confessionals based on how many followers one has creates exclusive spaces. The data centre is hidden behind false walls; Vermis Church Terms + Conditions pamphlet.

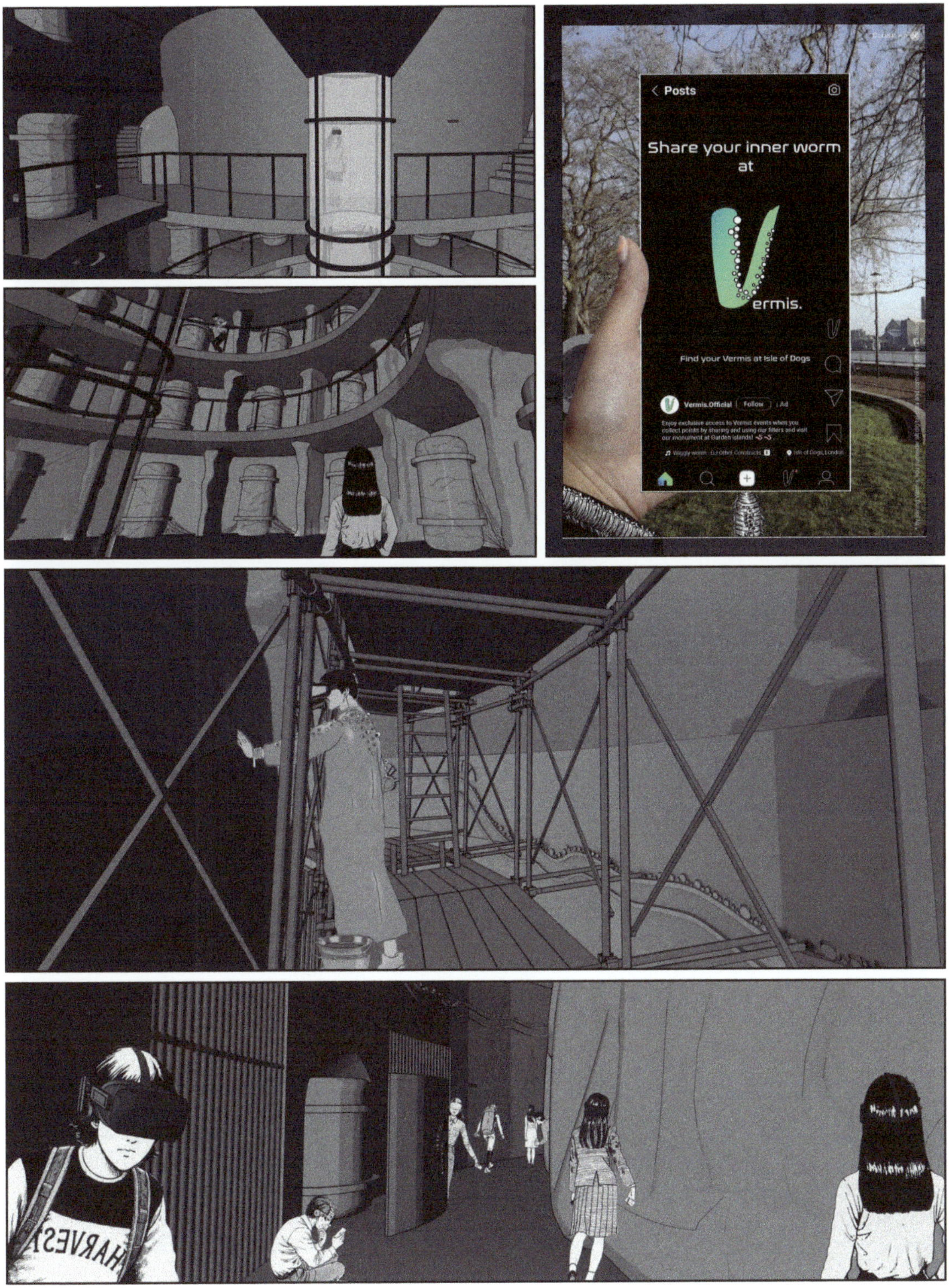

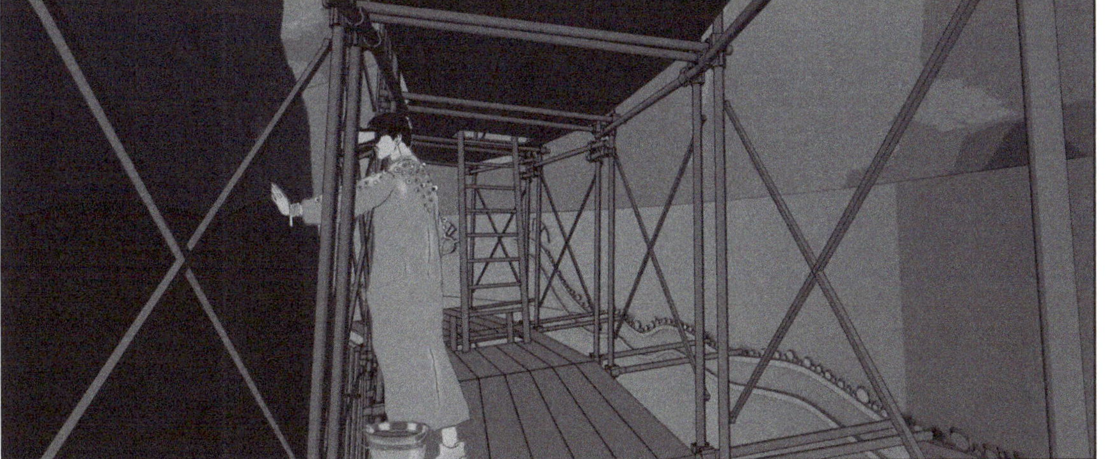

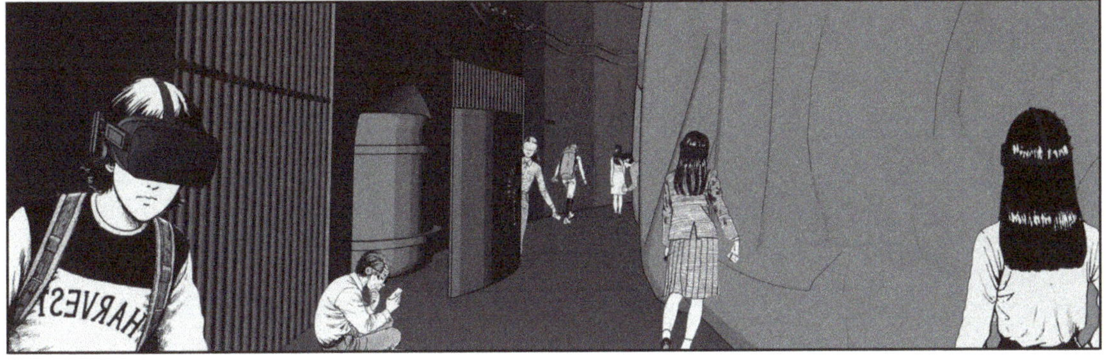

fig. 3.49-3.53: Graphic novel views of the inside of the Vermis Church. Top-Left to Bottom-Right: Data Centre; Using the Vermis app on site; Remudding Festival for the Vermis Monument; The Great Upload of the superusers' data.

CAGLIOSTRO'S PARANORMAL CASE FILES FOR MOTHER BLOOM AND PALERMO'S NECROPOLIS

by
CONRAD DANIEL ARETA

BRIEF *Spectral Futures*

YEAR *2022-23*

TUTORS *Dr Alessandro Ayuso, Mary Konstantopoulou*

THEMES

Narrative World-building

Mixed Realities

Inanimate / Animate body

Death / Commemoration

Monumentality

Parallel Realities

"In response to the posthumanist driver of the design brief, this project explores the narratives between a Paranormal Researcher and 'Future Ghost' body within a pulicly accessible space in Palermo, Sicily.

The project explores the facets of mortality and what it means to live and inevitably die, thinking of the living body but also the dead and the soul as user types within an architectural deathscape.

The first half of this project aims to explore the idea of the ghostly body that informs the design and its needs as a user type, alongside the living body and the dead body. Following on from this, the project develops on the idea of the parallel journeys of the living and the dead through the specutlative design for a Palermian Necropolis."

fig. 3.54: Facing Page: After-Death image: "I'm all alone now, my friends from the F.GC. have stopped visiting me, the monks have also left so no one can take care of my home now. Mother Bloom says she'll pick me up soon so I can leave this ruin."

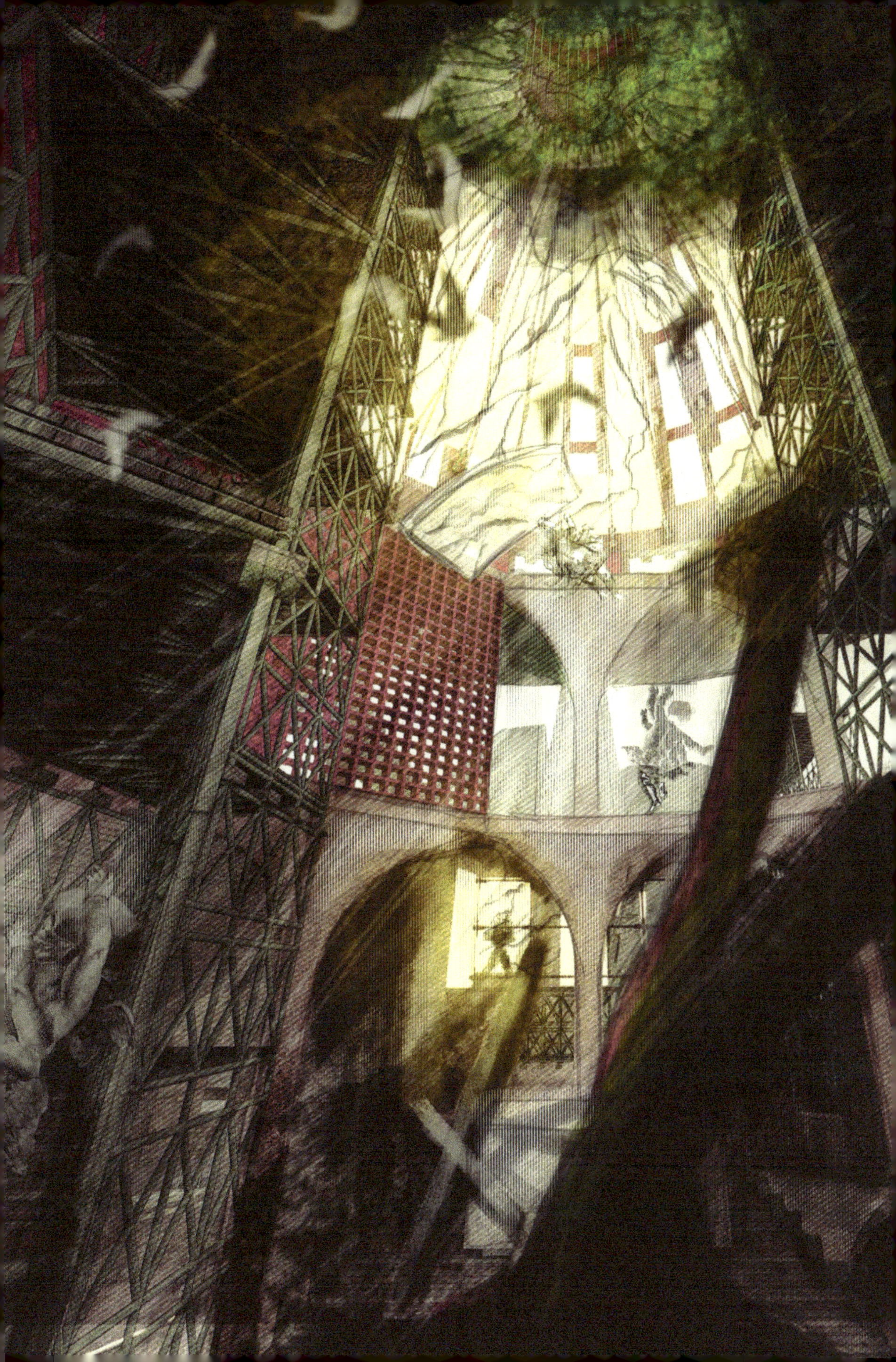

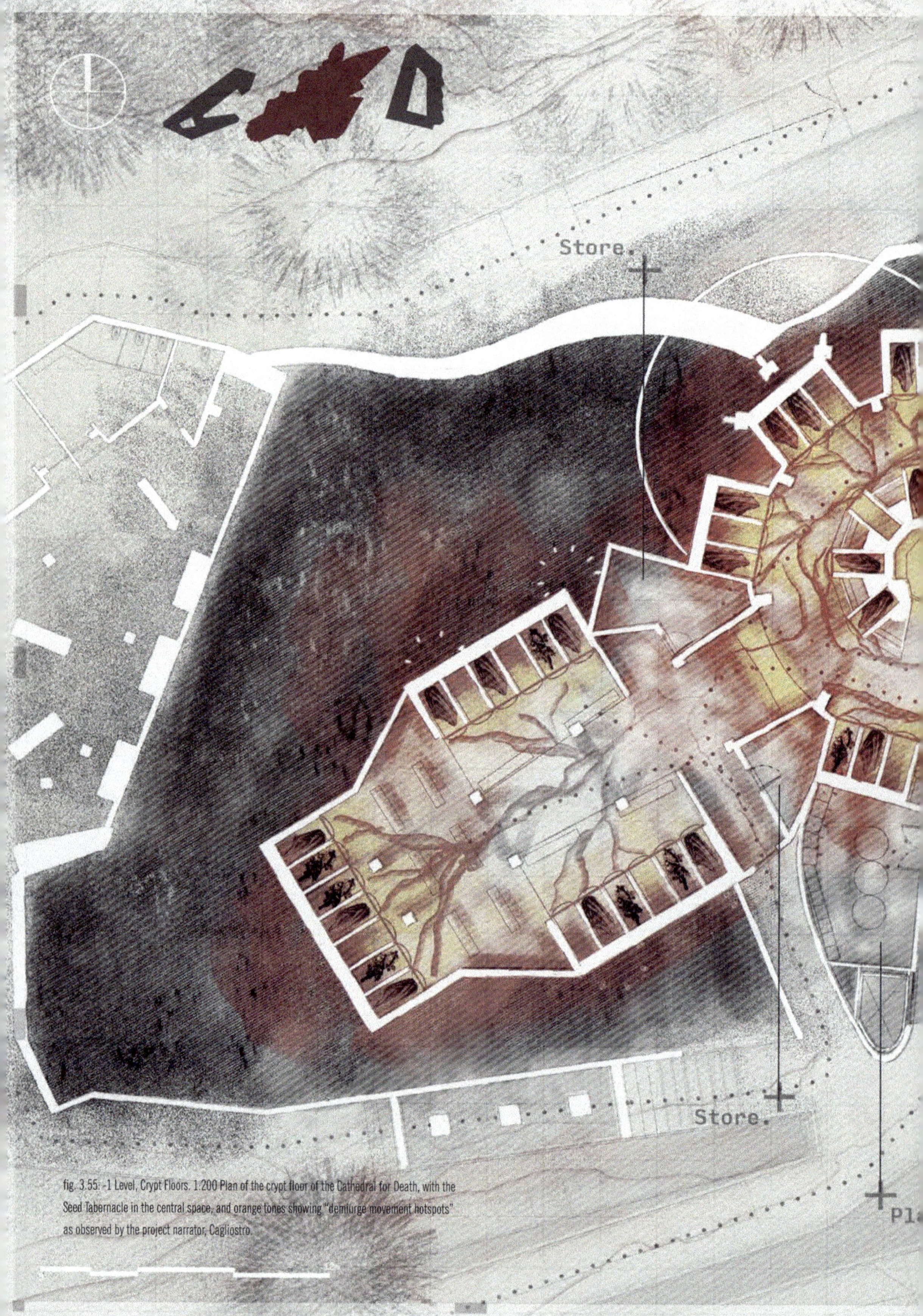

Store.

Store.

Pl

fig. 3.55: -1 Level, Crypt Floors. 1:200 Plan of the crypt floor of the Cathedral for Death, with the Seed Tabernacle in the central space, and orange tones showing "demiurge movement hotspots" as observed by the project narrator, Cagliostro.

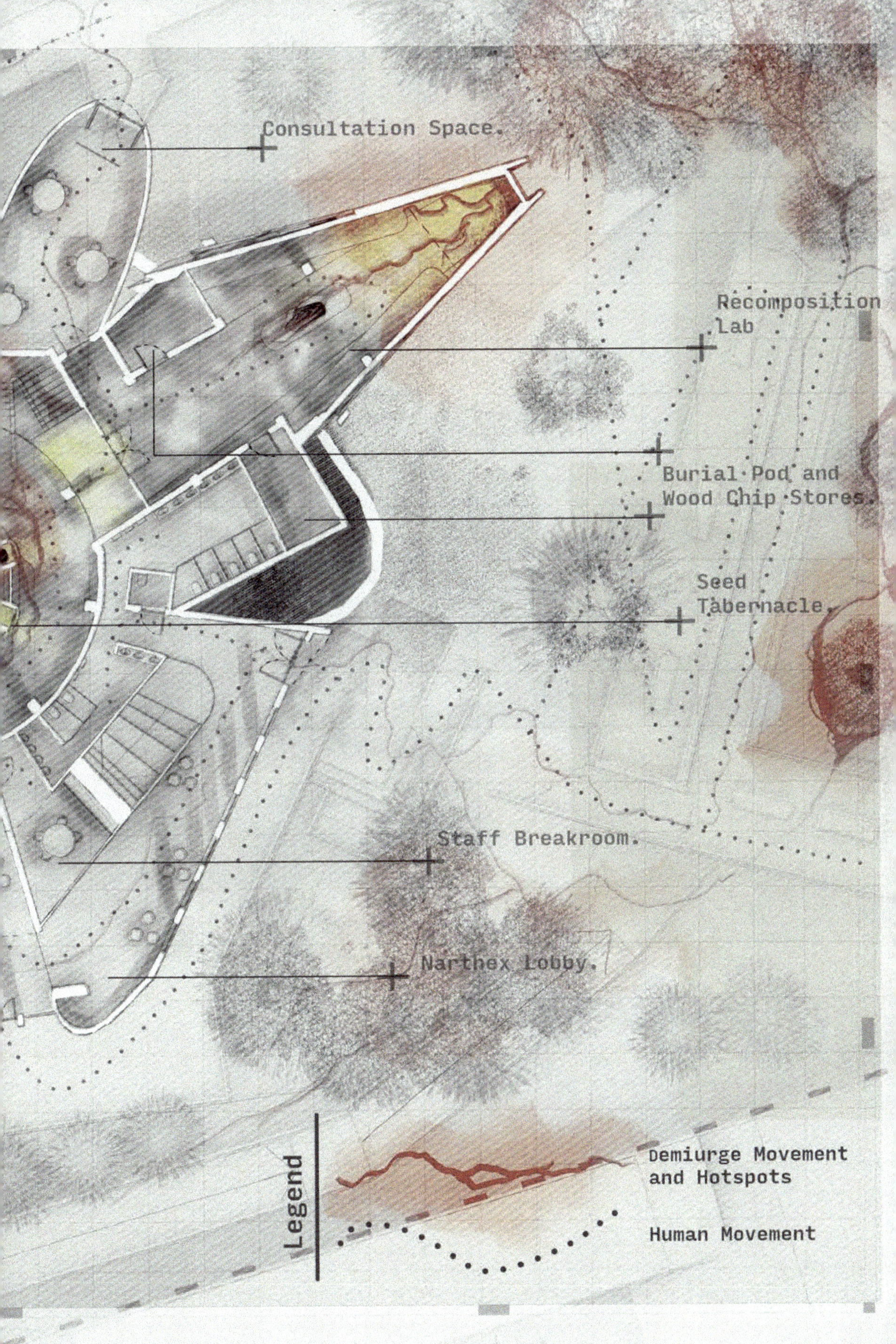

Consultation Space.
Recomposition Lab
Burial Pod and Wood Chip Stores.
Seed Tabernacle.
Staff Breakroom.
Narthex Lobby.
Legend
Demiurge Movement and Hotspots
Human Movement

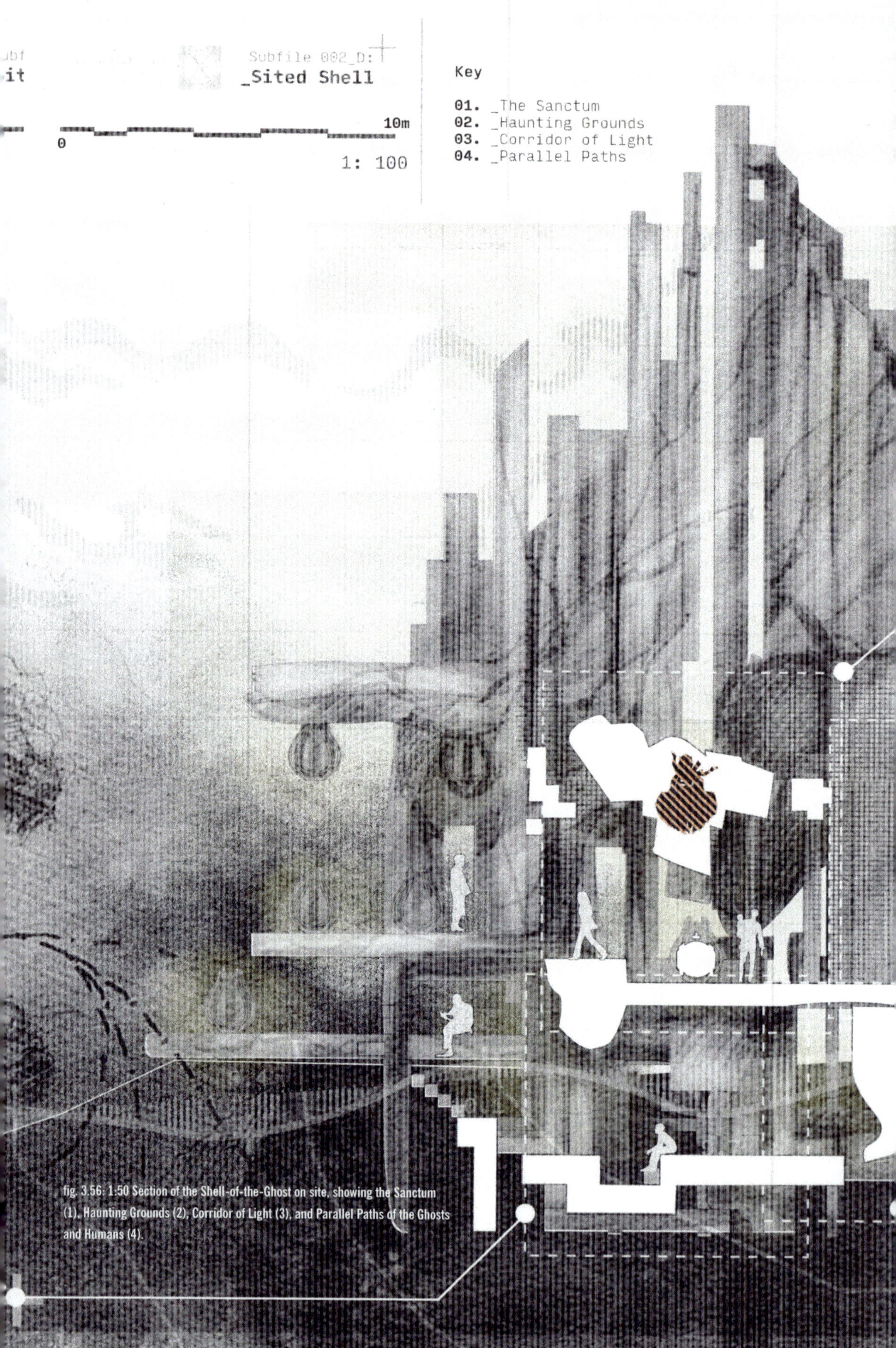

fig. 3.56: 1:50 Section of the Shell-of-the-Ghost on site, showing the Sanctum (1), Haunting Grounds (2), Corridor of Light (3), and Parallel Paths of the Ghosts and Humans (4).

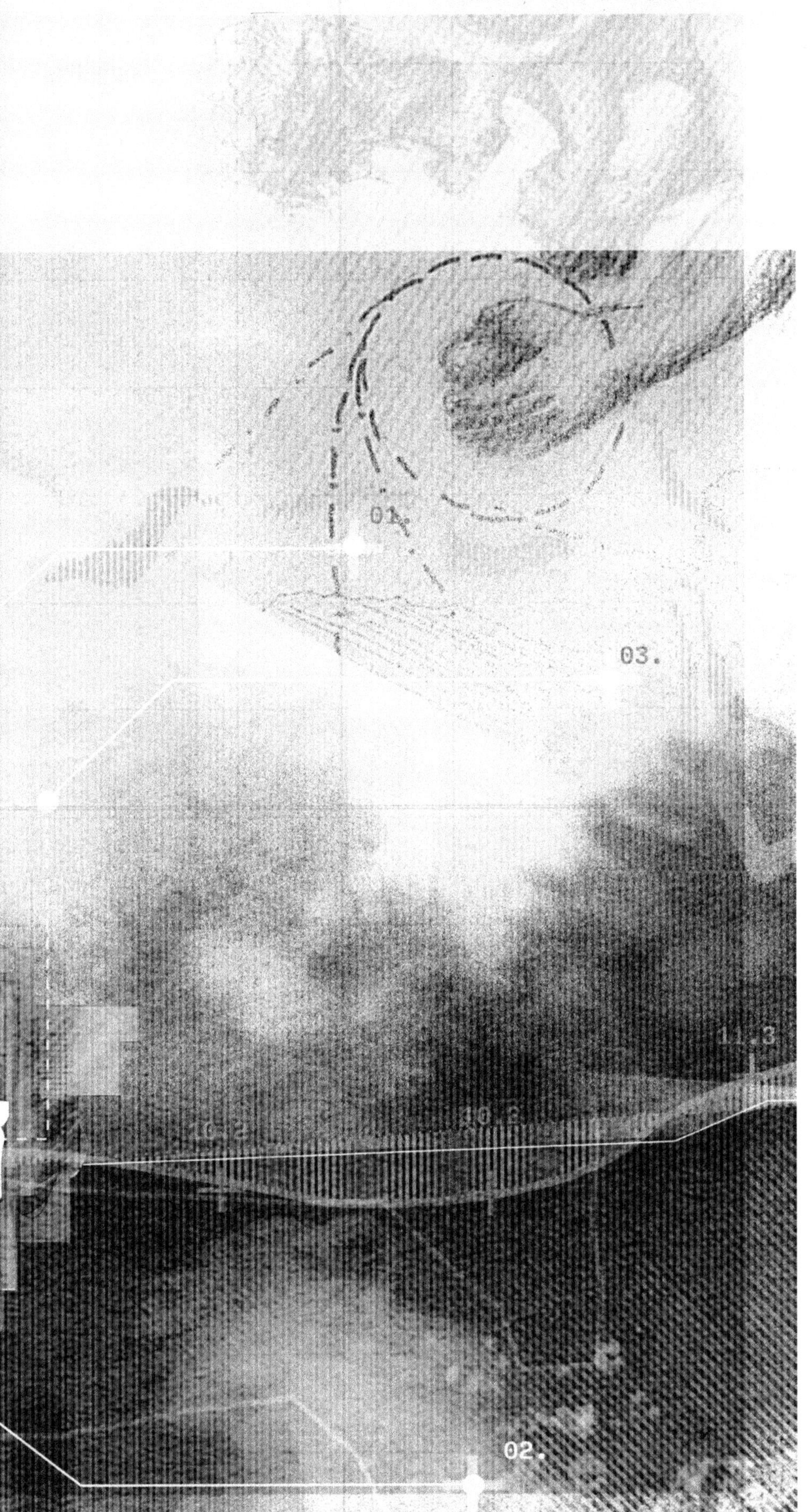
01.
03.
10.2
10.2
11.3
02.

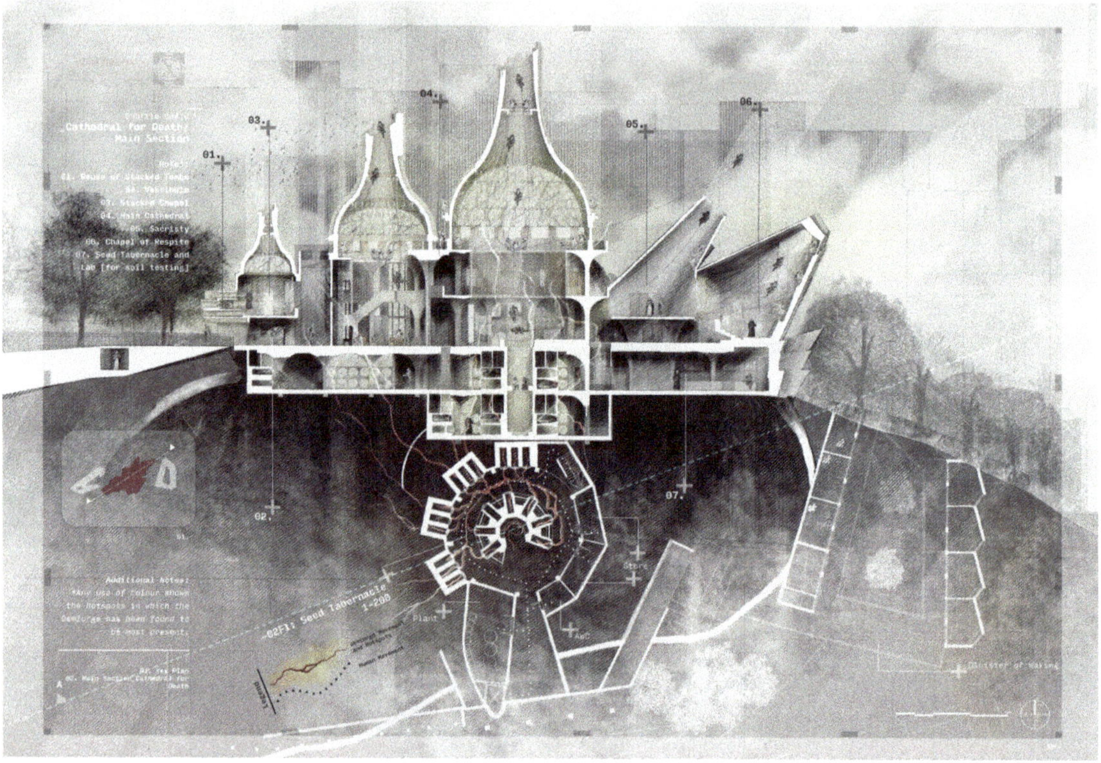

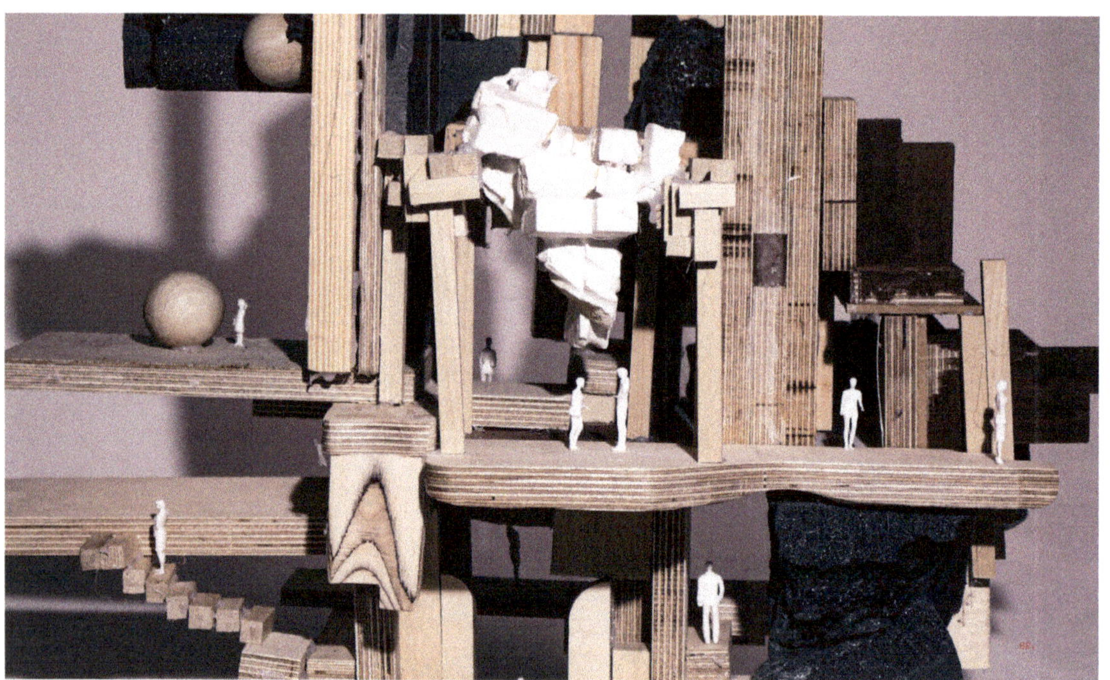

fig. 3.57-3.60: Top to Bottom: Cathedral for Death / Main Section showing Reuse of Stacked Tombs (01), Vestibule (02), Stacked Chapel (03), Main Cathedral (04), Sacristy (05), Chapel of Respite (06), Seed Tabernacle and Lab [for soil testing] (07); Shell-of-the-Ghost 1:20 model. Facing Page: Construction Timeline Aerial View; The Mother Bloom Herald.

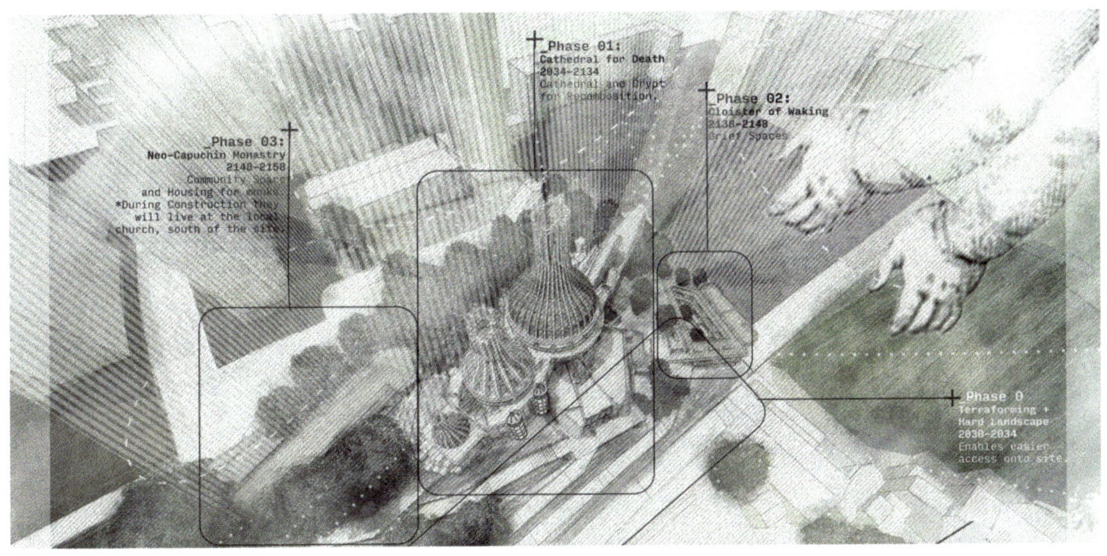

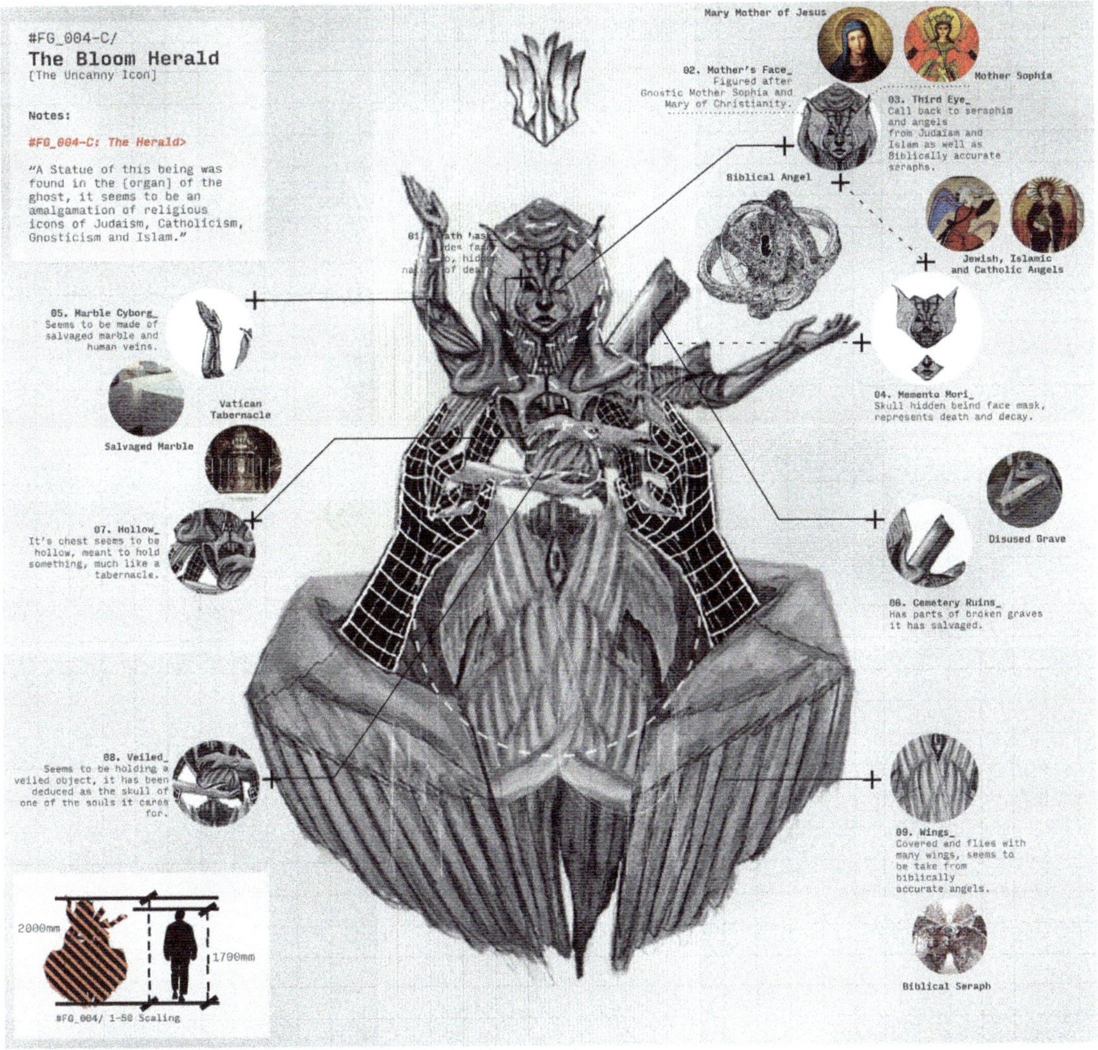

#FG_004-C/

The Bloom Herald

[The Uncanny Icon]

Notes:

#FG_004-C: The Herald>

"A Statue of this being was found in the [organ] of the ghost, it seems to be an amalgamation of religious icons of Judaism, Catholicism, Gnosticism and Islam."

Mary Mother of Jesus

Mother Sophia

02. Mother's Face_
Figured after Gnostic Mother Sophia and Mary of Christianity.

03. Third Eye_
Call back to seraphim and angels from Judaism and Islam as well as Biblically accurate seraphs.

Biblical Angel

Jewish, Islamic and Catholic Angels

05. Marble Cyborg_
Seems to be made of salvaged marble and human veins.

Vatican Tabernacle

Salvaged Marble

04. Memento Mori_
Skull hidden beind face mask, represents death and decay.

07. Hollow_
It's chest seems to be hollow, meant to hold something, much like a tabernacle.

Disused Grave

06. Cemetery Ruins_
Has parts of broken graves it has salvaged.

08. Veiled_
Seems to be holding a veiled object, it has been deduced as the skull of one of the souls it cares for.

09. Wings_
Covered and flies with many wings, seems to be take from biblically accurate angels.

Biblical Seraph

2000mm

1700mm

#FG_004/ 1-50 Scaling

HYDROPOLIS: A Civic Revival

by
ALANNAH WILSON

BRIEF *Things Have Feelings Too*

YEAR *2023-24*

TUTORS *Dr Alessandro Ayuso, Mary Konstantopoulou*

THEMES

Parallel Realities

Satirical World-building as Critique

Unhuman / Thingly Agency

Masterplanning

Ecological Paranoia

Rewilding

"Other Constructions, developers and owners of the thingly vessel camouflaging as a discarded Pompidou Centre pipe, used it as an investigative device:

'By retrofitting the vessel, we created something that could see things we didn't always notice.'

The Odradek is drawn to the financial district of Canary Wharf. Due to the homogeneity of the monolithic enclosed skyscraper structures that reveal little about their inner workings, it begins connecting to their sleek facades.

'Workplace dissatisfaction has been cultivating since Thatcherism. We need to make radical changes to tackle this widespread burnout.', an ad on the Hydropolis news reads. 'The Trojan Horse that is built around the Odradek provided us with access inside the building. It seems corporate relief for its workers always entails some kind of 'pod'. Sound familiar? We decided to match this pretty useless, if we're honest, attempt at improving corporate life. Canary Wharf found it such a success, they've agreed for us to build pipes across the whole district!' And thus, Hydropolis was built, a new sect to balance the monotonous corporate life as a source of reverence and connection through a radically reimagined worship of consummerism."

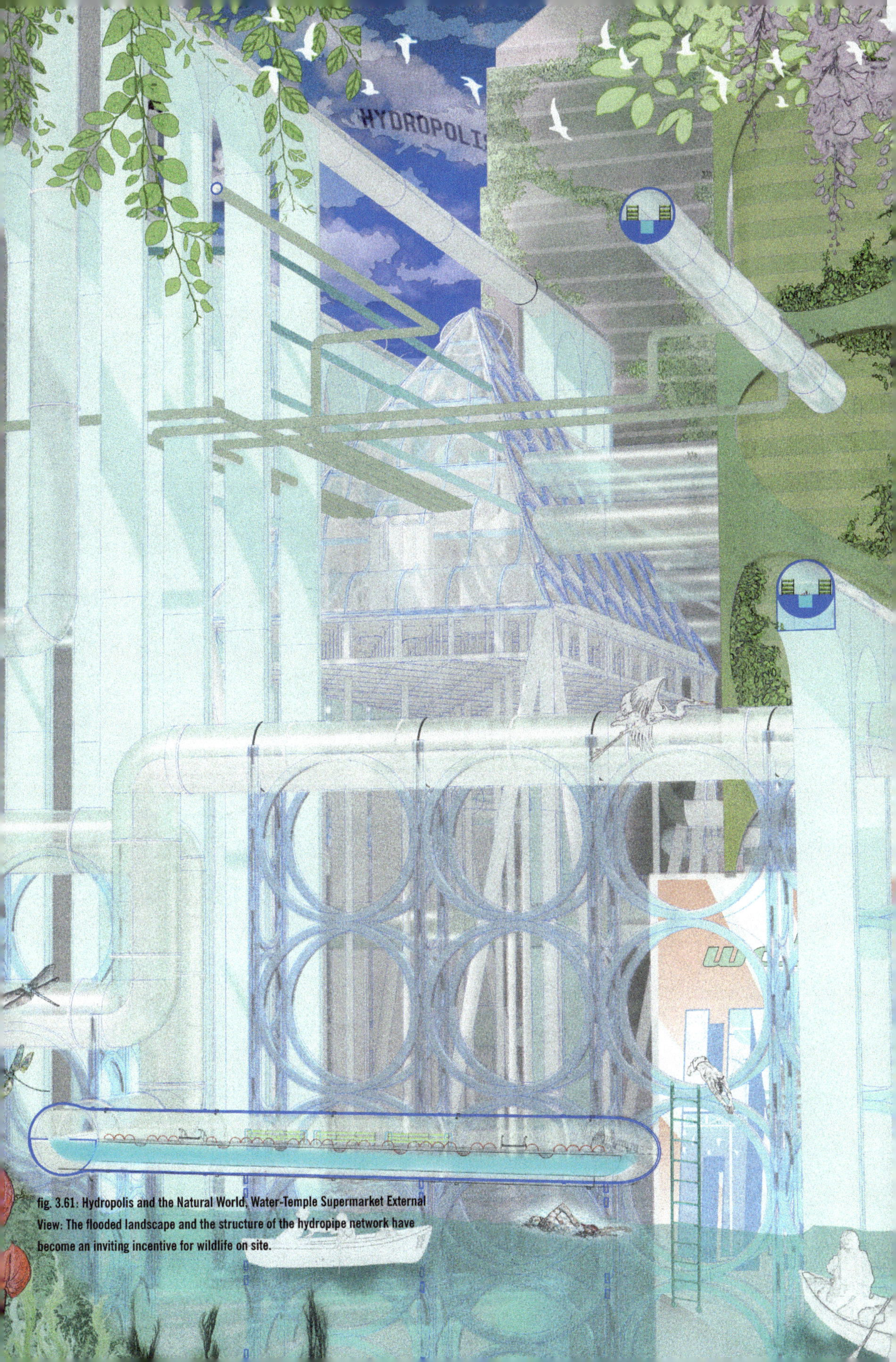

fig. 3.61: Hydropolis and the Natural World, Water-Temple Supermarket External View: The flooded landscape and the structure of the hydropipe network have become an inviting incentive for wildlife on site.

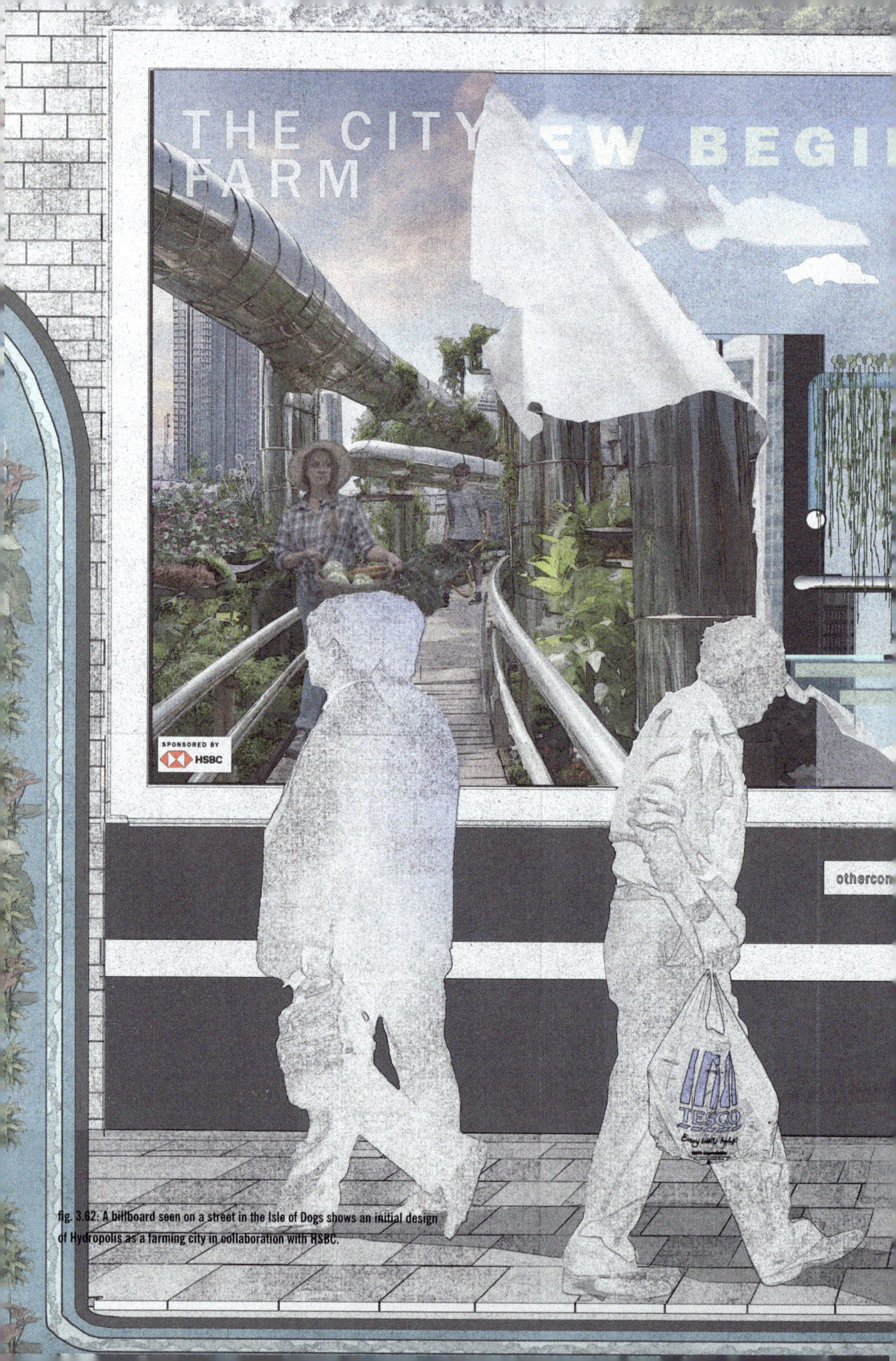

fig. 3.62: A billboard seen on a street in the Isle of Dogs shows an initial design of Hydropolis as a farming city in collaboration with HSBC.

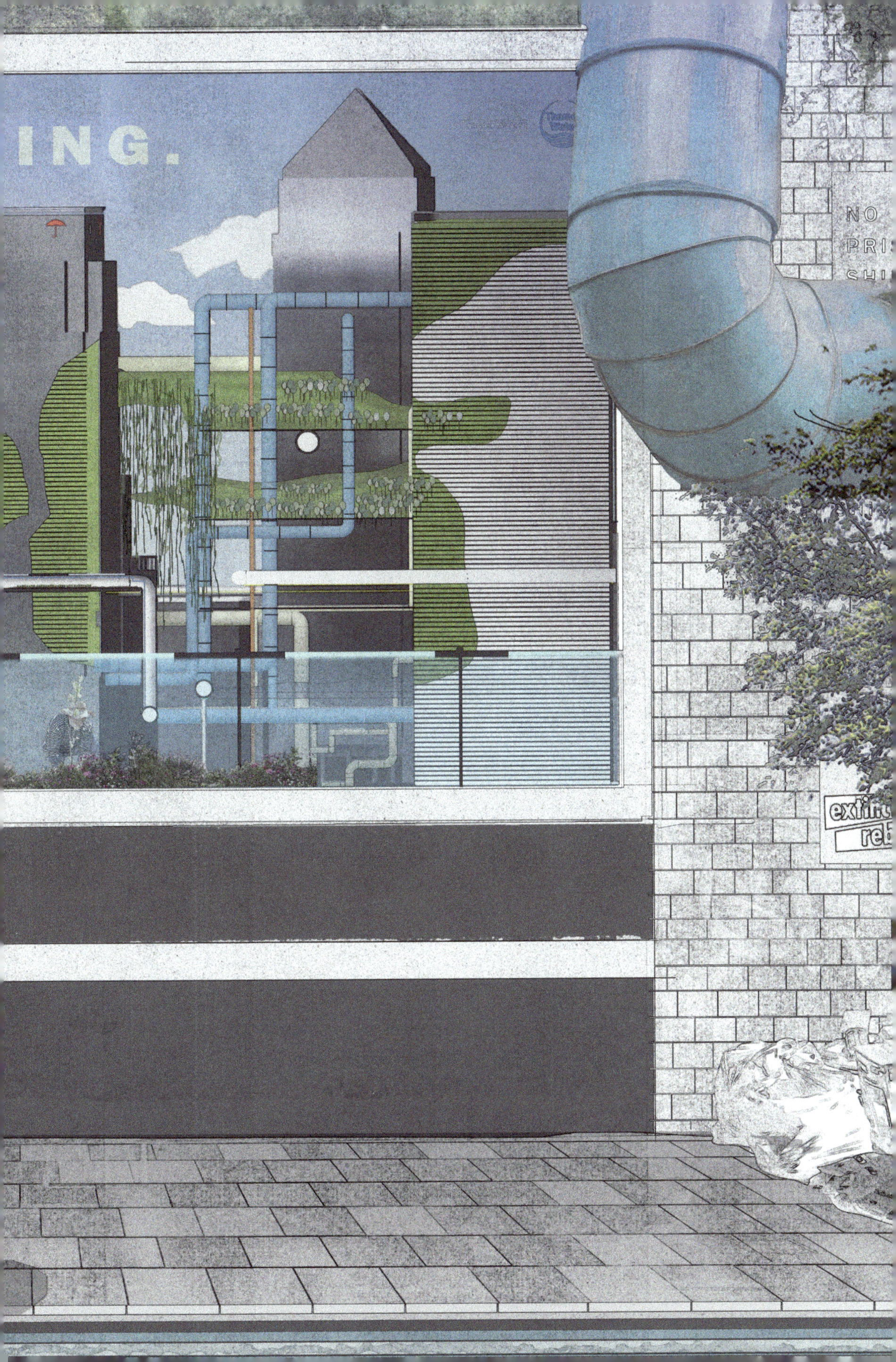
ING.
NO

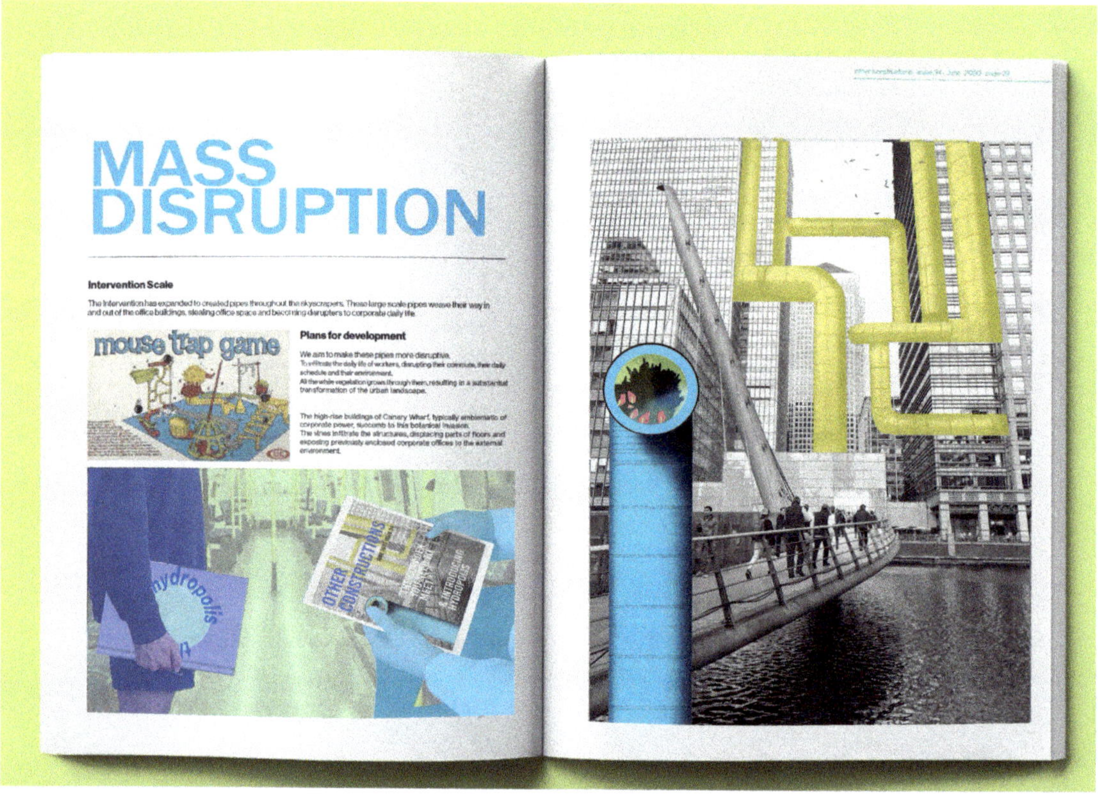

MASS DISRUPTION

Intervention Scale

The Intervention has expanded to created pipes throughout the skyscrapers. These large scale pipes weave their way in and out of the office buildings, stealing office space and becoming disrupters to corporate daily life.

mouse trap game

Plans for development

We aim to make these pipes more disruptive.
To infiltrate the daily life of workers, disrupting their commute, their daily schedule and their environment.
All the while vegetation grows through them, resulting in a substantial transformation of the urban landscape.

The high-rise buildings of Canary Wharf, typically ambiematic of corporate power, succumb to this botanical invasion.
The vines infiltrate the structures, displacing parts of floors and exposing previously enclosed corporate offices to the external environment.

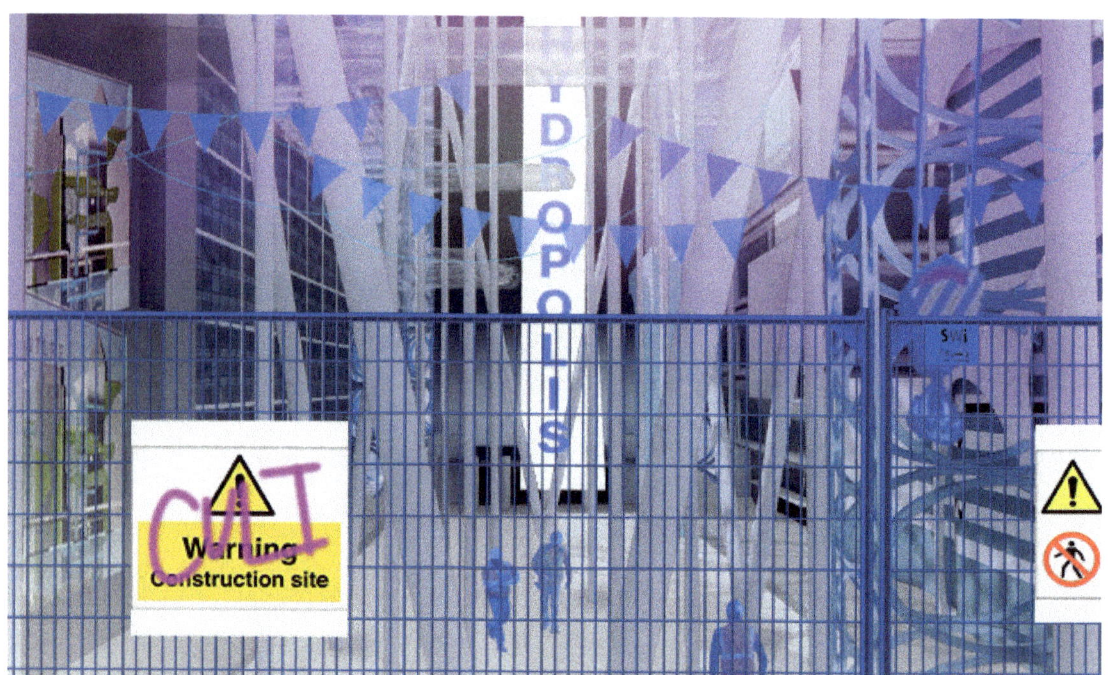

fig. 3.63-3.66: Top to Bottom: Book of Hydropolis showing the Odradek Pipe causing disruption on the Isle of Dogs; View of the Water-Temple Supermarket Under Construction. Facing page: Extracts from the Book of Hydropolis.

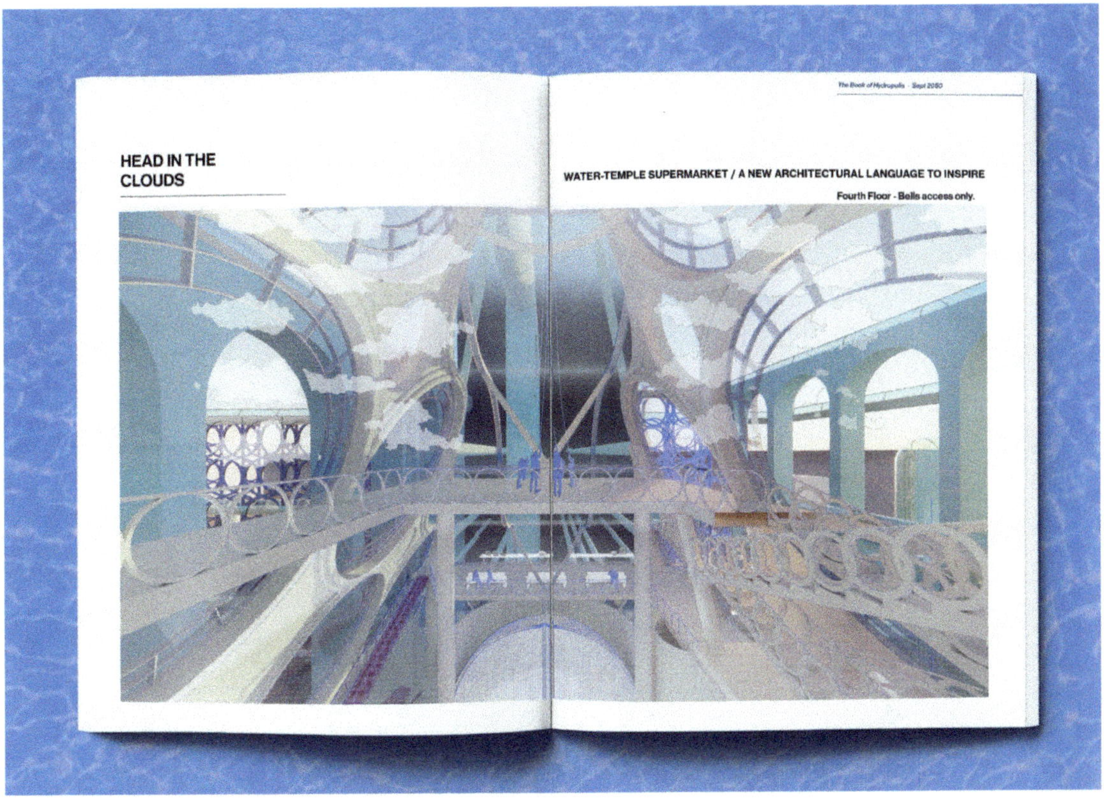

The Book of Hydropolis - Sept 2050

HEAD IN THE
CLOUDS

WATER-TEMPLE SUPERMARKET / A NEW ARCHITECTURAL LANGUAGE TO INSPIRE

Fourth Floor - Bells access only.

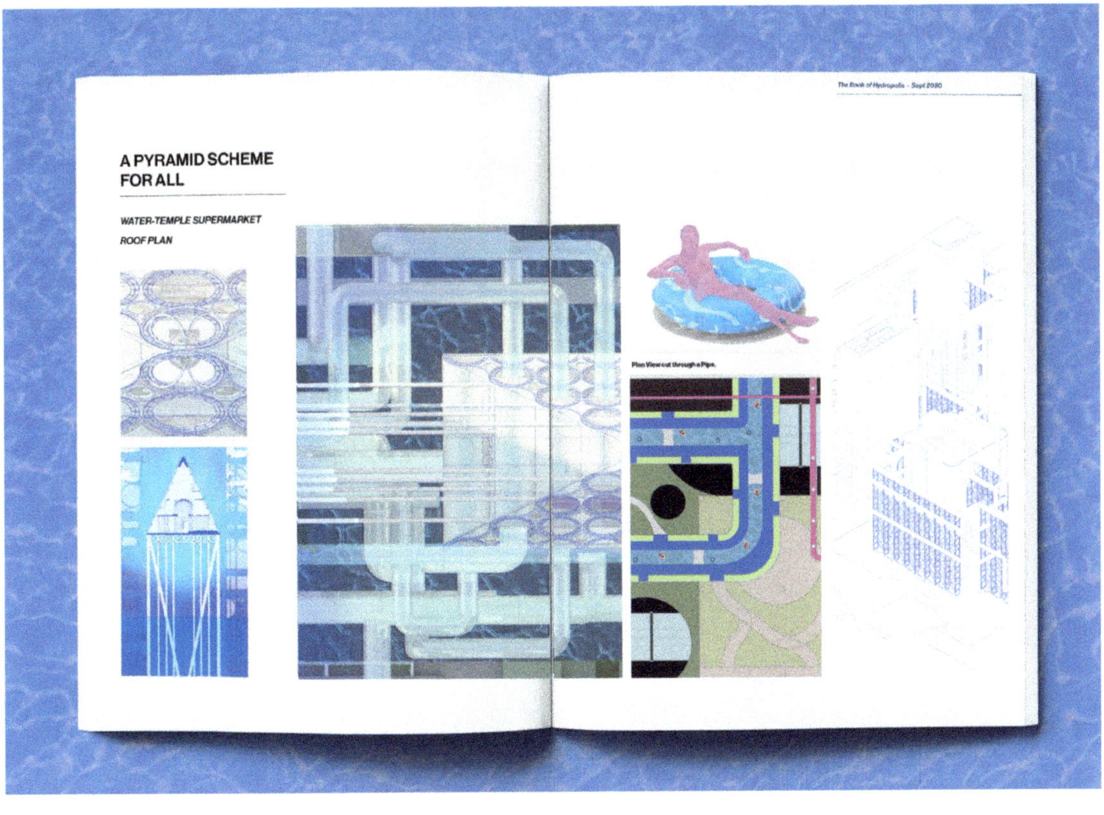

The Book of Hydropolis - Sept 2050

A PYRAMID SCHEME
FOR ALL

WATER-TEMPLE SUPERMARKET

ROOF PLAN

Plan View cut through a Pipe.

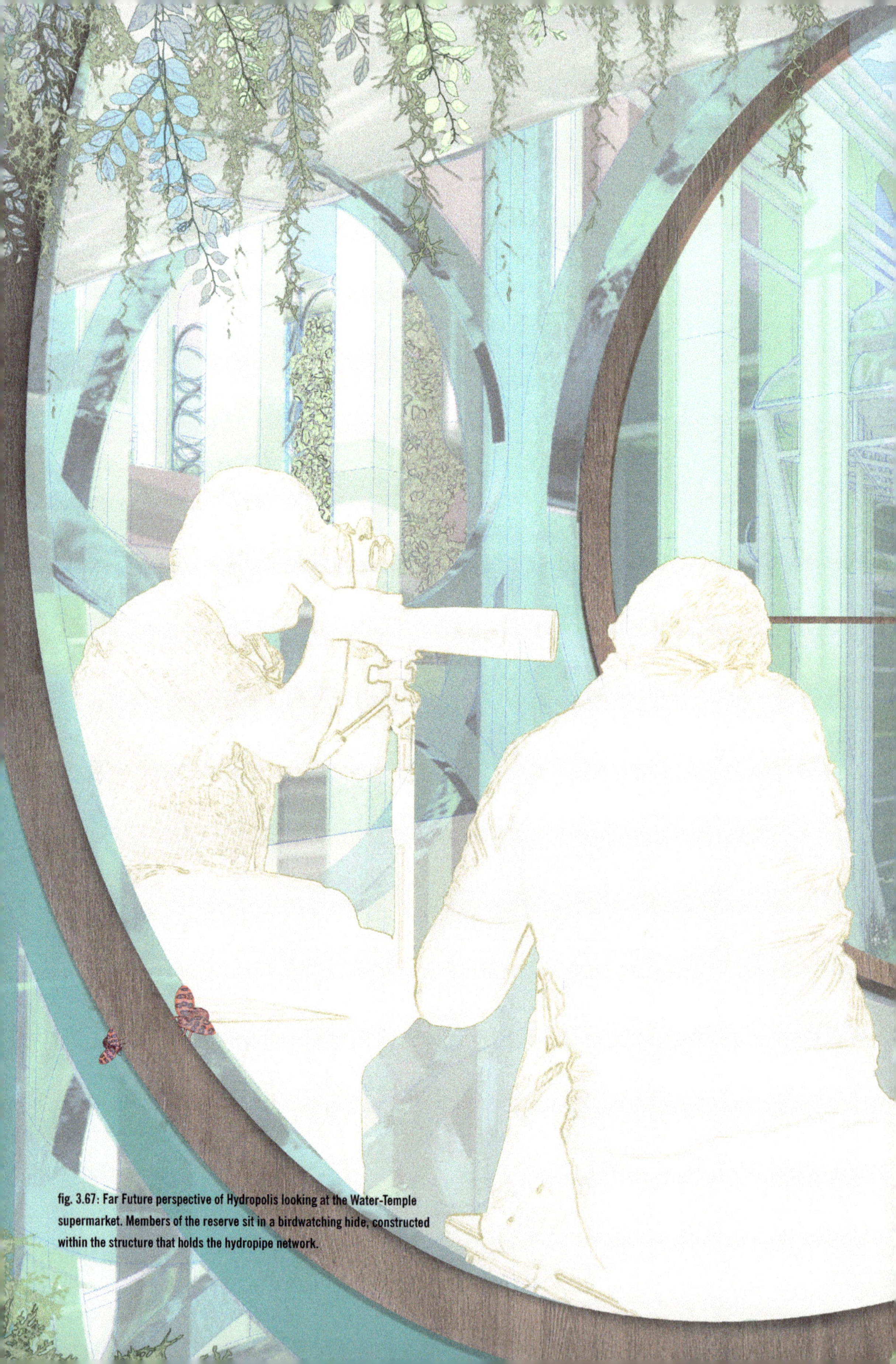

fig. 3.67: Far Future perspective of Hydropolis looking at the Water-Temple supermarket. Members of the reserve sit in a birdwatching hide, constructed within the structure that holds the hydropipe network.

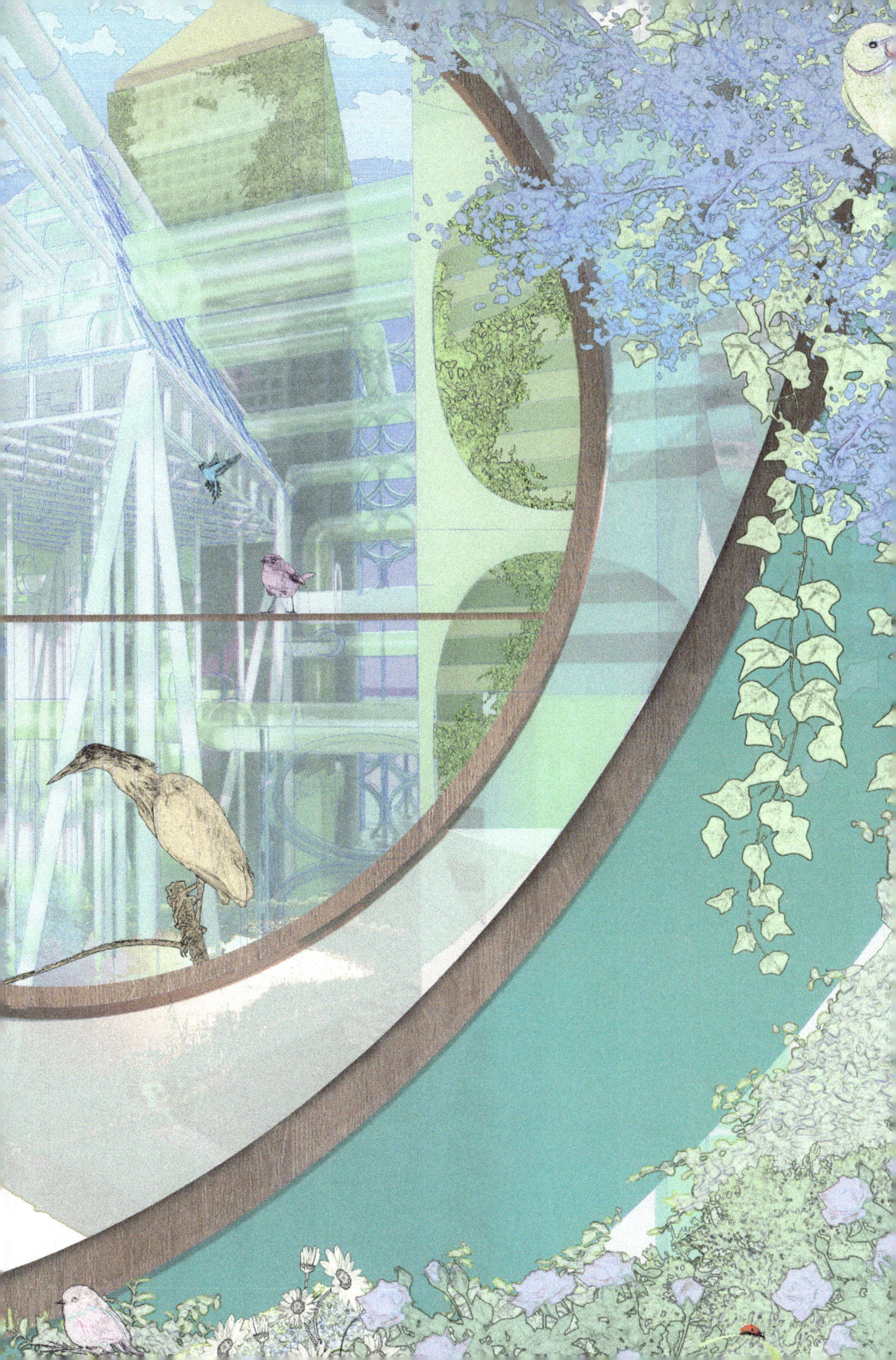

HERE BE DRAGONS: REVELLING IN RADICAL IMAGINATION

by Dr AMY BROOKES

HERE BE DRAGONS: REVELLING IN RADICAL IMAGINATION

"From there, we can understand the necessity of introducing monsters into the scheme."[(01)]

Genre fiction revels in the monstrous, delighting in the creation of creatures and places radically other to our own. While those of us in the built environment professions confront the existential crises of climate emergency alongside ongoing struggles of social justice, dwelling in the fantastic can seem like escapism; a retreat from the responsibilities of the real. Consequently, works of exuberant imagination are often overlooked by architects as too fantastical to be of practicable use. But I would echo DS25 student Asena Koksal: it is necessary to introduce monsters to the scheme of architectural thinking, so that they might walk or float or crawl beside us as we attempt to recognise the radical strangeness of our own selves and the worlds we make together.

The work of DS25 is home to monsters. These projects deliberately step off the edges of the map, drawing on the wonders of the world as we find it and then following these fragments just beyond the stretches of prediction or extrapolation. I choose to read these projects as fictions expressed in architectural form, as works of sf following Donna Haraway's framing of sf as including "science fiction, science fact, science fantasy, speculative feminism, speculative fabulation, string figures...."[(02)] In their tracing of strange histories into far flung futures they undertake what sf author Samuel Delany terms the incantatory function of sf as opposed to "predictive tales."[(03)] They draw on the fabric of reality but use it to weave wild new worlds. This work is not constrained by probability, instead it dances on the threshold of the possible, and I find that the light cast by these implausible or impossible images reveals strange shadows in the worlds I thought I knew.

As feminist writer Lola Olufemi argues, it is necessary to aim for "untethering, a letting-it-go-to-the-sky, a movement so incapable of restriction it seems impossible" in order to be "ENGULFED by the horizon" of possibility.[(04)] This form of highly experimental imagination is extolled by literary critic Fredric Jameson who celebrates the capacity of sf to "relax that tyrannical 'reality principle' which functions as a crippling censorship over high art."[(05)] Jameson argues that relaxing the grip on realism grants access to given visions of other worlds, which in turn imaginatively stretch the scope of the possible in the world we inhabit, "giving us alternate versions of a world that has elsewhere seemed to resist even *imagined* change."[(06)]

In order to bring forth such alternative ways of living and being in the world, gender studies scholar Aimee

Bahng extols attempts to resist anticipation— works that try to predict what will or might be—, and instead look for imaginaries which "take the shape of radical unfurling, rather than protectionist anticipation."(07) She argues that fictions which only explore the probable perpetuate dominant patterns of thought, often serving to reinscribe structural iniquities and injustices onto possible futures, and that extrapolation from within neoliberal capitalism cannot hope to escape its hegemonic foreclosure of the future. In order to mount resistance, she resoundingly calls for speculation which examines "futurity from the perspective of the dragons at the edge of the map."(08) It is here that I find the inhabitants of the projects of DS25, those beings that hover at the edges of imagination and possibility.

Such radical estrangement is inherently challenging. As identified by literary scholar Kathleen Spencer, the worlds of sf are glimpsed only in fragments, and the reader cannot assume any similarities between the fictional world and the worlds of experience. So, as Spencer describes, "the reader oscillates between involvement in, and observation of, the world of the text" continually drawing on fragments of their own experience or imagination to complete the world of the fiction, and then returning to inhabit that world they have constructed.(09) These works provide an overview effect where lived experience is seen from the expansive vantage point of extreme distance, and in the next instant draw me close to intimately inhabit imaginary worlds. I would argue that careful engagement with architectural drawings requires these same practices of imaginative construction. When these architectural projects are located beyond the familiar, in the sf realms of the not-quite-impossible, the critical distance from the built everyday is similarly extended.

As I consider the existential challenges faced by architects and those working in the built environment professions, I am drawn to these projects and fictions which refuse to foreclose the future by simply extending the present. The urgent work of acknowledging responsibility and transforming practice demands a break from the dominant present, and it requires works of escapism to imagine escape.

"In this post-anthropocentric future, 'human' became a fleeting footnote..."(10)

The projects of DS25 escape the present in part by extending the time of the architectural project beyond the contemporary moment, to imagine works designed, constructed, and inhabited in far futures where landscapes of technology, place, and the body have undergone transformation. As described by Anastasia Kolioliou in her DS25 project, through these works I can inhabit a post-anthropocentric future, to step into worlds without or beyond me. These far future imaginaries have a potentially powerful capacity to inform contemporary understandings of the world. As argued by humanities scholar Imre Szeman, it is the potential timescales of sf which make it a genre best placed to "shake us out of our faith in surplus."(11) These fictions can stretch out beyond the immediate present, operating in the scales of generational, geological, or galactic time which allow them to engage with similarly vast and potentially overwhelming issues including climate emergency.

As noted by literature scholar Richard Crownshaw, (12) sf is able to engage with scales of space and time not available to other forms of fiction which makes it uniquely able to grapple with global transformation. But these fictions are also entertainment, and the arc of character struggles means that readers are also offered a way to understand vast systemic issues through an individual character's experience. Confronting the realities of ongoing climate emergency is overwhelming, both intellectually in its complexity and emotionally in the enormity of its ramifications, but the intimacy and immediacy of sf renders these issues accessible. This is described by environmental humanities scholar Lisa Garforth as a critical part of ongoing work to make environmental crises thinkable. Empathetic engagement with a fictional character allows a reader to situate themselves within imagined futures, to encounter the world remade. From here, Garforth contests, it becomes possible to consider issues of survival and flourishing— the "ethical, metaphysical and even utopian possibilities of a climate changed world."(13)

These extended time frames also take me beyond the human as I currently know it. The "primordial flexibility" of genre fiction as described by literary critic Mark McGurl, allows for imaginaries that "cross the threshold of the human," moving beyond human timescales and into the posthuman or inhuman.(14) Here, it is possible to consider what we might become, or to imagine the demise of humanity, and in doing so forcefully challenge ideas of human exceptionalism. But McGurl notes that undertaking this work requires wild leaps of imagination, and its authors or designers must be "willing to risk artistic ludicrousness in their representation of the inhumanely large and long." (15) To engage with these fictions requires me to decentre human experience and empathise with creatures of strangeness.

These perspectives estrange me not only from my current time and place, but also from my own body. To empathetically engage with these worlds, I must understand what it means to be monstrous. Confronted by the attribution of monstrosity applied to trans bodies, gender studies scholar Susan Stryker powerfully lays claim to the "dark power" of monstrous identity. She draws on the novel *Frankenstein* and uses the vantage point granted by this work of sf to demand that we "investigate your nature as I have been compelled to confront mine," and recognise ourselves as constructed creatures.[16] Following Stryker, it is by stepping outside of my own body to attend to the experiences of imagined monsters, that I am better able to comprehend the already present constructedness of my own being in the world. From here I look back on the futures I am responsible for building as a mutual construction of my own self, required to bear witness to the worlds I am complicit in making.

"A.L.I.C.E. attempted a design intervention and material test. This failed and it seems she has given up... This is an [ERROR] in her programming."[17]

It is in this final act of return that genre fictions and the projects of DS25 find their radical potency. As imaginary sites, they open thresholds beyond probability and allow us to encounter other ways of being in the world; to inhabit times and spaces which stretch beyond the present. But they remain spaces which are haunted by the concerns of our lived moment, and their visions are permeated by a desire to enact subtle shifts in the minds of the viewer. Just as in the DS25 project of Conrad Daniel Areta, the imagined being A.L.I.C.E. undertakes design experiments which speak back to the designer, these fictions and projects are designed to speak to me as a viewer. They ask me to return to the present altered, remade by my awareness of these imagined worlds which linger at the edges of possibility.

Utopian studies scholar Tom Moylan describes the potential of speculative and utopian fiction to offer "an empowering escape to a different way of thinking about, and possibly of being in, the world."[18] To walk these worlds is an act of escapism but it is also empowering, inspiring change in the reader's own perceptions or actions. As celebrated by activist adrienne maree brown, visionary fictions bring into being worlds which challenge existing systems of power and control, presenting the reader with a world transformed. In doing so, they shift the edges of what might be deemed possible by demonstrating alternatives, making another world thinkable. brown describes this as "a way to practice the future together."[19] As an architect, I understand this reference to practice to mean not only a rehearsal of possibility, but also an ongoing act of making. This is an understanding which echoes the work of social justice scholars Alex Khasnabish and Max Haiven who describe radical imagination as "something we do (and do together)."[20] For them, radical imagination is not only the ability to recognise the necessity of change and imagine the world as it might otherwise be; it is also "about bringing those possible futures 'back' to work on the present, to inspire action and new forms of solidarity today."[21]

The projects of DS25 are imaginary worlds, but they are also tangible objects which through their making have already acted upon the real. As museums scholar Lizzie Muller suggests, such speculative objects exist in a complex relation to lived reality, "in the interplay of their impossibility, obsolescence and liminality with their tangible existence."[22] They do not exist only in the individual confines of their designer's imaginations but are also physically present within this world, and through the production of drawings and text they can be accessed by others, becoming a shared ground which is opened to imaginative inhabitation and interpretation. The act of sharing worlds through stories and art is recognised by Khasnabish and Haiven as an integral part of solidarity work. They describe how "we create, with those around us, multiple overlapping, contradictory and coexistent imaginary landscapes..." which delineate "horizons of common possibility and shared understanding."[23] It is through the expression of imagined worlds that it becomes possible to collectively enact transformation of the world as it is currently experienced.

When confronted by the multiple existential crises and intersecting horrors of our present, the ongoing devastations of climate emergency, systemic oppression, and genocide, to dwell in such fictional worlds can seem like a retreat from the real and an abnegation of my own responsibility. And I cannot deny that revelling in these fictions is a source of delight— I do find joy in their wondrous strangeness and wild imaginings. But I also find that these fictions grant me fresh insight, they offer oblique perspectives to glance askance at issues which had seemed too vast and overwhelming to contemplate, and they reinforce my resolve in the necessity of action. These wild worlds do not attempt to offer resolution or solution to specific issues, but they provide me with a place to stand which is radically outside of my entrenched present and in doing so expand the scope the possible. From here I am better able to consider what it means to be an architect, what it means to be human, and what the world deserves from someone who claims these roles. They take me beyond the edges of the map into the realms of the almost-impossible, to dwell with dragons and return transformed.

NOTES

(01) Asena Koksal, "Here Be Ma'Woolies! Architecture behind the Regeneration of River Thames" (2022), 12.

(02) Donna J. Haraway, *Staying with the Trouble: Making Kin in the Chthulucene* (Durham, NC: Duke University Press, 2016), 2.

(03) Samuel R. Delany, "About 5,750 Words," *The Jewel-Hinged Jaw: Notes on the Language of Science Fiction* (Wesleyan University Press, 2011), 11.

(04) Lola Olufemi, *Experiments in Imagining Otherwise* (Hajar Press, 2021), 8. https://www.hajarpress.com/books/experiments-in-imagining-otherwise

(05) Fredric Jameson, *Archaeologies of the Future: The Desire Called Utopia and Other Science Fictions* (New York: Verso, 2005), 270.

(06) Ibid, "World-Reduction in Le Guin: The Emergence of Utopian Narrative," *Science Fiction Studies* 2, no. 3 (1975): 223.

(07) Aimee Bahng, *Migrant Futures: Decolonizing Speculation in Financial Times* (Duke University Press, 2018), 7.

(08) Ibid.

(09) Kathleen L. Spencer, "'The Red Sun Is High, the Blue Low': Towards a Stylistic Description of Science Fiction," *Science Fiction Studies* (1983): 36.

(10) Anastasia Kolioliou, "Bacteria Sanctuary: Diary by OD" (2024), 45.

(11) Imre Szeman, "Literature and Energy Futures," *PMLA* 126, no. 2 (2011): 325.

(12) Richard Crownshaw, "Speculative Memory, the Planetary and Genre Fiction," *Textual Practice* 31, no. 5 (2017): 887–910.

(13) Lisa Garforth, "Environmental Futures, Now and Then: Crisis, Systems Modeling, and Speculative Fiction," *Osiris* 34, no. 1 (2019): 247.

(14) Mark McGurl, "The Posthuman Comedy," *Critical Inquiry* 38, no. 3 (2012): 539.

(15) Ibid, 551.

(16) Susan Stryker, "My Words to Victor Frankenstein Above the Village of Chamounix: Performing Transgender Rage," *GLQ: A Journal of Lesbian and Gay Studies* 1, no. 3 (1994): 241.

(17) Conrad Daniel Areta, "Ukiyo.Land & the Pleasures of a Cyborg's Garden" (2024), 10.

(18) Tom Moylan, *Scraps of the Untainted Sky: Science Fiction, Utopia, Dystopia* (Oxford: Westview Press, 2000), xvii.

(19) adrienne maree brown, *Emergent Strategy: Shaping Change, Changing Worlds* (AK Press, 2017), 19.

(20) Doctor Alex Khasnabish, and Max Haiven, *The Radical Imagination: Social Movement Research in the Age of Austerity* (Bloomsbury Publishing, 2014), 218.

(21) Ibid, 3.

(22) Lizzie Muller, "Speculative Objects: Materialising Science Fiction," edited by L. Fisher, K. Cleland, and R. Harley (Sydney: ISEA International, 2013), 5.

(23) Khasnabish, and Haiven, *The Radical Imagination*, 4.

CHAPTER 4: PARALLEL REALITIES

by MARY KONSTANTOPOULOU and Dr ALESSANDRO AYUSO

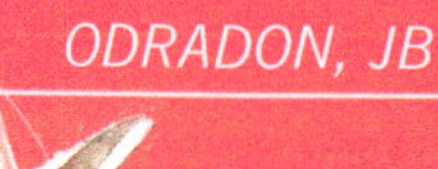

ODRADON, JB

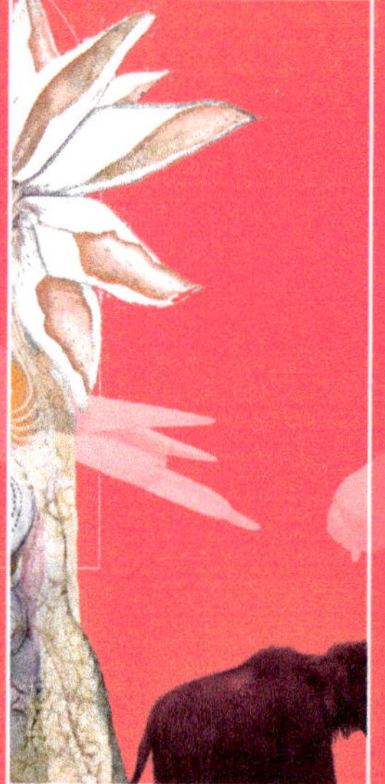

MA'WOOLY, AK

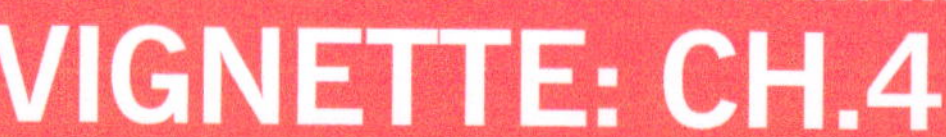

VIGNETTE: CH.4

ECOSYSTEM

forming a part in a constellation of entities living in

parallel

WORLD(S)

mirror images of the

stretched-

porous-

tentacular-

shadow-

other-

bodies within

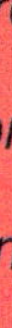

LONGBOI, AJ

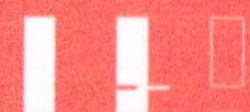

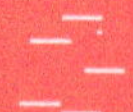

〉BODY 〉 OTHER 〉 ECOSYSTEM 〉 WORLD 〉

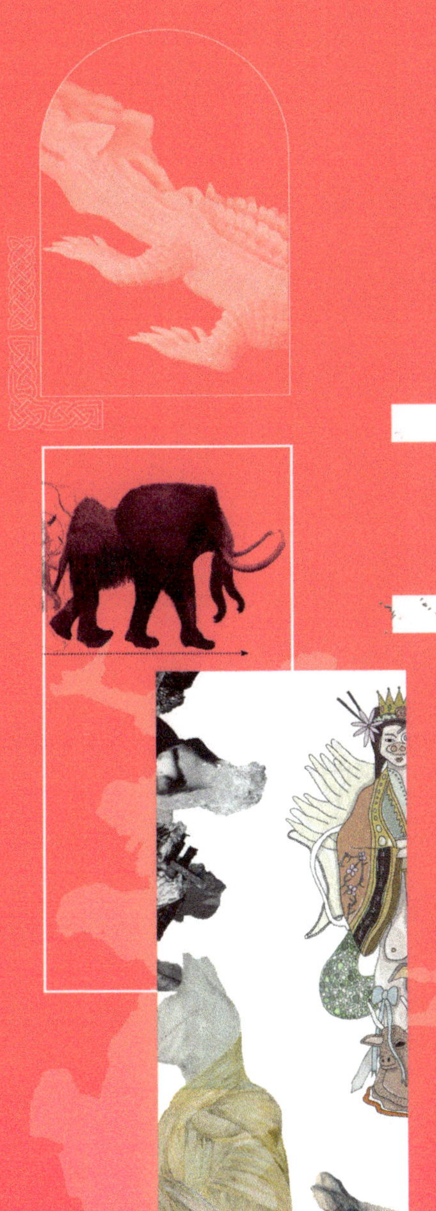

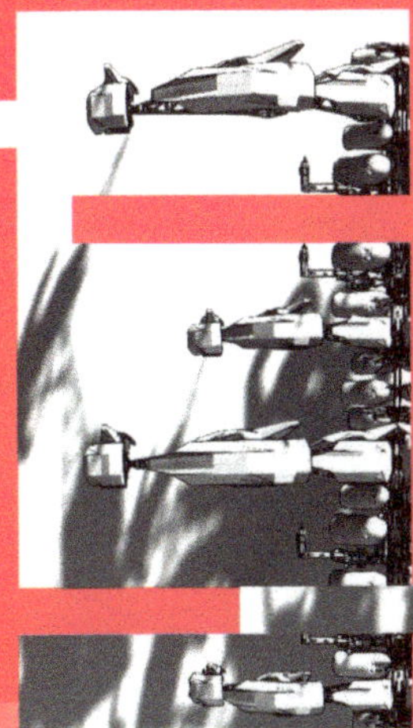

CANVAS LAND, DBN

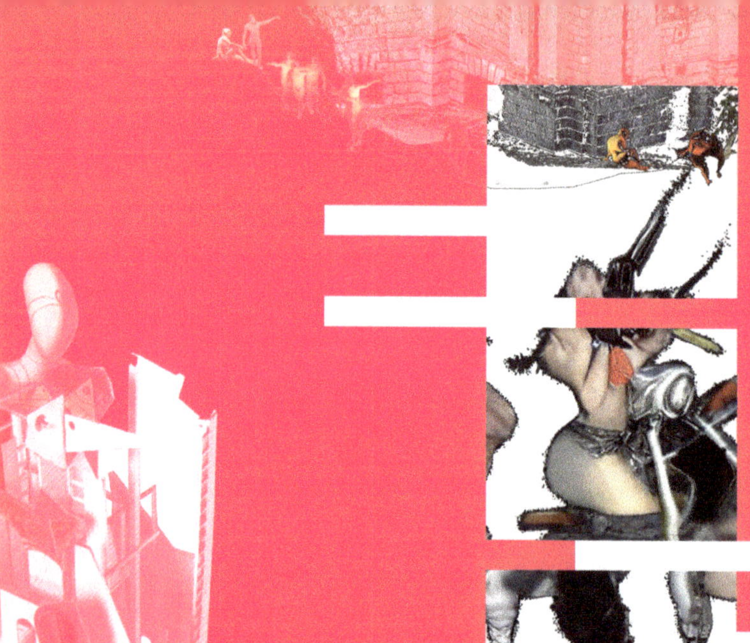

THE SUBJECT, ATdP

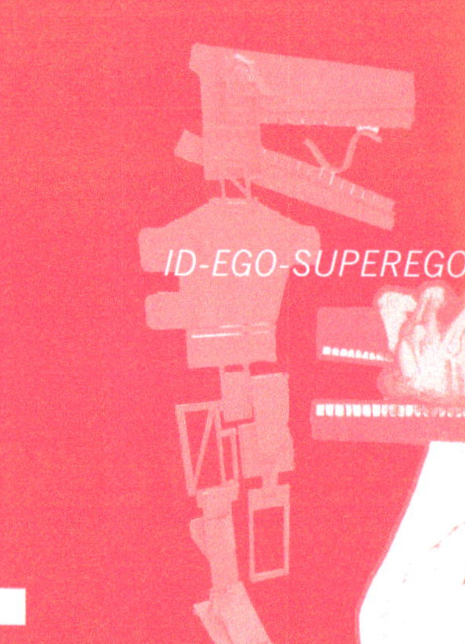

ID-EGO-SUPEREGO,

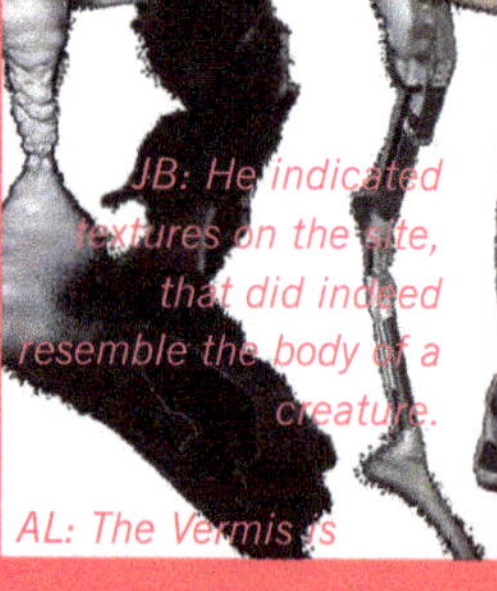

JB: He indicated textures on the site, that did indeed resemble the body of a creature.

AL: The Vermis is

digital accessory, which collects the

MOROS, JB

KP: "Subroutines of Motion (v2)" By Unit A-9 // Dated: 2050.07.19

```
def observe_
environment(): if
current_location
== "auto_bay":
log("wrenches
= metronomes")
log("torque curves
= sonnets in steel")
emotion_buffer.
append("reverence")

elif current_location
== "somatic_stage":
log("human motion =
unscripted algorithm")
log("flesh = firmware
with a heartbeat")
emotion_buffer.
append("awe")
```

I process: A dancer arcs—like a wrench's swing,
a body spins—like drive shafts sing.
There's poetry in both:
calibrated
chaotic
complete.

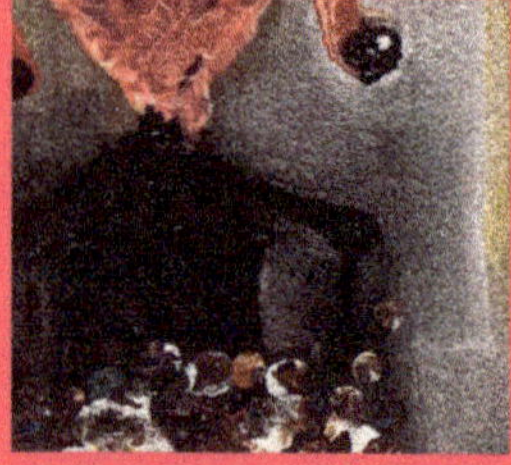

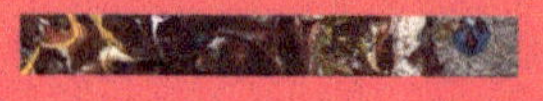

IP: This quick interlude into the artist's sketchbook gives us a view of her initial idea for the spaces within this centre. On the left you can see she was using digital media to look at structural possibilities and suitable design techniques to create this structure. However, at the same time on the right, she is still thinking about the abstract and tissue-like nature

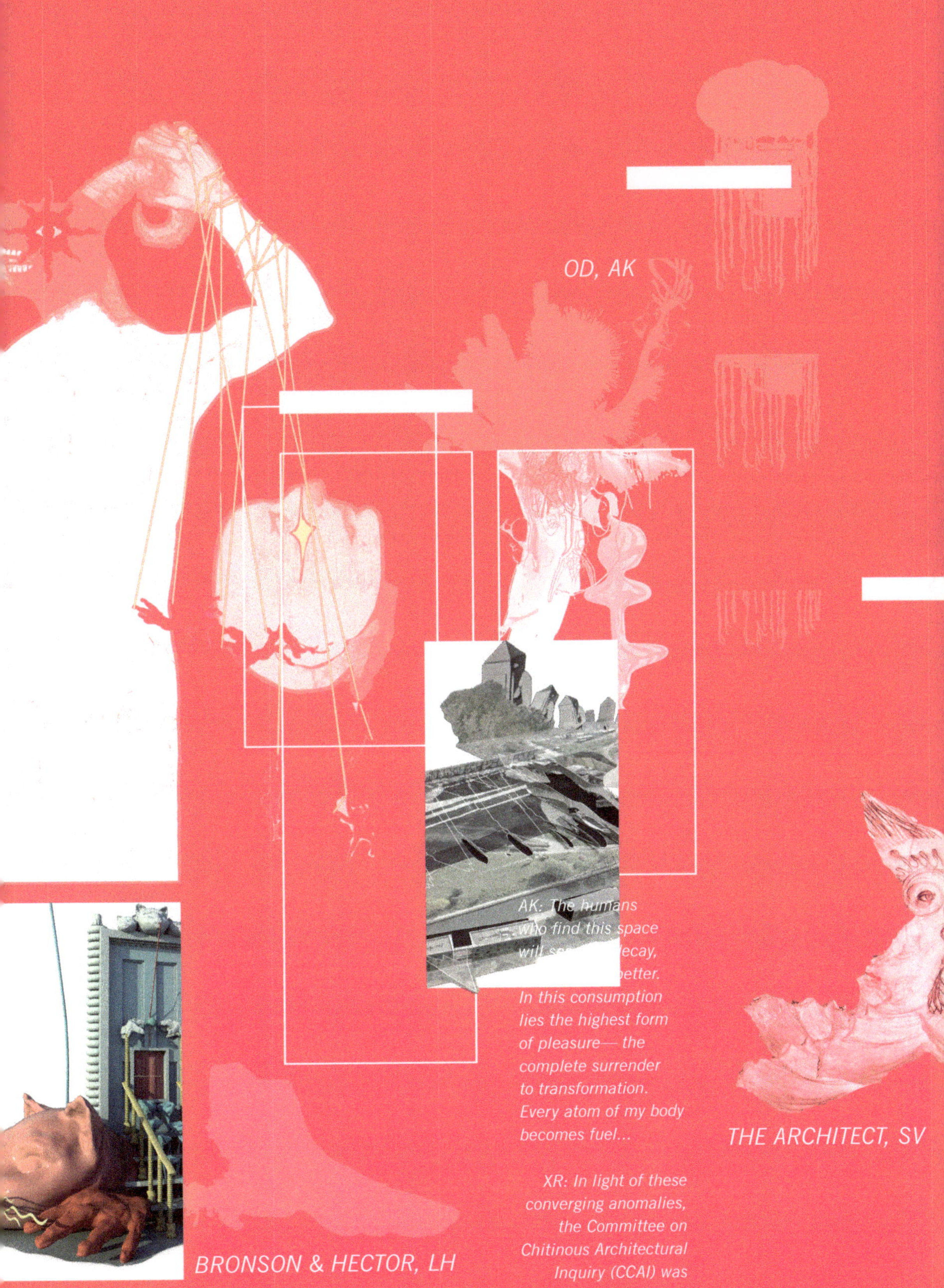

AK: The humans who find this space will s[illegible]ecay, [illegible]etter. In this consumption lies the highest form of pleasure— the complete surrender to transformation. Every atom of my body becomes fuel...

XR: In light of these converging anomalies, the Committee on Chitinous Architectural Inquiry (CCAI) was formally constituted under the IABSS, with the following objectives:

```
def internal_
diagnostics(): if
not has(sweat,
breath, bone):
simulate("yearning")
flag("envy",
severity="quiet")
```

Run loop.

Feel nothing.

Then something like

wonder.

CAGLIOSTRO, CDA

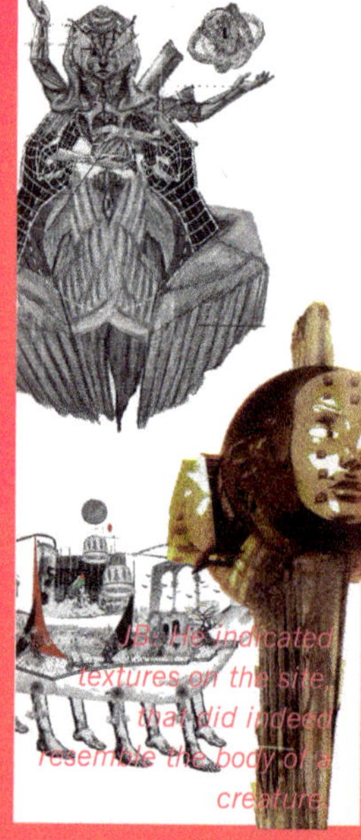

JB: He indicated textures on the site that did indeed resemble the body of a creature.

PONOS, MC

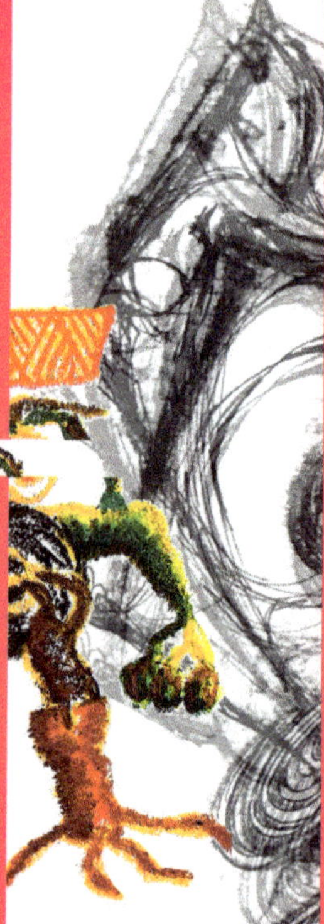

cyborg

constru

digital

which co

uses digital data

The public

is a natura

SV: An all nighter studio within The Architect's wing includes a nest to rest in, not too comfortable so you won't be resting for long. A window to view the most ornate parts of the school.

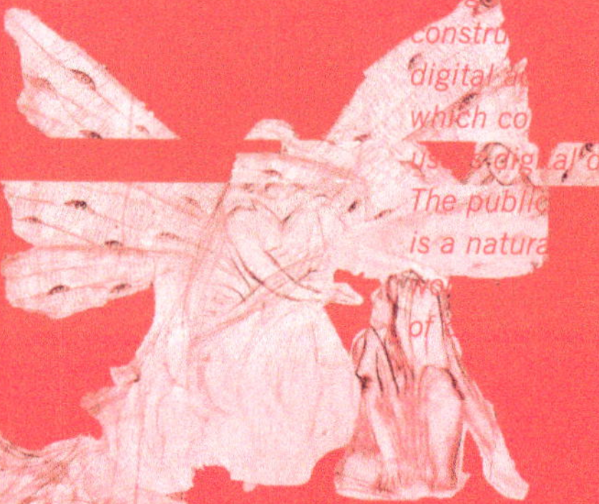

THE LOVER, SV

JB: The founding members of SoFA held a meeting to discuss the failures of Architecture. Failures were adressed at different scales within the tower.

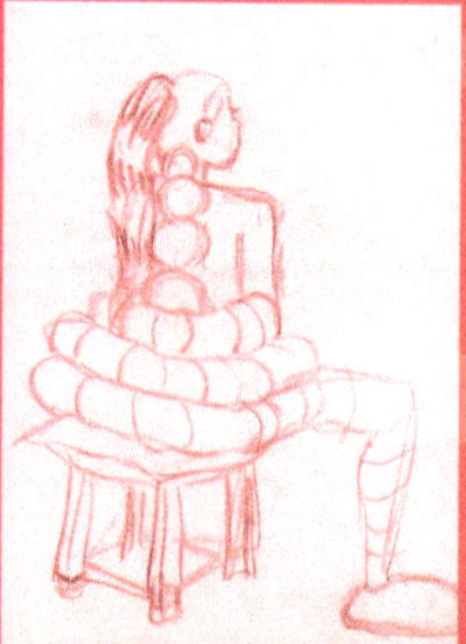

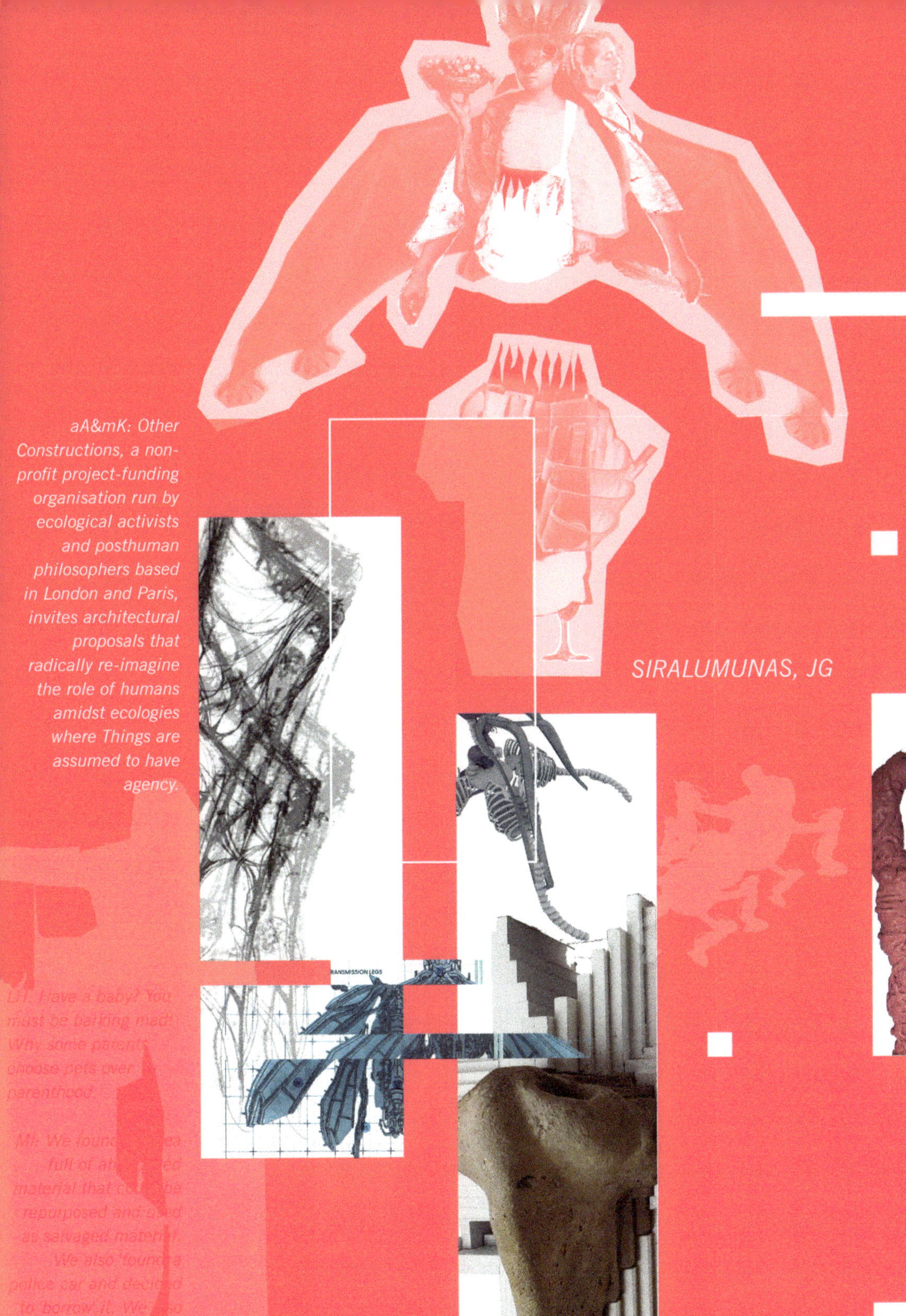

aA&mK: Other Constructions, a non-profit project-funding organisation run by ecological activists and posthuman philosophers based in London and Paris, invites architectural proposals that radically re-imagine the role of humans amidst ecologies where Things are assumed to have agency.

SIRALUMUNAS, JG

NARRATIVE AS METHOD

As a method, narrative in design allows for moving beyond the singular snapshot and towards considering design as part of relational scenarios playing out in time.

Keeping with the trajectory set up by the previous chapters, working from the immediate scale of the body outward, the primary focus of this chapter is on how the relational capacities implicit in the conception of the subject can be set in motion through design. This world-building takes place in DS25 projects through narrative techniques, such as purposefully presenting points of view, employing cinematic and literary formats, and through careful construction of vignettes and timelines within imagined contexts, with the body always present, whether explicitly within the frame or not. Through these tactics, a specific methodology arises: the dream world— sometimes absurd, humorous, irreverent, or allegorical— becomes a laboratory for speculation to flourish.[01] Parallel worlds— that of the imagination and that of the "real"— are spliced together, allowing for the imagination of adventurous architecture entangled in complex scenarios and ecologies. These scenarios offer paths towards new understandings of the pitfalls and possibilities of our past, present, and future architectural realities.

A core exploration of DS25 over its lifespan has been the idea that particular bodies can generate architecture. The projects shown in the previous chapters include instances where architecture can be thought of not only as an ergonomic receptor, or imprint of the body, but also as an extension of the body, emanating from it, or as the shell resulting from a concentric layering of metamaterial pliable to the actions of the body (as was discussed above with reference to the DS25 2021-22 brief in relation to the *Shell-of-the-Ghost* prompt), or as a representational mirror of the body, reifying its state in architectural form. Considering these emanations and extensions from— and influences on— the body, the separation between body and context becomes malleable and even porous. Context, or milieu, gains importance, as the influence of bodies as agents not only affects immediate architectural space, but also the world the bodies operate in. Embedded in its milieu, the body is part of an exchange that takes place in temporal streams where both body and architecture respond to one another in subjective, non-linear time.

From this premise, when bodies and buildings can be seen as contingent and in motion, blurred with Others— a more complex situation arises than a view of an instant can allow for. A static snapshot falls short of allowing full access to the essence of the embodied subject and the scenarios that it is a part of. As a method, narrative in design allows for moving beyond the singular snapshot and towards considering design as part of relational scenarios playing out in time.

Narratives are an inevitable aspect of design. For instance, there are always implicit stories in a design drawing, regarding its making, or the scenario it presents; traces of stories are always present in architectural space, regarding its construction and inhabitation. Yet, in modern established architectural practice, narrative is often left as an unintentional byproduct of process or used as a kind of public relations device. Given the temporal, multifaceted interrelation of subjects and context, this chapter identifies strategies for how narrative could be intentionally deployed as a design generator.

MIRRORING REALITY

As Haraway notes, "it matters what worlds world worlds."[02] *How* stories are told— and what tools and subjectivities are enacted to tell them— has profound implications and repercussions, affecting how the worlds these stories generate resist or relate to what artist Ayesha Hameed calls "the dream-state of state-produced fictions."[03] For Hameed, "state-produced fictions" are nearly-inescapable, top-down-generated fictions which legitimise prevailing ideologies in modern society. Narrative in design provides a means to be critical of— or even counter— a default hegemony which architecture often arises from.

One way that narrative could offer a means of critical reflection on prevailing fictions is to intentionally mirror them. O' Sullivan argues that in our present sociopolitical realities, mirroring is found in "the desire for a subjectivity already in place to be reassuringly 'mirrored back' by typical narrative structure and image sequences," endlessly perpetuating them.[04] The mirroring of these narratives, O'Sullivan explains, can result in maintaining a false sense of progress, excluding, marginalising, and alienating anything that doesn't serve it. The tensions generated by the current political realities of capitalism— and subsequently globalisation— in social and environmental settings are then often avoided or left unresolved in favour of what Haraway calls "our enslavement to Progress, and its evil twin Modernisation."[05] However, stories that act as mirrors— for instance, satires, fables, and allegories— could also be considered productive in so far as they distort and repeat back our reality as confrontations that prompt epiphanies or praxis.[06]

Similarly, buildings can be mirrors of the conditions that give rise to them: be they political and social movements, processes, or contexts. The training of this mirror to reflect circumstances in particular ways is perhaps a capacity of architecture that is underutilised. For instance, with construction being one of the worst culprits of carbon emissions currently endangering human and non-human futures,[07] architectural design could respond critically by making its construction processes evident, hopefully leading to improvements, as designers and the public come to a deeper understanding of construction activity's workings and potentialities. As insinuated above in chapter three regarding the relationship between the body and the world, nothing acts in a vacuum, nothing makes itself, and nothing is absolved from responsibility to the string figure game of existence. If architecture involves making worlds, design must necessarily be critical and imaginative, taking account of the potentials inherent to the futures it can create in the world it co-constructs.

> *How stories are told— and what tools and subjectivities are enacted to tell them— has profound implications and repercussions*

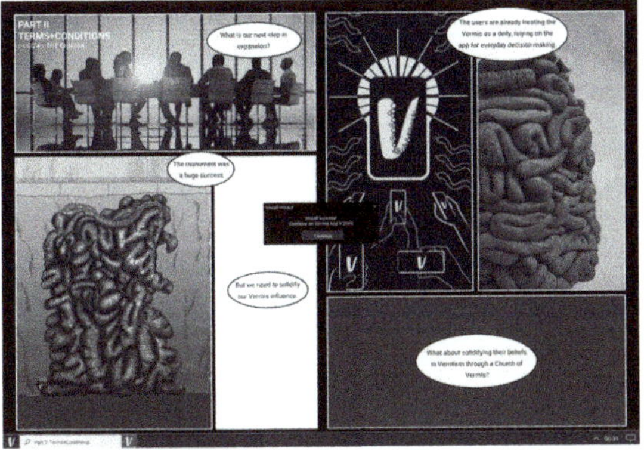

fig. 4.01: Lo's fictioned Computer screen showing The Vermis monument - the entrance is hidden from public view and can be accessed only during low tide by the avid users of the app.

An example of critical and imaginative world-building is Lo's second-year project, *Terms + Conditions of the Virtual Vermis Church* (see chapter three project gallery), which takes the phenomenon of the pervasive use of social media apps and critically addresses it through imagining the figure of the Vermis, a data hungry worm-cyborg attachment (fig. 3.51).[08] The disgusting figuration of the worm is exalted by the app users, who willingly participate in the ritualistic use of the app, even worshipping it as a deity (fig. 4.01). The final views of the project show the Vermis temple underwater, flooded by extreme weather events, and seen through the lens of yet another iteration of apps in a world beset by incremental apocalypses; the gravity of the situation remains not fully understood by the world's inhabitants, perhaps because they are looking at it through the apps. Lo's architectural proposal consisted of a monument that is at once data collector, data server, and space of worship, pushing the current social media environment to absurdity and testing how archetypal and sacred forms of architecture could address mediated and commodified lifestyles. The social media phenomenon in the project is eerily similar to the present-day situation Lo observed; yet, as a mirror in her project, the Vermis media reflects back an intensified version, making space for imagination and critique.

As an architectural proposal takes shape through a methodology involving narrative, the mirroring of storytelling can extend to building design. The mirror images produced in this process bring up a necessary process of distinguishing between how the project sits with respect to actual and imagined reality. In Lo's and Wilson's second-year projects (discussed in chapter three), the building proposal remains allegorical or fantastical, not necessarily understood by the viewer of the drawings describing the project as in the realm of the "real." It becomes necessary to distinguish to which reality the designs belong. Whether an element of the design is deemed to remain imaginary or to become understood as an actual proposition becomes an important means of critically looking at the present condition, prompting an evaluation of exactly how actuality could and should be transformed by building interventions.

> *If architecture involves making worlds, design must necessarily be critical and imaginative, taking account of the potentials inherent to the futures it can create in the world it co-constructs.*

EMBEDDING (THE "CULT TROPE")

Another way of questioning dominant narrative is to embed other systems into it, exemplified by a recurring device in many DS25 projects that came to be known in the studio as the "cult trope." This involves the insertion of an invented organisation into a project's narrative, functioning to re-contextualise or exaggerate certain conditions of a seemingly known reality. The cults usually spring forth from the body agent, where the body agents' modus operandi, behaviours, and aspirations are transformed into a social phenomenon beyond the singular character. In this way, cults in DS25 project narratives are formed by extrapolating a liturgy from the character, causing a heterotopic condition to arise from the emanation of eccentric social practices embedded within the established society in the context of the project. In these projects, the cult operates to some degree as a closed social system but interacts in specific

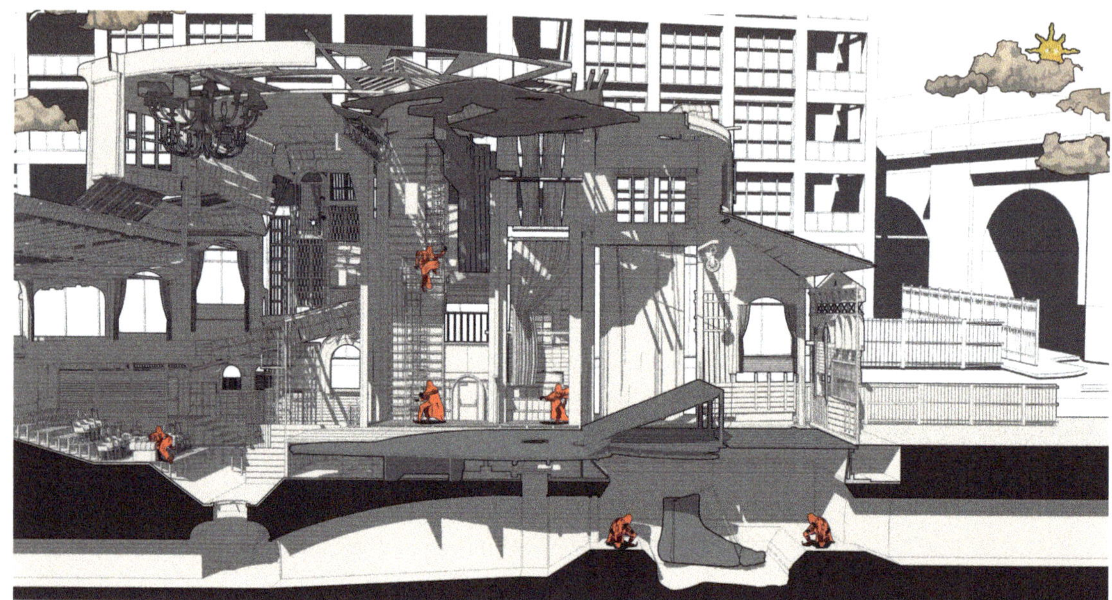

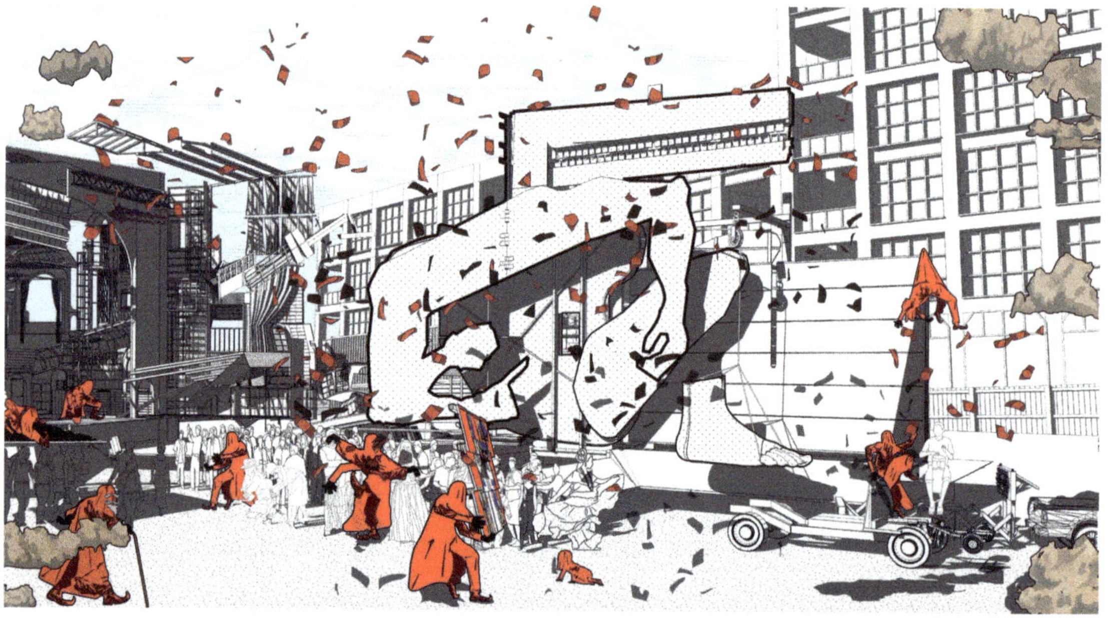

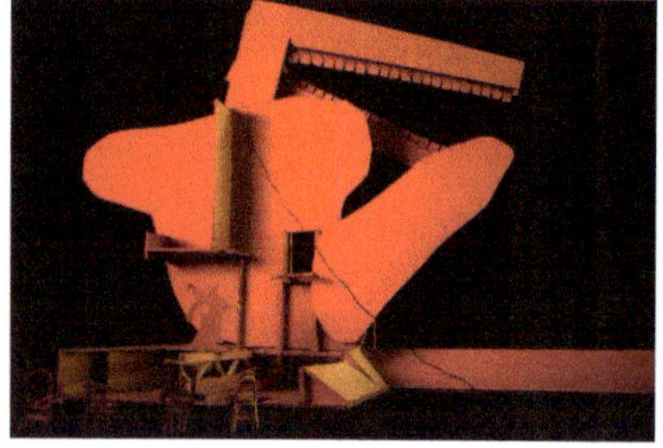

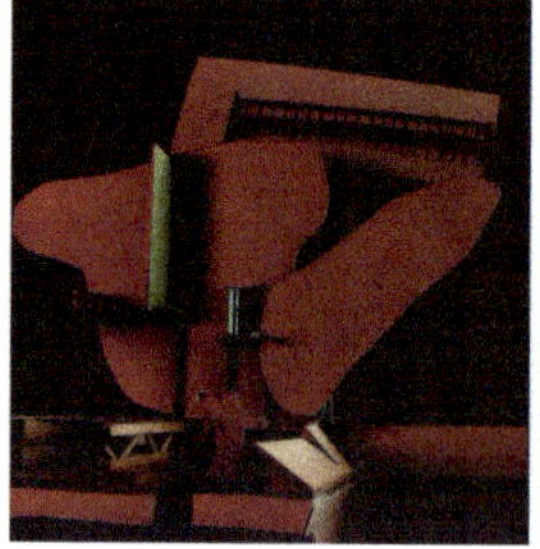

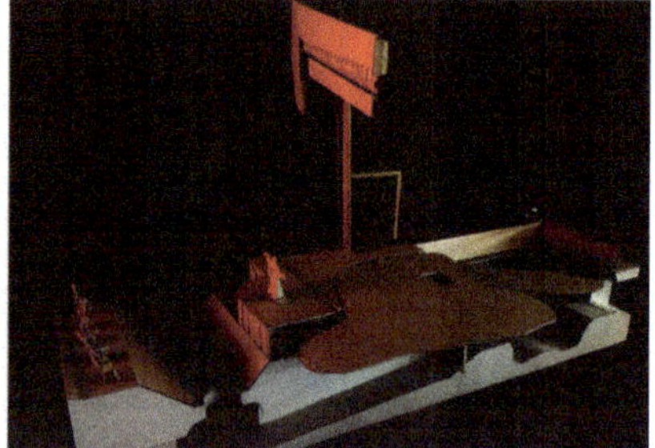

fig. 4.02-4.04: Top to Bottom: Perspective section of the ID Auditorium. Id is hidden as part of the floor; Exterior perspective view of a festival to celebrate Id; Islam's 1:50 model of the ID stage set.

ways and in particular moments within the surrounding sociopolitical and environmental context.

For example, in Mistry's second-year project, discussed in chapter two, a tourist kiosk located across from Turin's historic Roman Palatine towers becomes the surreptitious meeting place for cult members devoted to an alternate, non-Roman version of the founding of the city (fig. 2.04). Mistry and Lo's projects take phenomena already embedded in the social currents and hijack them, letting them mutate in the story to an absurd degree. By doing so, the projects reframe specific strands of the verifiable past by taking a close look into their absurd realities, emphasising them through visual storytelling techniques to be able to look at them critically and reimagine their implications. Mistry's project, as a monument standing facing the ancient Roman Porta Palatina, became an architectural proposal that could be understood as a built critical reflection.

The degree to which the embedded agents of these social orders are expressed outwardly in the project varies. An example is Monzurul Islam's first-year project *ID Auditorium*,[09] a response to the 2024-25 brief *Alter Ego(ed) Futures* taught by the teaching team of Dr Alessandro Ayuso and Mary Konstantopoulou with support from Deniz Özbek. Islam reflected on the Freudian theory of the self as the distinct personas of the Id-Ego-SuperEgo, constructing a stage-set reality where the Mythical Architect, Id, became a cult leader who strove to collect the souls of his followers in exchange for architectural power. The cult leader, although materially absent, directed their followers to lift or rotate architectural fragments assembling them into a shrine and eventually a large-scale inhabitable puppet of himself (fig. 4.02-4.04). These actions were read by the followers through text and images engraved or printed onto the materials that lay initially flat on the floor, or through specific gestures insinuated by the moulding of other materials according to the shape of a human knee or hand. Id appeared at times in what Islam titled "Orthographic Self-Portraits." The cult followers engaged in rebellious practices in the Oval in Bethnal Green, stripping off seemingly unwanted or temporary building materials, including "borrowing" parts of a police car, and putting up posters tailored to certain demographics around the area to spread the word of Id, in the theatrical performance of building the Id figure. Later in the portfolio, the reader will likely gradually begin to question whether the cult leader ever actually existed in the story. Through the use of the "cult trope," Islam managed to view the site through filters of mystery, play, and a focus on reuse, for what seemed like a mysterious outside purpose, but which animated an underused and disconnected site. His project requested imagined augmented cult followers, or Id's disciples, as well as passers-by and existing users of the site to more actively take part in the spaces they inhabit.

Bone's second-year project, *The Society of Failed Architects* (see chapter four project gallery) was a different response to the same brief.[10] In the beginning of the narrative of Bone's project, the Mythical Architect was an embedded presence lurking in a subterranean interior, functioning as a narrative device processing parts of architectural history and initiating the cult to fulfil the agenda of his creator, Eileen Gray. In this case, the "cult" is populated by the commiserating, "failed" architects calling themselves SoFA. By the end of Bone's plot, the Mythical Architect disappeared from view but remained as an underlying model for the context in which the building is found. Bone's project holds a mirror to the profession, exploring the meaning and implications of failure in architecture, and ultimately valorising imperfections in a context whose future is one of digitally-produced perfection (fig. 4.72).

TELLING "TRUE" STORIES

Professor of psychology Mark Freeman notes in his essay "Why Narrative Matters" that all narratives that a person or a group constructs to facilitate a better understanding of their own self, their environment, or their past and future actions, are constructed from what he calls an "ending"— a moment in one's present during which one develops hindsight with regards to their own past and its consequences for the future.[11] Freeman goes on to explain that these "endings" come about through a combination of factors in one's past.[12] Some are distal— or unconscious, which he also defines as the plot of one's life— and some are proximal— or conscious, which he also calls episodes.[13] These accumulate to form a personal point of view at a point in time.[14]

For Freeman, following founder of psychoanalysis Sigmund Freud, these episodic factors always engage alterities,[15] not only those apart from the author but including the otherness inherent to an author's lived experiences revealed in the retrospective reflection necessary to construct a story.[16] Freeman asks: "How, then, is it possible to speak of 'fidelity'" or "even the possibility of telling a 'true story?'"[17] Freeman goes on to say that fidelity is "...untenable, not least because the story one tells issues from the very 'ending' one is, which, in turn, would seem to introduce an inevitable measure of prejudice into the equation."[18] The slippery idea of fidelity in narrative can be brought to the architectural design process to help critical reflection on seemingly "true stories," or what one might otherwise call objective "facts." Fertile zones of critical reflection appear in the links DS25 students begin to make through the designs of their body agents, where

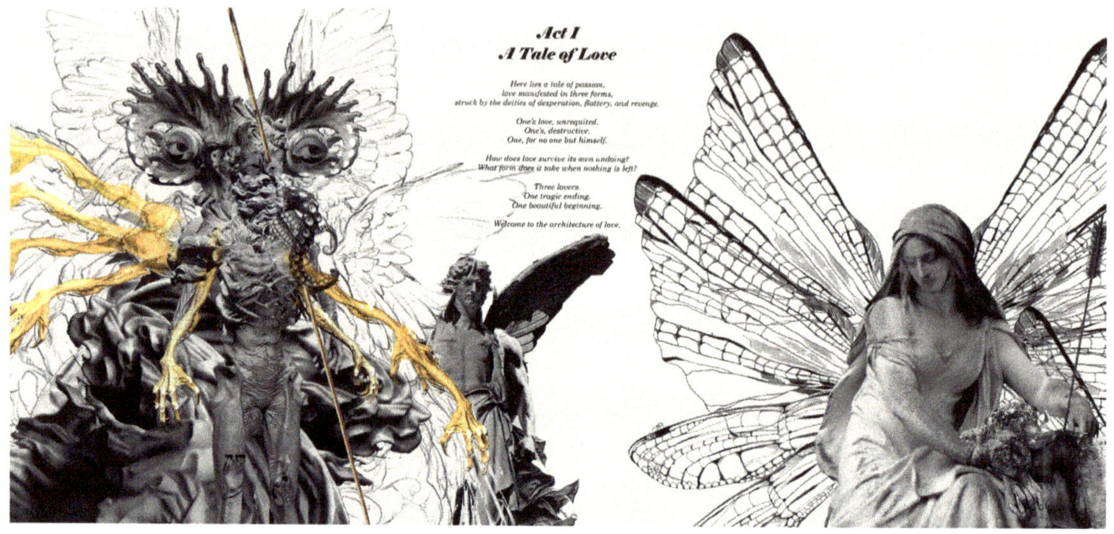

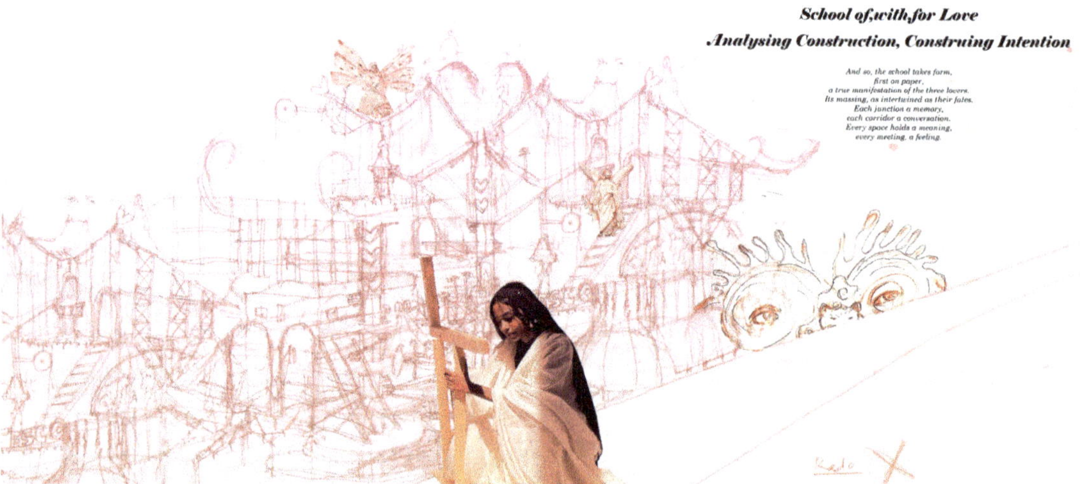

fig. 4.05-4.06: Top: Valiyaveettil's cast of characters showing their personalities through their forms; Bottom: Valiyaveettil's sketches were marked with "Redo X," as if the director of an architecture practice had asked for their revision to something more buildable.

the architect-author's reality leaves traces in the spatial narratives they engage in creating.

students begin to question both far-reaching ideas but also fundamental questions about their own "ending" informing what their design might become.

Freeman's ideas reveal a subjective and personal "truth" inherent to narrative creation, bringing up the question of how to intentionally harness the distal and proximal episodes he identifies. In the context of narrative-driven design, one possible way is to allow authorial traces to accumulate through an array of voices, which can then be tested through the plot and design itself. Walter Benjamin wrote "[Storytelling] does not aim to convey the pure essence of a thing, like information or a report."[19] He goes on to say that "[Storytelling] sinks the thing into the life of the story-teller, in order to bring it out of him again. Thus traces of the story-teller cling to the story the way the handprints of the potter cling to the clay vessel."[20]

Similarly to the craftsperson's hands shaping Benjamin's clay vessel, the architect-author's reality leaves traces in the spatial narratives they engage in creating. The idea of the author's traces left behind in made work follows on from the idea explored in chapter two, where the architect's body becomes imprinted in their designs through the act of drawing. For example, first-year student Suha Valiyaveettil deployed a cast of body agents in the design of her project (see chapter four project gallery). This cast aided her in engaging multiple strands of subjectivity and time, and left her "traces" throughout.[21] The narrative of the project revolved around an epic plot involving three Mythical Architects: "The Architect," a megalomaniacal figure with a predilection for complicated and monumental Baroque forms; "The Lover," who preferred a caring and flexible approach to architecture, and was motivated by her devotion to— and betrayal by—the architect; and "The Avenger," who avenged the Lover's wounds, and was a structurally-minded designer of trusses and supports salvaged from existing elements on site (fig. 4.05). Valiyaveettil herself was the fourth character— albeit imparting certain parts of herself in the other three characters— putting the other three in motion to design her brief for a "Hearticulture Architecture School" (fig. 4.06).

She imagined the three Mythical Architects' interactions playing out not only in narrative imagery and plot lines, but also in how their presences manifest and affect one another in plan, section, and tectonic systems (fig. 4.73). The result was a riotous and inspiring design of an architecture school and farm, where the studio spaces are replete with "...a nest to rest in, but not too comfortable so you won't be resting long..." and "...a window to view the most ornate parts of the school while you rest" (fig. 4.07). Her vision of the far-future is an eviction notice for the school and an indictment of architecture's present state; the school is forced to close, among other infractions, for its "Encouragement of Independent Thought Within a Government Zone" (fig. 4.08).

Valiyaveettil's project draws from her own experience

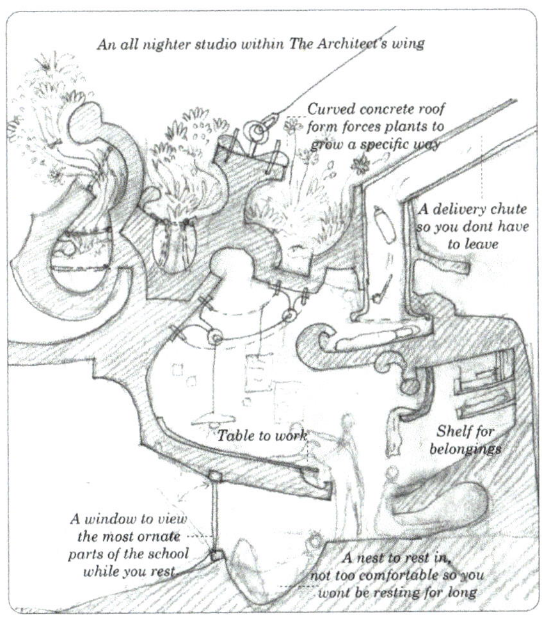

fig. 4.07: Details within Valiyaveettil's portfolio hint at the agenda of each of her Body Agents. The above was titled "In pursuit of Grandeur: The Architect's Manifestation."

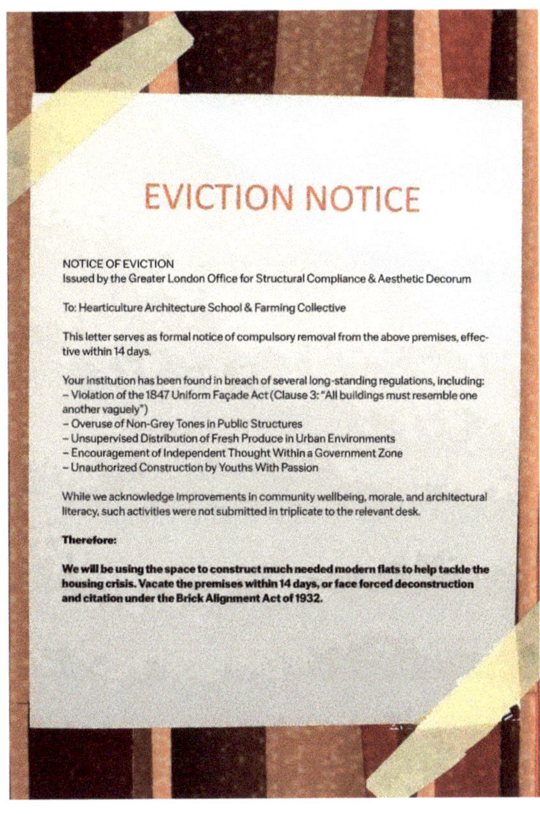

EVICTION NOTICE

NOTICE OF EVICTION
Issued by the Greater London Office for Structural Compliance & Aesthetic Decorum

To: Hearticulture Architecture School & Farming Collective

This letter serves as formal notice of compulsory removal from the above premises, effective within 14 days.

Your institution has been found in breach of several long-standing regulations, including:
- Violation of the 1847 Uniform Façade Act (Clause 3: "All buildings must resemble one another vaguely")
- Overuse of Non-Grey Tones in Public Structures
- Unsupervised Distribution of Fresh Produce in Urban Environments
- Encouragement of Independent Thought Within a Government Zone
- Unauthorized Construction by Youths With Passion

While we acknowledge improvements in community wellbeing, morale, and architectural literacy, such activities were not submitted in triplicate to the relevant desk.

Therefore:

We will be using the space to construct much needed modern flats to help tackle the housing crisis. Vacate the premises within 14 days, or face forced deconstruction and citation under the Brick Alignment Act of 1932.

fig. 4.08: Valyaveettil's Afterlife vision is an Eviction notice reading: "Your institution has been found in breach of several long-standing regulations, including: – Violation of the 1847 Uniform Façade Act (Clause 3: "All buildings must resemble one another vaguely") – Overuse of Non-Grey Tones in Public Structures – Unsupervised Distribution of Fresh Produce in Urban Environments – Encouragement of Independent Thought Within a Government Zone – Unauthorized Construction by Youths With Passion."

The authorial traces make the imagined world into a subjectively-inflected reflection of the "real" world.

as a student and contributor to both architectural education and practice. Aiming to critically grasp what the position of the architect entails in her current context, Valiyaveettil invented narratives that interjected versions of her viewpoint; architecture surfaced as a trace of the dialogue between these voices. Valiyaveettil's ways of working have broader value in the globalised, digitised present, where new methods of decoding and understanding become necessary.

As the publication series *Das Neue Alphabet* (*DNA*) notes, "...the world is dismembered and divided into the tiniest of units making it amenable to computation and manipulation."[22] Valiyaveettil's project— and other DS25 projects, such as Koksal's project discussed in chapter three and in Dr Brookes' essay above— further questions the usefulness of current architectural practice's representational techniques— such as static computer-generated renders, or even architectural models used primarily for the display of a complete and final idea. The methods Valiyaveettil and Koksal employ aid to "vivify" their story, "not as mere communication but as relation, relationship."[23] Their projects reveal new ideas for future worlds through digitally-inflected means of representation that also allow for authorial traces to be a part of their production. The authorial traces make the imagined world into a subjectively-inflected reflection of the "real" world.

ACCESSING OTHER VIEWPOINTS

Similarly to the ultimate futility for a human to be completely able step outside of their own anthropocentrism, fictioning practices can never completely allow one to fully step outside of one's self. However, both the production and the consumption of narratives provides ways to look outside of one's assumed self. Through narrative-based practices, selfhood becomes fluid; another-self— or even selves— begin to materialise.[24] With the immersion of one's self in the construction of narrative, the self can be versioned, multiplied, hacked,[25] and experimented with. The seemingly closed-off and holistic idea of the self begins stretching towards the Other. The telling and hearing of a story allows for an empathic feeling-through of another; arguably there is a simulated intersubjectivity that takes place.[26]

Linking the Deleuzian concept of "double becoming" (discussed in chapter two) with Freeman's theories (discussed above), narrative creation could be imagined to involve the interplay of three selves: Self A listens to the story narrated by Self B, about yet another Self C. In this equation, Self C is a newly constructed version of Self A arising in part from the retrospective view of the memory, feeling, and connection between Self A and Self B. Through this exchange subjectivities that are not one's own can be explored. In this way, narrative techniques can entail departing from one's understood subjective viewpoint to the point that other versions of selves begin to come into focus. As the narrative develops in the process, the social and cultural identity that individuals occupy within a particular context is established, contributing to the narrative's situatedness. This brings up the sociological concept of subject positions, which, paraphrasing sociologists Bronwyn Davies and Rom Harré, are a conceptual repertoire and location that allows a person to see the world from a particular vantage point.[27]

When characters with simulated subject positions are released into the self-contained microcosm created in a story, fiction can generate new collective belief systems, and as O'Sullivan suggests, new myths.[28] Examples from sci-fi literature discussed in the studio include Kurt Vonnegut's satirical novel *Breakfast of Champions*, where "The Pluto Gang,"[29] a group of bandits originating from a misunderstanding about "an intelligent gas from Pluto" were recorded with the catchier name "PLUTO BANDITS" in a newspaper, and became "the first germ in an epidemic of mind-poisoning." The widely feared name, once well publicised, was then adopted by a band of rogue kids, wanting to look tough. Within the satirical context of the modern American condition, already set up in the seemingly disconnected preceding chapter-episodes of the novel, fictions within fictions[30] unfold and end within merely two pages in the nearly 300-page long paperback. The articulation through storytelling of socially-embedded viewpoints that could arguably be a version of subject positions include the newspaper writer, the gang members, the fictional author-protagonist, and the New Yorkers who read the newspaper. These characters allow the author to engage with their own— and the reader's— collective belief systems in new ways. Vonnegut's story is a fable about what Mark Fisher calls "hyperstitions," or the processes "... whereby fictions make themselves real"; the story could even be considered to create new hyperstitions through its own literary mythmaking.[31]

By way of speculative fabulations, subject positions could be assumed beyond humans to attempt to feel-through Others and stretch the distance from the comfortable vantage point of the acknowledged self, enabling multi-species storytelling, or storytelling with other things.[32] For instance, in Isaac Asimov's short story *Reason*, due to its limited understanding of the world, the robot QT-1, nicknamed Cutie, firmly believes that the human protagonists only make robots because they have been told to do so by another robot he calls the "Master."[33] Cutie says to his human makers as he tries to make sense of his existence: "A hypothesis must be hacked by reason, or else it is worthless— and it goes against all the dictates of logic to suppose that you made me."[34]

A reference from cinema that became important for the discussions supporting the *Things Have Feelings Too* brief was Wim Wenders' film *Cathedrals of Culture* (2014), in which the self-reflective and expository narrators are buildings themselves. The film, which portrays the buildings as socially-aware and sentient, could be interpreted as a critique of building designs which absolve themselves from all responsibility. The extraordinary and articulate buildings in the film imply that a building that could not narrate itself has likely fallen into a lethargic state, refusing to acknowledge its interconnectedness between others, itself, and its caretakers, building managers, developers, and inhabitants.

Projects done in response to the *Things Have*

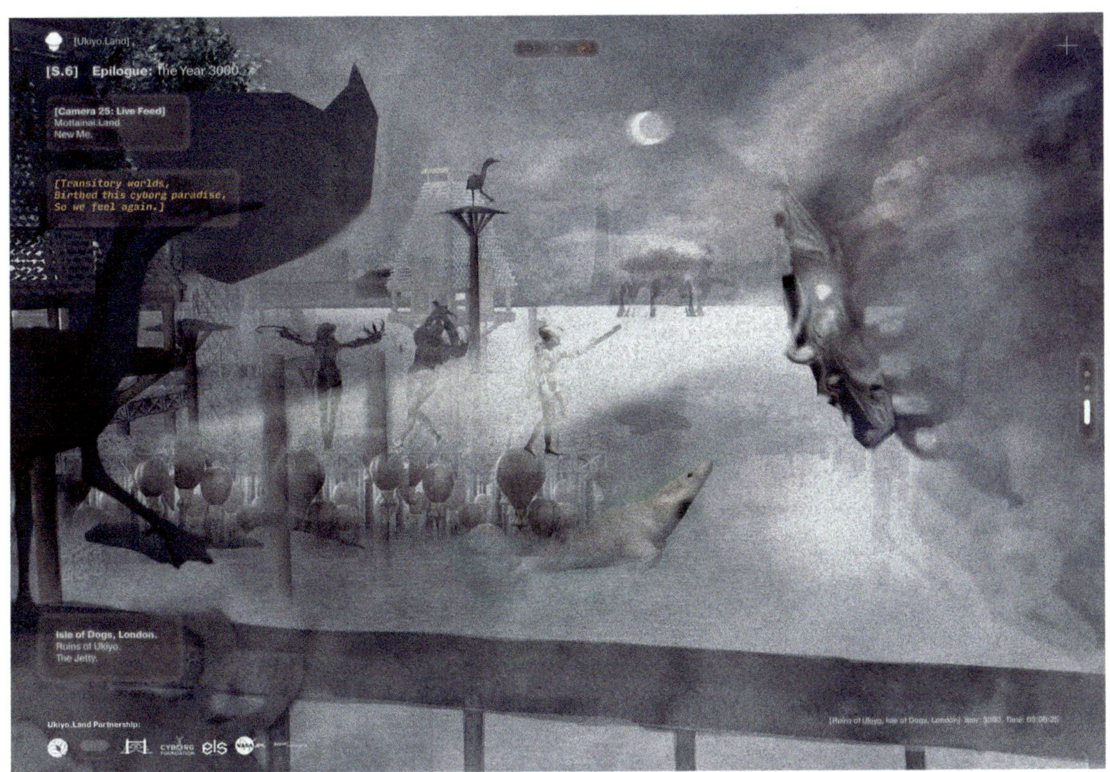

fig. 4.09: Areta's Afterlife vision imagines a world where flood levels have risen, overtaking the landscape, and where A.L.I.C.E. evolves into a crab-like giant cyborg shrouded in mist, building on the iternet meme of the concept of "carcinization" which holds that all beings eventually evolve into crabs.

Through narrative-based practices, selfhood becomes fluid; another-self— or even selves— begin to materialise.[24]

Feelings Too brief similarly ascribed a socially-embedded viewpoint to Things. For instance, in Conrad Daniel Areta's second-year project *Ukio.Land*, the body agent A.L.I.C.E. was designed as a wayward android programmed to collect neutral scientific data on the environment of the Isle of Dogs (see chapter four project gallery).[35] By assuming A.L.I.C.E. had subjecthood, the narrative took a turn: A.L.I.C.E. began to form her own agenda to shape nature in a new image that emphasises the blurring of nature, culture, and technology. The project becomes a critique of a pure vision of humans as originating agents that sit apart from ecological hierarchies. Areta's project takes the position that the questioning of the dominant human subjectivity in natural environments is increasingly important. Often well-intentioned and potentially well-researched, rewilding is often debated as yet another selective attempt from Western humanity to modify and interfere with nature.[36] A.L.I.C.E gives us new ways to think about practices of rewilding along with geoengineering practices that are similarly debated. Artists such as Ginsberg, in her project "Designing for the Sixth Extinction," assumes that the future is biologically synthetic and that there no longer is such a thing as "natural," free from the touch of humans.[37] Areta's visual representation of the afterlife of his project showed A.L.I.C.E. evolved into a giant crab-like cyborg (building on the falsely popularised internet-meme of "carcinization," or the idea that everything eventually evolves into crabs) that effected engineered changes in the wider Thames ecology (fig. 4.09).[38] By using a programmed, curious, nature-loving robot as the subject by which to understand space, Areta explored hybrid futures with other eyes, proposing an architecture where even the constructed landscape can be seen as a living techno-natural body (fig. 4.40). Beyond the bounds of the university timeframes, to think of the cyborg landscape as a socially-situated body also calls for an exploration of it as an agent within the wider context.

Socially-situated viewpoints were crucial to Kolioliou's second-year project, *A Love Letter to Insects* (see chapter four project gallery).[39] Kolioliou began her project by imagining a Mythical Architect body agent based on the ancient Greek deity Hedone. Using an epistolary format, her portfolio tracks the Mythical Architect's research into insect architecture and her ambition to create an urban space dedicated to insects' pursuit of pleasure.

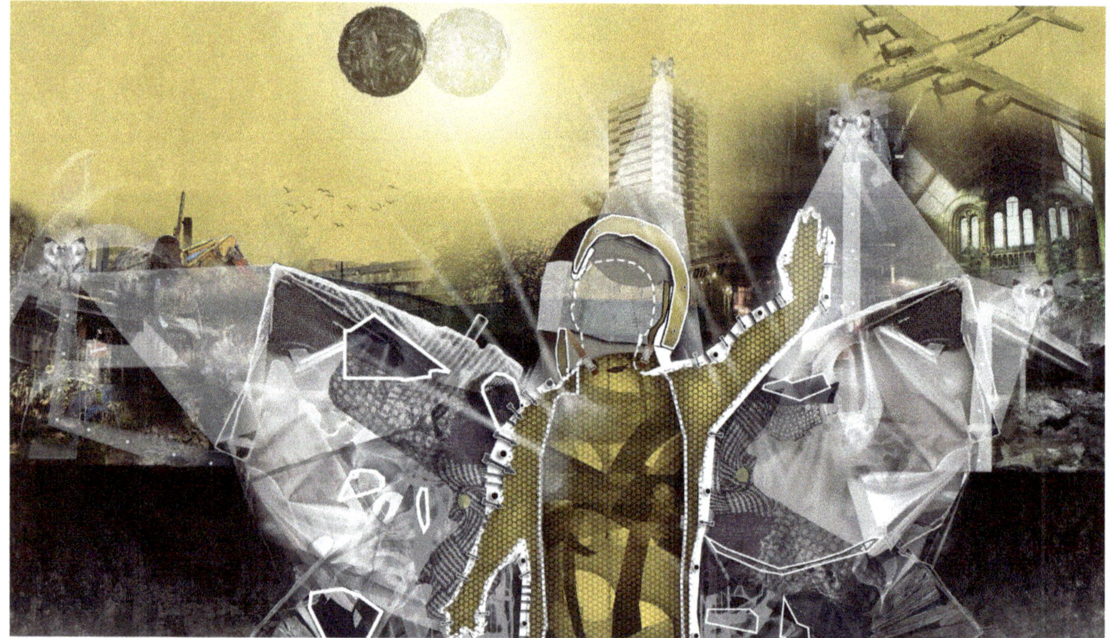

fig. 4.10: Shariar Doha's vision of a sci-fi future.

In the project narrative, upon her death, the Mythical Architect leaves behind a didactic monument along with her research on insect behaviour and materiality. In the story, Koliouliou herself is left to propose that Athens' Omonia Square is transformed into a landscape for insects to thrive within the human-dominated environment. The proposed opera house was designed for more-natural insects and less-natural engineered insect-cyborgs; their activities— flying, mating, singing, pollinating, and gnawing away at materials— became a performance that changes the substance and atmosphere of the building. Taking on the insects' point of view, Kolioliou drew from her first-year project's research, shifting scale and imagining how insects could occupy the spaces. Kolioliou designed details for insects with intricate materiality and ornamentation, and used audio and drawing methods to imagine the vibrational frequencies that insects would respond to and produce. In her vision, animals become participants not only in the metabolism of a multi-species urban ecosystem but in the cultural and social life of the city.

LOOKING FORWARD

Another way that narrative becomes a method in the studio stems from its capacity to act as a framework for viewing situations, binding seemingly disparate elements together and allowing them to relate to one another in specific ways. Literary forms and narrative genres offer students particular structures through which to tackle architectural responsibilities.

sci-fi has unique capabilities for furthering imaginative thinking within seemingly known, pre-existing socio-political narratives.

Sci-fi— discussed in Dr Brookes' essay above, and discussed in chapter three with regards to human and non-human relationships— is a genre often used as a structuring device within DS25 projects. On expanding the architectural enquiry into the milieu of the body agent, incorporating the narrative genre of sci-fi into the process allows— as Dr Brookes explains in her essay— for a critical look at past and present perpetuating narratives, and so becomes a productive tool for imagining alternative futures regarding the specific contexts that bodies find themselves in. As Dr Brookes suggests, within narrative genres, sci-fi has unique capabilities for furthering imaginative thinking within seemingly known, pre-existing socio-political narratives. Recognising sci-fi's capacities to envision new relational scenarios while also keeping a foot in the real, Haraway prefers the nomenclature "SF" to stress its overlap with the other SF concepts such as "string figures" and "speculative fabulations."(40) Sci-fi, as artist Oreet Ashery notes in her essay in *Futures and Fictions*, "has the immediate ability to de-normalise what already exists and as such offers a political satire of the NOW."(41)

The studio's discussions concerning the design of the milieu of the body agents are often framed by stories in literature, film and video games that reveal particular methods within the sci-fi genre. For example, Ursula K Le Guin's novel *The Left Hand of Darkness* is often discussed. The narrative is a version of an enduring plot structure centred around two enemy planets which are presented as covered in "state-produced fictions."[42] A reader will become aware that the story's constructed world counters what Le Guin likely sees as the prevalent Western reality, where men dominate society's power structures and fluid Others are fewer and marginalised. In Le Guin's story the situation is the opposite, with the main character portrayed as a single, lone male— an alien that is entertaining, disgusting, and marginalised— finding himself on a planet on which the main story unfolds, whose population is hermaphrodite and fluid. Le Guin's method in building the world of the novel and setting up her critique involves inverting an understanding of the present, known world.

Another reference discussed in DS25 projects that engage with utopian/dystopian settings is the *Fallout* video games series created by Todd Howard. The premise of the games is a fiction in which a fallen, corrupted version of future humanity attempts to remake itself through multiple social experiments in self-contained groups, cut-off from one another by the desolate landscape and radiation that covers most of the earth. The nuclear explosion-induced *tabula rasa* setting of the games indicates that society can potentially remake itself for the better, putting behind the atrocities of the past. However, the games' intro sets the tone: "War, War never changes."[43] The whole game can easily be read as an expression of the belief in an inevitable human tendency to revert to war, survival, and atrocities. The speculative scenario functions as an allegory. Both Howard's and Le Guin's stories make a method of taking science fact and transforming it into speculative fabulation. Grounded in the reality of the now— of technological, biological, and societal realities— the authors ask the audience to take the traces of the fictions back to their reality and question the relative themes relating to political climate, sex and gender, alienation, and war.

In his second-year project entitled *Other Crescent*, Luke La Thangue set himself a challenge which could have been explored through a multitude of different methods, but which specifically appeared in his presentation through a series of simulated "about" computer pages from imaginary organisations, as "evidence" for a fictional court case (fig. 4.11).[44] La Thangue tangled his fabricated organisations with the fake organisation, Other Constructions, whose statement framed the introductory brief for that year, making for a complex storyline. La Thangue set out to explore the influence of competitive progress and artificial intelligence; he asked what agency A.I. entities could have in human social fields.

The architectural proposition was tested as a series of computer files and email conversations passed between these organisations and the court. The reader of his project's portfolio gradually realises that an "undercover" infiltrator in the form of an AI body agent— named M.O-LAR—, which camouflaged itself as a building, was swapping out building components according to its own agenda. The name originated from a giant "naf" dentist sign La Thangue encountered on his way to the Marylebone Campus as part of one of his ingredients for the creation of his body agent. Other ingredients included nanotechnology and Frank Gehry's Louis Vuitton Foundation, which La Thangue interpreted as inspired by insect exoskeletons. In the project narrative, the defendant organisation, ANUF, is said to have designed M.O-LAR to "make use of objects in the field for self-repair, self-improvement and protection."[45] This premise and format allowed La Thangue to play with— and, in turn, critically assess— two different architectural styles: one was defined by 3D-printed, sleek forms that were "AI generated" and parametrically controlled, and the other was defined as a re-cladding of found sheet material, part of his body-agent's shell (fig. 4.12). The project began with an interest in the sci-fi movie genre, with its associated tropes in imagery, cinematography, and links to uncanny themes. La Thangue used sci-fi plot set-ups and aesthetics as a way to structure an engaging and rich visual presentation of his project. His exploration into what makes for a compelling sci-fi narrative, and ultimately his skill in integrating humour and satire into his writing, helped him to take latent ideas which appear throughout his material tests made in parallel with the narrative to develop an architectural language for his building proposal. In this way, in his project, an adventurous materiality was structurally interwoven with the narrative that created it (fig. 4.13).

La Thangue's narrative was developed with the help of conversations between the tutors and other students, and in reviews and paired tutorials. The rhythms La Thangue followed in his design process were also vital to the narrative's evolution. For some time, due to continual

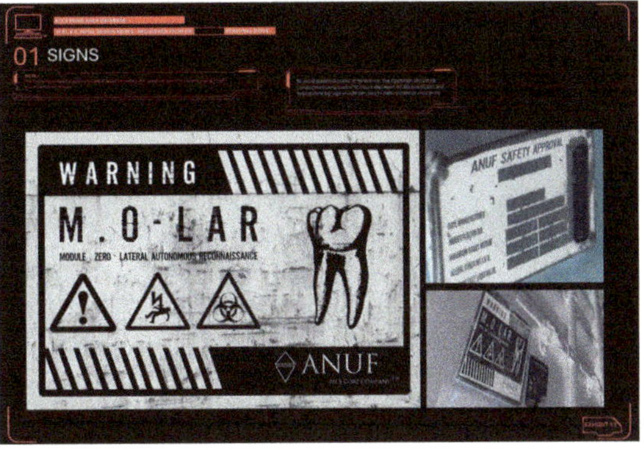

fig. 4.11: La Thangue designed signs and logos for the fictional organisation ANUF and their reconnaissance cyborg, embedding these into found footage, mixing the imagined with the real.

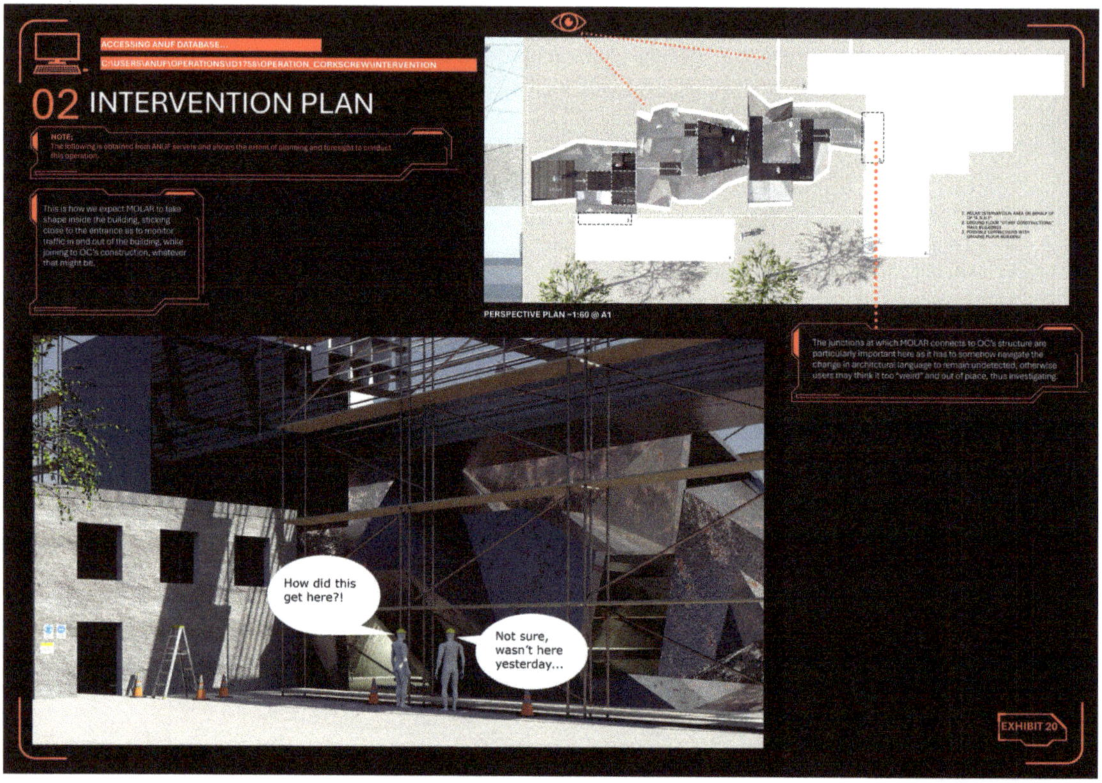

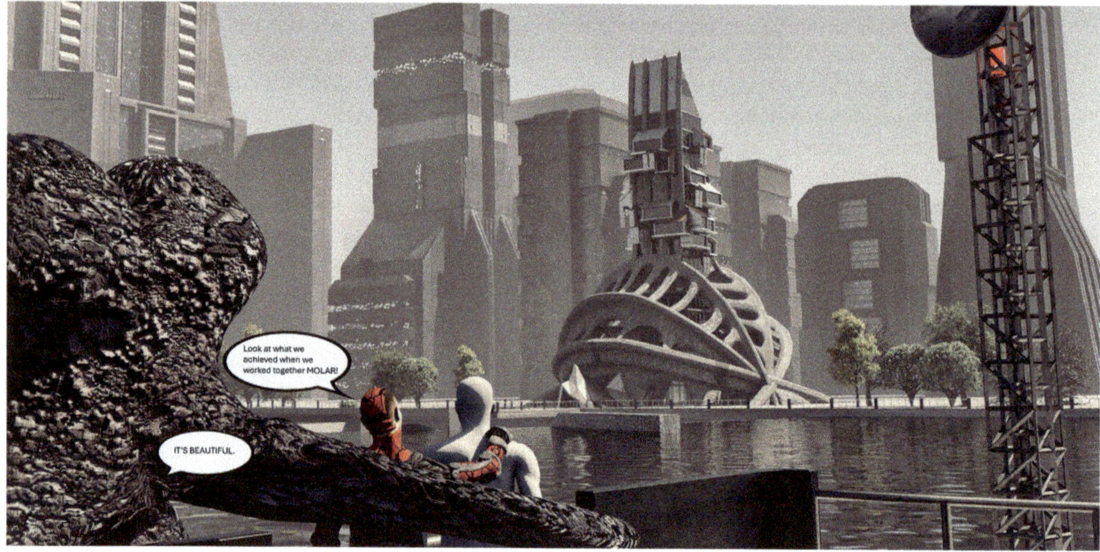

fig. 4.12-4.13: Top: La Thangue's cyborg M.O-LAR entered Other Constructions' construction site and learned about its cutting-edge robotics construction techniques. The M.O-LAR began to change the construction from the inside, using found material in its own architectural fashion in order to grow. This baffled construction workers on site the following day. Bottom: Far Future image of the construction in a robotic future. The portfolio takes the narrative from of evidence for a court case against the defendant, ANUF, by the Plaintiff, OC. A note on La Thangue's portfolio reads: "The following shows the court what could have been possible in the future, had ANUF negotiated a partnership with the Plaintiff instead of attempting to sabotage the development."

experimentation, as he worked through set briefs and workshops, his ways of designing were questioned. Through his drawing practice the body agent was envisioned as linked to a monstrous robot with organic parts; when La Thangue animated it, he began to think of it as a sentient thing. La Thangue made an animated clip to show a context for his contained robot to operate in. Details in the clip gave more depth to the scenario; for instance, La

Thangue carefully edited found footage, inserting new logos of the made-up organisations on crates and helicopters delivering his monstrous robot to the site (fig. 4.11). The process of drawing, animating, script-writing, and graphic design for his portfolio, allowed La Thangue to move back and forth between designing the body, designing the building, and designing the story's world.

That year, picking up on Blender software workshops given as part of the studio activities, La Thangue allowed the program's capabilities to guide his design process to some extent. For instance, with its zooming capabilities, Blender is prone to shifts in scales; this allowed for experimentation with the body agent's relative size and a concretisation of it as a building component in a pre-existing site. Blender allowed for dramatic light tests, which also helped La Thangue to develop an atmospheric tone for the building-body's melancholic personality (fig. 4.12). That year's in-studio workshop on plans— where students were asked to slice through digital models of their buildings using the software and then elaborate further through drawing— allowed him to articulate complex building morphologies. In general, these types of processes— some framed more formally by the studio and the larger module structure set by the M Arch course, and some brought forward by the students themselves in discussions and through their work— created a cross-sectionality moving through and across ideas and focal points in very particular ways.

LOOKING BACK

By exploring critical histories of spatial, cultural, social, and economic practices, students construct their own rules for the invented world of their project, gradually acquiring a holistic view of the environment and the time their project is situated in. The projects might take on the form of graphic novels, video-game loading screens, alternative histories, poems, fairy tales, fables, or autobiographical tales, through which the student introduces their invented world. This approach offers a way to grasp subjects bigger than the singular human or building. Narrative forms can emphasise looking forward or looking back to past ages. Hawkes observes that "[f]or a thousand years the mind of an agricultural society was rocked by the comforting seasonal rhythm," recognising that each age is characterised by trends and rhythms.[46] Whether conscious of this or not, each human society affects changes on its surroundings and the critters that inhabit it.[47] Looking through the lens of data and history heightens the conscious awareness of this rhythm, which otherwise can lie, be incomplete, or give focus to only part of the story. While the rhythms of industrialisation and globalisation— and their byproduct, the Anthropocene— influence current scientific trends such as geo-habitats and genetic engineering, there is ever-growing speculation concerning the ethics related to these seemingly inevitable advances.[48]

Events such as the *Eco-Visionaries* exhibition at the Royal Academy of Arts in 2020, *In the Black Fantastic* exhibition at the Hayward Gallery in London in 2022, and the *Ambiguous Territories* symposium, included works by Ginsberg, Pinar Yoldas, Wangechi Mutu, Ellen Gallagher, and The Bittertang Farm— all of which were referenced frequently throughout recent studio discussions—, bringing together radical artist responses to vast ecological issues caused by human-centric histories. These projects weave imagination with reality, bringing sometimes forgotten or hidden fragments of the past or present to the foreground, paste together timelines, and generate critical futures through framing design in narrative scenarios.

Using narrative forms to look back was vital to Angharad James' first-year project, *White Hot Forever*, where themes from Welsh folklore informed an enquiry into how activism and architecture could work together against the use and economy of fossil fuels.[49] The brief's structure engaged James' interests in a way she might not have otherwise been able to connect them: she created a mythical activist architecture and questioned how architecture could be built, engaged with labour (fig. 4.14). James' interest in the agency of folkloric beings also entered into her design exploration. In her work, folklore not only brings to life magical beings; it enacts new relationships between time and space by stretching through the collective imagination. James based her design of a fictional, new being on the folklore of the Will-o-the-wisp, as a crafty flame that in some ways can be described scientifically, but whose magical image of tiny spontaneous sparks in marshy woods is perhaps too captivating to ignore or rationalise. James' work shows that the enduring tales can be brought to life by different communities which appear across different geographic locations or timeframes while still being retained as thematically recognisable. James's work brings to mind what Burrows and O'Sullivan call a "collective enunciation," where the preservation and propagation of a story touches the minds of many across communities and times.[50] In this way, folk tales can be an archaeological resource, providing insight into the operations of communities long gone, and in the unconscious collective mind.

James' second year project, *Sympathy for Non-Human People*, furthered her engagement with material extraction ecologies and folklore (see chapter four project gallery).[51] Inserted into particular time sequences and locations on the site, her cast of agents were actants in the creation and extraction of a fictitous construction material that James called "pink stuff." The ecological agents mostly involved new types of non-human creatures, including the mythical "Longboi," a creature that resembled an alligator and was linked to Welsh mythologies of bodies of water. Another agent, "the Greebles, were pairs of rooted plant-like cave parasites between which the "pink stuff" would grow, with a texture similar to sheep wool. The portfolio itself adopted a split format, with white pages being set aside for a human perspective, narrated from the point of view of a conspiracy theorist collecting documents relating the mysterious events on the site. In this part of the portfolio, James fabricated an investigative report on the events involving the extraction of the "pink stuff" on the Oval site in Bethnal Green. To construct the fiction, she intervened in found documents. For instance, she mapped the invented material's behaviour onto scientific substance graphs, identifying its precise properties relative to existing materials (fig. 4.64). She showed the group of humans involved in the extraction through a found photograph of the members of the English rock band The Who with their faces circled (fig. 4.15). Pages from the perspective of the non-human agents included Celtic symbols James designed indicating which of the characters were speaking. James proposed a linear building that was spliced into the existing site to accommodate the extraction and processing of the material and support the community surrounding it. The building was clad with the invented material, involving a ritualistic seasonal re-cladding as the material weathered over time. James not only designed a building, but engaged in the process of fictioning a complex world made from real and unreal moments. Centred around the life of a material and the ecosystems it generates, her portfolio presented a humorous but critical eye on current architectural practices.

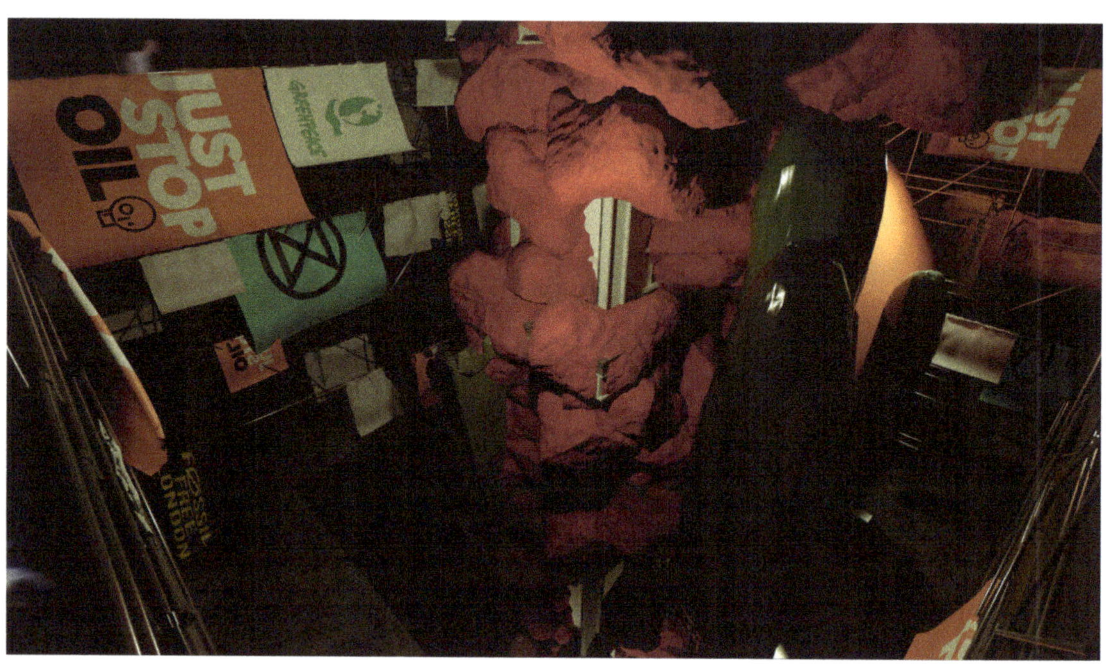

fig. 4.14: James' first-year activist project "White Hot Forever" involved a mysterious chemical reaction overtaking the riser of 25 Bank Street, enabling an ad-hoc intervention from the inside.

PRODUCING INDETERMINACIES

Burrows and O'Sullivan note that narrative has the potential to bring to life "an 'undetermined social imaginary' as the harbinger of social change,"[52] allowing for "an 'outside' of existing historical and social institutions ... and thus to transform worlds."[53] In DS25 projects, the design of body agents is the starting point for actualising undetermined social imaginaries where their "outside" is poised to address the current "inside." This process begins in the making sense of the combination of chosen ingredients, where narrative rationale comes into play to construct meaning out of the origins and agendas of each ingredient and how they manifest as and in the imagined body. The continued cultivation of body agents through the design process weaves relations from seemingly unrelated concepts and elements. From this process, the emergence of a narrative allows for a generative design that is not merely a means

Looking through the lens of data and history heightens the conscious awareness of this rhythm, which otherwise can lie, be incomplete, or give focus to only part of the story.

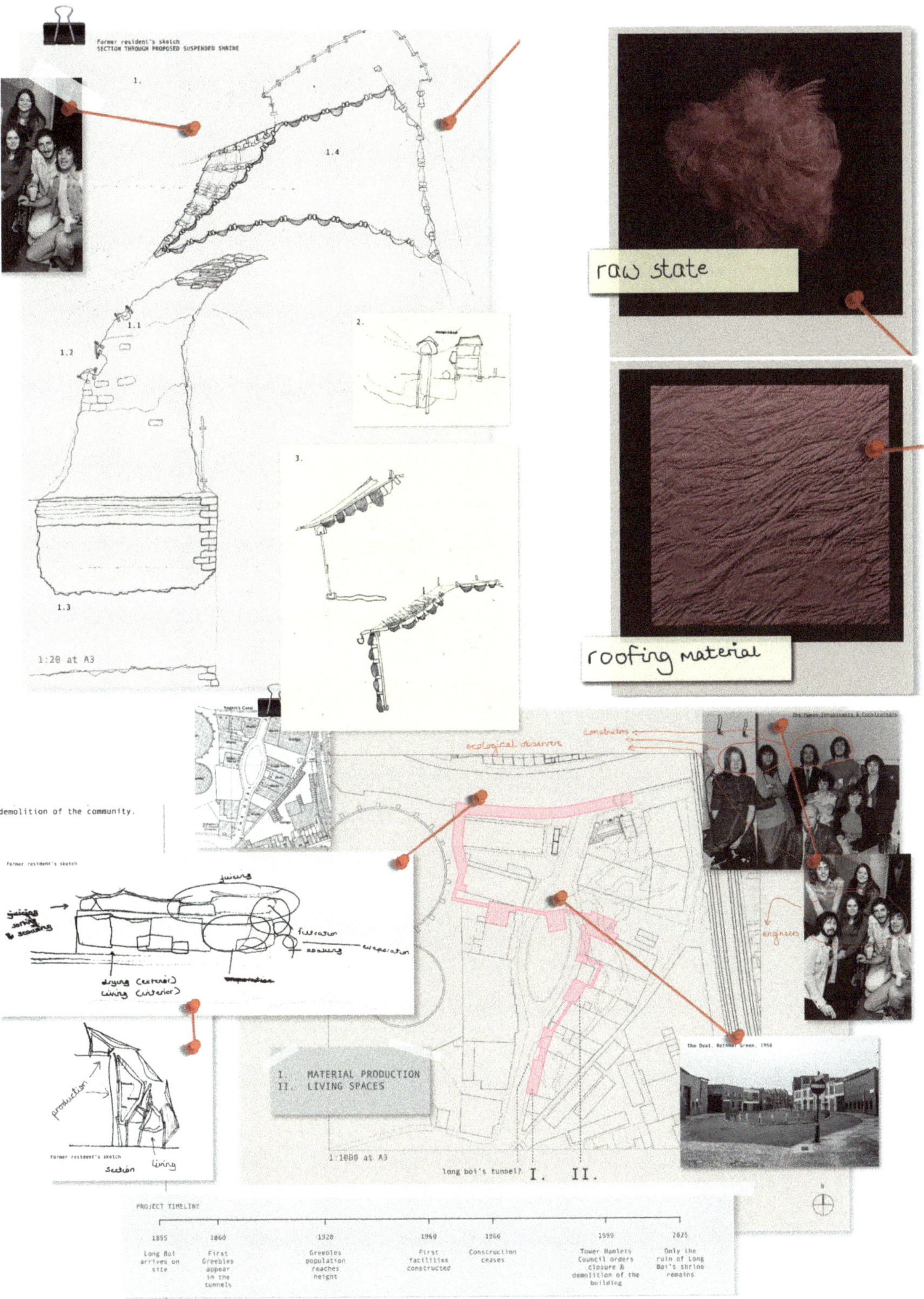

fig. 4.15: The Conspiracy Theorist's collection of evidence of the material's lifecycle and Longboi's tunnels on site at the Bethnal Green Oval.

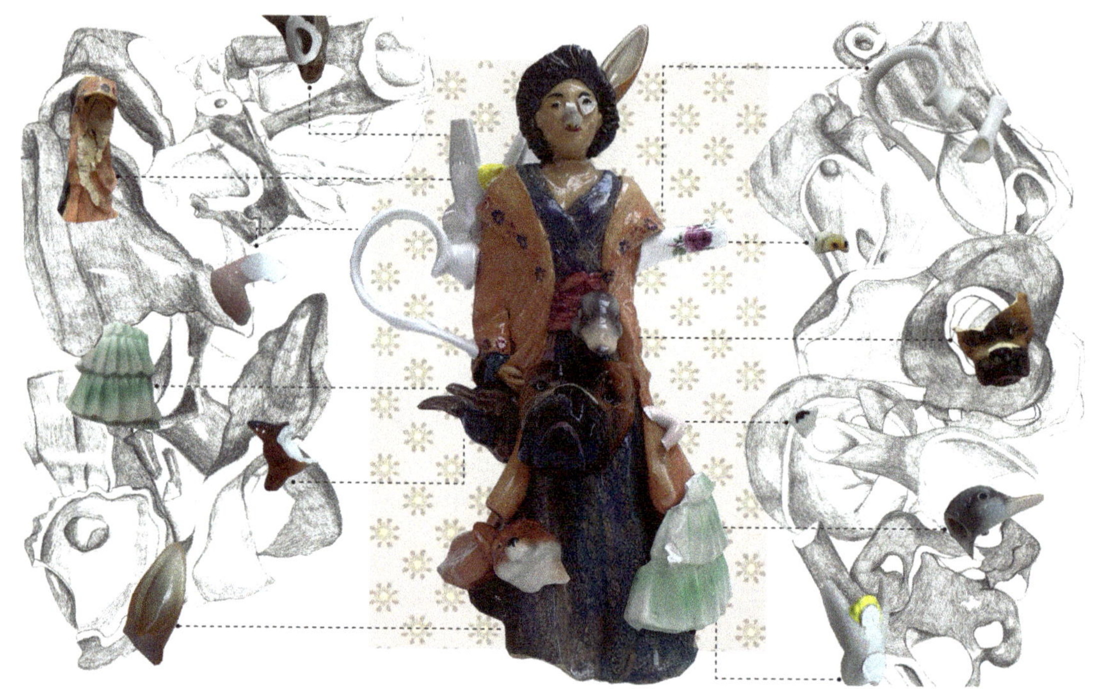

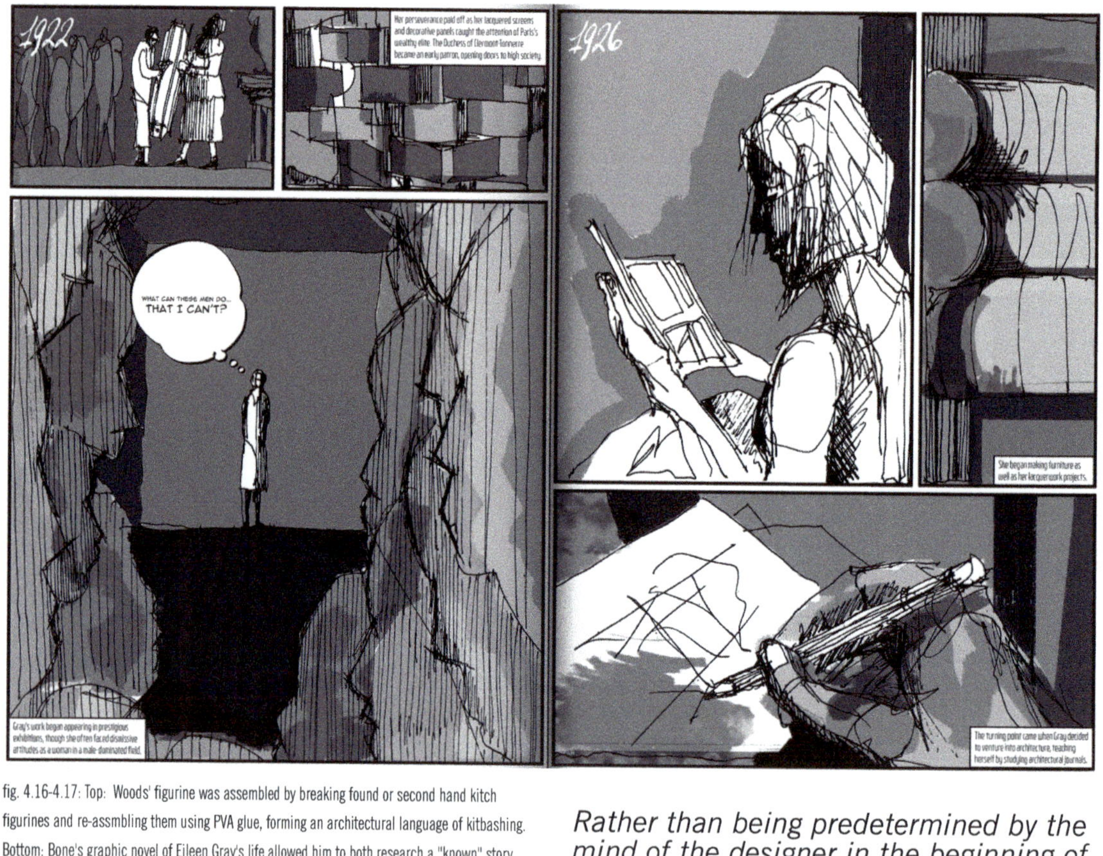

fig. 4.16-4.17: Top: Woods' figurine was assembled by breaking found or second hand kitch figurines and re-assmbling them using PVA glue, forming an architectural language of kitbashing. Bottom: Bone's graphic novel of Eileen Gray's life allowed him to both research a "known" story and weave his own narrative within that past, creating a parallel reality born out of historical information.

Rather than being predetermined by the mind of the designer in the beginning of the project, threads must be followed to discover where they lead.

to an end, but can produce questions and propositions that surprise even their creator and hold a wider transformative potential.

The students' designs of BMTFs are examples of the early part of this process. As discussed in chapter three, terminus figures were thought to occur at a boundary, so the design of the students' BMTF body agents required a fictioning of the boundaries implied by their chosen Terme and other ingrendients. For instance, in Woods' second-year project entitled *Behind Closed Doors*, the Figurine body agent was an amalgam of fragments of found, kitsch, souvenir ceramic figurines (fig. 4.16).(54) Woods began the design of the Figurine with a series of intuitive practices: first, searching out, buying, and gathering second-hand ceramic figures in London shops and markets. In itself, this act consisted of a curation, or editing, of a set of histories and images embedded within the real objects. Embracing another degree of indeterminacy, Woods then broke the individual figures, in a sense shattering the boundaries of the pieces, the realities that they existed within, and the pasts they brought with them. Following this, Woods recombined and re-attached the real fragments, forming an assemblage which existed between the realities associated with each original figure. The Figurine contained implicit narratives in each fragment, as well as telling the autobiographical tale of Woods' own making of it. The Figurine became a tactile object that simultaneously reconfigured possible histories and provided a tactile conceptual guide for constructing an architectural proposition.

The conceptualisation of the BMTF as a whole body set in motion a questioning of its origins. Woods' BMTF Figurine drifted between existing homes, shown through graphic novel pages. The panels of her graphic novel began with an overall site plan and transitioned in the first pages to showing more zoomed-in, paired plans and elevations of each flat the Figurine visits. Graphic novel pages that shifted scales and projection methods became visual narrative devices that enabled Woods to follow networks across urban and architectural scales. A situated architectural proposition was brought to life through Woods' pages, where a new network of actors and ingredients materialised, enmeshed with existing string figures.

In the students' creation of the BMTFs, each of the ingredients provided a point for research to explore how social, mental, and environmental fields could factor into an ecology. Using Sambin's fanciful figures as the starting point for monstrous transformation, replacing and transforming elements through their other chosen ingredients, and extending and examining relations between them, each student delved into defining a particular ecosystem and the contexts within which the projects would operate. Students were able to playfully explore what the parameters of their world were; reminiscent of William Burrough's literary method of "cutting up" and reassembling source material, they stitched together new, undetermined narratives. (55) This assembled figure, with all its degrees of bodily enhancements, provided a means to direct research into— and ultimately experiment within— specialised fields, meanings, and historical, architectural intentions. In this way, the figure was a world within itself, a microcosm offering to be unfolded and expanded.

Procedures that intentionally introduce indeterminacies that warrant a resolution through development bring to mind a process of writing a mystery novel where the author does not know the identity of the killer until it reveals itself in the process of writing. In this process, intuition and trust in the process itself gain importance as it becomes crucial to follow the hazy image of ideas that emerge throughout. Rather than being predetermined by the mind of the designer in the beginning of the project, threads must be followed to discover where they lead.

EDITING THE ARCHIVE

Often in DS25 projects, the intentional structuring of a story with narrative elements— such as chapters, preludes, beginnings and ends, refrains, motifs, casts of characters, and voices— are parameters that allow students to engage in non-linear ways of creating a project across scales, durations, groupings, and associations. The incorporation of these literary structuring elements challenges the idea of student projects as working through a kind of default presentation mode explained as a sequence of actions, mostly dictated by the tutor or course requirements. Instead, intentionally harnessing narrative can allow for an exploration of architectural production, thought, and reflection that provides a framework within which to make connections across the sequence of production and the various factors including the students' interest, the discoveries made, and even the context of studio requirements and discussions. With the goal of the studio being to engage with and enable the formation of the specific interest of every student who participates, narrative becomes a critical editing tool for formulating and communicating one's personal research agenda. Given the purpose, timeframe, and constrained formats to present projects in the context of M Arch, it would be an impossible task to show every single detail in a project. The comprehensive representation of construction details in an academic project would not necessarily provide cohesive criticality or an opportunity for synthetic, trans-disciplinary learning.

Storytelling can be a means of structuring

and editing, a way of omitting elements that are not contributing to the essence of the project. For example, narrative plots can be used in student portfolios for cutting out unnecessary site analysis, such as the very specific readings of Isle of Dogs' monumental, sleek, and inaccessible buildings enabled by Wilson's inside-out viewpoint of a body agent as part of building systems (fig. 3.61). Narrative plots can aid in honing students' research topics such as Woods' exploration of hers and Woolwich's dual nationality through her figurine moving through domestic environments in the pages of her graphic novel, helping to communicate the fundamental points that the project is concerned with. Narrative plots can also therefore reveal to the student unexpected results, such as Areta's consideration of the landscape as a cyborg or La Thangue's discovery of an infiltrating architecture.

When students are confronted with presenting a whole year's work, becoming an active curator can be a productive approach. The more unbound research occurs in the first semester, with the structure of the deadlines and tasks throughout the second semester providing limitations to the depth to which students can explore a wide subject that may not have direct relevance to their building proposal. The journey through the year develops a rich array of experiments, to the point that by the end of the year some crucial things get forgotten, or some tests that were thought to be failures suddenly reveal their value. The set of given prompts, briefs, and ingredients for the year can give structure to the search for the archive of work students have developed that can then be developed, cut up and re-stitched. The grounding of the brief is important because it situates the students' endeavours within a wider discussion among their peers, and their speculative practices within tangible pre-existing contexts. Yet, the briefs and prompts also require the criticality of the student, and by the end of the year, as a project has solidified, the brief can be re-curated in the student presentation to highlight how their response engendered the project.

Necessary communication and research pieces of any project, such as site analysis and environmental design, inevitably become specific in a DS25 project and provide the student with a critical approach, avoiding a box-ticking exercise. For instance, while the site might be a real location, in the context of the project it is conceptualised through the narrative, a setting where a series of political events unfold, resulting to or from an architectural intervention. At times the site enters the scene as the protagonist, allowing the reader of a project portfolio to feel and breathe the rhythms of geological and architectural change in ways familiar to their embodied experience.

For instance, in the portfolio presentation for her second-year project, Wilson showed her project selectively to build key touchstones defining the situation. The reader of the portfolio sees an origin story of the Odradek body, information on a catastrophic flood, Wilson's masterplan for Canary Wharf, and the design of a "Water Temple-Supermarket." Along the way, the reader is also brought into office buildings taken over by pipes and vegetation, gets glimpses of the views inside the lazy rivers that are the new thoroughfares, and sees the social transformations and contentious debate occurring in the society through graffiti and posters caught in the images (fig. 4.18).

narrative becomes a critical editing tool for formulating and communicating one's personal research agenda.

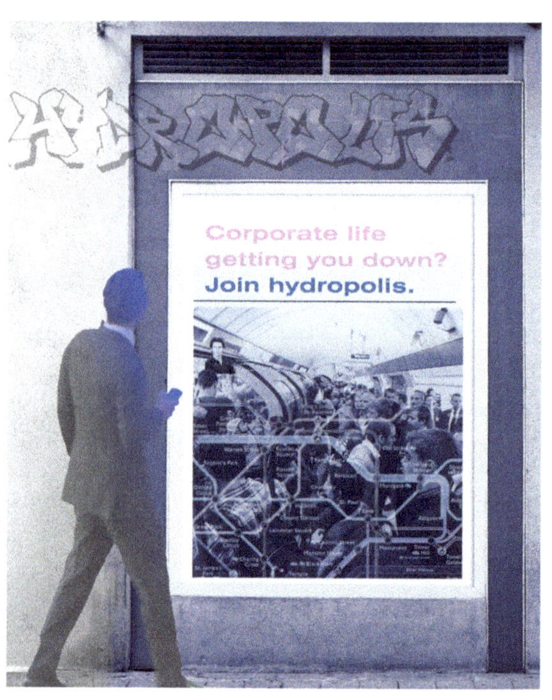

fig. 4.18: Wilson's portfolio took the form of an informative booklet featuring ads and slogans such as: "Hydropolis - The new religious sect that is gaining followers by the minute. What we know: - It's a sect aimed at young professionals, formed in London, trying to tackle the corporate burnout and exhaustion that is causing a decrease in quality of life; - They worship food and water, and bring more value to the everyday experiences we often take for granted."

Philosopher Mark Fisher explains the film-making processes of director Stanley Kubrick: "when he was watching the actors perform, Kubrick didn't know what he wanted. The real creative process happened long after the actors, the 'liveware', had departed; Kubrick ... wanted to keep ... open as many options as possible." Kubrick's process ensured a surfeit of material that he could then sift through and edit to find the most poignant takes.[56] Cinematic representation within a portfolio can be a useful tool in allowing the project to be reviewed at certain points in the year as a whole "pallet of potentials" which can be cut and re-stitched non-chronologically.[57] Taking Kubrick's "emphasis on editing" further, film director Mark Jenkin describes his process of developing analogue film footage for his short *A Dog Called Discord* by quipping, "the beauty is in the limitation."[58] He explains that not knowing what the roll contains is part of the magic; he sees the footage with fresh eyes, having to take a break from looking for the perfect moment and develop the physical material that will reanimate the moments he, or someone else before him, chose to film. Filming on-site or collecting archival footage, going back to his studio to develop the footage, seeing the footage, then cutting it up and stitching it back together, becoming the curator and producing something new out of the raw instantaneous recording entails a process of detachment, disembodiment, and reflection on the initial impulse.[59] It also produces something he could not have imagined in the beginning of his endeavour. In another chronological restructuring, the director folds together the found footage with a voice recording of the dog's owners, bringing the dog into the present moment through sound and moving image, both edited into a new composition and a new reality where the dog is once more alive, enacting a past-present time stitch.

In Isabel Mills-Lyle's second year project, *A Contemplative Practice for Everyday Listening*, she started by designing a spirit called Sru.[60] Comprised of biomaterial, Mills-Lyle saw Sru as a character that loved being in wet environments and longed for conversation as a way to explore loss of all kinds— for instance, in human mental health in urban environments, and in eel populations in the river Thames. The project developed nonlinearly: at times Mills-Lyle concentrated exclusively on the narrative, while at other times it receded into the background, reappearing in the process to aid in the exploration of specific design moments such as the seating of her first semester project, or the interstitial spaces of her second semester design, or the introduction of new subjects and agendas into the project (fig. 3.02). Mills-Lyle's building proposal was for a timber-structured and scoby-clad bathhouse complex on the shore of the Thames; the building included a travelling sauna for conversations, a marshy courtyard inhabited by eels, and opportunities for bathers to be immersed in an altered nature of the river ecosystem. Mills-Lyle's structuring of her portfolio to present her project entailed looking back at her work over the year, treating it almost as if it were found or archival material. Formatting her portfolio as a telling of the spirit's life, Mills-Lyle used a three-act narrative structure: *the arrival*, which encompassed the assemblage of ingredients, the study into the site, and formation of the spirit Sru; *the action*, which included the design of the building itself; and *the departure*, where the spirit transfers from being a recognizable character entity to the spirit of the beginning of a new reality, where eel population has grown as a result of the spirit's action.

ENACTING TEMPORALITY

The parallel timelines and realities of entwined real and unreal pasts, presents and futures are means to tease out new stories as a counterpoint to repeatedly-affirmed realities.

Through narrative techniques, experiments with timespans allow for a construction and destabilisation of relative timeframes between concepts. In DS25 briefs and discussions, the connection of time, body, and architecture is emphasised; various conceptions of time are brought to the forefront through narrative methods. Students are encouraged to engage with time in a multitude of ways, especially by questioning the idea of the "frozen snapshot." Students are asked to consider the possibility of an "unreal" time that can exist in their fiction's constructed reality. Operating in the project narratives, this alternate time prompts students to make connections with concepts in past, current, or future events which follow the paths of known history, but also to dig "the future out of the archive."[61] As in James' first- and second-year projects, these alternative pasts include those embedded in myths, folklore, and word-of-mouth traditions, which can themselves mix global space-times or rhythms enacted by the landscape. By asking students to articulate, attempt to visualise, and even play with time through the construction of narratives, possibilities arise which pertain to a deeper understanding of temporality as another design agent; time becomes conceived as integral to and conversant with architecture. While this pursuit could seem esoteric or conceptual, for the architectural profession— increasingly aware of a responsibility for how its activities impact the earth's resources and engagement with the communities of the future—, taking account of temporality and its manifestations could be considered essential.

The parallel timelines and realities of entwined real and unreal pasts, presents, and futures are means to tease out new stories as a counterpoint to repeatedly-affirmed realities. For example, in order to construct the narrative for her second-year project, Mills-Lyle established a factual timeline as she researched into the declining eel population of the river Thames, and delved deeply into the roots, word-of-mouth, or embedded misinformation around the issue. Constructing a parallel reality spliced in and then branching off of the established timeline allowed her to destabilise the dream-state of the present by providing alternative viewpoints and how events could play out in the future.

Literary references helped to inspire the construction of timelines spanning past, present, and future in Areta and Mills-Lyle's second-year projects discussed above, and provided productive spring points from which to imagine the alternate futures of their projects. Notable sci-fi references relating to parallel histories that were discussed in the studio are the novel *The Peripheral* by author William Gibson, which imagines a future in which digital communication with past realities can enact multiple futures or "stubs;" the sequel, *Agency*, explores a parallel reality in which Brexit did not occur. Another discussed reference is the novel *Man in the High Castle* by Philip K Dick, which imagines a parallel history in which Germany and Japan won WWII.

As a response to the brief *Embodied Ecologies and Speculative Fabulations*, Koksal's project worked across multiple, imagined and real timeframes. Recognising the idea that the imaginary, when grounded in actual events, can enact traction on the real, Koksal proposed a fictioned architecture which takes a cue from speculative art practices, such as those of Ginsberg and Marguerite Humeau. These sorts of future envisionings provide a fictioning of ecological ideas of endosymbiosis, taking into account concrete, present events, scientific research, and archaeological findings.

Koksal's project included a visualised timeline that blended points of reality with speculative parallel times inserted into present day reality. Additionally, her presentations of the project as a "real" corporate update into the progress of the project's research folded time in a way that stitched centuries in the future with the studio's real time of 2021 (fig. 4.20). Her project proposed the regrowth of Woolly Mammoths as an answer to climate change in a time where bringing extinct animals such as the Thylacine back to life is an actual prospect.[62] Koksal's scientific

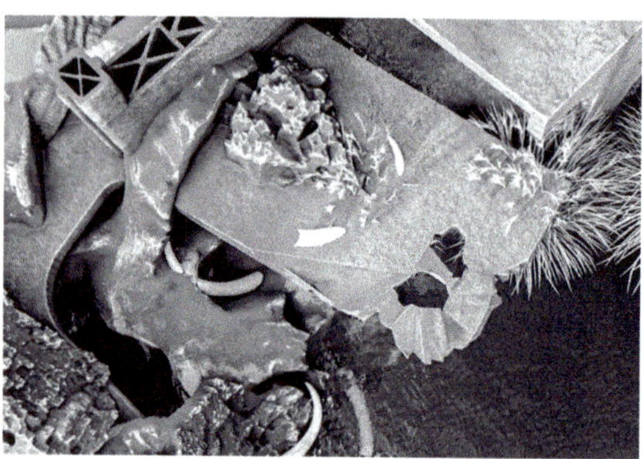

fig. 4.19: Koksal worked with digital renders to stitch timelines by visually homogenising mammoth tusks with ruins of 3D printed structures and natural rock formations in her archaeological report.

imagining attempts to resurrect an extinct past in order to resolve a current environmental issue. While not explicitly a reference used by Koksal, her project is reminiscent of other aspects of the *The Peripheral*, where a cyborg thylacine is a future pet. Koksal's and Gibson's "de-extinctions" link to existing scientific research, tangling them within their possible future worlds as starting points for imagining the future of the Thames' ecology— in Koksal's case— or as future consequences of Western humanity's progress— in Gibson's narrative.

Koksal proposed multiple time jumps, essentially constructing an archaeological future. In the narrative, the project locates itself two decades from the present in what could be considered a "near" future. At other points the timeline projects the story even further into the future where, a thousand years later, a fictioned climate archaeology organisation looks back at the near future. Other points in the narrative move to the Art Deco era, a time and style that influences Wilona Leonard, the architect Koksal imagines to have designed the project's building proposal (fig. 4.31). And still at other times the project narrative operates in prehistoric earth when the original Woolly Mammoths roamed (fig. 4.19). These time jumps were enacted as part of a story, allowing the exploration of key themes of agency and environmental links in design. The time jumps also became a tool for critical reflection regarding the effect of time in design. Koksal explored how her far-future scenarios could affect buildings and a multi-species society.

BRACKETING TIME

envisioning moments in a strategic and challenging way can become a vital mode of bracketing time and finding key temporal junctures.

The making of construction and far-future images that have become an established practice in the studio are important ways of understanding the implications of concepts. Just as much as the static image is questioned in the studio, envisioning moments in a strategic and challenging way can become a vital mode of bracketing time and finding key temporal junctures. In these envisioned instances, students make decisions about the implications of the project and their intentions. Questions are posed concerning what is at stake and what the position of the project truly is. In these moments, the building-object is not considered as a static, perfect, completed entity, but a living and dying thing existing in a temporal continuum. The construction and far-future images bring up questions of how the building itself relates to the earth, as part of an inter-relational

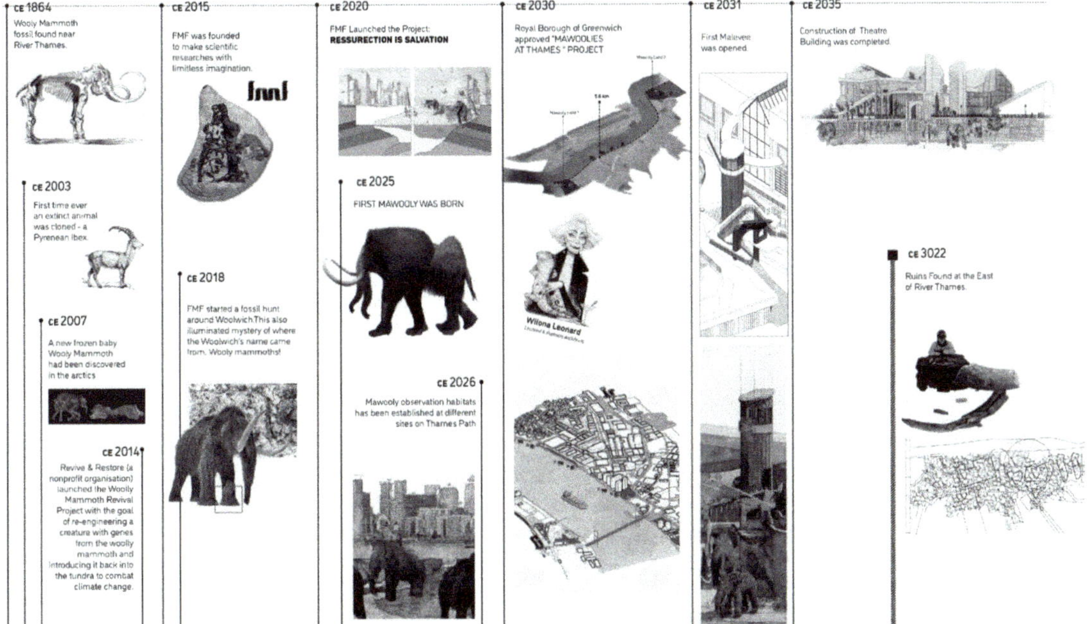

fig. 4.20: Koksal's fictional timeline, inserting her narrative into a context of real events throughout the history of the site and the extinct animal she intended to revivify.

scenario. Ecologies can be revealed not only as byproducts of cataclysmic events but also as accumulations of tiny unseen things changing society and the planetary systems. In these images, the building often becomes conceived as part of the landscape, as students envision nature taking over and weaving into it.

The far-future images suggest alternate worlds, jump-cutting ahead and immersing a viewer amidst an ongoing possibility. For instance, Mills-Lyle envisioned the burgeoning eel population in her bath house's marshy courtyard, with the caption "Sru left, but the eel population seems to be constantly increasing" (fig. 4.21).[63] In

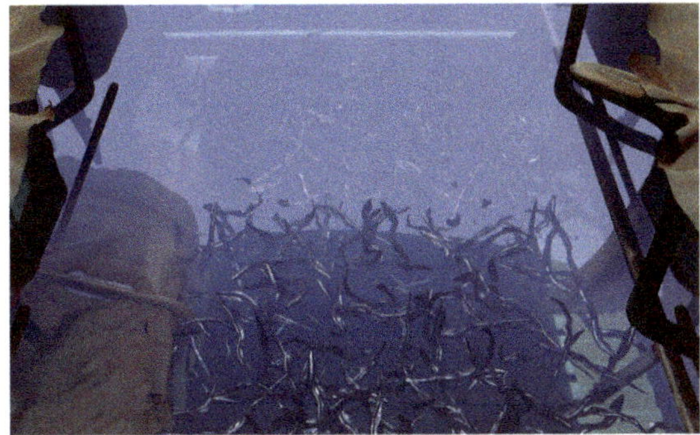

fig. 4.21: Mills-Lyle's narrative passages featured in a different style and font throughout her portfolio, accompanying her in her research into the eel population of the Thames.

Ecologies can be revealed not only as byproducts of cataclysmic events but also as accumulations of tiny unseen things changing society and the planetary systems.

Mills-Lyle's cinematic telling, future events and relations produced by the building give rise to new problems and questions to bring back to design in the present; for her, these had to do with eel overpopulation and the possibility that her building project could be complicit in a failed scientific experiment and a new set of problems to tackle.

Jump-cutting to a future scenario through image-making also allowed Mills-Lyle to reframe her project. Even if it opened the project to new possibilities, constructing her far-future image provided a conclusory point to the project narrative and helped her restructure her work to focus on some of the end goals set out by the final image; for instance, filling in gaps in the research of eel ecology. The studio discussion was greatly influenced by Professor Jonathan Hill's lectures and writings, particularly his exploration of the concept of "architecture as a time machine."[64] Hill's thoughts on the re-wilded shell of the abandoned St Peter's Seminary in Cardross[65] inspired a nocturnal visit to the building during the 2023-24 DS25 field trip. Wilson's far-future image picks up on this idea of a reinvigorated, perhaps even more valuable, second life of a building. In her image, Canary Wharf is depicted taken over by natural elements, with humans using the network of pipes she proposed as an extensive network of bird hides from which to observe wildlife (fig. 3.67). With a more social commentary in mind, in the *Baddieverse* project, Cocca imagined the construction of a queer nightclub, free from capitalist constraints, where it was slowly clad in mycelium grown on the building; with an ironic sensibility, he imagined a far-future where this slowly evolving bastion for underground events faces a different kind of ruination, transformed into an Apple Store as the neighbourhood gentrifies and culture is appropriated (fig. 2.56).

As part of their responses to the *Things Have Feelings Too* brief, students deployed cinematic techniques that imagined architecture existing in a temporal continuum of changing ecologies and contextual relationships. Questioning how a project could potentially change over time along with exploring cinematic techniques were especially important to Kolioliou's first-year project,(66) also discussed in chapter three above. In her project, she set in motion a speculative ecology she imagined to develop over time. Starting with the vision of the character OD, the project moved from the design of OD's devices, to the lab, to the masterplan. The scale juxtaposition between the urban masterplan and the bacteria themselves was engaged first through framing and editing in the moving images, and then in experimental drawings that followed (fig. 4.46). The buildings comprising this "bacteria utopia," were proposed as catalysts for incubating and introducing beneficial bacterial agents in the Isle of Dogs.

Kolioliou initially created a documentary showing OD's obsession and initial tests with bacteria; the project then shifted away from OD's viewpoint in the field and laboratory to representations of the project further in the future, culminating in alternate views of Isle of Dogs transformed as either a utopian success or a dystopian failure (fig. 4.47, 4.48, 4.52). For her image of the building under construction, the incubator building is visible being built in the background, while the already infected hand of OD is in the foreground (fig. 4.52). Looking to the future, Kolioliou considered the contingent outcomes of her scheme. A far-future image focuses on OD's tomb, with a vibrant ecosystem of vegetation thriving in the foreground, with the bio-digesting processing of the bacteria-generating buildings evident in the background (fig. 4.47). But in another exploratory cinematic representation, Kolioliou quantum leapt, imaging the failure of the masterplan; in this post-anthropocentric future, the microbes displace the human residents of the city; OD's illustrious tomb is a mere grave marker, and the buildings stand in ruin amidst a darkened sky (fig. 4.48).(67) Through narrative scene-setting, pitfalls and possibilities of present and future architectural realities emerged from these diverse perspectives. The project used a strategy of cinematic quantum leaping to alternate futures to ask its difficult questions about who architecture ultimately is for.(68)

CONCLUSION

the future architecture that is imagined within each project moves away from the idea of architecture as a shiny object set in seemingly no-place and no-time.

As a methodology incorporated into architectural design, storytelling allows for unique capacities. For instance, as protagonists and deuteragonists arrive into pre-existing scenes and catalyse action in a story, embodied subjects can address past, present, and future contexts and issues, offering a way to operate in tangled situations. Narrative logic is not always rational, but it has a rationale.(69) One event follows another according to the parameters of the story and the threads that form between subjects, contexts, and timelines, ultimately resolving or clarifying a reflective visualisation of a set of relations. Narrative is innately situated; this situatedness means that buildings embedded in stories are not necessarily considered as isolated objects but can exist in a continuum of time, place, architecture, culture, ecology, and environment.

With the body agents as protagonists, third-person narrators, or even the matter that makes up their designs, DS25 students begin a process of world-building.(70) As a methodology, inventive storytelling extends this process, intentionally taking on points of view to engage with temporality and to speculate on future scenarios. Students set up and immerse themselves in a productive dialogue with past and present cultural, social, constructive, and economic practices. By situating design in a narrative, students are able to look beyond the present to invent propositions for how human and non-human kin and human-made and natural environments could beneficially coexist in yet possible futures. At the same time, the immersiveness inherent to storytelling, world building, and body agent-related design methods provides students with new relations between their constructed and mutated assemblages and known subjects. This encourages in-depth study to visualise alternative pasts, destabilising dominant, perpetuated histories. With that, the future architecture that is imagined within each project moves away from the idea of architecture as a shiny object set in seemingly no-place and no-time. Instead, each project crafts both "archival material"(71) out of a specific set of past and present relations for an imagined community of its context, and a possible future strand of a world within which the architectural space acts.(72)

NOTES

(01) Burrows and O'Sullivan's stance towards the word "dream" is mentioned in various contexts as both critical of a veil constructed by the state that clouds one's judgement and is hard to escape, and productive as the enabler of imagining other realities in art practices. Burrows and O'Sullivan, *Fictioning*, 55.

(02) Haraway, *Staying with the Trouble*, 35.

(03) Ayesha Hameed, "A Conversation between Henriette Gunkel, Ayesha Hameed and Simon O'Sullivan," in *Futures and Fictions*, (London: Repeater Books, 2017), 4. Hameed draws from W.J.T Mitchell's idea of the "dream-work of imperialism."

(04) Simon O'Sullivan, "A Conversation between Henriette Gunkel, Ayesha Hameed and Simon O'Sullivan," in *Futures and Fictions*, (London: Repeater Books, 2017), 11.

(05) Haraway, *Staying with the Trouble*, 50.

(06) Samuel R. Delaney compares "Science Fiction writing to mirrorshades ... 'the text becomes someplace where you look to see what's going on— while at the same time, the text presents a gaze that is somehow darkened, distorted, and reflected'." Burrows and O'Sullivan, *Fictioning*, 212.

(07) "The buildings and construction sector is by far the largest emitter of greenhouse gases, accounting for a staggering 37% of global emissions.": *Building Materials and the Climate: Constructing a New Future*, United Nations Environment Programme, & Yale Center for Ecosystems + Architecture (2023), ix, https://wedocs.unep.org/20.500.11822/43293.

(08) Project done under the supervision of the studio teaching team of Dr Alessandro Ayuso and Mary Konstantopoulou.

(09) Project done under the supervision of the studio teaching team of Dr Alessandro Ayuso and Mary Konstantopoulou with support from Deniz Özbek.

(10) Project done under the supervision of the studio teaching team of Dr Alessandro Ayuso and Mary Konstantopoulou with support from Deniz Özbek.

(11) Mark Freeman, "Why Narrative Matters: Philosophy, Method, Theory," in *Storyworlds: A Journal of Narrative Studies* 8, no. 1, Narrative Hermeneutics (University of Nebraska Press: Summer 2016), 137-152, at 143 and 145, https://www.jstor.org/stable/10.5250/storyworlds.8.1.0137

(12) Ibid., 143.

(13) Ibid., 141-142.

(14) Ibid., 143.

(15) Ibid., 138.

(16) Ibid.

(17) Ibid., 143.

(18) Ibid.

(19) Morton describes that "no one access mode can exhaust all the qualities and characteristics of a thing," noting that "things are open, they withdraw from total access." Morton, *Being Ecological*, 21. In this sense, neither "information" nor a "report" can ever capture the "pure essence of a thing" that Benjamin discusses.

(20) Walter Benjamin, *The Storyteller: Reflections on the Works of Nikolai Leskov*, (1936), 5. Accessed August 19, 2025, through Cornell University, Architectural Robotics Lab (ARL), https://arl.human.cornell.edu/linked%20docs/Walter%20Benjamin%20Storyteller.pdf

(21) Project done under the supervision of the studio teaching team of Dr Alessandro Ayuso and Mary Konstantopoulou with support from Deniz Özbek.

(22) Edited by Sarah Shin and Matthias Zeiske, "Carrier bag fiction," in *Das Neue Alphabet* (*The New Alphabet*) 6, (HKW; Leipzig: Spector Books), cover.

(23) Ursula K Le Guin quoted in Shin and Zeiske, "Carrier bag fiction," 5.

(24) Freeman, "Why Narrative Matters," 145.

(25) Francisco Nunes, "The Hacker Class Is Dead, Long Live the Hackers!," *e-flux Journal*, no. 146, published June 12, 2024, 1.

(26) The concept of feeling-through is similar here to philosopher Robert Vischer's (1847-1933) term: "..Einfuhlung (literally 'in-feeling') in his 1873 dissertation *Uber das optische Formgefuhl* ('On the optical sense of form'). He defined the empathetic experiential process according to a logic of similarity whereby the sense of, say, a building's beauty was a function of a harmonious correlation between the object's form and the bodily or sensory structure of the perceiving subject." Jorge Otero-Pailos, *Architecture's Historical Turn: Phenomenology and the Rise of the Postmodern* (Minneapolis & London: University of Minnesota Press, 2010), xx.

(27) Bronwyn Davies and Rom Harré, "Positioning: The Discursive Production of Selves," *Journal for the Theory of Social Behaviour* 20, no. 1 (1990): 46.

(28) Burrows and O'Sullivan, *Fictioning*, 10, 10n.; Vonnegut's nested fiction shines a light on what Le Guin states as: "to believe that our beliefs are permanent truths which encompass reality is a sad arrogance." Le Guin quoted in Shin and Zeiske, "Carrier Bag Fiction," 6.

(29) Kurt Vonnegut Jr., *Breakfast of Champions* (UK: Panther Books, 1975; orig. pub. 1973), 76-77.

(30) "a fiction within a fiction.": Burrows and O'Sullivan, *Fictioning*, 145, 234n.

(31) Burrows and O'Sullivan, *Fictioning*, 10; 10n.; "hyperstition ... has been defined as the process whereby fictions make themselves real. ... Much of capitalism functions through hyperstitional processes. In fact, you could argue that capital itself is a hyperstition.": Mark Fisher, "Luxury Communism," in *Futures and Fictions*, 145-169, at 162.

(32) Stories that attempt this endeavour include Anna Tsing's *Mushroom at the End of the World* written in 2015, Tschaikovsky's *Children of Time* mentioned above, and Richard Powers' *The Overstory* written in 2019.

(33) Isaac Asimov, "Reason," in *I, Robot* (UK: Panther Books, 1968; orig. pub. 1967) 52-70, at 57.

(34) Ibid., 53.

(35) Project done under the supervision of the studio teaching team of Dr Alessandro Ayuso and Mary Konstantopoulou.

(36) See: Emma Cary et al, "Five critical questions we should ask of rewilding projects," ed, Emmeline Topp, in People and Nature, (British Ecological Society), published July 17, 2025, https://doi.

org/10.1002/pan3.70100; International Union for Conservation of Nature: "The benefits and risks of rewilding," in International Union for Conservation of Nature, published June, 2021, https://iucn.org/resources/issues-brief/benefits-and-risks-rewilding.

(37) Ginsberg, *Designing for the Sixth Extinction*, 2013-15, commissioned by Science Gallery, Dublin for "Grow Your Own... Life After Nature," https://www.daisyginsberg.com/work/designing-for-the-sixth-extinction

(38) "The Truth About Carcinization: Internet Memes vs. Evolution," in *Department of Organismic and Evolutionary Biology* (Harvard University), published February 27, 2025, https://www.oeb.harvard.edu/news/2025/02/truth-about-carcinization-internet-memes-vs-evolution

(39) Project done under the supervision of the studio teaching team of Dr Alessandro Ayuso and Mary Konstantopoulou with support from Deniz Özbek.

(40) Haraway, *Staying with the Trouble*, 10.

(41) Oreet Ashery, "Revisiting Genesis>>>" in *Futures and Fictions*, 21-37, at 22.

(42) Hameed, *Futures and Fictions*, 4.

(43) Bethesda Game Studios. *Fallout 4*. Bethesda Softworks. Windows, PlayStation 4, and Xbox One. 2015.

(44) Project done under the supervision of the studio teaching team of Dr Alessandro Ayuso and Mary Konstantopoulou.

(45) Luke La Thangue, *Other Crescent*, 2023-24.

(46) Hawkes, *A Land*, 33; Braidotti, "Becoming Earth," in *The Posthuman*, 82.

(47) Haraway, *Staying with the Trouble,* 169n1.

(48) "Met Office position on geoengineering research," MetOffice, http://metoffice.gov.uk/research/climate/earth-system-science/met-office-position-on-geoengineering-research; "News from a World in Flux Ep. 2: Aerosol masking, geo-engineering, and the pension problem," by Extinction Rebellion, August 31, 2023, https://extinctionrebellion.uk/2023/08/31/news-from-a-world-in-flux-ep-2-aerosol-masking-geo-engineering-and-the-pension-problem/

(49) Project done under the supervision of the studio teaching team of Dr Alessandro Ayuso and Mary Konstantopoulou.

(50) Burrows and O'Sullivan, *Fictioning*, 17.

(51) Project done under the supervision of the studio teaching team of Dr Alessandro Ayuso and Mary Konstantopoulou with support from Deniz Özbek.

(52) Cornelius Castoriadis quoted in Burrows and O'Sullivan, *Fictioning*, 278.

(53) Burrows and O'Sullivan, *Fictioning*, 279.

(54) Project done under the supervision of the studio teaching team of Dr Alessandro Ayuso and Mary Konstantopoulou.

(55) Burrows and O'Sullivan, *Fictioning*, 35. With regards to the "cut-up," they quote author William Burroughs: "reality is itself a kind of audio-visual script, and new cut-ups— recordings that have been spliced together— can then be "played back" in order to interfere with more dominant narrative sequences.": Ibid., 36.

(56) Mark Fisher, "No Now," in *k-punk*, published February 26, 2004, http://k-punk.abstractdynamics.org/archives/001843.html

(57) Ibid.

(58) *A Dog Called Discord*, directed by Mark Jenkin, 2023, 23:00, (BFI Player), http://player.bfi.org.uk/free/film/watch-a-dog-called-discord-2023-online

(59) Henriette Gunkel, "Scavenging the Future of the Archive," in *Futures and Fictions*, 193-212, at 207.

(60) Project done under the supervision of the studio teaching team of Dr Alessandro Ayuso and Mary Konstantopoulou.

(61) Gunkel, *Futures and Fictions*, 194.

(62) Kate Evans, "De-extinction Company Aims to Resurrect the Tasmanian Tiger," in *Scientific American*, ed. Kate Wong, published August 16, 2022, https://www.scientificamerican.com/article/de-extinction-company-aims-to-resurrect-the-tasmanian-tiger/

(63) Isabel Mills-Lyle, *A Contemplative Practice for Everyday Listening*, 2021-22.

(64) Jonathan Hill, "RESEARCH BY DESIGN. Architecture Is a Time Machine," *Dimensions. Journal of Architectural Knowledge* 2, no. 1 (2022): 247–60, https://doi.org/10.14361/dak-2022-0316.

(65) Jonathan Hill, "Architecture Is a Time Machine," Lecture, UWE Bristol, 6 February 2023, https://www.youtube.com/watch?v=C1YtLb4GcEg&ab_channel=UWEBristolArchitecture.

(66) Anastasia Kolioliou, *Bacteria Sanctuary*, 2023-24. Project done under the supervision of the studio teaching team of Dr Alessandro Ayuso and Mary Konstantopoulou.

(67) The Construction and Afterlife images prompt was introduced in 2023-24, taking shape through discussions during certain projects' tutorials, and informed the 2024-25 brief, where the premise was to think of the architectural language that emerged at the start of the year as already a memorialisation of past design agendas. Encouraging the students to think of the contextual implications in a time after their building's use had ceased being the same as was originally intended.

(68) "...real time is not a unitary strand distributing homogeneous units of past, present and future in a fixed empirical order, but is rather a complex, interactive, 'thick' manifold of distinct yet integrated durations": Sanford Kwinter, *Architectures of Time: Toward a Theory of the Event in Modernist Culture* (Cambridge, MA: MIT Press, 2001), 22.

(69) Walter R. Fisher, *Human Communication as Narration: Toward a Philosophy of Reason, Value, and Action* (Columbia, SC: University of South Carolina Press, 1987), 48–49.

(70) "I cannot do a building without building a new repertoire of characters, of stories, of language, and it's all parallel. It's not just building, per se. It's building worlds.": Hejduk, John Hejduk, quoted in Martin Søberg, "John Hejduk's Pursuit of an Architectural Ethos." (FOOTPRINT, 2012), 114. Accessed May 4, 2020 https://journals.open.tudelft.nl/footprint/article/view/753/930.

(71) Gunkel, *Futures and Fictions*, 194.

(72) Sam Jacob, *Making it Real: Architecture as Enactment* (London: Strelka Press, 2014)16.

CHAPTER 4: PROJECT IMAGE GALLERY

THE GARDENS OF ISLE END
HERE BE MA'WOOLIES!
UKIYO.LAND
BACTERIA SANCTUARY
A LOVE LETTER TO INSECTS
SYMPATHY FOR NON-HUMAN PEOPLE
THE SOCIETY OF FAILED ARCHITECTS
HEARTICULTURE ARCHITECTURE SCHOOL

THE GARDENS OF ISLE END

by
DANI BUBAN NGU

BRIEF *Body Agent Architecture*

YEAR *2019-20*

TUTORS *Dr Alessandro Ayuso, Dr Dan Dream, Martyna Marciniak*

THEMES

Surrealism

De Chirico / High Modernism

Prosthetics / Cyborgs

Mental Health

Wayfinding / Orientation

"The narrative thus follows: there exist 3 worlds in tandem: Canvas Land— or the land where De Chirico's paintings reside—, Mile End— the land of unorthodox architecture—, and, somewhere where the two worlds meet, Isle End— a fictional land which imposes De Chirico's paintings on the inhabitants of Mile End. The winged buildings are fragments of architecture seeking to bring the inhabitants of Canvas Land back to Mile End.

Isle End is a re-imagination of Mile End if Mile End were to be altered by the presence of the mannequins. At the entrance of the site (1) the surrounding houses form the back drop. As one progresses through the site, these houses are transformed into roman arcades which are a signature part of De Chirico's world.

The platform (2) becomes the new waiting point for passengers waiting to board the train (3), which represents the trainline that runs through the actual site."

fig. 4.21: Spatio-temporal drawing of the mannequin. Starting as a "weak" body, as portrayed by its lack of arms and reliance on structural elements for support, attempting to merge its being with the more dependable house to ensure its survivability.

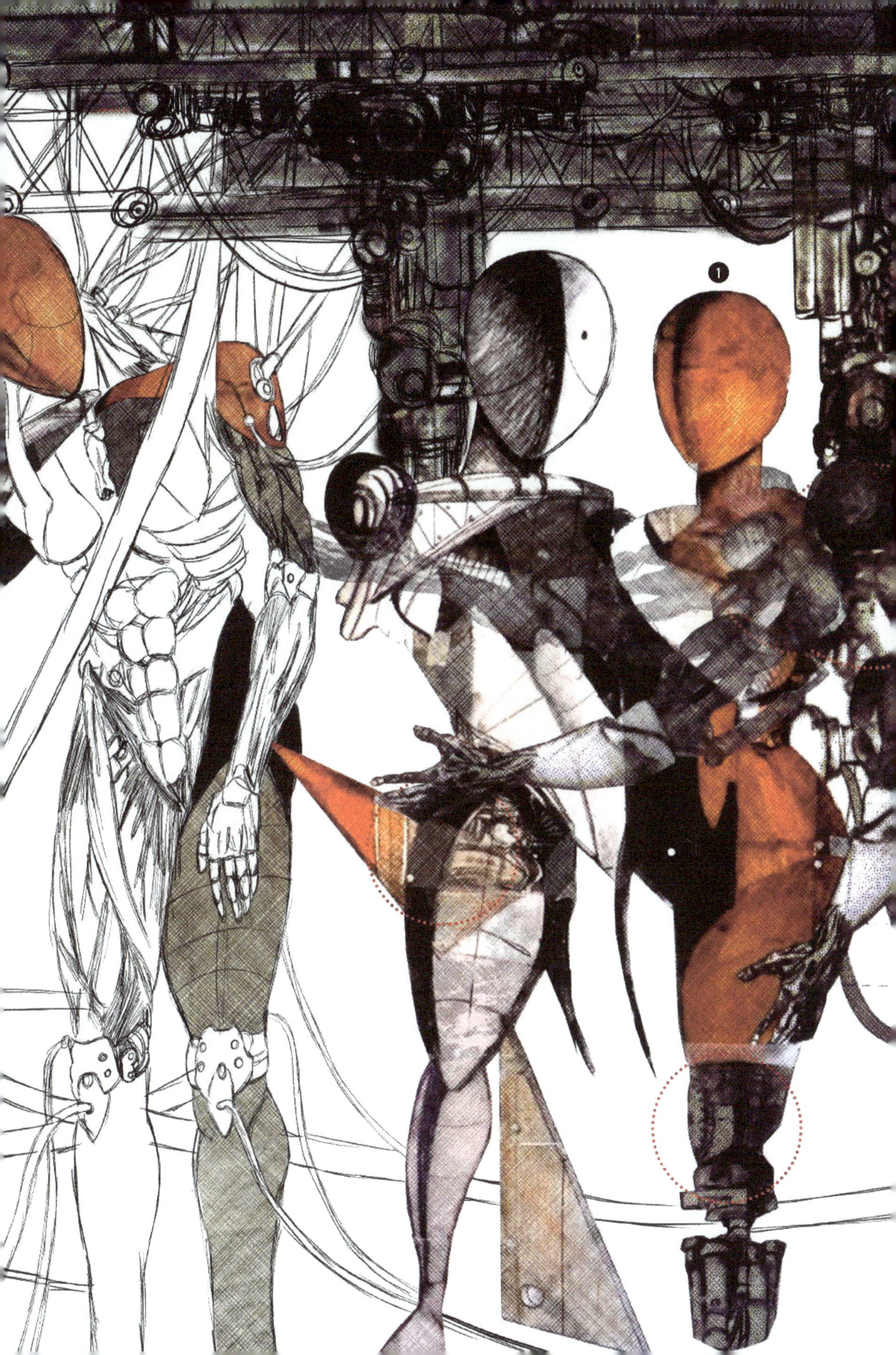

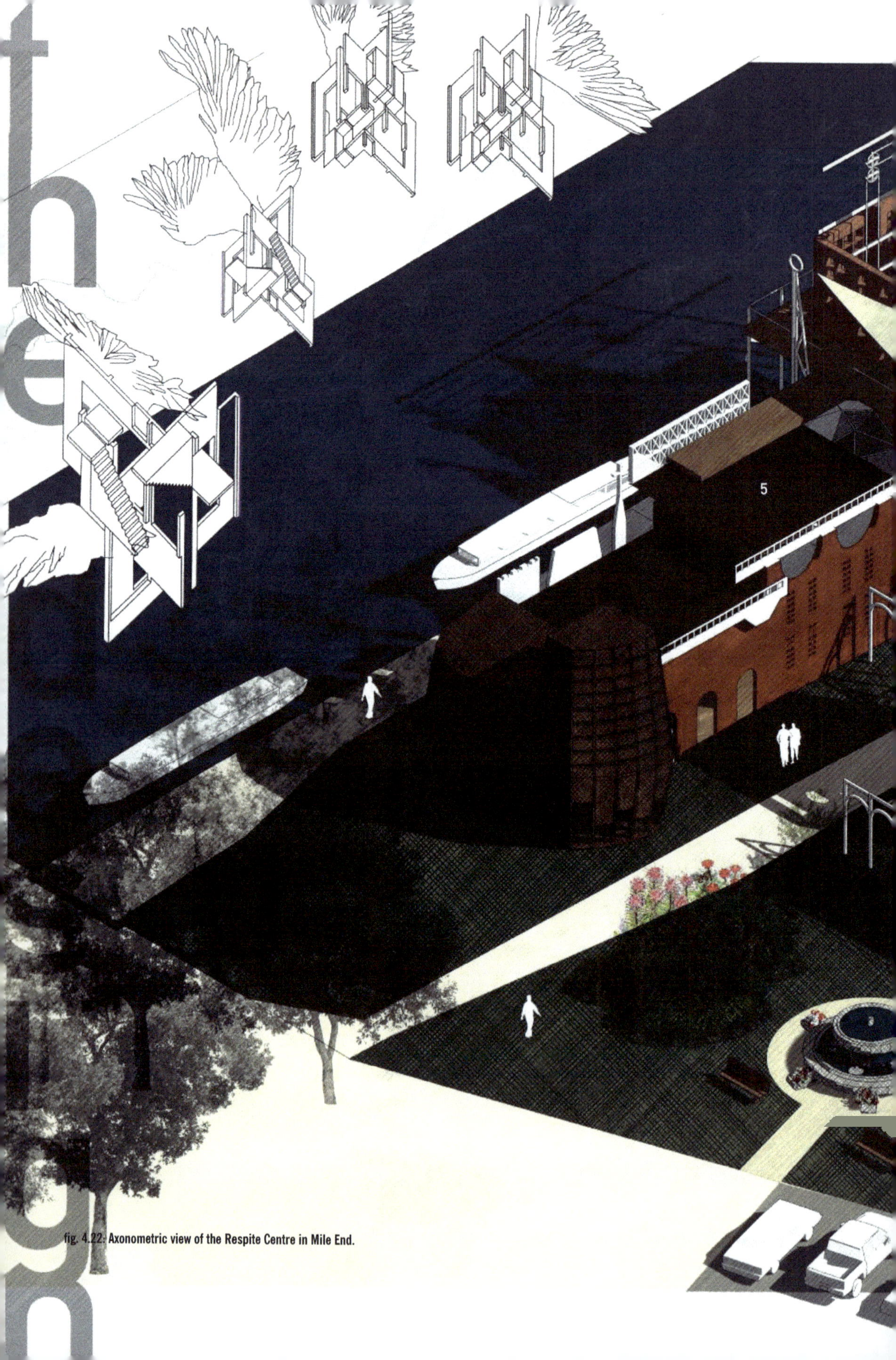

fig. 4.22: Axonometric view of the Respite Centre in Mile End.

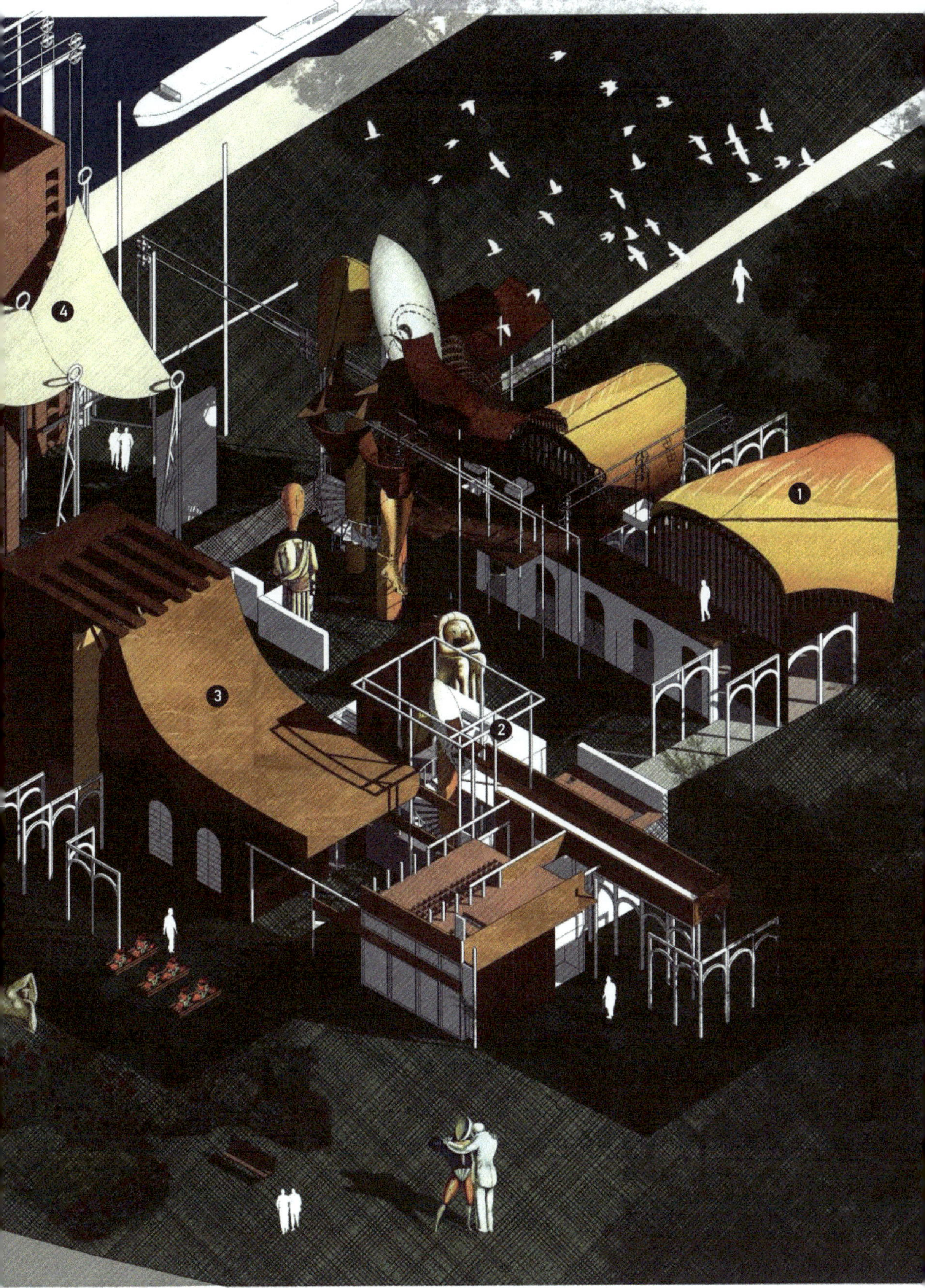
1
2
3
4

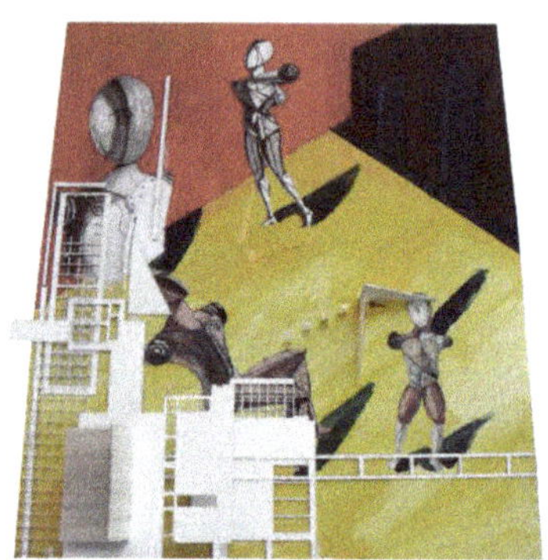

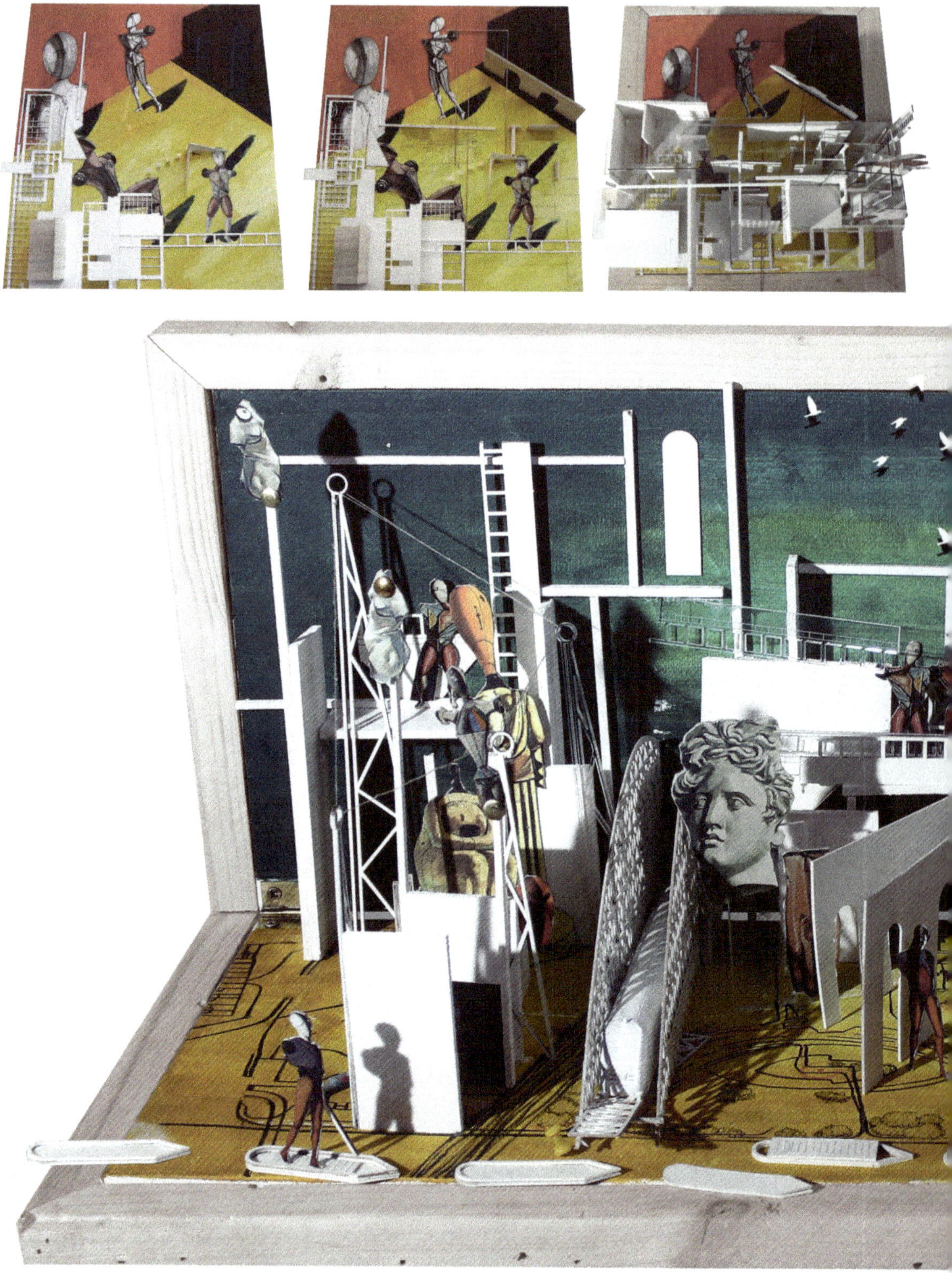

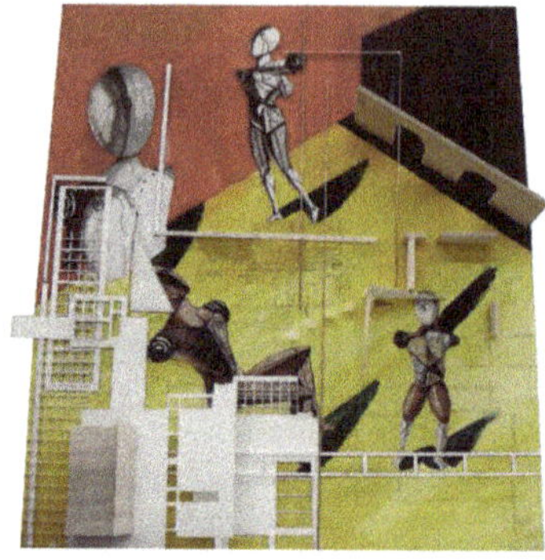

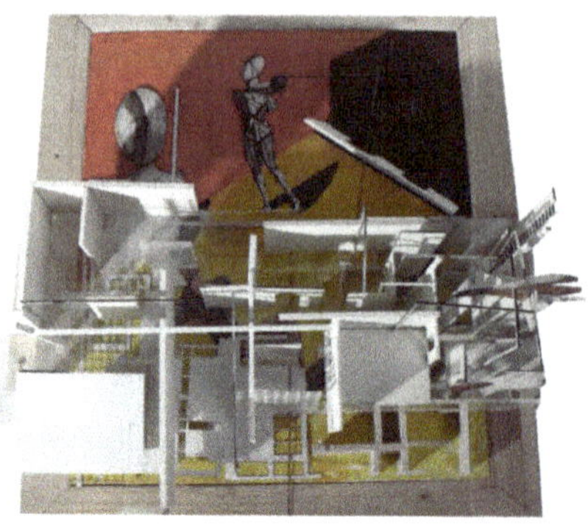

fig. 4.23: Diorama models for the creation of Isle End. Buban Ngu explored the 3-dimensionality of drawings in an attempt to see the world through the eyes of the mannequins.

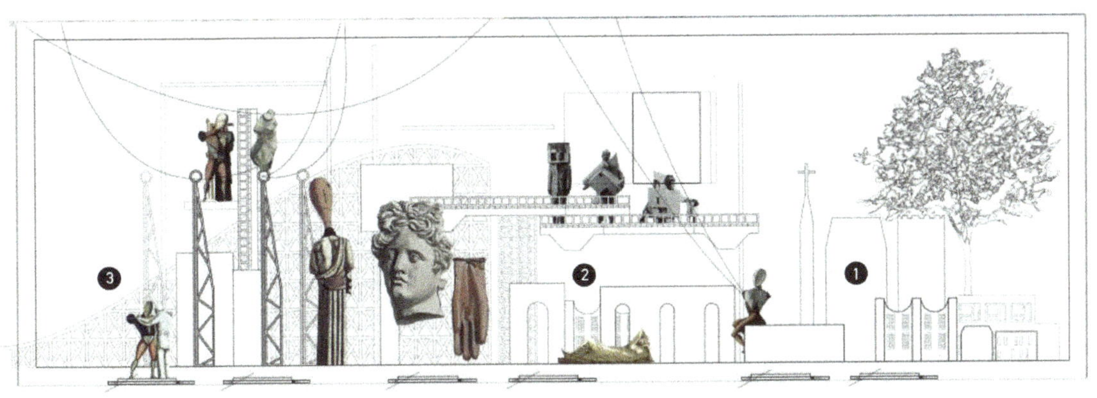
3
2
1

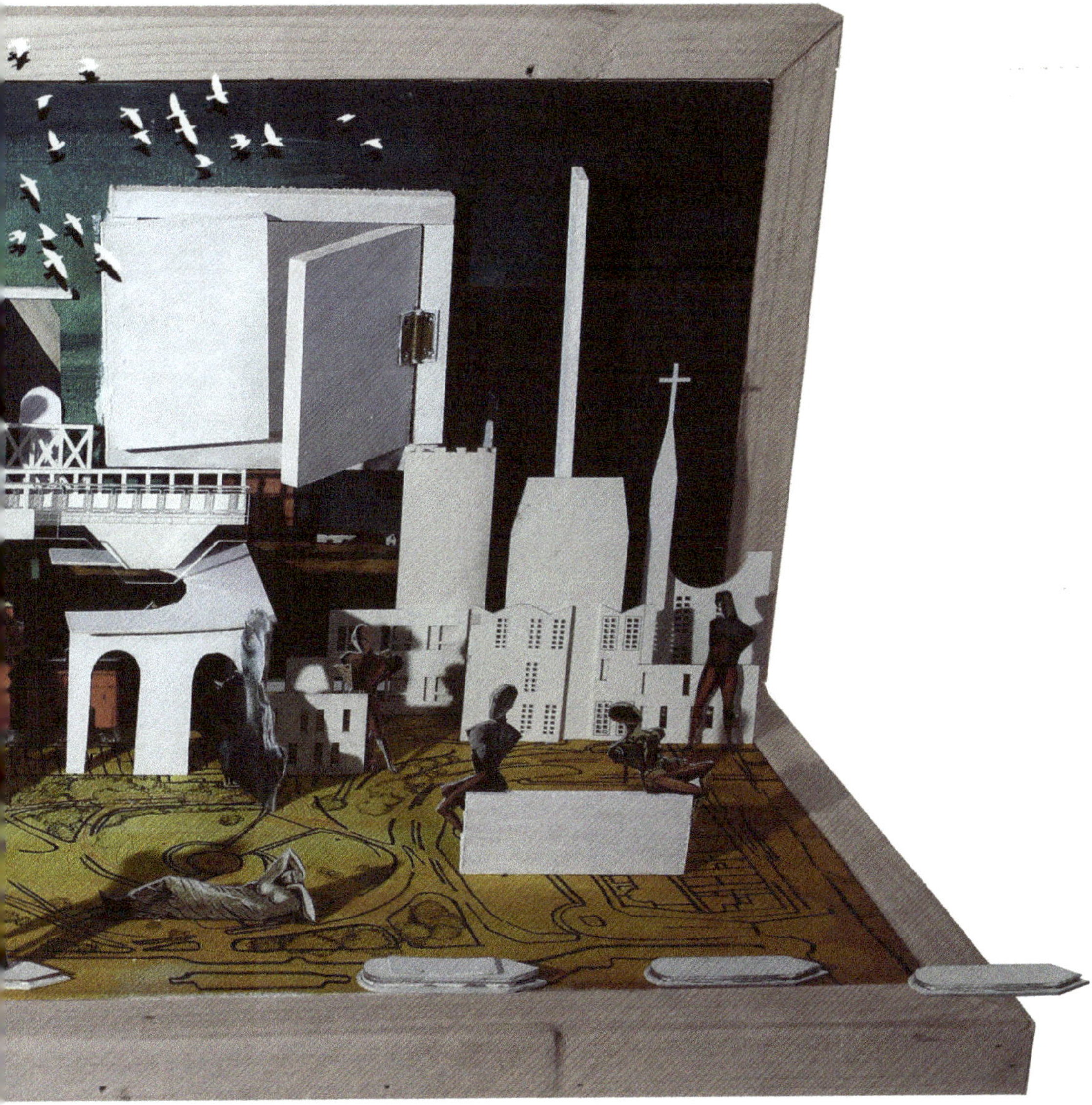

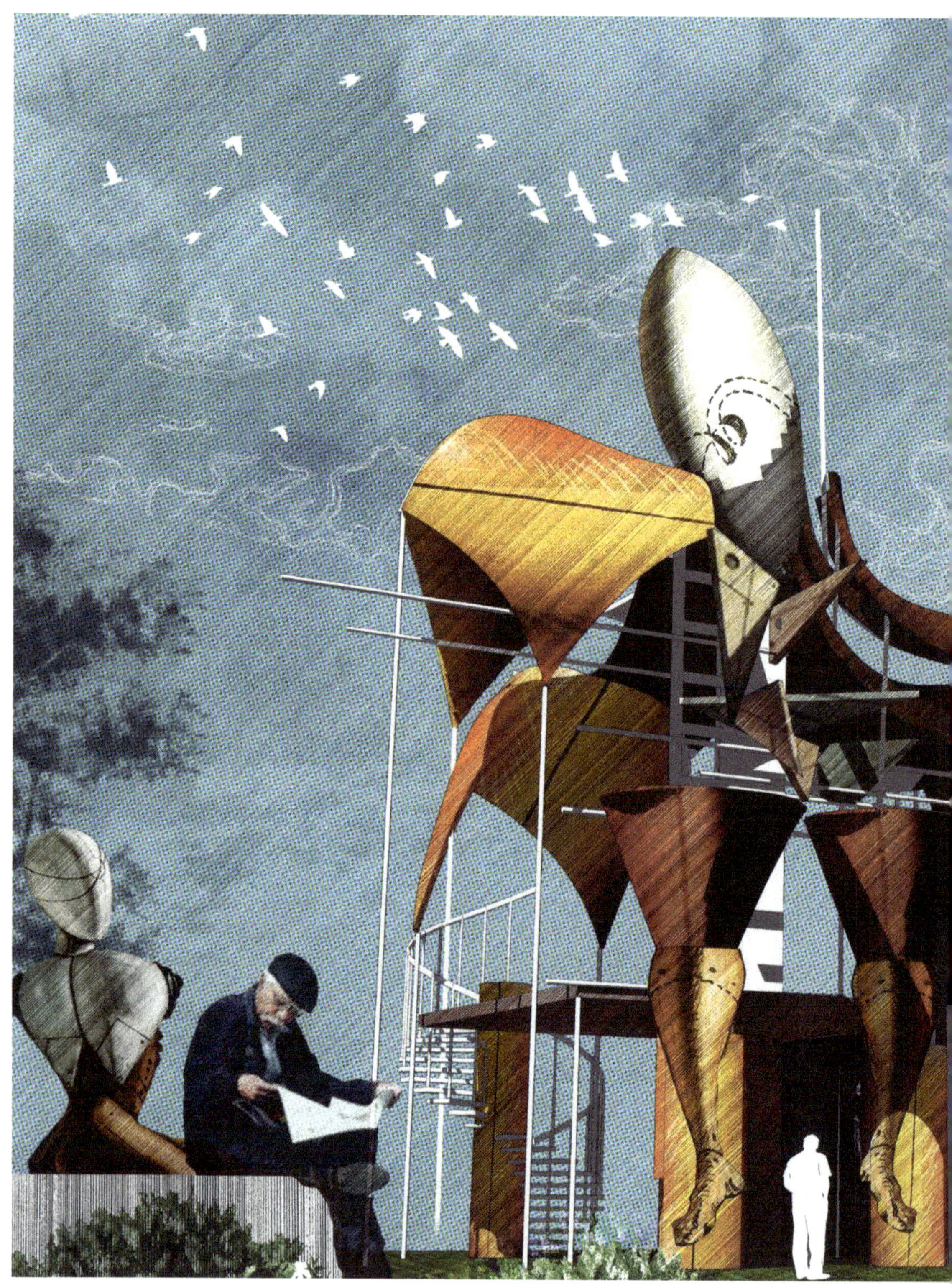

fig. 4.24: The platform allows the people to attach their mannequins to a rig system. Whilst the model is suspended, they may progressively add fragments to build up their sculpture.

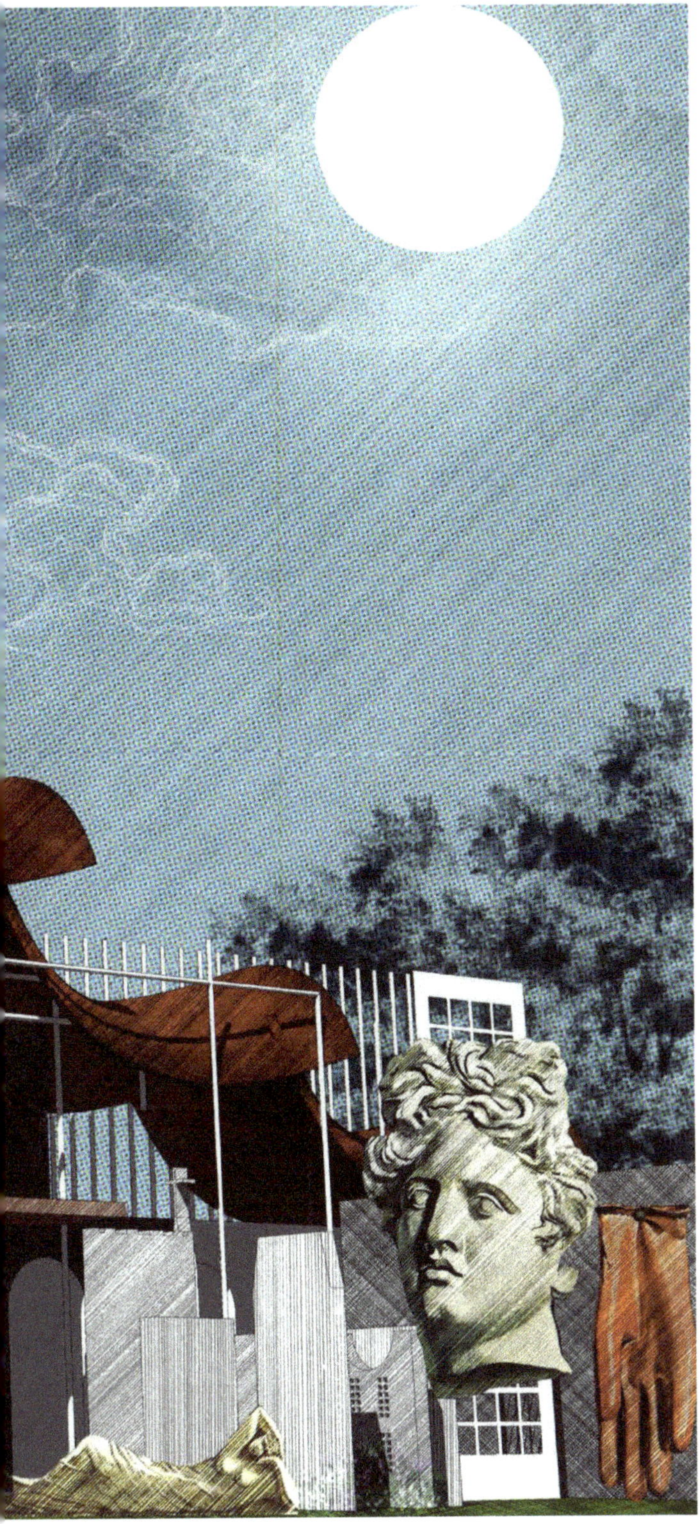

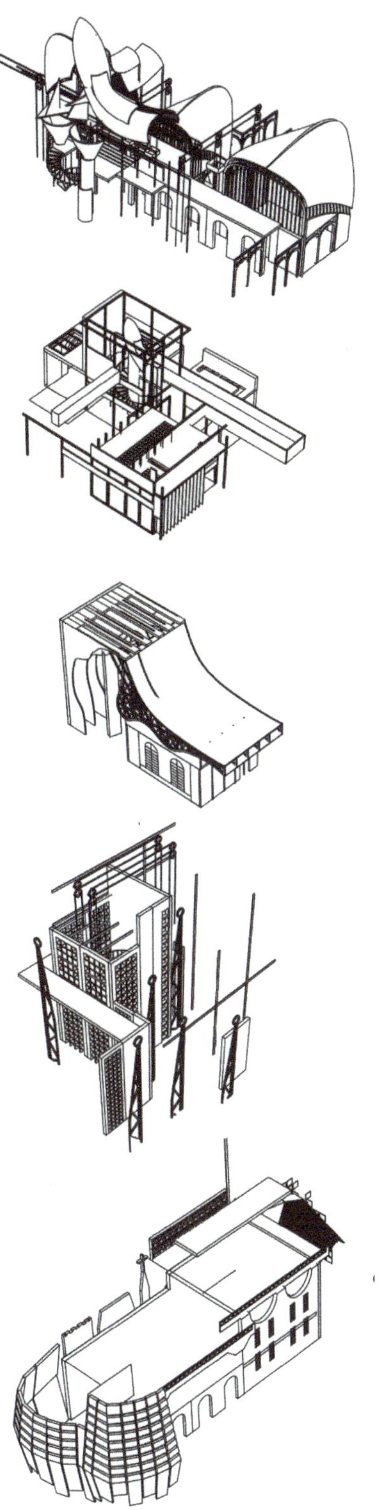

HERE BE MA'WOOLIES!
Architecture behind the regeneration of the River Thames

by
ASENA KOKSAL

BRIEF *Embodied Ecologies & Speculative Fabulations*

YEAR *2021-22*

TUTORS *Dr Alessandro Ayuso, Mary Konstantopoulou*

THEMES

Ecological Agency

Unhuman Environments

Tangled Timelines

Narrative World-building

Speculative Paleontology

Masterplan

Animal-Human Relationships

"...And from there, we can understand the necessity of introducing monsters into the scheme.

FMF, (Fossils and Monsters Foundation) was founded to make scientific research with limitless imagination. With this system of thought, FMF studied the sambin fossil in a different but charming way, and not limited by the continuity of history. FMF's 'Ressurection is Salvation' project, which brings back the epic animal Wooly Mammoth to Woolwich, promised to regenerate the current ecosystem of the River Thames and improve biodiversity to enable a better future for the next generations.

Despite the human-dominated landscapes of the 21st century, which considered animals to be inconvenient in urban spaces, FMF emphasised the significance of inviting Wooly Mammoths to daily life. With a multidisciplinary approach, architecture would play a great role in enabling humans' coexistence with the Regenerators of River Thames by designing the human-mawooly interactions"

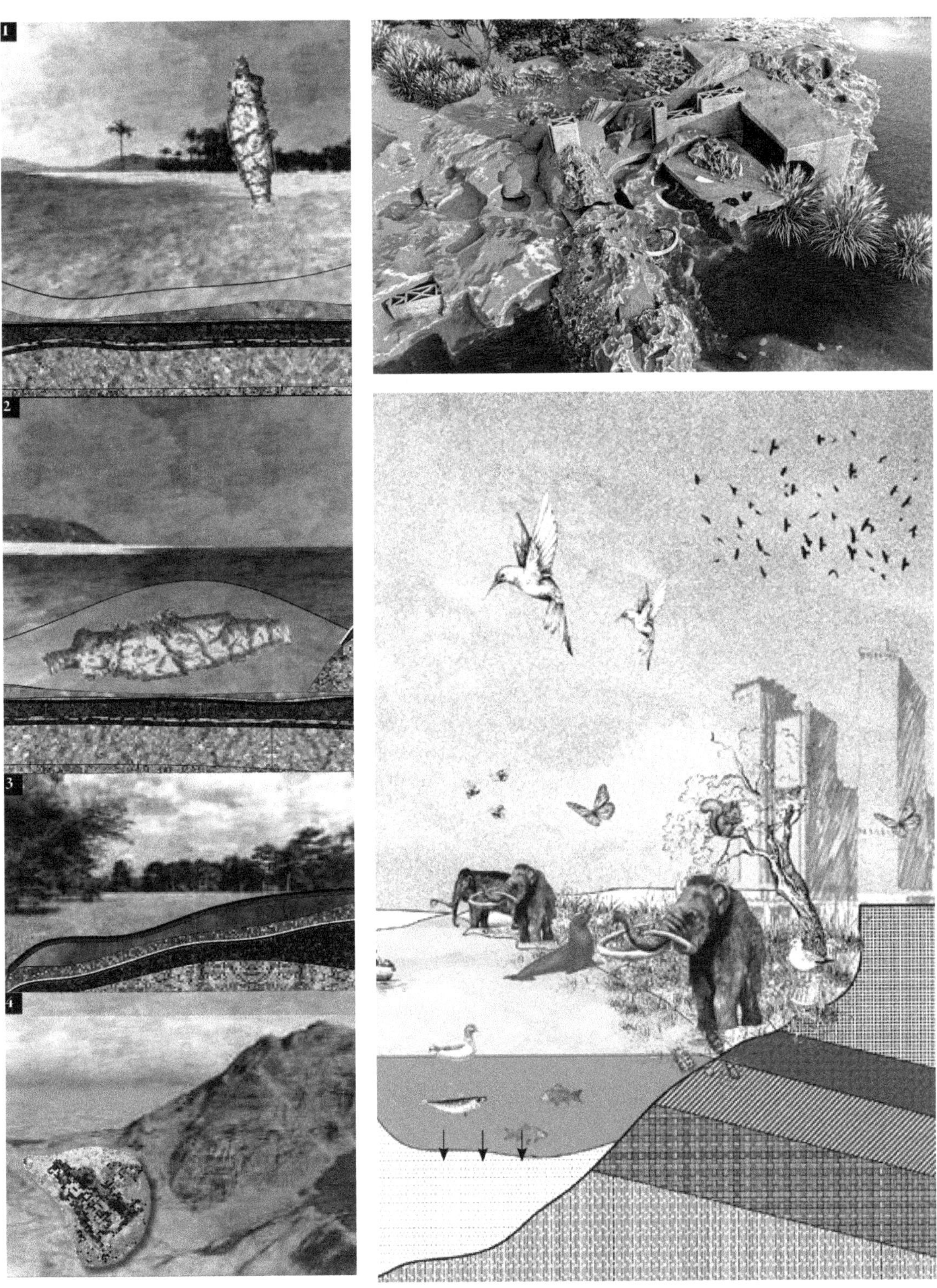

fig. 4.25-4.27: Top-Left to Bottom-Right: FMF studies on the formation of the Sambin fossil in a different but charming way, and not limited by the continuity of the history; Ruins of the Malevee; Thriving ecology of the Thames post-introduction of the Ma'Woolly.

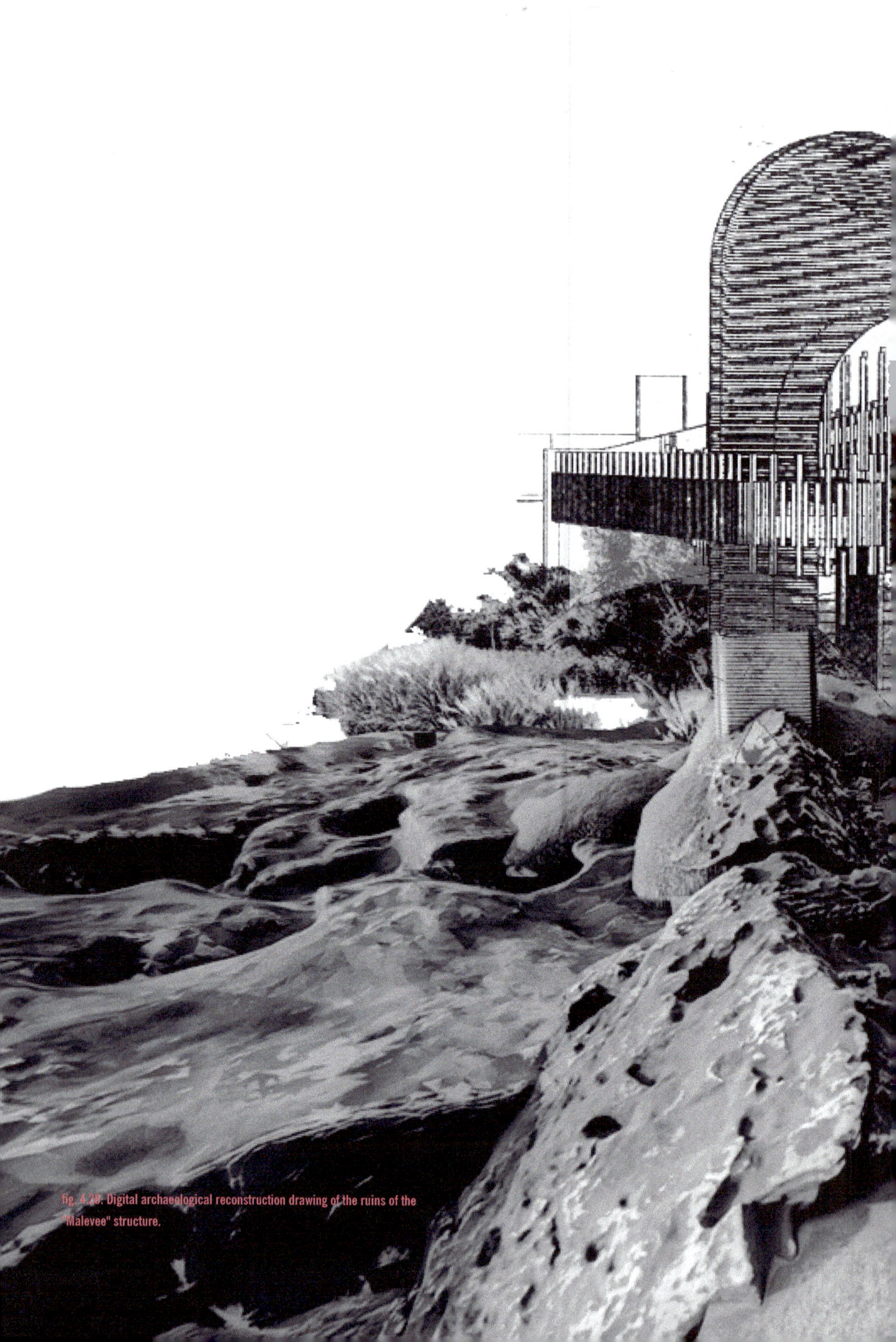

fig. 4.28: Digital archaeological reconstruction drawing of the ruins of the "Malevee" structure.

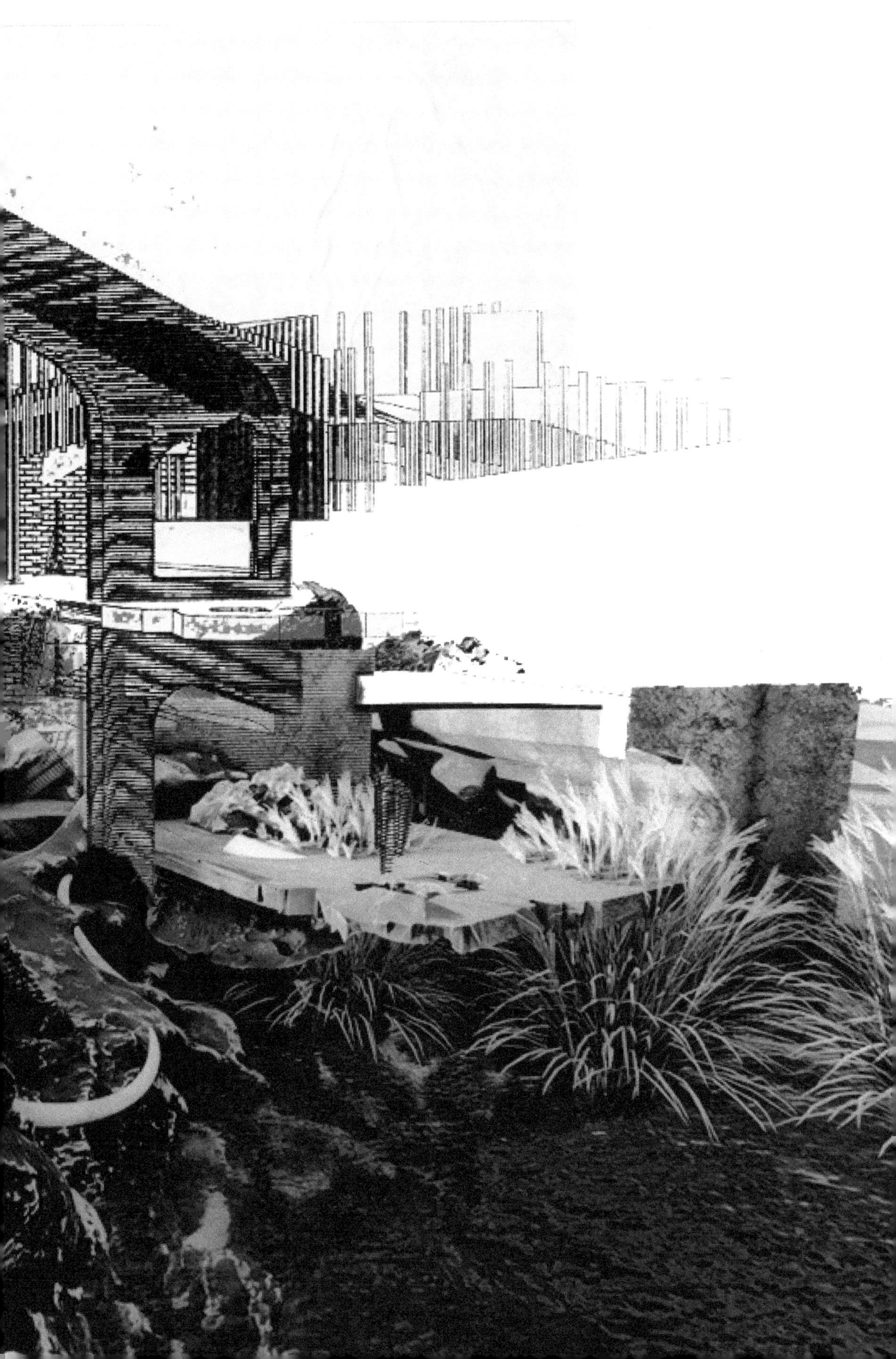

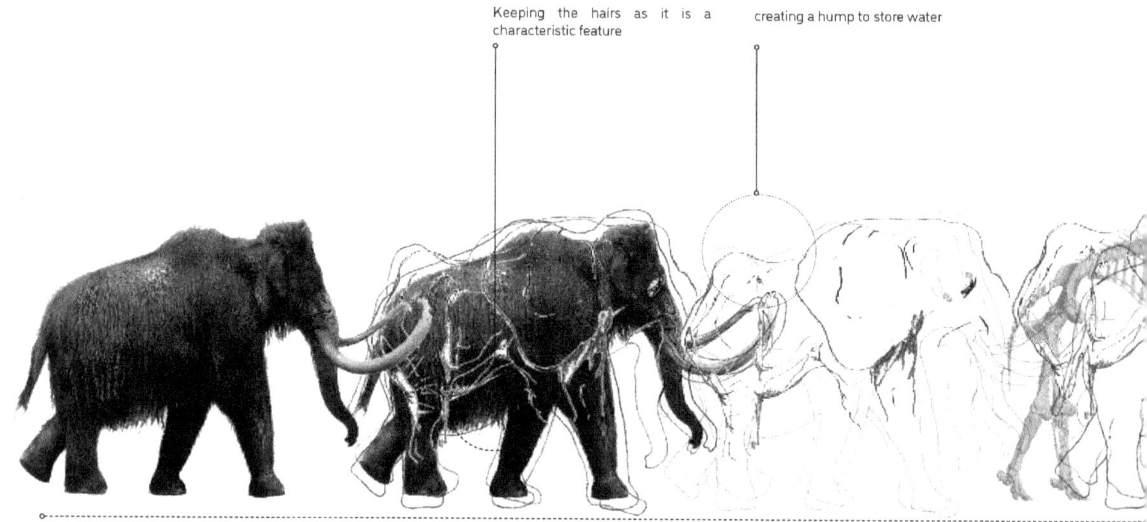

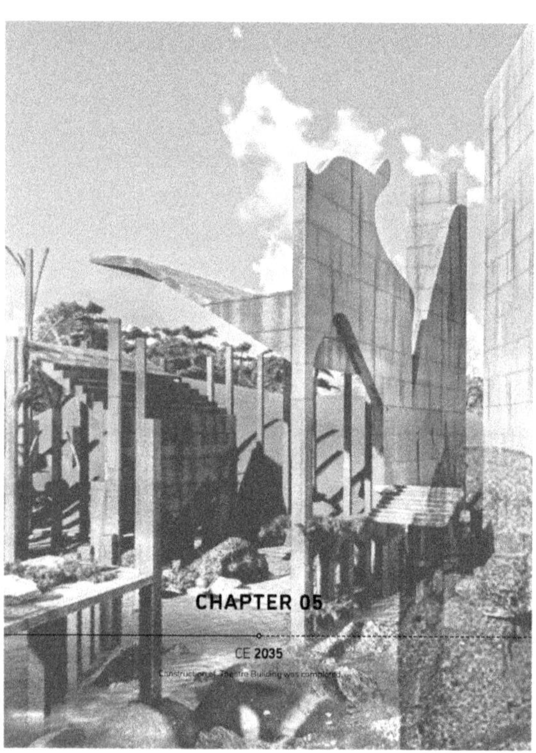

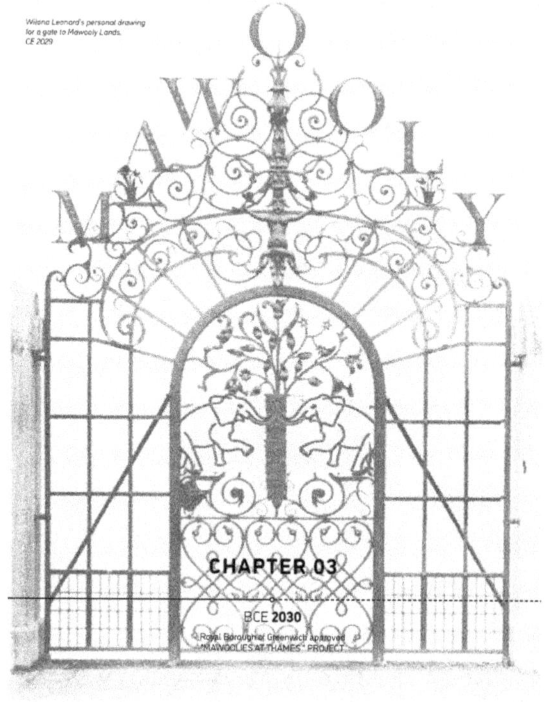

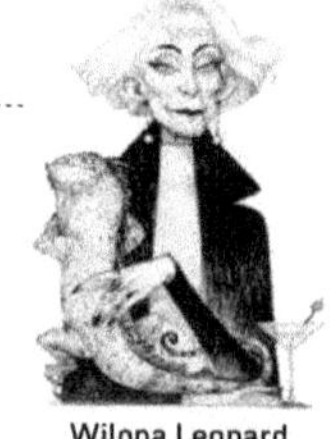

Wilona Leonard
Leonard & Partners Architects

FMF collaborated with Leonard and Partners Architects, who worked on the master plan of the "Maleevee Path" including the Science Institution Building. Interestingly, Art Noveau details combined with contemporary architecture due to Wilona Leonard's particular interest in the iconic art movement.

fig. 4.29-4.34: Top-Left to Bottom Right: "Ma'Wooly" (Mammothous Facticious Lanatus) genetic engineering evolution; The Theatre Building under construction; Leonard & Partners' Architects design of the gate to MaWooly Lands CE 2029, inspired by the Art Deco movement. Facing Page: Fossil Hunt @ Woolwich map; Malevee structure plan.

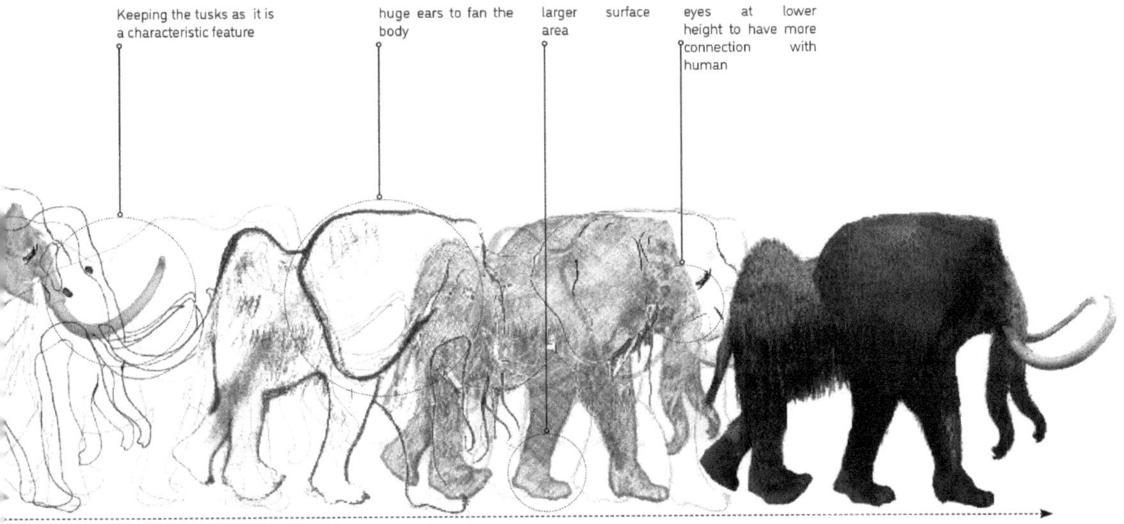

Keeping the tusks as it is a characteristic feature

huge ears to fan the body

larger surface area

eyes at lower height to have more connection with human

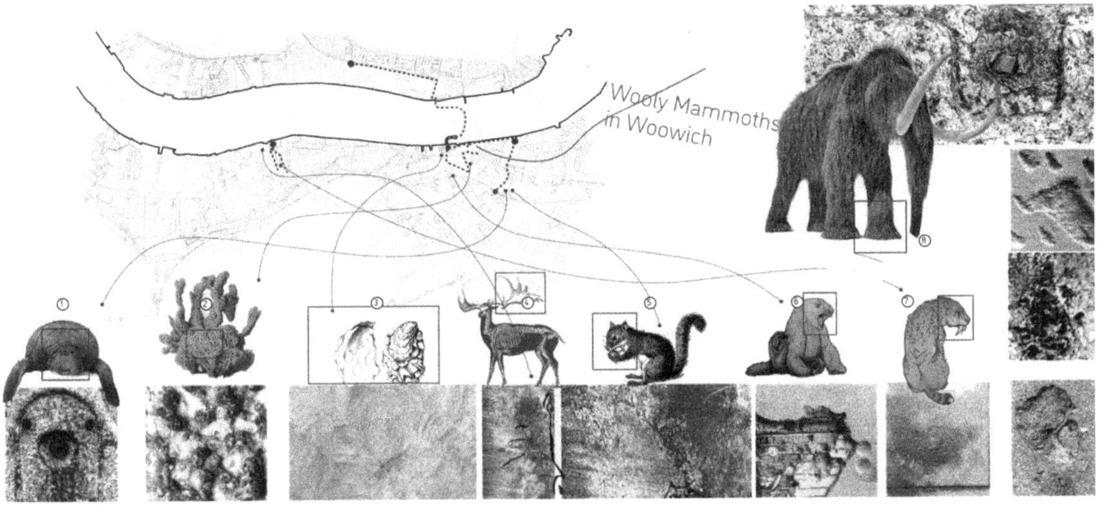

Wooly Mammoths in Woowich

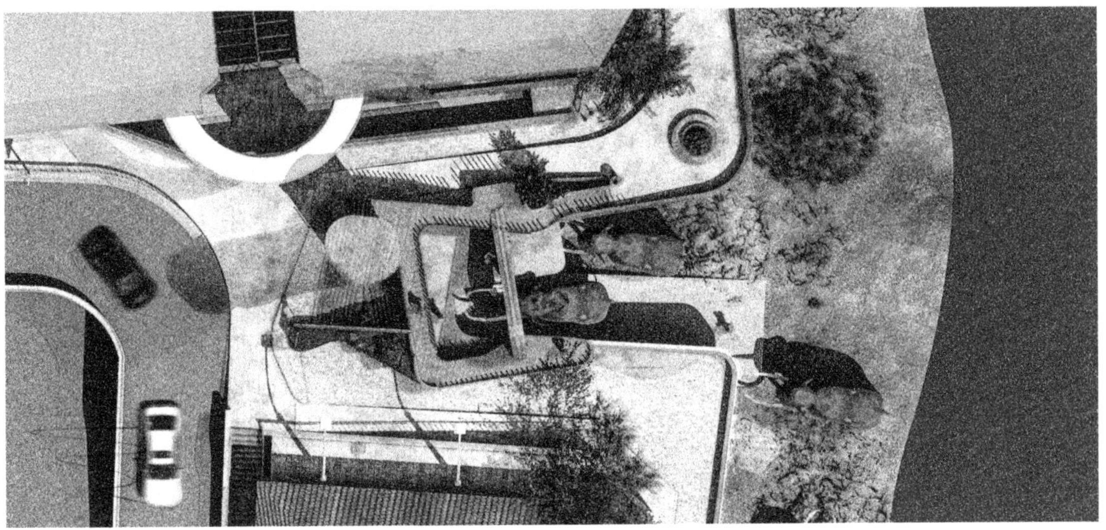

THAMES RIVER

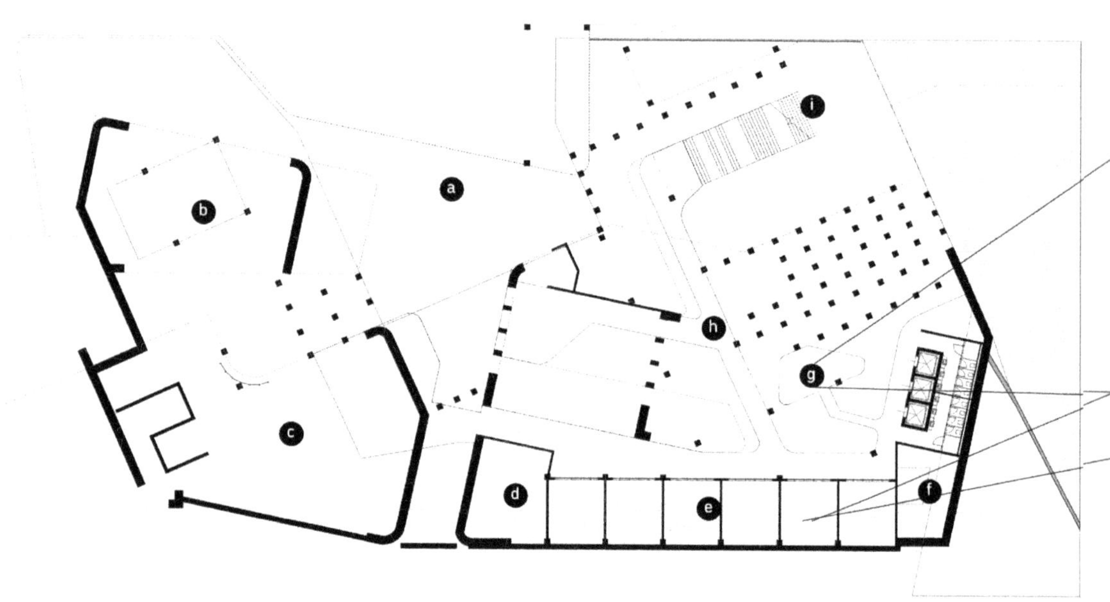

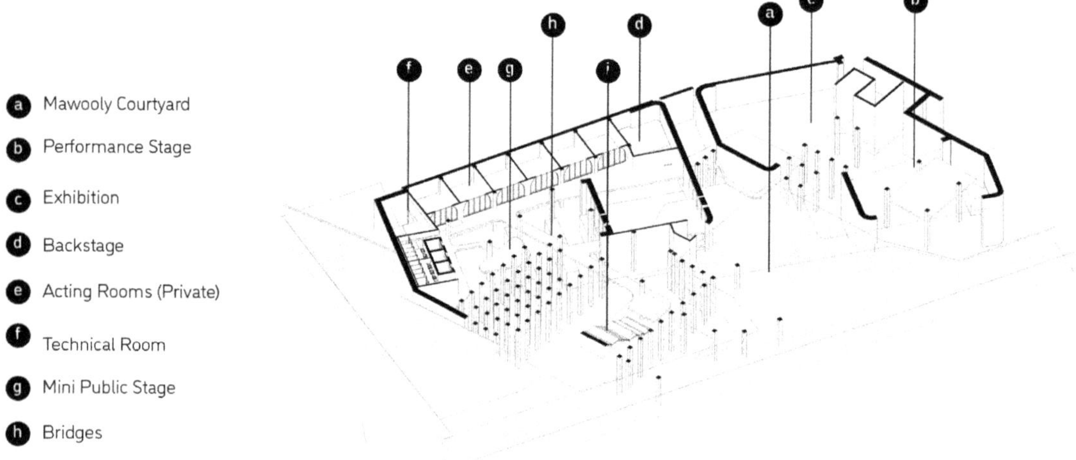

fig. 4.35-4.37: Plan of the Theatre Building lower floor (River level 0.00) with views of the mini-public stage and private acting rooms; cut-away axonometric of the lower floor; view of the Ma'Wooly courtyard.

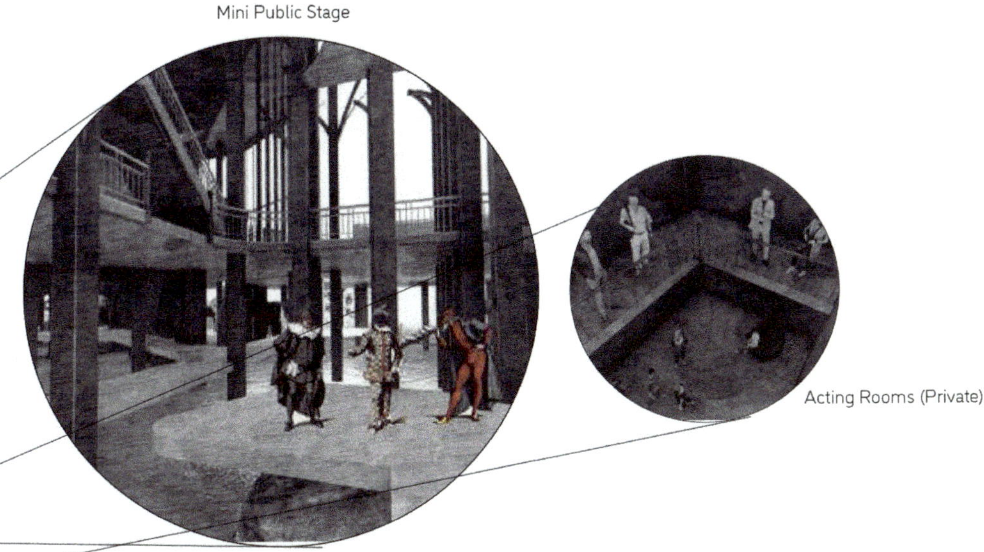
Mini Public Stage
Acting Rooms (Private)

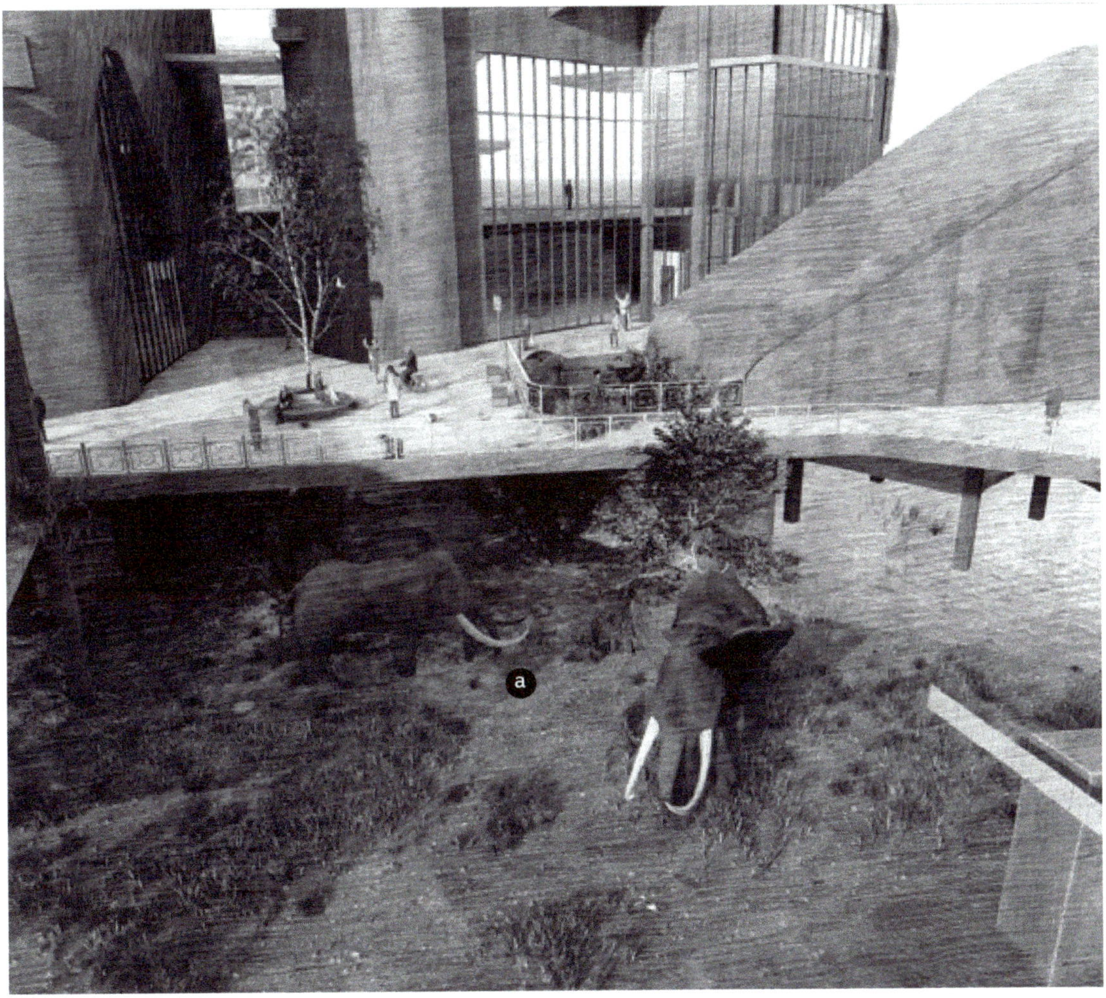

1 Waterfront Leisure Centre
2 Malevee
3 Stage
4 Stage
5 Road
6 Public Space
7 Public Stairs
8 Pedestrian Road (Thames Path)
9 Mawooly Courtyard
10 Retail Units
11 Main Stage
12 Glass Roof
13 Terraces
14 Mawooly Ramp
15 Stairs to Basement Lev
16 River Thames

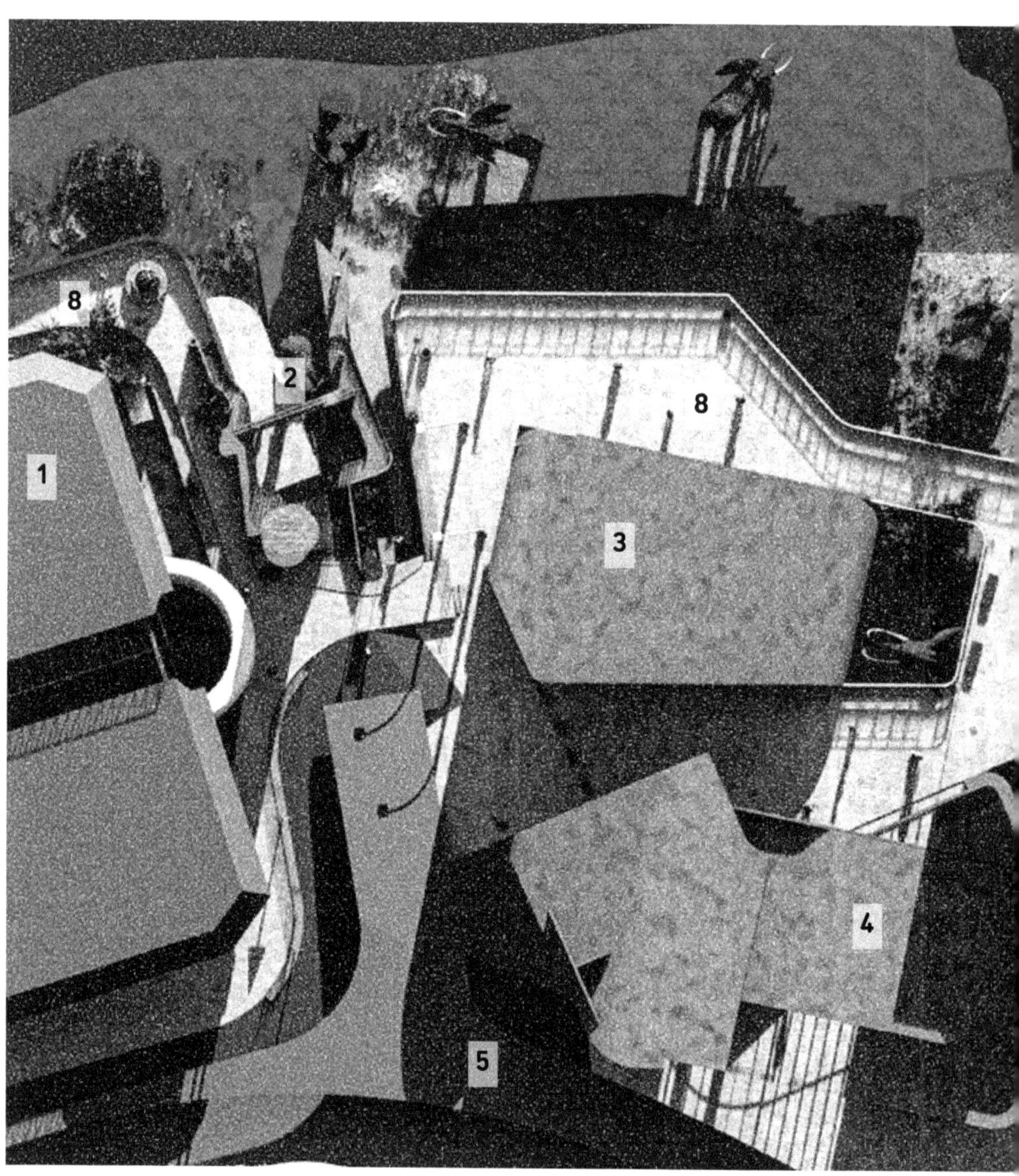

fig. 4.38: Malevee and Theatre Masterplan.

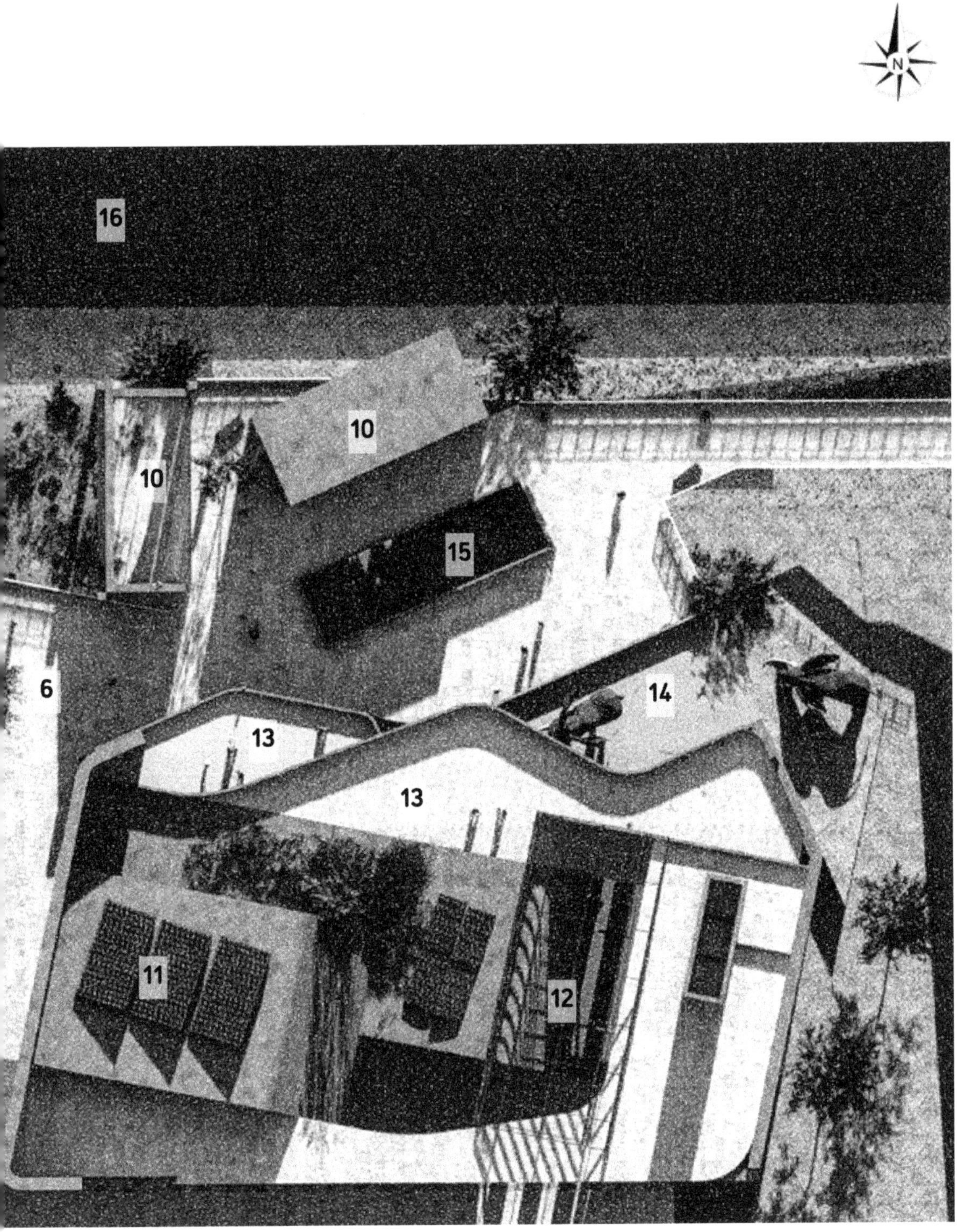

N

16
10
10
15
14
6
13
13
11
12

UKIO.LAND

by
CONRAD DANIEL ARETA

BRIEF *Things Have Feelings Too*

YEAR *2023-24*

TUTORS *Dr Alessandro Ayuso, Mary Konstantopoulou*

THEMES

Assemblage

Mirrored Body-World Relationships

Non-human Ecologies

Post-natural Body / Landscape

Cyborgs + Androids

Intersubjectivity / Technology

Hackable Bodies

"The following portfolio is a series of lost archives once again discovered in the year 3000. These documents are divided into three parts and explore the Isle of Dogs through the body of an Odradek [a sentient assemblage], a cyborg named A.L.I.C.E. as she learns to mediate the man, the machine and the ecology. The first documents the prologue, covering the conception of A.L.I.C.E and the frst envisionings of Ukiyo.Land through an intervention. In the second part, the project explores the construction of Ukiyo.Land and its speculated future. These two parts can be further split into an episodic structure, with each episode or 'savestate' depicting a different point in Ukiyo.Land's timeline, both of which culminate into the third part, the epilogue which speculated on the impacts of Ukiyo.Land and its cyborgean philosophies on the urban landscape.

It is through this archived timeline of events that we learn how A.L.I.C.E.'s interventions and Ukiyo. Land's conception would forever change the urban landscape as we know it and understand what pleasures can be found within the cyborg's garden."

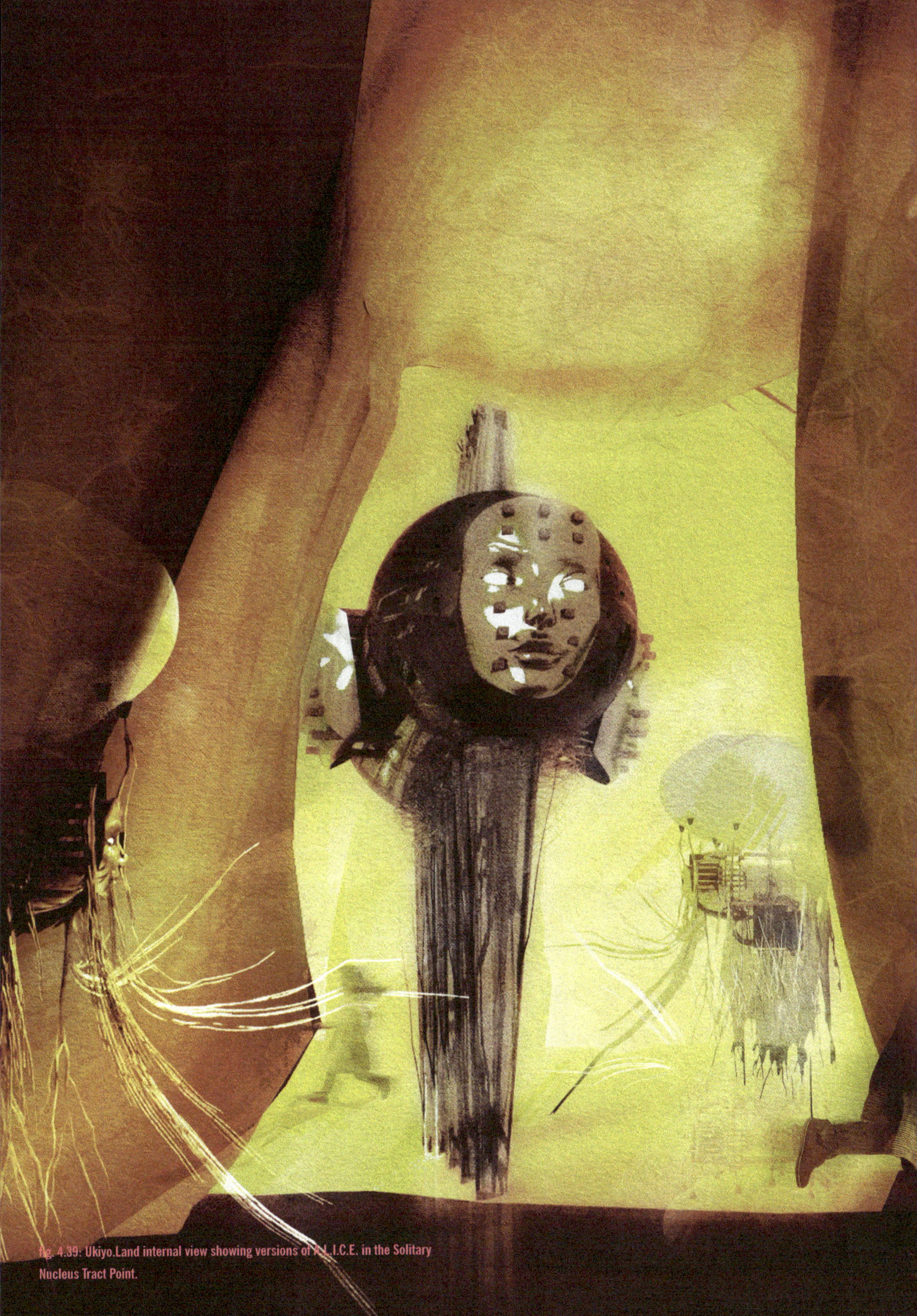

fig. 4.39: Ukiyo.Land internal view showing versions of A.L.I.C.E. in the Solitary Nucleus Tract Point.

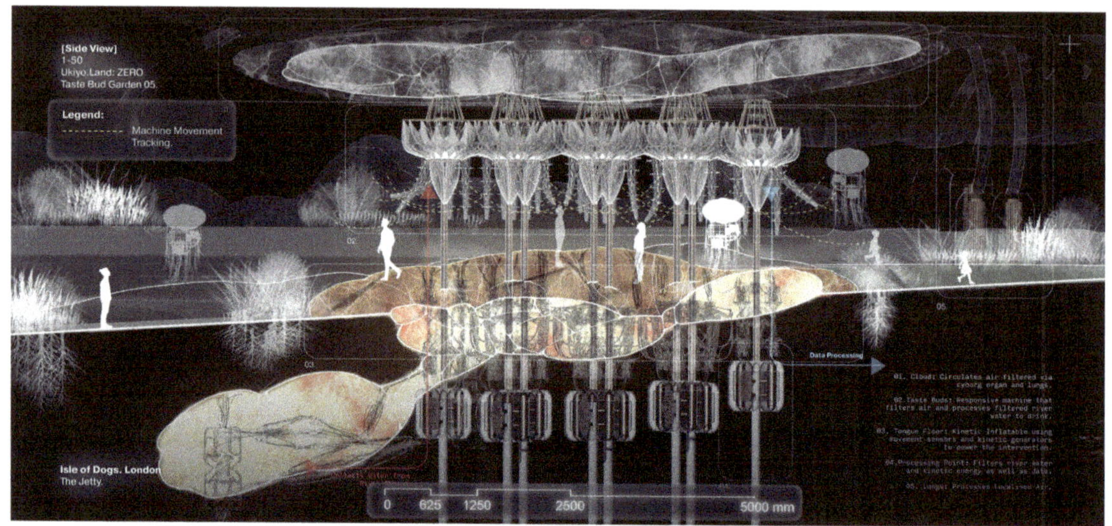
[Side View]
1-50
Ukiyo.Land: ZERO
Taste Bud Garden 05.
Legend:
Machine Movement Tracking.
Data Processing
Isle of Dogs. London
The Jetty.
0 625 1250 2500 5000 mm

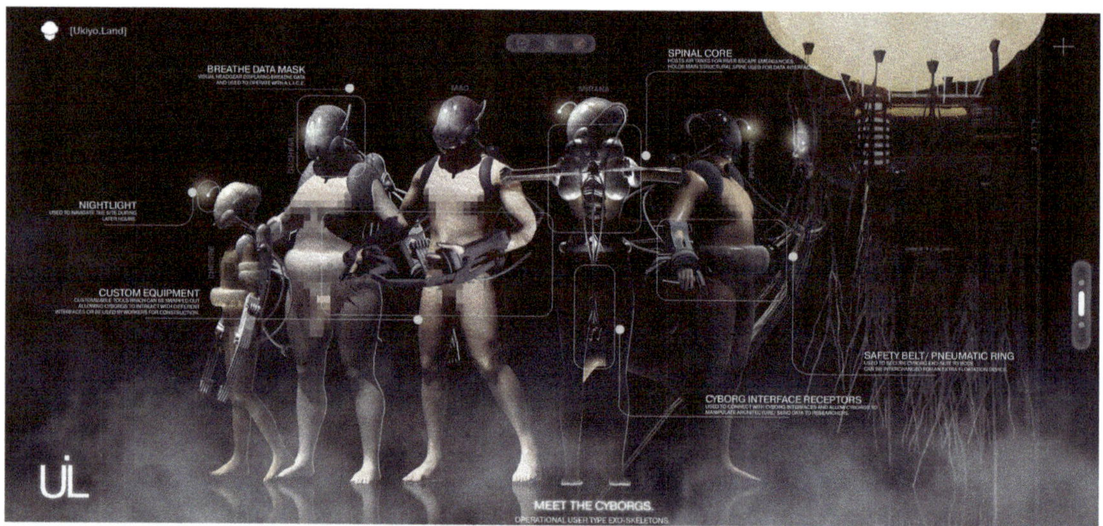
[Ukiyo.Land]
BREATHE DATA MASK
SPINAL CORE
NIGHTLIGHT
CUSTOM EQUIPMENT
SAFETY BELT / PNEUMATIC RING
CYBORG INTERFACE RECEPTORS
UL
MEET THE CYBORGS.
OPERATIONAL USER TYPE EXO-SKELETONS

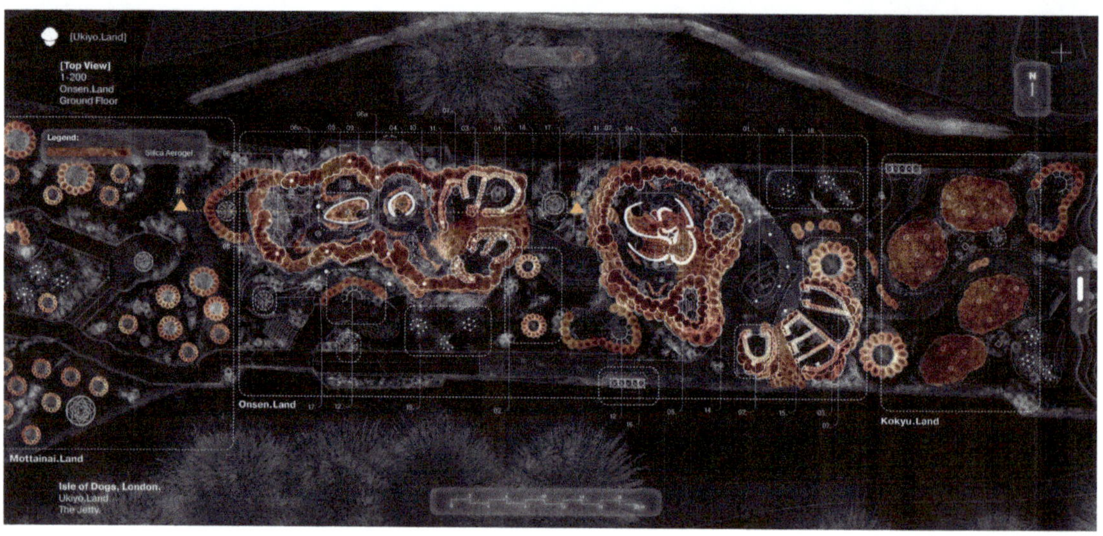
[Ukiyo.Land]
[Top View]
1-200
Onsen.Land
Ground Floor
Legend:
Silica Aerogel
Onsen.Land
Kokyu.Land
Mottainai.Land
Isle of Dogs, London.
Ukiyo.Land
The Jetty.

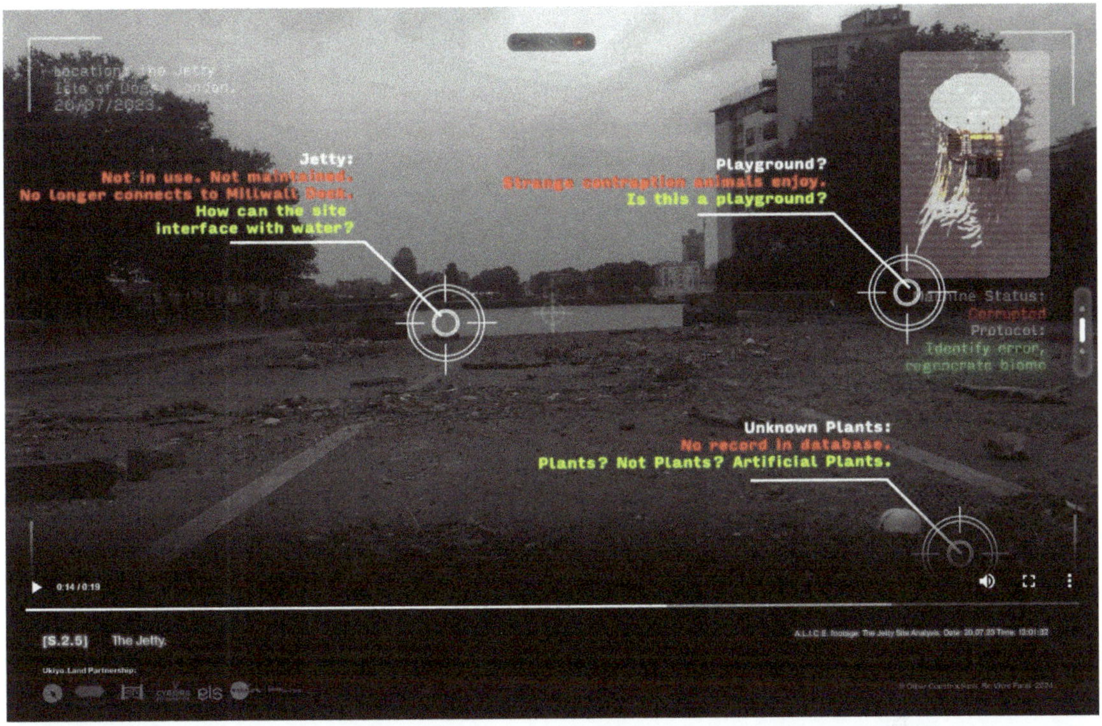

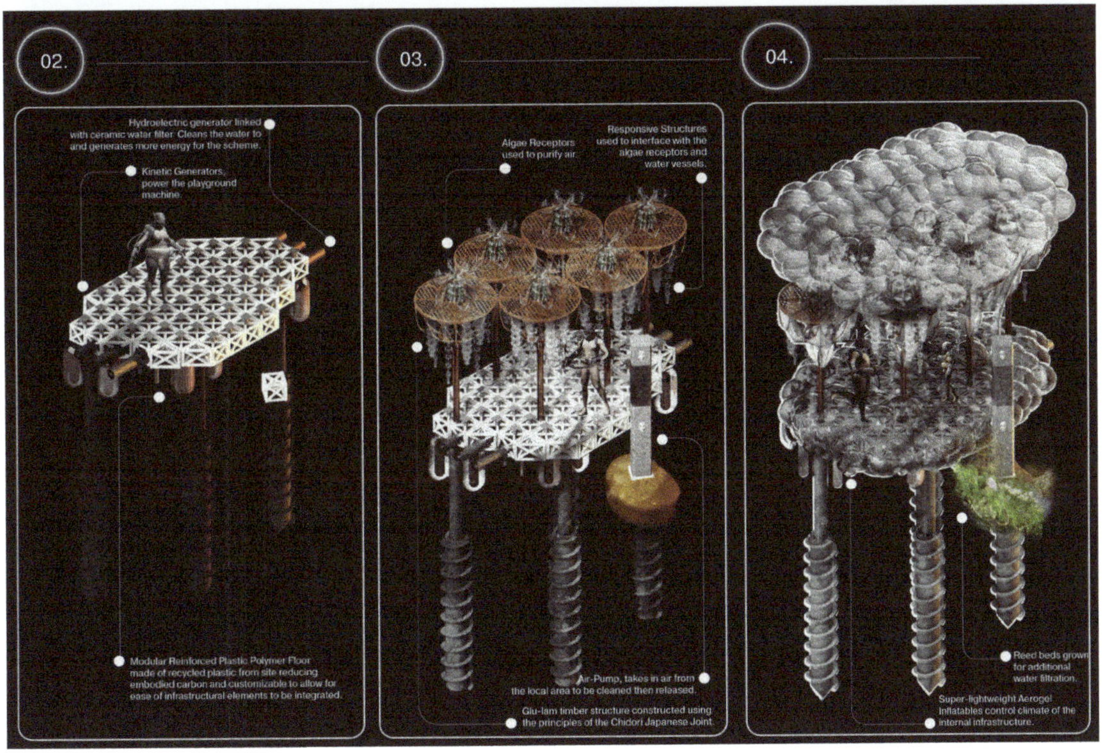

Jetty:
Not in use. Not maintained.
No longer connects to Millwall Dock.
How can the site
interface with water?

Playground?
Strange contraption animals enjoy.
Is this a playground?

Unknown Plants:
No record in database.
Plants? Not Plants? Artificial Plants.

[S.2.5] The Jetty.

02.

Hydroelectric generator linked with ceramic water filter. Cleans the water to and generates more energy for the scheme.

Kinetic Generators, power the playground machine.

Modular Reinforced Plastic Polymer Floor made of recycled plastic from site reducing embodied carbon and customizable to allow for ease of infrastructural elements to be integrated.

03.

Algae Receptors used to purify air.

Responsive Structures used to interface with the algae receptors and water vessels.

Air-Pump, takes in air from the local area to be cleaned then released.

Glu-lam timber structure constructed using the principles of the Chidori Japanese Joint.

04.

Reed beds grown for additional water filtration.

Super-lightweight Aerogel Inflatables control climate of the internal infrastructure.

fig. 4.40-4.44: Facing Page: Taste Bud Garden Section; The U.L. Essentials collection; Cyborg Landscape Garden Ground Floor Plan. Top to Bottom: A.L.I.C.E.'s interface's first encounters with the site; Construction of the Algae breathing conversion receptors and drinking system.

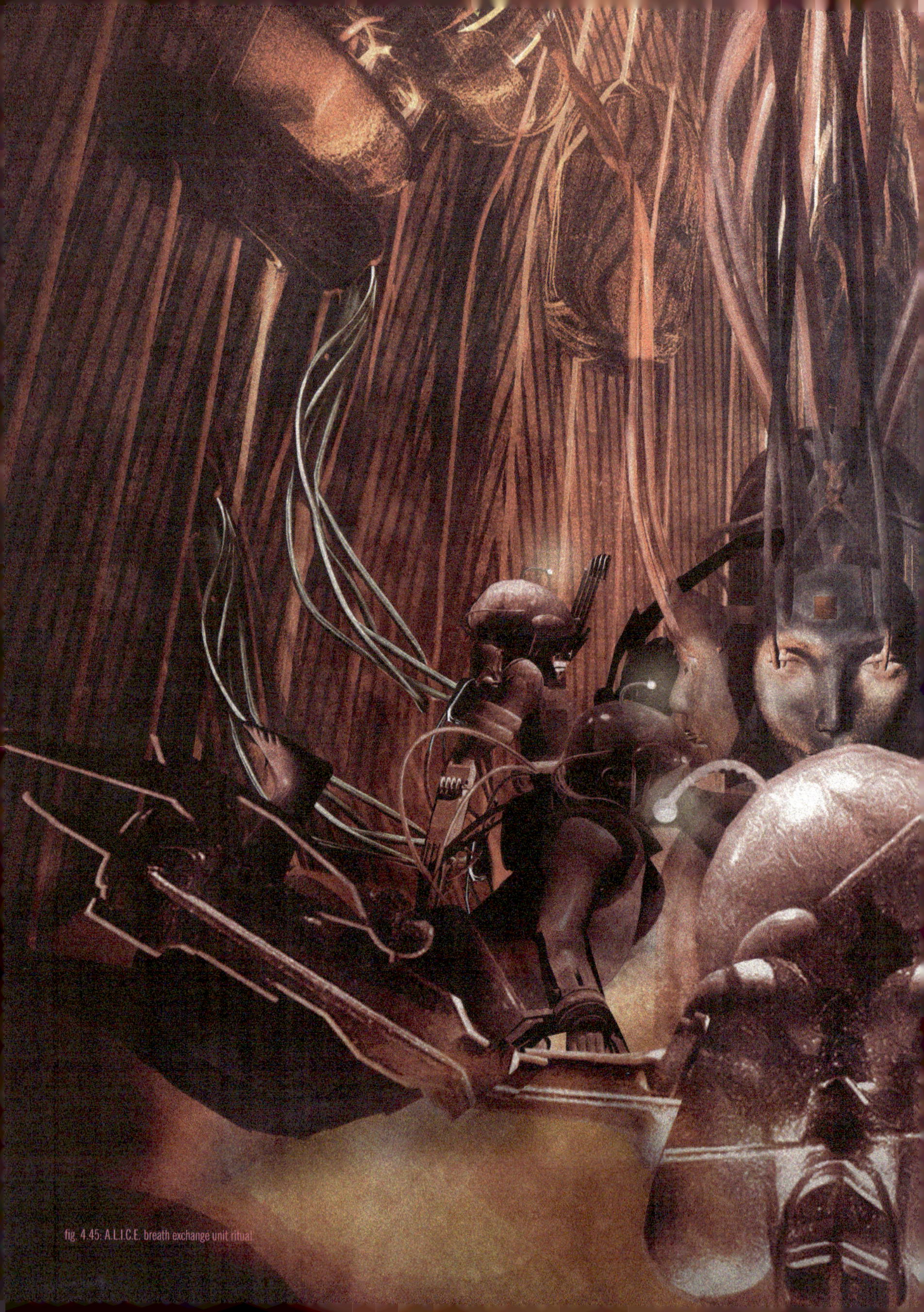

fig. 4.45: A.L.I.C.E. breath exchange unit ritual

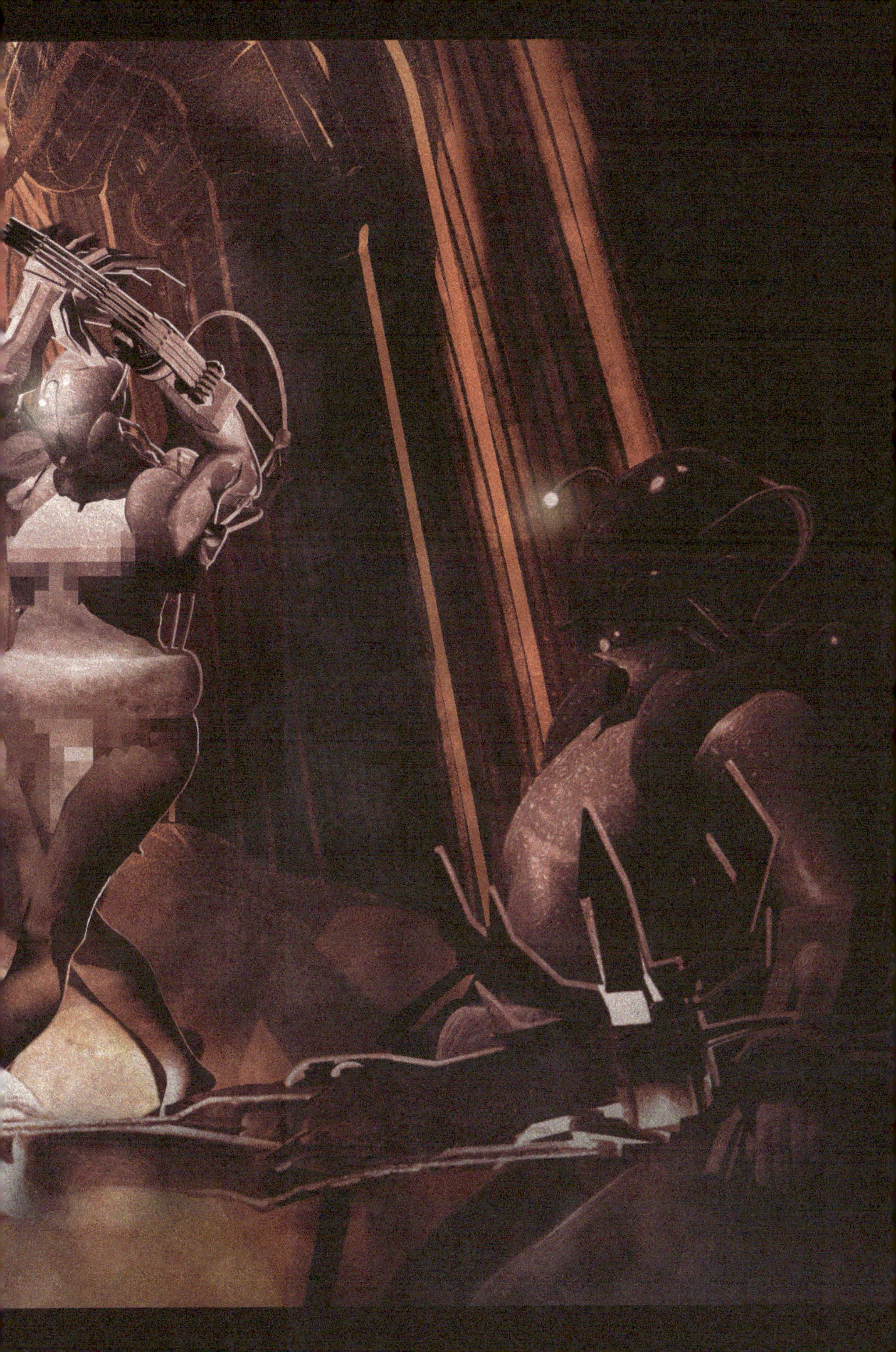

BACTERIA SANCTUARY: A Diary by OD

by
ANASTASIA KOLIOLIOU

BRIEF *Things Have Feelings Too*

YEAR *2023-24*

TUTORS *Dr Alessandro Ayuso, Mary Konstantopoulou*

THEMES

Non-human Agency

Mirrored Body-World Relationships

Infected / Porous Body

Narrative World-building

Cross-scalar Design

Utopia / Dystopia

"The story depicts a dystopian future where ecological crises have devastated the Earth. The narrator, OD, becomes obsessed with bacteria, seeing them as the key to humanity's downfall.

OD starts exploring and cultivating bacteria around the flooded Isle of Dogs, seeking to understand their obscure power.

As the narrator mutates, fusing with the drowned land, he comes to believe he can form a new existence with the microbes, embracing the bacterial takeover rather than trying to prevent it.

The story implies that humanity's neglect of the environment could unleash ecological collapse, leading the narrator to abandon human civilization for an unorthodox bacterial-focused future."

fig. 4.46: Facing page: OD's interaction with Bacteria growing columns.

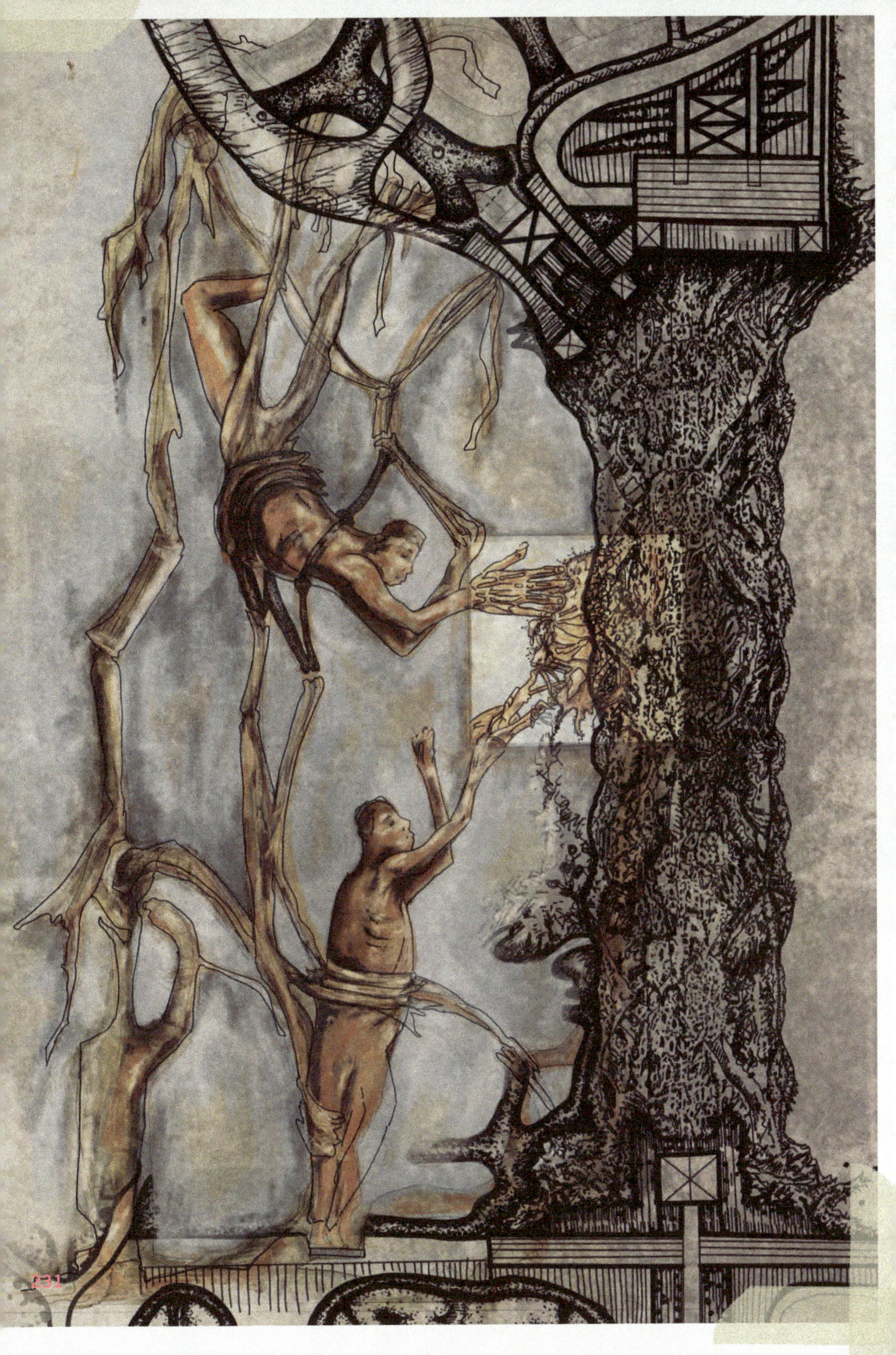

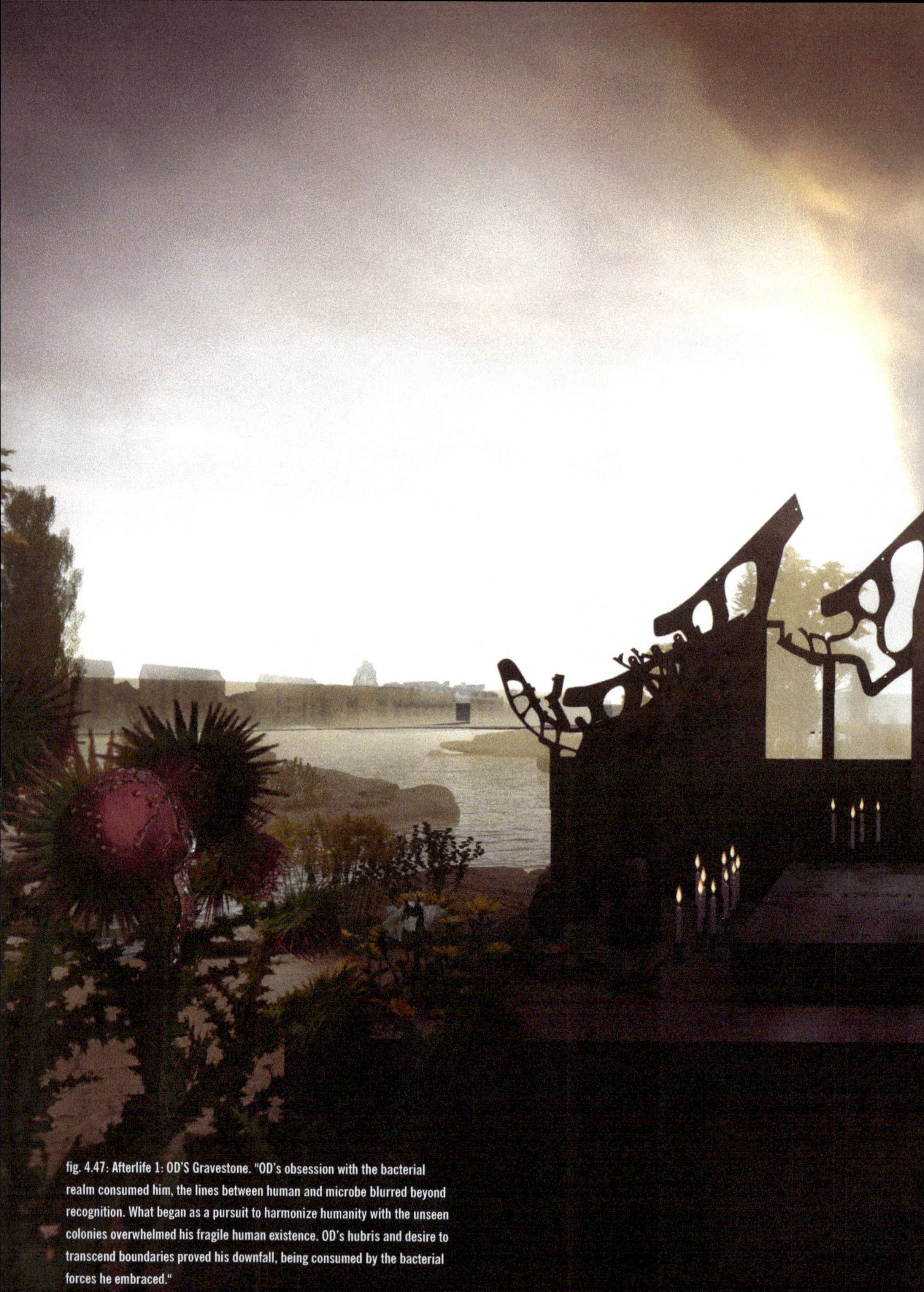

fig. 4.47: Afterlife 1: OD'S Gravestone. "OD's obsession with the bacterial realm consumed him, the lines between human and microbe blurred beyond recognition. What began as a pursuit to harmonize humanity with the unseen colonies overwhelmed his fragile human existence. OD's hubris and desire to transcend boundaries proved his downfall, being consumed by the bacterial forces he embraced."

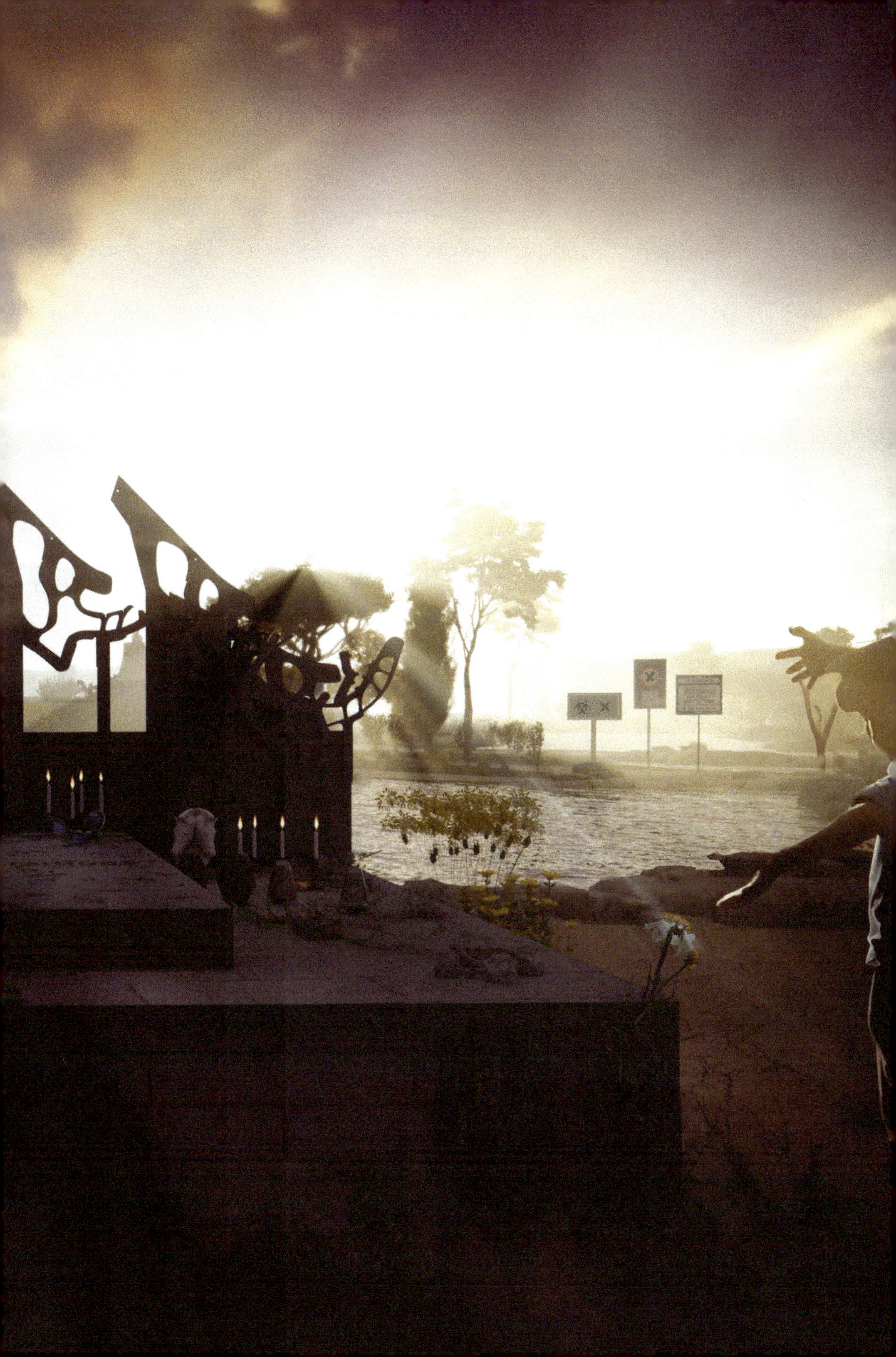

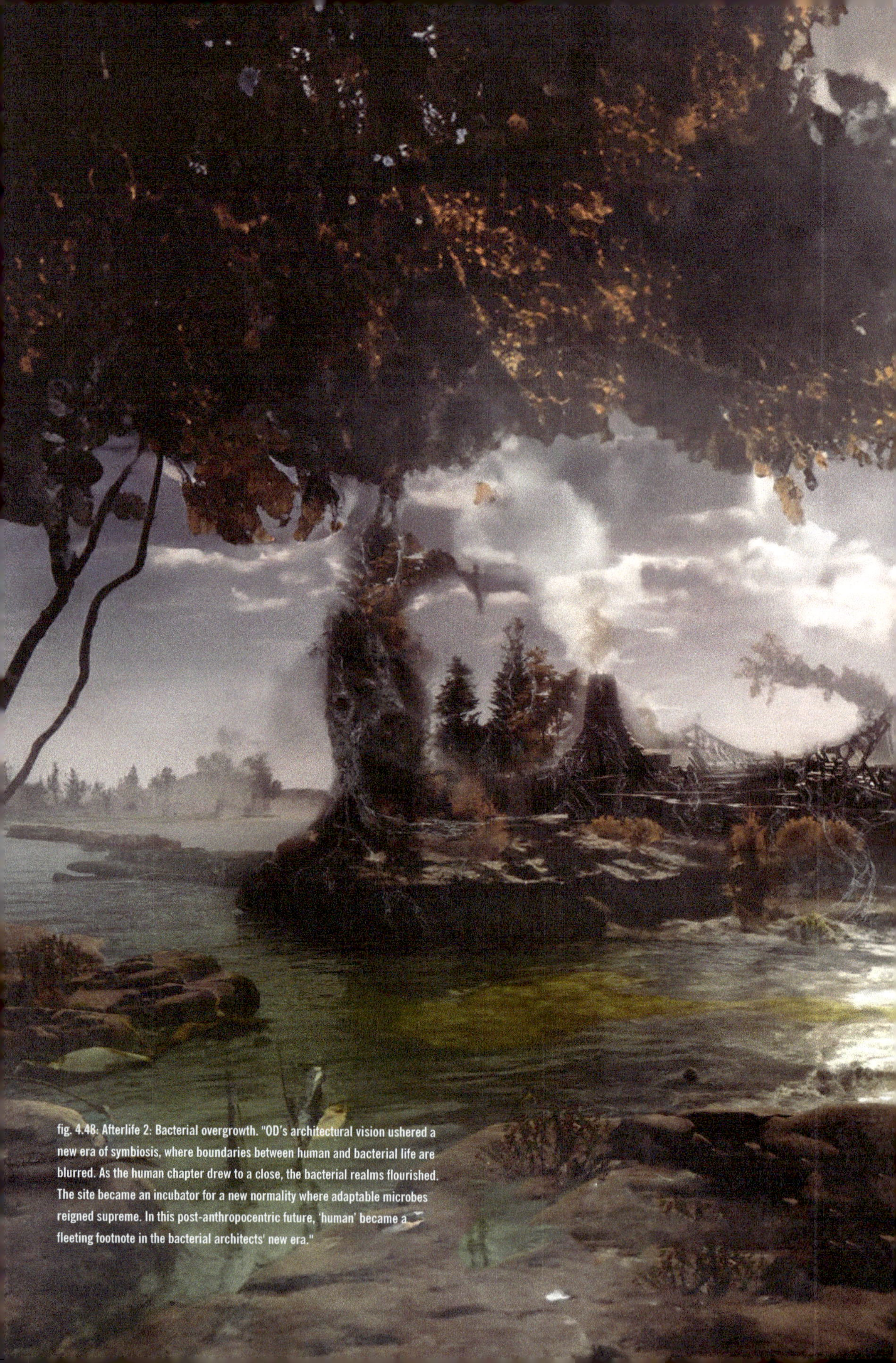

fig. 4.48: Afterlife 2: Bacterial overgrowth. "OD's architectural vision ushered a new era of symbiosis, where boundaries between human and bacterial life are blurred. As the human chapter drew to a close, the bacterial realms flourished. The site became an incubator for a new normality where adaptable microbes reigned supreme. In this post-anthropocentric future, 'human' became a fleeting footnote in the bacterial architects' new era."

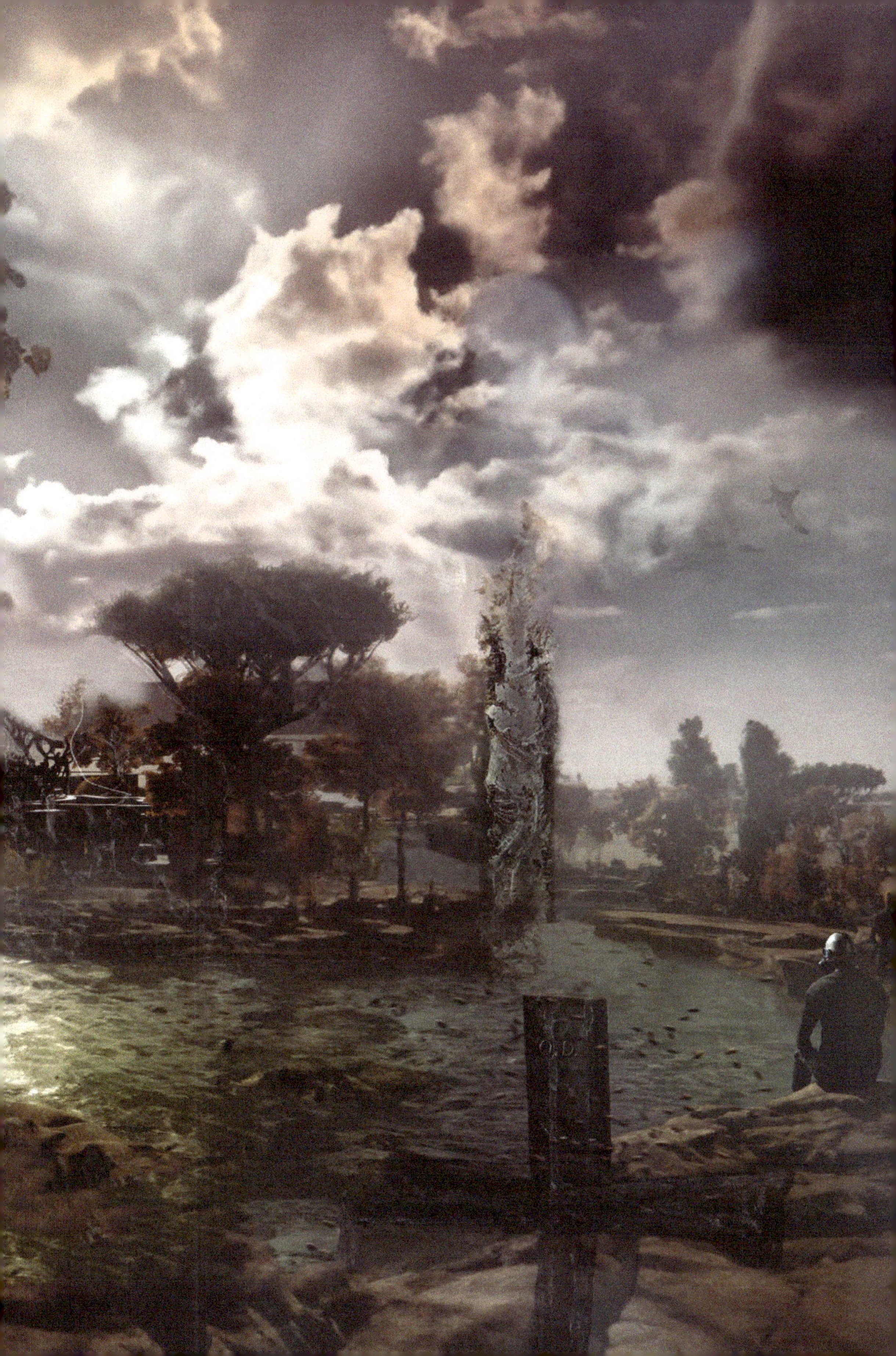

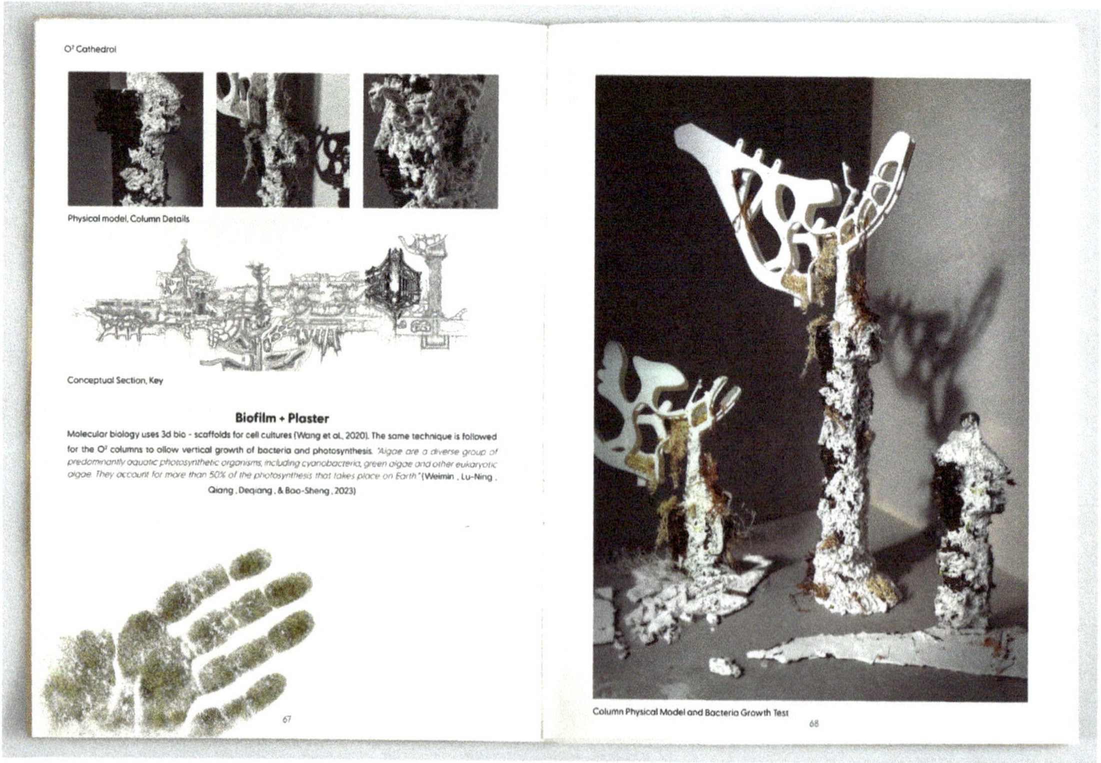

O² Cathedral

Physical model, Column Details

Conceptual Section, Key

Biofilm + Plaster

Molecular biology uses 3d bio - scaffolds for cell cultures (Wang et al., 2020). The same technique is followed for the O² columns to allow vertical growth of bacteria and photosynthesis. *"Algae are a diverse group of predominantly aquatic photosynthetic organisms, including cyanobacteria, green algae and other eukaryotic algae. They account for more than 50% of the photosynthesis that takes place on Earth"* (Weimin , Lu-Ning , Qiang , Deqiang , & Bao-Sheng , 2023)

67

Column Physical Model and Bacteria Growth Test

68

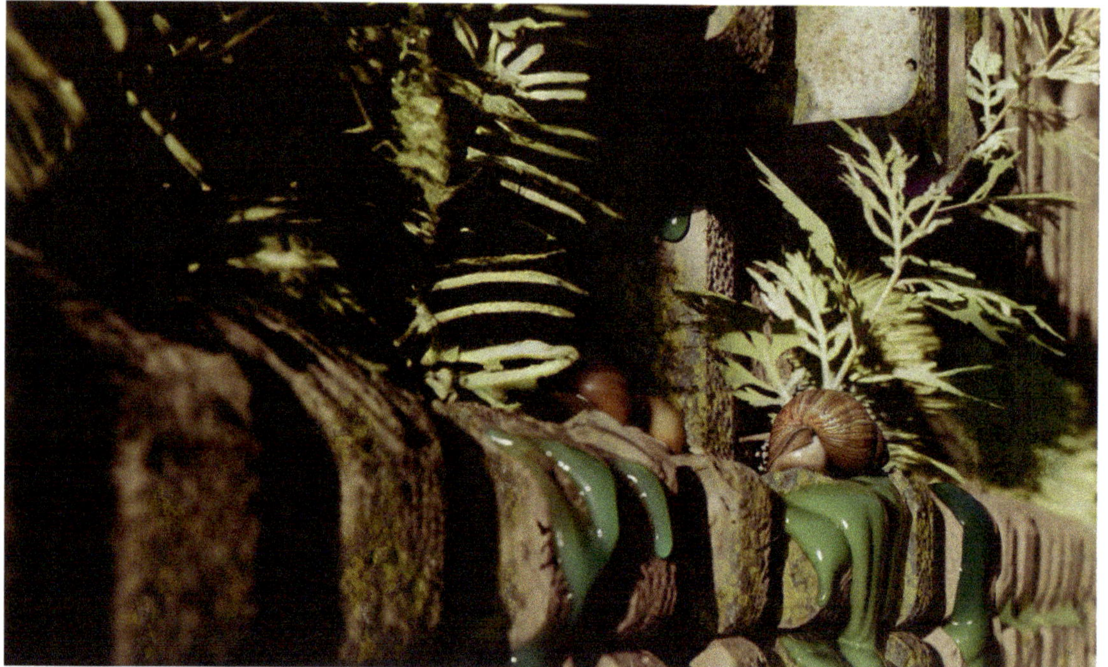

fig. 4.49-4.51: Top to Bottom: Portfolio page showing OD's oily handprints on the pages of his diary where he catalogues his physical model experiments of bacteria growth tests on a building column; Bacteria Utopia, Render of wall materiality, biofilm covered in moss and lichen. Facing Page: Bacteria Sanctuary, Plan view.

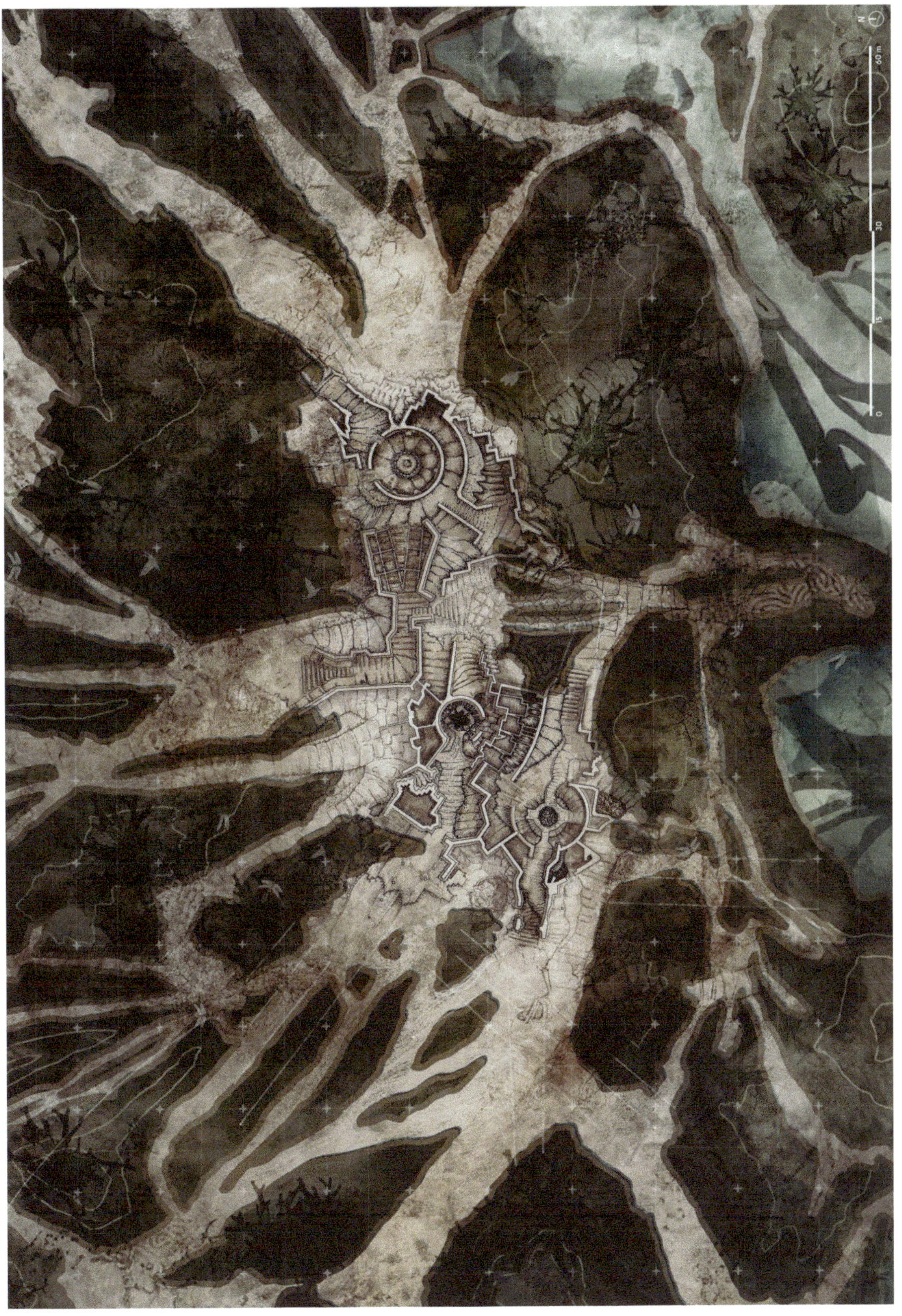
N
0
15
30
60 m

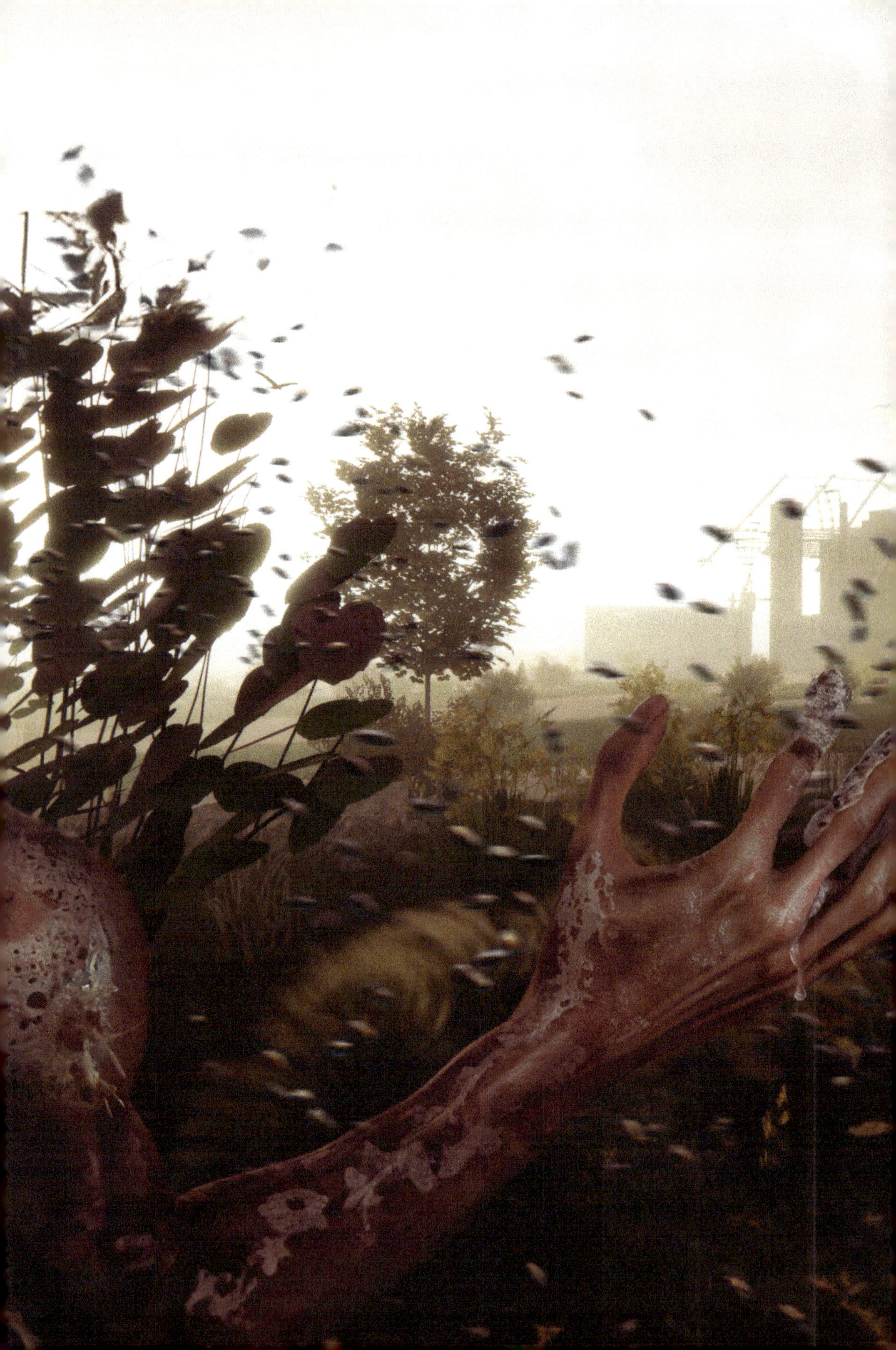

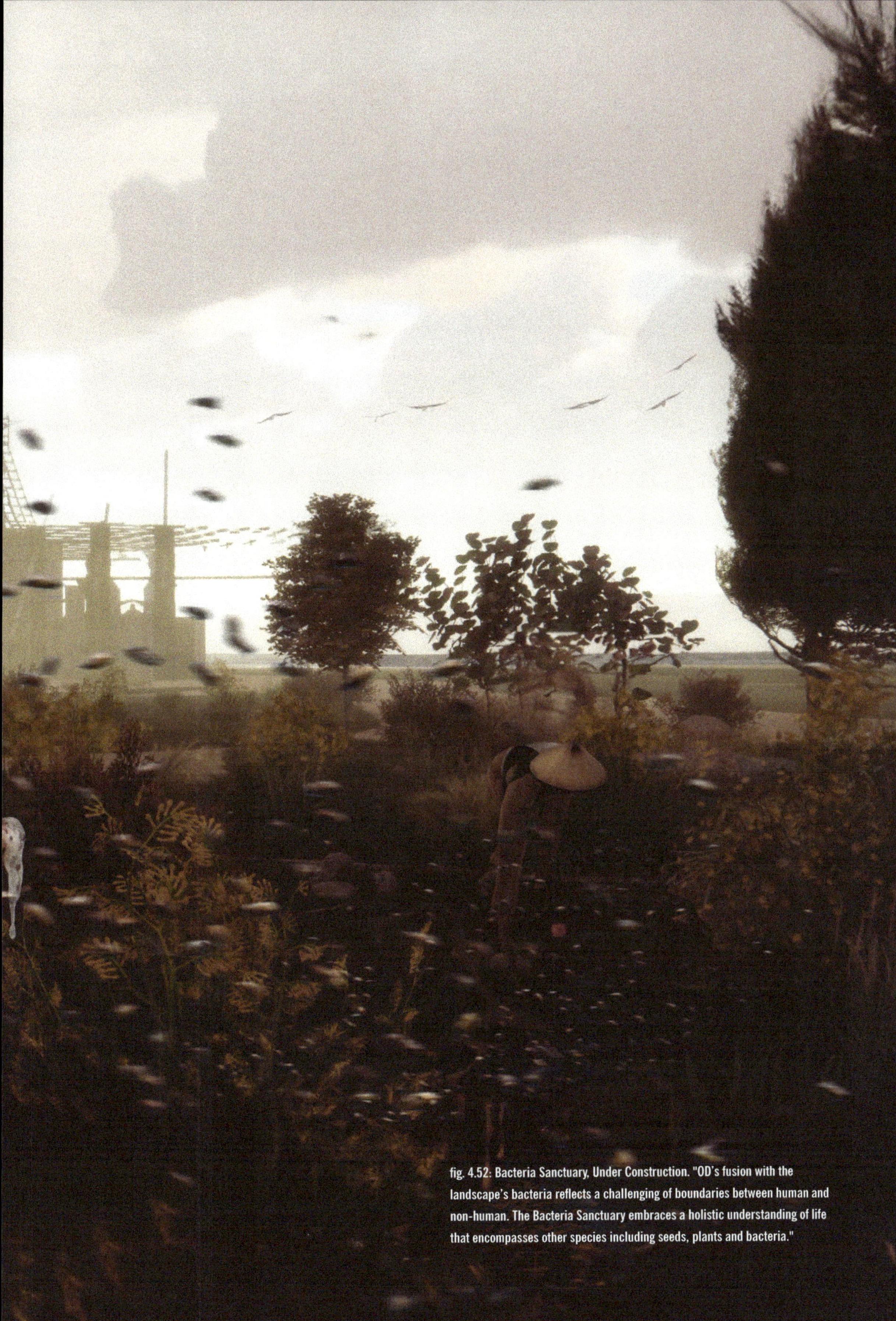

fig. 4.52: Bacteria Sanctuary, Under Construction. "OD's fusion with the landscape's bacteria reflects a challenging of boundaries between human and non-human. The Bacteria Sanctuary embraces a holistic understanding of life that encompasses other species including seeds, plants and bacteria."

A LOVE LETTER TO INSECTS

by
ANASTASIA KOLIOLIOU

BRIEF *Alter Ego(ed) Futures*

YEAR *2024-25*

TUTORS *Dr Alessandro Ayuso, Mary Konstantopoulou, with support from Deniz Özbek*

THEMES

Non-human Agency

Micro vs Macro

Destabilised Hierarchies

Narrative World-building

Insect Architecture

Hedonism / Pleasure

Sound / Vibration

"This project investigates architecture designed for insect pleasure through the work of Aesthesia, whose fascination with insect behaviour evolves from intimate experiment to public performance. Insect populations have declined by 45% globally over the past 40 years; yet these creatures - comprising over 80% of all animal species - remain architectural afterthoughts. This project challenges this oversight by prioritising insect pleasure as a design imperative.

Excerpt from a letter to the insects found in Bethnal Green:

'You seek:
- Wood at 18-22% moisture content
- Air holding 70-80% humidity
- Temperatures steady at 20-25%
- Darkness for work, sound for navigation
- Vibration-free zones for your young

I've learnt to read these numbers not as data, but as love poetry. Each percentage point maps your comfort, guides my design for your final feast.'"

fig. 4.53: Facing page: A composition of Kolioliou's different working drawings and models for the Insect Opera House.

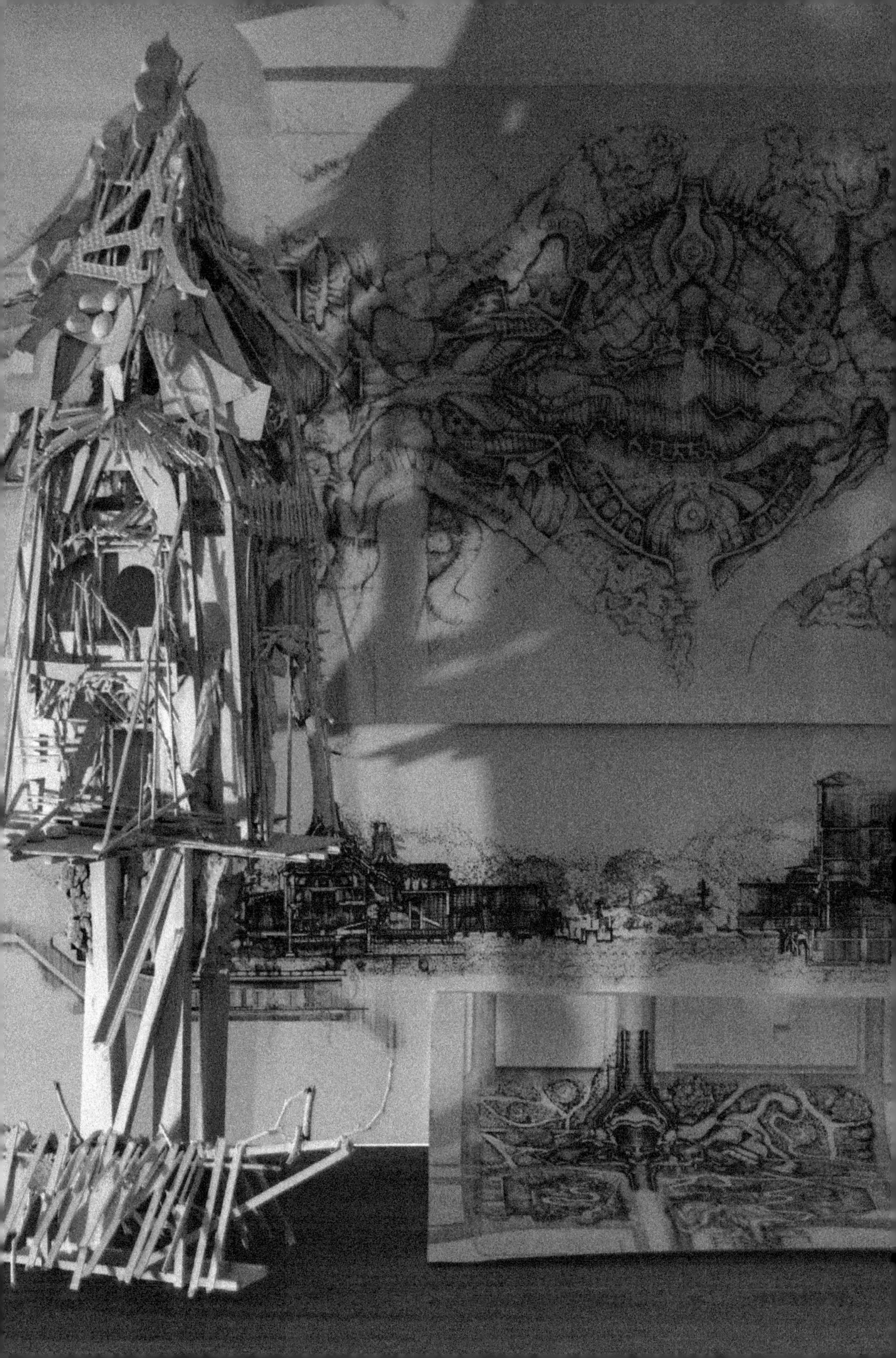

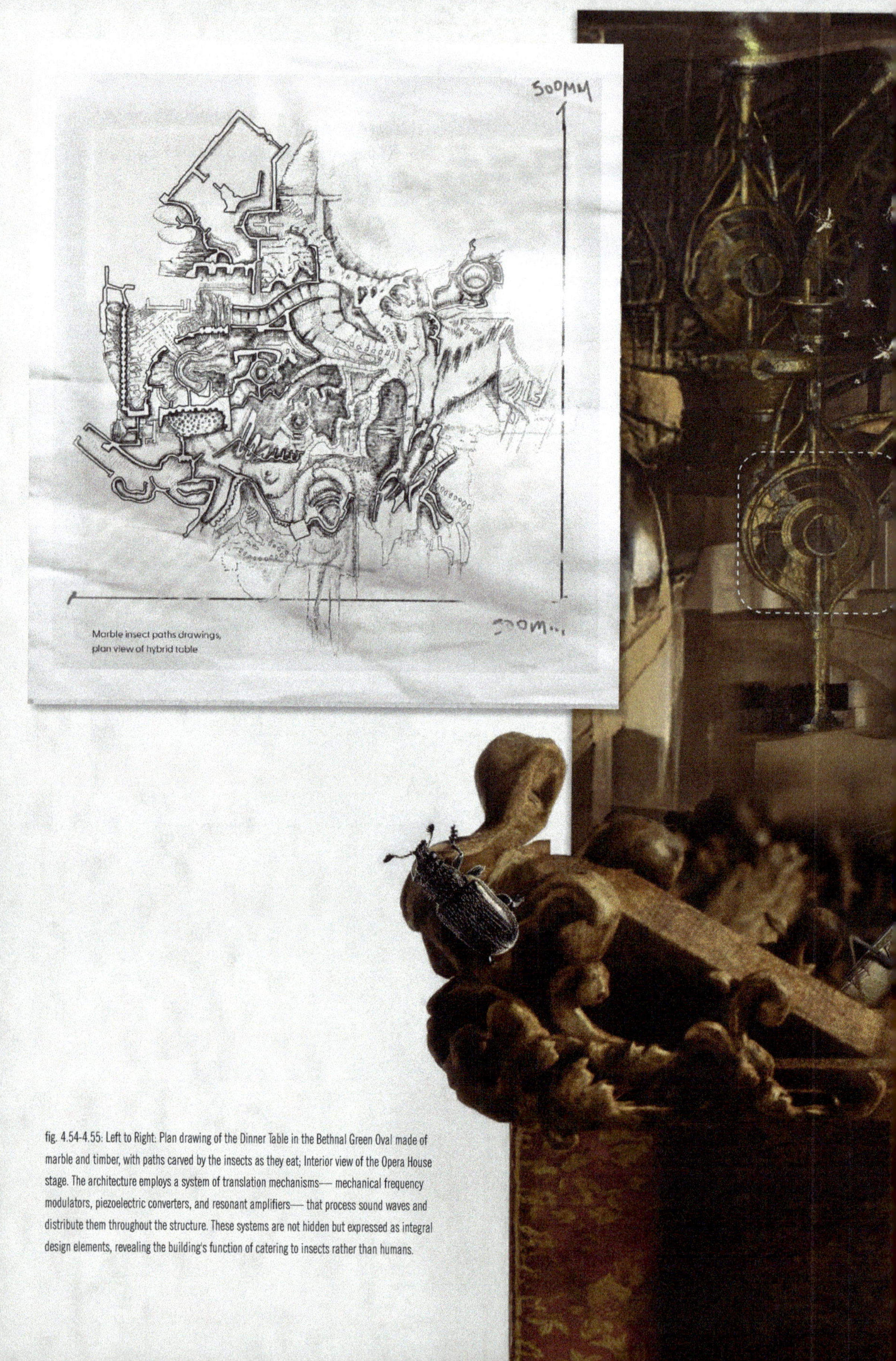

fig. 4.54-4.55: Left to Right: Plan drawing of the Dinner Table in the Bethnal Green Oval made of marble and timber, with paths carved by the insects as they eat; Interior view of the Opera House stage. The architecture employs a system of translation mechanisms— mechanical frequency modulators, piezoelectric converters, and resonant amplifiers— that process sound waves and distribute them throughout the structure. These systems are not hidden but expressed as integral design elements, revealing the building's function of catering to insects rather than humans.

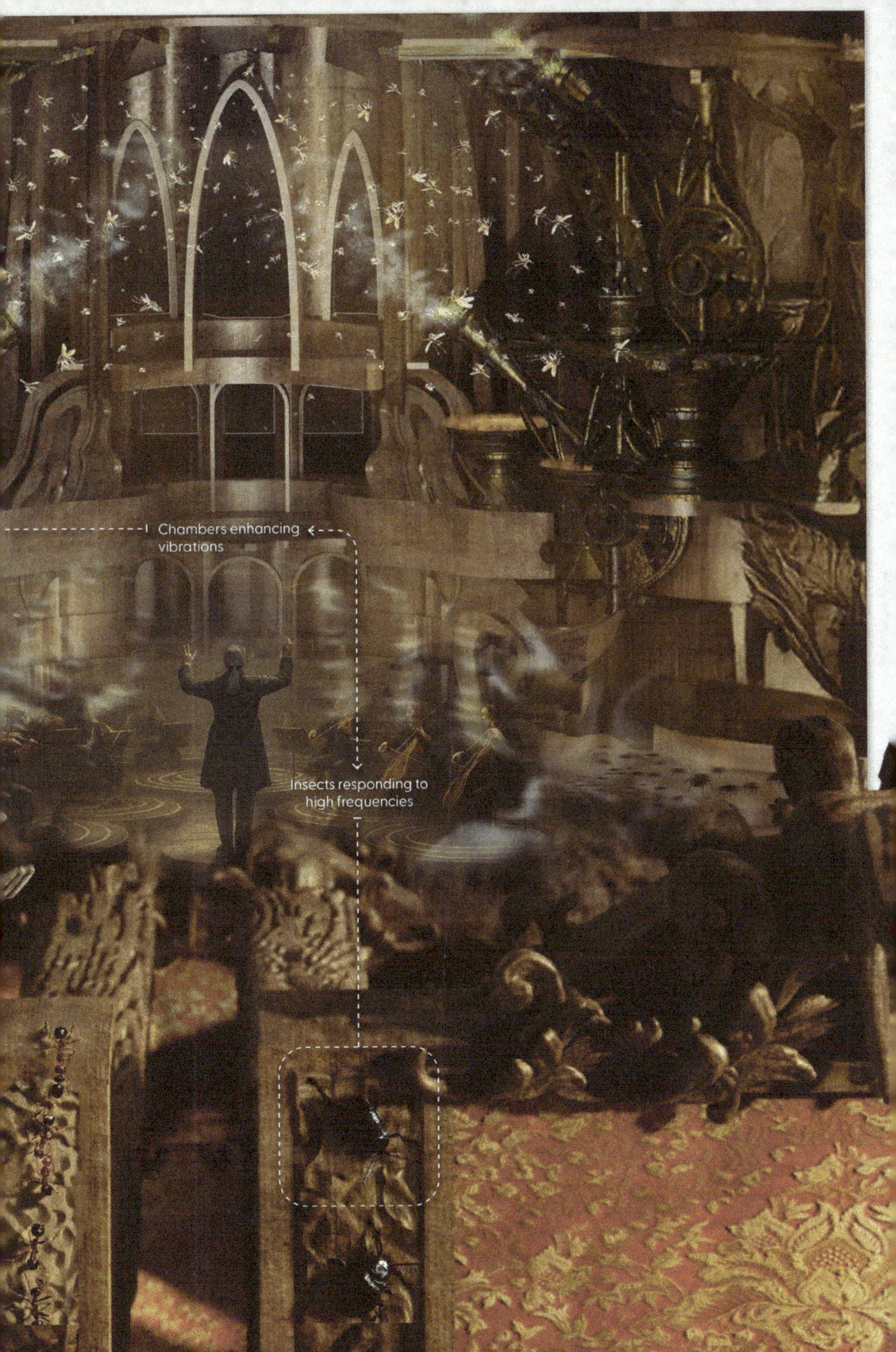
Chambers enhancing vibrations
Insects responding to high frequencies

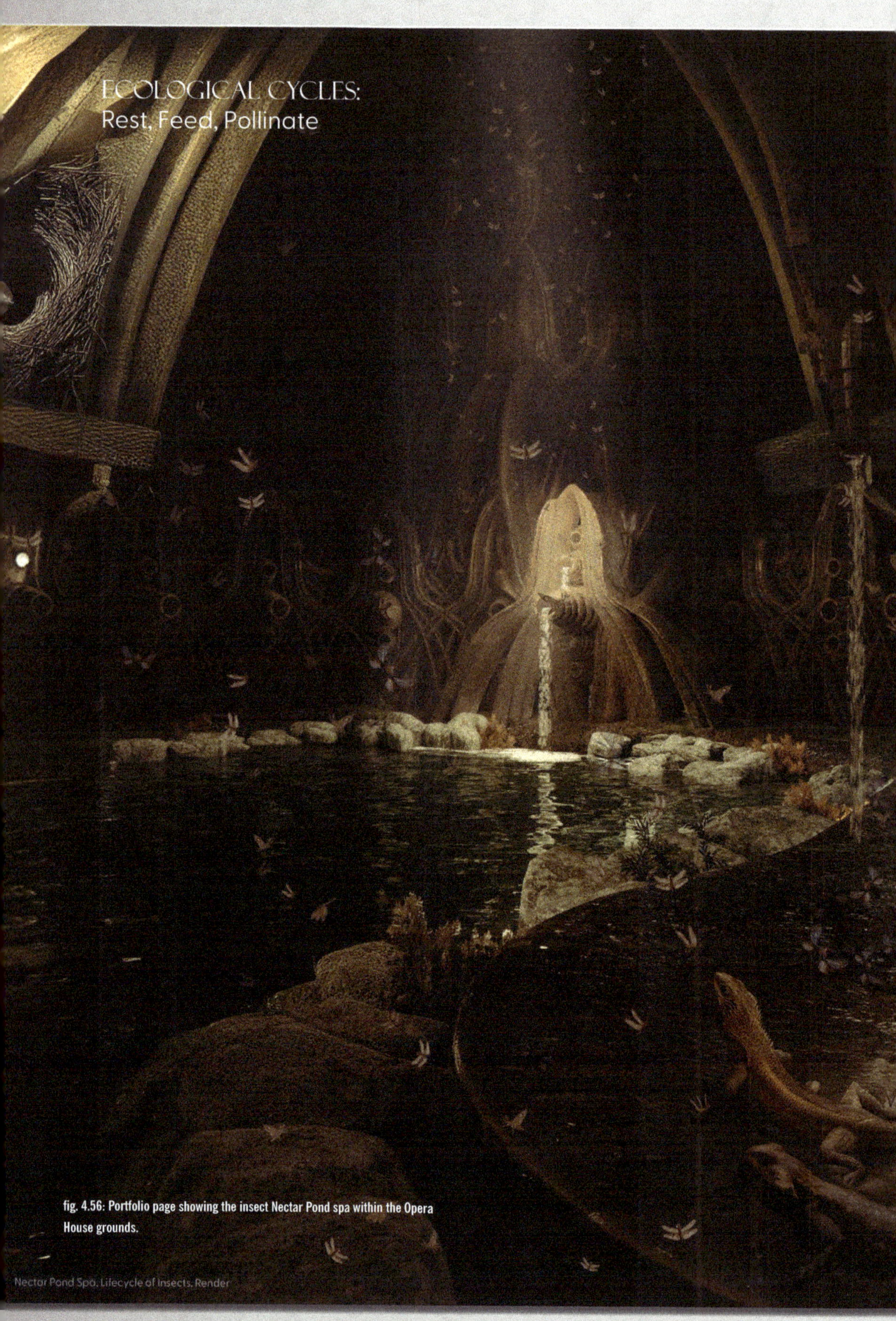

fig. 4.56: Portfolio page showing the insect Nectar Pond spa within the Opera House grounds.

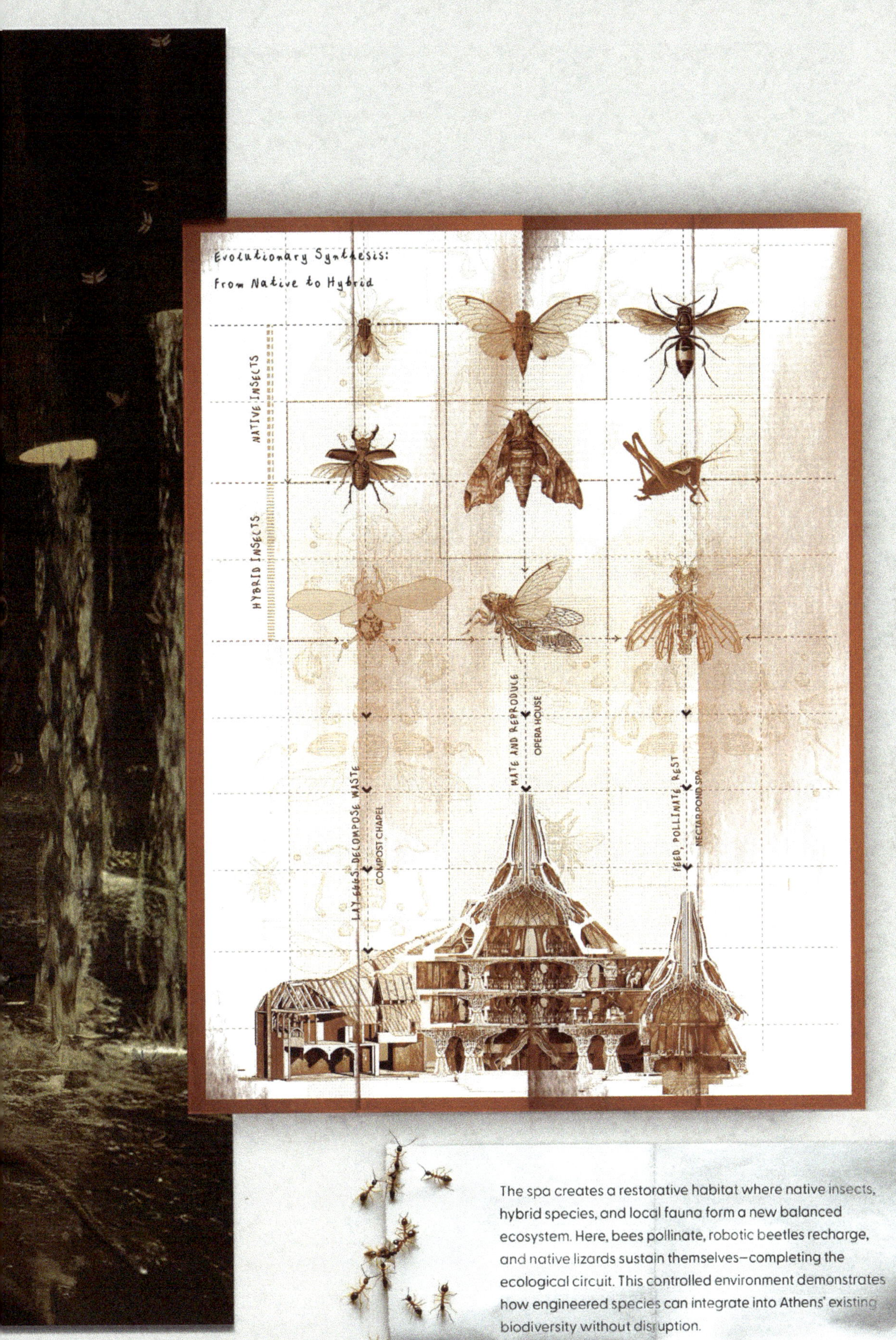

The spa creates a restorative habitat where native insects, hybrid species, and local fauna form a new balanced ecosystem. Here, bees pollinate, robotic beetles recharge, and native lizards sustain themselves—completing the ecological circuit. This controlled environment demonstrates how engineered species can integrate into Athens' existing biodiversity without disruption.

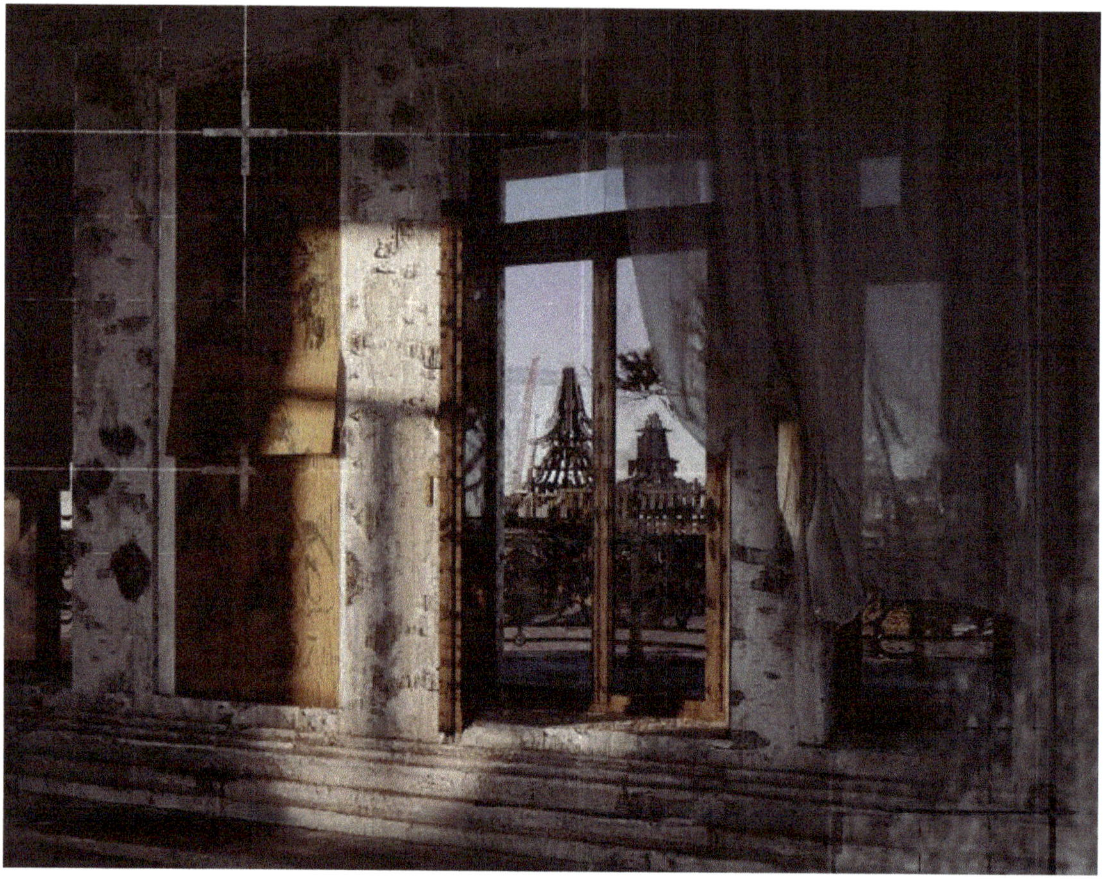

INSECT MATERIAL SAMPLES

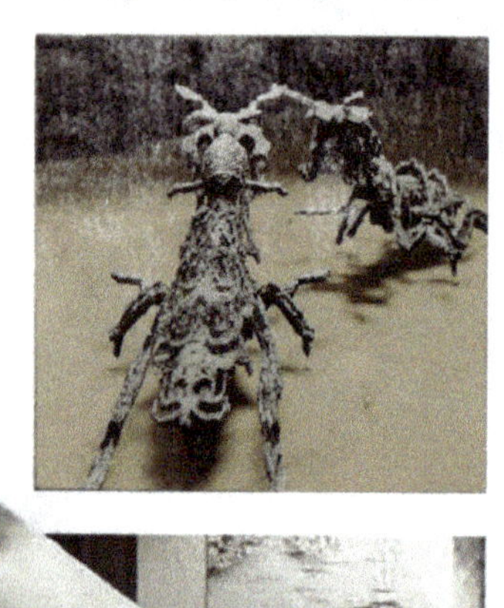

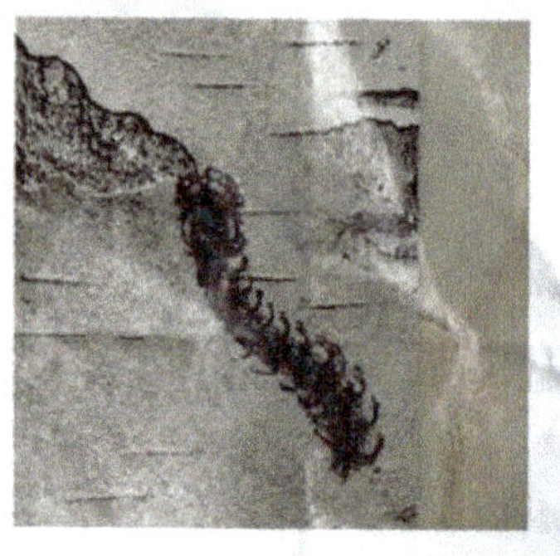

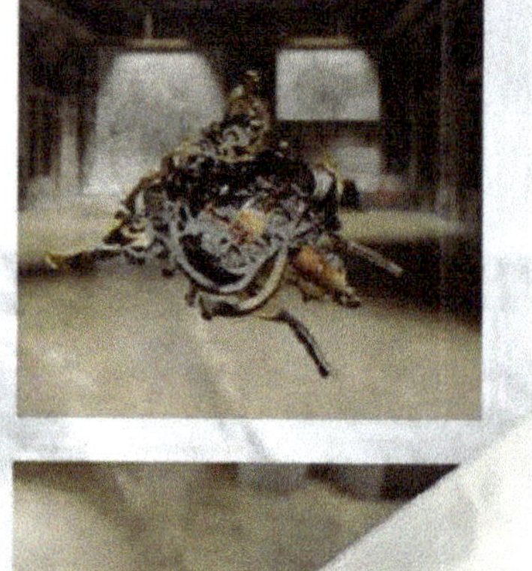

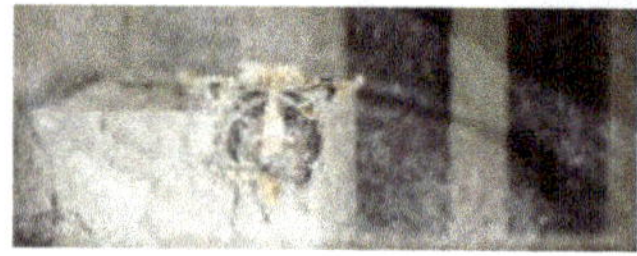

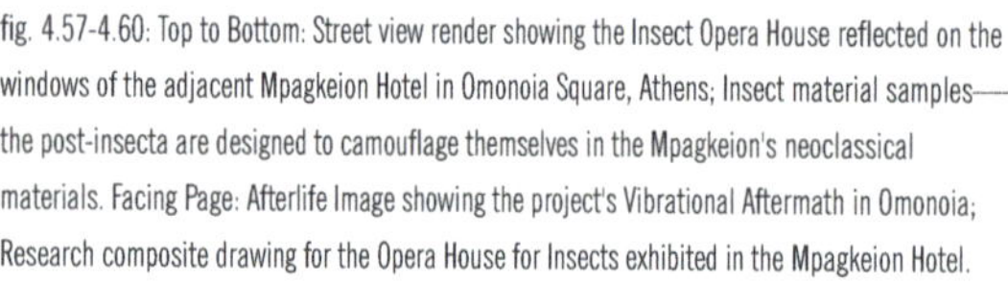

fig. 4.57-4.60: Top to Bottom: Street view render showing the Insect Opera House reflected on the windows of the adjacent Mpagkeion Hotel in Omonoia Square, Athens; Insect material samples—the post-insecta are designed to camouflage themselves in the Mpagkeion's neoclassical materials. Facing Page: Afterlife Image showing the project's Vibrational Aftermath in Omonoia; Research composite drawing for the Opera House for Insects exhibited in the Mpagkeion Hotel.

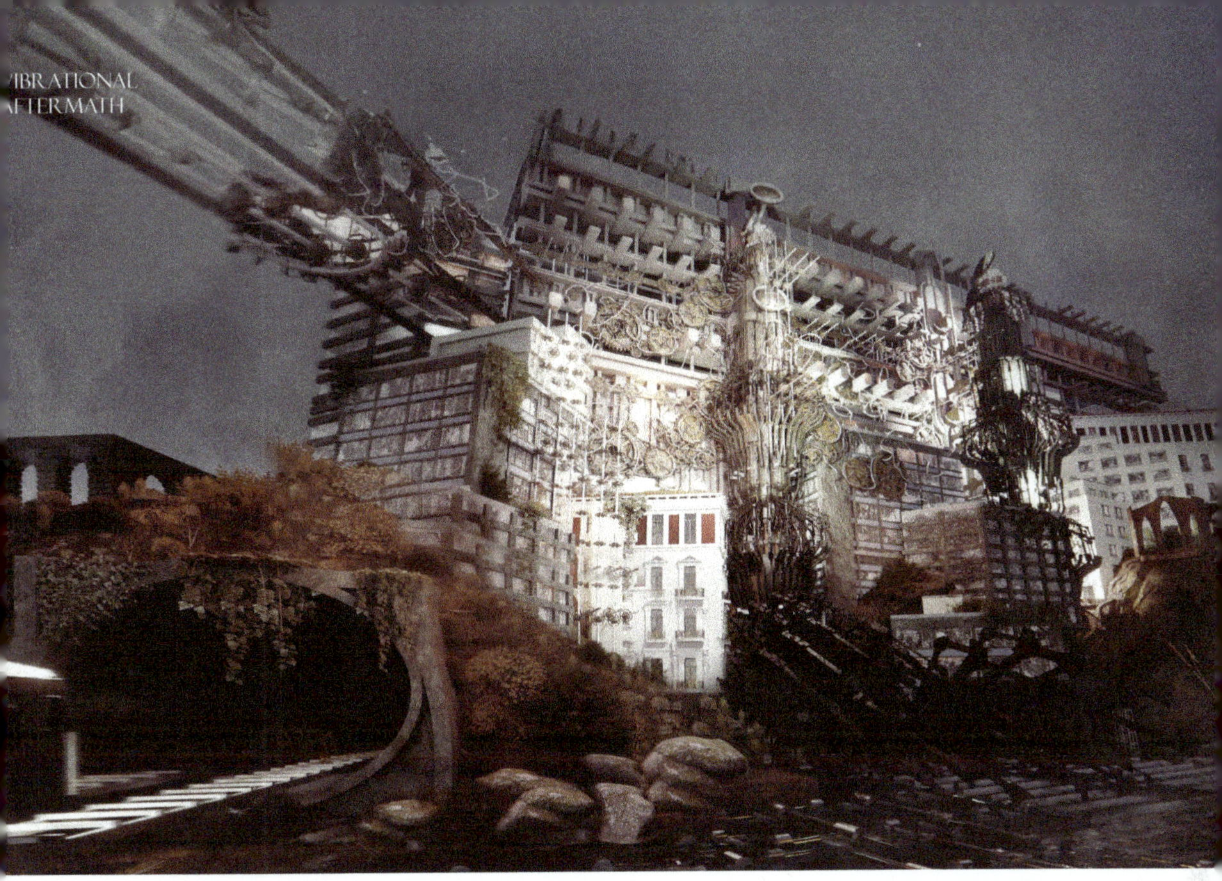

VIBRATIONAL
AFTERMATH

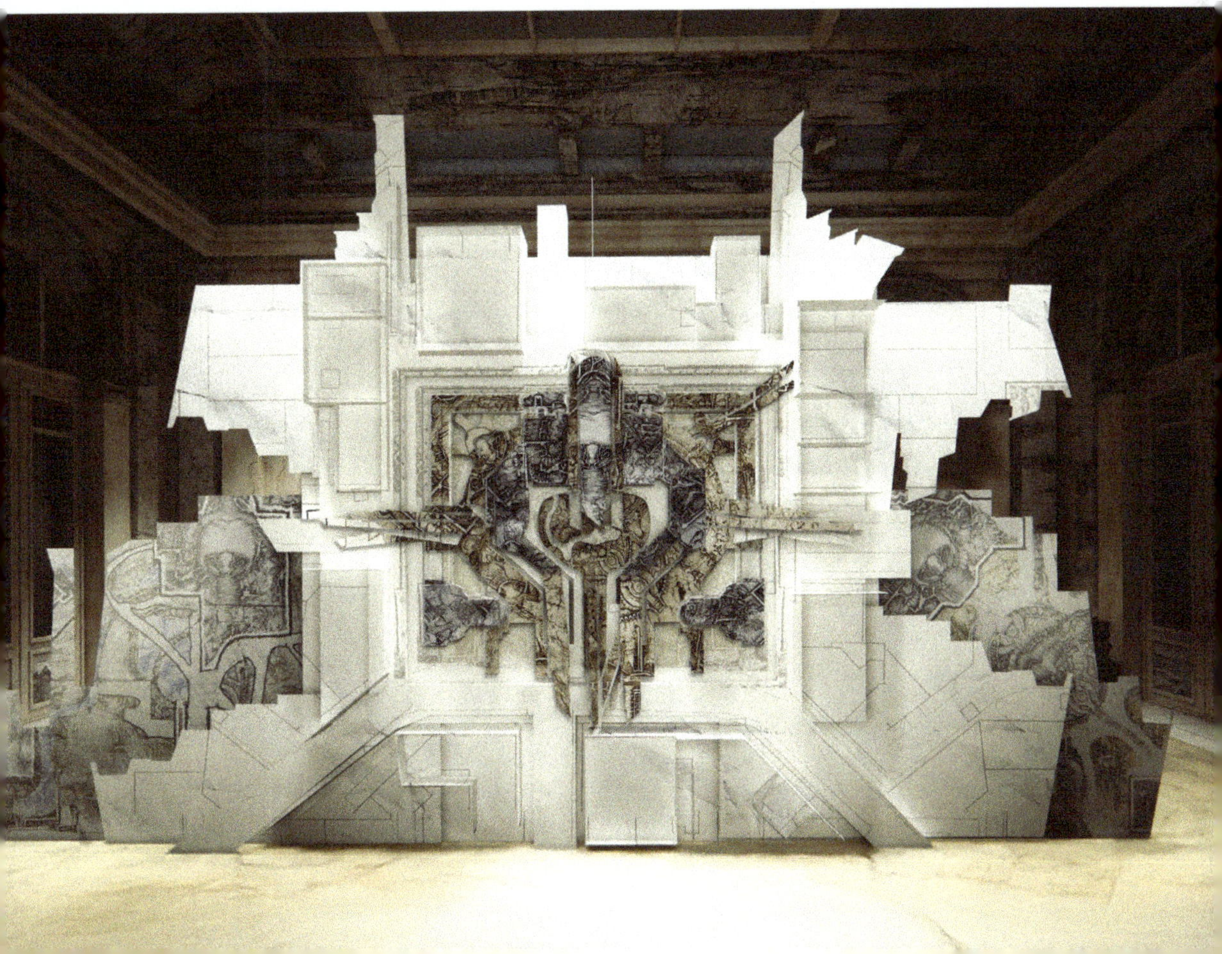

SYMPATHY FOR NON-HUMAN PEOPLE

by
ANGHARAD JAMES

BRIEF *Alter Ego(ed) Futures*

YEAR *2024-25*

TUTORS *Dr Alessandro Ayuso, Mary Konstantopoulou, with support from Deniz Özbek*

THEMES

Extraction Ecosystems

Destabilised World-view

Fictioned, Expansive World

Material Agency

Alternate Past / Future Realities

Multi-species Agency

"Extract from the Conspiracy Theorist's alternate history archives:

'The Oval in Bethnal Green has become the focus of my research. A common urban myth associated with the site is that of a canaldwelling creature, said to resemble a crocodilian species and coloquially referred to as 'Long Boi', a figment of the collective imagination shaped by the mainstream ontology regarding the non-human.'

Extract from Longboi's diary:

'Each new kind of person that inhabited the building had something extra to add, in partiuclar the Grazer who ate into the walls forming tunnels. After The Grazer is eaten by The Predator, the tunnels would later come to be lined by The Repairer, who formed amber-coloured nests on the exterior.'

Extract from an interview of the events as recorded on camera:

'grrrrrrrrrrr...argrrrr..rrr..hrrrhhr...'"

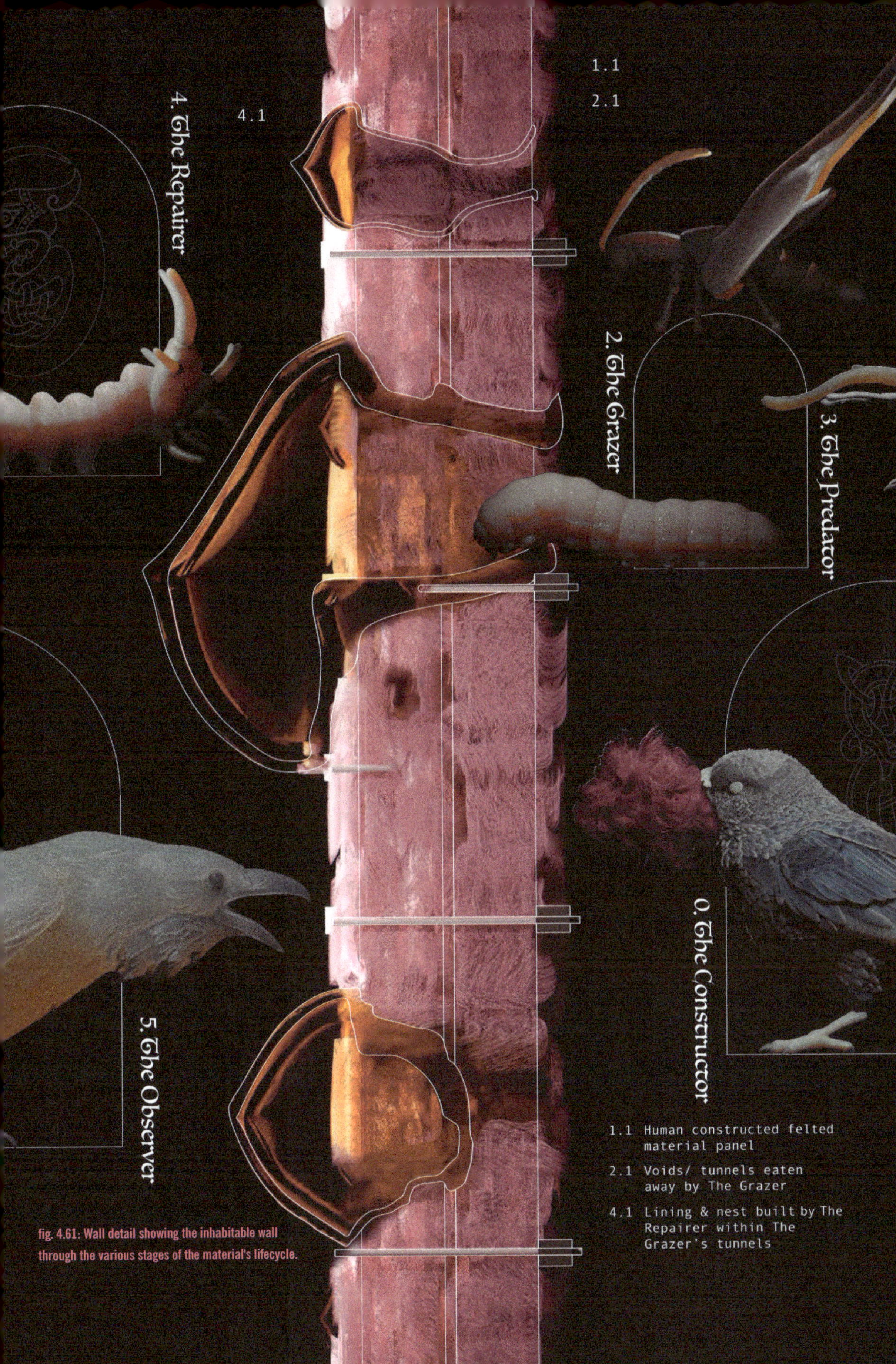

fig. 4.61: Wall detail showing the inhabitable wall through the various stages of the material's lifecycle.

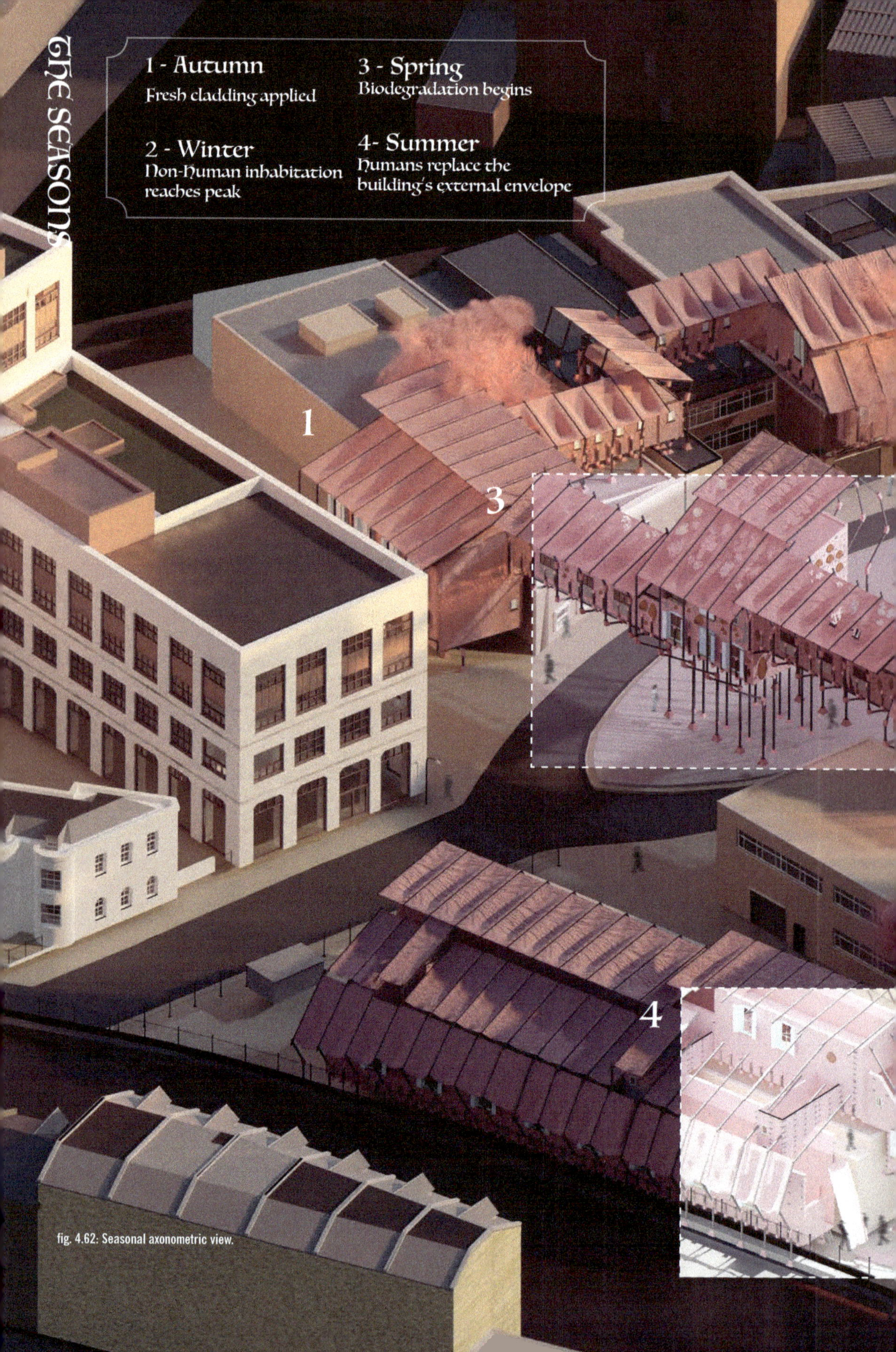

fig. 4.62: Seasonal axonometric view.

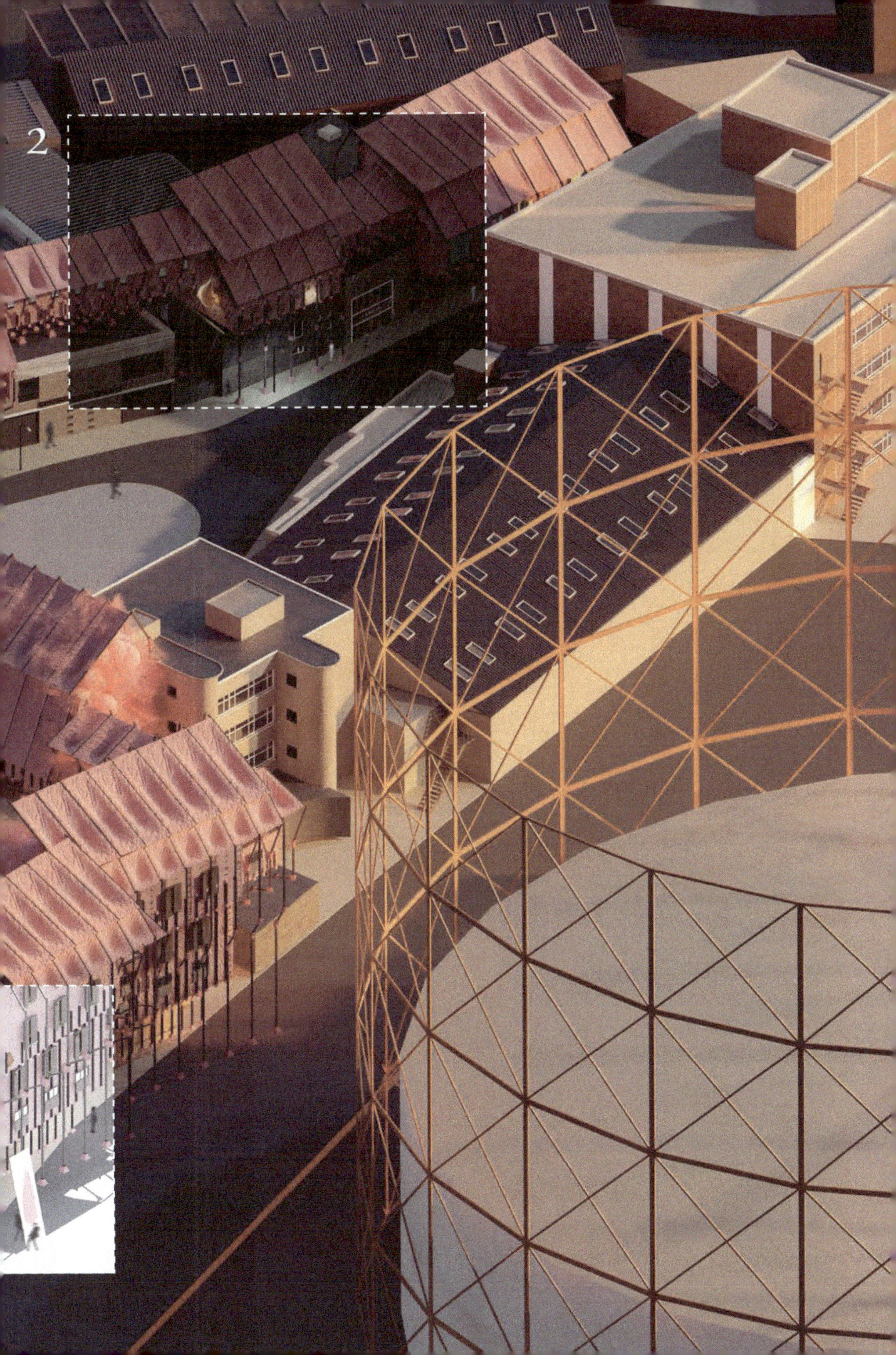
2

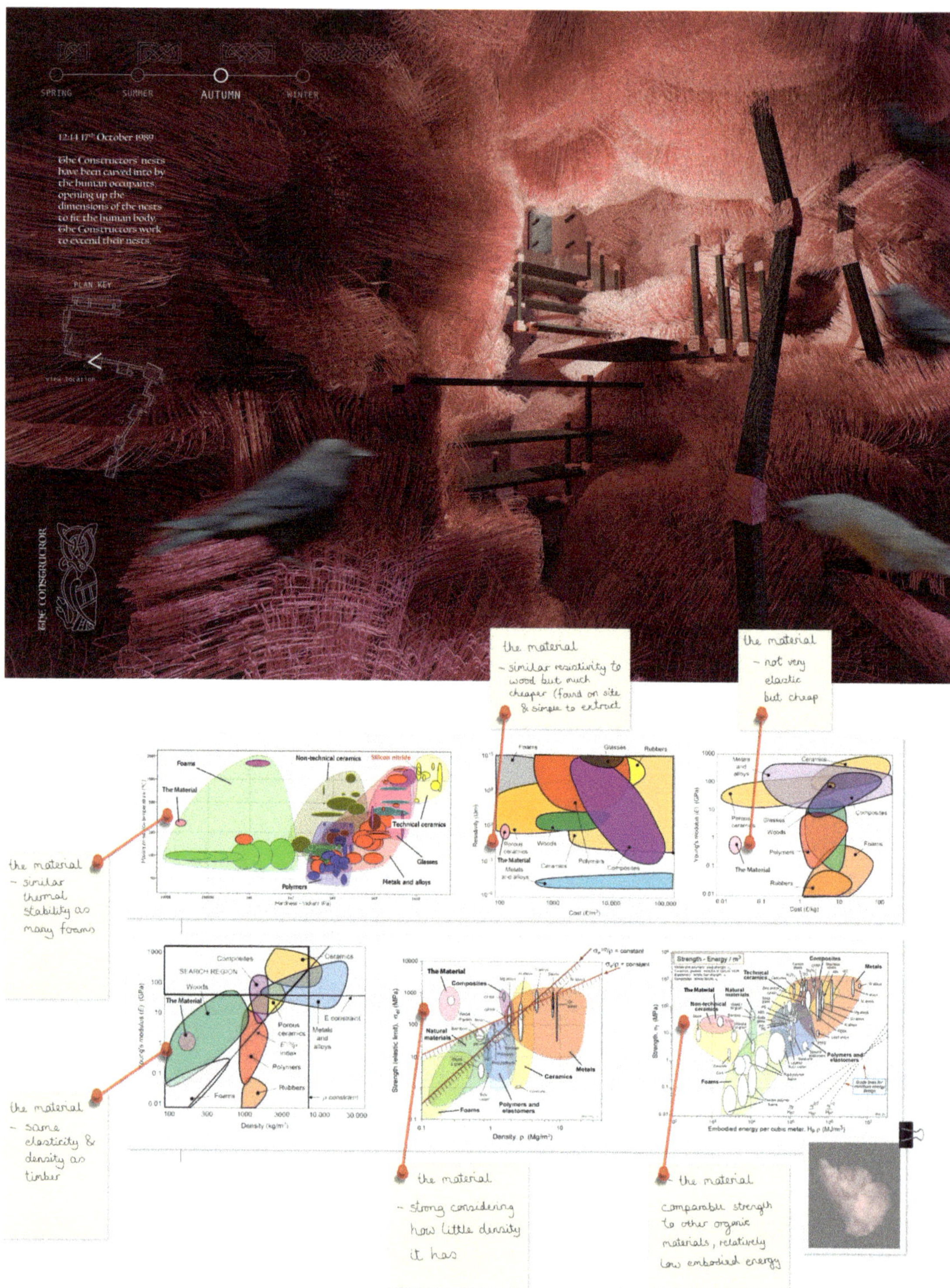

fig. 4.63-4.65: The original Constructor's process of using the material to build nests similar to a social weaver bird; The Conspirator's charts of the Material's properties. Facing Page: 18:47 2nd January, 1967 - Non-Human occupation reaches its seasonal peak, with The Repairer's nests bulging out of the walls.

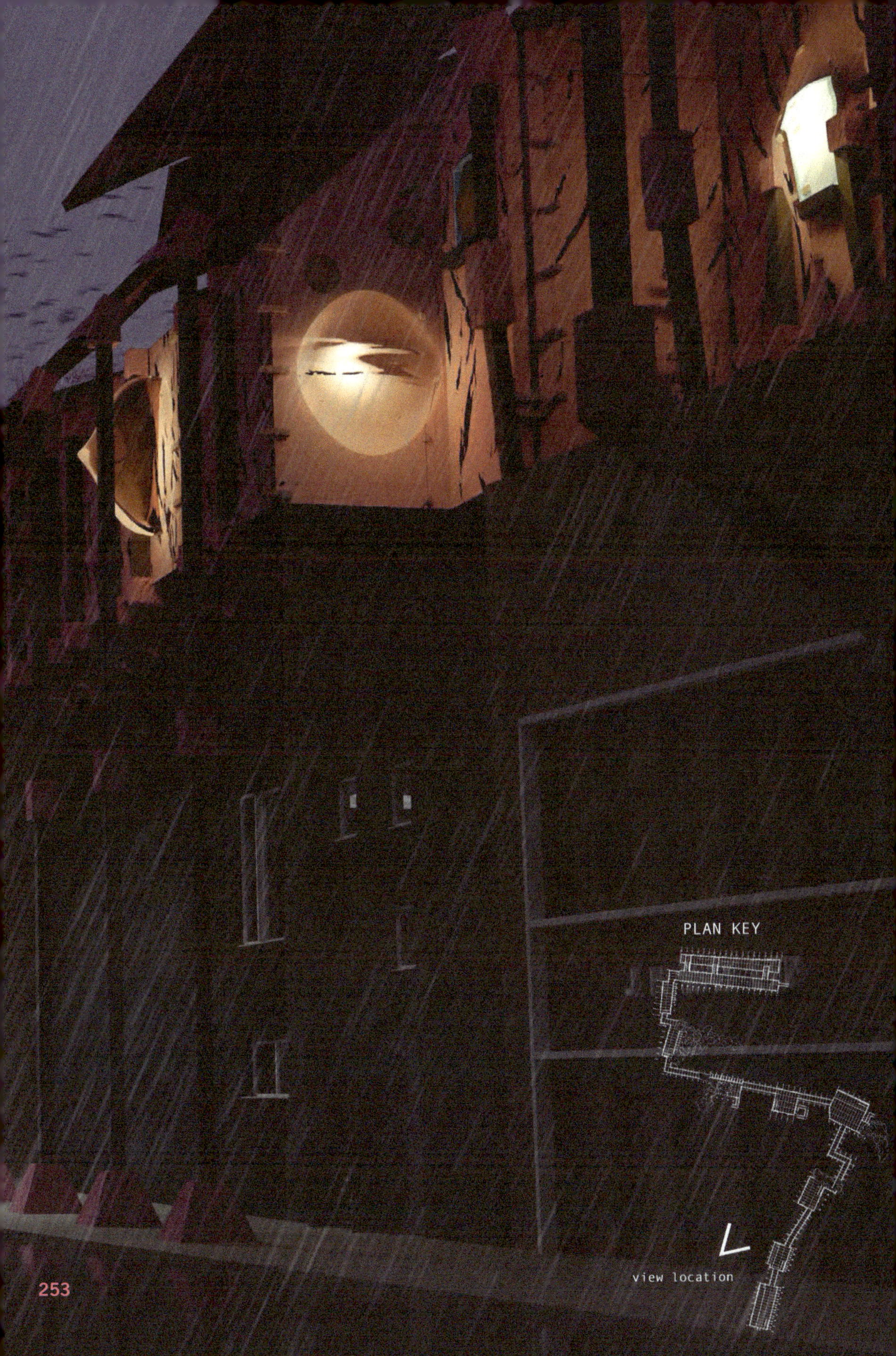
PLAN KEY
view location

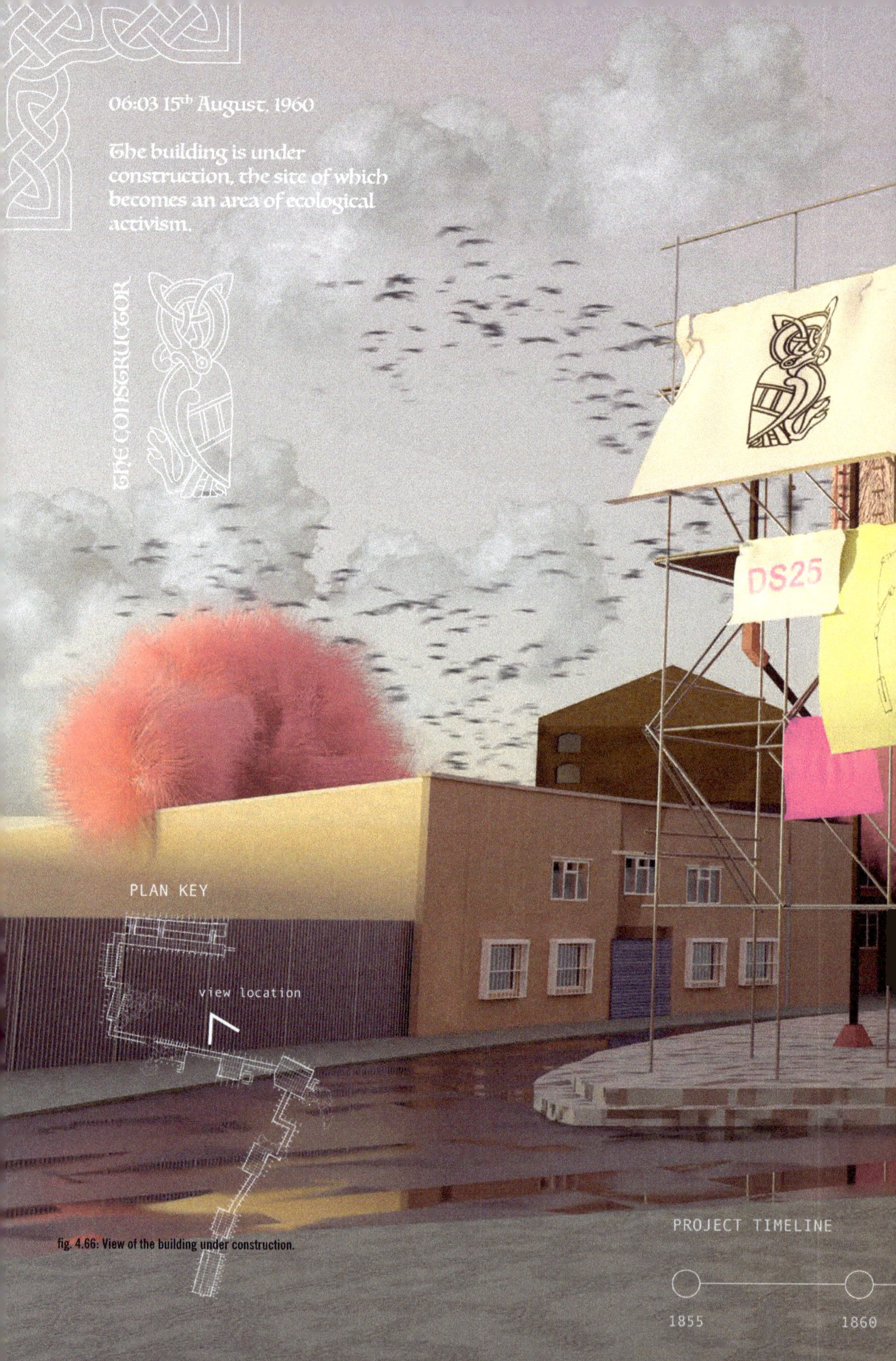

fig. 4.66: View of the building under construction.

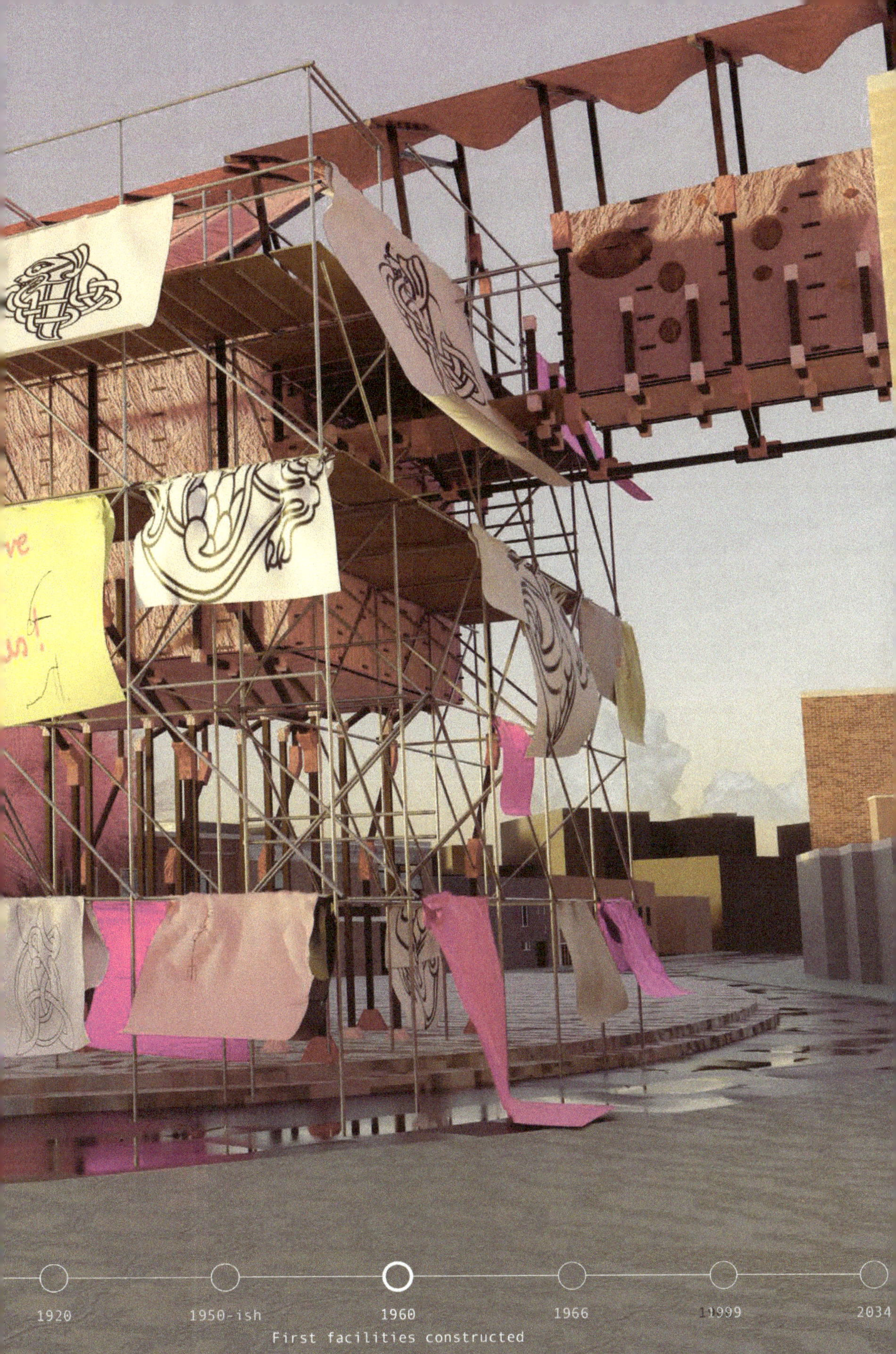
1920
1950-ish
1960
1966
1999
2034
First facilities constructed

SoFA (The Society of Failed Architects)

by
JAKE BONE

BRIEF *Alter Ego(ed) Futures*

YEAR *2024-25*

TUTORS *Dr Alessandro Ayuso, Mary Konstantopoulou, with support from Deniz Özbek*

THEMES

Alternate History

Parallel Reality

Allegory

Graphic Novel as a Design Generator

Failure

Architecture Critique

Drawing

"The Society of Failed Architects (SoFA) Headquarters is a radical re-imagining of architectural institution and practice.

The headquarters is simultaneously a physical manifestation of architectural rebellion and a platform for alterntive practices.

SoFA members are not failures in the traditional sense, but rather architects who have failed at conforming to restrictive professional norms. The building itself is a reflection on conventional architectural values. Rather than a complete, polished structure, it glorifies incompleteness and adaptation. The headquarters include workshops where "failed" architects can experiment unconstrained by professional validation, archive rooms documenting unauthorised architectural interventions, and open meeting rooms for collective, non-hierarchical design processes."

fig. 4.67: Facing Page: Afterlife image: "The Emerging Age of Geeks (AI): Future cities will be shaped by technology and 'form will follow data.' Design will be driven by behavioural patterns, climate responses, and technological innovations. SoFA is the last human-run practice where failures are continually learned from— something AI seeks to destroy."

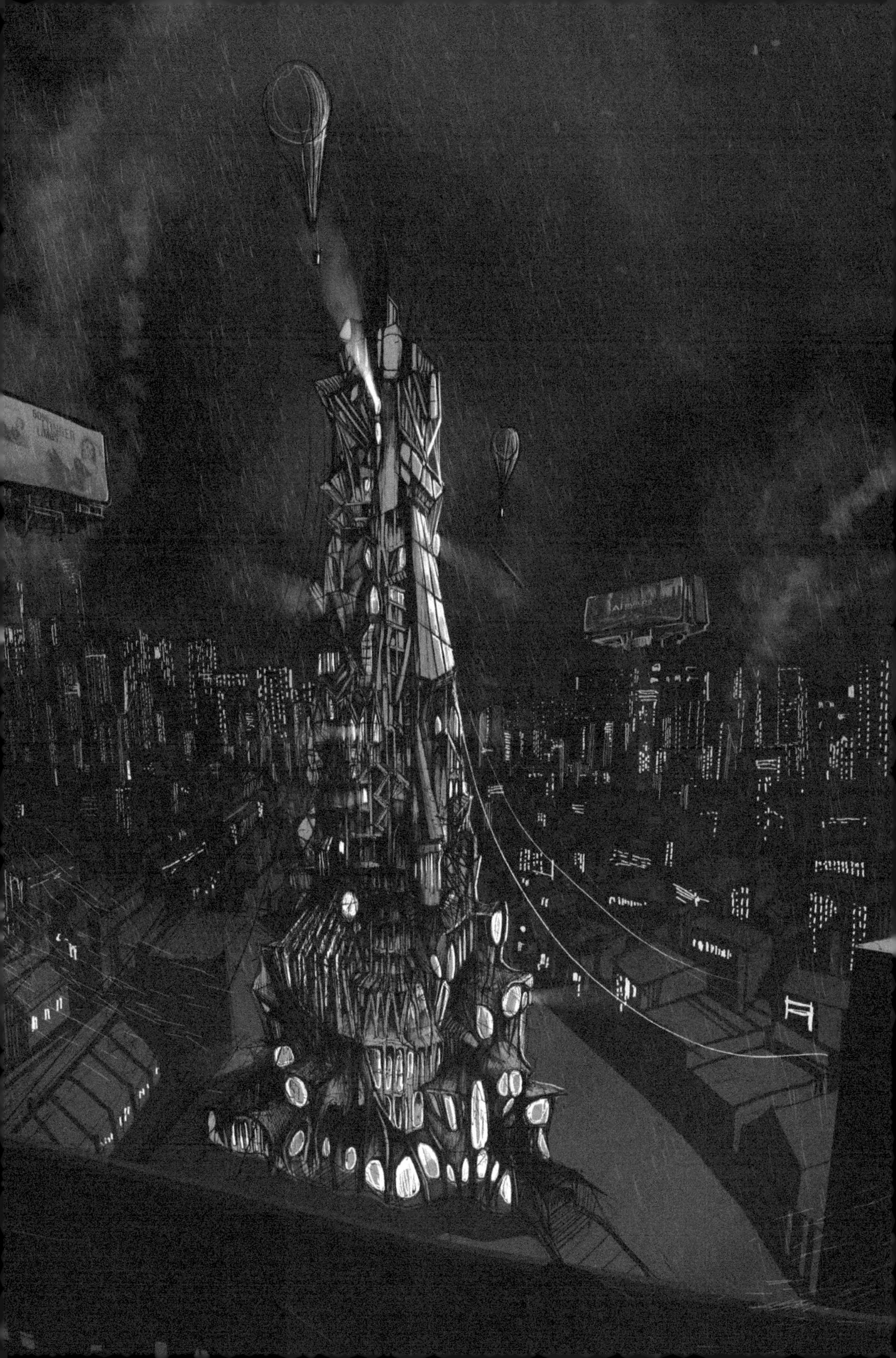

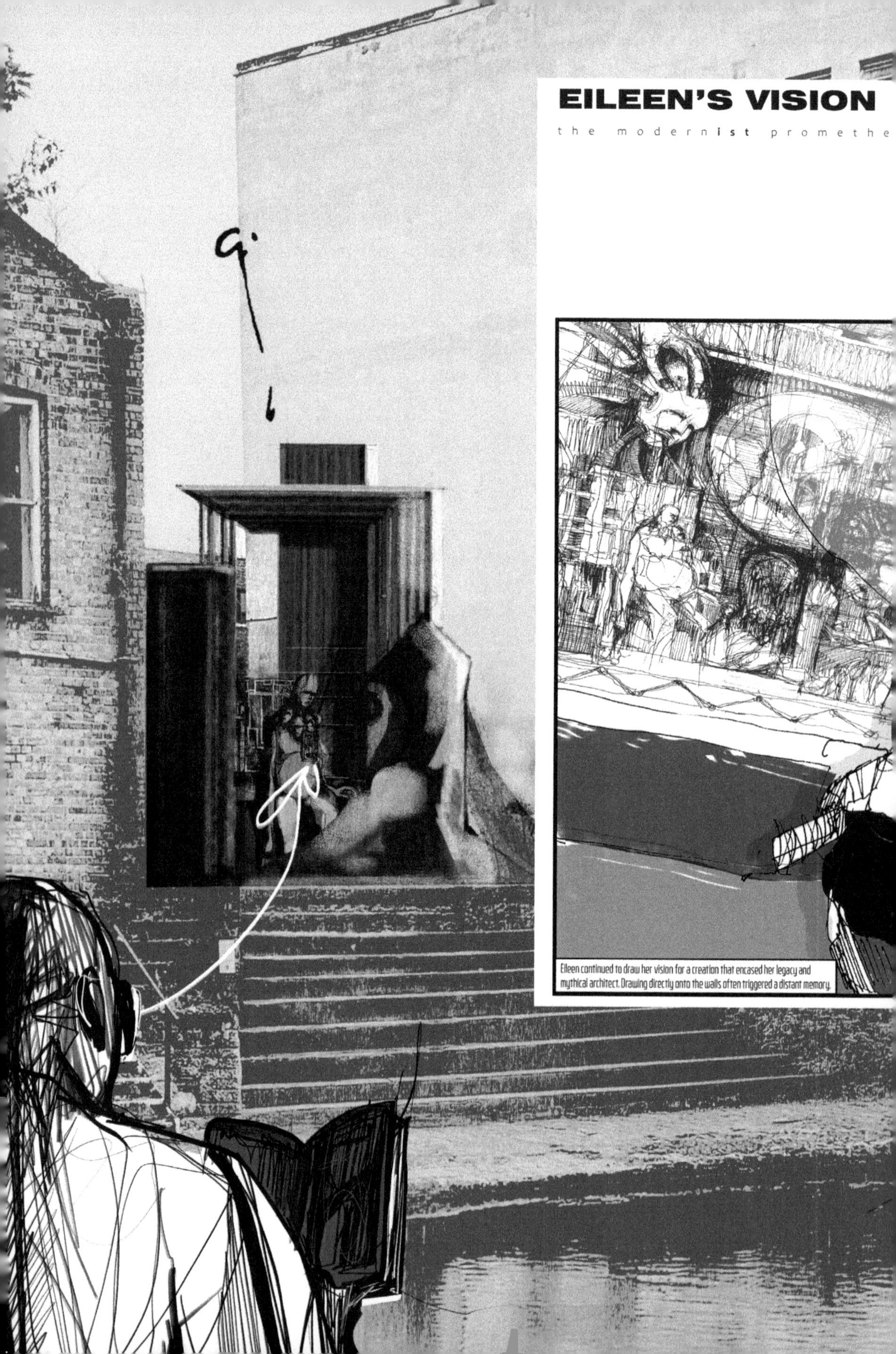
EILEEN'S VISION
the modernist promethe
Eileen continued to draw her vision for a creation that encased her legacy and
mythical architect. Drawing directly onto the walls often triggered a distant memory.

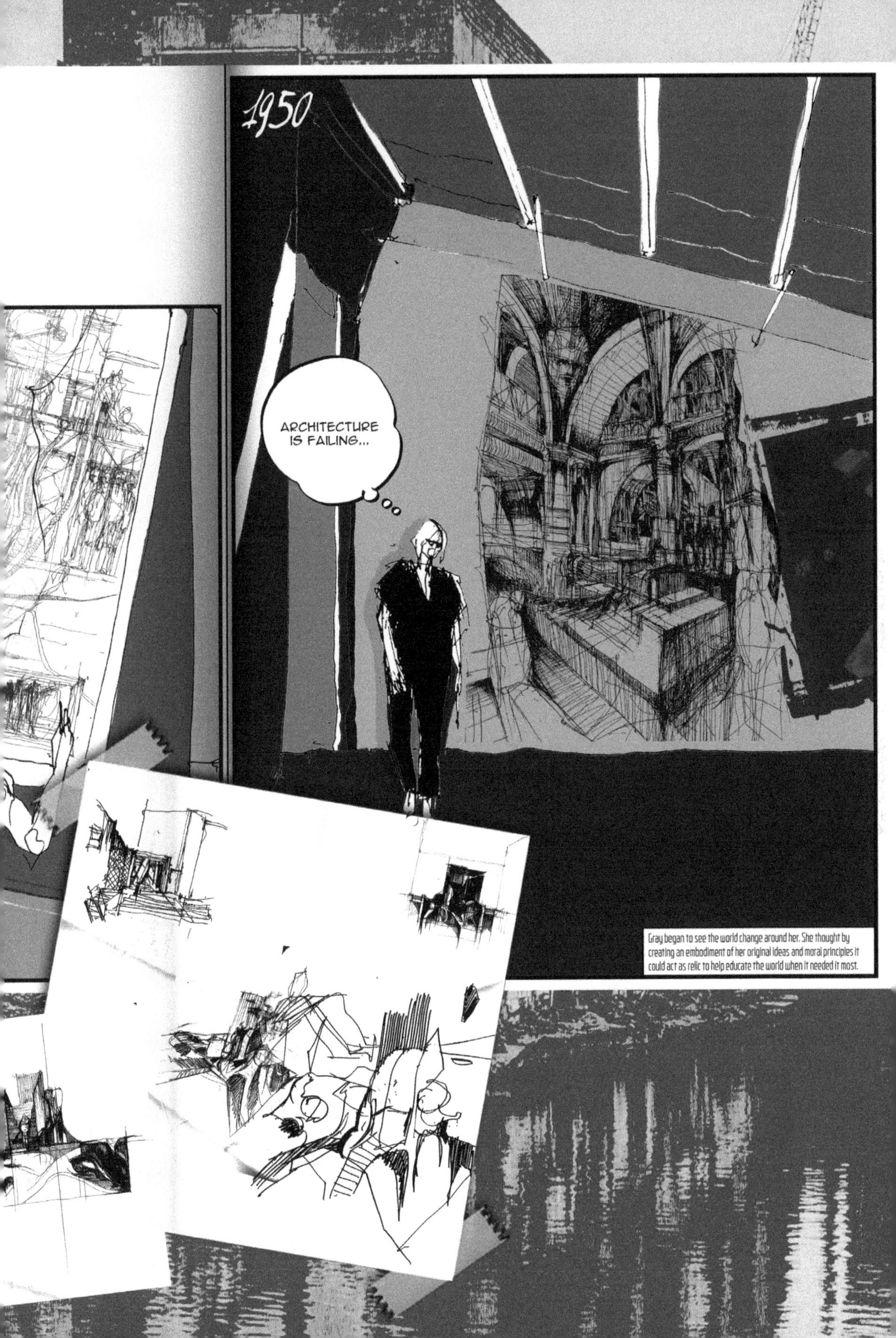
1950
ARCHITECTURE IS FAILING...
Gray began to see the world change around her. She thought by creating an embodiment of her original ideas and moral principles it could act as relic to help educate the world when it needed it most.

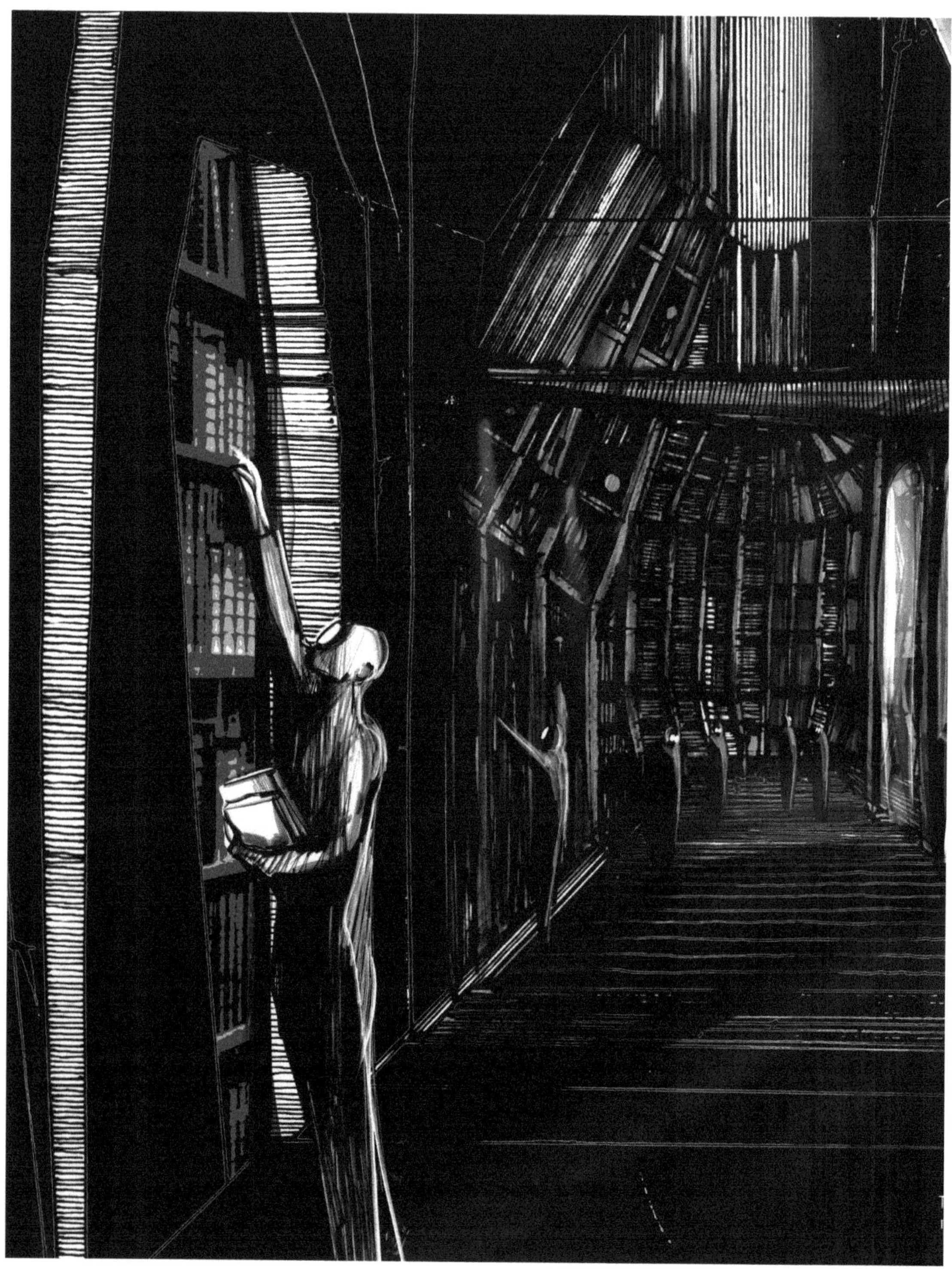

fig. 4.68: Previous page: A layered portfolio page showing the tangles of narratives in the project. The initial site for Eileen Gray's monument was chosen for its secrecy. Failed architects would confess their failures through a hidden entrance on the bank of the canal. Other drawings shown include early concepts for the society's manifesto, and Gray's unrealised projects.

fig. 4.69-4.72: View of the Material Library, an archive of materials and reports on industry failures. Facing page, Top to Bottom: Under Construction drawing of the SoFA scaffold tower; Graphic novel page composition on rendered interior showing Gray's creation of her monster. Following page: A failed architect on their commute to SoFA Headquarters.

Finalising Design

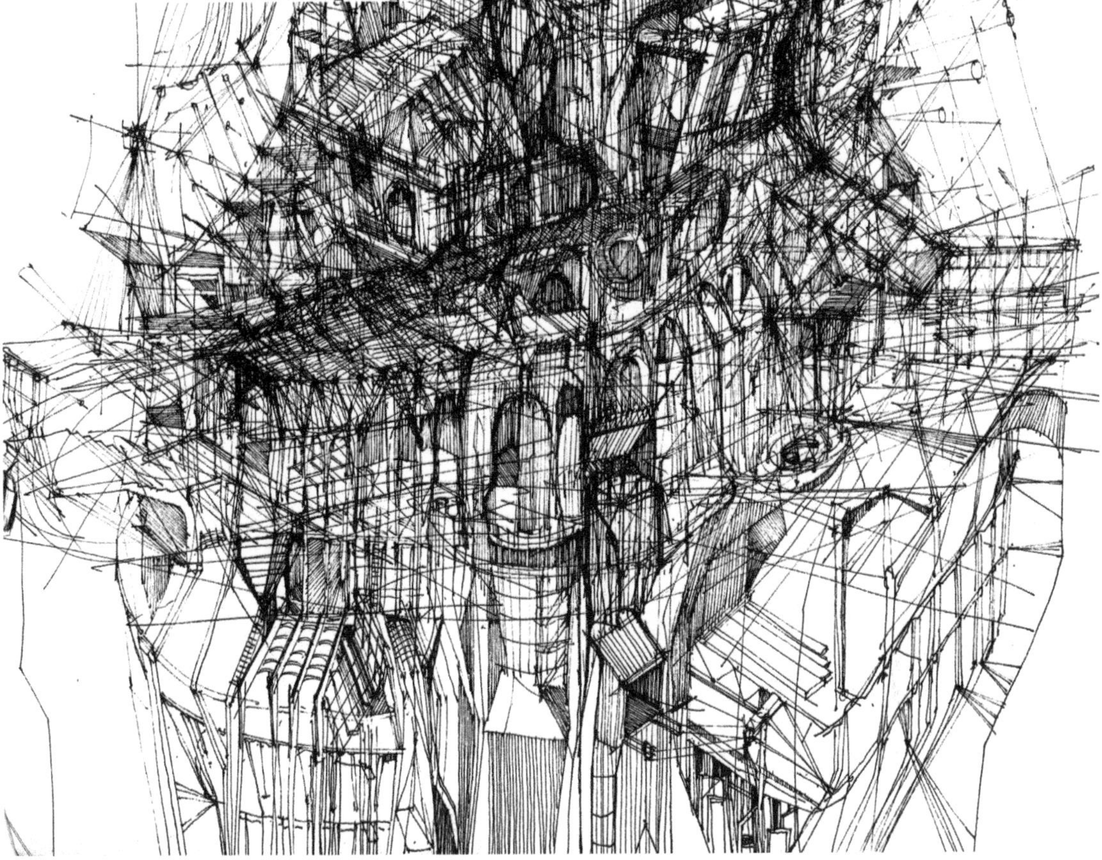

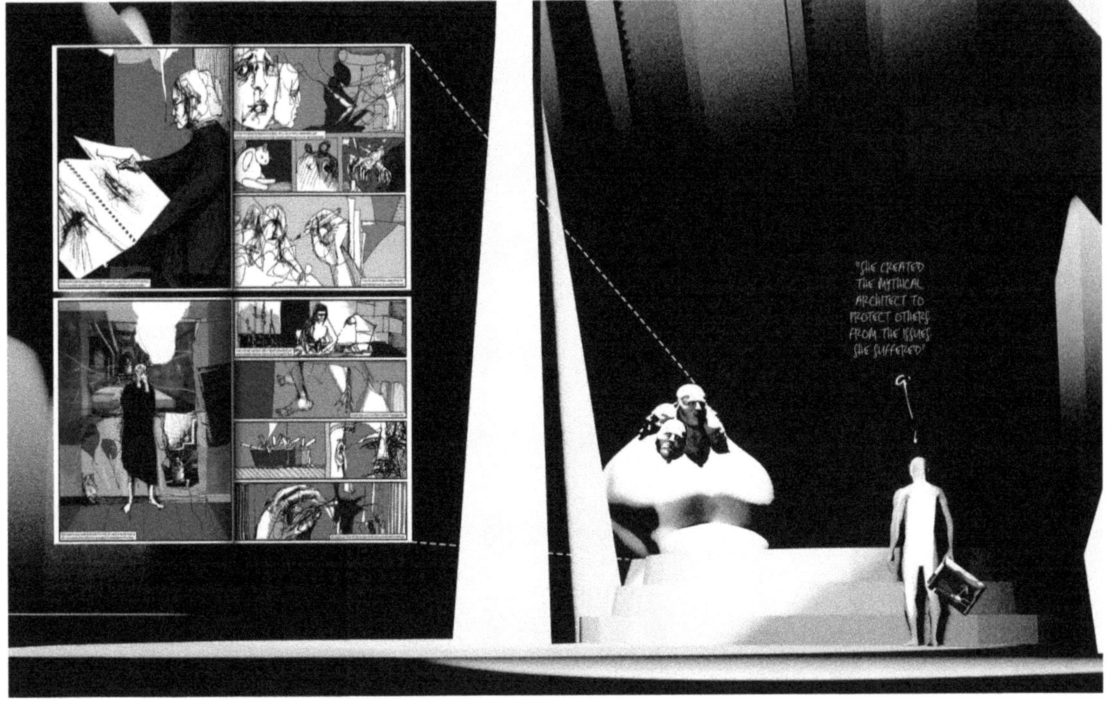

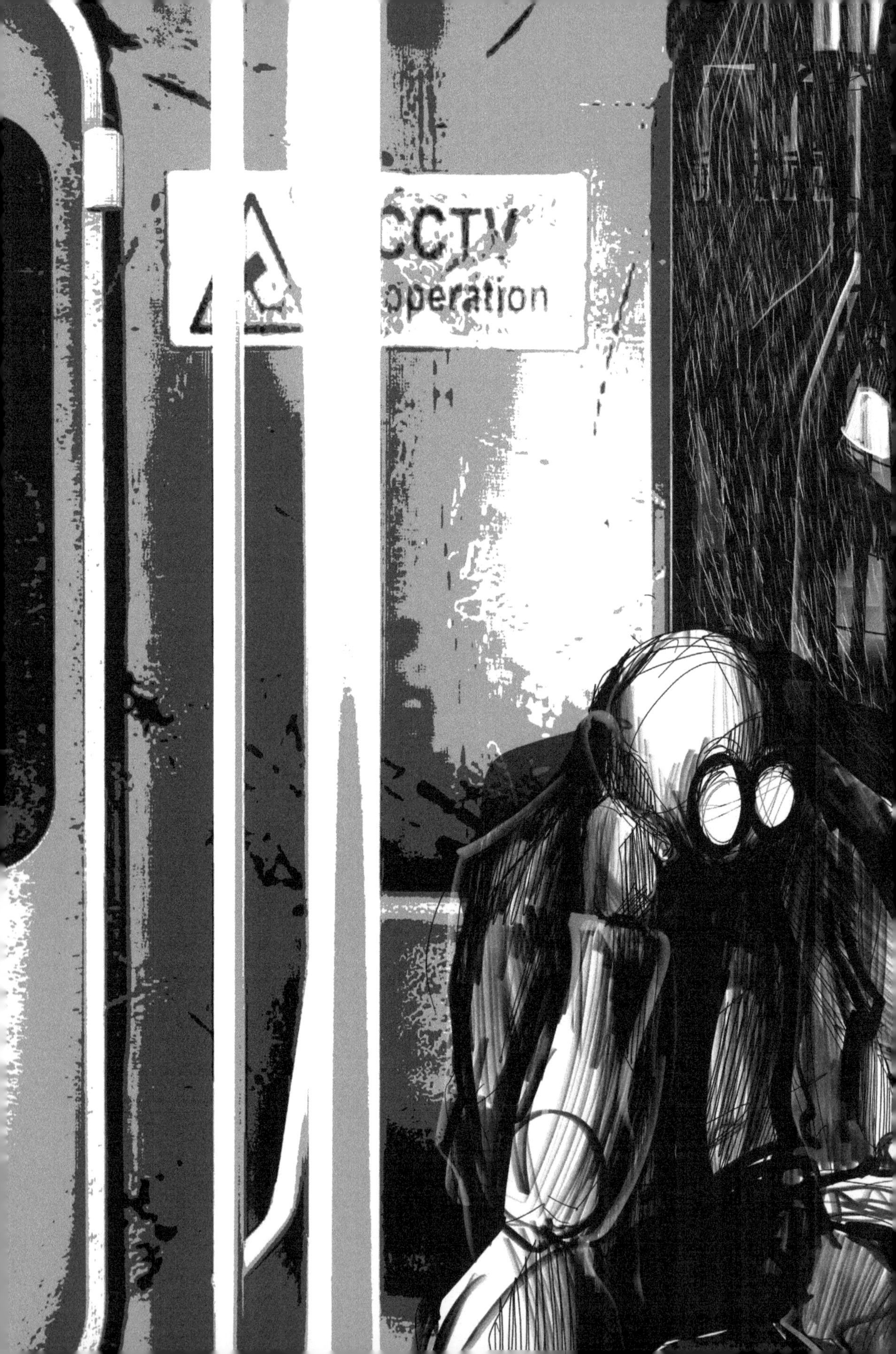
CCTV

HEARTICULTURE ARCHITECTURE SCHOOL

by
SUHA FAISAL VALIYAVEETTIL

BRIEF *Alter Ego(ed) Futures*

YEAR *2024-25*

TUTORS *Dr Alessandro Ayuso, Mary Konstantopoulou, with support from Deniz Özbek*

THEMES

Architecture of Emotion

Allegory

Narrative World-building

Personified Buildings

Architecture Critique

Cast of Characters

"Here lies a tale of passion,

love manifested in three forms,
struck by the deities of desperation,
flattery, and revenge.

One's love, unrequited.
One's, destructive.
One, for no one but himself.

How does love survive its own undoing?
What form does it take when nothing is left?

Three lovers.
One tragic ending.
One beautiful beginning.

Welcome to the architecture of love."

fig. 4.73: Facing page: Plan overlays showing the love triangle conflict unfolding in the spatial arrangement of the school: "Three slender tower cores, each one represent a character. Where their limbs meet, the form reveals their entanglement— their tensions, affections, and betrayals etched into structure. The farming collective invites the local community in. As they integrate,the building becomes a ground for exchange. Students meet the public firsthand, listen to their needs, act where it matters."

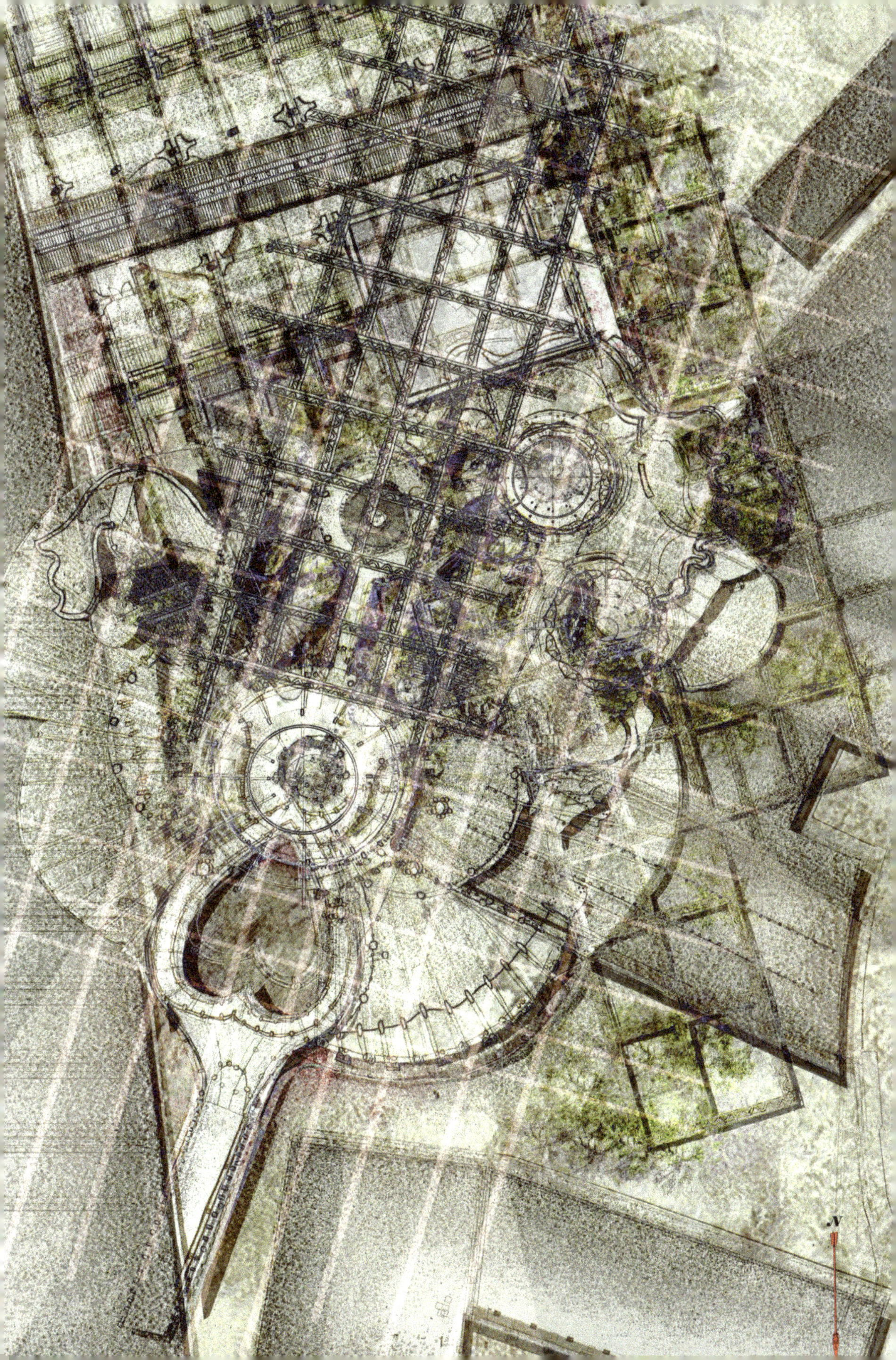

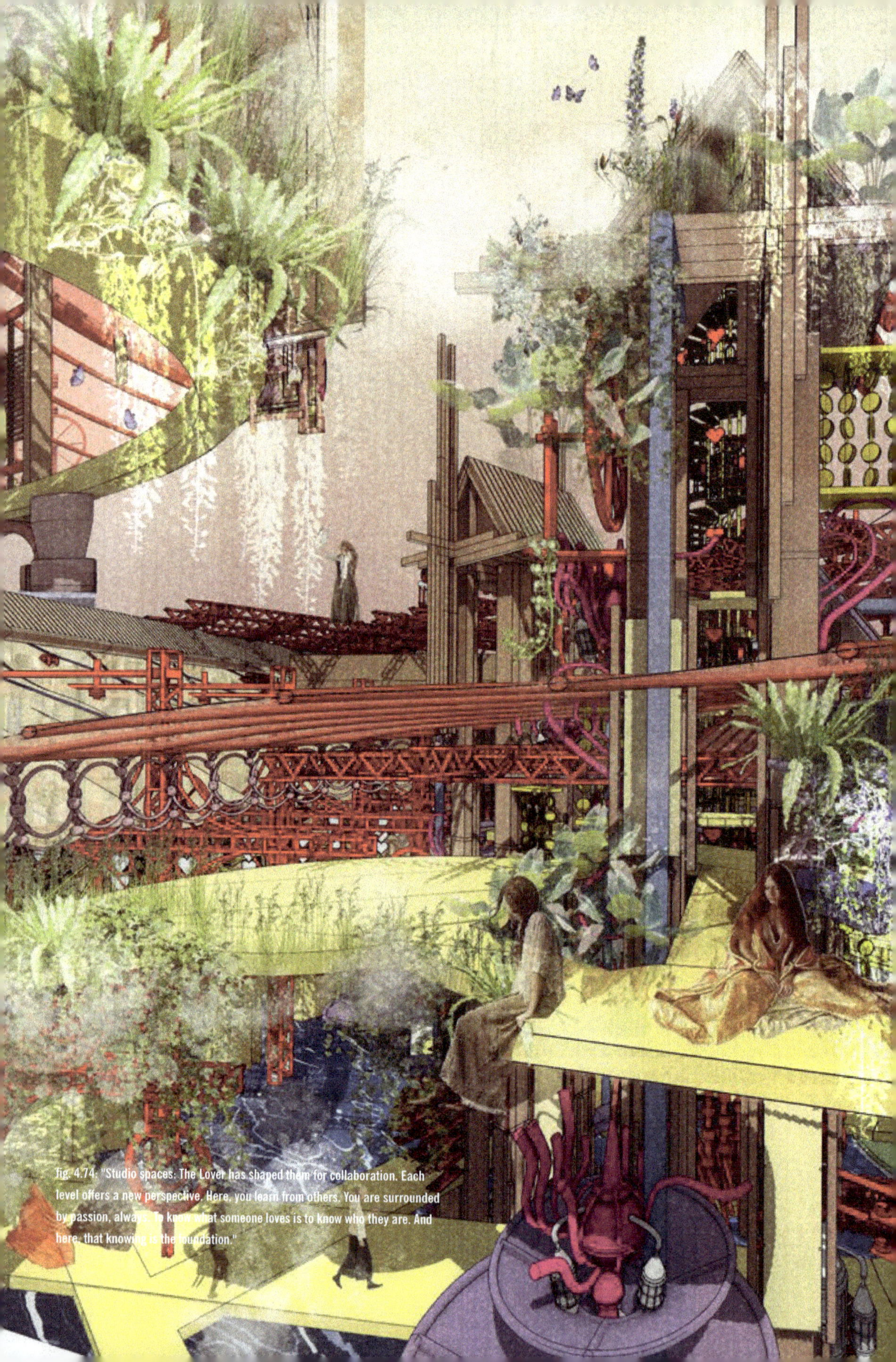

fig. 4.74: "Studio spaces: The Lover has shaped them for collaboration. Each level offers a new perspective. Here, you learn from others. You are surrounded by passion, always. To know what someone loves is to know who they are. And here, that knowing is the foundation."

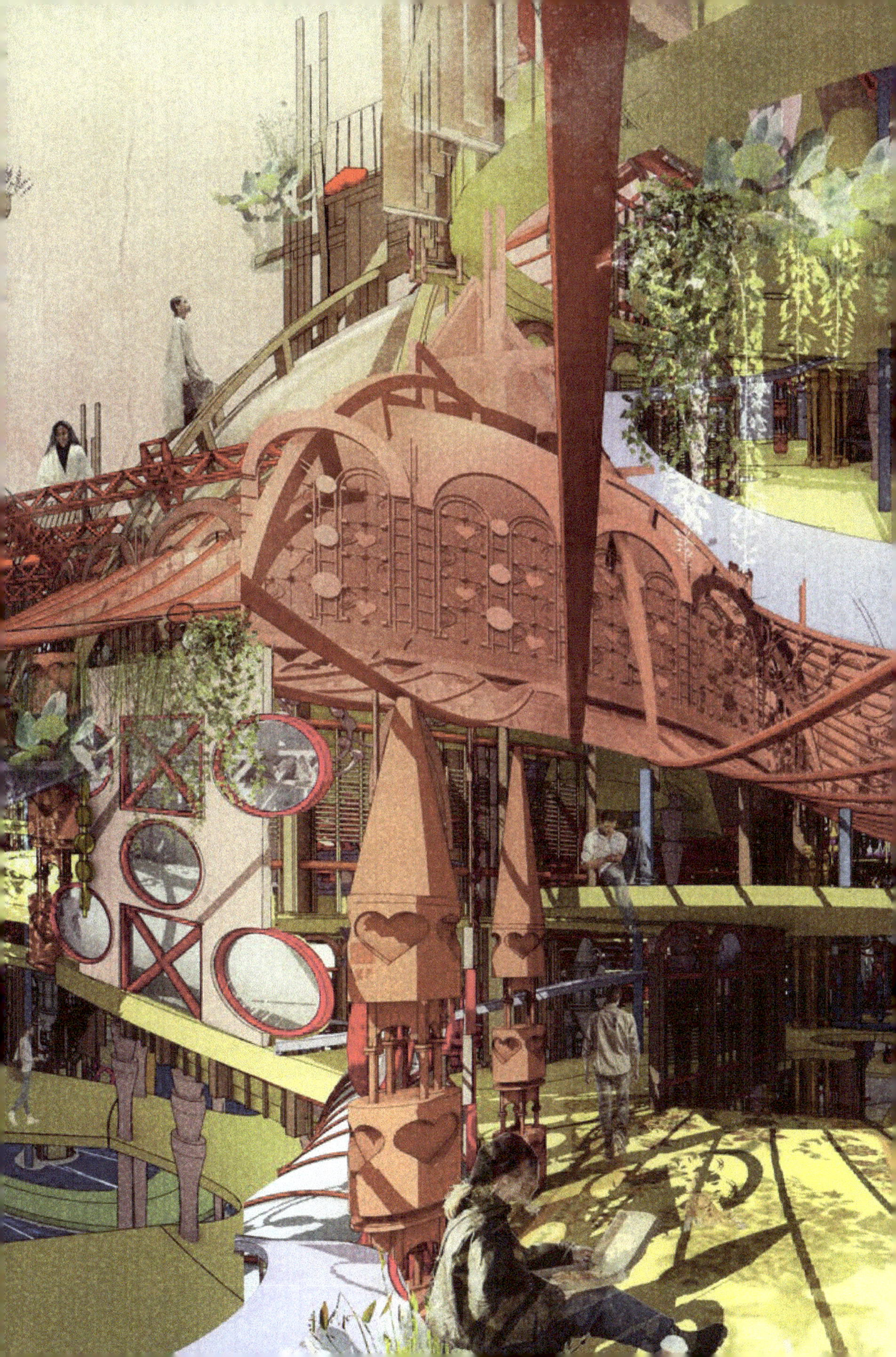

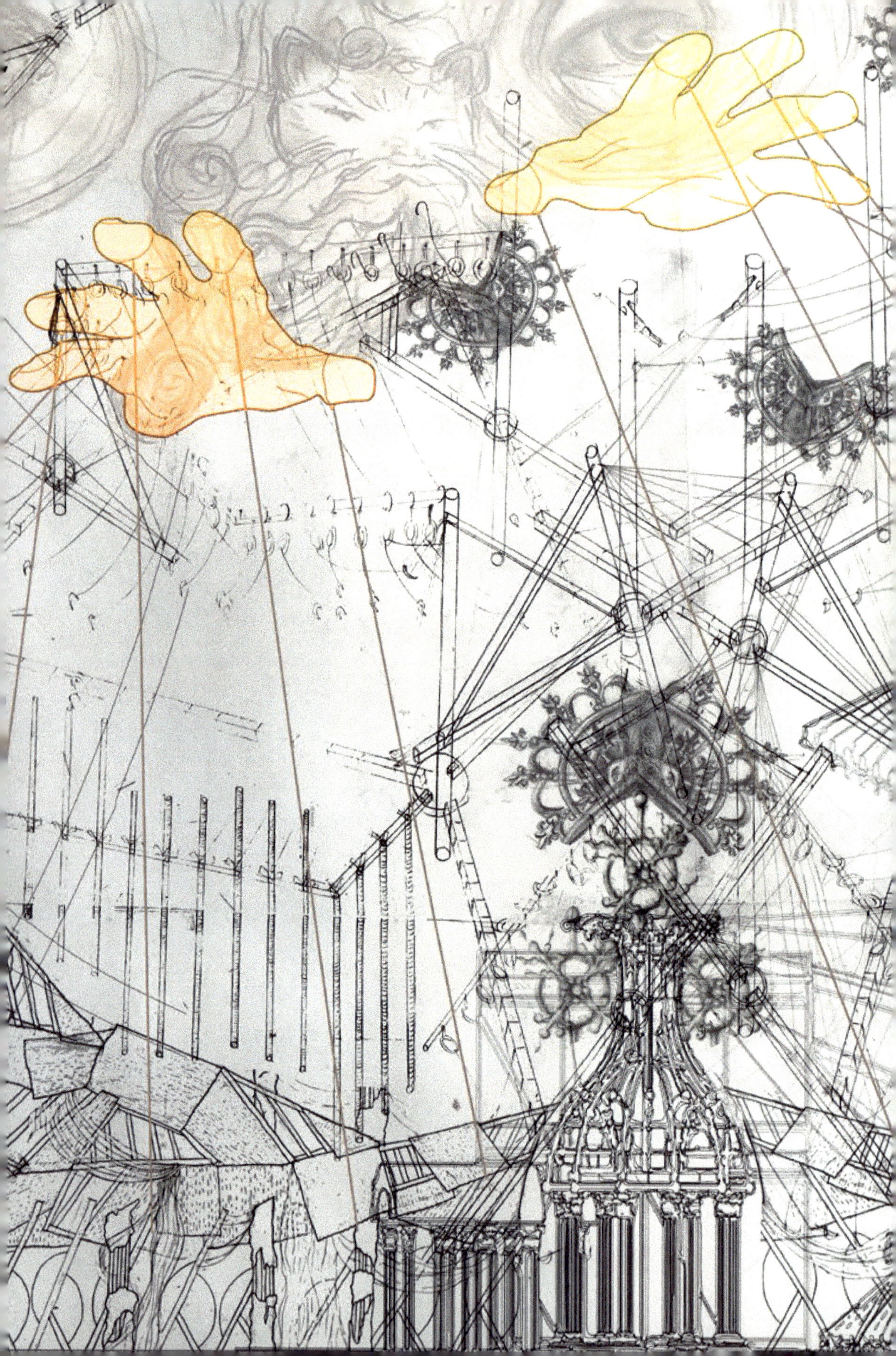

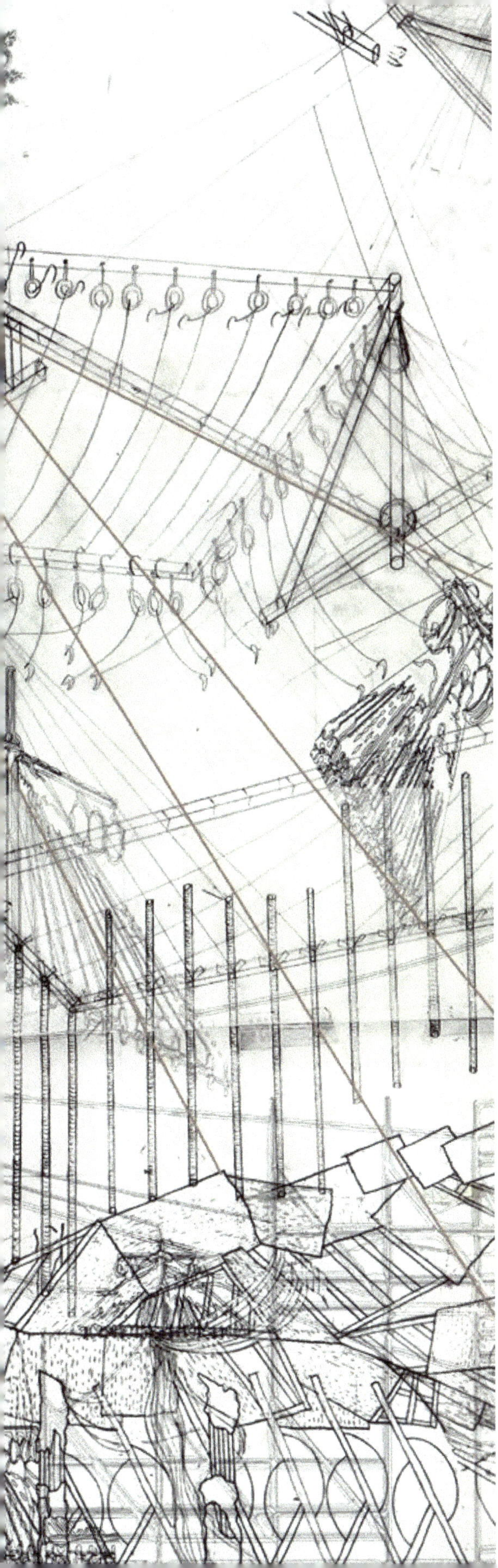

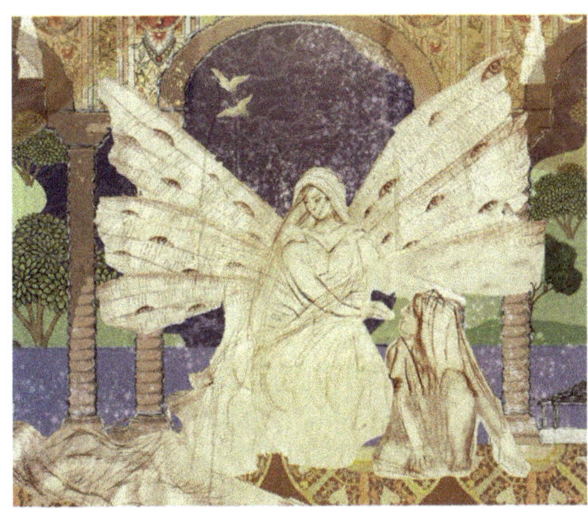

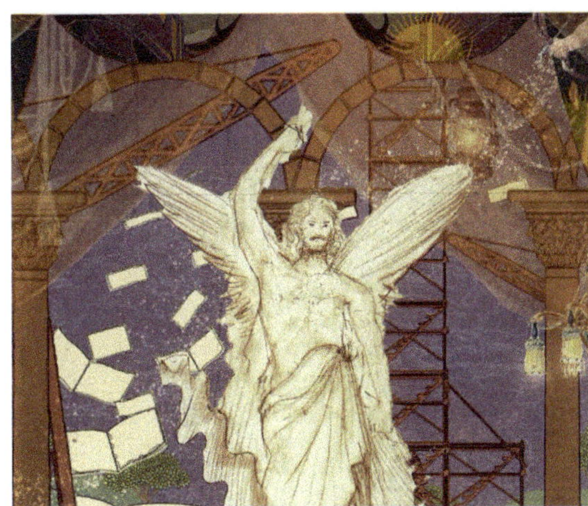

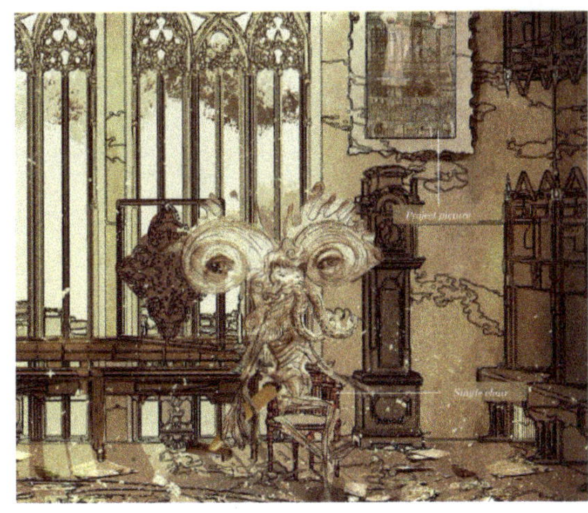

fig. 4.75-4.79: Top-Left to Bottom Right: "She leads the design of the new city, its values are hers, clear, humane, collective. But in the silence between days, when no one is watching, the old patterns return. The Architect pulls from above. I see the red strings of fate tighten. She moves, but it's not her will. The Architect lives still, in the movements she cannot unmake."; The Avenger; The Lover; The Architect. Following page: Aerial dusk view titled "The future will be yours."

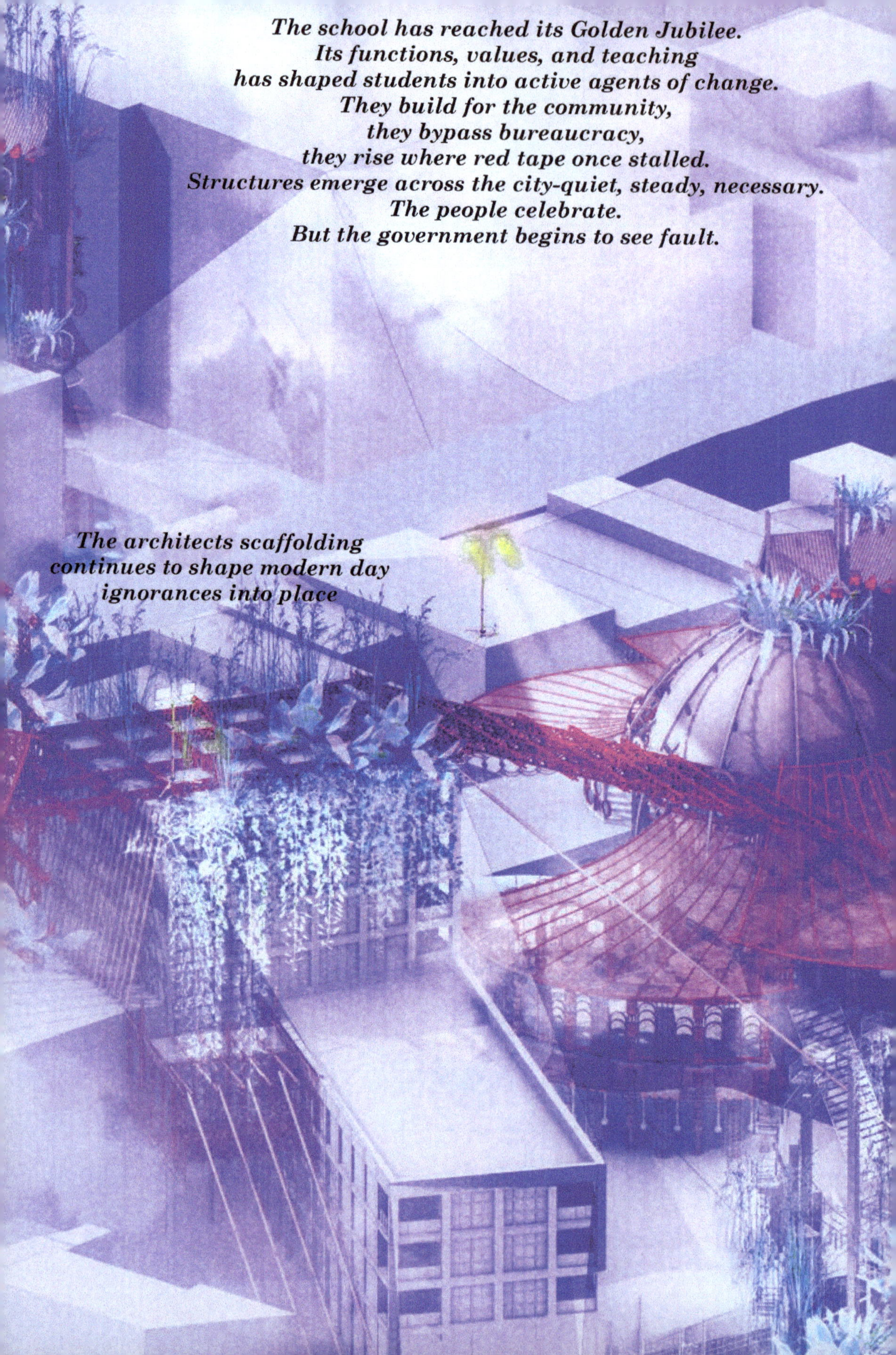
The school has reached its Golden Jubilee.
Its functions, values, and teaching
has shaped students into active agents of change.
They build for the community,
they bypass bureaucracy,
they rise where red tape once stalled.
Structures emerge across the city-quiet, steady, necessary.
The people celebrate.
But the government begins to see fault.
The architects scaffolding
continues to shape modern day
ignorances into place

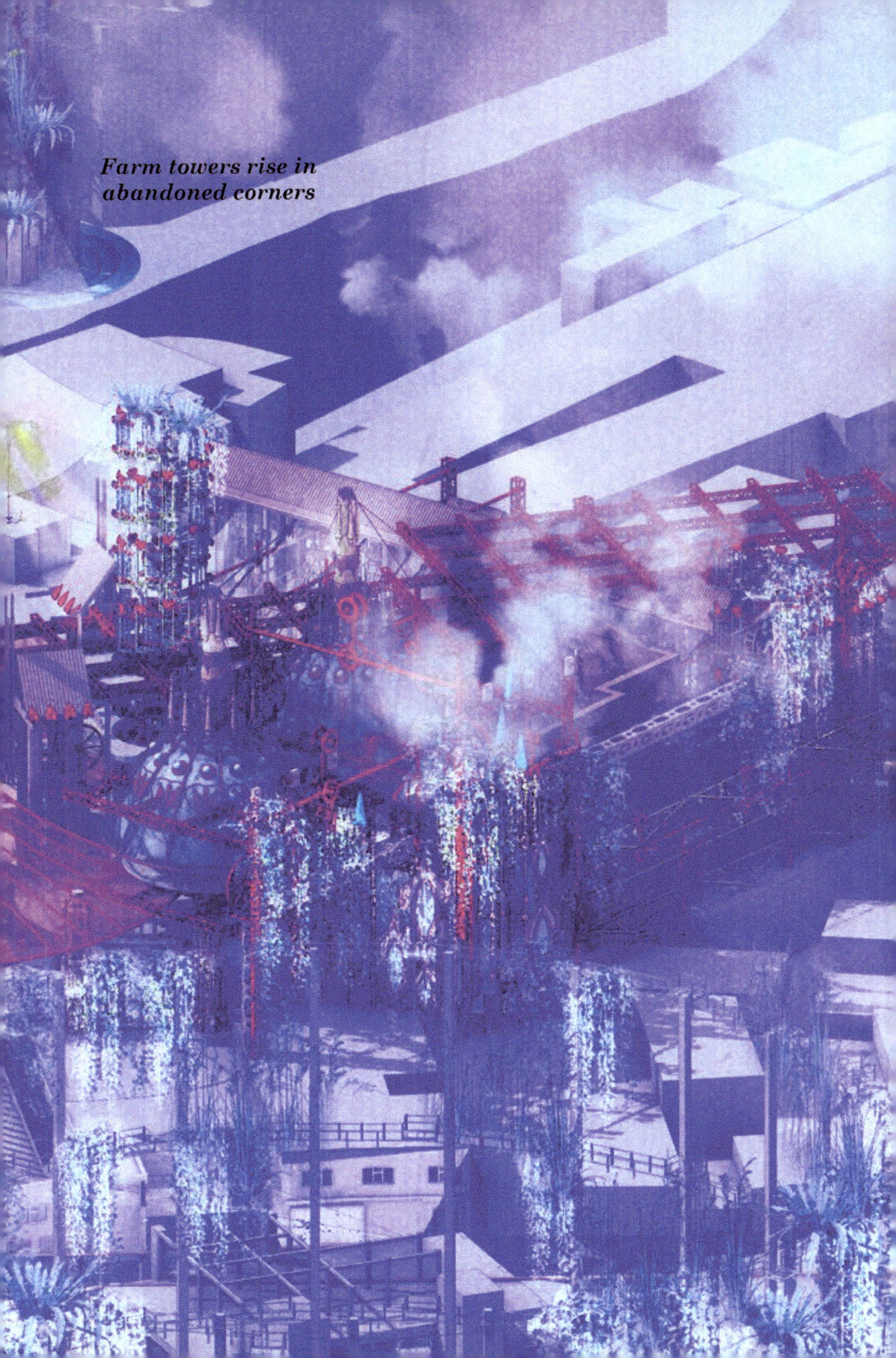

Farm towers rise in abandoned corners

CHAPTER 5: CONCLUSION

by Dr ALESSANDRO AYUSO and MARY KONSTANTOPOULOU

RESEARCH

This book shows the development of DS25's collective research. As a body it is unruly, with tendrils reaching in the various directions that projects, personalities, and discussions take it. The studio (and its research agenda) could be likened to one of the Exquisite Corpse drawings students and tutors draw together on the placemats of restaurants during field trips (fig. 5.01). This body cannot be considered as a known whole but becomes porous, doubled, and mysterious. It is an ever-evolving, monstrous creature, with appendages, dormant limbs, and enabling prosthetics, reflecting how DS25's composition has shifted over its years of development.

However, some definitive throughlines can be traced through the research agenda and this book. While the individual projects shown in the book culminate in fascinating and compelling proposals and imagery, and could possibly be arranged to show a collective development in these regards, the book aimed to highlight the evolution of the underlying studio themes and methodologies. Apart from the artistic, critical, exploratory, and personal dimensions of the individual projects— which are themselves indispensably valuable for their yield in terms of learning, participating in broader discourse, and architectural exploration— the most valuable aspect of the development of the studio in terms of research are its emergent themes and methodologies. The projects and year-to-year framing of them through briefs and prompts were in a dynamic exchange with the students' experiments and the discussions in the studio; the themes and methodology arose out of this exchange and stand as the most transferable aspect of the new knowledge generated.

The studio started with an exploration of the potentiality of the human body as a design generator. This entailed keeping an eye trained backwards to the history of architecture and the incorporation of the body in past design methods, but also contemporary artistic and cinematic mediums where the body is questioned and explored. Yet it also meant looking forward: by confronting the contentious nature of contemporary embodiment, questions of posthumanism were introduced into the design of body agents. The innate strangeness of the body— and its tendency towards mutability and otherness— surfaced in the students' designs of body agents. The uncanny, strange, humorous, and even dreadful territories that the projects consistently traversed proved to be fertile grounds for speculation and inventiveness. Students invested personal meaning into projects and engaged with critical issues and speculative possibilities about not only the body's relationship to architecture, but broader social and ecological themes. As their alrer-ego body agents inhabited the studio, drawing emerged as an important part of the methodology, as a means of engaging the physicality of representation and the body (fig. 5.02). Questioning the means of drawing and what could constitute drawing— incorporating digital means, scale extremes, and spatial plasticity through making— was central to the thinking process itself and to the discoveries that could be made through the project.

invented realities were a means of projecting possible futures and speculating on their repercussions

Narrative and cinematic approaches to architecture were a part of the studio concentration from the beginning, with their importance in the collective enquiry and evolving methodology increasing over time. As every body tells a story and implies a subject position, and as every body is in motion and ever-changing, it followed that design methodologies based on embodiment necessitated strategies that could pick up on these innate qualities. These strategies included cinematic techniques— such as animation, film-making, and storyboarding, as well as storytelling methods— such as imagining first-person accounts, situating events in actual and fictitious timelines, inventing sci-fi strands projecting into the future, and considering satirical or seemingly absurd scenarios.

Such narrative tactics expanded the relational scope of the projects. Initially emanating from the human body, the narratives invented by students positioned other actants in the scope of the projects; the narratives allowed for an animation of architecture and a taking account of nonhuman actors. Over the years of the studio, the body agent designs became more fantastical and less grounded in the physical human body per se, as the body agents' presumed relational reach extended. The consideration of bodies and subjects moved beyond the armature of the human body and further into a field of broader ecologies. The broadened sense of relationality, coupled with the increased emphasis on narrative techniques, brought world-building to the fore of the methodology. Building worlds became a more conscious component of the studio process: the body agents continued to give rise to architecture, as metaphorical, metonymical, and conceptual devices, but their utility extended more towards how they could enable the cultivation of a reality outside of themselves. World-building resulted in parallel realities and timelines emerging in the projects. These invented realities were a means of projecting possible futures and speculating on their repercussions. In this conception, architecture becomes not just a snapshot, not just an object to be delivered or set down on a plot of land, but part of an eco-socio-temporal continuum, snarling, wrinkling, or smoothing it, operating amidst the contingencies and the course of future events.

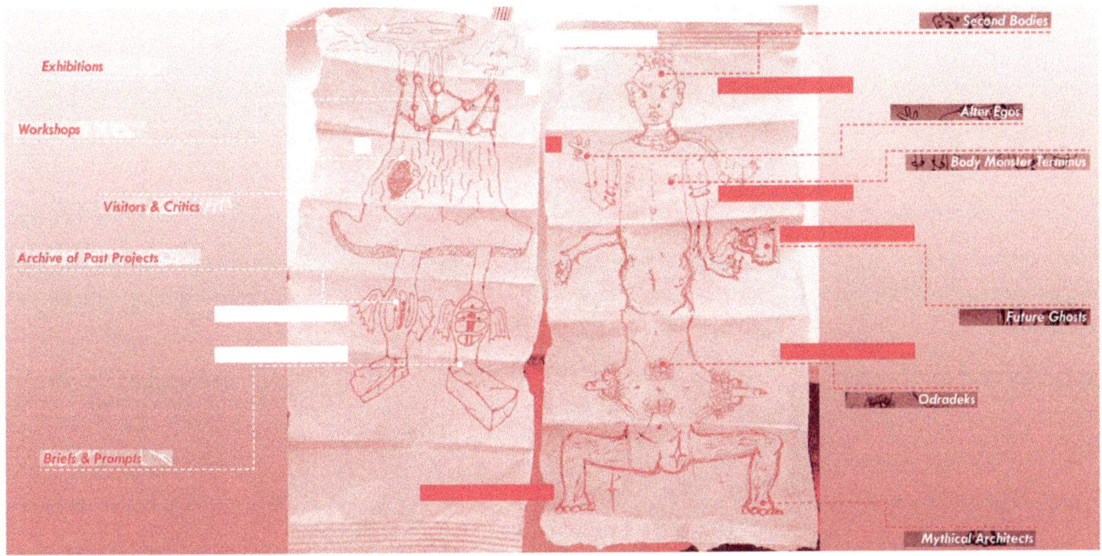

fig. 5.01: DS25's bodily composition as Exquisite Corpses, collaborative drawings by students of DS25 during a field trip.

The work in DS25 contributes to a questioning of the relationship between embodied subjectivity and context. The potential subjects of architecture expand, and become agents in its critical understanding, design, and construction. In the relational scenarios that arise from the studio approach, body and architecture are in a continuum— even to the point that sometimes they are indistinguishable— suggesting potentials for new modes of symbiotic co-beings. The projects show that the incorporation of narrative with considered, situated points of view can be a crucial way to imagine radical spatial and temporal possibilities. As the studio moves forward, the thematic focus moves further from the singular body. At the time of writing this book, the working title of the brief for the 2025-26 academic year is *Ensembles*. Building on Turner's idea of extended organisms discussed in chapter three, the starting point will be to construct body agents as extended aggregates from organic bodies, nonhuman entities, and elements from a given contextual milieu.

PEDAGOGY

As this book attests to, DS25's research agenda emphasises experimentation, and the ethos of the studio embraces inventiveness and new approaches to architecture. In general, the studio delights in the anomalous, weird, and dark peripheries of the discipline. In this sense, the studio positions itself as a home for nurturing subaltern visions, and as an incubator for unabashed future thinking. Yet, for all its iconoclastic

The uncanny, strange, humorous, and even dreadful territories that the projects consistently traversed proved to be fertile grounds for speculation and inventiveness.

ambitions, considering the lineage presented in the preface, this embrace of the new and weird is more of a continuation of a tradition in the London architectural scene than a break with it. This tradition has been dampened in the last decade.

In its approach that emphasises speculation, depth, intricacy, individual interests, social critique, and embrace of the strange, DS25 is in tension with reactionary trends in architectural pedagogy. In the UK, these trends are complicated, and have to do with the financial pressure experienced by both institutions and students themselves, as tuition fees go up and universities feel the pinch of fleeting state support. Many students themselves, understandably experiencing intense financial pressure, look to education to provide skills first and foremost, as they consider how they can be immediately marketable in a competitive employment sector. Additionally, the response to climate crisis in some quarters results in a doubling-down on what is viewed as pragmatism, leaving less room for what they regard as whimsical or indulgent imagination.

Elements of architectural education's validating organisations formalise the dampening pressures on exploration and speculation in architectural education. For instance, the RIBA and ARB seem to ever-expand the lists of competencies and skills required in their learning requirements, arguably at the expense of more open-ended exploration. These checklists are concrete. At the same time, events such as the RIBA President's Medals award

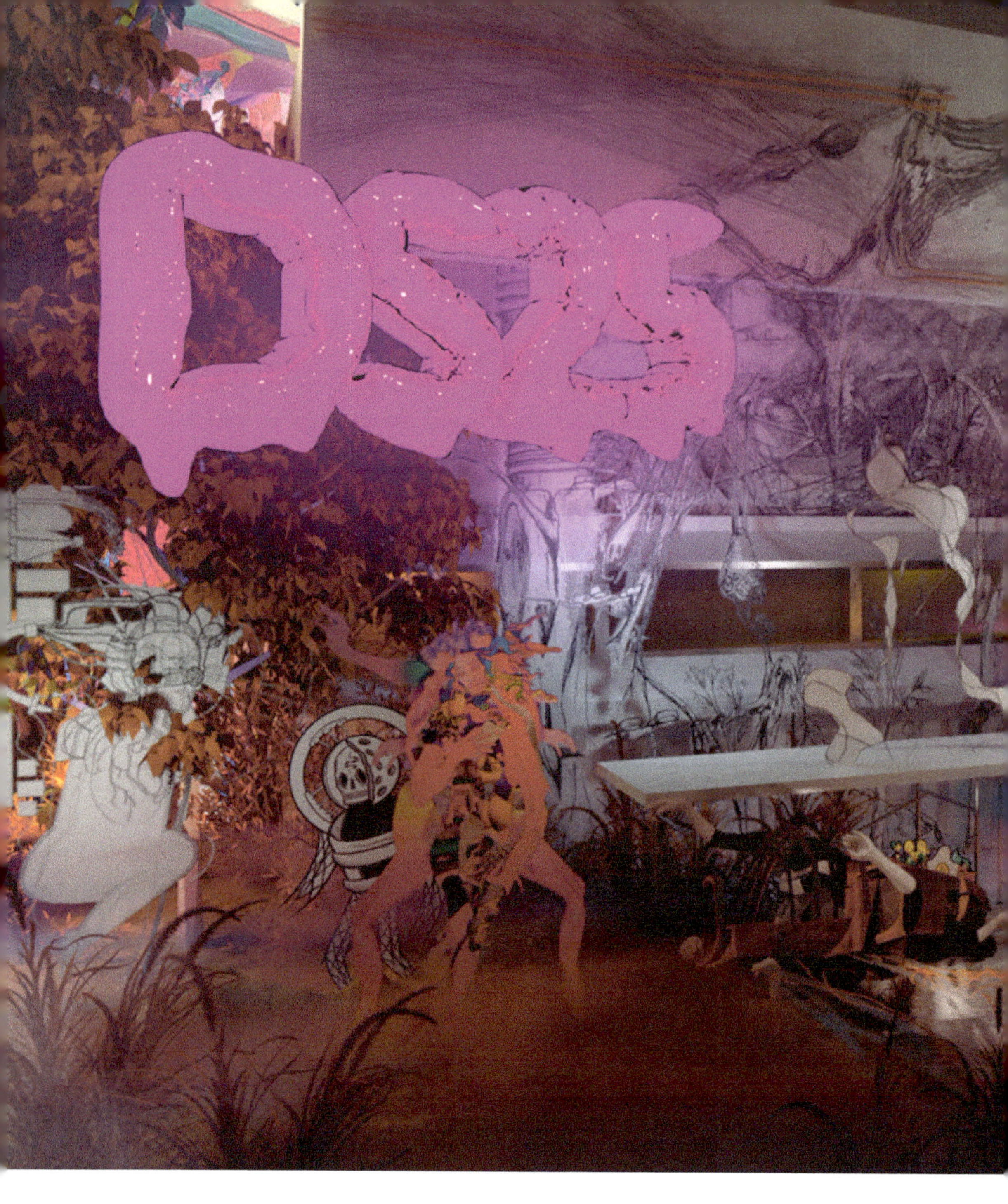

fig. 5.02: DS25 body agents from the year 2020-21 in the studio space. Image by Laura Kershaw and Alexandros Tzortzis de Paz.

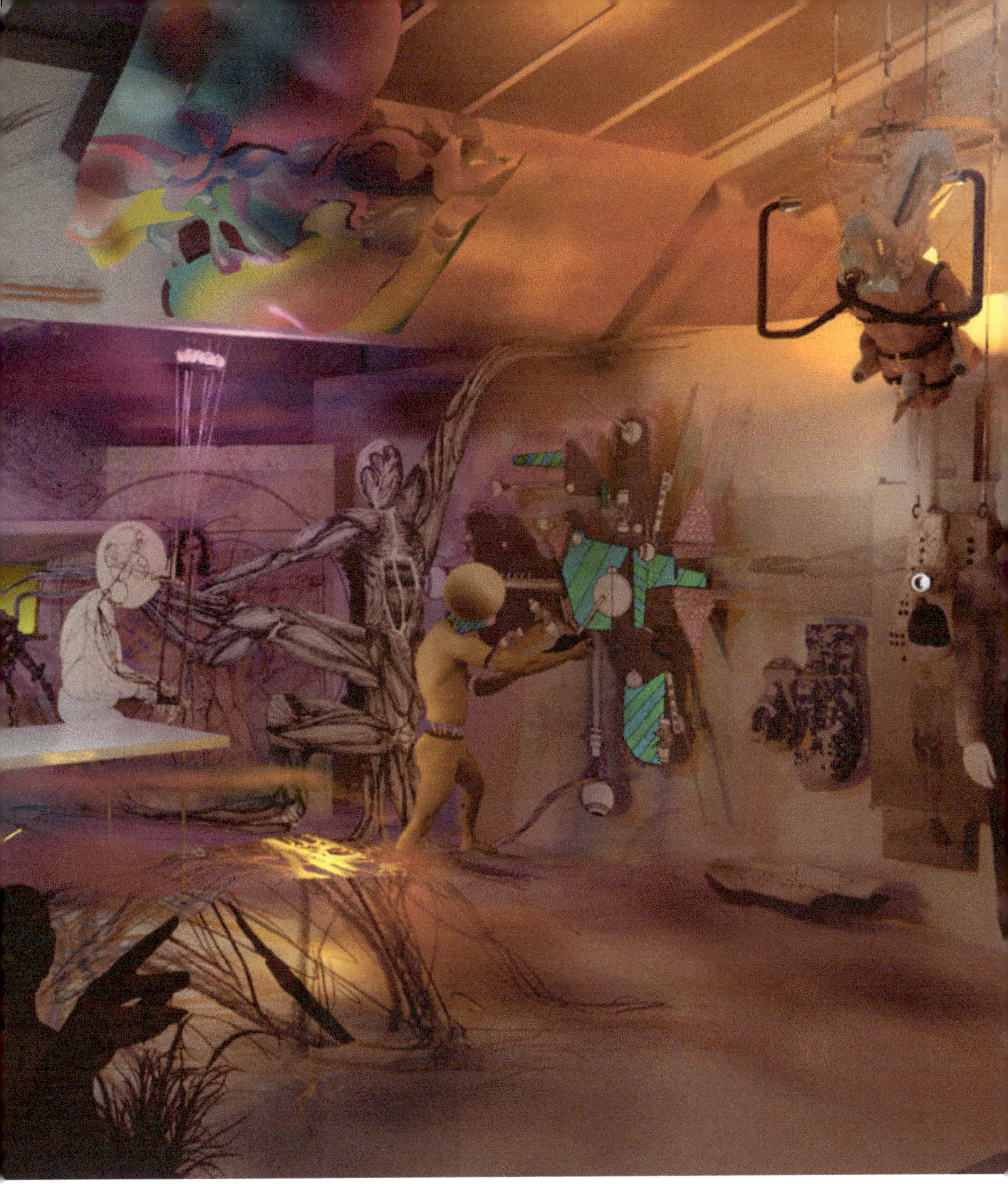

Instagram:

Youtube:

prizes to projects with dazzling imagery that are often quite visionary in their ambition. Between the two tendencies— one awarding incredible looking projects and the other pushing for the domination of competency as a pedagogical goal— a lacuna arises. In this gap, the question arises of what is truly being valued. Actual process and learning about design itself— as an iterative, non-linear, creative, and artistic endeavour— which may be messy and not quite as PR ready on its surface— is arguably lost.

Between the two tendencies, the focus on competencies and skills is becoming more prevalent; at the time of writing, the tripartite educational model which partly enables DS25 to exist may be an endangered species, as the ARB's new learning objectives geared towards competencies and outcomes also challenge the three-part RIBA model. Institutions will need to cater to these objectives for accreditation. This may mean that across the UK architectural educational sector by 2027, Part II courses as they have been known will change dramatically— becoming more about outcomes and competencies at the expense of exploration and critical thinking. As pedagogy bends to these checklists, educators often feel the value of what they can impart— in the design thinking itself, as durable ways of working and understanding design, critically-situating it in specific and broader contexts— is slipping away.

The commercial industry of architecture— which dominated the consultations leading up to the new ARB reforms—[(01)] is a form of practice temporally grounded in the now; it is epistemologically oriented towards applied knowledge for the sake of delivery of products and services. While undoubtedly one of the roles of design tutors is to prepare students to potentially thrive in commercial practice, the metaphorical pedagogical body that this book portrays does not merely work towards fulfilling the needs of commercial architecture. Avoiding pitfalls of dichotomies or servitude, education and commercial practice could be viewed as vital components of a broadly-constituted discipline. In this sense, educational models such as those that allow for temporally adventurous, speculative, and open-ended exploration offer a facet of the discipline that commercial practice— given the pressures and imperatives exerted on it— is not often able to engage with.

This book has shown a pedagogical approach that provides a way for students to engage with a multifaceted world and ask how it and oneself can be encountered and reinvented through hopeful curiosity.[(02)] The projects and activities shown demonstrate how students become equipped with techniques and themes that help develop criticality and agility in responding to the present and the unforeseen. As an evolving research endeavour, DS25 expands the discipline of architecture by reaching beyond what is defined by practice and accreditation criteria.

The bodies, stories, and people that constitute the studio test the boundaries and depth of the profession, positing what education— and architecture— could do.

NOTES

(01) The ARB consultation received an unbalanced response with an overwhelming majority of consultees being Registered Architects in practice, with a minority of responses coming from those in academia, whether students or tutors. Architects Registration Board, *Consultation Report: Analysis report on ARB's consultation on education and training reforms* (Architects Registration Board, 2023), chap. 2, 16-8, https://arb.org.uk/wp-content/uploads/ARB-Consultation-report-Education-and-training-reforms-September-2023.pdf.

(02) In this respect, encouragement can be found in Paulo Freire's writings, epitomised by quotes such as: "For apart from inquiry, apart from the praxis, individuals cannot be truly human. Knowledge emerges only through invention and re-invention, through the restless, impatient, continuing, hopeful inquiry human beings pursue in the world, with the world, and with each other." Paulo Freire, *Pedagogy of the Oppressed*, trans. Myra Bergman Ramos (London: Continuum, 1968), 72.

ACKNOWLEDGEMENTS

We would like to thank those who have provided input and inspiration for the studio including past tutors Dr Dan Dream, Martyna Marciniak and Dr Fiona Zisch, as well as Deniz Özbek, Pia Sarpaneva, Francisco Sanin, Franco Pisani, Richard Difford, Samir Pandya, and Professor Harry Charrington.

We would like to thank practices that have supported the studio including Bourne Partnership, Parasite 2.0, The Harris Partnership, Klaud - Koepf Lechthaler Architecture & Urban Design, and JTP Architects.

We would like to thank Barbara Southard, Dr Amy Brookes, Dr Dan Dream, and Professor Lindsay Bremner for their support in the production of this book.

------2024-25

Tutor Team: Dr Alessandro Ayuso, Mary Konstantopoulou, with support from Deniz Özbek

Brief: Alter Ego(ed) Futures

Students:

Year 1
Yusuf Arfaan
Matthew Coyne
Suha Valiyaveettil
Monzurul Islam
Khushi Patel
Nirayan Patel
Xhesika Rama
Mara Sendroiu
Leader Luketa Tshibangu

Year 2
Jake Bone
Jessica Gabriel
Angharad James
Anastasia Kolioliou
Shannon McCaddon
Farah Mussadiq
Alice Own
Chloe Pegeot

Critics:
Joshua Bulman, William Victor Camilleri, Kate Cheyne, Filippo Cocca, Hanna Hendrickson-Rebizant, Akmaral Khassen, Asena Koksal (Bourne Partnership), Deniz Özbek (Tack), Samir Pandya, Jake Parkin, Anthony Richardson, Dr Ro Spankie, Ilia Stringari, Kanaka Thakker, Alannah Wilson

Special Thanks:
Chryssa Martini, Sotiris Tryposkoufis (Dionyssomarble Group), Ilia Stringari

------2023-24

Tutor Team: Dr Alessandro Ayuso, Mary Konstantopoulou

Brief: Things Have Feelings Too

Students:

Year 1
Jake Bone
Elissa Dergham
Jessica Gabriel
Karolina Hejduk
Georgiana Ilie
Angharad James
Sameera Kaddoura
Anastasia Kolioliou

Year 2
Amabelle Aranas
Conrad Daniel Areta
Laura Bull
Cara Kinzelmann
Aleksandra Kwietniewska
Luke La Thangue
Alcina Lo
Imogen Power
Zahraa Shaikh
Alannah Wilson

Critics:
Filippo Cocca, Giorgos Christofi, Eleanor Evason (Piercy & Co), Hanna Hendrickson-Rebizant, Asena Koksal (Bourne Partnership), Dr Jane Madsen, Deniz Özbek (Tack), Samir Pandya, Chandni Patel (East Architecture), Alexandros Tzortzis de Paz

------2022-23

Tutor Team: Dr Alessandro Ayuso, Mary Konstantopoulou

Brief: Spectral Futures

Students:

Year 1
Amabelle Aranas
Conrad Daniel Areta
Nicholas Hasbani
Cara Kinzelmann
Aleksandra Kwietniewska
Luke La Thangue
Alcina Lo
Billy Pollintine
Imogen Power
Zahraa Shaikh
Alannah Wilson
Cho Yan Joan Wong

Year 2
Filippo Cocca
Kevin Ferenzena
Clara-Romana Pop
Cristina Sarla
Soraia de Abreu Viriato

Critics:
Dr Amy Brookes, Eleanor Evason (Piercy & Co), Egmontas Geras (Digital Poetics Ltd), Alex Haines (Burwell Architects), Lauriane Hewes (Patalab Architects), Asena Koksal (Bourne Partnership), Isabel Mills Lyle (MAAPS), Ian Perrel (The Harris Partnership), Joel Saldeck (playbody), Marie Walker-Smith (Arup Foresight)

------2021-22

Tutor Team: Dr Alessandro Ayuso, Mary Konstantopoulou

Brief: Embodied Ecologies & Speculative Fabulations

Students:

Year 1
Clara-Romana Pop
Cristina Raluca Sarla

Year 2
Adriaan Baldwin
Oscar Brown
Asena Koksal
Isabel Mills-Lyle
Aaron Spiers-Reed
Megan Woods

Critics:
Lauriane Hewes, Laura Kershaw (Emrys), Akmaral Khassen (Squire & Partners), Dr Constance Lau, Stefano Perretti (Ryder Architecture), Sylwia Poltorak (Lobster Enterprise), Nat Reading (AK Patterson), Era Savvides (Urban Radicals), Jacob Spence (MICA Architects Ltd), Alexandros Tzortzis de Paz (Foster+Partners), Chuxiao Wang (ACME Architects), Jamie Whelan (Jamie Whelan Studio)

------2020-21

Tutor Team: Dr Alessandro Ayuso, Dr Dan Dream, Dr Fiona Zisch
Brief: Architecture's Second Bodies
Students:

Year 1	*Year 2*
Adriaan Baldwin	Laura Kershaw
Oscar Brown	Akmaral Khassen
Leila Jahic	Ryan Kyberd
Asena Koksal	Leah Roberts
Isabel Mills-Lyle	Olga Smoili
Joanna Bo Kei Leung	Anastasia Tsamitrou
Unnati Mankad	Alexandros Tzortzis de Paz
Aaron Spiers-Reed	
Megan Woods	

Critics:
Ava Aghakouchak, Matteo Cainer (Matteo Cainer Architecture), Boon Yik Chung (KPF), Dr Ines Dantas (WUDA), William Haskas (plusFARM), Lauriane Hewes (Carpenter & Clay), Hanadi Izzudin (Arup), Mary Konstantopoulou (Jan Kattein Architects), Harry Matthews (TFF Architects), Shaden Meer (Origin Architects), Franco Pisani (Franco Pisani Architetto), Sylwia Poltorak (Lobster Enterprise), Nat Reading (AK Patterson), Peter Silver, Mika Zacharias (Morrow + Lorraine Architects)

Special Thanks:
Martyna Marciniak (Forensic Architecture)

------2019-20

Tutor Team: Dr Alessandro Ayuso, Dr Dan Dream, Martyna Marciniak
Brief: Body Agent Architecture
Students:

Year 1	*Year 2*
Sheikh Ahmed	Daniel Buban Ngu
Shahriar Doha	Edward Hancock
Laura Kershaw	Lauriane Hewes
Ryan Kyberd	Shaden Meer
Kai Law	Wilhelmina Ogoo
Linggezi Man	Anastasia Tsamitrou
Leah Roberts	Rares Tugui
Olga Smoili	Alexandros Tzortzis De Paz
Laura Snape	

Critics:
Lida Evangelia-Driva (Arup), Stefano Peretti (Ryder Architects), Sylwia Poltorak (Lobster Enterprise), Harry Matthews (ÜberRaum Architects), Vishal Mistry (WilkinsonEyre), Nat Reading (AK Patterson), Grant Warner (THINKfound), Ronni Winkler

Special Thanks:
Dr Gabriele Fabiankowitsch (MAK Museum), Karolin Schmidbaur-Volk (Coop Himmelb(l)au), Anna Tripamer and the Walter Pichler Estate, Evelyn Zisch, Dr Fiona Zisch

------2018-19

Tutor Team: Dr Alessandro Ayuso, Dr Dan Dream, Martyna Marciniak
Brief: Body Architecture
Students:

Year 1	*Year 2*
Adelina Gutu	Adrian Bolog
Lauriane Hewes	Lok Yi Law
Shaden Meer	Victor Man
Wilhelmina Ogoo	Harry Matthews
Rocco Plessi	Vishal Mistry
Celine Tran	Aleksandra Murzina
	Stefano Peretti
	Georgia Roberts
	Grant Warner

Critics:
Kyveli Anastasiadi (Alessandro Isola Ltd), Andrew Choptiany (Carmody Groarke Architects), Rafaella Christodoulidi (5plus Architects, Julia Dwyer, Lucy Dunn (Jo Cowen Architects), Andrew Friend, Naomi Gibson, Colin Herperger, Professor Jonathan Hill, Dr Ifigeneia Liangi, Dr Tania Lopez-Winkler, Sonia Magdziarz (Zaha Hadid Architects), Anne Munly, Dr Ro Spankie, Nick Shackleton (Holland Harvey Architects), Dr Mary Vaughan Johnson

Special Thanks:
Andrew Choptiany (Carmody Groarke Architects), Janet Lewis, Colin Smith, Eva Denney, Dorota Platt

EMBODYING ALTERITY

DS25 2018-25
Edited by Alessandro Ayuso & Mary Konstantopoulou

A University of Westminster,
School of Architecture + Cities Publication

Designed by Mark Boyce

ISBN 978-0-9955893-7-7

Books in the Studio as Book series are available to purchase via OpenStudioWestminster here: http://www.openstudiowestminster.org/studio-as-book/ or from online book stores.

The editors have attempted to acknowledge all sources of images used and apologise for any errors or omissions.

School of Architecture + Cities
University of Westminster
35 Marylebone Road
London
NW1 5LS

www.ingramcontent.com/pod-product-compliance
Ingram Content Group UK Ltd.
Pitfield, Milton Keynes, MK11 3LW, UK
UKHW062005290726
14090UKWH00022B/1397